# CONSTITUTION

OF THE

# STATE OF NORTH-CAROLINA,

TOGETHER WITH THE

# ORDINANCES AND RESOLUTIONS

OF THE

# CONSTITUTIONAL CONVENTION,

Assembled in the City of Raleigh, Jan. 14th, 1868.

RALEIGH:
JOSEPH W. HOLDEN, CONVENTION PRINTER.
1868.

# CONSTITUTION

OF

# NORTH-CAROLINA.

## CHAPTER I.

### PREAMBLE.

We the people of the State of North-Carolina, grateful to Almighty God, the Sovereign Ruler of Nations, for the preservation of the American Union, and the existence of our civil, political and religious liberties, and acknowledging our dependence upon Him, for the continuance of those blessings to us and our posterity, do, for the more certain security thereof, and for the better government of this State, ordain and establish this Constitution. Preamble.

## ARTICLE I.

### DECLARATION OF RIGHTS.

That the great, general and essential principles of liberty and free government, may be recognized and established, and that the relations of this State to the Union and government of the United States, and those of the people of this State to the rest of the American people, may be defined and affirmed, we do declare:

SECTION 1. That we hold it to be self-evident that all men are created equal; that they are endowed by their Creator with certain unalienable rights; that among these are life, liberty, the enjoyment of the fruits of their own labor, and the pursuit of happiness. The equality and rights of men.

Political power and government.

SEC. 2. That all political power is vested in, and derived from the people; all government of right originates from the people, is founded upon their will only, and is instituted solely for the good of the whole.

Internal government of the State.

SEC. 3. That the people of this State have the inherent, sole, and exclusive right of regulating the internal government and police thereof, and of altering and abolishing their Constitution and form of government, whenever it may be necessary to their safety and happiness; but every such right should be exercised in pursuance of law, and consistently with the Constitution of the United States.

That there is no right to secede.

SEC. 4. That this State shall ever remain a member of the American Union; that the people thereof are part of the American nation; that there is no right on the part of this State to secede, and that all attempts from whatever source or upon whatever pretext, to dissolve said Union, or to sever said nation, ought to be resisted with the whole power of the State.

Of allegiance to the U. S. government.

SEC. 5. That every citizen of this State owes paramount allegiance to the Constitution and Government of the United States, and that no law or ordinance of the State in contravention or subversion thereof, can have any binding force.

Public Debt.

SEC. 6. To maintain the honor and good faith of the State untarnished, the public debt, regularly contracted before and since the rebellion, shall be regarded as inviolable and never be questioned; but the State shall never assume or pay, or authorize the collection of, any debt or obligation, express or implied, incurred in aid of insurrection or rebellion against the United States, or any claim for the loss or emancipation of any slave.

Exclusive emoluments, &c

SEC. 7. No man or set of men are entitled to exclusive or separate emoluments or privileges from the community but in consideration of public services.

The Legislative, Executive and Judicial powers distinct.

SEC. 8. The Legislative, Executive, and Supreme judicial powers of the government ought to be forever separate and distinct from each other.

Of the power of suspending laws.

SEC. 9. All power of suspending laws, or the execution of laws, by any authority, without the consent of the representatives of the people, is injurious to their rights, and ought not to be exercised.

Elections free.

SEC. 10. All elections ought to be free.

In criminal prosecutions.

SEC. 11. In all criminal prosecutions, every man has the right to be informed of the accusation against him and to confront the accusers and witnesses with other testimony, and to have counsel for his defence, and not be compelled to give evidence against himself, or to pay costs, jail fees, or necessary witness fees of the defence, unless found guilty.

Answers to criminal charges

SEC. 12. No person shall be put to answer any criminal charge, except as hereinafter allowed, but by indictment, presentment, or impeachment.

Right of Jury.

SEC. 13. No person shall be convicted of any crime but by the unanimous verdict of a jury of good and lawful men in open court. The Legislature may, however, provide other means of trial, for petty misdemeanors, with the right of appeal.

Excessive bail

SEC. 14. Excessive bail should not be required, nor excessive fines imposed, nor cruel or unusual punishments inflicted.

General warrants.

SEC. 15. General warrants, whereby any officer or messenger may be commanded to search suspected places, without evidence of the act committed, or to seize any person or persons not named, whose offence is not particularly described and supported by evidence, are dangerous to liberty and ought not to be granted.

Imprisonment for debt.

SEC. 16. There shall be no imprisonment for debt in this State, except in cases of fraud.

No person to be taken, &c., but by law of the land.

SEC. 17. No person ought to be taken, imprisoned or disseized of his freehold, liberties or privileges, or outlawed, or exiled, or in any manner deprived of his life, liberty, or property, but by the law of the land.

Persons restrained of liberty.

SEC. 18. Every person restrained of his liberty, is entitled to a remedy to enquire into the lawfulness thereof, and to remove the same, if unlawful; and such remedy ought not to be denied or delayed.

Controversies at law respecting property.

SEC. 19. In all controversies at law respecting property, the ancient mode of trial by jury is one of the best securities of the rights of the people, and ought to remain sacred and inviolable.

Freedom of the Press.

SEC. 20. The freedom of the press is one of the great bulwarks of liberty, and therefore ought never to be restrained, but every individual shall be held responsible for the abuse of the same.

Habeas Corpus.

SEC. 21. The privilege of the writ of *habeas corpus* shall not be suspended.

Property qualification.

SEC. 22. As political rights and privileges are not dependent upon, or modified by property, therefore no property qualification ought to affect the right to vote or hold office.

Representation and taxation.

SEC. 23. The people of this State ought not to be taxed, or made subject to the payment of any impost or duty, without the consent of themselves, or their representatives in General Assembly, freely given.

Militia, and the right to bear arms.

SEC. 24. A well regulated militia being necessary to the security of a free State, the right of the people to keep and bear arms shall not be infringed; and, as standing armies, in time of peace, are dangerous to liberty, they ought not to be kept up, and the military should be kept under strict subordination to, and governed by, the civil power.

Right of the people to assemble together.

SEC. 25. The people have a right to assemble together to consult for their common good, to instruct their representatives, and to apply to the Legislature for redress of grievances.

Religious liberty.

SEC. 26. All men have a natural and unalienable right to worship Almighty God according to the dictates of their own consciences, and no human authority should, in any case whatever, control or interfere with the rights of conscience.

Education.

SEC. 27. The people have a right to the privilege of education, and it is the duty of the State to guard and maintain that right.

Elections should be frequent.

SEC. 28. For redress of grievances, and for amending and strengthening the laws, elections should be often held.

Recurrence to fundamental principles.

SEC. 29. A frequent recurrence to fundamental principles, is absolutely necessary to preserve the blessings of liberty.

SEC. 30. No hereditary emoluments, privileges, or honors, ought to be granted or conferred in this State. Hereditary emoluments, &c.

SEC. 31. Perpetuities and monopolies are contrary to the genius of a free State, and ought not to be allowed. Perpetuities, &c.

SEC. 32. Retrospective laws, punishing acts committed before the existence of such laws, and by them only declared criminal, are oppressive, unjust and incompatible with liberty, wherefore no *ex post facto* law ought to be made. No law taxing retrospectively, sales, purchases, or other acts previously done, ought to be passed. Expost factal laws.

SEC. 33. Slavery and involuntary servitude, otherwise than for crime whereof the parties shall have been duly convicted, shall be, and are hereby forever prohibited within this State Slavery prohibited.

SEC. 34. The limits and boundaries of the State shall be and remain as they now are. State boundaries.

SEC. 35. All courts shall be open, and every person for an injury done him in his lands, goods, person, or reputation, shall have remedy by due course of law, and right and justice administered without sale, denial, or delay. Courts shall be open, &c.

SEC. 36. No soldier shall, in time of peace, be quartered in any house without the consent of the owner; nor in time of war, but in a manner prescribed by law. Soldiers in time of peace.

SEC. 37. This enumeration of rights shall not be construed to impair or deny others, retained by the people; and all powers, not herein delegated, remain with the people. Other rights of the people.

## ARTICLE II.

### LEGISLATIVE DEPARTMENT.

SECTION 1. The Legislative authority shall be vested in two distinct branches, both dependent on the people, to wit: a Senate and House of Representatives. Two branches.

SEC. 2. The Senate and House of Representatives shall meet annually on the third Monday in November, and when assembled, shall be denominated the General Assembly. Time of assembling.

Neither House shall proceed upon public business, unless a majority of all the members are actually present.

Number of Senators.

SEC. 3. The Senate shall be composed of fifty Senators biennially chosen by ballot.

Senatorial districts.

SEC. 4. Until the first session of the General Assembly which shall be had after the year eighteen hundred and seventy-one, the Senate shall be composed of members elected from districts constituted as follows:

1st District—Perquimans, Chowan, Pasquotank, Currituck, Gates and Camden, shall elect two Senators.

2d District—Martin, Washington and Tyrrell, shall elect one Senator.

3d District—Beaufort and Hyde, shall elect one Senator.

4th District—Northampton, shall elect one Senator.

5th District—Bertie and Hertford, shall elect one Senator.

6th District—Halifax, shall elect one Senator.

7th District—Edgecombe shall elect one Senator.

8th District—Pitt, shall elect one Senator.

9th District—Nash and Wilson, shall elect one Senator.

10th District—Craven and Carteret, shall elect two Senators.

11th District—Jones and Lenoir, shall elect one Senator.

12th District—Duplin and Onslow, shall elect one Senator.

13th District—Brunswick and New Hanover, shall elect two Senators.

14th District—Bladen and Columbus, shall elect one Senator.

15th District—Robeson, shall elect one Senator.

16th District—Cumberland, Harnett and Sampson, shall elect two Senators.

17th District—Johnston, shall elect one Senator.

18th District—Greene and Wayne, shall elect one Senator.

19th District—Franklin and Wake, shall elect two Senators.

20th District—Warren, shall elect one Senator.

21st District—Granville and Person, shall elect two Senators.

22d District—Orange, shall elect one Senator.

23d District—Chatham, shall elect one Senator. Senatorial districts.

24th District—Caswell, shall elect one Senator.

25th District—Rockingham, shall elect one Senator.

26th District—Alamance and Guilford, shall elect two Senators.

27th District—Randolph and Montgomery, shall elect one Senator.

28th District—Moore and Richmond, shall elect one Senator.

29th District—Anson and Union, shall elect one Senator.

30th District—Mecklenburg, shall elect one Senator.

31st District—Cabarrus and Stanly, shall elect one Senator.

32d District—Davie and Rowan, shall elect one Senator.

33d District—Davidson, shall elect one Senator.

34th District—Forsythe and Stokes, shall elect one Senator.

35th District—Surry and Yadkin, shall elect one Senator.

36th District—Alexander and Iredell, shall elect one Senator.

37th District—Catawba, Gaston and Lincoln, shall elect one Senator.

38th District—Cleveland, Polk and Rutherford, shall elect one Senator.

39th District—Alleghany, Ashe and Wilkes, shall elect one Senator.

40th District—Buncombe, Henderson and Transylvania, shall elect one Senator.

41st District—Burke, Caldwell and Watauga, shall elect one Senator.

42d District—Madison, Mitchel, McDowell and Yancey, shall elect one Senator.

43d District—Clay, Cherokee, Haywood, Jackson and Macon, shall elect one Senator.

Regulations in relation to districting the State for Senators.

SEC. 5. An enumeration of the inhabitants of the State shall be taken under the direction of the General Assembly in the year one thousand eight hundred and seventy-five, and at the end of every ten years thereafter; and the said

Senate districts shall be so altered by the General Assembly, at the first session after the return of every enumeration taken as aforesaid, or by order of Congress, that each Senate district shall contain, as nearly as may be, an equal number of inhabitants, excluding aliens and Indians not taxed, and shall remain unaltered until the return of another enumeration, and shall at all times consist of contiguous territory; and no county shall be divided in the formation of a Senate district, unless such county shall be equitably entitled to two or more Senators.

Regulations in relation to apportionment of Representatives

SEC. 6. The House of Representatives shall be composed of one hundred and twenty Representatives, biennially chosen by ballot, to be elected by the counties respectively, according to their population, and each county shall have at least one Representative in the House of Representatives, although it may not contain the requisite ratio of representation; this apportionment shall be made by the General Assembly at the respective times and periods when the districts for the Senate are hereinbefore directed to be laid off.

Ratio of Representation.

SEC. 7. In making the apportionment in the House of Representatives, the ratio of representation shall be ascertained by dividing the amount of the population of the State, exclusive of that comprehended within those counties which do not severally contain the one hundred and twentieth part of the population of the State, by the number of Representatives, less the number assigned to such counties; and in ascertaining the number of the population of the State, aliens and Indians not taxed, shall not be included. To each county containing the said ratio and not twice the said ratio, there shall be assigned one representative; to each county containing twice but not three times the said ratio, there shall be assigned two representatives, and so on progressively, and then the remaining representatives shall be assigned severally to the counties having the largest fractions.

Apportionment of Representatives.

SEC. 8. Until the General Assembly shall have made the apportionment as hereinbefore provided, the House of Representatives shall be composed of members elected from the counties in the following manner, to-wit:

The county of Wake shall elect four members; the counties of Craven, Granville, Halifax and New Hanover shall elect three members each; the counties of Caswell, Chatham, Cumberland, Davidson, Duplin, Edgecombe, Franklin, Guilford, Iredell, Johnston, Mecklenburg, Northampton, Orange, Pitt, Randolph, Robeson, Rockingham, Rowan, Warren, and Wayne shall elect two members each; the counties of Alamance, Alexander, Alleghany, Anson, Ashe, Beaufort, Bertie, Bladen, Brunswick, Buncombe, Burke, Cabarrus, Caldwell, Camden, Carteret, Catawba, Cherokee, Chowan, Clay, Cleveland, Columbus, Currituck, Davie, Forsyth, Gaston, Gates, Greene, Harnett, Henderson, Haywood, Hertford, Hyde, Jackson, Jones, Lenoir, Lincoln, Macon, Madison, Martin, McDowell, Mitchell, Montgomery, Moore, Nash, Onslow, Pasquotank, Perquimans, Person, Polk, Richmond, Rutherford, Sampson, Stanly, Stokes, Surry, Transylvania, Tyrrell, Union, Washington, Watauga, Wilkes, Wilson, Yadkin and Yancey shall elect one member each.

SEC. 9 Each member of the Senate shall be not less than twenty-five years of age, shall have resided in the State as a citizen two years, and shall have usually resided in the district for which he is chosen, one year immediately preceding his election. Qualifications for Senators.

SEC. 10. Each member of the House of Representatives shall be a qualified elector of the State, and shall have resided in the county for which he is chosen, for one year immediately preceding his election. Qualifications for Representatives.

SEC. 11. In the election of all officers, whose appointment shall be conferred upon the General Assembly by the Constitution, the vote shall be *viva voce*. Election of officers.

SEC. 12. The General Assembly shall have power to pass general laws regulating divorce and alimony, but shall not have power to grant a divorce or secure alimony in any individual case. Powers in relation to divorce and alimony.

SEC. 13. The General Assembly shall not have power to pass any private law to alter the name of any person, Private laws in relation to names of persons, &c.

or to legitimate any person not born in lawful wedlock, or to restore to the rights of citizenship any person convicted of an infamous crime, but shall have power to pass general laws regulating the same.

Thirty days notice shall be given anterior to passage of private laws.

SEC. 14. The General Assembly shall not pass any private law, unless it shall be made to appear, that thirty days notice of application to pass such law shall have been given, under such direction, and in such manner as shall be provided by law.

Vacancies.

SEC. 15. If vacancies shall occur in the General Assembly by death, resignation or otherwise, writs of election shall be issued by the Governor under such regulations as may be prescribed by law.

Revenue.

SEC. 16. No law shall be passed to raise money on the credit of the State, or to pledge the faith of the State directly or indirectly for the payment of any debt, or to impose any tax upon the people of the State, or to allow the counties, cities or towns to do so, unless the bill for the purpose shall have been read three several times in each house of the General Assembly, and passed three several readings, which readings shall have been on three different days, and agreed to by each House respectively, and unless the yeas and nays on the second and third readings of the bill shall have been entered on the Journal.

Entails.

SEC. 17. The General Assembly shall regulate entails in such manner as to prevent perpetuities.

Journals.

SEC. 18. Each House shall keep a journal of its proceedings, which shall be printed and made public immediately after the adjournment of the General Assembly.

Protest.

SEC. 19. Any member of either House may dissent from, and protest against, any act or resolve, which he may think injurious to the public, or any individual, and have the reasons of his dissent entered on the Journal.

Officers of the House.

SEC. 20. The House of Representatives shall choose their own Speaker and other officers.

President of the Senate.

SEC. 21. The Lieutenant-Governor shall preside in the Senate, but shall have no vote, unless it may be equally divided.

SEC. 22. The Senate shall choose its other officers and also a Speaker (*pro tempore*) in the absence of the Lieutenant Governor, or when he shall exercise the office of Governor. Other Senatorial officers.

SEC. 23. The style of the acts shall be, "The General Assembly of North-Carolina do enact." Style of the acts.

SEC. 24. Each House shall be judge of the qualifications and elections of its own members, shall sit upon its own adjournment from day to day, prepare bills to be passed into laws, and the two Houses may also jointly adjourn to any future day, or other place. Powers of the General Assembly.

SEC. 25. All bills and resolutions of a legislative nature, shall be read three times in each House, before they pass into laws; and shall be signed by the presiding officers of both Houses. Bills and resolutions tobe read three times, &c.

SEC. 26. Each member of the General Assembly, before taking his seat, shall take an oath or affirmation that he will support the Constitution and laws of the United States, and the Constitution of the State of North-Carolina, and will faithfully discharge his duty as a member of the Senate or House of Representatives. Oath for members.

SEC. 27. The terms of office for Senators and members of the House of Representatives shall commence at the time of their election; and the term of office of those elected at the first election held under this Constitution shall terminate at the same time as if they had been elected, at the first ensuing regular election. Terms of office.

SEC. 28. Upon motion made and seconded in either House, by one-fifth of the members present, the yeas and nays upon any question shall be taken and entered upon the journals. Yeas and nays.

SEC. 29. The election for members of the General Assembly shall be held for the respective districts, and counties, at the places where they are now held, or may be directed hereafter to be held, in such manner as may be prescribed by law, on the first Thursday in August, in the year one thousand eight hundred and seventy, and every two years thereafter. But the General Assembly may change the time of holding the elections. The first election shall be Election for members of the General Assembly.

held when the vote shall be taken on the ratification of this Constitution by the voters of the State, and the General Assembly then elected, shall meet on the fifteenth day after the approval thereof by the Congress of the United States, if it fall not on Sunday, but if it shall so fall, then on the next day thereafter; and the members then elected shall hold their seats until their successors are elected at a regular election.

---

## ARTICLE III.

### EXECUTIVE DEPARTMENT.

Officers of the Executive Department.

SECTION 1. The Executive Department shall consist of a Governor, (in whom shall be vested the Supreme executive power of the State) a Lieutenant-Governor, a Secretary of State, an Auditor, a Treasurer, a Superintendent of Public Works, a Superintendent of Public Instruction, and an Attorney General, who shall be elected for a term of four years, by the qualified electors of the State, at the same time and places, and in the same manner as members of the General Assembly are elected. Their term of office shall commence on the first day of January next, after their election, and continue until their successors are elected and qualified: *Provided*, That the officers first elected shall assume the duties of their office ten days after the approval of this Constitution by the Congress of the United States, and shall hold their offices four years from and after the first day of January, 1869.

Term of office.

Qualifications of Governor and Lieutenant-Governor.

SEC. 2. No person shall be eligible as Governor or Lieutenant-Governor, unless he shall have attained the age of thirty years, shall have been a citizen of the United States five years, and shall have been a resident of this State for two years next before the election; nor shall the person elected to either of these two offices be eligible to the same office more than four years in any term of eight years unless the office shall have been cast upon him as Lieutenant-Governor or President of the Senate.

Returns of elections.

SEC. 3. The return of every election for officers of the Executive Department shall be sealed up and transmitted to the seat of Government by the returning officers, directed to the Speaker of the House of Representatives, who shall open and publish the same in the presence of a majority of the members of both Houses of the General Assembly. The persons having the highest number of votes respectively, shall be declared duly elected; but if two or more be equal and highest in votes for the same office, then one of them shall be chosen by joint-ballot of both Houses of the General Assembly. Contested elections shall be determined by a joint vote of both Houses of the General Assembly, in such manner as shall be prescribed by law.

Oath of office for Governor.

SEC. 4. The Governor, before entering upon the duties of his office, shall, in the presence of the members of both branches of the General Assembly, or before any Justice of the Supreme Court, take an oath or affirmation, that he will support the Constitution and laws of the United States and of the State of North-Carolina, and that he will faithfully perform the duties appertaining to the office of Governor to which he has been elected.

Duties of the Governor.

SEC. 5. The Governor shall reside at the seat of government of this State, and he shall, from time to time, give the General Assembly information of the affairs of the State, and recommend to their consideration such measures as he shall deem expedient.

Reprieves, commutations and pardons.

SEC. 6. The Governor shall have power to grant reprieves, commutations and pardons, after conviction, for all offences, (except in cases of impeachment,) upon such conditions as he may think proper, subject to such regulations as may be provided by law relative to the manner of applying for pardons. He shall annually communicate to the General Assembly each case of reprieve, commutation, or pardon granted; stating the name of each convict, the crime for which he was convicted, the sentence and its date, the date of commutation, pardon, or reprieve, and the reasons therefor.

Annual reports from officers of Executive Department and of Public Institutions.

SEC. 7. The officers of the Executive Department and of the Public Institutions of the State, shall at least five days previous to each regular session of the General Assembly severally report to the Governor, who shall transmit such reports, with his message, to the General Assembly; and the Governor may, at any time, require information in writing from the officers in the Executive Department upon any subject relating to the duties of their respective offices, and shall take care that the laws be faithfully executed.

Commander-in-chief.

SEC. 8. The Governor shall be Commander-in-Chief of the militia of the State, except when they shall be called into the service of the United States.

Extra Sessions of General Assembly.

SEC. 9. The Governor shall have power, on extraordinary occasions, by and with the advice of the Council of State, to convene the General Assembly in extra session by his proclamation, stating therein the purpose or purposes for which they are thus convened.

Officers whose appointments are not otherwise provided for.

SEC. 10. The Governor shall nominate, and, by and with the advice and consent of a majority of the Senators elect, appoint, all officers whose offices are established by this Constitution, or which shall be created by law, and whose appointments are not otherwise provided for, and no such officer shall be appointed or elected by the General Assembly.

Duties of the Lieutenant-Governor.

SEC. 11. The Lieutenant-Governor shall be President of the Senate, but shall have no vote unless the Senate be equally divided. He shall, whilst acting as President of the Senate, receive for his services the same pay which shall, for the same period, be allowed to the Speaker of the House of Representatives; and he shall receive no other compensation except when he is acting as Governor.

In case of impeachment of Governor, or vacancy caused by death or resignation.

SEC. 12. In case of the impeachment of the Governor, his failure to qualify, his absence from the State, his inability to discharge the duties of his office, or in case the office of Governor shall in anywise become vacant, the powers, duties and emoluments of the office shall devolve upon the Lieutenant-Governor until the disabilities shall cease, or a new Governor shall be elected and qualified. In every case in which the Lieutenant-Governor shall be unable to preside over the Senate, the Senators shall elect one of their own number President of their body; and the powers, duties and emoluments of the office of Governor shall devolve upon him whenever the Lieutenant-Governor shall, for any reason, be prevented from discharging the duties of such office as above provided, and he shall continue as acting Governor until the disabilities be removed or a new Governor or Lieutenant-Governor shall be elected and qualified. Whenever, during the recess of theGeneral Assembly, it shall become necessary for a President of the Senate to administer the government, the Secretary of State shall convene the Senate, that they may elect such President.

SEC. 13. The respective duties of the Secretary of State, Auditor, Treasurer, Superintendent of Public Works, Superintendent of Public Instruction, and Attorney General shall be prescribed by law. If the office of any of said officers shall be vacated by death, resignation, or otherwise, it shall be the duty of the Governor to appoint another until the disability be removed or his successor be elected and qualified. Every such vacancy shall be filled by election, at the first general election that occurs more than thirty days after the vacancy has taken place, and the person chosen shall hold the office for the remainder of the unexpired term fixed in the first section of this Article. Duties of other Executive officers.

SEC. 14. The Secretary of State, Auditor, Treasurer, Superintendent of Public Works, and Superintendent of Public Instruction, shall constitute *ex officio*, the Council of State, who shall advise the Governor in the execution of his office, and three of whom shall constitute a quorum: their advice and proceedings in this capacity shall be entered in a Journal, to be kept for this purpose exclusively, and signed by the members present, from any part of which any member may enter his dissent; and such Journal shall be placed Council of State.

2

before the General Assembly when called for by either House. The Attorney General shall be, *ex officio*, the legal adviser of the Executive Department.

Compensation of Executive officers.

SEC. 15. The officers mentioned in this Article shall, at stated periods, receive for their services a compensation to be established by law, which shall neither be increased nor diminished during the time for which they shall have been elected, and the said officers shall receive no other emolument or allowance whatever.

Seal of State.

SEC. 16. There shall be a seal of the State, which shall be kept by the Governor, and used by him, as occasion may require, and shall be called "the Great Seal of the State of North Carolina." All grants and commissions shall be issued in the name and by the authority of the State of North-Carolina, sealed with "the Great Seal of the State," signed by the Governor and countersigned by the Secretary of State.

Bureau of Statistics, Agriculture, and Immigration.

SEC. 17. There shall be established in the office of Secretary of State, a Bureau of Statistics, Agriculture and Immigration, under such regulations as the General Assembly may provide.

## ARTICLE IV.

### JUDICIAL DEPARTMENT.

Abolishes the distinction between actions at law and suits in equity.

SECTION 1. The distinction between actions at law and suits in equity, and the forms of all such actions and suits shall be abolished, and there shall be in this State but one form of action, for the enforcement or protection of private rights or the redress of private wrongs, which shall be denominated a civil action; and every action prosecuted by the people of the State as a party, against a person charged with a public offence, for the punishment of the same, shall be termed a criminal action. Feigned issues shall also be abolished, and the fact at issue tried by order of Court before a jury.

Feigned issues abolished.

Apportionment and duties of three Commissioners.

SEC. 2. Three Commissioners shall be appointed by this Convention to report to the General Assembly at its first session after this Constitution shall be adopted by the people, rules of practice and procedure in accordance with the provisions of the foregoing section, and the Convention shall provide for the commissioners a reasonable compensation.

Code of law.

SEC. 3. The same Commissioners shall also report to the General Assembly as soon as practicable, a code of the law of North-Carolina. The Governor shall have power to fill all vacancies occurring in this Commission.

Division of Judicial powers.

SEC. 4. The Judicial power of the State shall be veestd in a Court for the trial of Impeachments, a Supreme Court, Superior Courts, Courts of Justices of the Peace, and Special Courts.

Trial court of impeachment.

SEC. 5. The Court for the trial of Impeachments shall be the Senate. A majority of the members shall be necessary to a quorum, and the judgment shall not extend beyond removal from, and disqualification to hold office in this State; but the party shall be liable to indictment and punishment according to law.

Impeachment.

SEC. 6. The House of Representatives solely, shall have the power of impeaching. No person shall be convicted without the concurrence of two-thirds of the Senators present. When the Governor is impeached the Chief Justice shall preside.

Treason against the State.

SEC. 7. Treason against the State shall consist only in levying war against it or adhering to its enemies, giving them aid and comfort. No person shall be convicted of treason unless on the testimony of two witnesses to the same overt act, or on confession in open court. No conviction of treason or attainder shall work corruption of blood or forfeiture.

Five Supreme Court Justices.

SEC. 8. The Supreme Court shall consist of a Chief Justice and four Associate Justices.

Terms of Supreme Court.

SEC. 9. There shall be two terms of the Supreme Court held at the seat of Government of the State in each year, commencing on the first Monday in January, and first Monday in June, and continuing as long as the public interests may require.

Jurisdiction of Supreme Court.

SEC. 10. The Supreme Court shall have jurisdiction to review, upon appeal, any decision of the courts below, upon any matter of law or legal inference; but no issue of fact shall be tried before this court: and the court shall have power to issue any remedial writs necessary to give it a general supervision and control of the inferior courts.

Claims against the State.

SEC. 11. The Supreme Court shall have original jurisdiction to hear claims against the State, but its decisions shall be merely recommendatory: no process in the nature of execution shall issue thereon; they shall be reported to the next session of the General Assembly for its action.

Twelve Judicial Districts for Superior Courts.

SEC. 12. The State shall be divided into twelve judicial districts, for each of which a Judge shall be chosen, who shall hold a Superior Court in each county in said District, at least twice in each year, to continue for two weeks, unless the business shall be sooner disposed of.

Apportionment of said districts.

SEC. 13. Until altered by law, the following shall be the Judicial Districts:

FIRST DISTRICT.

| | | |
|---|---|---|
| Currituck, | Camden, | Pasquotank, |
| Perquimans, | Chowan, | Gates, |
| Hertford, | Bertie. | |

SECOND DISTRICT.

| | | |
|---|---|---|
| Tyrrell, | Hyde, | Washington, |
| Beaufort, | Martin, | Pitt, |
| Edgecombe. | | |

THIRD DISTRICT.

| | | |
|---|---|---|
| Craven, | Carteret, | Jones, |
| Greene, | Onslow, | Lenoir, |
| Wayne, | Wilson. | |

FOURTH DISTRICT.

| | | |
|---|---|---|
| Brunswick, | New Hanover, | Duplin, |
| Columbus, | Bladen, | Sampson, |
| Robeson. | | |

FIFTH DISTRICT.

Judicial districts.

| | | |
|---|---|---|
| Cumberland, | Harnett, | Moore, |
| Richmond, | Anson, | Montgomery, |
| Stanly, | Union. | |

SIXTH DISTRICT.

| | | |
|---|---|---|
| Northampton, | Warren, | Halifax, |
| Wake, | Nash, | Franklin, |
| Johnston, | Granville. | |

SEVENTH DISTRICT.

| | | |
|---|---|---|
| Person, | Orange, | Chatham, |
| Randolph, | Guilford, | Alamance, |
| Caswell, | Rockingham. | |

EIGHTH DISTRICT.

| | | |
|---|---|---|
| Stokes, | Forsyth, | Davidson, |
| Rowan, | Davie, | Yadkin, |
| Surry. | | |

NINTH DISTRICT.

| | | |
|---|---|---|
| Catawba, | Cabarrus, | Mecklenburg, |
| Lincoln, | Gaston, | Cleveland, |
| Rutherford, | Polk. | |

TENTH DISTRICT.

| | | |
|---|---|---|
| Iredell, | Wilkes, | Burke, |
| Alexander, | Caldwell, | McDowell. |

ELEVENTH DISTRICT.

| | | |
|---|---|---|
| Alleghany, | Ashe, | Watauga, |
| Mitchell, | Yancey, | Madison, |
| Buncombe. | | |

TWELFTH DISTRICT.

| | | |
|---|---|---|
| Henderson, | Transylvania, | Haywood, |
| Macon, | Jackson, | Clay, |
| Cherokee. | | |

Residences of Judges, and special terms of courts.

SEC. 14. Every Judge of a Superior Court shall reside in his District while holding his office. The Judges may exchange districts with each other with the consent of the Governor, and the Governor, for good reasons, which he shall report to the Legislature at its current or next session, may require any Judge to hold one or more specified terms of said Courts in lieu of the Judge in whose district they are.

Original jurisdiction of the Superior Courts.

SEC. 15. The Superior Courts shall have exclusive original jurisdiction of all civil actions, whereof exclusive original jurisdiction is not given to some other Courts; and of all criminal actions in which the punishment may exceed a fine of fifty dollars or imprisonment for one month.

Appellate jurisdiction.

SEC. 16. The Superior Courts shall have appellate jurisdiction of all issues of law or fact, determined by a Probate Judge or a Justice of the Peace, where the matter in controversy exceeds twenty-five dollars, and of matters of law in all cases.

Jurisdiction of Superior Court Clerks.

SEC. 17. The Clerks of the Superior Courts shall have jurisdiction of the probate of deeds, the granting of letters testamentary and of administration, the appointment of guardians, the apprenticing of orphans, to audit the accounts of executors, administrators and guardians, and of such other matters as shall be prescribed by law. All issues of fact joined before them shall be transferred to the Superior Courts for trial, and appeals shall lie to the Superior Courts from their judgments in all matters of law.

Right of appeal.

In case of waiver of trial by jury.

SEC. 18. In all issues of fact, joined in any court, the parties may waive the right to have the same determined by jury, in which case the finding of the Judge upon the facts, shall have the force and effect of a verdict of a jury.

SEC. 19. The General Assembly shall provide for the establishment of Special Courts, for the trial of misdemeanors, in cities and towns, where the same may be necessary. Special courts in cities.

SEC. 20. The Clerk of the Supreme Court shall be appointed by the Court, and shall hold his office for eight years. Clerk of Supreme Court.

SEC. 21. A Clerk of the Superior Court for each county, shall be elected by the qualified voters thereof, at the time and in the manner prescribed by law for the election of members of the General Assembly. Election of Superior Court Clerk.

SEC. 22. Clerks of the Superior Courts shall hold their offices for four years. Term of office.

SEC. 23. The General Assembly shall prescribe and regulate the fees, salaries, and emoluments of all officers provided for in this Article; but the salaries of the Judges shall not be diminished during their continuance in office. Fees, salaries and emoluments

SEC. 24. The laws of North-Carolina, not repugnant to this Constitution, or to the Constitution and laws of the United States, shall be in force until lawfully altered. What laws are and shall be in force.

SEC. 25. Actions at law, and suits in equity, pending when this Constitution shall go into effect, shall be transferred to the Courts having jurisdiction thereof, without prejudice by reason of the change, and all such actions and suits, commenced before, and pending at, the adoption by the General Assembly, of the rules of practice and procedure herein provided for, shall be heard and determined, according to the practice now in use, unless otherwise provided for by said rules. Disposition of actions at law and suits in equity pending when this Constitution shall go into effect, &c.

SEC. 26. The Justices of the Supreme Court shall be elected by the qualified voters of the State, as is provided for the election of members of the General Assembly. They shall hold their offices for eight years. The Judges of the Superior Courts shall be elected in like manner, and shall hold their offices for eight years; but the Judges of the Superior Courts elected at the first election under this Constitution, shall, after their election, under the superintendence of the Justices of the Supreme Court, be divided by Election, terms of office, &c., of Supreme and Superior Court Judges.

lot into two equal classes, one of which shall hold office for four years, the other for eight years.

Provision in relation to election of Superior Court Judges.

SEC. 27. The General Assembly may provide by law that the Judges of the Superior Courts, instead of being elected by the voters of the whole State, as is herein provided for, shall be elected by the voters of their respective districts.

Transaction of business in the Superior Courts.

SEC. 28. The Superior Courts shall be, at all times, open for the transaction of all business within their jurisdiction, except the trial of issues of fact requiring a jury.

Solicitors for each Judicial District.

SEC. 29. A Solicitor shall be elected for each judicial district by the qualified voters thereof, as is prescribed for members of the General Assembly, who shall hold office for the term of four years, and prosecute on behalf of the State, in all criminal actions in the Superior Courts, and advise the officers of justice in his district.

Sheriffs and Coroners.

SEC. 30. In each county a Sheriff and Coroner shall be elected by the qualified voters thereof, as is prescribed for members of the General Assembly, and shall hold their offices for two years. In each township there shall be a Constable, elected in like manner by the voters thereof, who shall hold his office for two years. When there is no Coroner in the county, the Clerk of the Superior Court for the county may appoint one for special cases. In case of a vacancy existing for any cause, in any of the offices created by this section, the Commissioners for the county may appoint to such office for the unexpired term.

Vacancies.

SEC. 31. All vacancies occurring in the offices provided for by this article of this Constitution, shall be filled by the appointment of the Governor, unless otherwise provided for, and the appointees shall hold their places until the next regular election.

Terms of office of first officers under this Article.

SEC. 32. The officers elected at the first election held under this Constitution, shall hold their offices for the terms prescribed for them respectively, next ensuing after the next regular election for members of the General Assembly. But their terms shall begin upon the approval of this Constitution by the Congress of the United States.

SEC. 33. The several Justices of the Peace shall have exclusive original jurisdiction under such regulations as the General Assembly shall prescribe, of all civil actions, founded on contract, wherein the sum demanded shall not exceed two hundred dollars, and wherein the title to real estate shall not be in controversy; and of all criminal matters arising within their counties, where the punishment cannot exceed a fine of fifty dollars, or imprisonment for one month. When an issue of fact shall be joined before a Justice, on demand of either party thereto, he shall cause a jury of six men to be summoned, who shall try the same. The party against whom judgment shall be rendered in any civil action, may appeal to the Superior Court from the same, and, if the judgment shall exceed twenty-five dollars, there may be a new trial of the whole matter in the appellate court; but if the judgment shall be for twenty-five dollars or less, then the case shall be heard in the appellate court, only upon matters of law. In all cases of a criminal nature, the party against whom judgment is given may appeal to the Superior Court, where the matter shall be heard anew. In all cases brought before a Justice, he shall make a record of the proceedings, and file the same with the Clerk of the Superior Court for his county. Jurisdiction of Justices of the Peace.

SEC. 34. When the office of Justice of the Peace shall become vacant, otherwise than by expiration of the term, and in case of a failure by the voters of any district to elect, the Clerk of the Superior Court for the County shall appoint to fill the vacancy for the unexpired term. Vacancies in office of Justices

SEC. 35. In case the office of Clerk of a Superior Court for a County shall become vacant, otherwise than by the expiration of the term, and in case of a failure by the people to elect, the Judge of the Superior Court for the County shall appoint to fill the vacancy until an election can be regularly held. Vacancies in office of Superior Court Clerk.

## ARTICLE V.

### REVENUE AND TAXATION.

Capitation tax. SECTION 1. The General Assembly shall levy a capitation tax on every male inhabitant of the State over twenty-one and under fifty years of age, which shall be equal on each, to the tax on property valued at three hundred dollars in cash. Exemptions. The Commissioners of the several counties may exempt from capitation tax in special cases, on account of poverty and infirmity, and the State and county capitation tax combined, shall never exceed two dollars on the head.

Application of proceeds of State and County capitation tax. SEC. 2. The proceeds of the State and County capitation tax shall be applied to the purposes of education and the support of the poor, but in no one year shall more than twenty-five per cent. thereof be appropriated to the latter purpose.

Taxation shall be by uniform rule and ad valorem. SEC. 3. Laws shall be passed taxing, by a uniform rule, all moneys, credits, investments in bonds, stocks, joint-stock companies or otherwise; and, also, all real and personal property, according to its true value in money. The General Assembly may also tax trades, professions, franchises, and incomes, provided that no income shall be taxed when the property from which the income is derived, is taxed.

Payment of interest on public debt. SEC. 4. The General Assembly shall, by appropriate legislation and by adequate taxation, provide for the prompt and regular payment of the interest on the public debt, and after the year 1880, it shall lay a specific annual tax upon the real and personal property of the State, and the sum thus realized shall be set apart as a sinking fund, to be devoted to the payment of the public debt.

Restriction upon the increase of the public debt, except in certain contingencies. SEC. 5. Until the bonds of the State shall be at par, the General Assembly shall have no power to contract any new debt or pecuniary obligation in behalf the State, except to supply a casual deficit, or for suppressing invasion or insurrection, unless it shall in the same bill levy a special tax to pay the interest annually. And the General Assembly shall have no power to give or lend the credit of the State in aid of any person, association or corporation, except to aid in the completion of such Rail Roads as may be unfinished at the time of the adoption of this Constitution, or in which the State has a direct pecuniary interest, unless the subject be submitted to a direct vote of the people of the State, and be approved by a majority of those who shall vote thereon.

Property exemptions from taxation.

SEC. 6. Property belonging to the State, or to municipal corporations, shall be exempt from taxation. The General Assembly may exempt cemetaries, and property held for educational, scientific, literary, charitable, or religious purposes; also, wearing apparel, arms for muster, household and kitchen furniture, the mechanical and agricultural implements of mechanics and farmers, libraries and scientific instruments, to a value not exceeding three hundred dollars.

Taxes levied by County Commissioners.

SEC. 7. The taxes levied by the commissioners of the several counties, for county purposes, shall be levied in like manner with the State taxes, and shall never exceed the double of the State tax, except for a special purpose, and with the special approval of the General Assembly.

Acts levying taxes shall state object, &c.

SEC. 8. Every act of the General Assembly, levying a tax, shall state the special object to which it is to be applied, and it shall be applied to no other purpose.

---

## ARTICLE VI.

### SUFFRAGE AND ELIGIBILITY TO OFFICE.

Qualification of an elector.

SECTION 1. Every male person born in the United States, and every male person who has been naturalized, twenty-one years old or upward, who shall have resided in this State twelve months next preceding the election, and thirty days in the county in which he offers to vote, shall be deemed an elector.

Registration of electors.

SEC. 2. It shall be the duty of the General Assembly to provide from time to time, for the registration of all electors, and no person shall be allowed to vote without registration, or to register, without first taking an oath or affirmation to support and maintain the Constitution and laws of the United States, and the Constitution and laws of North-Carolina, not inconsistent therewith.

Elections by people and Gen. Assembly.

SEC. 3. All elections by the people shall be by ballot, and all elections by the General Assembly shall be *viva voce*.

Oath of office.

SEC. 4. Every voter, except as hereinafter provided, shall be eligible to office; but before entering upon the discharge of the duties of his office, he shall take and subscribe the following oath: "I, ——, do solemnly swear (or affirm) that I will support and maintain the Constitution and laws of the United States, and the Constitution and laws of North-Carolina not inconsistent therewith, and that I will faithfully discharge the duties of my office. So help me God."

Disqualifications for office.

SEC. 5. The following classes of persons shall be disqualified for office: First, All persons who shall deny the being of Almighty God. Second, All persons who shall have been convicted of treason, perjury, or of any other infamous crime, since becoming citizens of the United States, or of corruption, or mal-practice in office, unless such person shall have been legally restored to the rights of citizenship.

---

## ARTICLE VII.

### MUNICIPAL CORPORATIONS.

County officers.

SECTION 1. In each county, there shall be elected, biennially, by the qualified voters thereof, as provided for the election of members of the General Assembly, the following officers: A Treasurer, Register of Deeds, Surveyor and Five Commissioners.

Duty of County Commissioners.

SEC. 2. It shall be the duty of the Commissioners to exercise a general supervision and control of the penal and charitable institutions, schools, roads, bridges, levying of taxes and finances of the county, as may be prescribed by law. The Register of Deeds shall be, *ex officio*, Clerk of the Board of Commissioners.

Counties to be divided into districts.

SEC. 3. It shall be the duty of the Commissioners first elected in each county, to divide the same into convenient districts, to determine the boundaries and prescribe the names of the said districts, and to report the same to the General Assembly before the first day of January, 1869.

Said districts shall have corporate powers as townships.

SEC. 4. Upon the approval of the reports provided for in the foregoing section, by the General Assembly, the said districts shall have corporate powers for the necessary purposes of local government, and shall be known as townships.

Officers of townships.

SEC. 5. In each township there shall be biennially elected, by the qualified voters thereof, a Clerk and two Justices of the Peace, who shall constitute a Board of Trustees, and shall, under the supervision of the County Commissioners, have control of the taxes and finances, roads and bridges of the Township as may be prescribed by law. The General Assembly may provide for the election of a larger number of Justices of the Peace in cities and towns and in those Townships in which cities and towns are situated. In every Township there shall also be biennially elected a School Committee consisting of three persons, whose duty shall be prescribed law.

Trustees shall assess property.

SEC. 6. The township Board of Trustees, shall assess the taxable property of their townships and make return to the County Commissioners, for revision, as may be prescribed by law. The Clerk shall also be *ex officio* Treasurer of the Township.

No debt or loan except by a majority of voters.

SEC. 7. No county, city, town, or other municipal corporation shall contract any debt, pledge its faith, or loan its credit, nor shall any tax be levied, or collected by any officers of the same, except for the necessary expenses thereof, unless by a vote of a majority of the qualified voters therein.

Drawing of money.

SEC. 8. No money shall be drawn from any County or Township Treasury, except by authority of law.

Taxes to be ad valorem.

SEC. 9. All taxes levied by any county, city, town, or township, shall be uniform and *ad valorem*, upon all property in the same, except property exempted by this Constitution.

When officers enter on duty.

SEC. 10. The county officers first elected under the provisions of this article shall enter upon their duties ten days after the approval of this Constitution by the Congress of the United States.

Governor to appoint Justices

SEC. 11. The Governor shall appoint a sufficient number of Justices of the Peace in each county, who shall hold their places until sections 4, 5, and 6 of this Article shall have been carried into effect.

Charters to remain in force until legally changed.

SEC. 12. All charters, ordinances and provisions relating to municipal corporations shall remain in force until legally changed, unless inconsistent with the provisions of this Constitution.

Debts in and of the rebellion not to be paid.

SEC. 13. No County, City, Town or other municipal corporation, shall assume or pay, nor shall any tax be levied, or collected, for the payment of any debt, or the interest upon any debt, contracted directly or indirectly in aid or support of the rebellion.

---

## ARTICLE VIII.

### CORPORATIONS OTHER THAN MUNICIPAL.

Corporations under general laws.

SECTION 1. Corporations may be formed under general laws, but shall not be created by special act, except for municipal purposes, and in cases where, in the judgment of the Legislature, the object of the corporations cannot be attained under general laws. All general laws and special acts passed, pursuant to this section, may be altered from time to time or repealed.

Debts of corporations, how secured.

SEC. 2. Dues from corporations shall be secured by such individual liabilities of the corporations and other means, as may be prescribed by law.

What corporations shall include.

SEC. 3. The term corporation, as used in this Article, shall be construed to include all associations and joint-stock companies, having any of the powers and privileges of corporations, not possessed by individuals or partnerships. And all corporations shall have the right to sue, and shall be subject to be sued in all courts, in like cases as natural persons.

Legislature to provide for organizing cities, towns, &c.

SEC. 4. It shall be the duty of the Legislature to provide for the organization of cities, towns and incorporated villages, and to restrict their power of taxation, assessments, borrowing money, contracting debts, and loaning their credit, so as to prevent abuses in assessments and in contracting debts by such municipal corporation.

---

## ARTICLE IX.

### EDUCATION.

Education shall be encouraged.

SECTION 1. Religion, morality, and knowledge being necessary to good government and happiness of mankind, schools and the means of education shall forever be encouraged.

General Assembly shall provide for schools.

SEC. 2. The General Assembly at its first session under this Constitution, shall provide by taxation and otherwise for a general and uniform system of Public Schools, wherein tuition shall be free of charge to all the children of the State between the ages of six and twenty-one years.

Counties to be divided into districts.

SEC. 3. Each County of the State shall be divided into a convenient number of Districts, in which one or more Public Schools shall be maintained, at least four months in every year; and if the Commissioners of any county shall fail to comply with the aforesaid requirements of this section, they shall be liable to indictment.

What property shall be devoted to educational purposes.

SEC. 4. The proceeds of all lands that have been, or hereafter may be granted by the United States to this State and not otherwise specially appropriated by the United States or heretofore by this State; also, all moneys, stocks, bonds, and other property now belonging to any fund for purposes of education; also, the net proceeds that may accrue to the State from sales of estrays, or from fines, penalties and forfeitures; also, the proceeds of all sales of the swamp lands belonging to the State; also, all money that shall be paid as an equivalent for exemption from military duty; also, all grants, gifts or devises that may hereafter be made to this State, and not otherwise appropriated by the grant, gift or devise, shall be securely invested, and sacredly preserved as an irreducible educational fund, the annual income of which, together with so much of the ordinary revenue of the State as may be necessary, shall be faithfully appropriated for establishing and perfecting in this State a system of Free Public Schools, and for no other purposes or uses whatsoever.

University and Public Schools not to be separated.

Sec. 5. The University of North-Carolina, with its lands, emoluments and franchises, is under the control of the State, and shall be held to an inseparable connection with the Free Public School system of the State.

Benefits of the University.

Sec. 6. The General Assembly shall provide that the benefits of the University, as far as practicable, be extended to the youth of the State free of expense for tuition; also, that all the property which has heretofore accrued to the State, or shall hereafter accrue from escheats, unclaimed dividends, or distributive shares of the estates of deceased persons, shall be appropriated to the use of the University.

Board of Education.

Sec. 7. The Governor, Lieutenant-Governor, Secretary of State, Treasurer, Auditor, Superintendent of Public Works, Superintendent of Public Instruction and Attorney General, shall constitute a State Board of Education.

President and Secretary.

Sec. 8. The Governor shall be President, and the Superintendent of Public Instruction shall be Secretary of the Board of Education.

Power of Board.

Sec. 9. The Board of Education shall succeed to all the powers and trusts of the President and Directors of the Literary Fund of North-Carolina, and shall have full power to legislate and make all needful rules and regulations in relation to Free Public Schools, and the Educational Fund of the State; but all acts, rules and regulations of said Board may be altered, amended or repealed by the General Assembly, and when so altered, amended or repealed, they shall not be re-enacted by the Board.

SEC. 10. The first session of the Board of Education shall be held at the Capital of the State, within fifteen days after the organization of the State government under this Constitution; the time of future meeting may be determined by the Board. First session of Board.

SEC. 11. A majority of the Board shall constitute a quorum for the transaction of business. Quorum

SEC. 12. The contingent expenses of the Board shall be provided for by the General Assembly. Expenses

SEC. 13. The Board of Education shall elect Trustees for the University, as follows: one Trustee for each County in the State, whose term of office shall be eight years. The first meeting of the Board shall be held within ten (10) days after their election, and at this and every subsequent meeting, ten Trustees shall constitute a quorum. The Trustees, at their first meeting, shall be divided, as equally as may be, into four classes. The seats of the first class shall be vacated at the expiration of two years; of the second class, at the expiration of four years; of the third class, at the expiration of six years; of the fourth class, at the expiration of eight years; so that one-fourth may be chosen every second year. Trustees for the University.

SEC. 14. The Board of Education and the President of the University, shall be *ex officio* members of the Board of Trustees of the University; and shall, with three other Trustees, to be appointed by the Board of Trustees, constitute the Executive Committee of the Trustees of the University of North-Carolina, and shall be clothed with the powers delegated to the Executive Committee under the existing organization of the Institution. The Governor shall be *ex officio* President of the Board of Trustees and Chairman of the Executive Committee of the University. The Board of Education shall provide for the more perfect organization of the Board of Trustees. Board of Trustees.

SEC. 15. All the privileges, rights, franchises and endowments heretofore granted to, or conferred upon, the Board Privileges and rights vested in new Board.

of Trustees of the University of North-Carolina by the charter of 1789, or by any subsequent legislation, are hereby vested in the Board of Trustees, authorized by this Constitution, for the perpetual benefit of the University.

Agricultural department.

SEC. 16. As soon as practicable after the adoption of this Constitution, the General Assembly shall establish and maintain in connection with the University, a Department of Agriculture, of Mechanics, of Mining, and of Normal Instruction.

Children must attend school.

SEC. 17. The General Assembly is hereby empowered to enact that every child of sufficient mental and physical ability, shall attend the Public Schools during the period between the ages of six and eighteen years, for a term of not less than sixteen months, unless educated by other means.

## ARTICLE X.

### HOMESTEADS AND EXEMPTIONS.

Exemption.

SECTION 1. The personal property of any resident of this State, to the value of five hundred dollars, to be selected by such resident, shall be, and is hereby exempted from sale under execution, or other final process of any court, issued for the collection of any debt.

Homestead.

SEC. 2. Every Homestead, and the dwelling and buildings used therewith, not exceeding in value one thousand dollars, to be selected by the owner thereof, or in lieu thereof, at the option of the owner, any lot in a city, town or village, with the dwelling and buildings used thereon, owned and occupied by any resident of this State, and not exceeding the value of one thousand dollars, shall be exempted from sale under execution, or other final process, obtained on any debt. But no property shall be exempt from sale for taxes, or for payment of obligations contracted for the purchase of said premises.

Homestead exempted from debt.

SEC. 3. The Homestead, after the death of the owner thereof, shall be exempt from the payment of any debt, during the minority of his children, or any one of them.

SEC. 4. The provisions of section one and two of this Article shall not be so construed as to prevent a laborer's lien for work done and performed for the person claiming such exemption, or a mechanic's lien for work done on the premises. Laborer's lien.

SEC. 5. If the owner of a Homestead die, leaving a widow, but no children, the same shall be exempt from the debts of her husband, and the rents and profits thereof shall inure to her benefit during her widowhood, unless she be the owner of a Homestead in her own right. Benefit of widow.

SEC. 6. The real and personal property of any female in this State, acquired before marriage, and all property, real and personal, to which she may after marriage, become in any manner entitled, shall be and remain the sole and separate estate and property of such female, and shall not be liable for any debts, obligations or engagements of her husband, and may be devised or bequeathed, and, with the written assent of her husband, conveyed, by her as if she were unmarried. Property of a married female secured to her.

SEC. 7. The husband may insure his own life for the sole use and benefit of his wife and children, and in case of the death of the husband the amount thus insured shall be paid over to the wife and children, or the guardian, if under age, for her, or their own use, free from all the claims of the representatives of the husband, or any of his creditors. Husband may insure his life for benefit of wife and children.

SEC. 8. Nothing contained in the foregoing sections of this Article shall operate to prevent the owner of a Homestead from disposing of the same by deed; but no deed made by the owner of a Homestead shall be valid without the voluntary signature and assent of his wife, signified on her private examination according to law. How deed for homestead may be made.

## ARTICLE XI.

### PUNISHMENTS, PENAL INSTITUTIONS AND PUBLIC CHARITIES.

Punishments. SECTION. 1. The following punishments only, shall be known to the laws of this State, viz: death, imprisonment, with or without hard labor, fines, removal from office and disqualification to hold and enjoy any office of honor, trust, or profit, under this State.

Death punishment. SEC. 2. The object of punishments, being not only to satisfy justice, but also to reform the offender, and thus prevent crime, murder, arson, burglary, and rape, and these only, may be punishable with death, if the General Assembly shall so enact.

Penitentiary. SEC. 3. The General Assembly shall, at its first meeting, make provision for the erection and conduct of a States' Prison or Penitentiary at some central and accessible point within the State.

Houses of correction. SEC. 4. The General Assembly may provide for the erection of Houses of Correction, where vagrants and persons guilty of misdemeanors shall be restrained and usefully employed.

Houses of refuge. SEC. 5. A House or Houses of Refuge may be established, whenever the public interest may require it, for the correction and instruction of other classes of offenders.

The sexes to be separated. SEC. 6. It shall be required, by competent legislation, that the structure and superintendence of penal institutions of the State, the county jails, and city police prisons, secure the health and comfort of the prisoners, and that male and female prisoners be never confined in the same room or cell.

Provision for the poor and orphans. SEC. 7. Beneficent provision for the poor, the unfortunate and orphan, being one of the first duties of a civilized and a Christian State, the General Assembly shall, at its first session, appoint and define the duties of a Board of Public Charities, to whom shall be intrusted the supervision of all charitable and penal State institutions, and who shall annually report to the Governor upon their condition, with suggestions for their improvement.

SEC. 8. There shall also, as soon as practicable, be measures devised by the State for the establishment of one or more Orphan Houses, where destitute orphans may be cared for, educated and taught some business or trade. Orphan houses.

SEC. 9. It shall be the duty of the Legislature, as soon as practicable, to devise means for the education of idiots and inebriates. Inebriates and idiots.

SEC. 10. The General Assembly shall provide that all the deaf mutes, the blind, and the insane of the State, shall be cared for at the charge of the State. Deaf mutes and insane.

SEC. 11. It shall be steadily kept in view by the Legislature, and the Board of Public Charities, that all penal and charitable institutions should be made as nearly self-supporting as is consistent with the purposes of their creation. Self-supporting.

---

## ARTICLE XII.

### MILITIA.

SECTION 1. All able bodied male citizens of the State of North-Carolina, between the ages of twenty-one and forty years, who are citizens of the United States, shall be liable to duty in the Militia: *Provided*, That all persons who may be adverse to bearing arms, from religious scruples, shall be exempt therefrom. Who are liable to militia duty.

SEC. 2. The General Assembly shall provide for the organizing, arming, equipping and discipline of the Militia, and for paying the same when called into active service. Organizing, &c.

SEC. 3. The Governor shall be Commander-in-Chief, and have power to call out the Militia to execute the law, suppress riots or insurrection, and to repel invasion. Governor Commander-in-Chief

SEC. 4. The General Assembly shall have power to make such exemptions as may be deemed necessary, and to enact laws that may be expedient for the government of the Militia. Exemptions.

## ARTICLE XIII.

### AMENDMENTS.

Convention, how called.

SECTION 1. No Convention of the people shall be called by the General Assembly unless by the concurrence of two-thirds of all the members of each House of the General Assembly.

How the Constitution may be altered.

SEC. 2. No part of the Constitution of this State shall be altered, unless a bill to alter the same shall have been read three times in each House of the General Assembly and agreed to by three-fifths of the whole number of members of each House, respectively; nor shall any alteration take place until the bill, so agreed to, shall have been published six months previous to a new election of members to the General Assembly. If, after such publication, the alteration proposed by the preceding General Assembly shall be agreed to, in the first session thereafter, by two-thirds of the whole representation in each House of the General Assembly, after the same shall have been read three times on three several days in each House, then the said General Assembly shall prescribe a mode by which the amendment or amendments may be submitted to the qualified voters of the House of Representatives throughout the State; and if, upon comparing the votes given in the whole State, it shall appear that a majority of the voters voting thereon have approved thereof, then, and not otherwise, the same shall become a part of the Constitution.

---

## ARTICLE XIV.

### MISCELLANEOUS.

Indictments

SECTION 1. All indictments which shall have been found, or may hereafter be found, for any crime or offence committed before this Constitution takes effect, may be proceeded upon in the proper Courts, but no punishment shall be inflicted, which is forbidden by this Constitution.

Penalty for fighting duel.

SEC. 2. No person who shall hereafter fight a duel, or assist in the same as a second, or send, accept, or knowingly carry a challenge therefor, or agree to go out of this State to fight a duel, shall hold any office in this State.

Drawing money.

SEC. 3. No money shall be drawn from the Treasury but in consequence of appropriations made by law, and an accurate account of the receipts and expenditures of the public money shall be annually published.

Mechanic's lien.

SEC. 4. The General Assembly shall provide, by proper legislation, for giving to mechanics and laborers an adequate lien on the subject matter of their labor.

Governor to make appointments.

SEC. 5. In the absence of any contrary provision, all officers in this State, whether heretofore elected, or appointed by the Governor, shall hold their positions only until other appointments are made by the Governor, or, if the officers are elective, until their successors shall have been chosen and duly qualified, according to the provisions of this Constitution.

Seat of government.

SEC. 6. The seat of government in this State shall remain at the City of Raleigh.

Holding office.

SEC. 7. No person shall hold more than one lucrative office, under the State, at the same time: *Provided*, That officers in the Militia, Justices of the Peace, Commissioners of Public Charities and Commissioners appointed for special purposes, shall not be considered officers within the meaning of this section.

Done in Convention at Raleigh, the sixteenth day of March, in the year of our Lord, one thousand eight hundred and sixty-eight, and of the Independence of the United States the ninety-second.

(SIGNED,) CALVIN J. COWLES,
*President of the Constitutional Convention.*

T. A. BYRNES, *Secretary.*
HENRY M. RAY,
JERE. SMITH,
HENRY E. CHILSON,

Signers names.

GEORGE TUCKER,
WILLIAM STILLY, Beaufort County,
WILL: B. RODMAN, Beaufort County,
PARKER D. ROBBINS,
WILLIAM A. MANN, of Cumberland,
BRYANT LEE,
ABIAL W. FISHER,
FRED. F. FRENCH,
JOHN S. PARKS,
T. J. CANDLER, Buncombe County,
W. T. BLUME,
CALVIN C. JONES,
ABRAHAM CONGLETON,
W. T. GUNTER,
GEORGE W. DICKEY,
JOHN R. FRENCH,
DAVID HEATON,
W. H. S. SWEET,
CLINTON D. PEARSON,
ISAAC KINNEY,
S. S. MULICAN,
WILSON CAREY,
MILTON HOBBS,
SAMUEL HIGHSMITH,
J. W. PETERSON,
E. B. TEAGUE,
H. C. CHERRY,
J. T. HARRIS,
M. J. AYDLOTT,
T. D. HOFFLER, of Gates,
JOHN M. PATRICK,
JOHN H. WILLIAMSON, of Franklin,
G. WILLIAM WELKER,
A. W. TOURGEE,
W. T. J. HAYES,
HENRY EPPS,
JAMES MADISON TURNER,
W. G. B. GARRETT,

J. H. DUCKWORTH, Signers names.
ANDREW J. GLOVER,
W. H. GEORGE,
JAMES HAY, Johnston County,
NATHAN GULLY, Johnston County,
DAVID D. COLGROVE,
GEO. W. GAHAGAN,
SAMUEL WASHINGTON WATTS,
W. A. B. MURPHY,
SILAS N. STILWELL, Mecklenburg,
EDWARD FULLINGS, Mecklenburg,
GEO. A. GRAHAM, of Montgomery,
LUCIEN M. S. McDONALD,
JACOB ING,
JOSEPH C. ABBOTT, New Hanover,
SAMUEL S. ASHLEY,
A. H. GALLOWAY,
ROSWELL C. PARKER, Northampton Co.
HENRY T. GRANT,
CHARLES C. POOL, Pasquotank County,
WILLIAM NICHOLSON, Perquimans Co.
D. J. RICH, Pitt County,
BYRON LAFLIN, Pitt County,
JESSE RHODES,
REUBEN F. TROGDEN, Randolph County,
TALTON L. L. COX,
R. T. LONG,
O. S. HAYES, Robeson County,
J. L. NANCE, Robeson County,
JOHN H. FRENCH,
ALLEN ROSE, Rowan County,
WILLIAM H. LOGAN, Rutherford County,
SYLVESTER CARTER, Sampson County,
LORENZO D. HALL, Sampson County,
LEVI C. MORTON, Stanly,
RILEY F. PETREE, of Stokes,
SAM'L FORKNER, Surry County,
JOHN M. MARSHALL, Surry County,

Signers names.

E. W. JONES, Washington and Tyrrel,
WILLIAM NEWSOM, Union County,
J. P. ANDREWS, Wake County,
STOKES D. FRANKLIN, Wake County,
J. H. HARRIS, Wake County,
JOHN A. HYMAN, Warren County,
JOHN READ, Warren County,
WILLIE DANIEL, Wilson County,
JESSE HOLLOWELL, Wayne County,
H. L. GRANT,
JOHN QUINCY ADAMS BRYAN, Wilkes Co.
E. BENBOW, Yadkin,
E. LEGG, of Brunswick,
B. S. D. WILLIAMS, of Wake,
J. W. HOOD, of Cumberland,
JOHN H. RENFROW, Halifax County,
MATCHET TAYLOR, Camden,
CUFFEE MAYO.

# ORDINANCES.

## CHAPTER II.

AN ORDINANCE IN RELATION TO THE PER DIEM AND MILEAGE OF MEMBERS AND OFFICERS OF THE CONSTITUTIONAL CONVENTION OF NORTH-CAROLINA.

Per diem and mileage.

SECTION 1. *Be it ordained by the people of North-Carolina in Convention Assembled*, That the Treasurer of the State of North-Carolina, upon the warrant of the President of this Convention, is hereby authorized and directed to pay the per diem and mileage of members and officers of this Convention.

Ratified the 24th day of January, A. D. 1868.

CALVIN J. COWLES, *President.*

T. A. BYRNES, *Secretary.*

---

## CHAPTER III.

AN ORDINANCE REDUCING THE AMOUNT OF BONDS AUTHORIZED TO BE ISSUED BY THE WILMINGTON, CHARLOTTE & RUTHERFORD RAIL ROAD COMPANY.

Preamble

WHEREAS, By an act of the General Assembly of the State of North-Carolina, ratified the 20th day of December, 1866, the Wilmington, Charlotte & Rutherford Rail Road Company was authorized to place upon its road way property and franchise, a first mortgage to secure an issue of bonds, not to exceed in amount four million of dollars, which mortgage has been duly executed and recorded according to the provisions of said act; and whereas, the State holds a second mortgage upon said road for two millions of dollars, to protect which interest it is manifestly essential that the bonds to be issued under said first mortgage should be reduced in amount and their value enhanced by the endorsement of the State, so that the Company may be enabled to complete its road: therefore,

Bonds for one million to be endorsed.

SECTION 1. *Be it ordained by the people of North-Carolina in Convention assembled, and it is hereby ordained by authority of the same*, That the President of this Convention, or the Governor, or the Public Treasurer of the State, or either of them, be, and they are hereby authorized and directed, in behalf of the State, to endorse the bonds authorized as aforesaid to the amount of one million dollars, which endorsement shall be in words and figures following, to-wit: "The principal and interest of this bond is guaranteed by the State of North-Carolina by ordinance of the Convention, ratified the 5th day of February, 1868"; *Provided*, That the amount of the bonds issued by authority of the said act of the General Assembly shall not exceed in the aggregate two million five hundred thousand dollars; and the remainder of the authorized to be issued, to-wit: one million five hundred thousand dollars, shall be delivered to the President of this Convention, or to the Governor, or to the State Treasurer, and by him or them cancelled and destroyed, or that said one million five hundred thousand dollars of bonds shall be cancelled and destroyed by the Trustees of said first mortgage, and a certificate shall be printed upon each of the remaining bonds, certifying that two million five hundred thousand dollars of bonds are all that are issued, or authorized to be issued, under the deed of trust or mortgage delivered to them, and that the additional one million five hundred thousand dollars of bonds have been cancelled and destroyed, and that the said certificate shall be signed by each of the trustees; *Provided further*, That five hundred thousand dollars of the remaining two millions five hundred thousand dollars of bonds be deposited with the Treasurer of the State, as collateral security of the State, for the above named endorsement, and if the said Wilmington, Charlotte & Rutherford Rail Road Com-

Proviso.

Further proviso.

pany shall fail to pay either interest or principal of said endorsed bonds, so that the State shall become liable for the same by reason of said endorsement, and shall pay the same, then the State shall become the owner of said five hundred thousand dollars of bonds; but if the said Rail Road Company shall pay both interest and principal of said endorsed bonds, so that the State shall not become liable for the same by reason of its endorsement, then the said five hundred thousand dollars of bonds shall be the property of said Rail Road Company.

SEC. 2. *Be it further ordained*, That this ordinance shall take effect from and after its ratification.

Ratified this 5th day of February, A. D. 1868.

CALVIN J. COWLES, *President*.

T. A. BYRNES, *Secretary*.

---

## CHAPTER IV.

### AN ORDINANCE RESPECTING THE JURISDICTION OF THE COURTS OF THE STATE.

No jurisdiction on certain contracts.

SECTION 1. *Be it ordained by the people of North-Carolina in Convention assembled*, That no Court of Law or Equity of this State shall have jurisdiction of any suit or action founded on any contract made prior to the first day of May, 1865, (except actions against public officers, executors, administrators, guardians, trustees, and others acting in a fiduciary capacity, and the sureties for breach of their respective duties, by the appropriation to their own use of money or property officially received by them, or other fraudulent act,) or of any action or process to revive or enforce any judgment heretofore recovered on any such contract, whether such action be now pending or shall be commenced hereafter, and whether such process has then already issued or shall be hereafter sued for; and the Sheriffs, Coroners and Constables of this State, having in their hands any final process issued upon any judgment founded on such cause of action, are hereby commanded to stay all proceedings upon the same, and return the same to the proper courts.

Ordinance, when in force.

Sec. 2. *Be it further ordained*, That this ordinance shall be in force from and after its ratification by this Convention, and shall continue in force until the first day of July, 1868, or until the Constitution, which this Convention has met to adopt, shall go into effect, whichever shall first happen.

Ratified this 5th day of February, A. D. 1868.

CALVIN J. COWLES, *President.*

T. A. Byrnes, *Secretary.*

*Resolved*, That a copy of the foregoing ordinance be sent to Brevet Major-General Canby, Commanding Second Military District, and that he be respectfully requested to cause the same to be enforced.

---

## CHAPTER V.

### AN ORDINANCE LEVYING A TAX FOR DEFRAYING THE EXPENSES OF THIS CONVENTION.

Tax of one-twentieth levied

Section 1. *Be it ordained by the people of North-Carolina in Convention assembled*, That, for the purpose of raising monies to pay the expenses of this Convention, according to the acts of Congress in such case made and provided, a tax of one-twentieth of one per cent. shall be levied on the land in North-Carolina according to its valuation in the year 1860, subject to such changes therein as have been since made by law, and on the personal property within said State, according to the valuation thereof to be made in the year 1868.

Sec. 2. *Be it further ordained*, That this tax shall be collected, paid and accounted for at the Treasury of the State at the time when and in the same manner as other State taxes are by law required to be.

Penalty.

Sec. 3. *Be it further ordained*, That the collecting officers shall be subject to the same penalties for failure to collect, pay and account for the taxes hereby levied as they now are for such failure in respect to other taxes.

SEC. 4. *Be it further ordained*, That the said collecting officer shall receive the like compensation for the collection of the tax hereby levied as for the collection of other taxes. Compensation.

SEC. 5. *Be it further ordained*, That this ordinance shall be in force from and after its passage.

Ratified this 6th day of February, A. D. 1868.

CALVIN J. COWLES, *President*.

T. A. BYRNES, *Secretary*.

---

## CHAPTER VI.

AN ORDINANCE IN FAVOR OF WILLIAM D. JUSTUS, SHERIFF OF HENDERSON COUNTY, N. C.

SECTION 1. *Be it ordained by the people of North-Carolina in Convention assembled*, That William D. Justus, Sheriff of Henderson County, be allowed two years from the first day of January, 1868, to collect arrears of taxes due for the year 1866.

Ratified this 6th day of February, A. D. 1868.

CALVIN J. COWLES, *President*.

T. A. BYRNES, *Secretary*.

---

## CHAPTER VII.

AN ORDINANCE AMENDING SECTION SECOND OF THE ACT OF THE LEGISLATURE OF 1866–'67, ENTITLED "AN ACT TO INCORPORATE THE TOWN OF COLUMBIA, IN THE COUNTY OF TYRREL."

SECTION 1. *Be it ordained by the people of North-Carolina in Convention Assembled*, That section second of the act of the Legislature, passed 1866–'67, entitled "An Act to incorporate the town oi Columbia, in the County of Tyrrel," be Amendment.

so amended as to read: "That said town of Columbia shall be embraced within the following boundaries in the County of Tyrrell, to-wit: Beginning at the Ferry Wharf on the east side of Scuppernong river, thence running up the said river south fifty poles, thence east one hundred and twenty-five poles, north one hundred poles, thence west one hundred and twenty-five poles to the river, then by the river's edge to the beginning."

Ratified this 10th day of February, A. D. 1868.

CALVIN J. COWLES, *President.*

T. A. Byrnes, *Secretary.*

---

## CHAPTER VIII.

### AN ORDINANCE IN FAVOR OF THE SHERIFFS OF NORTH-CAROLINA.

Sheriffs allowed to Jan., 1868, to collect taxes.

Section 1. *Be it ordained by the people of North-Carolina in Convention assembled, and it is hereby ordained by authority of the same,* That the Sheriffs of this State shall be allowed one year from and after the first day of January, 1868, to collect the unpaid taxes for the years 1866–'67.

Sec. 2. *Be it further ordained,* That this ordinance shall be in force from and after its passage, and that a copy of the same be printed and transmitted to each Sheriff in the State.

Ratified this 12th day of February, A. D. 1868.

CALVIN J. COWLES, *President.*

T. A. Byrnes, *Secretary.*

---

## CHAPTER IX.

### AN ORDINANCE PROHIBITING THE DISTILLATION OF GRAIN.

Preamble.

Whereas, In consequence of the rapid reduction of the small crops of corn in this State, the prices of food have already greatly advanced, and money being unusually scarce great destitution already exists and starvation must inevitably follow speedily: therefore, in order that all the grain still on hand may be reserved for bread, and famine at least in a degree averted,

Not to distill until Nov. 1868.

SECTION 1. *Be it ordained by the people of North-Carolina in Convention assembled*, That after the passage of this act until the 1st day of November, 1868, it shall not be lawful for any person or persons to still corn, or any other grain, into intoxicating liquors.

Penalty.

SEC. 2. *Be it further ordained*, That any person or persons who shall be guilty of a violation of this ordinance, on being convicted before a competent court, shall pay a fine of fifty dollars for the first offence, one hundred dollars for the second offence, and for the third offence his distillery shall be closed by the Sheriff. In this ordinance, each day in which the distillery is in operation shall be counted a separate offence.

Fines to go to the poor.

SEC. 3. *Be it further ordained*, That all fines recovered under this ordinance (after the lawful costs are deducted) shall be paid into the Treasury of the County in which the conviction takes place for the benefit of the poor supported by said County.

Ratified this 15th day of February, A. D. 1868.

CALVIN J. COWLES, *President.*

T. A. BYRNES, *Secretary.*

---

## CHAPTER X.

### AN ORDINANCE FOR THE APPOINTMENT OF A COLLECTOR OF TAXES FOR THE CITY OF NEWBERN.

Power to appoint.

SECTION 1. *Be it ordained by the people of North-Carolina in Convention assembled, and it is hereby ordained by the authority of the same*, That the Mayor and Council of the City of Newbern shall have power to appoint a Collector of Taxes for said city.

Duty of Collector.

SEC. 2. *Be it further ordained*, That it shall be the duty of said collector of taxes to collect taxes which may be levied agreeable to law by the Mayor and Council, and in the execution of such duty such collector of taxes shall have and exercise all the power given by law to Sheriffs in the collection of State or County taxes.

Bond. SEC. 3. *Be it further ordained*, That the collector of taxes for the City of Newbern shall, before entering upon the duties of his office, enter into a bond with securities, approved by the Mayor of said City, in the sum of five thousand dollars, payable to the Mayor and Council of the City of Newbern, with conditions for the due collection, payment and settlement of the taxes imposed by the Mayor and Council of said City, and shall be entitled to a compensation, to be fixed by the Mayor and Council, not to exceed five per cent. on the amount collected. Compensation.

SEC. 4. *Be it further ordained*, That it shall be the duty of such collector of taxes to pay over to the Treasurer of the City of Newbern, weekly, all taxes collected by him.

SEC. 5. *Be it further ordained*, That all laws and clauses of laws, or ordinances or clauses of ordinances conflicting with this ordinance are hereby repealed.

SEC. 6. *Be it further ordained*, That this ordinance shall take effect from the date of its ratiffcation.

Ratified this 15th day of February, A. D. 1868.

CALVIN J. COWLES, *President*.

T. A. BYRNES, *Secretary*.

---

## CHAPTER XI.

### AN ORDINANCE TO DIVIDE NORTH-CAROLINA IN SEVEN CONGRESSIONAL DISTRICTS.

Districts. SECTION 1. *Be it ordained by the people of North-Carolina in Convention assembled, and it is hereby ordained by the authority of the same*, That, for the purpose of electing Representatives in the Congress of the United States, the State shall be divided into seven districts as follows, to-wit: the first district shall be composed of the Counties of Currituck,

Camden, Pasquotank, Perquimans, Chowan, Hertford, Gates, Northampton, Halifax, Martin, Bertie, Washington, Tyrrell, Hyde and Beaufort; the second district of the Counties of Pitt, Craven, Jones, Lenoir, Wayne, Greene, Edgecombe, Wilson, Onslow, Carteret and Duplin; the third district of the Counties of Brunswick, Columbus, Bladen, New Hanover, Cumberland, Sampson, Robeson, Richmond, Harnett, Moore, Montgomery and Anson; the fourth district of the Counties of Wake, Warren, Franklin, Granville, Orange, Nash, Johnston and Chatham; the fifth district of the Counties of Alamance, Randolph, Guilford, Rockingham, Davidson, Forsyth, Stokes, Surry, Person, Stanly and Caswell; the sixth district of the Counties of Rowan, Cabarrus, Union, Mecklenburg, Gaston, Lincoln, Catawba, Iredell, Davie, Yadkin, Wilkes and Alexander; the seventh district of the Counties of Ashe, Alleghany, Watauga, Yancey, Mitchell, McDowell, Burke, Caldwell, Rutherford, Cleaveland, Polk, Henderson, Transylvania, Buncombe, Madison, Haywood, Jackson, Macon, Cherokee and Clay, each of which districts shall be entitled to elect one representative in the Congress of the United States. Districts

Sec. 2. *Be it further ordained*, That the first election for Representatives in Congress shall be held and conducted in every respect in conformity with the orders of the Commandant of the Second Military District, and all future elections for members of Congress shall be held as the Legislature may authorize. Election.

Sec. 3. *Be it further ordained*, That the first election under the provisions of the Constitution shall be held at the time when this Constitution shall be submitted to the people for their ratification, and the members of Congress then elected shall hold their offices during the Congress then current, and until their successors are duly elected. Election.

Ratified this 20th day of February, A. D. 1868.

CALVIN J. COWLES, *President*.

T. A. Byrnes, *Secretary*.

## CHAPTER XII.

AN ORDINANCE FIXING THE STATE TAXES ON THEATRICAL COMPANIES, &C.

What tax shall be.

SECTION 1. *Be it ordained by the people of North-Carolina in Convention assembled, and it is hereby ordained by the authority of the same,* That the State tax to be collected from theatrical companies shall be five dollars per night on each exhibition, or fifty dollars for a season of three months, and on concerts three dollars per night, or thirty dollars for a season of three months.

SEC. 2. *Be it further ordained,* That all laws and clauses of laws coming in conflict with the provisions of this ordinance are repealed, and that this ordinance shall go into effect from and after its passage, subject to amendment or repeal by the Legislature.

Ratified this 28th day of February, A. D. 1868.

CALVIN J. COWLES, *President.*

T. A. BYRNES, *Secretary.*

---

## CHAPTER XIII.

AN ORDINANCE IN REFERENCE TO SHERIFFS, CORONERS, &C.

Sheriffs not to be amerced in certain cases.

SECTION 1. *Be it ordained by the people of North-Carolina in Convention assembled,* That no Sheriff, or other officer in the State of North-Carolina, who, in performance of official duty, has obeyed and observed the provisions of an act of the General Assembly of the State of North-Carolina, entitled "An act to protect property sold under execution from sacrifice," ratified the 26th day of February, A. D. 1867, shall be liable to amercement or any other proceedings for failure to sell any property whatsoever to satisfy any execution or other process issued from a justice of the peace, or from any of the several courts of said State; and any judgment *nisi,* heretofore granted by any such amercements, and which may still be pending in any of said courts; and any action commenced, or which may hereafter be commenced, in any of said courts for failure to satisfy executions or other process as aforesaid, shall be dismissed upon notice duly made.

Ratified this 2d day of March, A. D. 1868.

CALVIN J. COWLES, *President.*

T. A. Byrnes, *Secretary.*

---

## CHAPTER XIV.

### AN ORDINANCE PROTECTING PROPERTY PURCHASED BY PERSONS HELD AS SLAVES.

Persons formerly slaves entitled to property purchased.

Section 1. *Be it ordained by the people of North-Carolina in Convention assembled,* That whenever it shall judicially appear that any person while held as a slave purchased and paid for any property, personal or real, and that conveyance thereof was made to him, or to any one for his use, such purchaser, or those lawfully representing him, shall be entitled to such property, anything in the former laws of this State forbidding slaves to acquire or hold property to the contrary notwithstanding.

Ratified this 6th day of March, A. D. 1868.

CALVIN J. COWLES, *President.*

T. A. Byrnes, *Secretary.*

---

## CHAPTER XV.

### AN ORDINANCE DISSOLVING THE BONDS OF MATRIMONY OF ROSA B. QUINLIVIN AND JOHN R. QUINLIVIN.

Section 1. *Be it ordained by the people of North-Carolina in Convention assembled,* That Rosa B. Quinlivin, formerly Rosa B. Chatterton, now the wife of John R. Quinlivin, be and she hereby is divorced from the bonds of matrimony with her said husband, and this ordinance shall be in force from and after its ratification.

Ratified this 6th day of March, A. D. 1868.

CALVIN J. COWLES, *President.*

T. A. BYRNES, *Secretary.*

---

## CHAPTER XVI.

### AN ORDINANCE IN RELATION TO THE DRAINING OF MATTAMUSKEET LAKE.

Preamble.

WHEREAS, The agricultural interests of Hyde County are greatly imperiled by the overflow of the waters of Lake Mattamuskeet; and whereas, the value of the lands in that County belonging to the Common School Fund of the State are greatly impaired thereby: therefore, for the purpose of draining said lake,

Commissioners appointed.

SECTION 1. *Be it ordained by the people of North-Carolina in Convention assembled,* That David M. Carter, Jones Spencer, George W. Swindell, Riley Murray, Joseph Mann and William L. Carter are hereby appointed Commissioners and invested with full power to locate one or more canals leading from Mattamusket Lake for the purpose of draining said lake, to contract for the execution of such canals, or to have the same contracted under their own superintendence. Said Commissioners are authorized to condemn the lands through which said canals may pass to the exclusive use of such canals, not to exceed one hundred feet wide and extending from one terminus of such canals to the other. Said Commissioners shall fix the price to be paid the owners of said land, who may appeal to the Superior Court of Hyde County if dissatisfied with the price fixed by said Commissioners upon said lands, and may have the value of the lands condemned for the use of said canals ascertained by jury; but the Commissioners, and in case of such appeal, the jury also shall estimate the benefit accruing to the other lands of said owners in fixing the compensation for so much as is appropriated to the canals. The title to the lands thus condemned, and to the canals and other appertenances, shall vest in said Commissioners and their successors. A majority of said Commissioners shall constitute a quorum for the transaction of any business whatever within the scope of their duties, and a majority of the quorum shall determine all questions which may arise.

Quorum.

SEC. 2. *Be it further ordained*, That an annual tax is hereby levied upon all the lands in the County of Hyde of one *per centum* of the value of said lands, as assessed for taxation in the year 1860, for the period of five years, unless the said canals are sooner completed and paid for; and also a further tax is hereby levied upon all other taxable subjects, is to be paid annually for the period of five years, of the same amount which the State of North-Carolina may levy for State purposes on the same subjects of taxation during that period, and the money thus raised by taxation of canals and other subjects, or so much as will be necessary, shall be faithfully expended by said Commissioners in the construction of one or more canals, for the purpose of draining the waters of Lake Mattamuskeet so as to prevent the overflow thereof.

Tax levied.

SEC. 3. *Be it further ordained*, That it shall be the duty of the proper officer who makes out the tax list for the County of Hyde also to make out and deliver to the Sheriff of that County a tax list by which the taxes herein levied may be collected annually at the same time with the other taxes, and under like penalties for any failure or neglect of duty, and it shall be the duty of the Sheriff of the County to collect and pay over to the Treasurer of the Board of Commissioners the taxes herein levied at the same time when the taxes for the State are payable to the Public Treasurer, under the same penalties for any failure or neglect of duty as are imposed in case of his failure to pay over the taxes levied for State purposes, and the sureties of his official bonds are to be held liable for the same.

Duty of the Sheriff.

SEC. 4. *Be it further ordained*, That said Commissioners shall appoint one of their number President of the Board,

Officers of the Board.

and shall also elect a Treasurer, who shall give bonds with two or more sufficient sureties in the sum of ten thousand dollars to keep safely and pay out properly under the requisition of the President, the moneys received by him from the Sheriff of Hyde County or from any other source which are appropriated to be expended by said Commissioners. Said bond shall be payable to the State of North-Carolina.

Vacancies.

SEC. 5. *Be it further ordained*, That whenever a vacancy may happen in said Board of Commissioners by death, resignation or expulsion for malfeasance of any of its members by said Board of Commissioners, such vacancies may be filled by the Commissioners at their first or any meeting thereafter. It shall also be the duty of said Commissioners to hold at least one meeting each year during the time of the construction of the canals. The President and Treasurer may receive such compensation for their services as a majority of the Commissioners shall fix.

Commissioners to value lands.

SEC. 6. *Be it further ordained*, That said Commissioners may value all the unclear swamp lands within two miles of said canals, and assess an amount of money to be paid for such lands in proportion to the advantage accruing to said lands by the canals, not exceeding five per cent. of their value as aforesaid in 1860, and in case of the refusal of the owners of said lands to pay said assessments, the said Commissioners may file their petition in the Superior Court of Hyde County and have a judgment condemning said lands to be sold to pay such assessment; *Provided*, That the question of the valuation of said lands may be received by a jury of said court.

Canal.

SEC. 7. *Be it further ordained*, That if a majority of the whole number of said Commissioners shall be of opinion that the best plan to drain said lake is by cutting a canal from the head of Broad Creek to the head of Aligator River, then said Commissioners may also expend any part of the moneys herein appropriated in cutting such canal.

Submitted to vote of the people.

SEC. 8. *Be it further ordained*, That this ordinance shall be submitted to the qualified voters of Hyde County for their approval or rejection under the direction of the County

Court of said County, or of the Commissioners for said County, and shall take the proper means for that purpose and declare the result; and if approved by a majority of the qualified voters who shall vote upon the question, shall go into force and effect from and after such approval.

Ratified this 9th day of March, A. D. 1868.

CALVIN J. COWLES, *President.*

T. A. Byrnes, *Secretary.*

---

## CHAPTER XVII.

### AN ORDINANCE TO INCORPORATE THE NORTH WESTERN NORTH-CAROLINA RAILROAD COMPANY.

Company incorporated.

Section 1. *Be it ordained by the people of North-Carolina in Convention assembled, and it is hereby ordained by authority of the same,* That for the purpose of constructing a Rail Road, of one or more tracks, from some point on the North-Carolina Rail Road, between the town of Greensboro', in Guilford County, and the town of Lexington, in Davidson County, running by way of Salem and Winston, in Forsyth County, to some point on the North Western boundary line of the State, to be hereafter determined, a company is hereby incorporated under the name and style of the North Western North-Carolina Rail Road Company, with a capital stock of two millions of dollars, which shall have a corporate existence as a body politic for the space of ninety-nine years, and by that name may sue and be sued, plead and be impleaded, in any Court of Law and Equity in the State of North-Carolina, and may have and use a common seal, and shall be capable in law and equity of purchasing, holding, leasing and conveying estates, real and personal and mixed, and acquiring the same by gift or devise so far as may be necessary for the objects herein contemplated and no further; and said Company may enjoy all other rights and immunities which other corporate bodies may lawfully exercise, and may make all necessary by-laws and regulations for its government not inconsistent with the Constitution and laws of the State of North-Carolina and of the United States.

Shares.

SEC. 2. *Be it further ordained*, That the capital stock of said Company may be created by subscriptions on the part of individuals, corporations and counties, in shares of one hundred dollars.

Commissioners to open books.

SEC. 3. *Be it further ordained*, That books of subscription to the capital stock of said Company shall be opened by the following Commissioners, to-wit: I. G. Lash, J. A. Vogler, H. W. Fries, in the town of Salem, and Thomas J. Wilson, Jos. Masten, R. A. Wilson, in the town of Winston, and by such other persons and in such other places as the aforesaid Commissioners may direct, and that ten days notice of the opening of said books shall be given in one or more newspapers of this State; and furthermore, that the said Commissioners, or any four of them, may, at any time after said books have been kept open for the space of thirty days, and the sum of thirty thousand dollars has been subscribed to the capital stock of said Company and five per cent. paid thereon, have power to call together the subscribers to said stock for the purpose of completing the organization of said Company; and the said subscribers shall be and are hereby declared incorporated into a company by the said name and style of the North Western North-Carolina Rail Road Company, and the said Company may, from time to time, receive other subscriptions to its capital stock as it may deem proper.

Election of Directors.

SEC. 4. *Be it further ordained*, That said Company may hold annual meetings of its stockholders, and oftener if necessary, and at its organization and the annual meetings subsequent thereto ten Directors shall be elected to hold office for one year, or until their successors shall be elected, and any of said meetings shall have power to make or alter the by-laws of the Company; *Provided*, That in all such meetings of the stockholders a majority of all the stock subscribed shall be represented in person or by proxy, which proxy shall be verified in the manner prescribed by the by-laws of the Company, and each share thus represented shall be entitled to one vote on all questions; that it shall be the duty of the Directors of the Company to elect one of their own number as President of said Company, and to fill all vacancies in their Board.

Location of the Road.

SEC. 5. *Be it further ordained*, That after the organization of said Company and the election of the President and other necessary officers, the officers so elected shall proceed, under the advice of the Directors, to locate the Eastern terminus of the North Western North-Carolina Rail Road, and shall proceed to construct said road, with one or more tracks, as speedily as practicable, in sections of five miles each, to the towns of Winston and Salem, in Forsyth County, which portion of said Rail Road, when completed, shall constitute its first division; *Provided*, That if the distance from the nearest section to the towns of Salem and Winston be less than five miles, the same shall be considered a section.

Powers of the Company.

SEC. 6. *Be it further ordained*, That said Company shall have the same power to call for and enforce the payment of stock subscribed as was heretofore granted to the North-Carolina Rail Road Company, by their charter of incorporation, and shall have power to condemn land for the use of the Company, when a contract of purchase cannot be made with the owner thereof, to the same extent and in the same manner and under the same rules, regulations and restrictions as the said North-Carolina Rail Road Company were authorized to do by their act of incorporation.

Contracts binding.

SEC. 7. *Be it further ordained*, That all contracts made and entered into by the President or Superintendent of the Company, whether with or without seal, shall be binding upon the Company; and the President shall, under the instruction of the Board of Directors, issue certificates of stock and the stockholders, which shall be transferable in the manner prescribed by the by-laws of the Company.

The State to loan to the Company.

SEC. 8. *Be it further ordained*, That whenever the President and Chief Engineer of said Company shall certify to the Governor of the State that the grading of any of the sections of said road, as mentioned in section 5th of this ordinance, is completed and ready for the superstructure, he shall direct the Public Treasurer of the State to loan in behalf of the State to the said Company the sum of fifty thousand dollars in coupon bonds, and in like manner the Governor will direct similar loans to be made to the Company, upon the completion of the grading of each and every section until the first division is graded entire, and said Company shall set aside the receipts of the road over and above its annual expenses, as a sinking fund to pay the said debts and interest, the whole amount of said debt and interest to be paid before the said Company shall order any dividends on the stock of the Company; and that said sinking fund so produced shall be semi-annually paid into the Public Treasury.

Mortgage.

Sec. 9. *Be it further ordained*, That no part of said loan or bonds shall be delivered to said Company until the President and Directors thereof shall execute and deliver to the Governor of the State a mortgage on the entire road and its property, conditioned to save the State harmless against the loss of both principal and interest of said loan.

Bonds.

Sec. 10. *Be it further ordained*, That the coupon bonds loaned as aforesaid shall be signed by the Governor, countersigned by the Treasurer and sealed with "the Great Seal of the State," bearing six per cent. interest, the principal payable at the end of thirty years from the date thereof, and the coupons for the interest payable semi-annually in such form as the Public Treasurer may direct.

Rights of Company.

Sec. 11. *Be it further ordained*, That said Company may have the exclusive right of transporting persons and freight upon said road at such rates of charges as the Board of Directors may fix, and may have power to farm or lease the same to any person or persons or corporation.

Stockholders may pay in money or labor.

Sec. 12. *Be it further ordained*, That the stockholders of the said Company may pay the stock subscribed by them either in money, labor or material for constructing said road, as the Board of Directors may determine, and that all counties and towns subscribing stock to said company shall do so in the same manner, and under the same rules, regulations and restrictions as are set forth and prescribed in the act incorporating the North-Carolina and Atlantic Rail Road Company for the government of such towns and counties as now allowed to subscribers to the capital stock of said Company.

Branch roads.

SEC. 13. *Be it further ordained*, That the Company shall have power to construct branches of said Rail Road, one of which shall run from said towns of Winston and Salem, by way of Mount Airy, in Surry County, to the line in the State of Virginia.

SEC. 14. *Be it further ordained*, That this ordinance shall be in force from and after its passage.

Ratified this 9th day of March, A. D. 1868.

CALVIN J. COWLES, *President*.

T. A. BYRNES, *Secretary*.

---

## CHAPTER XVIII.

### AN ORDINANCE INCORPORATING THE NEW BERNE TURPENTINE COMPANY.

Incorporated.

SECTION 1. *Be it ordained by the people of North-Carolina in Convention assembled, and it is hereby ordained by the authority of the same*, That Wm. H. S. Sweet, Chas. R. Dutton, Wm. Fowler, Jeremiah Sweet, James Dutton, Stephen Northop, and their associates, successors, and assigns, are hereby created and constituted a body corporate and politic, by the name, and style, and title, of the New Berne Turpentine Company, and by that name may sue and be sued, plead and be impleaded, appear, prosecute and defend, in any court of law and equity whatever, in all suits and actions; may have a common seal, and alter the same at pleasure, and may purchase, hold, and convey real and personal estate, to an amount not exceeding two hundred and fifty thousand dollars, ($250,000.)

Powers of corporation.

SEC. 2. *Be it further ordained*, That the first meeting of said corporation may be called by the persons named in this ordinance, or any of them, at such time and place as they may agree upon; and at such meetings, and at all other meetings, legally notified, said corporation may make, alter, and repeal such by-laws and regulations for the management of the business of said corporation, as a majority of the stock may direct, not repugnant to the laws of this State or of the United States.

Stock.

SEC. 3. *Be it further ordained*, That the said corporation may divide their original stock into such number of shares, and provide for the sale and transfer thereof, in such manner and form as said corporation shall, from time to time, deem expedient, and may levy and collect assessments, forfeit and sell delinquent shares, declare and pay dividends on the shares in such manner as the by-laws shall direct.

Books of record.

SEC. 4. *Be it further ordained*, That it shall be the duty of the directors, one of whom shall reside continually in the State, to have regular books of record, and transfer thereof, at all times open to the inspection of the stockholders.

SEC. 5. *Be it further ordained*, That this corporation shall continue in force thirty years from and after the passage of this ordinance.

Ratified this 10th day of March, A. D. 1868.

CALVIN J. COWLES, *President*.

T. A. BYRNES, *Secretary*.

---

## CHAPTER XIX.

### AN ORDINANCE TO AMEND THE CHARTER OF THE CHATHAM RAIL ROAD COMPANY.

Public Treasurer to issue bonds.

SECTION 1. *Be it ordained by the people of North-Carolina, in Convention assembled*, That to enable the Chatham Rail Road Company to finish its road, the Public Treasurer is hereby authorized and directed to deliver to the President and Directors of the said Rail Road Company, the coupon bonds of the State to an amount not exceeding twelve hundred thousand dollars, ($1,200,000,) signed by the Governor, countersigned by the Public Treasurer and sealed with "the Great Seal of the State," bearing six per cent. interest, the principal payable at the end of thirty years from the date thereof and the coupons of interest payable semi-annually, in such form as the Public Treasurer may direct, to be made payable at such time and place as may be agreed upon by the Public Treasurer.

Company to deposit its bonds with the Public Treasurer.

SEC. 2. *Be it further ordained*, That before the Public Treasurer shall deliver any of said bonds hereby authorized the said Chatham Rail Road Company [shall deposit] with the Public Treasurer the coupon bonds of said Company for the same amount and bearing the same interest and date, the principal and coupons payable at the same time and place as those of the State hereinbefore directed to be issued and paid over to the Chatham Rail Road Company, and to secure the principal and interest of said bonds issued by the Chatham Railroad Company, the State of North-Carolina shall by this ordinance have a lien upon all the estate of said Company, both real and personal, which they may now have or may hereafter acquire, between the city of Raleigh and the Gulf, the terminus of said Rail Road in the Coal-fields, including that at both points, together with all the rights, franchises and powers thereunto belonging or appertaining, or that may hereafter belong or appertain to said Company, which lien shall be more effectually secured by a first mortgage duly executed by said Company to the State and registered in the Register's office in the Counties of Wake and Chatham, and in case of failure of said Company to pay the semi-annual interest on its bonds for twenty-four months after such interest shall become due, or to pay the principal of said bonds for twelve months after their maturity, the Board of Internal Improvements for and in behalf of the State may enter upon and take possession of all the property hereinbefore specified and dispose of the same by sale so as to protect the State.

Lien by the State.

May take up bonds.

SEC. 3. *Be it further ordained*, That the Chatham Rail

Road Company may at any time before maturity take up the bonds of said Company deposited with the Public Treasurer by substituting in lieu thereof coupon bonds of the State or other indebtedness of the State.

Privilege reserved to the State.

Sec. 4. *Be it further ordained*, That the State shall have the privilege at any time within eight years from the passage of this ordinance to subscribe stock in said Company to the amount of six hundred thousand dollars ($600,000) in shares of one hundred dollars ($100) each, and upon certificate of stock being issued to the State by said Company for the same, to surrender the bonds of said Company which had previously been delivered to the State under the provisions of this ordinance.

Sec. 5. *Be it further ordained*, That this ordinance shall take effect and be in force from and after its passage.

Ratified this 11th day of March, A. D. 1868.

CALVIN J. COWLES, *President*.

T. A. Byrnes, *Secretary*.

---

## CHAPTER XX.

### AN ORDINANCE TO AID THE WILLIAMSTON AND TARBORO' RAIL ROAD COMPANY.

State loan to Williamston and Tarboro' R. R. Company.

Section 1. *Be it ordained by the people of North-Carolina in Convention assembled*, That when the President of the Williamston and Tarboro' Rail Road Company shall certify to the Governor of the State that said road is graded, he shall direct the Public Treasurer to loan in behalf of the State to said Company the sum of one hundred and fifty thousand dollars in coupon bonds, and said Company shall set aside the receipts of the road over and above its annual expenses as a sinking fund to pay said debt, and interest to be paid before the said Company shall order any dividends on the stock of the Company, and that said sinking fund so produced shall be semi-annually paid into the Public Treasury.

SEC. 2. *Be it further ordained*, That no part of said loan or bonds shall be delivered to said Company until the President and Directors thereof shall execute and deliver to the Governor of the State a first mortgage on the entire road and its property, conditioned to save the State harmless against the loss of both principal and interest of said loan.

Loan to be secured by mortgage.

SEC. 3. *Be it further ordained*, That the coupon bonds loaned as aforesaid shall be signed by the Governor, countersigned by the Treasurer and sealed with "the Great Seal of the State," bearing six per cent. interest, the principal payable at the end of thirty years from the date thereof, and the coupons for the interest payable semi-annually in such form as the Public Treasurer may direct.

Interest and payments.

SEC. 4. *Be it further ordained*, That said Company may have the exclusive right of transporting persons and freight upon said road at such rates of charges as the Board of Directors may fix, and may have power to farm or lease the same to any person or persons or corporation.

Power to fix rates and to lease.

SEC. 5. *Be it further ordained*, That the stockholders of said Company may pay the stock subscribed by them either in money, labor or material for constructing said road as the Board of Directors may determine, and that all counties and towns subscribing stock to said Company shall do so in the same manner and under the same rules, regulations and restrictions as are set forth and prescribed in the act incorporating said Company.

Payment of subscribedstock

SEC. 6. *Be it further ordained*, That this ordinance shall be in force and take effect from and after its passage.

Ordinance in force from its passage.

Ratified this 11th day of March, A. D. 1868.

CALVIN J. COWLES, *President.*

T. A. BYRNES, *Secretary.*

## CHAPTER XXI.

AN ORDINANCE TO DIVORCE WINNEY GRIBBLES AND JAMES GRIBBLES.

Jas. Gribbles and Winney Gribbles divorced.

SECTION 1. *Be it ordained by the people of North-Carolina in Convention assembled*, That the nuptial tie between Winney Gribbles and James Gribbles, be, and the same is hereby dissolved, and that the said Winney Gribbles be divorced from the bonds of matrimony contracted with the said James Gribbles, and that the said Winney Gribbles be from henceforth, to all intents and purposes, a *feme sole.*

SEC. 2. *Be it further ordained*, That this ordinance shall take effect from its ratification.

Ratified this 13th day of March, A. D. 1868.

CALVIN J. COWLES, *President.*

T. A. BYRNES, *Secretary*

## CHAPTER XXII.

AN ORDINANCE FOR THE DIVORCE OF ELIZA C. WAGNER.

Herman and Eliza C. Wagner divorced.

SECTION 1. *Be it ordained by the people of North-Carolina in Convention assembled*, That Eliza C. Wagner, of Alamance County, be, and she is hereby divorced from the bonds of matrimony with her husband, Herman Wagner.

Ratified this 13th day of March, A. D. 1868.

CALVIN J. COWLES, *President.*

T. A. BYRNES, *Secretary.*

## CHAPTER XXIII.

AN ORDINANCE FOR THE DIVORCE OF JOSEPHINE EMANUEL.

James W. and Josephine Emanuel divorced.

SECTION 1. *Be it ordained by the people of North-Carolina in Convention assembled*, That Josephine, wife of James M.

Emanuel, of Orange County, be, and is hereby divorced from the bonds of matrimony with her husband.

Ratified this 13th day of March, A. D. 1868.

CALVIN J. COWLES, *President.*

T. A. Byrnes, *Secretary.*

---

## CHAPTER XXIV.

### AN ORDINANCE FOR THE DIVORCE OF LAVINIA LEE AND WESLEY LEE.

Section 1. *Be it ordained by the people of North-Carolina in Convention assembled,* That Lavinia Lee, of Guilford County, be and she is hereby divorced from the bonds of matrimony with her husband, Wesley Lee.

Wesley and Lavinia Lee divorced.

Ratified this 13th day of March, A. D. 1868.

CALVIN J. COWLES, *President.*

T. A. Byrnes, *Secretary.*

---

## CHAPTER XXV.

### AN ORDINANCE FOR THE DIVORCE OF DEWITT C. WILSON AND NANCY C. WILSON.

Section 1. *Be it ordained by the people of North-Carolina in Convention assembled,* That Dewitt C. Wilson and Nancy C. Wilson, his wife, of Davie County, be and they are hereby divorced from the bonds of matrimony.

DeWitt C. and Nancy C. Wilson divorced.

Ratified this 13th day of March, A. D. 1868.

CALVIN J. COWLES, *President.*

T. A. Byrnes, *Secretary.*

## CHAPTER XXVI.

AN ORDINANCE FOR THE DIVORCE OF ESTHER V. TODD AND BENJAMIN W. TODD.

Benj. W. and Esther V. Todd divorced.

SECTION 1. *Be it ordained by the people of North-Carolina in Convention assembled*, That Esther V. Todd, formerly Esther V. Walton, now wife of Benjamin W. Todd, be and she is hereby divorced from the bonds of matrimony with her said husband, and that she shall be at liberty to resume her maiden name; and this ordinance shall take effect from and after its passage.

Ratified this 13th day of March, A. D. 1868.

CALVIN J. COWLES, *President.*

T. A. BYRNES, *Secretary.*

---

## CHAPTER XXVII.

AN ORDINANCE FOR THE DIVORCE OF JAMES OVERTON AND CHARLOTTE OVERTON.

Jas. and Charlotte Overton divorced.

SECTION 1. *Be it ordained by the people of North-Carolina in Convention assembled*, That James Overton and Charlotte, his wife, are hereby divorced from the bonds of matrimony.

Ratified this 13th day of March, A. D. 1868.

CALVIN J. COWLES, *President.*

T. A. BYRNES, *Secretary.*

---

## CHAPTER XXVIII.

AN ORDINANCE FOR THE DIVORCE OF WILLIAM J. HOPKINS AND MARTHA A. HOPKINS.

Wm. J. and Martha A. Hopkins divorced.

SECTION 1. *Be it ordained by the people of North-Carolina in Convention assembled*, That the bonds of matrimony between William J. Hopkins and Martha A., his wife, now of

Granville County, are hereby dissolved, and either party are at liberty to marry again.

Ratified this 12th day of March, A. D. 1868.

CALVIN J. COWLES, *President.*

T. A. Byrnes, *Secretary.*

---

## CHAPTER XXIX.

AN ORDINANCE IN RELATION TO THE PARDON OF OFFICERS AND SOLDIERS OF THE LATE CONFEDERATE SERVICE.

General Amnesty act repealed.

Section 1. *Be it ordained by the people of North-Carolina in Convention assembled, and it is hereby ordained by the authority of the same,* That an act of the General Assembly, ratified December the 22d, 1866, granting a general amnesty and pardon to all officers and soldiers of the State of North-Carolina, of the late Confederate States armies, or of the United States, or any person or class of persons to which said general amnesty was intended to apply, be and the same is hereby repealed, except so much of it as applies to females.

Ratified this 13th day of March, A. D. 1868.

CALVIN J. COWLES, *President.*

T. A. Byrnes, *Secretary.*

---

## CHAPTER XXX.

AN ORDINANCE TO CHANGE THE MANNER OF PAYMENT OF THE STATE'S SUBSCRIPTION TO THE CAPITAL STOCK OF THE WESTERN RAIL ROAD.

The Company authorized to return half million of mortgage bonds to the Treasurer.

Section 1. *Be it ordained by the people of North-Carolina in Convention assembled, and it is hereby ordained by the authority of the same,* That the Western Rail Road Company are hereby authorized to return to the Public Treasurer the sum of one-half million of dollars of the second mortgage bonds of the Wilmington, Charlotte and Rutherford Rail Road Company, which amount has heretofore been paid by the Public Treasurer to said Company, as the payment of the subscription of the State to the capital stock of said Company, under the authority of the third section of the act of the General Assembly, entitled "An act to enable the Western Rail Road Company to extend its road to and across the North-Carolina Rail Road to the Virginia line near Mt. Airy, in the County of Surry," ratified the 25th day of February, 1867; and in place thereof the Public Treasurer is hereby authorized and directed to make and deliver to said Western Rail Road Company one-half million dollars of the coupon bonds of the State of North-Carolina, signed by the Governor and countersigned by the Public Treasurer, bearing interest at the rate of six per cent. per annum, the principal and interest payable at such time and in such manner and place as the Governor or Public Treasurer may prescribe.

When the bonds shall be delivered.

SEC. 2. *Be it further ordained*, That no part of the five hundred thousand dollars ($500,000) of bonds herein appropriated as a loan to the Western Rail Road Company shall be delivered to said Company, until the President and Directors thereof shall have executed and delivered to the Governor of the State, a first mortgage on the entire road and its property, conditioned to save the State harmless against the loss of both principal and interest of said loan.

Act of the Legislature repealed

SEC. 3. *Be it further ordained*, That so much of the third section of the act of the General Assembly, entitled "An act to enable the Western Rail Road Company to complete its road from the Coalfields in Chatham County to some point on the North-Carolina Rail Road," ratified the 22d day of December, 1866, as prohibits said Company from negotiating its bonds at not less than par, be and the same is hereby repealed; and this ordinance shall be in force from and after its passage.

Ratified the 14th day of March, A. D. 1868.

CALVIN J. COWLES, *President.*

T. A. BYRNES, *Secretary.*

## CHAPTER XXXI.

AN ORDINANCE TO DIVORCE ADELIA E. SLATER AND JAMES A. SLATER.

SECTION 1. *Be it ordained by the people of North-Carolina in Convention assembled*, That Adelia E. Slater, of Rowan County, be and she is hereby divorced from the bonds of matrimony with her husband, James A. Slater, and that she shall be at liberty to assume her maiden name, said Adelia to have sole charge of her children.

James A. and Adelia E. Slater divorced.

Ratified this 16th day of March, A. D. 1868.

CALVIN J. COWLES, *President*.

T. A. BRYNES, *Secretary*.

---

## CHAPTER XXXII.

AN ORDINANCE TO AMEND AN ORDINANCE OF THIS CONVENTION ENTITLED "AN ORDINANCE TO CHANGE THE MANNER OF PAYMENT OF THE STATE'S SUBSCRIPTION TO THE CAPITAL STOCK OF THE WESTERN RAIL ROAD COMPANY."

SECTION 1. *Be it ordained by the people of North-Carolina in Convention assembled*, That section second of an ordinance of this Convention, entitled "An ordinance to change the manner of payment of the State's subscription to the capital stock of the Western Rail Road Company," ratified the 14th day of March, 1868, be and is hereby repealed and declared of no effect.

Ordinance repealed.

SEC. 2. *Be it further ordained*, That this ordinance shall be in force from and after its ratification.

Ordinance in force from its ratification.

Ratified this 17th day of March, A. D. 1868.

CALVIN J. COWLES, *President*.

T. A. BYRNES, *Secretary*.

## CHAPTER XXXIII.

AN ORDINANCE IN RELATION TO THE PRINTING OF THE CONSTITUTION, ORDINANCES AND RESOLUTIONS.

Ordinances to be in force from the date of their authentication.

SECTION 1. *Be it ordained by the people of North-Carolina in Convention assembled*, That every ordinance and resolution of this Convention, when the same shall have been enrolled, shall be authenticated by the signatures of the President and of the Principal Secretary of this Convention, and the date of its final passage shall be affixed thereto; and such ordinances and resolutions shall go into effect from such date, unless some other be prescribed or unless such ordinance or resolution shall be required to be submitted to the people for ratification.

Ordinances, resolutions, &c., to be deposited in the office of the Secretary of State.

SEC. 2. *Be it further ordained*, That all such enrolled ordinances and resolutions, and also the Journals of the Convention, and all the papers belonging to the Convention, immediately upon the adjournment thereof shall be deposited by the President and Secretary of the Convention in the office of the Secretary of State for the State of North-Carolina.

Constitution, &c., to be printed and distributed.

SEC. 3. *Be it further ordained*, That four thousand copies of the Constitution, ordinances and resolutions of this Convention, and three hundred copies of the Journals, shall be printed as soon as possible after the adjournment of the Convention, under the supervision of the Principal Secretary of the Convention, and that ten copies of the ordinances and resolutions and one copy of the Journals shall be given to each member of this Convention, and two bound copies of the ordinances and resolutions to each Clerk of the Superior Court, one copy to each Judge of the Supreme Court and to each Justice of the Peace and County Commissioner elected under the provisions of this Constitution, and the residue to the Secretary of State of North-Carolina for the use of the State.

SEC. 4. *Be it further ordained*, That as soon as possible after the adjournment of this Convention there shall be printed under the same supervision ten thousand copies of the Constitution adopted, and of all ordinances for the purposes of carrying the same into effect, or which shall be required to be submitted to the people for ratification at the same time, and that the same be distributed as rapidly as possible among them by the said Principal Secretary.

Ten thousand copies of Constitution and Ordinances to be printed.

Sec. 5. *Be it further ordained*, That the Constitution shall also be published in the following named newspapers of this State once a week for three weeks: *Newbern Republican; Wilmington Post; Raleigh Standard*, Raleigh, N. C.; *Union Republican*, Charlotte; *Pioneer*, Asheville.

Constitution to be published in newspapers.

Sec. 6. *Be it further ordained*, That the Secretary shall receive for his services under this ordinance six dollars per day while engaged.

Compensation of the Secretary.

Sec. 7. *Be it further ordained*, That the printed copies of the Constitution, and of all the ordinances and resolutions of the Convention printed by authority of the Convention, or which shall be hereafter printed by authority of the General Assembly of North Carolina, shall be admitted as evidence in all courts of this State.

Printed copies of the Constitution to be evidence in the courts.

Ratified this 13th day of March, A. D. 1868.

CALVIN J. COWLES, *President*,

T. A. Byrnes, *Secretary*.

---

## CHAPTER XXXIV.

### AN ORDINANCE IN RELATION TO THE CAPE FEAR AND DEEP RIVER NAVIGATION WORKS.

Whereas, The Cape Fear and Deep River Navigation Works are in a ruinous condition, and in their present condition utterly worthless to the State and highly injurious to the interests of the people residing in the valleys of said rivers; and whereas, it is expedient that said Works shall be made available in developing the resources of said valleys:

Preamble.

Interest of the State in Works transferred to Chatham R. R. Company.

SECTION 1. *Now therefore be it ordained by the people of North-Carolina in Convention assembled*, That for the purpose of aiding the Chatham Rail Road Company in [the] transportation of stone for building their bridges, culverts and other masonry, and for the carriage of materials and supplies to points needed, the interest of the State of North-Carolina in said Cape Fear and Deep River Navigation Works from the Gulf Dam, on Deep River, to Northing Dam, on Cape Fear River, both inclusive, is hereby transferred to the said Chatham Rail Road Company, with liberty to said Company to repair, use and make avail of said portion of said Works, and all franchises and privileges appurtenant thereto, to the same extent as is possessed by the State.

President and Directors have power of transfer and assignment.

SEC. 2. *Be it further ordained*, That the President and Directors of the Chatham Rail Road Company shall have power to transfer and assign said interests herein conveyed and transferred, or any portion thereof, for the purpose of improving the valleys of said rivers.

SEC. 3. *Be it further ordained*, That this ordinance shall be in force from its passage.

Ratified this 15th day of March, A. D. 1868.

CALVIN J. COWLES, *President.*

T. A. BYRNES, *Secretary.*

---

## CHAPTER XXXV.

AN ORDINANCE FOR THE SUBMISSION OF THE CONSTITUTION TO THE PEOPLE, AND THE ELECTION OF CERTAIN OFFICERS.

Constitution to be submitted.

SECTION 1. *Be it ordained by the people of North-Carolina in Convention assembled*, That the Constitution adopted by this Convention be submitted for ratification to the voters of this State, registered and qualified, as provided by the acts of Congress known as the Reconstruction Laws, on the 21st, 22d and 23d of April, 1868. The vote on said Constitution shall be "For the Constitution" and "Against the

Constitution." The said election shall be held at the places and under the regulations to be prescribed by the Commanding General of this military district, and the returns made to him as directed by law.

SEC. 2. *Be it further ordained*, That an election shall be held at the same time and place as the ratification of the Constitution, for Senators and Representatives in the General Assembly, and for all State and County officers, who are to be elected by the people under this Constitution. Election to be held.

SEC. 3. *Be it further ordained*, That an election for members of the United States Congress shall be held in each Congressional District as now established, at the same time and place as the election for ratification of the Constitution. Said election shall be conducted by the same persons and under the same regulations as before mentioned in this ordinance. The returns shall be made to the President of this Convention, who shall give the persons chosen certificates of election. Members of Congress.

SEC. 4. *Be it further ordained*, That the Commanding General of this Military District is requested to enforce this ordinance

SEC. 5. *Be it further ordained*, That the President of this Convention is hereby directed to forward a certified copy of this ordinance to the Commanding General of this Military District.

Ratified this 17th day of March, A. D., 1868.

CALVIN J. COWLES, *President.*

T. A. BYRNES, *Secretary.*

---

## CHAPTER XXXVI.

AN ORDINANCE TO PREVENT THE INTIMIDATION OF VOTERS.

SECTION. 1. *Be it ordained by the people of North-Carolina in Convention assembled, and it is hereby ordained as follows:* Any person who shall prevent, or endeavor to prevent, any qualified elector of this State from the free ex- Misdemeanor to intimidate or bribe voters.

ercise of the elective franchise, by violence or bribery, or by threats of violence or injury to his person or property, or by depriving an elector of employment or threatening to deprive him of employment, shall be deemed guilty of a misdemeanor, and upon conviction thereof shall be punished by imprisonment for not less than one month, nor more than six months, or by fine of not less than one hundred dollars nor more than five hundred dollars for each offence, and one half of the fine shall go to the prosecutor.

Hiring of laborer to vote, bribery.

SEC. 2. *Be it further ordained*, That the hiring of any laborer upon the condition that the same shall vote, or not vote, for any special candidate, or any particular party, or in any specific manner shall be deemed bribery within the meaning of this act, upon the part of the person demanding the said condition.

SEC. 3. *Be it further ordained*, That this ordinance shall be published and circulated with this Constitution for the information of voters, and shall be in force from and after the date of its passage.

CALVIN J. COWLES, *President.*

T. A. BYRNES. *Secretary.*

---

## CHAPTER XXXVII.

### AN ORDINANCE FOR THE RELIEF OF THE SHERIFF OF ORANGE COUNTY.

Preamble.

WHEREAS, The Sheriff of Orange County was delinquent in paying a portion of the taxes for 1866, and judgment was obtained against him by the State for said balance, one thousand dollars penalty, and no commissions for collecting were allowed him, which commissions, if allowed, would have amounted to two hundred and sixty-seven dollars and ninety-eight cents; and whereas, all the taxes due the State for that year have since been paid, including said penalty and commissions, and owing to the extraordinary poverty of the people and difficulty of collections, in the opinion of this Convention relief should be granted said Sheriff,

SECTION 1. *Be it ordained by the people of North-Carolina in Convention assembled*, That the said Hugh B. Guthrie, Sheriff of Orange County, be allowed the sum of one thousand two hundred and sixty-seven dollars and ninety-eight cents, ($1,267.98,) to be credited upon any taxes still owing by said Sheriff, in the order of the dates wherein the same were due. Allowed a certain amount.

Ratified this 6th day of March, A. D. 1868.

CALVIN J. COWLES, *President*.

T. A. BYRNES, *Secretary*.

---

## CHAPTER XXXVIII.

AN ORDINANCE TO EXEMPT MINISTERS OF THE GOSPEL AND JUSTICES OF THE PEACE IN THE COUNTY OF CUMBERLAND FROM THE PENALTY IMPOSED BY THE ACT OF THE GENERAL ASSEMBLY OF NORTH-CAROLINA FOR CELEBRATING THE RITES OF MATRIMONY IN SAID COUNTY WITHOUT A LICENSE THEREFOR.

WHEREAS, There is no Clerk of the County Court in Cumberland County, (by reason of death of the late incumbent,) and therefore no one legally authorized to issue a license to persons desiring to intermarry; and whereas, D. G. McRae, J. W. Lett, and E. L. Pemberton, three of the Justices of the Peace in and for said County, have issued commissions to Ministers of the Gospel, and Justices of the Peace authorizing and empowering them to celebrate the rites between certain parties: now, therefore, Preamble.

SECTION 1. *Be it ordained by the people of North-Carolina in Convention assembled, and it is hereby ordained by the authority of the same*, That those Ministers of the Gospel and Justices of the Peace in said County, who have, or may hereafter, solemnize the rites of matrimony under a commission from the aforesaid Justices of the Peace be, and Ministers and Magistrates released from penalty.

they are hereby released from the penalty imposed by law for celebrating the rites of matrimony without having a license from the Clerk of the County Court of said County.

SEC. 2. *Be it further ordained,* That this power and authority given to said D. G. McRae, J. W. Lett and E. L. Pemberton, shall cease and be of no effect from and after the time that a Clerk of the County Court in said County shall be appointed and shall qualify according to law.

Ratified this 22d day of February, A. D. 1868.

CALVIN J. COWLES, *President.*

T. A. BYRNES, *Secretary.*

---

## CHAPTER XXXIX.

AN ORDINANCE FOR THE DIVORCE OF JOHN ROBERTS AND CAMELIA ROBERTS.

John and Camelia Roberts divorced.

SECTION 1. *Be it ordained by the people of North-Carolina in Convention assembled,* That John Roberts, of Chowan County, be and he hereby is divorced from the bonds of matrimony with Camelia, his wife: *Provided,* That it shall be lawful for the said Camelia to apply to the proper Court, and obtain such alimony as may be proper.

SEC. 2. *Be it further ordained,* That this ordinance shall go into effect from and after its ratification.

Ratified this 5th day of March, A. D. 1868.

CALVIN J. COWLES, *President.*

T. A. BYRNES, *Secretary.*

---

## CHAPTER XL.

AN ORDINANCE CONCERNING WIDOWS WHO HAVE QUALIFIED AS EXECUTRIX TO THE LAST WILL AND TESTAMENT OF THEIR DECEASED HUSBANDS.

SECTION 1. *Be it ordained by the people of North-Carolina*

*in Convention assembled, and it is hereby ordained by the authority of the same,* That the widow of any testator, whose last will and testament has been admitted to probate in this State, since the first day of January, one thousand eight hundred and sixty-two, and before the first day of May, one thousand eight hundred and sixty-five, notwithstanding such widow may have qualified to such last will and testament as Executrix, be, and she is hereby allowed to enter her dissent to the same, according to the same forms as are now provided by law for the dissent of widows.

Widow may dissent.

SEC. 2. *Be it further ordained,* That in all cases where a widow shall dissent from the last will and testament of her husband, as provided for in the foregoing section, she shall be entitled to the same rights of dower as if her husband had died intestate: *Provided, however,* That no widow shall be entitled to the benefit of this ordinance, unless such dissent shall be entered within six months from and after the passage of this ordinance, nor in any case where the real estate of the deceased husband has been sold subsequent to his death, or has been divided between his devisees or heirs at law.

What she shall be entitled to.

SEC. 3. *Be it further ordained,* That this ordinance shall be in force from and after its ratification.

Ratified this fifth day of March, A. D. 1868.

CALVIN J. COWLES, *President.*

T. A. BYRNES, *Secretary.*

---

## CHAPTER XLI.

AN ORDINANCE APPOINTING COMMISSIONERS TO PREPARE A CODE OF PRACTICE AND PROCEDURE IN THE DIFFERENT COURTS OF THE STATE.

SECTION. 1. *Be it ordained by the people of North-Carolina in Convention assembled, and it is hereby ordained as follows:* That Victor C. Barringer, A. W. Tourgee and Wm. B. Rodman are hereby appointed Commissioners, whose

Commissioners

duty it shall be to prepare a Code of Practice and Procedure in the different Courts of the State, and to reduce into a written and systematic Code the whole body of law of the State, or such parts thereof as shall seem to them practicable and expedient, and consistent with the provisions of the Constitution.

Code in two parts.

SEC. 2. *Be it further ordained*, That the Commissioners shall divide the Code of Practice and Procedure into two parts, the one as a Code of Criminal Procedure, with the requisite forms, the other a Code of Civil Procedure, with forms thereof.

What the Code shall contain.

SEC. 3. *Be it further ordained*, That the first division of the Code of Law must embrace the laws respecting the government of the State, its civil polity, the functions of its public officers and duties of its citizens. The second must embrace the laws of personal rights and relations of property and obligations. The third shall define crimes and prescribe their punishments.

Term of office.

SEC. 4. *Be it further ordained*, That the Commissioners shall hold their offices for three years; but the General Assembly may continue their term if it shall be deemed necessary.

Commissioners shall report.

SEC. 5. *Be it further ordained*, That the Commissioners shall report to the General Assembly at its first session after the adoption of this Constitution a general analysis of the Code projected by them and the progress made by them therein, and shall continue to report at each succeeding session of the General Assembly the progress made to that time.

Code to be printed and distributed.

SEC. 6. *Be it further ordained*, That whenever the Commissioners shall have prepared the Code, or any portion of the same, they shall contract with the printer of the State for printing of the same, and cause the same to be distributed among the Justices of the Supreme Court, Judges of the Superior Courts, and other competent persons, for examination, after which the Commissioners shall re-examine their work and consider such suggestions as may have been made to them. They shall then cause the Code as finally agreed upon by them to be reprinted under the contract as aforesaid and distributed to all the Justices of the Supreme Court, the Judges of the Superior Courts and Clerks of the Superior Courts thirty days before being presented to the General Assembly; and the Penal Code in like manner to be distributed to the Solicitors of the State.

Amendments.

SEC. 7. *Be it further ordained*, That the Commissioners shall from time to time specify such amendments, alterations and revision of the law as to them may seem necessary to carry into effect the provisions of the Constitution, and report the same to the General Assembly.

Salary of Commissioners.

SEC. 8. *Be it further ordained*, That each of said Commissioners shall receive a salary of two hundred dollars per month, while actually engaged in the performance of his duties as such. A suitable room in the capital shall be assigned to said Commissioners as an office, and the necessary printing and stationery allowed the same.

SEC. 9. *Be it further ordained*, That this ordinance shall be in force from and after its ratification.

Ratified this 13th day of March, A. D. 1868.

CALVIN J. COWLES, *President.*

T. A. BYRNES, *Secretary.*

---

## CHAPTER XLII.

### AN ORDINANCE TO INCORPORATE THE CHARLOTTE CITY HALL ASSOCIATION.

Incorporated.

SECTION 1. *Be it ordained by the people of North-Carolina in Convention assembled*, That John L. Morehead, Robert M. Oates, Jonas Rudicill, Samuel Taylor, Thomas W. Dewey, Charles W. Alexander, W. I. Sater, and their associates, successors and assigns, be and they are hereby incorporate a body in law and fact, by the name and style of the Charlotte City Hall Association, for the purpose of erecting buildings and other improvements in the City of Charlotte, and shall possess and enjoy all rights and privileges and immunities of a corporation, a body politic in law necessary to carry on said business.

Capital stock.

SEC. 2. *Be it further ordained*, That the said Company may employ such an amount of capital not exceeding one hundred thousand dollars as may be deemed necessary to carry on the business aforesaid, which may be divided into shares of one hundred dollars or such other amounts as the stockholders in general meeting may determine, for obtaining which books of subscription may be opened by the corporation aforesaid, and the sum paid in in such manner and such time as the Board of Directors may require; and if any subscriber shall fail to pay any instalment at the time required, he shall pay interest thereon at the rate of ten per cent. per annum, and his stock may be forfeited and sold by the Directors, and the proceeds applied to the payment of the aforesaid deficient instalment. Certificates of stock may be issued, and the same made transferable and assignable as the by-laws of the Company may prescribe.

Board of Directors.

SEC. 3. *Be it further ordained*, That the affairs of said Company shall be managed by a Board of five Directors, chosen from among the stockholders, who shall elect one of their number to be the President of the Company. Three of the Board shall be a quorum to transact business, one of whom shall be the President.

Powers of Company.

SEC. 4. *Be it further ordained*, That the said Company shall have power to make by-laws not inconsistent with the laws of the United States and this State, appointing all necessary officers and employees, fixing salaries, taking bonds, filling vacancies and making regulations for the transaction of any matters necessary for the successful carrying on of the business of the Company.

General meeting of stockholders.

SEC. 5. *Be it further ordained*, That as soon after the ratification of this act as they may think proper, said corporation or a majority of them may call a general meeting of the subscribers to the stock in said Company, for the purpose of adopting by-laws for, and electing Directors of, said Company, which Directors shall continue in office until their successors shall be duly elected by a succeeding meeting.

SEC. 6. *Be it further ordained*, That the said corporation shall have full power and authority to purchase and hold lots and parcels of land in said city or its vicinity, and erect thereon buildings and other improvements, and to sell, rent, lease or dispose of the same as may be ordered by the stockholders of said Company. May purchase lands.

SEC. 7. *Be it further ordained*, That the said corporation, for the purpose of carrying on their purchases of lots or lands, and of erecting buildings and other improvements, may issue bonds on the faith and credit of said corporation in such amounts, at such times and at such rates, as they may deem right and proper, and shall have power to make mortgages or deeds of trust to secure said bonds. May issue bonds.

SEC. 8. *Be it further ordained*, That this ordinance shall be in force from and after its ratification, and continue for fifty years.

Ratified this 13th day of March, A. D. 1868.

CALVIN J. COWLES, *President.*

T. A. BYRNES, *Secretary.*

---

## CHAPTER XLIII.

### AN ORDINANCE TO INCORPORATE THE HALCYON STEAM BOAT COMPANY.

SECTION. 1. *Be it ordained by the people of North-Carolina in Convention assembled, and it is hereby ordained by the authority of the same*, That Robert M. Orrell, James A. Orrell and John R. Dailey, and such others as they may hereinafter associate with them, their successors and assigns, shall be and are hereby created, constituted and declared a body corporate and politic by the name of "The Halcyon Steam Boat Company," and by that name shall be in law capable of sueing and being sued, pleading and being impleaded, shall have a common seal and be invested with all the rights and privileges and be subject to all the regulations and restrictions contained in the 26th chapter of the Revised Body corporate.

Code, so far as the same are applicable to such a corporation, that are not inconsistent with the provisions of this act.

Capital stock. SEC. 2. *Be it further ordained*, That the capital stock of said Company shall consist of fifteen thousand dollars, with the privilege of increasing the same to twenty thousand dollars, divided into shares of one thousand dollars each.

Other steamers. SEC. 3. *Be it further ordained*, That said Company may build another steamer or barge or flats if required for the interest of the Company.

Real estate. SEC. 4. *Be it further ordained*, That said Company shall have power to hold, possess, acquire and enjoy such real estate as may be necessary for the transaction of its business, and from time to time to make all necessary rules, regulations and by-laws for the government and direction of the concerns thereof, not inconsistent with the Constitution and laws of the State of North-Carolina and of the United States, and said Company to have corporate existence for twenty years, unless surrendered to the Legislature at an earlier date by a majority of the stock.

SEC. 5. *Be it further ordained*, That this ordinance shall be in force from and after its ratification.

Ratified this 13th day of March, A. D. 1868.

CALVIN J. COWLES, *President*.

T. A. BYRNES, *Secretary*.

---

## CHAPTER XLIV.

### AN ORDINANCE TO PROVIDE FOR THE PAYMENT OF THE INTEREST ON THE PUBLIC DEBT.

Directions to the Legislature. SECTION 1. *Be it ordained by the people of North-Carolina in Convention assembled, and it is hereby ordained by the authority of the same*, That the first General Assembly which shall be convened under the provisions of the Constitution framed by this body, be and the same is hereby directed to make the following provisions for the payment of the interest upon the public debt:

SEC. 2. It shall provide for the payment in cash of the interest falling due on and after the first day of January, 1869, upon that portion of the bonds of the State which are dated prior to May 20th, 1861.

Interest on public debt to January, 1869.

SEC. 3. It shall provide for the payment in cash of the interest falling due on and after the first day of July, 1869, upon that portion of the bonds of the State which are dated on and after January 1st, 1866.

Do. to July, 1869.

SEC. 4. It shall provide for funding all such coupons upon the above specified classes of bonds as are now due, or which may become due, prior to the time when the payment of interest shall be resumed as above directed; and for such purposes the General Assembly shall authorize the issue of bonds of the State bearing six per cent. interest, which shall be given at par in exchange for such coupons as are now due, or may become due prior to the time when such resumption of the payment of interest shall take place.

Other provisions in relation to public debt.

SEC. 5. This ordinance shall be in force and take effect from and after its passage.

Ratified this 14th day of March, A. D. 1868.

CALVIN J. COWLES, *President.*

T. A. BYRNES, *Secretary.*

---

## CHAPTER XLV.

### AN ORDINANCE PROVIDING FOR AUDITING THE ACCOUNTS OF THE CONVENTION.

SECTION 1. *Be it ordained by the people of North-Carolina in Convention assembled*, That Calvin J. Cowles, after the adjournment of this Convention, shall audit the accounts thereof, and also the accounts for all expenditures for the printing ordered by this Convention, and the Treasurer of this State is hereby required to pay from any money in the Treasury of the State, upon the warrant of said Cowles, any sum necessary for the purpose of paying such expenses. He shall receive for his services six dollars per day while ac-

Accounts shall be audited by the President.

tually employed therein, to be paid in like manner upon his own warrant. The Comptroller of the State is hereby requested to audit the accounts of said Cowles, and the said accounts so audited shall be deposited in the office of the Comptroller of the State of North-Carolina.

Ratified this 14th day of March, A. D. 1868.

CALVIN J. COWLES, *President.*

T. A. BYRNES, *Secretary*

---

## CHAPTER XLVI.

### AN ORDINANCE IN RELATION TO MARRIAGES AUTHORIZED BY MILITARY AUTHORITY.

Declared legal and valid.

SECTION 1. *Be it ordained by the people of North-Carolina in Convention assembled, and it is hereby ordained by the authority of the same,* That all marriages authorized by military authority since April 1st, 1862, are hereby declared legal and valid.

Ratified this 14th day of March, A. D. 1868.

CALVIN J. COWLES, *President.*

T. A. BYRNES, *Secretary.*

---

## CHAPTER XLVII.

### AN ORDINANCE FOR THE DIVORCE OF PALMER AND LUCIND C. BABCOCK.

Palmer and Lucind C. Babcock divorced.

SECTION 1. *Be it ordained by the people of North-Carolina in Convention assembled,* That Palmer Babcock be and he hereby is divorced from the bonds of matrimony with his wife, Lucind C. Babcock, and that this ordinance shall take effect from and after its passage.

Ratified this 14th day of March, A. D. 1868.

CALVIN J. COWLES, *President.*

T. A. BYRNES, *Secretary.*

# CHAPTER XLVIII.

AN ORDINANCE AMENDING THE CHARTER OF THE CITY OF WILMINGTON.

WHEREAS, Certain provisions of an act to incorporate the inhabitants of the town of Wilmington, ratified February 1st, A. D. 1866, are inconsistent with and contrary to section 22d of the Bill of Rights as adopted by this Convention, and proposed to be incorporated in the Constitution of the State of North-Carolina: Preamble

SECTION 1. *Be it ordained by the people of North-Carolina in Convention assembled*, That so much of section third of the aforesaid act to incorporate the inhabitants of the town of Wilmington, as requires a freehold situated in the city of the value of one thousand ($1,000) dollars, according to assessment for taxation, as a qualification to hold the office of Mayor and Alderman of said city, be and the same is hereby repealed. Amends sec. 3 of former charter.

SEC. 2. *Be it further ordained*, That so much of section fifth of the aforesaid act of incorporation, as requires the inspector of elections in each ward to be a freeholder, be and hereby is repealed. Amends section 5th.

SEC. 3. *Be it further ordained*, That within fifteen days after the organization of the State Government, under the Constitution adopted by this Convention, the Sheriff of the County of New Hanover, with such assistants as he may appoint, shall hold an election for Mayor and two (2) Aldermen for each of the four wards of the City of Wilmington, which election shall be in conformity with the provisions of this ordinance and in the manner prescribed by the seventeenth (17th) section of the beforementioned act of incorporation. The person elected Mayor shall hold office until the first Monday in January, 1869; and until his successor is qualified. Of the persons elected Aldermen of each ward, one shall hold office until the first Monday in January, 1869, and until his successor shall be qualified, and the other shall hold office until the first Monday in January, 1870, and Election for Mayor, &c.

until his successor shall be qualified. The classification of the Aldermen shall be made by the aforesaid Sheriff, in the manner prescribed for the classification of the first Board of Aldermen, by section seventeenth (17th) of the aforesaid act of incorporation.

SEC. 4. *Be it further ordained*, That this ordinance shall be in force from and after the approval by the Congress of the United States of the Constitution framed by this Convention.

Ratified this 14th day of March, A. D. 1868.

CALVIN J. COWLES, *President*.

T. A. BYRNES, *Secretary*.

---

## CHAPTER XLIX.

### AN ORDINANCE TO INCORPORATE THE DAN RIVER COALFIELD RAIL ROAD COMPANY.

Name and style.

SECTION 1. *Be it ordained by the people of North-Carolina in Convention assembled, and it is hereby ordained by the authority of the same*, That a Company by the name and style of the "Dan River Coalfield Rail Road Company" be and the same is hereby incorporated, with a capital stock of twelve hundred and fifty thousand dollars, divided into shares of one hundred dollars each, for the purpose of constructing a Rail Road from some point on the Virginia line, near the town of Danville, in Virginia, to the Coalfields of Dan River.

Capital stock.

General Commissioners.

SEC. 2. *Be it further ordained*, That for the purpose of increasing the capital stock of said Company heretofore subscribed, and renewing and sealing all former subscriptions to said Company, the following persons be and are hereby appointed general Commissioners, viz: John W. Broadnax, President, George L. Akin, Jones Burton, Wm. Carter, J. Turner Morehead, Gen. Alfred M. Scales, Marshall Black, Wm. A. Lash, Benj. Baley, Andrew H. Joyce, Reubin D. Golding, Joseph Willis, Robert Matthews, Wm.

W. McCanlass and James Davis, whose duty it shall be to direct the opening of books for subscription of stock at such times and places and under such persons as they, or a majority of them, may deem proper; and said general Commissioners may have power to appoint a Chairman of their body, Treasurer, and all other officers their organization may require, and to sue for and recover all lands and sums of money that ought, under this act, be recovered by them.

SEC. 3. *Be it further ordained*, That all persons who may be hereafter by the general commissioners authorized to open books of subscription, may do so at any time after the ratification of this act, upon giving twenty days notice of the time and place when said books will be opened, and said books shall be kept open for the space of thirty days at least, and as long thereafter as the general commissioners shall direct; and that all subscriptions of stock shall be in shares of one hundred dollars in money or its value in land, the subscriber paying at the time of making his subscription five dollars on each share by him subscribed to the person or persons authorized to receive such subscriptions; and in case of failure to pay said sum all such subscriptions shall be void and of no effect; and upon closing the books all such sums as shall have been thus received of subscribers on the first cash or land instalment, shall be paid over to the general commissioners by the persons receiving the same; and in case of failure to pay as aforesaid such person or persons receiving said money or lands shall be personally liable to said general commissioners, before the organization of said Company, and to the Company itself after the organization, to be recovered in the Superior Courts of Law within this State in the County where such delinquent resides, or if he resides in another State, then in any court in such State having competent jurisdiction. The general commissioners shall have power to call on all persons empowered to receive subscriptions of stock at any time, and from time to time, as a majority of them may think proper, to make a return of the stock by them respectively received, and to make payment of all lands or sums of money paid by sub- Subscriptions of stock, &c.

scribers; that all persons receiving subscriptions of stock shall pass a receipt to the subscriber or subscribers for the payment of the first instalment, as heretofore required to be paid; and upon their settlement with the general commissioners as aforesaid, it shall be the duty of said general commissioners in like manner to pass their receipt for all sums thus received to the person from whom received, and such receipt shall be taken and held to be good and sufficient vouchers to the persons holding them; that subscriptions of stock may be received as aforesaid, or as hereinafter provided for, to the amount of twelve hundred and fifty thousand dollars.

Duty of General Commissioners.

SEC. 4. *Be it further ordained*, That it shall be the duty of said general commissioners to direct and authorize said books of subscription to be kept open until the sum of fifty thousand dollars at least shall be subscribed in the manner aforesaid, and as soon as the sum of fifty thousand dollars or upwards shall be subscribed in the manner aforesaid, and the sum of five dollars on each share paid in as aforesaid, the subscribers to said stock shall be and are hereby declared to be a body politic and corporate in fact and in law, by the name and style of "the Dan River Coalfield Rail Road Company," with all the corporate powers and authority hereby created and granted, to be held and exercised by said Company and their successors and assigns in perpetuity, and by that name shall be capable in law and in equity to purchase, hold, lease, rent, sell or convey estates, real, personal and mixed, and to acquire the same by gift, devise or otherwise, so far as shall be necessary for the purposes embraced within the scope, object and intent of this charter, and shall have perpetual succession and a common seal, which they may use, alter or renew at pleasure, and by their corporate name may sue and be sued, plead and be impleaded in any Court of Law or Equity in this State or any other State, and shall have, possess and enjoy all the rights, privileges and immunities which corporate bodies may and of the right do exercise, and may make all such by-laws, rules and regulations as are necessary for the government of the corporation, or for effecting the object for which it is created not inconsistent with the laws of this State or of the United States.

SEC. 5. *Be it further ordained*, That as soon as the sum of fifty thousand dollars or upwards shall be subscribed as aforesaid, it shall be the duty of the general commissioners to appoint a time for the stockholders to meet in Madison, in the County of Rockingham, which they shall cause to be previously published for the space of thirty days in one or more newspapers, at which time and place the said stockholders, in person or by proxy, [shall] proceed to elect by ballot nine Directors of the Company, and to enact all such regulations and by-laws as may be necessary for the government of said corporation and the transaction of business. The persons elected Directors of this meeting shall serve such period, not exceeding one year, as the stockholders may direct, and at this meeting the stockholders shall fix on a day and place or places where the subsequent election of Directors shall be held; and such elections shall henceforth be annually made, and if the day of the annual election should pass without any election of Directors, the corporation shall not thereby be dissolved, but it shall be lawful on any other day to hold and make such elections in such manner as may be prescribed by a by-law of the corporation. Meeting of stockholders.

SEC. 6. *Be it further ordained*, That the affairs of said Company shall be managed by a general board to consist of nine Directors, to be elected by the stockholders from among themselves at their first and subsequent general annual elections, and no stockholder shall be elected as Director, nor serve as such, unless he be, at the time of his election, the *bona fide* owner and legal holder of ten shares of said stock, and shall continue to hold the same during the term of his service. Board of Directors.

SEC. 7. *Be it further ordained*, That the President of said Company shall be chosen by ballot by a majority of the Directors from among themselves, with a salary to be fixed by the stockholders in general meeting. President.

SEC. 8. *Be it further ordained*, That all stockholders be-

Representation of stock in ballots.

ing citizens of the United States shall be entitled to vote either in person or proxy, the proxy being a stockholder, at all general meetings, and the vote to which each stockholder shall be entitled according to the number of shares he may hold in the proportions following, that is to say: for one share and not more than two, one vote; for every two shares above two and not exceeding ten, one vote; for every four shares above ten and not exceeding thirty, one vote; for every six shares over thirty and not exceeding sixty, one vote; for every eight shares over sixty and not exceeding one hundred, one vote; for every ten shares over one hundred and not exceeding two hundred, one vote; and for every twenty shares over two hundred, one vote.

First meeting of stockholders.

SEC. 9. *Be it further ordained*, That at the first general meeting of the stockholders under this act, a majority of all the shares subscribed shall be represented before proceeding to business, and if a sufficient number do not appear on the day appointed, those who do attend shall have power to adjourn from time to time until a regular meeting be thus formed; and at such regular meeting the stockholders may provide a by-law as to the number of stockholders and the amount of stock to be held by them, which shall constitute a quorum for transacting business at all subsequent regular or occasional meetings of stockholders and Directors.

Duty of General Commissioners.

SEC. 10. *Be it further ordained*, That the general commissioners shall make their return of the shares of the stock subscribed for at the first general meeting of the stockholders, and pay over to the Directors elected at their meeting, or their authorized agents, all sums of money and all lands received from subscribers; and on failure to do so they shall be personally liable to said Company, to be recovered at the suit of said Company in any of the Superior Courts of Law in this State in the County where the delinquent resides, and in case of his death the same shall be recovered of his executors or administrators.

Vacancies in Board.

SEC. 11. *Be it further ordained*, That the Board of Directors may fill all vacancies which may occur in it during the period for which they have been elected, and in the absence of the President may fill his place by electing a President *pro tempore* from among their number.

Power of Board to open books, &c.

SEC. 12. *Be it further ordained*, That the said Board of Directors shall have power and authority to open books for further subscription to the stock of said Company, at such times and under such persons as they may designate, in the event that the whole stock be not subscribed before the first general meeting of the stockholders, and to open and keep open said books from time to time until the whole amount of the capital stock be subscribed.

Construction of railway.

SEC. 13. *Be it further ordained*, That said Company shall have power and may proceed to construct, as speedily as possible, a Rail Road, with one or more tracks, from some point on the Virginia line, near the town of Danville, in Virginia, to the Coalfields of Dan River.

Right of conveyance and transportation.

SEC. 14. *Be it further ordained*, That said Company shall have the exclusive right of conveyance or transportation of persons, goods, merchandise and produce over the road constructed by them, at such charges as may be fixed upon by a majority of the Directors; and the said Company [may] farm out their right of transportation over their said Rail Road, subject to the rules above mentioned, and said Company, and every person who may have received from them the right of transportation of goods, wares and produce on said Rail Road, shall be deemed and taken to be a common carrier, as respects everything entrusted to them or him for transportation.

Payments of subscriptions, &c.

SEC. 15. *Be it further ordained*, That the Board of Directors may call for the payment of the sum or bond subscribed as stock in said Company, in such instalments as the interests of said Company may, in their opinion, require; the call for each payment shall be published in one or more newspapers in this State, for the space of one month before the day of payment, and on failure of any stockholder to pay each instalment as thus required, the directors may sell at public auction, on a previous notice of ten days, for cash, all the stock subscribed for in said Company, by such stockholders, and convey the same to the purchaser at said sale, discharged from all further liability, and if said sale of stock does not produce a sum sufficient to pay off the incidental expenses of the sale, and the entire amount owing by such stockholders to the Company for such subscription of stock, then, and in that case, the whole of such balance shall be held and taken as due at once to the Company, and may be recovered of such stockholder, or of his executors, administrators or assignees at the suit of said Company, either by summary motion in any court of superior jurisdiction in the County where the delinquent resides, on previous notice of ten days to said subscriber, or by action of assumpsit in any Court of competent jurisdiction, or by warrant before a Justice of the Peace, where the sum does not exceed one hundred dollars, and in all cases of assignment of stock before the whole amount has been paid to the Company, then, for all sums due on such stocks, both the original subscribers and the first and all subsequent assignees shall be liable to the Company, and the same may be recovered as above described.

Debts due to Company for stock.

SEC. 16. *Be it further ordained*, That the debt of stockholders due to the Company for stock therein, either as original proprietor or as first or subsequent assignee, shall be considered of equal dignity with judgments in the distribution of assets of a deceased stockholder by his legal representative.

Certificate of stock.

SEC. 17. *Be it further ordained*, That said Company shall issue certificates of stock to its members, and said stock may be transferred in such manner and form as may be directed by the by-laws of the Company.

Board of Directors shall report.

SEC. 18. *Be it further ordained*, That the Board of Directors shall once every year at least, make a full report of the stock of the Company and its affairs to a general meeting of the stockholders, and oftener if required by a by-law, and shall have power to call a general meeting of the stockholders when the Board may deem it expedient, and the Company may provide in their by-laws for occasional meetings being called and prescribe the mode thereof.

SEC. 19. *Be it further ordained*, That said Company may

purchase, have and hold in fee, or for a term of years, any land tenaments or hereditaments, which may be necessary for the said road or the appurtenances thereof, or for the erection of depositories, store houses, houses for the officers, servants or agents of the said Company, or for work shops or foundaries, to be used for said Company, or for procuring stone or other materials necessary to the construction of the road, or for effecting transportation thereon.

Lands, tenements, &c.

SEC. 20. *Be it further ordained*, That the Company shall have the right, when necessary, to conduct the said road across or along any public road or water course: *Provided*, That the said Company shall not obstruct any public road without constructing another equally as good and convenient.

Crossing public roads.

SEC. 21. *Be it further ordained*, That when any lands or right of way may be required by said Company, for the purpose of constructing their road, and for want of agreement as to the value thereof, or for any other cause, the same cannot be purchased from the owner or owners, the same may be taken at a valuation to be made by the five Commissioners, or three of them, to be appointed by any court of record having common law jurisdiction in the County where some part of the land or right of way is situated. In making the said valuation, the said Commissioners shall take into consideration the loss or damage which may accrue to the owner or owners in consequence of the land or right of way being surrendered, and the benefit and advantage, general or special which he, she or they may receive by the general increased value of the land, or any special benefit which may arise from the location of a depot, or otherwise on said land, or any benefit which may accrue in any way whatever, by the establishment of said Rail Road or works, and shall state particularly the amout and value of each, and the excess of the loss and damage, over and above the advantage and benefit, shall form the measure of valuation of the said land or right of way: *Provided, nevertheless*, That if any person or persons, over whose land the road may pass, or if said company should be dissatisfied with the valuation of

Right of way.

said Commissioners, then, and in that case, the party so dissatified, may make an appeal to the Superior Court, in the County where said valuation has been made, or in either County in which the land may lie, when it shall be in more than one County, under the same rules, regulations and restrictions in other cases of appeals. The proceedings of said Commissioners, accompanied with a full description of said land or right of way, shall be returned under the hands and seal of a majority of them, to the Court from which the Commission issued, there to remain a matter of record, and the lands or right of way so valued, shall vest in the said Company so long as the same shall be used for the purpose of the Rail Road, so soon as the valuation shall have been paid, or when refused, may have been tendered: *Provided*, That on application for the appointment of Commissioners, under this section, it shall be made to appear to the satisfaction of the Court, that at least ten day's previous notice has been given by the applicant to the owner or owners of the said land, so proposed to be condemned, or if the owner or owners be infants or *non compos mentis*, then to the guardian of such owner or owners, if such guardian can be found within the County, or if he can not be so found, then such appointment shall not be made, unless notice of the application shall have been published at least one month next preceeding, in some newspaper printed as convenient as may be to the Court House of the County, and shall have been posted at the door of the Court House, on the first day at least of the term of said court to which the application is made; *Provided further*, That the valuation provided for in this section shall be made on oath, or by the commissioners aforesaid, which oath any justice of the peace or Clerk is authorized to administer: *Provided further*, That the right of condemnation herein granted shall not authorize the said Company to invade the dwelling house, yard, garden or burying ground of any individual without his consent.

Right to condemn land.

SEC. 22. *Be it further ordained*, That the right of said Company to condemn land in the manner aforesaid shall extend to the condemning of one hundred feet on each side of the main track of the road, measuring from the centre of the same, unless in case of deep cuts and fillings, when said Company shall have power to condemn as much in addition thereto as may be necessary for the purpose of constructing said road, and the Company shall also have power to condemn and appropriate lands in like manner for the constructing and building of depots, shops, warehouses, buildings for servants, agents and persons employed on the road, not exceeding two acres in any one lot or station.

Corporation to have good title.

SEC. 23. *Be it further ordained*, That in the absence of any contract or contracts with said Company in relation to lands through which the said road may pass, signed by the owner thereof, or his agent, or any claimant or person in possession thereof, which may be confirmed by the owner thereof, it shall be presumed that the land upon which said road may be constructed, together with the space of one hundred feet on each side of the centre of the said road, had been granted to the said Company by the owner thereof, shall have good right and title thereto, and shall have, hold and enjoy the same as long as the same be used for the purposes of said road, and no longer, unless the person or persons owning the said land at the time that part of the said road which may be on said land was finished, or the claiming under him, her or them, shall apply for an assessment of the value of said lands as hereinbefore directed, within two years next after that part of the said road which may be on the said land was finished; and in case the said owner or those claiming under him, his, her or them, shall not apply within two years next after the said part was finished, he, she or they shall be forever barred from recovering said land, or having any assessment or compensation therefrom: *Provided*, That nothing herein contained shall affect the rights of *feme coverts* or infants until two years after the removal of their respective disabilities.

Lands not granted to vest.

SEC. 24. *Be it further ordained*, That all lands not heretofore granted to any person within one hundred feet of the centre of the said road, shall vest in the company as soon as the line of the road is definitely laid out through it, and any grant of said land thereafter shall be void.

Intruders may be indicted.

SEC. 25. *Be it further ordained*, That if any person or persons shall intrude upon the said Rail Road by any manner of use thereof, or of the rights and privileges connected therewith without the permission, or contrary to the will of the said company, he, she or they may be indicted for misdemeanor, and upon conviction fined and imprisoned by any court of competent jurisdiction.

Penalty for injuring property of corporation.

SEC. 26. *Be it further ordained*, That if any person shall wilfully and maliciously destroy, or in any manner hurt, or damage, or destroy, or obstruct, or shall wilfully or maliciously cause, or aid, or assist, or counsel, or advise any other person or persons to destroy or in any manner to hurt, damage, injure or obstruct the said Rail Road, or any bridge or vehicle used for or in the transportation thereon, any water tank, warehouse, or any other property of said Company, such person or persons so offending shall be liable to be convicted therefor, and on conviction shall be imprisoned not more than six nor less than one month, and pay a fine not exceeding five hundred dollars nor less than twenty dollars, at the discretion of [the] court before which said conviction shall take place and shall be further liable to pay all expenses for repairing the same, and it shall not [be] competent for any person so offending against the provisions of this clause to defend himself by pleading or giving in evidence that he was the owner, agent or servant of the owner of the land where such destruction, hurt, damage, injury or obstruction was done at the time the same was done or caused to be done.

Obstructions to be removed.

SEC. 27. *Be it further ordained*, That every obstruction to the safe and free passage of vehicles on the said road shall be deemed a public nuisance, and may be abated as such by any officer, agent or servant of said Company, and the person causing such obstruction may be indicted for erecting a public nuisance.

Rights of corporation in its business.

SEC. 28. *Be it further ordained*, That the said Company shall have the right to take at the store-house they may establish, on or annexed to their Rail Road, all goods, wares, merchandise and produce intended for transportation, to prescribe the rules of priority and charge, and receive such just and reasonable compensation for storage as they by rules may establish, (which they shall cause to be published,) or as may be fixed by agreement with the owner, which may be distinct from the rates of transportation: *Provided*, That the said Company shall not charge or receive any storage on goods, wares, merchandise, or produce which may be delivered to them at their regular depositories for immediate transportation, and which the Company may have power to transact immediately.

SEC. 29. *Be it further ordained*, That the profits of the Company, or so much thereof as the general board may deem advisable, shall, when the affairs of the Company will permit, be semi-annually divided amongst the stockholders in proportion to the stock each may own. Annual dividends.

SEC. 30. *Be it further ordained*, That the following officers and servants, and persons in the actual employment of the said Company, be, and they are hereby exempt from the jury, and ordinary militia duty: the President and Treasurer, the Board of Directors, Chief and Assistant Engineers, the Secretary and accountants of this Company, keepers of the depositories, guards stationed on the road and at the bridges, and such persons as may be working the locomotive engines and traveling with the cars for the purpose of attending to transportation of produce, goods and passengers on the road. Exemptions.

SEC. 31. *Be it further ordained*, That for the purpose of constructing said road, the Company are hereby authorized and empowered, by a vote of the stockholders in general meeting assembled, to increase their capital stock to an amount sufficient in their opinion to effect the object, and to raise money, by loan or otherwise, sufficient to complete the main track or road, upon such securities and in such a manner as the stockholders may direct. May increase capital stock.

SEC. 32. *Be it further ordained*, That for the purpose of ascertaining the best route for said road, and to locate the May make surveys.

same, it shall be lawful for said Company, by its engineers, servants and agents, to enter upon, examine and survey any land or lands that they may wish to examine for such purpose, free from any liability whatever.

Not to run within 20 miles of N. C. Road.

SEC. 33. *Be it further ordained*, That said road shall not run within twenty miles of the North-Carolina Rail Road, and if the Company hereby incorporated violate the provisions of this section, it shall work a forfeiture of their charter.

Ratified this March 5th, A. D. 1868.

CALVIN J. COWLES, *President.*

T. A. BYRNES, *Secretary.*

---

## CHAPTER L.

AN ORDINANCE FOR THE COMPLETION OF THE WESTERN NORTH-CAROLINA RAIL ROAD.

Use of appropriations.

SECTION 1. *Be it ordained by the people of North-Carolina in Convention assembled, and it is hereby ordained by the authority of the same*, That the proceeds of no appropriations or subscriptions which the State of North-Carolina has made or may hereafter make to, or in aid of, the Western North-Carolina Rail Road Company, shall be used in the construction of any branch road except that of French Broad until the main trunk line of said Rail Road shall have been completed to Copper Mine, at or near Ducktown.

Further appropriations.

SEC. 2. *Be it further ordained*, That the General Assembly, when the interest of said corporation (the Western North-Carolina Rail Road Company) requires it, shall be and the same is hereby authorized and directed to make such further appropriation or subscription to the capital stock of said Rail Road Company as will insure the completion of said road at the earliest practicable day.

Ratified this 14th day of March, A. D. 1868.

CALVIN J. COWLES, *President.*

T. A. BYRNES, *Secretary.*

## CHAPTER LI.

ORDINANCE FOR THE DIVORCE OF ANN UNDERDUE AND WILLIAM UNDERDUE.

SECTION 1. *Be it ordained by the people of North-Carolina in Convention assembled*, That Ann Underdue, formerly Ann Smith, wife of William Underdue, be and she is hereby divorced from the bohds of mrtrimony with her said husband and that this ordinance shall be in force from and after its passage.

Dissolves the bonds of matrimony.

Ratified this 14th day of March, A. D. 1868.

CALVIN J. COWLES, *President.*

T. A. BYRNES, *Secretary.*

---

## CHAPTER LII.

AN ORDINANCE APPOINTING COMMISSIONERS TO INVESTIGATE THE ACCOUNTS AND AFFAIRS OF THE ALBEMARE AND CHESAPEAKE CANAL COMPANY.

SECTION 1. *Be it ordained by the people of North-Carolina in Convention assembled, and it is hereby ordained by the authority of the same*, That E. W. Jones, C. C. Pool, and Gesbourne J. Cherry be, and the same are hereby appointed a Committee to investigate the accounts and affairs of the Albemarle and Chesapeake Canal Company with authority to send for persons and papers, to examine and take testimony, to fill vacancies in said Commission, should any occur, and to report the result of their investigations together with such recommendations as they may deem proper to protect the interest of the State, to the next meeting of the Convention or Legislature, and that said Commissioners be paid therefor the sum of six dollars per day each when actually employed, together with such travelling and inciden-

Committee.

Powers.

Report.

tal expenses that may be incurred in prosecuting said investigation.

Ratified this 16th day of March, A. D. 1868.

CALVIN J. COWLES, *President.*

T. A. Byrnes, *Secretary.*

---

## CHAPTER LIII.

### AN ORDINANCE AMENDING THE CHARTER OF THE CITY OF RALEIGH.

Amends section 4.

Section 1. *Be it ordained by the people of North-Carolina in Convention assembled, and it is hereby ordained by the authority of the same*, That Section 4 of the Charter of the City of Raleigh be so amended as to read as follows:

"Sec. 4. *Be it further ordained*, That any qualified elector shall be eligible as Mayor or Commissioner, and every Commissioner shall be a resident of the Ward for which he shall be chosen."

Sec. 2. *Be it further ordained*, That this ordinance shall be in force from and after its passage.

Ratified this 17th day of March, A. D. 1868.

CALVIN J. COWLES, *President.*

T. A. Byrnes, *Secretary.*

---

## CHAPTER LIV.

### AN ORDINANCE COMPENSATING C. J. COWLES.

Per diem and mileage.

Section 1. *Be it ordained by the people of North-Carolina in Convention assembled, and it is hereby ordained by the authority of the same*, That Calvin J. Cowles shall receive a compensation of six dollars per day and mileage while engaged in the performance of the duties imposed on him by the several ordinances of this Convention, and that the same be paid by the Treasurer of the State, on the warrant of said Cowles.

SEC. 2. *Be it further ordained*, That this ordinance shall be in effect from and after its passage.

Ratified this 17th day of March, A. D. 1868.

CALVIN J. COWLES, *President.*

T. A. BYRNES, *Secretary.*

---

## CHAPTER LV.

### AN ORDINANCE DIVORCING EDWARD SHROYER AND MARY P. SHROYER.

Dissolves the bonds of matrimony.

SECTION 1. *Be it ordained by the people of North-Carolina in Convention assembled, and it is hereby ordained by the authority of the same*, That Edward Shroyer be and he hereby is divorced from the bonds of matrimony with his wife, Mary P. Shroyer, and this ordinance shall be in force from and after its passage.

Ratified this 17th day of March, A. D. 1868.

CALVIN J. COWLES, *President.*

T. A. BYRNES, *Secretary*

---

## CHAPTER LVI.

### AN ORDINANCE EXTENDING THE TIME FOR REGISTRATION OF DEEDS.

Two years to register.

SECTION 1. *Be it ordained by the people of North-Carolina in Convention assembled, and it is hereby ordained by the authority of the same*, That no grant or conveyance of lands heretofore made shall be void by reason of the nonregistration thereof previous to this time, but the grantees in such deeds shall have two years from the ratification of this ordinance wherein to register the same: *Provided*, That nothing herein contained shall extend to mortgages, deeds in trust or marriage settlements.

SEC. 2. *Be it further ordained*, That all persons who

Purchasers to have till January, 1869.

have made entries of vacant land and paid the purchase money to the State for the same since the first day of January, 1861, shall have until the first day of January, 1869, to perfect titles to the same.

Sec. 3. *Be it further ordained*, That all persons who have heretofore made entries of lands according to law within the time aforesaid, and have not paid the purchase money into the Treasury, shall have until the first day of January, 1869, to make said payment and perfect their titles to said lands: *Provided*, That nothing herein contained shall be so construed as to affect the titles of persons who have heretofore obtained grants for said lands, or the rights of junior enterers, or extending to swamp lands vested in the Literary Board.

Proviso.

Ratified this 17th day of March, A. D. 1868.

CALVIN J. COWLES, *President*.

T. A. Byrnes, *Secretary*.

---

## CHAPTER LVII.

### AN ORDINANCE OF DIVORCE IN FAVOR OF ARCHIBALD HANEY, OF RANDOLPH COUNTY.

Archibald Haney divorced from his wife.

Section 1. *Be it ordained by the people of North-Carolina in Convention assembled, and it is hereby ordained by the authority of the same*, That Archibald Haney, of Randolph County, be and he hereby is divorced from the bonds of matrimony with Cornelia, his wife, and this ordinance shall go into effect from its ratification.

Ratified this 17th day of March, A. D. 1868.

CALVIN J. COWLES, *President*.

T. A. Byrnes, *Secretary*.

## CHAPTER LVIII.

AN ORDINANCE RESPECTING THE JURISDICTION OF THE COURTS OF THIS STATE.

Repeals sections of former acts.

SECTION 1. *Be it ordained by the people of North-Carolina in Convention assembled*, That sections one and two of the ordinance of the Convention adopted June 23d, 1866, entitled "An ordinance to change the jurisdiction of the courts and the rules of pleading therein," be and are hereby repealed.

Amends section 3.

SEC. 2. *Be it further ordained*, That section three of the above entitled ordinance be amended to read as follows: Sec. 3. That all actions of debt, covenant, assumpsit and account now pending in the Superior Courts shall be continued to Spring Term, 1869, and that the several Superior Courts at the Spring Term thereof only, unless otherwise herein provided, shall have exclusive original jurisdiction of all such causes of action except where jurisdiction has been or shall be given to a Justice of the Peace by the Constitution or laws of North-Carolina. Should the defendant at the Spring Term, 1869, on writs which shall be returned to that Term or in any suit, for the above causes of action then pending in the Superior Court, pay or confess judgment to the plaintiff for one-tenth of the debt, and demand principal and interest and all costs to that time, he shall be allowed until next Spring Term to plead. At the said Spring Term should the defendant pay to the plaintiff or confess judgment for one-fifth of the residue of the said debt or demand and cost, he shall be allowed until the succeeding Spring Term to plead. At the said Spring Term should the defendant pay to the plaintiff or confess judgment for one-half of the residue of the debt or demand, he shall be allowed until the succeeding Spring Term to plead. At the said Spring Term the plaintiff shall have judgment for the residue of his debt or demand: *Provided, however*, That the plaintiff, if required, shall file his debt or demand in writing, and if the defendant

Proviso.

shall make oath that the whole or any part thereof is not justly due, or that he has a counter demand, all of which shall be particularly set forth by affidavit, then the defendant shall only pay the instalment required of what he admits to be due, and the court shall order a jury at the same or some subsequent term to try the matters in dispute between the parties, and at the next Spring Term the defendant shall be allowed time to plead only upon paying or confessing judgment for one-fifth of the residue of the admitted amount, and whatever the jury finds him indebted over and above the same: *Provided further*, That should the defendant fail to pay or confess judgment for the first or any subsequent installment, then and in that case the plaintiff shall be entitled to proceed to judgment and execution for such installment, unless the defendant shall put in pleas, in which case the suit shall proceed according to the course of the court in 1860: *Provided further*, That by consent of the plaintiff the defendant at any term of the court may confess judgment for a stipulated sum in full and final discharge of all further demand or liability upon such claim.

Proviso.

Proviso.

Amends section 10.

SEC. 3. *Be it futher ordained*, That section 10 of the above recited act shall be amended to read as follows: Sec. 10. That executions on judgments in actions of debt, assumpsit, covenant or account, or decrees for money demands in equity, which have been, or shall be issued on judgments or decrees heretofore obtained, shall be levied on the property of the defendant and returned without sale: *Provided*, such return shall not prejudice any lien the plaintiff may acquire or then have by virtue of said *fi. fa.* or *venditioni exponas.* At Spring Term, 1869, execution on all such judgments or decrees shall issue for only one-tenth of the amount then due; at Spring Term, 1870, for one-fifth of the residue; at Spring Term, 1871, for one-half of the residue, and at Spring Term, 1872, for the balance of the debt; and no execution shall issue from the Fall Term on any such judgment or decree except by consent of the defendant. That no mortgagee or trustee shall

Proviso.

expose to sale the property conveyed in such mortgage or trust deed, without the consent of the grantor, before first of March, 1869. Should the mortgagor or trustor at that time pay one-tenth of the debts mentioned, the sale shall be postponed to first of March, 1870; at that time should the mortgagor or trustor pay one-fifth of the residue, the sale shall be postponed to the first of March, 1871; at that time should the trustor or mortgagor pay one-half of the residue, the sale shall be postponed to first of March, 1872; and at that time the trustee or morgagee shall sell the property or so much of it as will realize the balance of the debts: *Provided, however*, That should the trustor or mortgagor fail to pay the first or any subsequent installment, then, and in that case, the trustee or mortgagee shall sell at six months credit so much of the property conveyed as will realize such installment. Proviso.

Sec. 4. *Be it further ordained*, That section 11 of the above entitled act be amended to read as follows: That no warrants before Justices of the Peace shall issue or be returnable until January 1st, 1869. Should the defendant upon such return pay to the plaintiff, or to the collecting officer, for his use, or confess judgment before the magistrate for one-tenth of the debt and demand, (principal and interest) he shall be allowed twelve months to plead; at the expiration of that time, should the defendant pay to the plaintiff or confess judgment for one-fifth of the residue of the said debt or demand, he shall be allowed twelve months more to plead; at the expiration of that time should the defendant pay to the plaintiff or confess judgment for one half of the residue of said debt or demand, he shall be allowed twelve months more to plead; at the expiration of that time the plaintiff shall have judgment for the residue of his debt or demand: *Provided, however*, That the plaintiff, if required, shall file his claim in writing, and if the defendant shall make oath that the whole or any part thereof is not justly due, or that he has a counter demand, all of which he shall particularly set forth by affidavit, then the defendant shall only pay the installment required

Amends section 11.

Proviso.

of what he admits to be due, and the justice shall proceed to try the matters in dispute between the parties; and at the expiration of twelve months the defendant shall be allowed time to plead only upon payment of one-fifth of the amount admitted to be due, and whatever the justice may have found him indebted over and above the same: *Provided*, That should the defendant fail to pay or confess judgment for the first or any subsequent installment, then and in that case, the plaintiff shall be entitled to proceed to judgment and execution for such installment: *Provided further*, That by consent of the plaintiff the defendant may at any time confess judgment for a stipulated sum in full and final discharge of all further demand or liability upon such claim. That all executions on judgments in actions of debt, covenant, assumpsit or account which have been, or shall be issued on judgments heretofore obtained before any magistrate, shall be levied on the property of the defendant and returned without sale; at the expiration of twelve months from such return execution on all such judgments shall issue for only one-tenth of the amount then due; at the expiration of twelve months from that time for one-fifth of the residue; at the expiration of twelve months more for one-half of the residue, and at the expiration of twelve months more for the balance of the debt.

Proviso.

Proviso.

Amends section 17.

SEC. 5. *Be it further ordained*, That section 17 of the above entitled ordinance be amended to read as follows: Sec. 17. That the provisions of this ordinance shall not be construed to extend to any debts or demands contracted or penalties incurred since the first day of May, A. D. 1865, or which may hereafter be contracted or incurred, except actions founded on any bond, promissory note, bill of exchange, or any other instrument of writing, or parol promise made since first May, 1865, in renewal of, or substitution for, a contract made prior to first of May, 1865, to the full amount of the principal and interest of a debt existing prior to said day, and without other consideration than such pre-existent debt; and except also, actions, suits, or process to revive, continue or enforce any judgment heretofore recovered upon any such bond, promissory note, bill of exchange or other instruments of writing or parol promise as is hereinbefore mentioned.

SEC. 6. *Be it further ordained*, That this ordinance shall be in force from and after its ratification.

In force from ratification.

Ratified this 14th day of March, A. D. 1868

CALVIN J. COWLES, *President*.

T. A. BYRNES, *Secretary*.

---

AN ORDINANCE ADMITTING MEMBERS OF THE BAR OF OTHER STATES TO PRACTICE IN THIS STATE.

SECTION 1. *Be it ordained by the people of North Carolina in Convention assembled, and it is hereby ordained by the authority of the same*, That any person who shall produce a certificate of admission to the Bar of any other State, and satisfactory evidence of good moral character, before the Supreme Court of the State, shall be admitted to the practice of law in the several courts of this State, upon payment of the fees prescribed by law; and this ordinance shall be in force from and after the date of its passage.

Persons admitted to the bar in other States may practice in this State.

Ratified this 4th day of February, A. D. 1868.

CALVIN J. COWLES, *President*.

T. A. BYRNES, *Secretary*.

---

I, T. A. BYRNES, Secretary of the State Constitutional Convention of North Carolina, do hereby certify that the foregoing are true copies of the original Ordinances of the State Constitutional Convention, session of 1868.

T. A. BYRNES, *Secretary*.

# RESOLUTIONS.

RESOLUTION INSTITUTING THE OATH TO BE TAKEN BY DELEGATES TO THE CONSTITUTIONAL CONVENTION OF NORTH-CAROLINA.

*Resolved*, That the delegates to this Convention take the following oath, and that N. J. Riddick, Clerk of the Circuit Court of the United States, be requested to administer the same oath: Oath taken by delegates.

OATH.

You do solemnly swear [*or*, affirm] that you will support the Constitution of the United States, and faithfully discharge your duties as members of this Convention. So help you God.

Adopted January 14th, A. D. 1868.

---

RESOLUTION APPOINTING T. A. BYRNES SECRETARY.

*Resolved*, That T. A. Byrnes be appointed permanent Secretary of this Convention. Secretary.

Adopted January 15th, A. D. 1868.

---

RESOLUTION FIXING THE RULES OF ORDER FOR THE CONVENTION.

*Resolved*, That the rules of order of the Convention of this State for 1865-'66 be adopted by this Convention, so far as practicable, until further ordered. Rules of order.

Adopted January 15th, A. D. 1868.

RESOLUTION APPOINTING A COMMITTEE ON FRAMING A CONSTITUTION.

Plan of government.

*Resolved*, That a Committee of two members from each Judicial District be appointed by the President, whose duty it shall be to consider and report, at the earliest practicable moment, [the best plan] to frame a Constitution and Civil Government, according to the provisions of the Acts of Congress.

Adopted January 15th, A. D. 1868.

---

RESOLUTION IN REGARD TO FRAMING RULES FOR THE GOVERNMENT OF THE CONVENTION.

Rules of order.

*Resolved*, That the President appoint a Committee of Five to frame Rules of Order for the government of the Convention.

Adopted January 15th, 1868.

---

RESOLUTION REGARDING SERGEANT AT ARMS.

Sergeant at Arms.

*Resolved*, That this Convention do now proceed to an election of Sergeant at Arms.

Adopted January 16th, A. D. 1868.

---

RESOLUTION IN REGARD TO REPORTERS, &C.

Reporters excluded for disrespectful language.

*Resolved*, That no reporter for any newspaper shall hereafter be allowed upon this floor who, in his reports, shall treat the Convention or any of its members with disrespect, but that they shall, in case of offence in this respect, be excluded from the floor of the hall, and from the galleries, by the President.

Adopted January 16th, A. D. 1868.

RESOLUTION INSTRUCTING THE PRESIDENT OF THE CONVENTION IN REGARD TO CLERGYMEN.

*Resolved*, That the President of this Convention invite the Clergymen of the City of Raleigh to open the services of this Convention each morning with prayer. Prayer by Raleigh Clergymen.

Adopted January 16th, A. D. 1868.

---

RESOLUTION IN REGARD TO ASCERTAINING THE VOTES OF COUNTIES, &C.

*Resolved*, That the Secretary apply to General Canby for a full statement of the votes, by Counties, for and against a Convention, cast in this State and received by each candidate for this Convention. Vote on Convention.

Adopted January 17th, A. D. 1868.

---

REPORT OF COMMITTEE ON THE BEST MODE OF FRAMING A CONSTITUTION AND CIVIL GOVERNMENT.

The Committee appointed to consider and report upon the best mode of proceeding to frame a Constitution and Civil Government, according to the Acts of Congress, respectfully report as follows: Committees on various subjects.

*Resolved*, That the. Standing Committees be appointed by the President to report on each of the following subjects, viz:

1st. On a Preamble and Bill of Rights.

2d. On a Governor and other Necessary State Executive Officers, their Election or Appointment, Tenure of Office, Compensation, Powers and Duties.

3d. On the Legislature, its Organization, the Number, Apportionment, Election, Tenure of Office of its Members, its Powers and Duties, except as otherwise referred.

4th. On the Judiciary Department.

5th. On the Finances of the State, the Public Debt,

Committees on various subjects.

Revenues, Expenditures and Taxation, and Restrictions on the Powers of the Legislature in respect thereto.

6th. On Internal Improvements.

7th. On Counties, Cities, Towns and Villages, their Officers, Organization, Government and Powers.

8th. On Corporations other than Municipal.

9th. On Punishments and Penal Institutions.

10th. On Militia.

11th. On Education, Common Schools, Universities, and the Means of their Support.

12th. On Suffrage and Eligibility to Office.

13th. On Homestead.

The Committee also recommend [that] the different Standing Committees as named shall each consist of thirteen members.

DAVID HEATON, *Chairman*,
W. NICHOLSON,
W. B. RODMAN,
J. H. HARRIS,
T. L. L. COX,
J. W. HOOD,
M. HOBBS,
GEO. W. BRADLEY,
E. W. JONES,
H. A. DOWD,
A. W. TOURGEE,
J. C. ABBOTT,
S. FALKNER,
C. C. JONES,
G. W. GRAHAM,
W. G. B. GARRETT.

Adopted January 17th, A. D. 1868.

### RESOLUTION PROCURING AN AMERICAN FLAG.

*Resolved*, That the Secretary of this Convention is hereby authorized and instructed to procure an American flag to be suspended from the dome of the capitol.

Instructs the Secretary.

Adopted January 16th, A. D. 1868.

---

### RESOLUTION INFORMING GEN. CANBY OF THE ORGANIZATION OF THE CONVENTION.

*Resolved*, That the President of the Convention be requested to inform Major-General E. R. S. Canby, of this Military District, that this Convention is permanently organized, and is proceeding to the dispatch of business.

To General Canby.

Adopted this January 17th, A. D. 1868.

---

### RESOLUTION REQUESTING THE PROVISIONAL SECRETARY OF STATE TO FURNISH COPIES OF THE CONSTITUTION, 1865–'66.

*Resolved, by the delegates of the people of North-Carolina in Convention assembled*, That the Provisional Secretary of State furnish each delegate of this Convention a copy of the Constitution adopted by the Convention of 1865–'66 for the use of the delegates.

To the Secretary.

Adopted January 18th, A. D. 1868.

---

### RESOLUTION APPOINTING A COMMITTEE OF THREE TO WAIT ON THE GOVERNOR OF THE STATE.

*Resolved*, That a Committee of three be appointed to wait on his Excellency, the Governor of North-Caralina, and inform him of the organization of the Convention, and that the Convention is now ready to receive any communication he may desire to make.

Instructs Committee.

Adopted January 20th, A. D. 1868.

RESOLUTION APPOINTING A COMMITTEE TO PROCURE COPIES OF PROCEEDINGS OF THE GENERAL ASSEMBLY, SES. 1866–'67.

To the Secretary of State.

*Resolved*, That the President of this Convention be directed to appoint a Committee of two to request the Provisional Secretary of State to furnish twelve copies of the proceedings of the General Assembly during the session of 1866–'67 for the use of the members of this Convention.

Adopted January 20th, A. D. 1868.

---

RESOLUTION FIXING THE PER DIEM AND MILEAGE OF MEMBERS.

Per diem and mileage.

*Resolved*, That each delegate to the Convention, and each elective officer (the President excepted,) receive eight dollars ($8.00) per day, and twenty cents mileage to and from the Convention, and that the President receive twelve dollars ($12.00) per day, and twenty cents per mile.

Adopted January 22d, A. D. 1868.

---

RESOLUTION REQUESTING GEN. CANBY TO VISIT THE CONVENTION.

To General Canby.

*Resolved*, That the delegates of the Constitutional Convention of North-Carolina, now assembled, request Maj. Gen. E. R. S. Canby, Commanding Second Military District, composed of the States of North and South-Carolina, to visit this Convention and communicate anything he may deem for the good of the people of North-Carolina.

Adopted January 24th, A. D. 1868.

---

RESOLUTION REGARDING THE COMMITTEE ON PRINTING.

Power of Chairman.

*Resolved*, That the Chairman of the Committee on Printing have power, on the request of the chairman of any committee, to cause to be printed for the use of this Convention, any matter prepared by a committee and necessary for the information of the delegates.

Adopted January 25th, A. D. 1868.

RESOLUTION REQUESTING THE TREASURER OF STATE TO FURNISH THE CONVENTION WITH A STATEMENT OF THE INDEBTEDNESS OF THE STATE.

*Resolved*, That the Treasurer of the State of North-Carolina be requested to furnish this Convention with a statement of the indebtedness of said State; to what parties, or sources; what amount to each; what is the amount of her endorsement for railroad or other improvements; what further endorsement of railroad bonds is she directed to make under any existing law or regulation, and when passed; what property or assets or securities the State holds for or on account of said indebtedness; what amount of stock the State holds in the several corporations of the State; and what amount of dividend or interest she receives from each source? To Treasurer of State.

Adopted January 25th, A. D. 1868.

---

RESOLUTION REQUESTION TREASURER OF STATE TO FURNISH CERTAIN INFORMATION.

*Resolved*, That the Treasurer of the State of North-Carolina be requested to furnish this Convention with a statement of what amount of stock said State owns in the Albemarle and Chesapeake Canal Company, what amount she has paid, or agreed to pay, or is under any obligation in the future to pay, what is the entire amount of the capital stock of said Company, and where owned, and whether said State has received any divided or interest for, or on account of its investments, subscription or endorsement of said Company, or its bonds, and how much, or whether it is now paying its interest or dividend regularly to the State. To Treasurer of State.

Adopted January 25th, A. D. 1868.

---

RESOLUTION INSTRUCTING THE JUDICIARY COMMITTEE.

*Resolved*, That the Standing Committee on the Judiciary,

Instructs Judiciary Committee.

is hereby requested, if deemed advisable, to report such a provision to the new Constitution as will clearly authorize the first Legislature convened under it, to pass suitable laws giving mechanics and artizans an ample lien as indemnity for their labor.

Adopted January 27th, A. D. 1868.

---

RESOLUTION INVITING UNITED STATES OFFICERS TO THE FLOOR OF THE CONVENTION.

To the Secretary.

*Resolved*, That the Secretary be directed to invite the United States officers on duty at this Post to the floor of this House.

Adopted January 22d, A. D. 1868.

---

RESOLUTION INSTRUCTING THE COMMITTEE TO CONFER WITH GENERAL CANBY.

Inquiry concerning enforcement of an ordinance.

*Resolved*, That the Committee appointed to confer with General Canby, be instructed to inquire of him whether he would enforce an ordinance of this Convention, or upon its recommendation would issue an order staying the collection of all debts except in casses of fraud, and wages for labor performed since May 1st, 1868.

Adopted January 23d, A. D. 1868.

---

RESOLUTION APPOINTING A COMMITTEE OF THREE TO CONFER WITH GENERAL CANBY.

Powers of Committee.

*Resolved*, That a Committee of Three be appointed by the Chair, to confer with Major-General E. R. S. Canby, Commanding the second Military District, which committee shall be empowered to consult upon any subject relating to the public interest, and to report the result of their consultations to the Convention.

Adopted January 22d, A. D. 1868.

## RESOLUTION AUTHORIZING THE COMMITTEE ON FINANCE TO NEGOTIATE A LOAN.

*Resolved*, That the Committee on Finance, either in the name of the whole Committee or in the name of a sub-Committee, be authorized to negotiate a loan, not to exceed ten thousand dollars, in order to pay the mileage of members.

Instructing Committee on Finance.

Adopted January 29th, A. D. 1868.

---

## RESOLUTION REQUESTING CERTAIN INFORMATION OF SHERIFFS.

*Resolved*, That the Sheriffs of the several counties of this State are directed to inform this Convention at the earliest practicable moment, of the number of executions now in their hands, and the total amount of moneys therein ordered to be collected.

Sheriffs' requested to give information respecting number of executions in his hands.

Adopted January 30th, A. D. 1868.

---

## RESOLUTION APPOINTING A COMMITTEE OF EIGHT TO REPORT NAMES OF PERSONS TO BE PARDONED.

WHEREAS, The fourteenth article of the Constitution of the United States, which disfranchises a certain class of citizens for participation in the late rebellion, also provides that Congress may by a two third vote of each house, remove such disability; and whereas, there are many whose sentiments are in hearty accord with the reconstruction measures, who are injuriously effected by said disfranchisement: therefore,

Preamble.

*Resolved*, That a Committee of Eight, to consist of one from each judicial district, be appointed by the Chair, whose duty it shall be to gather such information as will enable them to report at an early day to this Convention, a list of such persons as may be presented to Congress to be relieved.

Committee to report a list of persons to be recommended for relief from disabilities.

Adopted January 30th, A. D. 1868.

RESOLUTION INSTRUCTING THE COMMITTEE TO CONFER WITH GENERAL CANBY.

Committee instructed to confer with General Canby in reference to certain debts.

*Resolved*, That the Committee appointed to confer with General Canby be directed to enquire whether Notes and Bonds given since May 1st, 1865, in renewal of debts contracted prior to that date are subject to the power of General Order, No. 164.

Adopted February 1st, A. D. 1868.

---

RESOLUTION IN RELATION TO MILAGE.

A list to be prepared.

*Resolved*, That the Secretary be directed to prepare a list of the members of this Convention which shall show the number of miles travelled by each, and the amount of mileage due.

Adopted February 4th, A. D. 1868.

---

RESOLUTION INSTRUCTING THE COMMITTEE ON FINANCE TO NEGOTIATE A LOAN FOR CONTINGENT EXPENSES.

Committee on finance to negotiate a loan.

*Resolved*, That the Committee on Finance be instructed to negotiate a loan of $500,00 for contingent expenses, and be also instructed to insert in the tax bill that amount in addition to the estimated ordinary expenses of the Convention.

Adopted February 5th, A. D. 1868.

---

RESOLUTION INSTRUCTING THE COMMITTEE APPOINTED TO CONFER WITH GEN. CANBY.

Committee to confer with General Canby on the subject of staying executions.

*Resolved*, That the Committee appointed to confer with General Canby, be authorized to request him to stay the ruinous executions on new debts contracted since the first of May, 1865, so that property may not be sacrificed for less than its intrinsic value, and make an order to that effect for for the temporary relief of our people.

Adopted February 6th, A. D. 1868.

---

RESOLUTION IN REGARD TO TRANSMITTING COPIES OF THE RELIEF BILL.

*Resolved*, That the President of this Convention order a copy of the Relief Bill to be sent to the Sheriffs, the County and Superior Court Clerks of each County in the State.

Copy of the relief bill to be sent to Superior Court Clerks and Sheriffs.

Adopted February 7th, A. D. 1868.

---

RESOLUTION TENDERING THE THANKS OF THE CONVENTION TO GENERAL NELSON A. MILES, &C.

*Be it Resolved by this Convention*, That the thanks of the people of North-Carolina are due, and are hereby tendered to General Nelson A. Miles, the Assistant Commissioner for the Freedman's Bereau in this State, for the efficient impartial, and faithfull, manner in which he has discharged his duties.

Thanks of the Convention tendered to General Miles.

*Resolved*, That the Secretary of this Convention transmit a copy of this resolution to General Miles.

Secretary to forward a copy of resolution.

Adopted February 10th, A. D., 1868.

---

RESOLUTION APPOINTING THE COMMITTEE TO PREPARE A MEMORIAL TO CONGRESS IN RELATION TO THE TOBACCO TAX.

*Resolved*, That a Committee of five be appointed to draw up a memorial to be sent to the Congress of the United States, praying that the Revenue tax on tobacco be reduced, setting forth the reasons therefor.

Praying for the reduction of the tax on tobacco.

Adopted February 10th, A. D., 1868.

## RESOLUTION EXPRESSING THE SENSE OF THE CONVENTION IN REGARD TO THE RACES.

Adverse to intermarriages and mixed schools.

*Resolved*, That it is the sense of this Convention that intermarriages and illegal intercourse between the races should be discountenanced, and the interests and happiness of the two races would be best promoted by the establishment of separate schools.

Adopted March 16th, A. D. 1868.

---

## RESOLUTION IN RELATION TO THE FORMATION OF A NEW COUNTY.

Referred to the Legislature.

*Resolved*, That it is the sense of this Convention that it is impracticable to take any definite action, at this late period of the session, on the petition in relation to the formation of a new County out of Iredell, Rowan and Cabarrus Counties, and that said petition is hereby respectfully referred to the earnest attention and consideration of the next Legislature.

Adopted March 16th, A. D. 1868.

---

## RESOLUTION AUTHORIZING THE SENDING OF COPIES OF THE CONSTITUTION TO CONGRESS AND THE DEPARTMENTS.

One copy to each.

*Resolved*, That one printed copy of the new Constitution be sent to the Secretary of State of the United States, one copy to each of the heads of the Departments of the United States, one to each member of Congress, and one to the General Commanding the armies of the United States.

Adopted March 17th, A. D. 1868.

---

## RESOLUTION PROVIDING FOR ASSISTANT CLERK.

One clerk.

*Resolved*, That the Secretary be authorized to employ a clerk to assist him in completing his duties.

Adopted March 17th, A. D. 1868.

## RESOLUTION INSTRUCTING THE JUDICIAL COMMITTEE.

WHEREAS, This Convention has passed an ordinance allowing men of legal profession, of a good moral character, by exhibiting a certificate granted by the Courts of other States, to the bar in the Courts of North-Carolina; and whereas, many of the States requiring nothing more than the establishment of a good moral character, to admit men to the bar; and that citizens of this State should be on equality with those of other States; therefore, Preamble.

*Be it Resolved*, That the Committee on the Judiciary be instructed to report an ordinance or clause for the Constitution, which will allow citizens of North Carolina to practice, and plead law in the Courts of the State by establishing a good moral character and paying necessary fees. Committee instructed to report an ordinance allowing all persons to practice law.

Adopted February 12th, A. D., 1868.

---

## RESOLUTION IN RELATION TO ACTIONS AT LAW AND SUITS IN EQUITY.

*Resolved*, That it is the sense of this Convention that the distinctions between actions at law and suits in equity and the forms of all such actions and suits shall be abollished and there should be but one form of civil action. Distinction between law and equity abolished.

Adopted February 12th, A. D., 1868.

---

## RESOLUTION RELATING THE CALL FOR THE PREVIOUS QUESTION.

*Resolved*, That no one shall move the previous question except the Chairman of a Committee, whose report is under consideration, the mover of a resolution or the author of a minority report. In reference to the previous question.

Adopted February 12th, A. D., 1868.

---

## RESOLUTION IN RELATION TO CONTINGENT EXPENSES.

*Resolved*, That the contingent expenses of this Convention, including those for labor, be not paid until audited by In relation to contingent expenses.

the Committee on Contingent Expenses, and approved by the President and Secretary,

Adopted February 17th, A. D., 1868.

---

RESOLUTION REQUESTING THE SECRETARY OF STATE TO FURNISH STATIONERY, &c.

Pramble.

WHEREAS, By section 5th of the 104th chapter of the Revised Code of North-Carolina, it is made the duty of the Secretary of State to furnish suitable stationary, and the necessary fuel for all Legislative bodies of the State; therefore,

Secretary of State requested to furnish stationery.

*Resolved*, That from and after this date, the Secretary of State be, and is hereby requested to supply the officers and members of this Convention with the necessary stationery and suitable fuel, and that the officers of this Convention, whose duty it is to look after the stationery and fuel, are hereby directed to call upon the Secretary of State.

Adopted February 21st, A. D. 1868.

---

RESOLUTION IN RESPECT TO THE MEMORY OF WASHINGTON, &c.

Reverence for the memory of George Washington.

*Resolved*, That with profound reverence for the memory of George Washington, we will honor the day of his birth, not by adjourning, but by proceeding to ingraft upon the Constitution the great principles of justice and liberty, which has made his name illustrious.

Adopted February, 22d, A. D. 1868.

---

RESOLUTION REGARDING CONTINGENT EXPENSES, &C.

Pay of servants.

*Resolved*, That the Committee on Contingent Expenses, be instructed to allow three servants of this Convention, two dollars per day, for their services during the session of this Convention.

Adopted February 24th, A. D. 1868.

RESOLUTION REGARDING THE PAY OF MEMBERS OF THE CONVENTION.

*Resolved*, That each member of this Convention is entitled to pay from the first day of the session, and no member shall be deprived of pay for overstaying the leave granted by this Convention, for any valid reason. Pay of the members.

Adopted February 24th, A. D. 1868.

---

RESOLUTION TO CARRY OUT A CERTAIN ORDINANCE.

WHEREAS, It is understood that some of the Judges of the Superior Courts of the State are rendering and are about to render judgment in cases intended to be exempted by the ordinance for relief, entitled "An ordinance respecting the jurisdiction of the Courts of this State;" therefore, Preamble.

*Resolved*, That the President of this Convention is hereby instructed to communicate immediately with the Commanding General of this Military District, and request of him the issuing of such orders as will ensure the full observance of said ordinance. Instructs a Committee to request General Canby to enforce an ordinance.

Adopted February 29th, A. D. 1868.

---

RESOLUTION VACATING SEAT OF JOHN G. MARLER, IN FAVOR OF JOHN M. MARSHALL.

*Resolved*, That the seat now occupied by John G. Marler be vacated, and John M. Marshall be admitted to his seat. Vacating the seat John G. Marler.

Adopted March 2d, A. D. 1868.

---

RESOLUTION INSTRUCTING THE COMMITTEE ON REVISION.

*Resolved*, That the Committee on Revision be directed and impowered to procure parchment for the purpose of having the Constitution enrolled for signature by the members of this Convention. Instructing the Committee on Revision.

Adopted March 7th, A. D. 1868.

## RESOLUTION TENDERING THE THANKS OF THE CONVENTION.

Preamble.

WHEREAS, the people of North-Carolina, through their representatives in Convention assembled, have viewed with not less indignation than apprehension, the efforts on the part of the Executive branch of this government to throttle, circumscribe and over rule its co-ordinate and Legislative branch of the same: and whereas, in the opinion of this Convention, success in such efforts would lead to an agrarianism alike dangerous to the liberties of the people, and subversive of that good feeling and correct principle of Republicanism, which should be viewed not only with extreme jealousy and horror, but be marked by the unqualified condemnation of all lovers of good order and stable government: be it therefore

Thanks of the Convention tendered to Congress.

*Resolved*, That the thanks of this Convention are due, and are hereby tendered to these noble representatives who have so promptly stepped forth in their power of impeachment, to check and correct the evil threatened by the acts of an usurpative Executive.

Copy of these resolutions to be forwarded to Congress.

*Be it further resolved*, That a copy of these resolutions, duly engrossed, be transmitted to the Honorable, the President of the Senate, and the Speaker of the House of Representatives of the people of the United States.

Thanks of the Convention tendered to General Canby.

*Be it further resolved*, That this Convention tender to Brevet Major General E. R. S. Canby and the officers of his command its thanks for the bold, fearless, unprejudiced and manly manner in which they, each and all, have discharged the onerous and delicate duties devolving upon them under the Reconstruction Acts of Congress.

Adopted March 12th, A. D. 1868.

---

## A RESOLUTION APPOINTING A COMMITTEE OF THREE TO DRAFT AN ADDRESS TO THE PEOPLE OF NORTH-CAROLINA.

Committee appointed to draft an address to the people of North-Carolina.

*Resolved*, That a Committee of Three be appointed immediately, whose duty it shall be to draft an address to the people of North-Carolina, explanatory of the Constitution adopted by this Convention, which, if approved by the Convention, shall be appended to the Constitution and published therewith.

Adopted March 12th, A. D. 1868.

---

RESOLUTION DIRECTING THE PRESIDENT OF THE COVENTION TO INFORM GANERAL CANBY OF CERTAIN OFFICES TO BE FILLED.

*Resolved*, That the President of this Convention is hereby instructed to inform Major General Canby, without delay, that the following offices have been created under the Constitution of North-Carolina, to be submitted to the registered voters of the State, on the 21st, 22d and 23d of April, at which time persons to fill said offices will be elected by the voters aforesaid, viz: Informing Gen. Canby of the offices to be filled.

STATE AT LARGE.

*Executive.*

Executive offices.

One Governor.
One Lieutenant-Governor.
One Secretary of State.
One Auditor.
One Treasurer.
One Superintendent of Public Works.
One Superintendent of Public Instruction.
One Attorney General.

*Judiciary.*

Judicial offices.

One Chief Justice of the Supreme Court.
Four Associate Justices of the Supreme Court.
Twelve Judges of the Superior Court.

*Legislative.*

Fifty State Senators, to be elected in their respective Districts. Legislative offices.

One hundred and twenty members of the House of Representatives, to be elected in their respective Counties.

Twelve Solicitors, to be elected in their respective Judicial Districts.

In each County, one Sheriff, one Clerk of the Superior Court, one Surveyor, one Register of Deeds, one Treasurer, and Five Commissioners.

Seven Representatives in the Congress of the United States, to be elected in their respective Districts.

Adopted March 16th, A. D. 1868.

---

### RESOLUTION AUTHORIZING THE SECRETARY TO EMPLOY ONE OR MORE CLERKS.

Secretary authorized to employ one or more clerks.

*Resolved*, That for the purpose of completing the enrolment of the ordinances and resolution of this Convention, the Secretary be, and he is, authorized to employ one or more clerks.

Adopted March 14th, A. D. 1868.

---

### RESOLUTION INSTRUCTING THE COMMITTEE ON CONTINGENT EXPENSES.

Committee instructed to allow the account of W. H. S. Sweet.

*Resolved*, That the Committee on Contingent Expenses be instructed to audit and allow the accounts of W. H. S. Sweet for expenses to Charleston, S C., and return, said expenses having been incurred by order of this Convention.

Adopted March 16th, 1868.

---

### RESOLUTION IN FAVOR OF LORENZO D. HALL AND JOHN MARSHALL.

Resolution in favor of Lorenzo D. Hall and others.

*Resolved*, That Lorenzo D. Hall, of Sampson County, and John Marshall, of Surry County, be allowed pay and mileage from the commencement of the session, and that the President and Secretary be authorized and directed to sign vouchers for the same.

Adopted March 16th, A. D. 1868.

RESOLUTION IN RELATION TO THE LANDLESS.

*Resolved*, That it is the sense of this Convention that the next Legislature take into consideration the condition of the landless population of this State, and if practicable devise some means by loan or otherwise so that all citizens of the State can be permanently located on a small freehold, so that all will be fully identified with the interest of the State. Instructions to next Legislature.

Adopted March 17th, A. D. 1868.

---

I, T. A. BYRNES, Secretary of the State Constitutional Convention of North-Carolina, do hereby certify that the foregoing are true copies of the original Resolutions of the State Constitutional Convention, session of 1868.

T. A. BYRNES, *Secretary*.

# INDEX.

PAGE.
CONSTITUTION OF NORTH-CAROLINA, - - - - - - 3 Session 1868.

ORDINANCES.

An ordinance in relation to the per diem and mileage of members and officers of the Constitutional Convention of North-Carolina, - - 43
An ordinance reducing the amount of bonds authorized to be issued by the Wilmington, Charlotte and Rutherford Rail Road Company, - 43
An ordinance respecting the jurisdiction of the Courts of the State, - 45
An ordinance levying a tax for defraying the expenses of the Convention, 46
An ordinance in favor of William D. Justus, Sheriff of Henderson County, North-Carolina, - - - - - - - - - - - 47
An ordinance amending section second of the act of the Legislature of 1866–'67, entitled "An act to incorporate the town of Columbia, in the County of Tyrrell," - - : - - - - - - - 47
An ordinance in favor of the Sheriffs of North-Carolina, - - - - 48
An ordinance prohibiting the distillation of grain, - - - - 48
An ordinance for the appointment of a Collector of Taxes for the City of Newbern, - - - - - - - - - - - - - 49
An ordinance to divide North-Carolina in seven Congressional Districts, 50
An ordinance fixing the State Taxes on Theatrical Companies, &c., - 52
An ordinance in reference to Sheriffs, Coroners, &c., - - - - 52
An ordinance protecting property purchased by persons held as slaves, 53
An ordinance dissolving the bonds of matrimony of Rosa B. Quinlivin and John R. Quinlivin, - - - - - - - - - - 53
An ordinance in relation to the draining of Mattamuskeet Lake, - - 54
An ordinance to incorporate the North-Western North-Carolina Rail Road Company, - - - - - - - - - - - 57
An ordinance to incorporate the New Berne Turnpike Company, - - 61
An ordinance to amend the Charter of the Chatham Rail Road Company, 62
An ordinance to aid the Williamston and Tarboro' Rail Road Company, 64
An ordinance to divorce Winney Gribbles and James Gribbles, - - 66
An ordinance for the divorce of Eliza C. Wagner, - - - - - - 66
An ordinance for the divorce of Josephine Emanuel, - - - - 66
An ordinance for the divorce of Lavina Lee and Wesley Lee, - - - 67
An ordinance for the divorce of DeWitt C. Wilson and Nancy C. Wilson, 67
An ordinance for the divorce of Esther V. Todd and Benj. W. Todd, - 68
An ordinance for the divorce of James Overton and Charlotte Overton, 68
An ordinance for the divorce of Wm. J. Hopkins and Martha A. Hopkins, 68

PAGE.

Session 1868. An ordinance in relation to the pardon of officers and soldiers in the late Confederate service, - 69

An ordinance to change the manner of payment of the State's subscription to the capital stock of the Western Rail Road, - 69

An ordinance to divorce Adelia E. Slater and James A. Slater, - 71

An ordinance to amend an ordinance of the Convention, entitled "An ordinance to change the manner of payment of the State's subscription to the capital stock of the Western Rail Road Company," - 71

An ordinance in relation to the printing of the Constitution, Ordinances and Resolutions, - 72

An ordinance in relation to the Cape Fear and Deep River Navigation Works, - 73

An ordinance for the submission of the Constitution to the people, and the election of ceartain officers, - 74

An ordinance to prevent the intimidation of voters, - 75

An ordinance for the relief of the Sheriff of Orange County, - 76

An ordinance to exempt Ministers of the Gospel, and Justices of the Peace in thé County ot Cumberland from the penalty imposed by the act of the General Assembly of North-Carolina for celebrating the Rites of Matrimony in said County without a license therefor, - 77

An ordinance for the diverce of John Roberts and Camelia Roberts, - 78

An ordinance concerning widows who have qualified as Executrix to the last will and testament of their deceased husbands, - 78

An ordinance appointing Commissioners to prepare a Code of Practice and Procedure in the different Courts of the State, - 79

An ordinance to incorporate the Charlotte City Hall Association, - 81

An ordinance to incorporate the Halcyon Steam Boat Company, - 83

An ordinance to provide for the payment of the interest on the public debt, - 84

An ordinance providing for Auditing the Accounts of the Convention - 85

An ordinance in relation to Marriages authorized by Military authority, 86

An ordinance for the divorce of Palmer and Lucind Babcock, - 86

An ordinance amending the Charter of the City of Wilmington, - 87

An ordinance to incorporate the Dan River Coalfield R. R. Company, 88

An ordinance for the completion of the Western North-Carolina Rail Road, - 100

An ordinance for the divorce of Ann Underdue and William Underdue, 101

An ordinance appointing Commissioners to investigate the accounts and affairs of the Albemarle and Chesapeake Canal Company, - 101

An ordinance amending the Charter of the City of Raleigh, - 102

An ordinance compensating C. J. Cowles, - 102

An ordinance divorcing Edward Shroyer and Mary P. Shroyer, - 103

An ordinance extending the time for Registration of Deeds, - 103

An ordinance of divorce in favor of Archibald Haney, of Randolph County, - 104

An ordinance respecting the jurisdiction of the Courts of this State, - 105

## RESOLUTIONS.

PAGE.

Resolution instituting the Oath to be taken by delegates to the Constitutional Convention of North-Carolina, - - - - - - - - 111 Session 1868.
Resolution appointing T. A. Byrnes Secretary, - - - - - - 111
Resolution fixing the Rules of Order of the Convention, - - - 111
Resolution appointing a Committee on Framing a Constitution, - - 112
Resolution in regard to framing rules for the government of the Convention, - - - - - - - - - - - - - - 112
Resolution regarding Sergeant at Arms, - - - - - - - 112
Resolution in regard to Reporters, &c., - - - - - - - 112
Resolution instructing the President of the Convention in regard to Clergymen, - - - - - - - - - - - - - - 113
Resolution in regard to ascertaining the votes of Counties, &c., - - 113
Report of Committee on the best mode of framing a Constitution and Civil Government, - - - - - - - - - - - 113
Resolution procuring an American Flag, - - - - - - - 115
Resolution informing Gen. Canby of the organization of this Convention, 115
Resolution requesting the Provisional Secretary of State to furnish copies of the Constitution, 1865–'66. - - - - - - - 115
Resolution appointing a Committee of three to wait on the Governor of the State, - - - - - - - - - - - - - - 115
Resolution appointing a Committee to procure copies of proceedings of the General Assembly, ses. 1866–'67, - - - - - - - 116
Resolution fixing the per diem and mileage of members, - - - 116
Resolution requesting Gen. Canby to visit the Convention, - - 116
Resolution regarding the Committee on Printing, - - - - 116
Resolution requesting the Treasurer of State to furnish the Convention with a Statement of the indebtedness of the State, - - - 117
Resolution requesting the Treasurer of State to furnish certain information, - - - - - - - - - - - - - - 117
Resolution instructing the Judiciary Committee, - - - - 117
Resolution inviting United States officers to the floor of the Convention, 118
Resolution instructing the Committee to confer with General Canby, - 118
Resolution appointing a Committee of three to confer with Gen. Canby, 118
Resolution authorizing the Committee on Finance to negotiate a loan, 119
Resolution requesting certain information of Sheriffs, - - - 119
Resolution appointing a Committee of eight to report names of persons to be pardoned. - - - - - - - - - - - - - 119
Resolution instructing the Committee to confer with General Canby, - 120
Resolution in relation to mileage, - - - - - - - - 120
Resolution instructing the Committee on Finance to negotiate a loan for Contingent Expenses, - - - - - - - - - - - 120
Resolution instructing the Committee appointed to confer with General Canby, - - - - - - - - - - - - - - 120
Resolution in regard to transmitting copies of the Relief Bill, - - 121

PAGE.

Session 1868.

Resolution tendering the thanks of the Convention to General Nelson A. Miles, &c., - - - - - - - - - - - - - - 121
Resolution appointing the Committee to prepare a memorial to Congress in relation to the Tobacco Tax, - - - - - - - 121
Resolution expressing the sense of the Convention in regard to the races, 122
Resolution in relation to the formation of a new County, - - - 122
Resolution authorizing the sending of copies of the Constitution to Congress and the Departments, - - - - - - - - - 122
Resolution providing for Assistant Clerk, - - - - - - - 122
Resolution instructing the Judicial Committee, - - - - 123
Resolution in relation to actions at Law and suits in Equity, - - 123
Resolution relating to the call for the previous question, - - - 123
Resolution in relation to Contingent Expenses, - - - - - - 123
Resolution requesting the Secretary to furnish Stationery, &c., - 124
Resolution in respect to the memory of Washington, &c., - - - 124
Resolution regarding Contingent Expenses, &c., - . - 124
Resolution regarding the pay of members of the Convention, - - 125
Resolution to carry out a certain ordinance, - - - - 125
Resolution vacating the seat of John G. Marler in favor of John M. Marshall, - - - - - - - - 125
Resolution instructing the Committee on Revision, - - - 125
Resolution tendering the thanks of the Convention, - - - 126
A resolution appointing a Committee of three to draft an address to the people of North-Carolina, - - - - - - - 126
Resolution directing the President of the Convention to inform General Canby of certain offices to be filled, - - - - - - 127
Resolution authorizing the Secretary to employ one or more Clerks, - 128
Resolution instructing the Committee on Contingent Expenses, - 128
Resolution in favor of Lorenzo D. Hall and John Marshall, - - 128
Resolution in relation to the landless, - - - - - - 129

# JOURNAL

OF THE

# CONSTITUTIONAL CONVENTION

OF THE

# STATE OF NORTH-CAROLINA,

AT ITS

## SESSION 1868.

RALEIGH:
JOSEPH W. HOLDEN, CONVENTION PRINTER.
1868.

# JOURNAL

OF THE

# CONSTITUTIONAL CONVENTION.

## NORTH-CAROLINA STATE CONSTITUTIONAL CONVENTION.

The Convention of delegates, elected by the people of the several counties of the State of North-Carolina, in pursuance of the laws of Congress and the orders thereunder issued by the General Commanding the Second Military District, assembled in the Commons Hall of the Capitol, in the City of Raleigh, on the fourteenth day of January, in the year of our Lord one thousand eight hundred and sixty-eight, and of the independence of the United States, the ninety-third, under and by the following anthority:

HEADQUARTERS SECOND MILITARY DISTRICT,
CHARLESTON, S. C., December 31, 1867.

GENERAL ORDERS,
NO. 165.

At the election held in the State of North-Carolina, on the 19th and 20th days of November, 1867, pursuant to General Orders, No. 101, from these Headquarters, dated October 18, 1867, a majority of the registered voters of the said State having voted on the question of holding a Convention, and a majority of the votes cast being in favor of holding such Convention, the delegates elected thereto, and hereinafter named, are hereby notified, in conformity with the provisions of the fourth section of the act of Congress of March 23, 1867, to assemble in Convention in the City of Raleigh, North-Carolina, at noon, on Tuesday, the 14th day of January, 1868, for the purpose of framing a constitution and civil government according to the provisions of the aforesaid Act of the 23d day of March, 1867, and of the Act of the 2d day of March, 1867, to which it is supplementary.

A copy of this order will be furnished to each of the persons hereinafter named, and shall be the evidence of his having been elected as a delegate to the aforesaid Convention.

## DELEGATES:

COUNTIES OF BURKE AND McDOWELL.—John S. Parks, W. A. B. Murphy.

COUNTIES OF RUTHERFORD AND POLK.—W. H. Logan, Jesse Rhodes.

COUNTIES OF YANCEY AND MITCHELL.—Julius S. Garland.

COUNTIES OF MADISON, BUNCOMBE, HENDERSON AND TRANSYLVANIA.—Geo. W. Gahagan, J. H. Duckworth, Thos. J. Candler.

COUNTIES OF HAYWOOD AND JACKSON.—W. G. B. Garrett.

COUNTIES OF MACON, CLAY AND CHEROKEE.—Mark May, Geo. W. Dickey.

COUNTIES OF ALLEGHANY, ASHE, SURRY, WATAUGA AND YADKIN.—Saml. Forkner, Evan Benbow, Geo. W. Bradley, Edwin C. Bartlett.

COUNTIES OF CALDWELL, WILKES, IREDELL AND ALEXANDER.—Calvin J. Cowles, Calvin C. Jones, Wesley H. George, John Q. A. Bryan, Jerry Smith.

COUNTIES OF DAVIE AND ROWAN.—Allen Rose, Dr. Milton Hobbs, Isaac M. Shaver.

COUNTY OF CLEVELAND.—Plato Durham.

COUNTY OF CATAWBA.—James R. Ellis.

COUNTY OF LINCOLN.—Joseph H. King.

COUNTY OF GASTON.—Milot J. Aydlott.

County of Mecklenburg.—Edward Fullings, Silas N. Stilwell.

County of Union.—Wm. Newsom.

County of Cabarrus.—W. T. Blume.

County of Stanley.—Levi C. Morton.

County of Anson.—George Tucker, Henry Chillson.

County of Stokes.—R. F. Petree.

County of Forsythe.—E. B. Teague.

County of Davidson.—Isaac Kinney, S. Mullican.

County of Randolph.—T. L. L. Cox, R. F. Trogden.

County of Guilford.—G. W. Welker, A. W. Tourgee.

County of Rockingham.—H. Barnes, John French.

County of Caswell.—Wilson Carey, P. Hodnett.

County of Alamance.—Henry M. Ray.

County of Person.—William Merritt.

County of Orange.—E. M. Holt, J. W. Graham.

County of Chatham.—J. A. McDonald, W. T. Gunter.

County of Wake.—S. D. Franklin, J. P. Andrews, B. S. D. Williams, James H. Harris.

County of Granville.—J. W. Ragland, J. J. Moore, C. Mayo.

County of Warren.—John Hyman, John Read.

County of Franklin.—John H. Williamson, James T. Harris.

County of Cumberland.—W. A. Mann, J. W. Hood.

County of Harnett.—J. M. Turner.

County of Moore.—S. S McDonald.

County of Montgomery.—Geo. A. Graham.

County of Richmond.—R. T. Long, Sr.

County of Wayne.—H. L. Grant, J. Hollowell.

County of Johnston.—Dr. James Hay, Nathan Gulley.

County of Greene.—J. M. Patrick.

County of Wilson.—W. Daniel.

County of Nash.—Jacob Ing.

County of Halifax.—Henry Epps, J. H. Renfrow, W. J. T. Hayes.

County of Northampton.—R. C. Parker, H. T. Grant.

County of Edgecombe.—J. H. Baker, Henry A. Dowd, Henry C. Cherry.

County of Lenoir.—R. W. King.

County of Brunswick.—Edwin Legg.

County of Columbus.—Haynes Lennon.

County of Robeson.—Joshua L. Nance, O. S. Hayes.

County of Bladen.—A. W. Fisher, F. F. French.

County of New Hanover.—General J. C. Abbott, S. S. Ashley, A. H. Galloway.

County of Duplin.—J. W. Peterson, Samuel Highsmith.

County of Sampson.—Sylvester Carter, Alexander Williams.

Counties of Tyrrell and Washington.—E. W. Jones.

County of Martin.—Samuel W. Watts.

County of Bertie.—P. D. Robbins, Bryant Lee.

County of Hertford.—J. B. Hare.

County of Gates.—Thomas L. Hoffler.

County of Chowan.—John R. French.

County of Perquimans.—Dr. Wm. Nicholson.

Counties of Pasquotank and Camden.—C. C. Pool, M. Taylor.

County of Currituck.—Thomas Sanderlin.

County of Craven.—David Heaton, W. H. S. Sweet, C. D. Pierson.

County of Onslow.—Jasper Etheridge.

County of Carteret.—Abraham Congleton.

County of Jones.—David D. Colgrove.

County of Beaufort.—W. B. Rodman, William Stilley.

County of Pitt.—Byron Laflin, D. J. Rich.

County of Hyde.—Andrew J. Glover.

By Command of Brevet Major-General Ed. R. S. Canby:

LOUIS V. CAZIARC,
*Aid-de-Camp,*
*Actg. Asst. Adjt. Genl.*

Official:

Jacob F. Churr,
*Actg. Asst. Adjutant General.*

At 12 o'clock, the delegates to the State Constitutional Convention, assembled in the Commons Hall, and proceeded to organize temporarily.

Mr. Kinney, of Davidson, called the Convention to order.

Mr. Heaton, of Craven, moved that Mr. Kinney be authorized to call the Convention to order, which motion was carried.

Mr. Kinney assumed the Chair, and moved that Mr. King, of Lenoir, be made temporary President, which motion was carried.

The Chair called upon Rev. G. W. Welker, from Guilford, for Prayer.

On motion of Mr. Heaton, it was ordered that Mr. J. P. Andrews, of Wake, be appointed Secretary *pro tem.*

On motion of Mr. Abbott, the Secretary called the roll. The following delegates answered to their names:

Messrs. Abbott, Andrews, Ashley, Aydlott, Barnes, Bradley, Carey, Carter, Candler, Cherry, Colgrove, Congleton, Cowles, Cox, Daniel, Dowd, Duckworth, Ellis, Eppes, Etheridge, Fisher, Forkner, Franklin, French of Bladen, French of Rockingham, French of Chowan, Fullings, Gahagan, Galloway, Garrett, George, Graham of Montgomery, Graham of Orange, Grant of Wayne, Grant of Northampton, Gully, Gunter, Hare, Harris of Wake, Harris of Franklin, Hay, Hayes of Robeson, Hayes of Halifax, Heaton, Highsmith, Hobbs, Hodnett, Hoffler, Hollowell, Holt, Hood, Hyman, Ing, Jones of Caldwell, Jones of Washington, King of Lincoln, King of Lenoir, Kinney, Lee, Lennon, Logan, Mann, Mayo, McDonald of Chatham, McDonald of Moore, Moore, Morton, Mullican, Murphy, Nance, Newsom, Patrick, Parker, Parks, Petree, Peterson, Pierson, Pool, Ragland, Ray, Read, Renfrow, Rhodes, Rich, Robbins, Rodman, Rose, Smith, Stilly, Stilwell, Sweet, Taylor, Teague, Tourgee, Trogden, Tucker, Turner, Watts, Welker and Williamson.

Total present, 100.

Mr. Rodman offered the following resolution, which was adopted:

*Resolved,* That the the delegates to this Convention take

the following Oath, and that N. J. Riddick, Clerk of the Circuit Court of the United States, be requested to administer the same:

OATH.

You do solemnly swear (or affirm,) that you will support the Constitution of the United States, and faithfully discharge your duties as members of this Convention. So help you God.

Mr. Hood moved that the Oath be administered to the members rising from their seats in their places, with raised hands.

Amended by Mr. Sweet, so that members be sworn by twelves; names to be taken alphabetically from the list at the Secretary's desk. Adopted.

Mr. Welker moved that a committee of three be appointed to wait on the Post Commander, and obtain a correct list of delegates to the Convention. The motion was lost.

The following communication was received from Post Headquarters and read by the Secretary to the Convention:

HEADQUARTERS MILITARY POST OF RALEIGH.

*To the President of the Convention, Raleigh, N. C.*

SIR:—I have the honor to transmit herewith the enclosed dispatch from Headquarters Second Military District, for the information of the State Convention.

I am your obedient servant,

DANIEL T. WELLS,
*1st Lieutenant 8th U. S. Infantry.*
*Post Adjutant.*

CHARLESTON, S. C., Jan. 13th, 1868.

*To Commanding Officer, Post of Raleigh.*

General Orders, No. 165, is amended as follows: insert Jas. McCubbins in place of Isaac M. Shaver, as delegate from Davie and Rowan counties, and John G. Marler in place of Edwin P. Bartlett, for Ashe, Alleghany, Wautauga, Surry and Yadkin counties. Order by mail informs all parties.

By Command of GENERAL CANBY:

(Signed,) LOUIS V. CAZIARC,
*A. D. C. and A. A. A. G.*

Delegates present were called up by twelves, and sworn by Mr. Riddick, Clerk of the Circuit Court.

On motion of Mr. Abbott, it was ordered that when the Convention adjourned, it re-assemble to-morrow at 12 o'clock.

On motion the Convention adjourned.

---

WEDNESDAY, JANUARY, 15th, 1868.

Convention called to order at 12 o'clock, noon, by Mr. King of Lenoir, President *pro tem.*

Prayer by Rev. W. H. Logan.

The roll was called by Mr. Andrews, Secretary *pro tem.* when the President announced a qourum, ninety seven members answering to their names, as follows:

Messrs. Abbott, Andrews, Ashley, Barnes, Blume, Bradley, Carey, Carter, Candler, Cherry, Chillson, Colgrove, Cox, Daniel, Duckworth, Durham, Ellis, Epps, Etheridge, Fisher, French of Bladen, French of Rockingham, French of Chowan, Fullings, Gahagan, Galloway, Garrett, George, Graham of Montgomery, Graham of Orange, Grant of Wayne, Gully, Gunter, Hare, Harris of Wake, Harris of Franklin, Hay, Hayes of Robeson, Hayes of Halifax, Heaton, Highsmith, Hobbs, Hodnett, Hoffler, Hollowell, Hood, Hyman, Ing, Jones of Washington, King of Lincoln, King of Lenoir, Kinney, Laflin, Lee, Lennon, Logan, Long, Mann, Mayo, McCubbins, McDonald of Chatham, McDonald of Moore, Moore, Morton, Mullican, Murphy, Nance, Newsom, Nicholson, Patrick, Parker, Parks, Petree, Peterson, Pierson, Pool, Ragland, Ray, Read, Renfrow, Rhodes, Rich, Robbins, Rodman, Rose, Sanderlin, Smith, Stilly, Stillwell, Sweet, Taylor, Teague, Tourgee, Trogden, Tucker, Watts, Welker and Williams of Wake.—97.

The following delegates were sworn in by Mr. C. J. Rogers:

Messrs. Durham, Laflin, Hayes of Robeson, Long, Nance, Chillson, Sanderlin, McCubbins, Benbow, Bryan, Blume, George, Nicholson and Turner.

On motion of Mr. Abbott, the Convention proceeded to the election of permanent officers.

On motion of Mr. Abbott, Mr. Tourgee was chosen Assistant Secretary *pro tem.*

Mr. Harris, of Wake, nominated Mr. Calvin J. Cowles, of Wilkes, as permanent President of the Convention.

Mr. Hodnett nominated Mr. Plato Durham, of Cleaveland.

On motion of Mr. Heaton, it was ordered that the roll of members be called, and each delegate announce his choice.

The roll was called with the following result:

For Mr. Cowles—Messrs. Abbott, Andrews, Ashley, Aydlott, Barnes, Benbow, Blume, Bradley, Bryan, Carey, Carter, Candler, Cherry, Chillson, Colgrove, Congleton, Cox, Daniel, Duckworth, Eppes, Etheridge, Fisher, Forkner, Franklin, French of Bladen, French of Rockingham, French of Chowan, Fullings, Gahagan, Galloway, Garrett, George, Graham of Montgomery, Grant of Wayne, Grant of Northampton, Gully, Gunter, Harris of Wake, Harris of Franklin, Hay, Hayes of Robeson, Heaton, Highsmith, Hobbs, Hoffler, Hollowell, Hood, Hyman, Ing, Jones of Caldwell, Jones of Washington, King of Lincoln, King of Lenoir, Kinney, Laflin, Lee, Logan, Long, Mann, Mayo, Marler, McDonald of Chatham, McDonald of Moore, Moore, Morton, Mullican, Murphy, Nance, Newsom, Nicholson, Patrick, Parker, Parks, Petree, Peterson, Pierson, Pool, Ragland, Ray, Read, Renfrow, Rhodes, Rich, Robbins, Rodman, Rose, Smith, Stilly, Stillwell, Sweet,

Taylor, Teague, Tourgee, Trogden, Tucker, Turner, Watts, Welker, Williams of Wake and Williamson.—101.

For Mr. Durham—Messrs. Graham of Orange, Hare, Hodnett, McCubbins and Sanderlin—5.

For Mr. Bradley—Mr. Ellis—1.

For Mr. Rodman—Mr. Lennon—1.

For Mr. Hodnett—Mr. Durham—1.

Messrs. Heaton and Abbott were appointed to conduct the President to his seat.

On motion of Mr. Heaton, the Convention proceeded to the election of a permanent Secretary.

Mr. Galloway nominated Mr. T. A. Byrnes, of Cumberland.

Mr. Heaton offered the following resolution.

*Resolved*, That T. A. Byrnes, of Cumberland, be appointed permanent Secretary of this Convention. Adopted.

Mr. Abbott nominated Mr. John H. Boner, Assistant Secretary.

Vote was taken and Mr. Boner declared elected.

On motion of Mr. Hood the Convention proceeded to the election of Doorkeepers.

Mr. Galloway nominated Mr. James H. Jones, of Wake, for Principal Doorkeeper.

Mr. Ellis nominated Mr. Alexander, of Lincoln, for Principal Doorkeeper.

Mr. King withdrew the name of Mr. Alexander.

Mr. Heaton offered the following resolution:

*Resolved*, That James H. Jones be appointed Principal Doorkeeper to the Convention.

Mr. Heaton called for the yeas and nays upon this resolution. The roll was called and resulted yeas 95, nays 10.

Those who voted in the affirmative are:

Messrs. Abbott, Andrews, Ashley, Aydlott, Benbow, Blume, Bryan, Carey, Carter, Candler, Chillson, Colgrove, Congleton, Cox, Daniel, Dowd, Duckworth, Eppes, Etheridge, Fisher, Forkner, Franklin, French of Bladen, French of Rockingham, French of Chowan, Fullings, Gahagan, Galloway, Garrett, George, Graham of Montgomery, Grant of Wayne, Grant of Northampton, Gully, Gunter, Harris of Wake, Harris of Franklin, Hay, Hayes of Robeson, Hayes of Halifax, Heaton, Highsmith, Hobbs, Hoffler, Hollowell, Hood, Hyman, Ing, Jones of Caldwell, Jones of Washington, King of Lincoln, King of Lenoir, Kinney, Laflin, Lee, Logan, Long, Mann, Mayo, McDonald of Chatham, McDonald of Moore, Moore, Morton, Mullican, Murphy, Nance, Newsom, Nicholson, Patrick, Parker, Petree, Pierson, Pool, Ragland, Ray, Read, Rentrow, Rhodes, Rich, Robbins, Rodman, Rose, Smith, Stilly, Stilwell, Sweet, Taylor, Teague, Tourgee, Trogden, Tucker, Turner, Watts, Welker, Williams of Wake, and Williamson—95.

Those who voted in the negative are:

Messrs. Barnes, Bradley, Durham, Ellis, Graham of Orange, Hare, Hodnett, Lennon, McCubbins and Sanderlin—10.

Mr Jones was declared duly elected.

Mr. Hood moved that Mr. J. T. Ball be elected Assistant Doorkeeper.

Mr. Ball was chosen by acclamation.

Mr. Abbott offered the following resolution:

*Resolved*, That the rules of order of the House of Commons of the Legislature of this State for 1865–'66 be adopted by this Convention, so far as practicable, until otherwise ordered.

Mr. King moved to amend by snbstituting "Rules of Order of the Convention of this State for 1865–66," which was accepted, and the resolution as thus amended, was adopted.

Mr. Smith moved that the new elected officers be sworn, which was done by Mr. C. J. Rogers, whereupon they took their positions, and entered on the discharge of their duties.

Mr. Heaton offered the following resolution:

*Resolved*, That a Committee of two members from each Jndicial District be appointed by the President, whose duty it shall be to consider and report at the earliest practicable moment, the best mode of proceeding to frame a Constitution, and Civil Government according to the provisions of the Acts of Congress.

The resolution was read and adopted.

Mr. Sweet offered the following resolution, which was adopted:

*Resolved*, That the President appoint a Committee of five to frame Rules of Order for the government of the Convention.

Mr. Pool offered the following resolution:

*Resolved*, That this Convention being called for the purpose of framing a Constitution Republican in form, no proposition purely legislative shall be entertained until the Constitution shall have been adopted.

Mr. Jones moved to lay the resolution on the table.

Mr. Forkner moved to adjourn.

Mr. King moved to amend by adding the words 10 o'clock to-morrow.

The motion of Mr. King was put and lost.

When the question recurring on the motion to lay on the table,

The yeas and nays being demanded, resulted yeas 44, nays 53. The motion was lost.

Mr. Abbott moved that the resolution of Mr. Pool be referred to a Committee of three.

On motion of Mr. Garrett, the Convention adjourned to meet to-morrow at 10 o'clock.

---

THURSDAY January 16th, 1868.

The Convention was called to order at 10 o'clock by the President.

Prayer by the Rev. G. W. Welker.

Roll called by the Assistant Secretary. The following members answered to their names:

Messrs. Abbott, Andrews, Ashley, Aydlott, Barnes, Benbow, Blume, Bradley, Carey, Carter, Candler, Cherry, Chillson, Colgrove, Congleton, Cox, Daniel, Duckworth, Durham, Ellis, Eppes, Etheridge, Fisher, Forkner, Franklin, French of Bladen, French of Rockingham, French of Chowan, Gahagan, Galloway, Garrett, George, Graham of Montgomery, Graham of Orange, Grant of Wayne, Grant of Northampton, Gully, Gunter, Hare, Harris of Wake, Harris of Franklin, Hay, Hayes of Robeson, Hayes of Halifax, Heaton, Highsmith,

Hodnett, Hoffler, Hood, Ing, Jones of Caldwell, Jones of Washington, King of Lenoir, Kinney, Laflin, Lee, Legg, Lennon, Logan, Long, Mann, Mayo, McCubbins, McDonald of Moore, Moore, Morton, Mullican, Murphy, Nance, Patrick, Parker, Parks, Petree, Peterson, Pierson, Pool, Ragland, Ray, Read, Renfrow, Rhodes, Rich, Robbins, Rodman, Rose, Smith, Stilly, Stilwell, Sweet, Taylor, Teague, Tourgee, Trogden, Tucker, Turner, Watts, Welker, Williams of Wake, Williams of Sampson and Williamson—100.

The Journals of Tuesday 14th, and Wednesday 15th, were read and approved.

Ordered by the President, that the order of General Canby, (No. 165,) calling this Convention, be entered on the record of the 1st day's proceedings.

In accordance with the resolution of Mr. Heaton, Wednesday 15th, the Chair appointed the following Committee.

1st Judicial District—Wm. Nicholson, E. W. Jones.

2d Judicial District—David Heaton, W. B. Rodman.

3d Judicial District—James H. Harris, Henry A. Dowd.

4th Judicial District—A. W. Tourgée, T. L. L. Cox.

5th Judicial District—J. C. Abbott, J. W. Hood.

6th Judicial District—Samuel Forkner, Milton Hobbs.

7th Judicial District—G. W. Bradley, C. C. Jones.

8th Judicial District—G. W. Gahagan, W. B. G. Garrett.

The Chair in accordance with the resolution of Mr. Sweet, passed Wednesday 15th, appointed the following Committee on Rules of Order:

Messrs. W. H. S. Sweet, A. H. Galloway, C. C. Pool, J. W. Graham and E. Fullings.

Mr. Julius Garland, of Yancey and Mitchell,

Mr. Alex. Williams, of Sampson,

Mr. J. H. Baker, of Edgecombe,

Were duly qualified by the Chairman, and took their seats in the Convention.

Mr. Abbott referred to his motion made Wednesday, viz: That the resolution on Legislation offered by Mr. Pool, viz: That the Convention being called for the purpose of framing a Constitution Republican in form, no proposition purely

Legislative shall be entertained until the Constitution shall have been adopted, be referred to a Committee of three.

This motion was amended by Mr. French, of Chowan, by referring to a Committee of 16, on Constitution and Civil Government, appointed by the Chair.

The motion as amended, passed.

Mr. Jones presented the following resolution, which was adopted:

*Resolved*, That the President of this Convention invite the Clergymen of the City of Raleigh to open the services of this Convention each morning with Prayer.

Mr. Abbott offered the following resolution:

*Resolved*, That no Reporter for any newspaper shall hereafter be allowed upon this floor, who in his reports shall treat the Convention, or any of its members with disrespect, but that they shall, in case of offence in this respect be excluded from the floor of the Hall and from the Galleries, by the President.

After considerable discussion, the resolution was submitted to the House.

Mr. Moore, of Granville, moved to lay the resolution on the table.

Mr. Graham, of Orange, called for the yeas and nays.

Those who voted in the affirmative, are:

Messrs. Andrews, Aydlott, Baker, Benbow, Blume, Bradley, Chillson, Daniel, Dowd, Durham, Ellis, Franklin, Graham of Orange, Grant of Northampton, Gully, Hare, Harris of Franklin, Hobbs, Hodnett, Moore, Nicholson, Parker and Rich—28.

Those who voted in the negative are:

Messrs. Abbott, Ashley, Barnes, Bryan, Carey, Carter, Candler, Cherry, Colgrove, Congleton, Cox, Duckworth, Fisher, Forkner, French of Bladen, French of Rockingham, French of Chowan, Fullings, Gahagan, Galloway, Garrett, George, Graham of Montgomery, Grant of Wayne, Gunter, Harris of Wake, Hay, Hayes of Robeson, Hayes of Halifax, Heaton, Highsmith, Hoffler, Hood, Hyman, Ing, Jones of Caldwell, Jones of Washington, King of Lenoir, Kinney, Lee,

Logan, Long, Mann, Mayo, McDonald of Chatham, McDonald of Moore, Morton, Mullican, Murphy, Nance, Newsom, Patrick, Parks, Petree, Peterson, Pierson, Pool, Ragland, Ray, Read, Renfrow, Rhodes, Robbins, Rodman, Rose, Smith, Stilwell, Sweet, Taylor, Teague, Tourgee, Trogden, Turner. Watts, Welker and Williamson—76.

Mr. Hood moved the previous question.

Mr. Forkner moved to suspend the rules and put the resolution to a final reading. Carried.

Mr. Graham, of Orange, called for the yeas and nays.

Those who voted in the affirmative are:

Messrs. Abbott, Andrews, Ashley, Aydlott, Barnes, Benbow, Blume, Bryan, Carey, Carter, Candler, Chillson, Colgrove, Congleton, Cox, Duckworth, Eppes, Etheridge, Fisher. Forkner, Franklin, French of Bladen, French of Rockingham, French of Chowan, Fullings, Gahagan, Galloway, Garrett, George, Graham of Montgomery, Grant of Wayne, Gully, Gunter, Harris of Wake, Hay, Hayes of Robeson, Hayes of Halifax, Heaton, Highsmith, Hood, Hyman, Ing, Jones of Caldwell, Jones of Washington, King of Lenoir, Kinney, Laflin, Lee, Logan, Long, Mann, Mayo, McDonald of Chatham, Morton, Mullican, Murphy, Nance, Newsom, Patrick, Parks, Petree, Peterson, Pierson, Pool, Ragland, Ray, Read, Renfrow, Rhodes, Rich, Robbins, Rodman, Rose, Smith, Stilwell, Sweet, Taylor, Teague, Tourgee, Trogden, Tucker, Turner, Watts, Welker and Williamson—86.

Those who voted in the negative are:

Messrs Bradley, Daniel, Durham, Ellis, Graham of Orange, Grant of Northampton, Hare, Harris of Franklin, Hobbs, Hodnett, McCubbins, Moore, Nicholson, Parker, Sanderlin and Williams of Sampson—16.

Mr. Durham offered the following protest, to be entered on the Journals:

As this resolution is a step towards restricting the liberties of the Press, and of keeping information from the people, we protest against its passage.

(Signed,) P. DURHAM,
JAMES R. ELLIS,
J. S. McCUBBINS,
HAYNES LENNON,
ALEXANDER WILLIAMS,
JOHN W. GRAHAM,
J. B. HARE,
PHILLIP HODNETT,
THOMAS SANDERLIN.

Mr. Heaton offered the following resolution, which was adopted:

*Resolved*, That the Secretary of this Convention is hereby authorized and instructed to procure an American Flag to be suspended from the dome of the Capitol.

Mr. French, of Chowan, offered the following resolution:

*Resolved*, That 11 o'clock, A. M., until otherwise ordered, be the hour for the daily meeting of this Convention.

Mr. King, of Lenoir, offered to amend, so as to read 10 o'clock.

The amendment was not sustained by the House, and the original resolution was adopted.

Mr. Graham, of Orange, moved to adjourn.

The motion was put to the House and lost.

Mr. Abbott moved that the Convention enter into the election of a Sergeant at Arms.

Mr. Abbott withdrew his motion, and offered the following resolution:

*Resolved*, That this Convention does hereby create the office of Sergeant at Arms, and will proceed immediately to the election of that officer.

Mr. Ashley moved a suspension of the rules, to bring the resolution before the House.

Mr. King, of Lenoir, called for the yeas and nays.

Those who voted in the affirmative are:

Messrs. Abbott, Andrews, Ashley, Aydlott, Bryan, Carey, Carter, Candler, Chillson, Colgrove, Congleton, Cox, Duckworth, Fisher, Forkner, Franklin, French of Bladen, French of Rockingham, French of Chowan, Fullings, Gahagan, Galloway, Garrett, Grant of Wayne, Grant of Northampton, Gully, Harris of Wake, Harris of Franklin, Hay, Hayes of Robeson, Hayes of Halifax, Heaton, Highsmith, Hobbs, Hoffler, Hood, Hyman, Ing, Jones of Caldwell, Jones of Washington, Kinney, Laflin, Lee, Logan, Long, Mann, Mayo, McCubbins, McDonald of Moore, Murphy, Nance, Newsom, Nicholson, Patrick, Parker, Parks, Petree, Pierson, Pool, Ragland, Ray, Read, Renfrow, Rhodes, Rich, Robbins, Rodman, Rose, Smith, Stilly, Stilwell, Sweet, Taylor, Teague, Tourgee, Trogden, Tucker, Turner, Watts, Welker, Williams of Wake and Williamson—82.

Those who voted in the negative are:

Messrs. Baker, Barnes, Daniel, Durham, Ellis, Etheridge, Graham of Orange, Gunter, Hodnett, King of Lenoir, Lennon, McDonald of Chatham, Moore, Mullican, Peterson, Sanderlin and Williams of Sampson—17.

Mr. Abbott then offered the following substitute:

*Resolved*, That this Convention do now proceed to an election of Sergeant at Arms.

Which was adopted.

Mr. Rodman moved to reconsider.

Pending which the House adjourned.

---

FRIDAY JANUARY 17TH, 1868.

The Convention was called to order at 11 o'clock, by the President.

Prayer by the Rev. Mr. Lennon.

The Roll was called by the Secretary, 106 members answering to their names.

Messrs. Abbott, Andrews, Ashley, Aydlott, Baker, Barnes, Benbow, Blume, Bradley, Bryan, Carey, Carter, Chillson, Colgrove, Congleton, Cox, Daniel, Dowd, Duckworth, Durham, Ellis, Eppes, Etheridge, Fisher, Franklin, French of Bladen, French of Rockingham, French of Chowan, Fullings,

Gahagan, Galloway, Garland, Garrett, George, Graham of Montgomery, Graham of Orange, Grant of Wayne, Grant of Northampton, Gully, Gunter, Hare, Harris of Franklin, Hay, Hayes of Robeson, Hayes of Halifax, Heaton, Hobbs, Hodnett, Hoffler, Hollowell, Holt, Hood, Hyman, Ing, Jones of Caldwell, Jones of Washington, King of Lincoln, King of Lenoir, Kinney, Lee, Lennon, Logan, Long, Mann, Mayo, McCubbins, Merritt, McDonald of Chatham, McDonald of Moore, Moore, Morton, Mullican, Murphy, Nance, Newsom, Nicholson, Patrick, Parker, Parks, Petree, Peterson, Pierson, Pool, Ragland, Read, Renfrow, Rhodes, Rich, Robbins, Rodman, Rose, Sanderlin, Smith, Stilly, Stilwell, Sweet, Taylor, Teague, Tourgee, Trogden, Turner, Watts, Welker, Williams of Sampson and Williamson—105.

The Journals of Thursday was read and approved.

On motion of Mr. Welker, Mr. J. C. L. Harris was appointed Secretary *pro tem.*, during the illness of Assistant Secretary, Mr. Boner.

Mr. Rodman's motion to reconsider the vote taken the day previous, on Mr. Abbott's resolution for the election of Sergeant at Arms, was taken up.

Mr. Rodman withdrew his motion to reconsider.

Mr. E. M. Holt, delegate from Orange, and Mr. W. H. Merritt, of Person, were properly qualified by the President, and took their seats in the Convention.

The rules having been suspended Thursday, for the election of Sergeant at Arms, the House proceeded to an election.

Mr. Abbott nominated Mr. I. A. Peck.

Mr. Ellis, of Catawba, nominated Mr. C. J. Rogers.

Mr. Smith moved that the Roll be called, and each delegate announce his choice.

For Mr. Peck—Messrs. Abbott, Andrews, Ashley, Aydlott, Barnes, Benbow, Bryan, Carey, Carter, Candler, Cherry, Chillson, Colgrove, Congleton, Cox, Duckworth, Eppes, Fisher, Forkner, Franklin, French of Bladen, French of Rockingham, French of Chowan, Fullings, Gahagan, Galloway, Garland, Garrett, George, Graham of Montgomery, Gully, Harris of

Wake, Hay, Hayes of Robeson, Hayes of Halifax, Heaton, Highsmith, Hoffler, Hood, Hyman, Ing, Jones of Caldwell, Jones of Washington, King of Lincoln, King of Lenoir, Lee, Logan, Long, Mann, Mayo, Merritt, McDonald of Moore, Morton, Mullican, Murphy, Nance, Newsom, Patrick, Petree, Peterson, Pierson, Pool, Ragland, Read, Renfrow, Rhodes, Rich, Robbins, Rodman, Rose, Smith, Stillwell, Sweet, Taylor Teague, Tourgee, Trogden, Turner, Watts, Welker, Williams of Sampson and Williamson.—82.

For Mr. Rogers—Messrs. Blume and Moore—2.

For Mr. Ball—Mr. Graham, of Orange—1.

Mr. Peck being declared elected, was properly qualified by the Secretary, and entered upon his duties.

Mr. Sweet, as Chairman of the Committee on Rules of Order, presented the following report :

## REPORT OF THE SELECT COMMITTEE ON RULES.

The "Select Committee appointed to prepare and report to the Convention a code of rules for the regulation of its proceedings" submit the following report :

### CHAPTER I.

#### OF THE POWERS AND DUTIES OF THE PRESIDENT.

*Rule* 1. The President shall take the Chair each day at the hour appointed for the meeting of the session.

*Rule* 2. He shall possess the powers and perform the duties herein prescribed, viz :

1. He shall preserve order and decorum.

2. He shall decide all questions of order, subject to appeal to the Convention. On every appeal, he shall have the right, in his place, to assign his reasons for his decision.

3. He shall appoint all committees except where the Con-ntion shall otherwise order.

'. He may substitute any member to perform the duties of

the Chair for a period not exceeding two consecutive legislative days.

5. When the Convention shall be ready to go into Committee of the Whole, he shall name a Chairman to preside therein.

## CHAPTER II.

### OF THE DAILY ORDER OF BUSINESS.

*Rule* 3. The first business of each day's session shall be the reading of the Journal of the preceding day and the correction of any errors that may be found to exist therein. After which, except on days and at times set apart for the consideration of special orders, the order of business, which shall not be departed from except by unanimous consent, shall be as follows, viz :

1. The presentation of memorials. Under which head shall be included petitions, remonstrances and communications from individuals and from public bodies.
2. Notices.
3. Reports of Standing Committees.
4. Reports of Select Committees.
5. Resolutions.
6. Unfinished business of the General Orders.
7. Special Orders.
8. General Orders.

## CHAPTER III.

### OF THE RIGHTS AND DUTIES OF MEMBERS.

*Rule* 4. The President, or any member, when he shall be recognized in his place, may present, under the proper order of business, any paper of a respectful character, addressed to the Convention, and the same, unless the Convention shall otherwise order, shall be referred to the appropriate Committee.

*Rule* 5. Every member presenting a paper shall endorse the same; if a petition, memorial, remonstrance, or communication in answer to a call for information, with a concise statement of its subject, adding his name; if a notice or resolution, with his name; if the report of a committee, with a statement of its subject, the name of the committee and of the member making the report; if a proposition of any other kind for the consideration of the Convention, with a statement of its subject, the proposer's name, and the reference, if any, desired.

*Rule* 6. Every member who shall be within the bar of the Convention when a question shall be stated from the Chair, shall vote thereon unless he be excused by the Convention or be personally interested in the question. No member shall be obliged to vote on any question unless within the bar when the question shall be put, or in the case of a division by yeas and nays, before the last name shall be called. The bar of the Convention shall be deemed to include the semi-circle of colnmns.

*Rule* 7. Any member desiring to be excused from voting, must make his request before his name is passed. He may then state concisely, without argument, his reasons for asking to be excused, and the question of excusing shall be taken without debate.

## CHAPTER IV.

### OF ORDER AND DECORUM.

*Rule* 8. No member rising to debate, to give a notice, make a motion or present a paper of any kind, shall proceed until he shall have addressed the President, and been recognized by him as entitled to the floor.

*Rule* 9. Where a member shall have the floor for any purpose, no member shall entertain any private discourse or pass between him and the Chair.

*Rule* 10. While the President shall be putting a question, or a division by counting shall be had, no member shall leave his place, or speak, unless to make a privileged motion or state a question of privilege demanding immediate attention.

*Rule* 11. When a motion to adjourn, or for a recess, shall be affirmatively determined, no member or officer shall leave his place till the adjournment or recess shall be declared by the President.

## CHAPTER V.

### OF ORDER IN DEBATE.

*Rule* 12. No member shall speak more than once to the same question, without leave of the Convention, until every member desiring to speak on the question pending shall have spoken.

*Rule* 13. No remark reflecting personally upon the action of any member shall be in order in debate, unless preceded by a motion or resolution of investigation or censure.

*Rule* 14. If any member, in speaking, shall transgress the rules of the Convention, the President shall, or any member may call to order, in which case the member so called to order, shall not rise, unless to explain or proceed in order.

## CHAPTER VI.

### OF COMMITTEES AND THEIR DUTIES.

*Rule* 15. Standing Committees shall be appointed by the President, to consider and report severally upon the following subjects, and such others as may be referred to them, viz:

*To consist of five members:*

Privileges and Elections.
Printing.
Contingent Expenses.
Engrossment and Enrollment.

*Rule* 16. All Reports of Committees embracing proposition pertaining to the formation of a Constitution, shall be referred, as of course, to the Committee of the Whole for consideration therein before final action by the Convention.

## CHAPTER VII.

### OF GENERAL AND SPECIAL ORDERS.

*Rule* 17. The matters referred to the Committee of the Whole shall constitute the General Orders, and shall be recorded by their titles or subjects in a calandar to be kept for that purpose by the Secretary, in the order in which they shall be referred respectively.

*Rule* 18. Any particular report or other matter on the General Orders, may be made a Special Order for any particular day or from day to day, with the assent of two-thirds of the members voting, and no Special Order shall be postponed or rescinded except by a similar vote.

## CHAPTER VIII.

### OF THE COMMITTEE OF THE WHOLE.

*Rule* 19. The same rules shall be observed in Committee of the Whole as in the Convention, as far as applicable, except that the previous question shall not apply, nor shall the yeas and nays be taken on a division.

*Rule* 20. A motion to rise and report progress shall be in order at any stage, and shall be decided without debate.

*Rule* 21. Subjects shall be taken up in Committee of the Whole in the order in which they shall stand on the General Orders, unless the Committee, by a two-third's vote, shall, in any case, otherwise direct. The paper under consideration shall first be read at length, unless the Committee shall otherwise order, and shall then be read and considered by sections. All amendments made in Committee of the Whole shall be reported to the Convention for action.

*Rule* 22. If at any time, in the Committee of the Whole, it shall appear that no quorum be present, the Committee shall immediately rise, and the Chairman shall report the fact to the Convention.

## CHAPTER IX.

### OF MOTIONS AND THEIR PRECEDENCE.

*Rule* 23. When a question shall be under consideration, no motion shall be received except as herein specified, and motions shall have precedence in the order stated, viz:

1. For an adjournment.
2. For a recess.
3. A call of the Convention.
4. For the previous question.
5. To lay on the table.
6. To postpone indefinitely.
7. To postpone to a day certain.
8. To commit to a Committee of the Whole.
9. To commit to a Standing Committee.
10. To commit to a Select Committee.
11. To amend.

*Rule* 24. The motion to adjourn for the day, for the previous question and to lay on the table, shall be decided without amendment or debate. The respective motions to postpone or commit shall preclude debate on the main question.

*Rule* 25. Every motion or resolution shall, after presentation, be first stated by the President, or, on his order, read by the Secretary before debate, and again, if desired by any member, immediately before putting the question. And every resolution and amendment shall be reduced to writing, if the President or any member desires it.

*Rule* 26. After a proposition shall have been stated by the President, it shall be deemed to be in possession of the Convention, but may be withdrawn at any time before it shall be decided or amended.

*Rule* 27. The motions to adjourn or to take a recess shall be always in order when made by a member entitled to the floor.

*Rule* 28. No motion for the reconsideration of any vote shall be in order, unless made on the same day, or the next following legislative day, on which the decision proposed to be reconsidered shall have taken place; nor unless moved by one who shall have voted in the majority. After a motion for a reconsideration shall have been put and lost, it shall not be renewed without the unanimous consent of the Convention.

*Rule* 29. The motion for the previous question shall be put without debate, and until it be decided shall preclude further amendment. The question shall be, "Shall the main question be now put;" and if determined in the affirmative, no further debate or amendment shall be in order, and the main question shall be on the passage of the resolution or other matter under consideration; but when amendments shall be pending, the question shall be first taken on the amendments in their order; and when amendments shall have been recommended by the Committee of the Whole, and not acted on by the Convention, the question shall be taken upon such amendments in like order.

## CHAPTER X.

### OF RESOLUTIONS.

*Rule* 30. The following classes of resolutions shall lie over one day for consideration, after which they may be called up, as of course, under their appropriate order of business:

1. Resolutions giving rise to debate, except such as shall relate to the disposition of business immediately before the Convention, to the business of the day on which they may be offered, or to adjournment or recess.

*Rule* 31. All resolutions for the printing of an extra number of documents, shall be referred, as of course, to the Standing Committee on Printing, for their report thereon before final action by the Convention.

*Rule* 32. All resolutions authorizing or contemplating expenditures for the purpose of the Convention, shall be referred to the Standing Committee on Contingent Expenses, for their report thereon before final action by the Convention.

*Rule* 33. In case of the absence of a quorum at any session of the Convention, the members present, if exceeding one-fifth of the whole number, may take such measures as they may deem necessary to secure the presence of a qnorum, and may inflict such censure or pecuniary penalty as they may deem just, on those who on being called on for that purpose shall render no sufficient excuse for their absence.

*Rule* 34. If any question contain several distinct propositions, it shall be divided by the President, at the request of any member: *Provided*, Each sub-division, if left to itself, shall form a substantive proposition; but the motion to strike out and insert shall be indivisible.

*Rule* 35. The yeas and nays shall be taken and recorded in the journal on any question when demanded by one-fifth of the members present, except in cases where such a division shall have been already ordered on a pending question.

*Rule* 36. No standing rule of the Convention shall be suspended, amended or rescinded, unless one day's notice of the motion therefor shall have been given; nor shall any amendment or repeal be then made, except by the vote of a majority of all the members elected to the Convention. But such notice shall not be required on the last day's session. The notice and motion for a suspension, shall each state specifically the number of the rule and the object of the proposed suspension; and every suspension, on such notice and motion, shall be held to apply only to the partitular object or objects specied therein.

*Rule* 37. All questions relating to the priority of business, that is, the priority of one subject matter over another, under the same order of business, the postponement of any special order, or the suspension of any rule, shall be decided without debate.

*Rule* 38. There shall be printed, as of course, and without any special order, one hundred and fifty copies of all reports of committees on the subject of the formation of a Constitution, and of all reports and communications made in pursuance of the order or request of the Convention.

*Rule* 39. The Sergeant-at-Arms shall receive from the printer all matter printed for tne use of the Convention, and shall keep a record of the time of the reception of each document, and the number of copies received, and shall cause a copy of each to be placed on the desks of the members, officers and reporters entitled to receive them, immediately after their reception by him.

*Rule* 40. The Sergeant-at-Arms shall perform to duties of Postmaster of the Convention, and as such shall receive, distribute and dispatch such mail matter as shall be deposited in his office, addressed to or by the members of the Convention.

All of which is respecfully submitted.

W. H. S. SWEET, *Chairman.*
A. H. GALLOWAY,
C. C. POOL,
JOHN W. GRAHAM,
EDWARD FULLINGS.

Mr. Sweet, of Craven, offered the following resolution, which was adopted:

*Resolved*, That the rules be read separately, and except where a vote is demanded, or an amendment offered, each shall be declared adopted without a formal vote.

The Rules were read separately and adopted by the House.

Mr. Durham moved to strike out the previous question from the Rules, but was not sustained by the House.

Mr. C. C. Jones offered the following resolution, which was adopted:

*Resolved*, That the President of the Convention be requested to inform Major Gen. E. R. S. Canby, of this Military District, that this Convention is permanently organized, and is peoceeding to the dispatch of business.

Mr. Ashley offered the following order:

*Ordered*, That no person, except members and officers of the Convention, be permitted to come upon the floor, except by invitation of one of the members of the Convention.

Put to the House and lost.

Mr. Heaton, of Craven, as Chairman of the Committee on best mode of proceeding to frame a Constitution and Civil Government according to the acts of Congress submitted the following report:

The Committee appointed to consider and report upon the best mode of proceeding to frame a Constitution and Civil Government according to the Acts of Congress respectfully report as follows:

*Resolved*, That the Standing Committees be appointed by the President to report on each of the following subjects, viz:

1. On a Preamble and Bill of Rights.
2. On a Governor and other necessary State Executive Officers, their election or appointment, tenure of office, powers, compensation and duties.
3. On the Legislature, its organization, the number, appointment, election, tenure of office of its members, its powers and duties, except as otherwise referred.
4. On the Judicial Department.
5. On the finances of the State, the public debt, revenues, expenditures and taxation, and restrictions on the powers of the Legislature in respect thereto.
6. On Internal Improvement.
7. On counties, cities, towns and villages, their officers, organization, government and powers.
8. On Corporations other than municipal.
9. On Punishments and Penal Institutions.
10. On Militia.
11. On Education, Common Schools, University and the means of their support.
12. On Suffrage and Eligibility to Office.
13. On Homesteads.

The Committee also recommend the different Standing

Committees, as named, shall each consist of thirteen members.

DAVID HEATON, *Chairman.*
W. NICHOLSON,
E. W. JONES,
W. B. RODMAN,
H. A. DOWD,
J. H. HARRIS,
A. W. TOURGEE,
T. L. L. COX,
J. C. ABBOTT,
J. W. HOOD,
S. FORKNER,
M. HOBBS,
C. C. JONES,
GEO. W. BRADLEY,
G. W. GAHAGAN,
W. G. B. GARRETT,
*Committee.*

On motion of Mr. Tourgee, the report was adopted.

On motion of Mr. Mann, the Committee on Rules was discharged.

On motion of Mr. Tourgee, the Sergeant at Arms was ordered to cause to be printed one hundred and fifty copies of the Rules of Order.

Mr. Ashley introduced the following preamble and resolution:

WHEREAS, The Committee of Sixteen was directed to consider and report the best practicable plan for establishing a Constitution and Civil Government loyal to the Union; and whereas, the report now presented only provides a plan for the establishment of a Constitution, entirely ignoring anything like a plan for the adoption and carrying into effect that Constitution: therefore,

*Resolved*, That the Committee be instructed as soon as practicable to consider and report upon the best method of carrying into effect the Constitution, or establishing a civil government in North-Carolina.

Mr. Heaton moved the resolution be returned for revision,

When it was decided that the resolution should lie over one day.

The following resolution, introduced by C. C. Jones, was read and adopted:

*Resolved*, That the President of this Convention be requested to inform Major-General E. R. S. Canby, Commander of this Military District, that this Convention is permanently organized and is proceeding to the dispatch of business.

Mr. Forkner offered the following resolution:

*Resolved, by the delegates of the people of North-Carolina, in Convention assembled*, That the Secretary of State furnish each delegate of this Convention a copy of the Constitution adopted by the Convention of 1865–'66 for the use of the delegates.

On motion, the rules were suspended.

On motion of Mr. Hood, the resolution was amended by inserting the words "*be requested to*" before the word furnish.

Mr. Watts moved to amend by striking out the word "*State*" and insert "*North-Carolina.*"

Mr. Tourgee moved to insert the word "Provisional" before Secretary, which was agreed to, and the resolution as amended was adopted.

Mr. Rich offered the following resolution:

*Resolved*, That the Secretary apply to General Canby for a full statement of the votes for and against a Convention in the several Counties of this State.

On motion, the rules were suspended.

Mr. Rodman moved to amend by adding, "also for a statement of the vote by Counties received by each candidate for this Convention."

The amendment was adopted.

The resolution as amended was adopted.

Mr. McDonald, of Chatham, offered the following resolution:

*Resolved*, That a Committee of Eight, to consist of one member from each Judicial District, be raised by this Convention, whose duty it shall be to devise and report to the Convention some plan to relieve the people of the State from the pressure of debts under which they labor, and which must, unless some remedy be afforded, result in general bankruptcy and thus add very greatly not only to the present general distress, but operate to the serious injury of all our industrial pursuits.

Mr. Rodman offered the following ordinance as a substitute to the resolution of Mr. McDonald:

SECTION 1. *Be it ordained by the people of North-Carolina in Convention assembled*, That no court of law or equity of this State shall have jurisdiction of any suit or action founded on any contract made prior to the first day of May, 1865, (except actions against public officers, executors, administrators, guardians, trustees, and others acting in a fiduciary capacity, and their sureties for breach of their respective trusts,) or of any action or process to revive or enforce any judgment heretofore recovered on any such contracts, whether such action be now pending or shall be commenced hereafter, and whether such process has been already issued or shall be hereafter sued for; and the Sheriffs, Coroners and Constables of this State, having in their hands any final process issued upon any judgment founded on such cause of action, are hereby commanded to stay all proceedings upon the same, and to return the same to the proper court.

SEC. 2. This ordinance shall be in force from and after its ratification by this Convention, and shall continue in force until the Constitution which this Convention has met to form shall go into effect.

Mr. Tourgee moved to refer this entire subject to the Committee of the Whole, and make it the Special Order for Tuesday next at 12 o'clock, which was agreed to.

Mr. Durham offered the following resolutions:

*Resolved*, That it is the sincere desire of the people of North-Carolina to restore the State to her Constitutional relations with the Federal Government at the earliest day practicable, upon terms just and honorable, both to the Government of the United States and to the State.

*Resolved*, That, recognizing the helpless condition of North Carolina and the power of the Federal Government to force the acceptance of the terms of reconstruction proposed by Congress, it is nevertheless the sense of this Convention that these measures known as the Reconstruction Acts are unconstitutional, unwise, unjust and oppressive; subversive of the rights and liberties of eight millions of people, and calculated to hasten and complete the destruction of that wise system of government, which, when faithfully adherred to, secured so much happiness and prosperity to the American people.

*Resolved*, That the white and black races are distinct by nature, and that any and all efforts to abolish or abridge such distinction, and to degrade the white to the level of the black race, are crimes against the civilization of the age and against God.

*Resolved*, That the Government of the United States and of the Southern States were instituted by white men, and that while the lives, liberty and property of the black race should be protected by just laws, these governments ought to be controlled by white men only.

*Resolved*, That we appeal to the sense of justice of the masses of the Northern people to remove from the intelligent American citizens of the Southern States the degradation now heaped upon them, and to consider the dire results to the whole country if the policy of depriving eight millions of people of the services of these statesmen, disfranchising intelligent whites and transferring political power to ignorant blacks should be continued.

After some discussion the House, on motion, adjourned.

---

## SATURDAY, JANUARY 18TH, 1868.

The Convention was called to order at 11 o'clock, by the President.

Prayer by the Rev. Dr. Smith.

The roll was called by the Secretary. One hundred and eight delegates answered to their names.

Mr. Tourgee presented a Memorial from the Friends Association of Philadelphia and its vicinity, for the relief of colored Freedmen.

The petition was read and referred to the Committee on Education.

Mr. Heaton, Chairman of the Committee of sixteen, presented the following report, viz:

The Committee of sixteen, to whom was referred the following resolution, viz:

*Resolved*, That this Convention has been convened for the purpose of framing a Constitution Republican in form, and that no proposition purely legislative, shall be entertained until the Constitution shall have been adopted;

Have had the same under consideration, and report the following as a substitute therefor:

*Resolved*, That this Convention being called to frame a Constitution and Civil Government in accordance with the Acts of Congress, will proceed in the discharge of that duty as speedily as practicable.

All of which is respectfully submitted.

D. HEATON, *Chairman.*

On motion of Mr. Tourgee, the report was adopted.

Mr. Bradley, of Wautauga, offered the following resolution:

*Resolved*, That a Committee of three be appointed to wait on his Excellency, the Governor of North-Carolina, and inform him of the organization of the Convention, and that the Convention is now ready to receive any communication he may desire to make.

Laid over under the rules.

Mr. King, of Lenoir, offered the following resolution:

*Resolved*, That the word "suspended," in rule 36, lines 1st and 2d, be stricken out.

Laid over under the rule.

Mr. Ashley's resolution offered the day previous was taken up, when

Mr. Ashley offered the following as a substitute:

*Resolved*, That the Committee of sixteen, be instructed to further consider, and report as soon as practicable, upon the best method of carrying into effect the Constitution, or establishing a Civil Government in North-Carolina.

On motion of Mr. Abbott, the resolution was adopted.

The resolutions offered by Mr. Durham yesterday, were taken up.

Mr. Durham moved to make his resolutions a Special Order for Wednesday next, at 12 o'clock.

Mr. King, of Lenoir, moved to lay the resolution on the table.

On this motion, Mr. Durham demanded the yeas and nays. The demand was sustained.

The motion was lost by the following vote:

Those who voted in the affirmative are:

Messrs. Andrews, Candler, Colgrove Daniel, Dowd, Franklin, Gahagan, George, Graham of Montgemery, Gunter, King of Lenoir, Logan, Morton, Newsom, Nicholson, Peterson, Pool, Rhodes, Rich, Robbins and Rose—21.

Those who voted in the negative are:

Messrs. Abbott, Ashley, Aydlott, Baker, Barnes, Benbow, Blume, Bradley, Bryan, Carey, Carter, Cherry, Chillson, Congleton, Cox, Dickey, Duckworth, Durham, Ellis, Etheridge, Fisher, Forkner, French of Bladen, French of Rockingham, French of Chowan, Fullings, Galloway, Garland, Garrett, Graham of Orange, Grant of Northampton, Gully, Hare, Harris of Wake, Harris of Franklin, Hay, Hayes of Robeson, Hayes of Halifax, Heaton, Highsmith, Hobbs, Hodnett, Hollowell, Holt, Hood, Hyman, Ing, Jones of Caldwell, Jones of Washington, King of Lincoln, Kinney, Laflin, Lee, Legg, Lennon, Long, Mann, Mayo, McCubbins, Merritt, McDonald of Chatham, DcDonald of Moore, Moore,Murphy, Nance, Patrick, Parker, Parks, Petree, Pierson, Ragland, Ray, Read, Renfrow, Rodman, Sanderlin, Smith, Stilly, Stilwell, Sweet, Taylor, Teague, Tourgee, Trogden, Tucker, Turner, Watts, Welker, Williams of Sampson and Williamson—90.

Mr. King, of Lenoir, moved to amend the motion of Mr.

Durham, to postpone to Wednesday next, at 12 o'clock, M., by postponing to the 20th of May, 1868.

Mr. Andrews moved to amend by substituting 1869 for 1868.

Mr. Tourgee called for the previous question, which was on Mr. King's amendment. The call was sustained.

Mr. Graham, of Orange, called for the yeas and nays. The call was sustained.

The amendment was lost by the following vote:

Those who voted in the affirmative are:

Messrs. Andrews, Candler, Graham of Montgomery, King of Lenoir, Morton, Newsom and Pool—7.

Those who voted in the negative are:

Messrs. Ashley, Aydlott, Baker, Barnes, Benbow, Blume, Bradley, Bryan, Carey, Carter, Cherry, Chillson, Colgrove, Congleton, Cox, Daniel, Dowd, Duckworth, Durham, Ellis, Eppes, Etheridge, Fisher, Forkner, Franklin, French of Bladen, French of Rockingham, French of Chowan, Fullings, Gahagan, Galloway, Garland, Garrett, George, Graham of Orange, Grant of Northampton, Gunter, Hare, Harris of Franklin, Hayes of Robeson, Hayes of Halifax, Heaton, Highsmith, Hobbs, Hodnett, Hollowell, Holt, Hood, Hyman, Ing, Jones of Caldwell, Jones of Washington, King of Lincoln, Kinney, Laflin, Lee, Legg, Lennon, Logan, Long, Mann, Mayo, McCubbins, Merritt, McDonald of Chatham, McDonald of Moore, Moore, Mullican, Murphy, Nance, Nicholson, Patrick, Parker, Parks, Petree, Peterson, Pierson, Ragland, Ray, Read, Renfrow, Rhodes, Rich, Robbins, Rodman, Rose, Sanderlin, Stilly, Stilwell, Sweet, Taylor, Teague, Tourgee, Trogden, Tucker, Turner, Watts, Welker, Williams of Sampson and Williamson—100.

The question recurring on the motion of Mr. Durham, to postpone to Wednesday next.

On which motion the yeas and nays were ordered.

The motion was lost by the following vote:

Those who voted in the affirmative are:

Messrs. Aydlott, Baker, Bradley, Candler, Cherry, Chillson, Colgrove, Congleton, Daniel, Dickey, Dowd, Duckworth,

Ellis, Eppes, Etheridge, French of Chowan, Galloway, Hodnett, Hollowell, Hood, Ing, Jones of Washington, Legg, Mayo, McCubbins, McDonald of Chatham, Moore, Ragland, Read, Rich, Robbins and Taylor—32.

Those who voted in the negative are:

Messrs. Andrews, Ashley, Barnes, Benbow, Blume, Bryan, Carey, Carter, Cox, Durham, Fisher, Forkner, Franklin, French of Bladen, Fullings, Gahagan, Garland, Garrett, George, Graham of Montgomery, Graham of Orange, Grant of Wayne, Grant of Northampton, Gunter, Hare, Harris of Wake, Harris of Franklin, Hay, Hayes of Robeson, Heaton, Highsmith, Hobbs, Holt, Hyman, Jones of Caldwell, King of Lincoln, King of Lenoir, Kinney, Lee, Lennon, Logan, Long, Mann, Merritt, Morton, Mullican, Murphy, Nance, Newsom, Nicholson, Patrick, Parker, Parks, Petree, Peterson, Pierson, Pool, Ray, Renfrow, Rhodes, Rodman, Rose, Sanderlin, Smith, Stilly, Stilwell, Sweet, Teague, Tourgee, Trogden, Tucker, Turner, Watts, Welker, Williams of Sampson and Williamson—75.

The Resolution being before the House.

Mr. Tourgee moved to amend the 1st resolution so as to read, "That it is the sincere desire of the people of North-Carolina to be restored to their Constitutional relations."

Instead of, "That it is the desire of the people of North-Carolina to restore the State to her Constitutional relations."

Also, strike out the word "State," in the last part of the resolution and insert "people."

Mr. Heaton moved to refer the whole matter to a Committee of three.

The motion was put to the House and lost.

Mr. Tourgee called for the previous question on his amendment.

The call was sustained.

The vote was taken and the amendment was lost.

Mr. King, of Lincoln, moved to postpone indefinitely.

The motion prevailed.

Mr. Peterson offered the following resolution:

*Resolved*, That the President of the Convention be directed to appoint a Committee of *two* to request the Provisional Secretary of North-Carolina to furnish one hundred and twenty copies of the proceedings of the General Assembly during the sessions of 1866–'67, for the use of the members of the Convention.

Laid over under the rules.

On motion of Mr. Heaton, the Convention proceeded to the election of an Engrossing Clerk.

Mr. Heaton nominated Mr. James E. O'Hara, who was elected by acclamation.

Mr. Turner moved that the Convention proceed to the election of an Enrolling Clerk.

Mr. Jones, of Washington, moved that it is not absolutely necessary to have an Enrolling Clerk, since we have an Engrossing Clerk, under whose direction a Clerk can do what Enrolling may be required by the Convention and at less cost.

Pending which motion, the House adjourned.

---

MONDAY JANUARY 20TH, 1868.

The Convention was called to order at 11 o'clock, by the President.

Prayer by the Rev. Mr. Hudson.

The President announced a quorum.

The Journal of Saturday read and approved.

Mr. J. G. Marler, delegate from Yadkin, was sworn by the Secretary, and took his seat in the Convention.

Mr. O'Hara, the Engrossing Clerk, was properly sworn and entered upon the discharge of his duties.

Mr. Abbott offered a communication from Mr. Calton Sessoms, of Owensville, in regard to the late election in Sampson County.

Referred to the Committee on Elections and privileges.

Mr. Abbott also offered a statement from Mr. M. D. Pearsall, of Kenansville, Duplin County, in regard to the injustice arising from certain sales of property during the War, asking redress.

Referred to Committee on the Judicial Department.

Mr. D. D. Colgrove presented a petition from the citizens of Jones County, to change the boundary between the counties of Jones and Lenoir.

Referred to the Committee of sixteen.

Mr. L. C. Morton presented the following resolution:

*Resolved*, That the President appoint a Special Committee of twelve to enquire and report to this Convention the best practicable means of relief for the debtors of North-Carolina.

Laid over under the rules.

Mr. Hodnett presented the following preamble and resolution:

WHEREAS, Protection to the rights of persons and property, the fruits of industry and prudence, are the corner stones on which Civil Liberty is built, as recognized in our Constitution of 1776; therefore,

*Resolved*, That the action of this Convention should recognize the axiom, by providing that the legislative power consist of two branches, the one representing persons, and the other representing property, each of said branches having co-equal powers, so that no act of the Legislature, not approved by each Branch, should have validity. The Electors for the Commons, to consist of all male citizens above the age of twenty-one years; and the Electors for the Senate to consist of citizens of like age, who have listed property for taxation, at the listing next before such election, of the value of two hundred and fifty dollars or upwards, and who have paid the taxes assessed thereon.

Laid over under the rules.

Mr. Abbott offered the following resolution:

*Resolved*, That the Committee of sixteen be instructed to enquire into the propriety of appointing a Committee on Immigration, and to report the result of their deliberations to the Convention.

Laid over under the rules.

Mr. McDonald, of Chatham, offered a petition for relief from the citizens of Chatham.

Referred to a Committee of the Whole, and made a Special Order for Tuesday at 12 o'clock.

Mr. G. W. Welker introduced an Ordinance providing for the admission of members of the Bar from other States, to practice in the Courts of North-Carolina.

Referred to the Committee of the Whole.

Mr. W. A. Mann offered the following preamble and resolution:

WHAREAS, In consequence of the constant annoyance of the delegates occupying seats in the back part of this House, by conversation on the part of visitors in the lobbies, and the impossibility of keeping that portion of the House comfortably warm, and as the Galleries are capacious and well suplied with seats, be it

*Resolved*, That no person not a delegate, be admitted to the lobbies of this House, without an invitation from a delegate or an officer of this Convention.

Laid over under the rules.

Mr. Mann also presented the following resolution:

*Resolved*, That the Secretary be directed to invite the United States Officers on duty at this post to the floor of this House.

Laid over under the rules.

Mr. Logan offered an Ordinance in relation to a Court of Pleas and Quarter Sessions for the County of Rutherford.

Laid over under the rules.

Mr. Hood, of Cumberland, offered the following resolution:

*Resolved*, That each delegate to this Convention, and each elective officer, (the President excepted,) receive six dollars per day and twenty cents mileage to and from the Convention, and that the President receive ten dollars per day and twenty cents mileage.

Laid over under the rule.

UNFINISHED BUSINESS.

The motion of C. C. Jones to amend the motion of Mr. Turner, of Harnett, to proceed to an election of an enrolling clerk, by taking the sense of the House, as to whether the office of enrolling clerk should be created, put to the House and was lost.

Mr. Jones called the yeas and nays, which resulted yeas 32, nays 77.

Those who voted in the affirmative are:

Messrs. Ashley, Baker, Candler, Colgrove, Daniel, Dowd, Durham, Ellis, Fisher, Garrett, Graham of Orange, Grant of Northampton, Gunter, Hare, Harris of Franklin, Hayes of Robeson, Hobbs, Holt, Jones of Washington, King of Lenoir, Lee, Lennon, Logan, Mayo, Marshall, McCubbins, Merritt, McDonald of Chatham, Nicholson, Parker, Peterson and Sanderlin—32.

Those who voted in the negative are:

Messrs. Abbott, Andrews, Aydlott, Barnes, Benbow, Blume, Bryan, Carey, Carter, Cherry, Chillson, Congleton, Cox, Dickey, Duckworth, Eppes, Etheridge, Forkner, Franklin, French of Bladen, French of Rockingham, French of Chowan, Fullings, Gahagan, Galloway, Garland, George, Graham of Montgomery, Grant of Wayne, Gully, Hay, Hayes of Halifax, Heaton, Highsmith, Hoffler, Hollowell, Hood, Hyman, Ing, Jones of Caldwell, King of Lincoln, Kinney, Long, Mann, McDonald of Moore, Moore, Morton, Mullican, Murphy, Nance, Newsom, Parks, Petree, Pierson, Pool, Ragland, Ray, Read, Renfrow, Rhodes, Rich, Robbins, Rodman, Rose, Smith, Stilly, Stilwell, Taylor, Teague, Tourgee, Trogden, Tucker, Turner, Watts, Welker, Williams of Sampson, and Williamson—77.

Mr. Morton nominated Mr. Ashworth, of Randolph, as enrolling clerk.

On motion of Mr. Rich, Mr. Ashworth was declared enrolling clerk for the Convention.

Mr. Ashworth being properly qualified by the Secretary, entered upon his duties.

Mr. King's resolution to amend Rule No. 36, was on motion recommitted to the committee on Rules.

Mr. Bradley's Resolution to appoint a committee to wait on His Excellency, "Gov. Worth," was taken up.

Mr. Tourgee moved to amend by striking out "His Excellency the Governor of North-Carolina," and substitute the words "Governor Worth."

The amendment was put and lost.

The original resolution was taken up and adopted.

The resolution of Mr. Peterson to appoint a Committee of two to call on the Provisional Secretary to furnish one hundred and fifty copies of the Acts of the General Assembly of 1866–'67.

Amended by Mr. Durham, so as to read Provisional Secretary of State. Adopted.

On motion of Mr. Harris, of Wake, it was ordered that the Committee on Printing confer with the military authorities in relation to the printing for this Convention.

Mr. Galloway introduced a bill on Equal Rights and Privileges in conveyances and all business places.

Referred to the Committee on Preamble and Bill of Rights.

Mr. Rodman offered the following Resolution:

*Resolved*, That the Committee on Contingent Expenses be directed to contract with some competent person to report the proceedings of this Convention in a condensed form, and to cause such reports to be published in some daily newspaper of this City. And it shall be a part of such contract that if the Convention before the final adjournment thereof shall determine to publish such reports in book form, then the property therein shall be in the State; but if the Convention shall not so determine, then the property in such reports shall be in the Reporter and he shall be at liberty to apply for a Copy Right.

*Resolved further*, That such Reporter shall receive a compensation not greater than the daily pay of a member.

Laid over under the rules.

On motion of Mr. Rich, the Convention adjourned to 3 o'clock, P. M.

AFTERNOON SESSION, JANUARY 20TH, 1868.

The Convention was called to order, and on motion of Mr. Heaton, Mr. Welker was called to the Chair.

Mr. Tourgee submitted an Ordinance "to prevent oppressive costs in Criminal cases," which was placed upon the General Orders of the Committee of the Whole.

Mr. Patrick offered an Ordinance in relation to the sale of property under executions.

Made a General Order and referred to a Committee of the Whole.

Mr. Tourgee offered an Ordinance "Regarding the Jurisdiction of Courts," which he asked to have referred to the Committee of the whole, and made a part of the special order for Tuesday, January 22d at 12 M., as he desired at that time to offer it as a substitute for Mr. Rodman's Ordinance introduced on Tuesday last.

The Convention received an invitation from the President of the Deaf and Dumb Asylum, to visit the Institution, which was accepted.

On motion of Mr. Welker, Friday evening was agreed upon.

On motion of Mr. Heaton the Convention took a recess until 4 o'clock.

At 4 o'clock the business was resumed. The President in the Chair.

Mr. Cowles announced the following committees:

*On a Preamble and Bill of Rights.*—Messrs. Heaton, Harris, of Wake, Nicholson, French of Chowan, Patrick, Gahagan, Pool, Etheridge, Fisher, Baker, Durham, Carter and Garland.

*On a Governor, &c.*—Messrs. Nicholson, May, Morton, Franklin, Hoffler, Petree, Forkner, Gunter, Williamson, Newsom, George, Trogden and Stilwell.

*On Legislature, &c.*—Messrs. Sweet, Marler, May, Forkner, Lennon, Mullican, Chillson, French, of Rockingham, Mayo, Williams, of Duplin, Turner, Taylor, and Smith.

*On the Judicial Department.*—Messrs. Rodman, Sweet,

Tourgee, Jones of Washington, Pool, Durham, Fisher, Watts, Welker, King of Lenoir, Cox, Galloway and Teague.

*On the Finances of the State, &c.*—Messrs. Abbott, Heaton, Rodman, Jones, of Caldwell, Forkner, Hobbs, McCubbins, King of Lenoir, Long, Hare, Peterson, Carey, and Read.

*On Internal Improvements.*—Messrs. Garrett, Abbott, Mann, French, McCubbins, Heaton, Bradley, Williams of Wake, Hayes of Robeson, Hyman, Candler, Fullings and Teague.

*On Counties, Cities, &c.*—Messrs. Tourgee, Fullings, Ray, McCubbins, Andrews, Aydlott, Moore, Congleton, Galloway, Laflin, Ing, Hollowell and Franklin.

*On Corporations other than Municipal.*—Messrs. Jones of Washington, Ashley, Grant of Northampton, Harris of Franklin, King, Merritt, Holt, Hay, Robbins, Dickey, Tucker, Murphy and Parker.

*On Punishments and Penal Institutions.*—Messrs. Welker, Cox, Long, Glover, Parks, Murphy, Lee, Pierson, Daniel, Duckworth, Hobbs, Bradley and Watts.

*On Militia.*—Messrs. Bryan, Laflin, Ellis, Graham of Montgomery, Dowd, Grant of Wayne, Ragland, Legg, Gully, Hayes of Halifax, Highsmith, Colgrove and Stilley.

*On Education, Common Schools, &c.*—Messrs. Ashley, Welker, Rose, Blume, Read, Sweet, Hood, Hayes of Halifax, Graham of Orange, Ellis, French of Chowan, Logan and Fisher.

*On Suffrage and Eligibility to Office.*—Messrs. Pool, Jones of Caldwell, French of Chowan, Rich, Candler, Durham, Graham of Orange, Harris of Wake, McDonald of Chatham, Andrews, Benbow, Congleton and Cherry.

*On Homesteads.*—Messrs. Jones of Caldwell, Hood, Gahagan, Duckworth, Renfrow, Sanderlin, Nance, Hodnett, Kinney, McDonald of Moore, Barnes, Eppes, Rhodes and Cox.

On motion of Mr. Tourgee, one hundred and fifty copies were ordered to be printed for the use of the members.

On motion of Mr. Heaton, the Convention adjourned.

TUESDAY, January 21st, 1868.

The Convention was called to order at 11 o'clock by the President.

A quorum was announced by the President.

Prayer by the Rev. Mr. Eppes.

The Journal of Monday was read and adopted.

Mr. Mark May, delegate from Macon, was properly qualified by the Secretary, and took his seat in the Convention.

In accordance with the resolution of Mr. Bradley, passed Monday, the President announced the following Committee to wait on his Excellency, Governor Worth:

Messrs. Bradley, Abbott and Andrews.

The Committee on Corporations other than Municipal, was altered by striking out "Watts," and inserting "Parker."

The Committee on Preamble and Bill of Rights was changed by striking out "Dowd" and inserting "Baker."

The Committee on the Judicial Department was altered by striking out "Jones, of Caldwell," and substituting "C. C. Pool."

Committee on Suffrage and Eligibility to Office, was altered to read "Harris of Wake," instead of "Harris of Franklin."

Mr. Fisher presented a Memorial from the Citizens of Bladen County, asking "that obligations incurred in the purchase of slaves be annulled."

Referred to the Committee on the Judicial Department.

Mr. Abbott offered a resolution providing for a Committee to confer with General Canby.

Lies over under the rules.

Mr. Harris, of Wake, offered a resolution defining the status of citizens of North-Carolina.

Referred, by the Chair, to the Committee on Preamble and Bill of Rights.

Mr. Congleton offered a resolution in relation to property qualification.

Referred to a Committee on Suffrage.

Mr. Welker offered a Preamble and Resolution, relating to the election of Commissioner of Public Works.

Referred to a Committee on Governor and other necessary State Executive Officers.

Mr. Welker also introduced a resolution "Limiting the power of Legislation."

Referred to a Committee on Legislature.

Mr. Tourgee introduced a resolution in relation to the Rights of Electors.

Referred to the Committee on Suffrage.

Mr. Dowd introduced a resolution "Declaring the unconstitutionality of Stay Laws."

Referred to the Committee on the Judicial Department.

Mr. Tourgee offered a resolution to amend Rule 3d, Chapter 2d.

Lies over under the rules.

Mr. Parker introduced a resolution to confer "the Elective Franchise on all male citizens."

Referred to the Committee on Suffrage.

Mr. Legg offered a resolution in relation to Suffrage and Eligibility to Office.

Referred to the Committee on Suffrage and Eligibility to Office.

Mr. Harris, of Wake, presented a resolution in relation to the School Funds.

Referred to the Committee on Education, &c.

Mr. Galloway introduced an Article in relation to Suffrage and Elective Franchise.

Referred to the Committee on Suffrage.

UNFINISHED BUSINESS.

Mr. Hodnett's resolution in relation to the qualification of Electors, was submitted to the House, and referred to the Committee on Suffrage.

The resolution of Mr. Morton on relief, was referred to a Committee of the Whole.

Mr. Mullican's resolutions declaring certain amendments to the Bill of Rights, was referred to the Committee on Preamble and Bill of Rights.

On motion of Mr. Abbott, the House resolved itself into a Committee of the Whole.

The President called Mr. Sweet to the Chair.

The resolution of Mr. McDonald, of Chatham, and

The ordinance of Mr. Rodman, which were made a Special Order for 12 o'clock, were taken up.

Mr. Abbott moved that when this Committee rise, they report to the House the following resolution:

*Resolved*, That this Committee recommend that the whole subject under consideration be referred to a Special Committee of eight, to consist of one from each Judicial District, who shall have authority to call for persons and papers.

Adopted.

Mr. Graham, of Orange, offered a substitute to the ordinance of Mr. Rodman, which was referred to the Committee of eight mentioned on the resolution of Mr. Abbott.

Under General Orders, the ordinance of Mr. Tourgee to prevent oppression in costs in criminal cases was taken up.

Mr. Tourgee moved to refer to the Committee on Preamble and Bill of Rights, with instructions to report the same as one of the sections of the Bill of Rights.

Mr. Jones, of Washington, moved to amend by referring to the Committee on the Judicial Department. Adopted.

On motion of Mr. Abbott, the President took the Chair and Mr. Sweet, Chairman, of the Committee of the Whole reported as follows on the subject of Relief made a Special Order for this day:

That this Committee recommend that the whole subject under consideration be referred to a Special Committee of eight to consist of one from each Judicial District, who shall have authority to call for persons and papers.

On ordinance of Mr. Tourgee to prevent oppression in costs of Criminal Cases, under General Order.

The Committee recommend that it be referred to the Committee on the Judicial Department.

On motion of Mr. Tourgee, the report was accepted.

Mr. Hodnett's resolutions on qualification of Electors, was,

On motion, referred to the Committee on Suffrage.

Mr· Mann's resolutions excluding persons uninvited from

the Lobbies and extending invitations to the United States Officers at this Post, were laid over in consequence of Mr. Mann's absence.

Mr. Logan's ordinance on Pleas and Quarter Sessions, was,

On motion of Mr. Durham, referred to the Committee on Judicial Department.

The resolution of Mr. Hood, on Pay and Mileage of members, was taken up.

Mr. Rich moved to amend by inserting eight dollars per day for Officers and Members, except the President, who shall receive twelve.

Mr. Bryan moved to amend by inserting four dollars for Officers and Members and seven for President.

Mr. Dickey moved to adjourn.

The yeas and nays were called.

The motion was lost by the following vote, yeas 26 nays 87:

Those who voted in the affirmative are:

Messrs. Andrews, Baker, Blume, Cherry, Colgrove, Daniel, Dickey, Durham, Etheridge, Fisher, French of Bladen, Graham of Orange, Hall, Hare, Holt, Jones of Caldwell, Legg, Lennon, Long, Merritt, Moore, Morton, Newsom, Ragland, Rich and Tourgee—26

Those who voted in the negative are:

Messrs. Abbott, Ashley, Aydlott, Barnes, Benbow, Bradley, Bryan, Carey, Carter, Candler, Chillson, Congleton, Cox, Dowd, Duckworth, Ellis, Eppes, Forkner, Franklin, French of Rockingham, French of Chowan, Fullings, Gahagan, Galloway, Garland, Garrett, George, Graham of Montgomery, Grant of Wayne, Gully, Gunter, Harris of Wake, Harris of Franklin, Hay, Hayes of Robeson, Highsmith, Hobbs, Hodnett, Hollowell, Hood, Hyman, Ing, Jones of Washington, King of Lincoln, King of Lenoir, Kinney, Laflin, Lee, Logan, Mayo, Marshall, McCubbins, McDonald of Chatham, McDonald of Moore, Mullican, Murphy, Nance, Nicholson, Patrick, Parker, Parks, Petree, Peterson, Pierson, Pool, Ray, Read, Renfrow, Rhodes, Robbins, Rodman, Rose, Sanderlin, Smith, Stilly, Stilwell, Sweet, Taylor, Teague, Trogden, Tucker,

Turner, Watts, Welker, Williams of Wake and Williamson—87.

Mr. Tourgee offered the following substitute:

That all Members and Officers, except the President, receive eight dollars per day, for thirty days, and four dollars per day thereafter, and the President ten dollars per day, and all twenty cent per mile going and returning.

Pending which the House adjourned.

---

WEDNESDAY, January 22d, 1868.

The Convention was called to order at 11 o'clock, by the President.

Prayer by the Rev. Mr. Brodie.

The Chair announced a quorum.

The Journal of yesterday was read and approved.

Mr. Glover, of Hyde County, being present, was sworn by the Secretary and took his seat in the Convention.

Mr. Patrick presented a resolution relative to the suspension of debts.

Laid over under the rules.

Mr. Galloway offered a resolution asking for a postponement of the sale of property for debt.

Referred to a Committee on Relief.

Mr. Abbott offered an ordinance reducing the amount of Bonds authorized to be issued by the Wilmington, Charlotte and Rutherford Rail Road Company.

Referred to the Committee on Internal Improvements.

Mr. Parker introduced a resolution in relation to property qualification of the Members of the House of Commons and State Senate.

Referred to the Committee on Suffrage.

Mr. McDonald, of Chatham, offered a resolution instructing the Committee on Judicial Department.

Lies over under the rules.

Mr. Pool offered a resolution that a Committee of sixteen

be instructed to report an Article on the subject of Impeachment.

Referred to a Committee on Judicial Department.

Mr. Tourgee offered a resolution instructing a Committee to confer with General Canby.

Laid over under the rules.

Mr. Tougee also offered a resolution relative to the rights of persons accused of crime, asking that it be made a section of the Bill of Rights.

Referred to the Committee on Bill of Rights.

Mr. King offered a resolution in relation to the per diem of delegates.

Lies over under the rules.

Mr. Welker offered a resolution relative to the formation of a Miscellaneous Committee.

Referred to the Committee of sixteen.

Mr. Tourgee submitted a resolution amending the title of the Committee on Punishments and Penal Institutions.

Lies over under the rules.

Mr. Mann offered a resolntion relative to the organization of the Militia.

Referred to the Committee on Militia.

Mr. Smith offered a resolution in regard to the reading of Bills in the Legislature.

Lies over under the rules.

The Committee authorized to confer with his Excellency, Governor Worth, submitted the following report:

The undersigned Committee, appointed by the President, in compliance with the resolution of the gentleman from Watauga, to inform his Excellency, Governor Worth, that this Convention is organized and ready to receive any communication he may deem fit to make, beg leave to report that they have performed that duty, and that his Excellency, Governor Worth, informs this body that he will communicate with them to-morrow, Thursday, at 12 o'clock.

(Signed,) G. W. BRADLEY,
JOSEPH C. ABBOTT,
J. P. ANDREWS.

UNFINISHED BUSINESS.

The amendment of Mr. Bryan to Mr. Rich's amendment of Mr. Hood's per diem resolution offered Monday, was submitted to the House and lost.

The amendment of Mr. Rich was taken up by the House and adopted.

Mr. King, of Lenoir, called for the yeas and nays.

The call was sustained.

The resolution was adopted by the following vote, yeas 61, nays 55:

Those who voted in the affirmative are:

Messrs. Abbott, Andrews, Ashley, Baker, Barnes, Benbow, Blume, Carey, Carter, Candler, Cherry, Chillson, Colgrove, Congleton, Cox, Daniel, Dickey, Dowd, Duckworth, Eppes, Fisher, Franklin, French of Bladen, French of Rockingham, Fullings, Garland, Glover, Graham of Montgomery, Graham of Orange, Grant of Northampton, Gully, Hare, Hay, Hayes of Robeson, Highsmith, Hoffler, Holt, Ing, Laflin, Logan, Long, Mayo, Moore, Murphy, Nicholson, Parker, Parks, Ragland, Read, Renfrow, Rhodes, Rich, Rose, Stilly, Stilwell, Taylor, Tourgee, Trogden, Watts, Welker and Williamson—61.

Those who voted in the negative are.

Messrs Aydlott, Bradley, Bryan, Durham, Ellis, Etheridge, Forkner, French of Chowan, Gahagan, Galloway, Garrett, Gunter, Hall, Harris of Wake, Harris of Franklin, Heaton, Hobbs, Hodnett, Hollowell, Hood, Hyman, Jones of Caldwell, Jones of Washington, King of Lincoln, King of Lenoir, Kinney, Lee, Legg, Lennon, Mann, May, Marshall, McCubbins, Merritt, McDonald of Chatham, McDonald of Moore, Morton, Mullican, Nance, Newsom, Patrick, Petree, Peterson, Pierson, Pool, Ray, Robbins, Rodman, Sanderlin, Smith, Sweet, Teague, Tucker, Turner and Williams of Wake—55.

Mr. Rich moved to reconsider the vote.

Mr. Tourgee moved to lay the motion to reconsider on the table. Adopted.

Mr. Mann's resolution excluding visitors uninvited from the lobbies of the House was withdrawn.

Mr. Mann's resolution introduced Monday, inviting the United States Officers now on duty at this Post to the floor of the House, was submitted to the House and adopted.

The following resolution offered by Mr. Abbott on Tuesday, was adopted:

*Resolved*, That a Committee of three be appointed by the Chair to confer with Major General E. R. S. Canby, Commanding the second Military District, which Committee shall be empowered to consult upon any subject relating to the public interests and to report the result of their consultations to the Convention.

Mr. Tourgee's resolution to amend rule 3d chapter 2d, was, On motion of Mr. King, of Lenoir, laid on the table.

The President, in accordance with the resolution of Mr. Peterson, to appoint a Committee to wait on the Provisional Secretary of State, appointed Messrs. Peterson and Mann.

The President appointed the following Committees:

*On Privileges and Elections.*—Messrs. Abbott, McCubbins, Sweet, Forkner and Fullings.

*On Printing.*—Messrs. Ashley, Andrews, Tourgee, Marler and Duckworth.

*On Contingent Expenses.*—Messrs. King of Lenoir, Hood, Morton, Read and Trogden.

*On Engrossment and Enrollment.*—Messrs. C. C. Pool, Durham, Jones of Washington, French of Chowan and Harris of Wake.

Mr. Rodman's resolution offered Monday, relative to the appointment of a Reporter, was brought before the House.

Mr. Holt moved to lay them on the table, which was not agreed to.

Mr. Durham demanded the yeas and nays.

The motion was lost by the following vote, yeas 24, nays 83:

Those who voted in the affirmative are:

Messrs. Baker, Bradley, Daniel, Durham, Ellis, Etheridge, Graham of Orange, Gunter, Hall, Hare, Hobbs, Hodnett, Hollowell, Holt, Lennon, Mann, May, Marshall, McCubbins,

Merritt, McDonald of Chatham, McDonald of Moore, Peterson and Sanderlin—24.

Those who voted in the negative are:

Messrs. Abbott, Andrews, Ashley, Barnes, Benbow, Blume, Bryan, Carey, Carter, Candler, Cherry, Chillson, Colgrove, Congleton, Cox, Dickey, Duckworth, Eppes, Forkner, Franklin, French of Bladen, French of Rockingham, Fullings, Gahagan, Galloway, Garland, Garrett, George, Glover, Graham of Montgomery, Grant of Northampton, Gully, Harris of Wake, Hay, Hayes of Robeson, Hayes of Halifax, Highsmith, Hoffler, Hood, Hyman, Ing, Jones of Caldwell, Jones of Washington, King of Lenoir, Kinney, Laflin, Lee, Legg, Logan, Long, Mayo, Morton, Mullican, Murphy, Nance, Nicholson, Patrick, Parker, Parks, Petree, Pierson, Ragland, Ray, Read, Renfrow, Rhodes, Rich, Robbins, Rodman, Rose, Smith, Stilly, Stillwell, Taylor, Teague, Tourgee, Trogden, Tucker, Turner, Watts, Welker, Williams of Wake and Williamson.—83.

Mr. Durham moved to amend by striking out the second resolution, which was not sustained by the House.

The resolutions were then submitted to the House.

Mr. Durham demanded the yeas and nays.

The resolutions were adopted by the following vote, yeas 79 nays 25:

Those who voted in the affirmative are:

Messrs. Abbott, Andrews, Ashley, Barnes, Benbow, Blume, Bryan, Carey, Carter, Candler, Chillson, Colgrove, Congleton, Cox, Dickey, Duckworth, Eppes, Forkner, Franklin, French of Rockingham, Fullings, Gahagan, Galloway, Garland, Garrett, Glover, Graham of Montgomery, Grant of Northampton, Gully, Harris of Wake, Hay, Hayes of Robeson, Hayes of Halifax, Highsmith, Hoffler, Hyman, Ing, Jones of Caldwell, Jones of Washington, King of Lenoir, Kinney, Laflin, Lee, Legg, Logan, Long, May, Mayo, Morton, Mullican, Murphy, Nance, Patrick, Parker, Parks, Petree, Pierson, Ragland, Ray, Renfrow, Rhodes, Rich, Robbins, Rodman, Rose, Smith, Stilly, Stilwell, Taylor, Teague, Tourgee, Trogden, Tucker, Turner, Watts, Welker, Williams of Wake and Williamson—79.

Those who voted in the negative are:

Messrs. Baker, Bradley, Cherry, Daniel, Durham, Ellis, Etheridge, George, Graham of Orange, Gunter, Hall, Hare, Hobbs, Hodnett, Hollowell, Holt, Lennon, Mann, Marshall, McCubbins, Merritt, McDonald of Chatham, DcDonald of Moore, Moore and Sanderlin—25.

Mr. Durham offered the following preamble and resolution, which he desired placed on the calendar:

WHEREAS, It is a matter of first importance to the prosperity of States to preserve untarnished their public credit, and whereas, the disastrous effect of the late War, renders the present payment of the interest accrued on the public debt of this State impracticable; Therefore,

*Be it resolved*, That the public debt of this State shall be inviolate, and it shall, by a provision in the State Constitution, be made the duty of the Legislature after the year 1870, to provide funds for the payment of the interest accruing thereon, and for the extinguishment of the same as fast as it matures, and for the funding of the interest which has accrued or may accrue up to that time.

Lies over under the rules.

Mr. Abbott offered a resolution in relation to the granting of the Commons Hall to the Rev. Dr. Smith.

Lies over under the rules.

Mr. Tourgee offered a resolution in relation to eligibility of members.

Referred to the Committee on Privileges and Elections.

On motion of Mr. Galloway, the Convention adjourned.

---

## THURSDAY, JANUARY 23D, 1868.

The Convention was called to order at 11 o'clock, by the President.

Prayer by the Rev. J. W. Hood.

The President announced a quorum.

The Journal of Wednesday was read and approved.

Mr. Rich offered a Petition of Divorce from Dewitt C. Wilson and Nancy C. Wilson, of Richmond County.

Referred to the Commttee on Judicial Department.

The following communication from General E. R. S. Canby was read:

HEADQUARTERS SECOND MILITARY DISTRICT.
CHARLESTON, S. C., JANUARY 20TH, 1868.

CALVIN J. COWLES, ESQ.,
*Chairman of the Constitutional Convention of North-Carolina, Raleigh, N. C.:*

SIR:—I am instructed by the Commanding General to acknowledge the receipt of your letter of the 17th inst., reporting the organization of the Convention of North-Carolina.

Very respectfully,
Your obedient servant,
LOUIS V. CAZIARC,
*A. D. C. & A. A. G.*

Mr. McDonald, of Chatham, offered a resolution aksing Congress for the loan of money, for the benefit of certain Rail Roads.

Lies over under the rules.

Mr. Parker, of Northampton, introduced a resolution relative to the qualification of voters.

Referred to the Committee on Suffrage.

Mr. Tourgee introduced a resolution in relation to Political Rights.

Referred to the Committee on Suffrage and Eligibility to Office.

Mr. Duckworth presented a resolution in regard to a Poll Tax for Educational purposes.

Referred to the Committee on Education.

Mr. Mullican introduced a resolution respecting the Compensation of members of the State Legislature.

Referred to the Committee on Legislature.

Mr. Hayes, of Halifax, presented a resolution respecting the qualification of Governor and Lieutenant-Governor.

Referred to the Committee on Suffrage.

Mr. Renfrow offered a resolution relative to the rights of citizenship.

Referred to the Committee on Suffrage.

Mr. Ashley submitted a resolution instructing the Committee of sixteen to report a standing Committee on Industrial Resources.

Lies over under the rules.

Mr. Abbott presented a communication from J. W. Etheridge, of Roanoke Island, in regard to the election in Currituck County.

Referred to the Committee on Elections.

Mr. Hayes, of Halifax, offered a resolution in relation to Amendments to the Constitution.

Referred to the Committee on Legislature.

Mr. Ragland submitted an ordinance Regulating the Jurisdiction of the Courts of Law and Equity, and all persons who hold any judiciary position or office, relative to the payment of all debts, liabilities and contracts made by individuals of the State of North-Carolina, prior to the first day of May, 1865.

Referred to the Committee on Finance.

Mr. Mann introduced an ordinance to aid the Fayetteville and Florence Rail Road Company.

Referred to the Committee on Internal Inprovements.

Mr. Welker introduced an ordinance respecting the liabilities of Banks.

Made General Order and referred to the Committee of the Whole.

Mr. Teague introduced an ordinance respecting Registration Boards of the State.

Referred to the Committee on Suffrage.

Mr. Franklin, of Wake, introduced an ordinance for the Relief of the People.

Referred to the Committee on Homesteads.

UNFINISHED BUSINESS.

The following resolution introduced by Mr. Tourgee, was adopted.

*Resolved*, That the Committee appointed to confer with General Canby be instructed to enquire of him whether he would enforce an ordinance of this Convention, or upon its recommendation would issue an order staying the collection of all debts, except in cases of fraud, and wages for labor performed since May first, 1865.

Mr. Patrick's resolution asking the suspension of debts, was referred to the Committee on Relief.

Mr. McDonald's resolution instructing the Committee on Judicial Department, was taken up, and

Referred to the Committee on the Judiciary Department.

The resolution of Mr. King, of Lenoir, regarding the pay of members and officers of the Convention, was taken up, and declared by the Chair to be out of order.

Mr. King appealed from the decision of the Chair, and demanded the yeas and nays, which was not agreed to.

The House sustained the decision of the Chair.

The following resolution of Mr. Tourgee, was adopted:

*Resolved*, That the title of the Committee on Punishments and Penal Institutions be amended by striking out the word "and," and inserting the words, "and Public Charities," and all matters relating to public charities shall be referred to that Committee.

Mr. Durham's resolution declaring that the Public Debt of North-Carolina shall be held inviolate, was taken up, and

Referred to the Committee on Finance.

The following communication from Governor Worth, was received and read to the Convention, and

On motion of Mr. Tourgee, was placed upon the Records:

STATE OF NORTH-CAROLINA,
EXECUTIVE DEPARTMENT,
Raleigh, January 23d, 1868.

*Gentlemen of the Convention:*

I had the honor, on yesterday, to be informed through your Committee, that your body is duly organized, and ready to receive any communication that I may be willing to make.

I desire you to accept my thanks for this mark of your courtesy.

I regard your resolution simply as an official notification of your organization, with a view to such future official intercourse and communication as may be deemed necessary; as it seems to me that it would be improper, if not indecorous, that I present to you any view of mine touching the object for which you are assembled, unless in due response to a specific inquiry.

Upon due notice of your wish to be furnished with any information contained in the archives of the State under my control, such information will be promptly supplied.

May a superintending Providence inspire you with wisdom to conduct your labors to results beneficial to our unhappy and distracted people.

JONATHAN WORTH.

The following resolution of Mr. Abbott, was taken up and adopted:

*Resolved*, That the use of this Hall be granted to the Rev. Dr. Smith, of Raleigh, for the purpose of addressing the members of this Convention, on the subject of Normal Schools.

The resolution of Mr. Smith, respecting the reading of Bills in the Legislature, was taken up and

Referred to the Committee on Legislation.

Mr. Heaton was allowed to record his vote in the negative on the resolution of Mr. Hood, as amended by Mr. Rich, fixing the per per diem at eight dollars per day.

Mr. Pool presented a request from the Chairman of several Committees for a Clerk to act conjointly.

On motion of Mr. Heaton, the request was referred to the Committee on Contingent Expenses.

Mr. Rodman introduced an amendment to an ordinance respecting the jurisdiction of the Courts of this State, offered by himself.

Refered to a Committee of eight on Relief.

The President appointed the following Committee on Relief.

1st Judicial District, Pool.
2d " " Rodman.
3d " " Read.
4th " " McDonald, of Chatham.
5th " " French, of Bladen.
6th " " Forkner.
7th " " Bradley.
8th " " Duckworth.

In conformity with the resolution of Mr. Abbott, passed Wednesday, the following Committee was appointed to consult with General Canby on matters of public interest:

Messrs. Abbott, Ragland and Durham.

On motion of Mr. Smith, the House adjourned.

---

## FRIDAY, January 24th, 1868.

The Convention was called to order at 11 o'clock by the President.

Prayer by the Rev. Mr. Warrick.

The President announced a quorum.

The Journal of Thursday was read and approved.

The following communication from Major General Canby, was read, and

On motion of Mr. C. C. Jones, entered on the Journal.

HEADQUARTERS SECOND MILITARY DISTRICT,
CHARLESTON, S. C., JANUARY 20TH, 1868.

HON. CALVIN J. COWLES,
*President of the Constitutional Convention,*
*Raleigh, N. C:*

SIR:—I have the honor to acknowledge the receipt of your communication of the 17th inst., informing me of the permanent organization of the Constitutional Convention assembled in North-Carolina, under the authority of the laws of the United States.

In expressing my gratification, I desire to add my conviction that from the character of your body, the result of its labors will be such as to commend it to the favor of all who aspire to the speedy restoration of your State to its full relations in the Union. I desire, also, to give you the assurance of my hearty co-operation with the Convention, whenever that co-operation may be necessary or proper.

Very respectfully,
Your obedient servant,
EDWARD CANBY,
*Major General.*

The following report of the Committee of sixteen, of which David Heaton is Chairman, was received, and

On motion of Mr. Rodman, was adopted:

The Committee of sixteen, to whom was referred the resolution on Immigration and other matters, hereby report as follows:

*Resolved*, That the President of this Convention proceed to appoint the following additional Standing Committees:

1st. A Committee on Immigration and the resources and statistics of the State, said Committee to consist of five members.

2d. A Standing Committee of five members on Miscellaneous Affairs.

3d. A Standing Committee of three members on the revision and adjustment of the Articles of the Constitution.

All of which is respectfully submitted.

D. HEATON, *Chairman.*

The report of the Committee on a Governor and other necessary State Executive Officers, of which Mr. Nicholson was Chairman, was received, and

On motion of Mr. Heaton, was ordered to be printed.

The following report of the Committee on the Judicial Department was received.

The Committee on the Judicial Department, respectfully report:

That they have duly considered the matters set forth in the petition of C. D. Pearsall, and are of the opinion that this Convention should take no action therein, and request to be discharged from its further consideration.

On motion the report was adopted, and the Committee discharged from further consideration of this subject.

The following reports of the Committee on Contingent Expenses, were read, and

On motion of Mr. Rodman, were adopted.

## REPORT OF THE COMMITTEE ON CONTINGENT EXPENSES.

The undersigned Committee, to whom was referred the resolution of the delegate from Beaufort, in relation to contracting with some competent person to report the proceedings and debates of this Convention, beg leave to report.

That we have contracted with Joseph W. Holden, Esq., to report the proceedings and debates of this Convention, in a condensed form, as contemplated by said resolution, for the sum of six dollars per diem, to be published in some daily newspaper in this city, and it is further agreed, as a part of said contract, that if the Convention, before its adjournment, shall determine to publish such reports in book form, then the property thereof shall be in the State, but if the Convention, shall not so determine, then the property of such reports shall be in the Reporter, and he shall be at liberty to apply for a copy right.

All of which is respectfully submitted.

R. W. KING,
R. F. TROGDEN,
J. W. HOOD,
JNO. READ,
L. C. MORTON.
*Committee.*

## REPORT OF THE COMMITTEE ON CONTINGENT EXPENSES.

The undersigned Committee to whom was referred the petition in relation to the Chairman of various Committees requesting that they be allowed to employ a Clerk conjointly, beg leave to report that they have had the same under consideration, and have come to the conclusion that the duties can be performed by some member of each of said Committees, and therefore deem it inexpedient to grant said request.

All of which is respectfully submitted.

R. W. KING,
R. F. TROGDEN,
L. C. MORTON,
J. W. HOOD,
JNO. READ,
*Committee.*

The following report of the Committee appointed to wait on the Provisional Secretary of State was received:

The Committee appointed to wait on the Provisional Secretary of State, and request him to furnish this Convention with one hundred and twenty copies of the laws of the State passed by the General Assembly of 1866–'67, beg leave to report that they called upon the Secretary, who informed the

Committee that he had in his possession but sixteen copies, which he furnished.

Very respectfully,

W. A. MANN,
J. W. PETERSON,
*Committee.*

On motion of Mr. Heaton, the word Provisional was stricken out, and the report as amended, was adopted.

Mr. McDonald, of Chatham, introduced the following resolution:

*Resolved,* That the delegates of the Constitutional Convention of North-Carolina, now assembled, request Major General Edward R. S. Canby, Commanding Second Military District, composed of the States of North and South-Carolina, to visit this Convention and communicate anything he may deem for the good of the people of North-Carolina.

On motion of Mr. McDonald, the rules were suspended and the resolution adopted.

Mr. Turner offered a resolution in relation to the Senatorial Districts of North-Carolina, which was referred to the Committee on Counties, Towns, &c.

Mr. Parker introduced a resolution on Taxation.

Referred to the Committee on Finance.

Mr. Jones, of Washington, presented a resolution requesting information of the State Treasurer in regard to the Albemarle and Chesapeake Canal Company.

Lies over under the rules.

Mr. Jones, of Washington, also introduced a resolution requesting the State Treasurer to furnish information of the State's indebtedness, &c.

Lies over under the rules.

Mr. Peterson introduced a resolution in relation to Public Schools.

Referred to the Committee on Education.

Also, a resolution in relation to Commissioners of Public Schools.

Referred to the Committee on Education.

Also, a resolution in relation to Militia.

Referred to the Committee on Militia.

Mr. Rodman offered a resolution for establishing a Bureau of Immigration and Statistics.

Referred to the Committee on Legislature.

Mr. Hare introduced a resolution providing that the notes and accounts of deceased persons shall be paid *pro rata*.

Referred to the Committee on Judicial Department.

Mr. Watts offered an ordinance for Relief from Debt.

Referred to the Special Committee on Relief.

Mr. Robbins introduced a resolution in relation to the observance of the Sabbath.

Lies over under the rules.

Mr. Dickey introduced an ordinance authorizing the Western North-Carolina Rail Road Company to endorse its Capital Stock for other purposes.

Referred to the Committee on Internal Improvements.

UNFINISHED BUSINESS.

The resolution of Mr. McDonald, of Chatham, asking Congress for the loan of money, was taken up, and

On motion of Mr. Abbott, was referred to the Committee on Internal Improvements.

The following resolution of Mr. Ashley, was taken up and adopted.

*Resolved*, That the Committee of of sixteen be, and is hereby instructed to consider the expediency of constituting a Standing Committee on Industrial Resources, and report as soon as practicable.

The report of the Committee on Internal Improvements was presented, and

On motion was ordered to be printed.

Mr. Rodman introduced a resolution in relation to Printing.

Lies over under the rules.

Mr. Heaton introduced the following ordinance:

*Be it ordained by the people of North-Carolina, in Convention assembled*, That the Treasurer of the State of North-Carolina, upon the warrant of the President of this Convention is hereby authorized and directed to pay the per diem and mileage of members and officers of this Convention.

After considerable discussion, Mr. Sweet moved the previous question, which the House sustained.

Mr. Durham demanded the yeas and nays, which was agreed to.

The yeas and nays were called and the ordinance was adopted by the following vote, yeas 104, nays 12.

Those who voted in the affirmative are:

Messrs. Abbott, Andrews, Ashley, Aydlott, Barnes, Benbow, Blume, Bradley, Bryan, Carey, Carter, Candler, Cherry, Chillson, Colgrove, Congleton, Cox, Dickey, Duckworth, Ellis, Eppes, Fisher, Forkner, Franklin, French of Bladen, French of Rockingham, French of Chowan, Fullings, Gahagan, Galloway, Garland, Garrett, George, Glover, Graham of Montgomery, Grant of Waye, Grant of Northampton, Gully, Gunter, Harris of Wake, Hay, Hayes of Robeson, Hayes of Halifax, Heaton, Highsmith, Hobbs, Hodnett, Hoffler, Hollowell, Hood, Hyman, Ing, Jones of Caldwell, Jones of Washington, King of Lincoln, King of Lenoir, Kinney, Laflin, Lee, Legg, Logan, Long, Mann, May, Mayo, Marshall, McCubbins, McDonald of Chatham, McDonald of Moore, Moore, Morton, Mullican, Murphy, Nance, Newsom, Nicholson, Parker, Parks, Petree, Peterson, Pierson, Pool, Ragland, Ray, Read, Renfrow, Rhodes, Rich, Robbins, Rodman, Rose, Smith, Stilly, Stilwell, Sweet, Taylor, Teague, Trogden, Tucker, Turner, Watts, Welker, Williams of Wake and Williamson—104.

Those who voted in the negative are:

Messrs. Baker, Daniel, Dowd, Durham, Etheridge, Graham of Orange, Hall, Holt, Lennon, Merritt, Sanderlin and Tourgee—12.

On motion the House adjourned.

---

## SATURDAY January 25th, 1868.

The Convention was called to order at 11 o'clock, by the President.

Prayer by the Rev. Dr. Mason.

The President announced a quorum.

The Journal of Friday read and approved.

Mr. Ragland offered a petition from Martha A. Hopkins, of the County of Granville.

Referred to the Committee on Judicial Department.

Mr. Garrett offered a memorial praying the Convention to petition Congress for the relief of certain men banned by the Howard Amendment.

Referred to the Committee on Suffrage.

Mr. Harris, of Wake, presented a petition from the people of the neighborhood of Jacob Sorrells, in the County of Wake.

Referred to the Committee on Relief.

The Committee on Finance, to whom was referred an ordinance regulating the jurisdiction of the Courts of Law and Equity for the payment of all debts contracted prior to May 1st, 1865, reported as follows:

Returned to the House with the recommendation that the ordinance do not pass.

J. C. ABBOTT, *Chairman.*

On motion the report was adopted.

The report of the Committee on Militia was presented, and

On motion of Mr. Abbott was referred, together with the report of the Committee on Governor and other necessary State Executive Officers, to a Committee of the Whole, and made the Special Order for Monday at 12 o'clock, M.

Mr. Daniel presented a resolution indemnifying Mechanics and Artizans for their labor.

Lies over under the rules.

Mr. Gunter presented the following resolution:

*Resolved*, That the thanks of this Convention be tendered to the managers of the Deaf and Dumb Asylum for the courtesy extended to the members of this Convention.

On motion the rules were suspended and the resolution adopted.

Mr. Hayes, of Halifax, presented a resolution regarding the qualification for office.

Referred to the Committee on the Judicial Department.

Mr. Grant, of Wayne, presented a resolution respecting the relief of the people.

Referred to the Committee on Relief.

Mr. Kinney introduced a resolution with regard to persons banned by the Howard Amendment.

Referred to the Committee on Suffrage.

Mr. Heaton asked leave of absence until Wednesday, A. M., for Mr. Daniel, of Wilson. Granted.

Mr. Gully received leave of absence from the House until Monday next.

Mr. Mullican introduced the following resolution:

*Resolved*, That if any member of this Convention shall absent himself without leave of this Convention, that their per diem shall cease during their absence.

On motion of Mr. Dowd, the resolution was laid on the table.

Leave of absence was granted to Mr. Hay, of Johnson, also to Mr. Mann, of Cumberland, until Tuesday next.

Mr. Galloway presented a resolution instructing the Committee on the Judicial Department.

Referred to the Committee on the Judicial Department.

Mr. Peterson introduced a resolution in relation to County Officers.

Referred to a Committee on Counties, Towns, &c.

Mr. Watts introduced a resolution to relieve political disability.

Referred to the Committee on Suffrage.

Mr. Congleton introduced a resolution declaring all laws passed heretofore by any Legislature or Convention, null and void.

Referred to the Committee on Legislature.

Mr. George presented a resolution in favor of Edwin C. Bartlett.

Referred to the Committee on Contingent Expenses.

Mr. Renfrow introduced a resolution in relation to the sale of land.

Referred to the Committee on Relief.

Mr. Peterson introduced a resolution in relation to Justices of the Peace.

Referred to the Committee on Counties, Towns, &c.

On motion of Mr. Rodman, the Journal was amended by striking out "referred to the Committee on Elections and Privileges," after the resolution of Mr. Tourgee instructing the Committee on Elections.

At the request of the President, Mr. Rodman took the Chair.

The resolution of Mr. Tourgee was then taken up, and after some discussion, was,

On motion of Mr. Harris, of Wake, laid on the table.

The following communication from Post Headquarters was received and read, and,

On motion of Mr. King, of Lenoir, was entered on the Journal:

HEADQUARTERS MILITARY POST OF RALEIGH.
RALEIGH, N. C., JANUARY 24TH, 1868.

MR. T. A. BYRNES,
*Secretary of State Convention, Raleigh, N. C.:*

SIR:—The Colonel Commanding directs me to acknowledge the receipt of a resolution passed by the Constitutional Convention of the State, January 22d, inviting the officers of the United States on duty at this Post to the floor of the House of said Convention, and to thank the members of the Convention for the honorable compliment.

I am sir,
Very respectfully,
Your obedient servant,
DANIEL T. WELLS,
1*st Lt* 8*th Infantry, Brevet Major.*
*Post Adjutant.*

Mr. Gunter introduced an ordinance in relation to Suffrage.

Referred to the Committee on Suffrage.

Mr. Ragland introduced an ordinance in relation to Deeds and Conveyances.

Referred to the Committee on the Judicial Department.

UNFINISHED BUSINESS.

The report of the Committee on Internal Improvements presented yesterday, was laid over until Monday.

The following resolution of Mr. Jones, of Washington, was taken up, and

On motion was adopted:

*Resolved*, That the Treasurer of the State of North-Carolina be requested to furnish this Convention with a statement of what amount of stock said State owns in the Albemarle and Chesapeake Canal Company, what she has paid or agreed to pay, or is under any obligation in the future to pay, what is the entire amount of the capital stock of said Company, and where owned, and whether said State has received any dividend or interest for or on account of its investment, subscription or endorsement of said Company, or its bonds, and how much, or whether it is now paying its interest or dividends regularly to the State?

The following resolution of Mr. Jones, of Washington, was also taken up, and,

On motion, was adopted:

*Reeolved*, That the Treasurer of the State cf North-Carolina be requested to furnish this Convention with a statement of the indebtedness of said State, to what parties or sources, what amount to each? What is the amount of her endorsement for Rail Roads or other improvements, what further endorsement of Rail Road Bonds she is directed to make under any existing laws or regulations, and when passed, what property, or assets, or securities the State holds for or on account of said indebtedness, what amount of stock the State holds in the several Corporations of this State, and what amount of dividend or interest she receives from each source?

The resolution of Mr. Robbins respecting the observance of the Sabbath, was,

On motion of Mr. King, of Lenoir, laid on the table.

The following resolution introduced by Mr. Rodman was taken up, and,

On motion, adopted:

*Resolved*, That the Chairman of the Committee on Printing have power, on the request of the Chairman of any Committee to cause to be printed for the use of this Convention, any matter prepared by a Committee and necessary for the information of the delegates.

The ordinance of Mr. Welker providing for the admission of members at the bar from other States to practice in the Courts of North-Carolina was taken up and referred to the Committee on the Judicial Department.

The ordinance of Mr. Welker regarding the liabilities of Banks was taken up, and referred to the Committee on Finance.

On motion the House adjourned.

---

MONDAY, JANUARY 27TH, 1868.

The Convention was called to order at 11 o'clock, by the President.

Prayer by the Rev. Dr. Smith.

The Chair announced a quorum.

The Journal of Saturday was read and approved.

Mr. Laflin asked and obtained leave of absence for Mr. Legg until Thursday next.

Mr. King, of Lenoir, presented a petition from the citizens of Lincoln, asking the removal of rebel State officers.

Referred to the Committee on the Judicial Department.

Mr. Hood presented a memorial from the citizens of Sampson County, respecting the late election in that County.

Referred to the Committee on Elections.

Mr. Hood presented a resolution relative to the appointment of a Committee to gather such information as would enable them to report the names of persons to be presented to Congress for relief from disability.

Lies over under the rules.

Mr. Legg introduced a resolution in reference to Schools and School Funds.

Referred to the Committee on Education.

Mr. Legg also introduced a resolution in relation to the taxation of real and personal property.

Referred to the Committee on Finance.

Mr. Andrews introduced a resolution in regard to the rights of the community.

Referred to the Committee on Bill of Rights.

Mr. Glover introduced an ordinance to revive debts.

Lies over under the rules.

Mr. Duckworth introduced an ordinance in regard to admission to the bar.

Lies over under the rules.

Mr. French, of Bladen, offered a resolution in relation to taxes.

Lies over under the rules.

Mr. Candler presented an ordinance repealing the granting of a general amnesty and pardon to soldiers, &c., ratified by the General Assembly, Dec. 22d, 1866.

Lies over under the rules.

Mr. Jones, of Caldwell, offered a resolution in regard to increasing the indebtedness of the State.

Lies over under the rules.

Mr. Welker introduced an ordinance on the distillation of grain.

Lies over under the rules.

Mr. Rodman presented a resolution respecting Contingent Expenses.

Lies over under the rules.

Mr. Tourgee introduced a resolution in regard to Banks of Issue.

Referred to the Committee on Corporations other than Municipal.

Mr. King, of Lenoir, offered a resolution amending rule 36.

Lies over under the rules.

Mr. Mullican introduced an ordinance declaring that contracts shall be held sacred and inviolate.

Lies over under the rules.

Mr. Laflin introduced a resolution on relief.

Referred to the Committee on Relief.

Mr. Pierson introduced a resolution requesting the consideration of some just and practicable plan for the admission of all races to the benefits of the Deaf and Dumb Asylum.

Referred to the Committee on Penal Institutions.

Mr. Cherry introduced a resolution on Suffrage.

Referred to the Committee on Suffrage.

UNFINISHED BUSINESS.

The report of the Committee on Internal Improvements, was laid over until Tuesday at the request of Mr. Abbott, the Chairman.

The following resolution of Mr. Daniel, of Wilson, was taken up and put upon its passage:

*Resolved*, That the Standing Committee on the Judiciary are hereby requested to report such a provision to the new Constitution as will clearly authorize the first Legislature convening under it to pass suitable laws giving Mechanics and Artizans an ample lean as indemnity for their labor.

Mr. Heaton moved to amend by inserting after the word requested the words, "if deemed advisable."

The resolution as amended, was, on motion, adopted.

At 12 o'clock the Convention resolved itself into a Committee of the Whole.

Mr. Jones, of Washington, in the Chair.

The following report of the Committee on a Governor and other necessary State Executive Officers was read:

## REPORT OF THE COMMITTEE ON A GOVERNOR AND OTHER NECESSARY STATE EXECUTIVE OFFICERS.

The Committee to whom was confided that portion of the proposed Constitution which relates to the officers of the Executive Department of the State, beg leave to submit the following Article, as within, in eighteen sections:

W. NICHOLSON, *Chairman*.

SECTION 1. The Executive Department shall consist of a Governor, in whom shall be vested the supreme Executive power of the State, a Lieutenant-Governor, a Secretary of State, an Auditor, a Treasurer, a Superintendent of Public Works, a Superintendent of Public Instruction, and an Attorney-General, who shall be elected for the term of two years, by the qualified electors of the State, at the same times and places, and in the same manner, as members of the General Assembly are elected. Their term of office shall commence on the first day of January next after their election, and continue until their successors are elected and qualified.

SEC. 2. No person shall be eligible as Governor, or as Lieutenant-Governor, unless he shall have been a citizen of the United States for twenty years, shall have attained the age of thirty years, and shall have been a resident of this State for two years next before the day of election ; nor shall the person elected to either of these two offices be eligible to the same office more than four years in any term of six years, unless the office shall have been cast upon him as Lieutenant-Governor or President of the Senate.

SEC. 3. The returns of every election for officers of the Executive Department shall be sealed up and transmitted to the seat of government by the returning officers, directed to the Speaker of the House of Commons, who shall open and publish the same in the presence of a majority of the members of both Houses of the General Assembly. The persons having the highest number of votes respectively shall be declared duly elected; but if two or more be equal and highest in votes for the same office, then one of them shall be chosen by joint ballot of both Houses of the General Assembly. Contested elections shall be determined by a joint vote of both Houses of the General Assembly, in such manner as shall be prescribed by law.

SEC. 4. The Governor before entering upon the duties of his office, shall, in the presence of the members of both branches of the General Assembly, or before any Justice of the Supreme Court, take an oath or an affirmation that to the best of his knowledge and belief, he is eligible under the Constitution and laws of this State, to the office to which he has been elected; that he will faithfully execute the duties appertaining to the office of Governor of the State of North-Carolina; and that he will, to the best of his ability, preserve, protect and defend, the Constitution, of this State and the Constitution of the United States.

SEC. 5. The Governor shall reside at the seat of Government of this State, and he shall, from time to time, give the General Assembly information of the affairs of the State and and recommend to their consideration such measures as he shall deem expedient.

SEC. 6. The Governor shall have power to grant reprieves, commutations, and pardons, after conviction, for all offences, (except treason and cases of impeachment,) upon such conditions and with such restrictions and limitations as he may think proper, subject to such regulations as may be provided by law relative to the manner of applying for pardons. In every case of conviction for treason, he shall have power to suspend the execution of the sentence, until the case shall be reported to the General Assembly at its next meeting, when the General Assembly shall pardon the convict, commute the sentence, direct the execution thereof, or grant a further reprieve. He shall biennally communicate to the General Assembly each case of reprieve, commutation, or pardon granted, stating the name of the convict, the crime for which he was convicted, the sentence and its date, and the date of commutation, pardon or reprieve, and the reasons therefor.

SEC. 7. The officers of the Executive Department and of the public Institutions of the State shall at least five days previous to each reguler session of the General Assembly, severally report to the Governor, who shall transmit such reports, with his message, to the General Assembly; and the Governor may, at any time, require information in writing from the officers in the Executive Department, upon any subject relating to the duties of their respective offices, and shall take care that the laws be faithfully executed.

SEC. 8. The Governor shall be Commander-in-Chief of the

Militia of the State, except when they shall be called into the service of the United States.

Sec. 9. The Governor shall have power, on extraordinary occasions, by and with the advice of the Council of State, to convene the General Assembly in extra session by his proclamation, stating therein the purpose or purposes for which they are thus convened.

Sec. 10. The Governor shall nominate, and, by and with the advice and consent of a majority of the Senators elect, appoint all officers whose offices are established by this Constitution, or which may be created by law and whose appointments are not otherwise provided for, and no such officer shall be appointed or elected by the General Assembly.

Sec. 11. The Lieutenant-Governor shall, by virtue of his office, be President of the Senate, but shall have no vote unless the Senate be equally divided. He shall, whilst acting as President of the Senate, receive for his services the same pay which shall, for the same period, be allowed to the Speaker of the House of Commons, and he shall receive no other compensation except when he is acting as Governor.

Sec. 12. In case of the impeachment of the Governor, his failure to qualify, his absence from the State, his inability to discharge the duties of his office, or in case the office of Governor shall in anywise become vacant, the powers, duties and emoluments of the office shall devolve upon the Lieutenant-Governor until the disabilities shall cease or a new Governor shall be elected and qualified. In every case in which the Lieutenant-Governor shall be unable to preside over the Senate, the Senators shall elect one of their own number President of their body; and the powers, duties and emoluments of the office of Governor shall devolve upon him whenever the Lieutenant Governor shall, for any reason, be prevented from discharging the duties of such office as above provided, and he shall continue as acting Governor until the disabilities be removed or a new Governor or Lieutenant-Governor shall be elected and qualified. Whenever, during a recess of the General Assembly, it shall become necessary for a President of the Senate to administer the government, the Secretary of

State shall convene the Senate, that they may elect such President.

SEC. 13. The respective duties of the Secretary of State, Auditor, Treasurer, Superintendent of Public Works, Superintendent of Public Instruction, and Attorney General, shall be prescribed by law. If the office of any of said officers shall be vacated by death, resignation, or otherwise, it shall be the duty of the Governor to appoint another until the disability be removed, or his successor be elected and qualified. Every such vacancy shall be filled by elction at the first general election that occurs more than thirty days after the vacancy has taken place, and the person chosen shall hold the office for the remainder of the unexpired term fixed in the first section of this article.

SEC. 14. The Secretary of State, Auditor, Treasurer, Superintendent of Public Works and Superintendent of Public Instruction, shall constitute, *ex officio*, the Council of State, who shall advise the Governor in the execution of his office and three of whom shall constitute a quorum; their advice and proceedings, in this capacity, shall be entered in a journal to be kept for this purpose exclusively, and signed by the members present, against any part of which any member may enter his dissent; and such journal shall be placed before the General Assembly when called for by either house. The Attorney General shall be, *ex officio*, the legal adviser of the Executive Department.

SEC. 15. The officers mentioned in this article shall, at stated periods, receive for their services a compensation to be established by law, which shall neither be increased nor diminished during the time for which they shall have been elected; and the said officers shall receive no other emolument or allowance whatever.

SEC. 16. There shall be a seal of the State, which shall be kept by the Governor, and used by him as occasion may require, and shall be called "the Great Seal of the State of North-Carolina." All grants and commissions shall be issued in the name and by the authority of the State of North-Carolina, sealed with "the Great Seal of the State," signed by the Governor and countersigned by the Secretary of State.

SEC. 17. All fees that may hereafter be made payable by law for any services performed by any officer provided for in this Article of the Constitution, shall be paid in advance directly into the Treasury of the State.

SEC. 18. There may be established in the office of Secretary of State a Bureau of Statistics and of Agriculture, under such regulations as the General Assembly may provide.

On motion of Mr. Abbott, it was agreed that the report be adopted by sections.

After considerable discussion on the first section, the Committee arose and reported progress, and asked leave to sit again, which was granted.

A communication was received from Mr. Battle, State Treasurer, and read to the House.

The following motion of Mr. Heaton was adopted:

That the report of the Treasurer of the State be referred to the Committee of three consisting of Messrs. Abbott, Ragland and Durham, to consult with General Canby on matters of public interest, with directions that the said Committee forward the same to General Canby, and request him to order the Treasurer to comply with the ordinance.

On motion the House adjourned.

---

## TUESDAY, JANUARY 28TH, 1868.

The Convention was called to order at 11 o'clock by the President.

Prayer by the Rev. Dr. Ellis.

The President announced a quorum.

The Journal of Monday was read and approved.

The report of the Committee on Relief was received, and,

On motion of Mr. Tourgee, was ordered to be printed and made the Special Order for Wednesday at 12 o'clock.

Mr. Rich offered a resolution amending the Rules of Order. Lies over under the rules.

Mr. Gunter introduced a resolution instructing the Committee on Relief to report an ordinance declaring void certain contracts, &c.

Lies over under the rules.

Mr. Laflin presented a resolution retiring present outstanding State Bonds and issuing new ones in their places.

Lies over under the rules.

Mr. Parker introduced a resolution in relation to the session and adjournment of the Convention.

Lies over under the rules.

Mr. Read introduced a resolution in regard to the hour of meeting of the Convention.

Lies over under the rules.

Mr. Hyman introduced a resolution instructing certain committees as to the revision or framing of the Constitution.

Referred to the Committee on Suffrage.

Mr. Eppes introduced a resolution in relation to the taxation of Cattle, &c.

Referred to the Committee on Towns, Counties, &c.

Mr. May submitted a resolution to proceed immediately with the framing of the Constitution and dispensing with other business.

Referred to the Committee of sixteen.

Mr. Baker offered a resolution in relation to Test Oaths.

Referred to the Committee on Suffrage and Eligibility to Office.

Mr. Ellis introduced a resolution in relation to the Reconstruction Acts.

Lies over under the rules.

Mr. Harris, of Wake, submitted a resolution in relation to Congressional Districts.

Lies over under the rules.

Mr. Hayes, of Robeson, introduced an ordinance to encourage the establishment of Manufactories.

Referred to the Committee on Finance.

UNFINISHED BUSINESS.

The resolution of Mr. Hood regarding the removal of disabilities, was taken up and discussed.

The hour of 12 having arrived, the House,

On motion of Mr. Abbott, resolved itself into a Committee of the Whole.

Mr. Jones, of Washington, was called to the Chair.

At 3 o'clock the Committee arose, and Mr. Jones, of Washington, Chairman, reported progress, also that section first of the report of the Committee on a Governor and other necessary State Executive Officers, had been adopted, by adding after the word qualified in the eleventh line the following words:

"*Provided*, That the officers first elected, shall assume the duties of their office thirty days after the ratification of this Constitution by the Congress of the United States, and shall hold their offices for two years from and after the first day of January, 1869."

Also, that the following had been submitted for section 2d.

"Sec. 2. No person shall be eligible as Governor or Lieutenant-Governor unless he shall have attained the age of thirty years, and shall have been a resident of the United States for twenty years, and of the State of North-Carolina for two years, next before the day of this election; nor shall the person elected to either of these two offices be eligible to the same office more than four years in any term of six years, unless the office shall have been cast upon him as Lieutenant-Governor, or President of the Senate."

The Committee asked leave to sit again, which was granted.

On motion the House adjourned.

---

## WEDNESDAY, January 29th, 1868.

The Convention was called to order at 11 o'clock, by the President.

Prayer by the Rev. Mr. Ashley.

The President announced a quorum.

The Journal of Tuesday was read and approved.

The following communication from the State Treasurer was read to the Convention:

STATE OF NORTH-CAROLINA,
TREASURY DEPARTMENT,
RALEIGH, January 27th, 1868.

HON. C. J. COWLES,
*President of Constitutional Convention of North-Carolina:*

SIR:—I have the honor to acknowledge the reception of the following resolution of your honorable body, viz:

"*Resolved*, That the Treasurer of the State of North-Carolina, be requested to furnish this Convention with a statement of what amount of stock said State owns in the Albemarle and Chesapeake Canal Company; what she has paid or agreed to pay, or is under any obligation in the future to pay; what is the entire amount of the Capital Stock of said Company and where owned; and whether said State has received any dividend or interest for, or on account of its investment, subscription or endorsement of said Company or its Bonds, and how much, or whether it is now paying its interest, or dividends regularly, to the State."

I take pleasure in answering as far as my information extends the qustions therein, *seriatum:*

1st. The stock of the State in the Albemarle and Chesapeake Canal Company is $350,000.

To pay for said stock the State issued $350,000, six per cent coupon bonds, running thirty years from April 1st, 1857, and April 1st, 1859, coupons and interest payable in New York. Of these $26,000 have been paid in to the State for Raleigh and Gaston Rail Road Company stock, leaving outstanding $324,000.

3rd. By Act of 1860–'61, chap. 121, ratified February 6th, 1861, the State agrees to exchange with said Company $200,-00 , State six per cent bonds, for the amount of seven per cent first mortgage bonds of the Company. This exchange has not been applied for by the Company. Indeed, I do not know that this amendment to the charter of the Company has ever been accepted.

4th. I learn from a late report made to the Stockholders of the Company that on September 30th, 1866, the authorized capital was $1,500.000, of which the following has been paid up, viz :

| | |
|---|---|
| By State of North Carolina, | $350,000 |
| Currituck County, | 44,000 |
| Individuals, | 494,100 |
| | 888,100 |

I have no other information than rumor as to the residences of individuals owning stock.

5th. This Company has never paid anything to the State for interest or dividend. I think there is no prospect of any such payment in any reasonable time. All the property of the company is mortgaged for $400,000 bonds issued by the company.

Very respectfully,

KEMP P. BATTLE,
*Public Treasurer.*

Mr. Jones, of Washington, moved to refer the communication to the Committee on Finance, with instruction to report what steps to take in reference to the Corporation.

Mr. Watts presented a communication from the County of Sampson.

Referred to the Committee on Elections.

Mr. Abbott read a communication from the President of the Wilmington, Charlotte and Rutherford Rail Road Company.

Mr. Harris, of Wake, presented a communication from Sampson County, contesting the seat of a delegate.

Referred to the Committee on Elections with instructions to report at an early day.

The Committee on Homesteads, presented a majority and a minority report, which was ordered to be printed.

Mr. Harris, of Wake, introduced a resolution requiring immediate action on the Constitution, and a bill for the relief of the people.

Lies over under the rules.

Mr. Mann introduced an ordinance to change the manner of payment of the State's subscription to the capital stock of the Western Rail Road Company.

Referred to the Committee on Internal Improvements.

Mr. King presented a resolution respecting the action of this Convention.

Lies over under the rules.

Mr. Congleton introduced a resolution in reference to immediate action on the Constitntion, and a bill of Relief.

Lies over under the rules.

Mr. Rich introduced a resolution in regard to sheriffs.

Lies over under the rules.

The hour of twelve o'clock having arrived, the following report of the Select Committee on Relief, being made a special order, was taken up.

## REPORT OF SELECT COMMITTEE ON RELIEF.

*To the Constitutional Convention of North-Carolina:*

The undersigned, a majority of the Select Committee on Relief, respectfully report the following Ordinance and Resotion and recommend their passage:

## AN ORDINANCE RESPECTING THE JURISDICTION OF THE COURTS OF THIS STATE.

SECTION 1. *Be it ordained by the people of North-Carolina in Convention assembled,* That no Court of law or equity of this State shall have jurisdiction of any suit or action founded on any contract made prior to the first day of May, 1865, (except actions against public officers, executors, administrators, guardians, trustees, and others acting in a fiduciary capacity, and their surities for breach of their respective duties, by the appropriation to their own use of money or property officially received by them or other fraudulent act,) or of any action or process to revive or enforce any judgment heretofore recovered on any such contract, whether such action be now pending, or shall be commenced hereafter, and whether such process has been already issued or shall be hereafter sued for; and the sheriffs, coroners and constables of this State, having in their hands any final process issued upon any judgment founded on such cause of action, are hereby commanded to stay all proceeding upon the same, and return the same to the proper courts.

SEC. 2. This Ordinance shall be in force from and after its ratification by this Convention, and shall continue in force until the first day of July, 1868, or until the Constitution, which this Convention has met to adopt, shall go into effect, whichever shall first happen.

*Resolved*, That a copy of the forgoing Ordinance be sent to Major-General Canby, Commanding, &c., and that he be respectfully requested to cause the same to be enforced.

Mr. McDonald, one of the Committee, agrees in recommending the foregoing, with the exception of the exception in the first section, which he thinks should be stricken out.

WILL. B. RODMAN, *Chairman.*
JOHN A. McDONALD,
JOHN READ,
G. W. BRADLEY,
J. H. DUCKWORTH.

Mr. Watts offered the following amendment:

Strike out in section 1st, all included in exceptions and insert after the word "except," "contracts or engagements entered into for the purchase of real estate where one half of the purchase money has not been paid."

The Committee on Preamble and Bill of Rights reported through their Chairman, Mr. Heaton.

The report was ordered to be printed.

The house granted leave of absence to Mr. King, of Lenoir.

Mr. French, of Chowan, presented the following resolution:

*Resolved*, That the Committee on Finance, either in the

name of the whole Committee or in the name of a sub committee, be authorized to negotiate a loan not to exceed ten thousand dollars (10,000) in order to pay the mileage of members.

On motion the rules were suspended and the resolution adopted.

On motion the house adjourned.

---

THURSDAY, January 30th, 1868.

The Convention was called to order at 11 o'clock, by the President.

Prayer by the Rev. Mr. Lennon.

A quorum was announced by the President.

The Journal of Wednesday was read and approved.

A communication from Dr. Fisher was read, inviting the delegates of the Convention to visit the Insane Asylum.

Mr. Galloway introduced a resolution pertaining to the City of Wilmington.

Referred to the Committee on Counties, Towns, &c.

Mr. Ashley introduced a resolution instructing the Committee on Corporations other than Municipal.

Referred to the Committee on Corporations.

Mr. Ashley also introduced a resolution instructing the Committee on the Legislature.

Referred to the Committee on Legislature.

Mr. Harris, of Wake, presented an ordinance providing means of relief.

Lies over under the rules.

Mr. Gunter introduced a resolution to change the hour of daily meeting of the Convention.

Lies over under the rules.

Mr. McDonald, of Chatham, introduced an ordinance levying a tax of seventy-five per cent on old debts.

On motion, was ordered to be printed.

Mr. Teague presented a resolution instructing the Committee of three to enquire of General Canby how far he will recognize legislation by this Convention.

Lies over under the rules.

The Committee on Privileges and Elections submitted their report, through Mr. Abbott.

On request it was laid over.

The Committee on relief presented a report, and,

On motion, was ordered to be printed.

The majority and minority reports of the Committee on Suffrage was presented, and,

On motion, was ordered to be printed, and made Special Order for Thursday next, at 12 o'clock, M.

The following communication was received from the State Treasurer, which was ordered to be printed, six copies to each member:

STATE OF NORTH-CAROLINA,
TREASURY DEPARTMENT,
RALEIGH, January 29th, 1868.

HON. CALVIN J. COWLES,
*President of Constitutional Convention of North-Carolina:*

SIR:—I have the honor in response to the resolution of your honorable body, requesting me to furnish the Convention a "statement of the indebtedness of the State, to what parties or sources, what amount to each, what is the amount of her endorsement for Rail Road or other improvements, what further endorsement of Rail Road Bonds she is directed to make under any existing law or regulation and when passed, what property or assets, or securities said State holds for, or on account of said indebtedness—what amount of stock the State holds in the several corporations of this State, and what amount of dividend or interest she receives annually from each source?"

I enclose a tabular statement giving in detail,

1st. A list of the bonds and certificates of indebtedness of the State, outstanding on the first day of October, 1867, aggregating principal and interest $13,970,000, and adding internal improvement bonds issued during the war, $15,238,000, showing under what acts the debts were incurred and for what purpose, where and when the different classes of debt and interest thereon are payable, when the principal will become due and what rate of interest is payable. Since October first, 1867, the alteration in the status of the debt has been inconconsiderable.

2d. A list showing the stocks and other securities owned by the State.

I have also given a list of bonds issued for internal improvement purposes during the war. Of these, all except those for the benefit of the Chatham Rail Road Company, were issued under acts passed before the war.

The interest due and unpaid, estimated is only approximate, as during the war, coupons of old and new bonds were paid at the Treasury without a separate account of each being kept, but the estimate is substantially correct.

Owing to the fact, that $682,500, bonds of the State, were surrendered in exchange for State stock in the Raleigh and Gaston Rail Road Company, and $304,600, bonds belonging to Literary Board were likewise surrendered in exchange for registered certificates, the amounts in the tables do not exactly represent the amounts originally issued.

As nearly all of the debt of the State is evidenced by coupon bonds payable to bearer and negotiable by delivery, I regret that it is impossible for me to state the names of the owners of said bonds.

The State is not responsible as endorser of any bonds, strictly speaking. As stated in the table $74,500 bonds issued by the Cape Fear and Deep River Navigation Company were originally company bonds endorsed by the State, but the same have since been assumed by the State, and stand on the same footing as regular State Bonds.

The large amount of stock in the Western Rail Road Company results from the transfer to that Company of $1,000,000, second mortgage bonds of the Wilmington, Charlotte and

Rutherford Rail Road Company, in exchange for that amount of stock in the former company, under the act of February 26th, 1867, entitled "An act to enable Western Rail Road Company to extend its road across the North-Carolina Rail Road to the Virginia line near Mt. Airy in the County of Surry."

By Act of December 20th, 1866, entitled "An Act to enable the Western Rail Road Company to complete its road from the Coal Fields in Chatham County to some point on the North-Carolina Rail Road," the State relinquished to said Western Rail Road Company the bonds and mortgage, held on said Company, amounting to $600,000, in exchange for the same amount of stock of that Company. It is claimed that this act likewise extinguishes the liability of the Company to the State by reason of the coupons amounting to $225,000 on said $600,000 of bonds, prior to the exchange authorized, but I have not yielded to this claim.

The interest due by the Wilmington, Charlotte and Rutherford Rail Road Company on the first of October, 1867, amounted to $187,500, that Company having regularly paid the interest due the State for many years.

This claim for interest as well as for the $1,000,000, bonds of this Company, transferred to the Western Rail Road Company, is secured by the second mortgage on the property of the Company, by act of December 20th, 1866, entitled "An act to enable the Wilmington, Charlotte and Rutherford Rail Road Company, to complete its Road, pay its debt to the State, and extend its road to the Tennessee line," the Company being authorized to issue first, mortgage bonds to the amount of $4,000,000.

The contingent liabilities of the State for Rail Roads are so far as I can learn as follows:

1ST, THE WESTERN NORTH-CAROLINA RAIL ROAD COMPANY.

The charter of the Western North-Carolina Rail Road Company, granted at the session of 1854 and 1855, has been amended at various times. The last amendments are, the "Act to enhance the value of the bonds to be issued for the completion of the Western North-Carolina Rail Road and for other purposes," ratified December 19th, 1866, and the "Act to authorize the President and Directors of the Western North-Carolina Rail Road Company to put said road under contract, ratified February 27th, 1867." By these Acts whenever the estimated cost of any portions or sections, such portions or sections to embrace at least $50,000 worth of work at the estimated cost has been subscribed by solvent individuals, &c., the Treasurer of the State is authorized and directed to issue bonds of the State for the remaining two-thirds, as provided in the former of the above mentioned acts. Upon the certificate of the President of said road to the Board of Internal Improvements, that the stock has been subscribed as above required, by the preamble of said act of December, 19th, 1856, it is recited that the faith of the State is pledged for $4,000,000, in bonds of the State. Of these $2,268,000, have been issued, leaving a contingent liability of $1,732,000.

2. By Act of 1860 and 61, chap. 121, ratified February 26th, 1861, the State agreed to give $200,000, State six per cent bonds, in exchange for a like amount of seven per cent first mortgage bonds of the Albemarle and Chesapeake Canal Company. This exchange has not been called for by the Company.

3. By section 1 of an Act to enable the Western Rail Road Company to extend their road from the Coal Fields to the North-Carolina Rail Road, ratified February 16th, 1866, $10,000 for every ten miles graded and ready for superstructure, are granted, on condition that the iron, rails, chains and spikes shall have been purchased, and moreover that the rails shall be the product and manufacture of North-Carolina. This appropriation is not to exceed $500,000, and is for the Western Division of the road, that is for the Division between Deep River and the North-Carolina Rail Road, and the loan by the State is to be secured by lien on the said Western Division.

By an ordinance of the Convention of 1861, entitled "An ordinance to enable the Western Rail Road Company to complete their road," ratified 10th May, 1862, the above restrictions in regard to rails, chains, and spikes are repealed, and the lien is to extend over both divisions of the road and all other property of the Company.

By an ordinance of the Convention of 1865, entitled "An ordinance declaring what laws and ordinances are in force and for other purposes," ratified 18th October, 1865, all laws and ordinances passed since May 20th, 1861, compatible with the allegiance of the citizens of this State to the Government of the United States, and not since repealed or modified, and which are consistent with the Constitutions of the State and the United States, are declared to be in full force.

Of course I no not pretend to say whether the aforesaid ordinance of May 10th, 1862, is in force or not by virtue of the ordinance of October 18th, 1865. I can only say that it has not been "repealed or modified."

THE CHATHAM RAIL ROAD COMPANY.

4. On the 5th day of February, 1863, an act was passed to amend the charter of the Chatham Rail Road Company, by which the State was to subscribe to the stock of said Company $10,000 for each mile graded, not to exceed $250,000. No part of this subscription has been called for or paid.

The question whether the Act has been ratified by the above recited ordinance of October 18th, 1865, has not yet been acted on.

I am not aware that the State is under any further contingent liability to Rail Road or other corporations. The obligation to advance money to the Wilmington, Charlotte and Rutherford Rail Road Company has been repealed by the aforesaid act of 1866 and 67, chap. 108, entitled "An act to enable the Wilmington, Charlotte and Rutherford Rail Road Company to complete its road, pay its debt to the State and extend its road to the Tennessee line."

The State has not since the close of the war received any interest or dividends from stocks or bonds owned by her, nor have I been notified that any such payment is shortly contemplated.

The following stocks in corporations are owned by the Literary Fund:

| | |
|---|---|
| Bank of North-Carolina, | $502,700 |
| Bank of Cape Fear, | 544,400 |
| Wilmington and Weldon Rail Road Company, | 400,000 |
| Wilmington and Manchester Rail Road " | 200,000 |
| Cape Fear Navigation Company, | 32,500 |
| Total, | $1,679,600 |

None of these corporations have paid any dividends since the war.

I have the honor to be,

Very respectfully,

KEMP P. BATTLE,

*Public Treasurer.*

Mr. Rich called for a suspension of the rules, to call up his resolution offered Wednesday, which was agreed to.

Whereupon the following resolution was brought before the House and adopted:

*Resolved*, That the Sheriffs of the several counties of this State be directed to inform this Convention, at the earliest practicable moment, of the number of executions now in their hands, and the total amount of money therein ordered to be collected.

### UNFINISHED BUSINESS.

The following preamble and resolution of Mr. Hood, was taken up and put upon its passage:

WHEREAS, The 14th Article of the Constitution of the United States, which disfranchises a certain class of citizens for participation in the late rebellion, also provides that Congress may, by a two-thirds vote of each House remove such disability, and whereas, there are many whose sentiments are in hearty accord with the Reconstruction measures, who are injuriously effected by said disfranchisement; Therefore

*Resolved*, That a Committee of five be appointed by the Chair, whose duty it shall be to gather such information as will enable them at an early day, to report to this Convention a list of such persons as may be presented to Congress to be relieved.

On motion of Mr. Pool amended so as to read, the Committee to consist of eight, one from each Judicial District.

The yeas and nays were demanded.

The resolution as amended, was adopted by the following vote, yeas 90, nays 16:

Those who voted in the affirmative are:

Messrs. Abbott, Andrews, Ashley, Aydlott, Barnes, Benbow, Blume, Bradley, Bryan, Carter, Candler, Chillson, Colgrove, Congleton, Cox, Daniel, Dickey, Duckworth, Fisher, Forkner, Franklin, French of Bladen, French of Rockingham, French of Chowan, Fullings, Gahagan, Galloway, Garland, Garrett, George, Glover, Graham of Montgomery, Grant of

Waye, Gully, Gunter, Harris of Wake, Harris of Franklin, Hay, Hayes of Robeson, Hayes of Halifax, Heaton, Highsmith, Hobbs, Hood, Hyman, Ing, Jones of Caldwell, Jones of Washington, King of Lenoir, Kinney, Laflin, Lee, Logan, Mann, May, Mayo, McDonald of Chatham, McDonald of Moore, Moore, Morton, Mullican, Murphy, Nance, Newsom, Patrick, Parks, Petree, Peterson, Pierson, Pool, Ragland, Ray, Renfrow, Rhodes, Rich, Robbins, Rodman, Rose, Smith, Stilly, Sweet, Taylor, Teague, Trogden, Tucker, Turner, Watts, Welker, Williams of Wake and Williamson—96.

Those who voted in the negative are:

Messrs. Durham, Ellis, Etheridge, Graham of Orange, Grant of Northampton, Hall, Hare, Hodnett, Holt, Lennon, McCubbins, Merritt, Nicholson, Parker, Read, and Tourgee—16.

The report of the Committee on Relief was taken up, and,

On motion, was postponed until Saturday.

On motion of Mr. Abbott, the House resolved itself into a Committee of the Whole, and,

On motion, it was also agreed that the House on each day at 12 o'clock, resolve itself into a Committee of the Whole.

Mr. Jones, of Washington, took the Chair.

At 3 o'clock the Committee arose and reported progress.

Mr. Jones, Chairman, reported the adoption of the 3d section of the report of the Committee on a Governor and other necessary State Executive Officers, also the adoption of section 4th, with the following amendments, viz: Striking out after the word "affirmation," "that to the best of his knowledge and belief, he is eligible under the Constitution and laws of this State, to the office to which he has been elected," and inserting, "that he will support the Constitution of the United States and of the State of North-Carolina;" also striking out after the word "Governor" the eighth line, the words, "of the State of North-Carolina," and inserting, "to which he has been elected."

Section 5th was also adopted.

Section 6th was adopted with the following amendments, viz: by striking out the words, "treason and" in the 3d line and inserting the word "in;" also striking out all after the word "pardon," in the 7th line to the word "reprieve," inclusive, in the 12th line; also by striking out the word "biennially," and inserting "annually."

Section 7th was adopted as read.

Section 8th " " "

Section 9th " " "

Section 10th " " "

Section 11th " " "

Section 12th " " "

Section 13th " " "

Section 14th " " "

Section 15th " " "

Section 16th " " "

Section 17th was stricken out.

Section 18th was adopted with the following amendments, viz: by striking out in the first line the word "may," and inserting "shall," and line 22d to read "a Bureau of Statistics, of Agriculture and of Immigration."

The following substitute was adopted for section 2d, as adopted Tuesday:

SEC. 2. No person shall be eligible as Governor, or Lieutenant Governor, unless he shall have attained the age of thirty years, shall have been a citizen of the United States for five years, and shall have been a resident of this State for two years next before the day of election, nor shall the person elected to either of these new offices be eligible to the same office more than four years in any term of six years, unless the office shall have been cast upon him as Lieutenant Governor, or President of the Senate.

Section 2d, as was reported, amended and adopted Tuesday, was again amended and adopted by striking out the word "ratification" and inserting the word "approval;" also striking out the words "thirty days," and inserting instead "ten days."

The committee also reported the following action on the report of the Committee on Millitia, viz:

The adoption of section 1st, with the following amendments in the 4th line, striking out the word "such" and inserting "provided that all;" in the 6th line by sriking out the word "exempted," and insert the word "exempt," and by striking out the balance of the section after the word therefrom; also striking out the word "military" in the 4th line.

Section 2d was adopted as read.

The committee asked and obtained leave to sit again.

The President in pursuance of the report of the Committee of Sixteen appointed the following committees:

*Committee on Immigration and Resources and Statistics of the State.*—Messrs. Rich, Gahagan, Hood, Ellis and Ashley.

*A Standing Committee on Miscellaneous Affairs.*—Messrs. Laflin, Baker, Eppes, Aydlott and May.

On motion the House adjourned.

---

FRIDAY, JANUARY 31ST, 1868.

The Convention was called to order at 11 o'clock by the President.

Prayer by the Rev. Mr. Warwick.

A quorum was announced by the President.

Mr. Parker was allowed to change his vote of yesterday on Mr. Hood's resolution as amended by Mr. Pool, from nay to yea.

Mr. Bryan presented a memorial in reference to disabilities and their removal.

Referred to the Committee on Miscellaneous Affairs.

Mr Tourgee, Chairman, of the Committee on Counties, Towns, &c., reported as follows:

The Committee on Counties, Towns, &c., have instructed me to report, that they have carfully considered the accompanying resolutions introduced by the delegate from Halifax, Mr. Eppes, and have concluded that the subject matter thereof, does not properly come within their power and they would respectfully ask to be discharged from its further consideration, and suggest that it be referred to the Committee on Suffrage.

A. W. TOURGEE, *Chairman.*

The report was accepted.

Mr. Rich presented a resolution relative to "the control of the veto power upon the Governor."

Lies over under the rules.

Mr. Tourgee introduced the following resolution.

*Resolved*, That the committee provided for, by the resolution of the delegate from Cumberland, to consider the preparation of a list of persons who should be recommended to Congress for the relief of disabilities imposed by the proposed amendment to the Constitution of the United States, known as Article XIV, be also instructed to consider the propriety of petitioning Congress for the relief of such persons as were, during the war, in hearty accord with the Government of the United States, though the same be not now in favor of the Reconstruction measures of Congress.

On motion, the rules were suspended.

Mr. Durham offered the following amendment:

Strike out all after the word "instructed," and insert the following:

"To ascertain and report the names of all citizens of the State, who are disfranchised by the Reconstruction Acts of Congress, that this Convention may recommend the same to Congress for a removal of political disabilities."

The hour of twelve having arrived, the house resolved itself into a Committee of the Whole.

Mr. Sweet in the Chair.

The following report of the Committee on Militia was considered:

## REPORT OF COMMITTEE ON MILITIA.

The Committee appointed on Militia met pursuant to instruction, and respectfully submit the following:

SECTION 1. All able bodied male citizens of the State of North-Carolina, between the ages of twenty-one and forty years, who are citizens of the United States, shall be liable to military duty in the militia. Such persons who may be adverse to bearing arms, from religious scruples, may be exempted therefrom upon such conditions as shall be prescribed by law.

SEC. 2. The General Assembly shall provide for the organizing, arming, equipping and discipline of the militia, and for paying the same when called into active service.

SEC. 3. All officers shall be elected by their respective commands, and commissioned by the Governor, with the consent of the General Assembly; the commissions of such officers to expire with the Governor's term of service.

SEC. 4. The Governor shall be Commander-in-Chief, and have power to call out the militia to execute the law, suppress riots or insurrections.

SEC. 5. The Governor shall have power to appoint and commission an Adjutant-General and such staff officers as he may deem necessary for the public good.

SEC. 6. The officers and men organized as militia shall not receive any pay or emolument except when in active service.

SEC. 7. The General Assembly shall have power to make such exemptions as may be deemed necessary, and to enact laws that may be expedient for the government of the same

J. Q. A. BRYAN, *Chairman.*
BYRON LAFLIN,
J. W. RAGLAND,
J. J. HAYES,
H. L. GRANT,
D. D. COLGROVE,
WM. STILLY,
SAMUEL H. HIGHSMITH,
G. A. GRAHAM,
E. LEGG.

At 2 o'clock the committee arose, and Mr. Sweet, Chairman, reported that the Committee of the Whole had the report of the Committee on Militia under consideration and report progress:

Reported section 3 stricken out.

Section 4 adopted.

Section 5 stricken out.

Section 6 stricken out.

Section 7 adopted as amended, viz: by striking out the word "same" and inserting "militia."

On motion of Mr. Heaton, it was ordered that the report of the Committee on a Governor and other necessary State executive officers as amended by the Committee of the Whole be engrossed for final reading and passage.

On motion of Mr. Heaton, the report of the Committee on Militia, as amended by the Committee of the Whole, be engrossed for final reading and passage.

Fabius Haywood Busbee, Reporter for the *North-Carolinian*, was expelled from the Convention by the President, by authority of a resolution passed January 16th, he having purposely and avowedly insulted the Convention by presenting at the desk of the President, a paper purporting to be a report of the current proceedings abounding in flouts, sneers and insults.

The resolution of Mr. Tourgee was taken up; also the amendment proposed by Mr. Durham.

Mr. Mann moved to lay the resolution on the table.

Mr. McDonald, of Chatham, demanded the yeas and nays. Granted.

The resolution and amendment were laid on the table by the following vote:

Those who voted in the affirmative are:

Messrs. Abbott, Andrews, Ashley, Aydlott, Barnes, Benbow, Blume, Bryan, Carey, Carter, Candler, Chillson, Colgrove, Congleton, Cox, Dickey, Duckworth, Eppes, Etheridge, Fisher, French of Bladen, French of Rockingham, French of Chowan, Fullings, Gahagan, Galloway, Garland, Garrett, George, Glover, Graham of Montgomery, Grant of Wayne, Grant of Northampton, Gully, Harris of Wake, Harris of Franklin, Hay, Hayes of Robeson, Hayes of Halifax, Heaton, Highsmith, Hobbs, Hyman, Ing, Jones of Caldwell, King of Lincoln, Kinney, Lee, Logan, Long, Mann, May, Mayo, Moore, Morton, Mullican, Murphy, Nance, Nicholson, Patrick, Parker, Parks, Petree, Pool, Ragland, Ray, Renfrow, Rhodes, Robbins, Rose, Smith, Stilwell, Sweet, Taylor, Teague, Tourgee, Trogden, Tucker, Turner, Watts, Welker, and Williams of Wake—82.

Those who voted in the negative are.

Messrs. Baker, Bradley, Cherry, Daniel, Dowd, Durham, Ellis, Forkner, Graham of Orange, Gunter, Hall, Hare, Hodnett, Hollowell, Holt, Jones of Washington, Laflin, Lennon, Marshall, McCubbins, Merritt, McDonald of Chatham, McDonald, of Moore, Newsom, Rich, Rodman, Sanderlin, Stilly and Williamson—29.

On motion the report of the Committee on a Preamble and Bill of Rights was made a special order for Monday at 12 o'clock.

On motion it was ordered that the report of the Committee on Internal Improvements be made a special order for Saturday at 12 o'clock.

Mr. Sweet asked and obtained leave of absence for Mr. Moore, of Granville, for two days.

Mr. Colgrove obtained leave of absence until Monday.

On motion the House adjourned.

---

SATURDAY FEBRUARY 1ST, 1868.

The Convention was called to order at 11 o'clock, by the President.

Prayer by the Rev. Mr. Brewer.

The Journal of Friday was read and approved.

The following communication was received from General Canby, giving the number of votes in the State for and against a Convention; also the number of votes received for each candidate to the Convention in each County.

On motion it was ordered that 200 copies be printed.

## STATEMENT

*Of votes cast for delegates to Convention in the election districts of North-Carolina at the election held on the* 19*th and* 20*th days of November*, 1867, *as returned by the superintendents of election.*

| ELECT. DIST. | COUNTY. | CANDIDATES. | VOTES POLLED |
|---|---|---|---|
| 1st. | Burke, and McDowell. | John S. Parks, | 1,287 |
| | | W. A. B. Murphy, | 1,281 |
| | | Woodville W. Fleming, | 441 |
| | | Robert V. Keely, | 420 |
| | | Geo. G. McCoy, | 33 |
| | | Scattering, | 11 |
| | | Total, | 3,473 |
| 2d. | Polk, and Rutherford. | W. H. Logan, | 1,459 |
| | | Jesse Rhodes, | 1,385 |
| | | R. A. Shotwell, | 81 |
| | | Jas. W. Adams, | 18 |
| | | Scattering, | 1 |
| | | Total, | 2,944 |
| 3d. | Mitchell and Yancey. | Julius S. Garland, | 652 |
| | | Andrew J. Roberts, | 225 |
| | | William J. Silver, | 35 |
| | | Scattering, | 5 |
| | | Total, | 917 |
| 4th. | Buncombe, Madison, Henderson and Transylvania. | Geo. W. Gahagan, | 2,307 |
| | | Thos. J. Candler, | 2,287 |
| | | Jas. H. Duckworth, | 2,304 |
| | | Sam'l. B. Gudger, | 702 |
| | | O. L. Erwin, | 684 |
| | | Dr. Jesse Wallen, | 699 |
| | | Total, | 8,983 |

| Elect. Dist. | County. | Candidates. | Votes polled |
|---|---|---|---|
| 5th. | Jackson and Haywood. | W. B. Garrett, | 663 |
| | | Wm. P. Welch, | 537 |
| | | Total, | 1,200 |
| 6th. | Cherokee, Clay and Macon. | Mark May, | 776 |
| | | Geo. W. Dickey, | 623 |
| | | David Malonee, | 369 |
| | | John M. Galloway, | 379 |
| | | John R. Simonds, | 291 |
| | | Scattering, | 27 |
| | | Total, | 2,465 |
| 7th. | Alleghany, Ashe, Surry, Yadkin and Watauga. | Samuel Forkner, | 1,928 |
| | | George W. Bradly, | 1,809 |
| | | Evan Benbow, | 1,974 |
| | | Belson Burham, | 49 |
| | | John G. Marler, | 1,030 |
| | | Edwin C. Bartlett, | 982 |
| | | James C. Gilmer, | 843 |
| | | John Jones, | 703 |
| | | John M. Marshall, | 1,123 |
| | | William Burke, | 58 |
| | | Wm. M. Caloway, | 455 |
| | | James G. Marler, | 155 |
| | | Marion Marshall, | 110 |
| | | Bilson B. Benham, | 220 |
| | | Johiel Smith, | 48 |
| | | B. B. Benham, | 34 |
| | | Scattering, | 36 |
| | | Total, | 11,562 |

| Elect. Dist. | County. | Candidates. | Votes polled |
|---|---|---|---|
| 8th. | Alexander, Caldwell, Iredell and Wilkes. | Calvin J. Cowles, | 3,120 |
| | | John Q. A. Bryan, | 3,066 |
| | | Wesley H. George, | 3,098 |
| | | Jerry Smith, | 3,042 |
| | | Calvin C. Jones, | 3,114 |
| | | Andrew A. Scroggs, | 1,568 |
| | | James H. Hill, | 1,502 |
| | | John H. McLaughlin, | 1,552 |
| | | Rev. Wm. Church, | 1,505 |
| | | Rev. Stafford C. Miller, | 1,325 |
| | | Samuel C. Miller, | 224 |
| | | John H. Hill, | 33 |
| | | Scattering, | 21 |
| | | Total, | 23,170 |
| 9th. | Rowan and Davie. | William M. Robbins, | 1,470 |
| | | Jas. S. McCubbins, | 1,523 |
| | | Robert F. Johnston, | 1,493 |
| | | Dr. Milton Hobbs, | 1,524 |
| | | Allen Rose, | 1,545 |
| | | Isaac M. Shaver, | 1,504 |
| | | Total, | 9,059 |
| 10th. | Cleveland. | Edward Elliott, | 630 |
| | | Plato Durham, | 653 |
| | | Total, | 1,283 |
| 11th. | Catawba. | James Ransom Ellis, | 638 |
| | | I. B. Killiam, | 426 |
| | | Total, | 1,064 |
| 12th. | Lincoln. | Joseph H. King, | 573 |
| | | W. A. Graham, Jr., | 386 |
| | | Total, | 359 |

| Eeect. Dist. | County. | Candidates. | Votes polled |
|---|---|---|---|
| 13th. | Gaston. | Milot J. Aydlott, | 735 |
| | | Robert Holland, | 159 |
| | | Scattering and informal, | 20 |
| | | Total, | 914 |
| 14th. | Mecklenburg. | Silas N. Stillwell, | 1,443 |
| | | Edward Fullings, | 1,503 |
| | | Thomas Gluyas, | 920 |
| | | John Hunter, | 917 |
| | | E. Stillwell, | 67 |
| | | Scattering, | 3 |
| | | Total, | 4,853 |
| 15th. | Union. | Wm. Newsom, | 875 |
| | | Edmond L. Davis, | 308 |
| | | Edmund Davis, | 41 |
| | | Scattering, | 3 |
| | | Total, | 1,227 |
| 16th. | Cabarrus. | William T. Blume, | 859 |
| | | John Hileman, | 463 |
| | | Informal, | 2 |
| | | Total, | 1,314 |
| 17th. | Stanly. | Levi C. Morton, | 417 |
| | | J. M. Redwine, | 278 |
| | | Total, | 695 |
| 18th | Anson. | George Tucker, | 1,128 |
| | | Henry Chillson, | 1,111 |
| | | Townley Redfearn, | 650 |
| | | R. T. Bennett, | 656 |
| | | Total, | 3,545 |

| Elect. Dist. | County. | Candidates. | Votes polled |
|---|---|---|---|
| 19th. | Stokes. | R. F. Petree, | 526 |
| | | R. W. Hill, | 114 |
| | | Total, | 640 |
| 20th. | Forsyth. | Elijah B. Teague, | 892 |
| | | James E. Mathews, | 175 |
| | | Scattering, | 7 |
| | | Total, | 1,074 |
| 21st. | Davidson. | Isaac Kinney, | 1,016 |
| | | Spencer Mullican, | 976 |
| | | Thos. P. Allen, | 272 |
| | | Samuel Jones, | 204 |
| | | D. W. C. Johnston, | 44 |
| | | Green Lambeth, | 63 |
| | | Scattering, | 6 |
| | | Total, | 2,581 |
| 22d. | Randolph. | T. L. L. Cox, | 1,272 |
| | | R. F. Trogdon, | 1,082 |
| | | W. S. Tomlinson, | 362 |
| | | Scattering, | 53 |
| | | Total, | 2,769 |
| 23d. | Guilford. | G. W. Welker, | 1,347 |
| | | A. W. Tourgee, | 1,231 |
| | | N. Mendenhall, | 1,188 |
| | | J. Harris, | 1,044 |
| | | Scattering, | 14 |
| | | Total, | 4,824 |

| Elect. Dist. | County. | Candidates. | Votes polled |
|---|---|---|---|
| 24th. | Rockingham. | Henry Barnes, | 756 |
| | | John French, | 741 |
| | | Wm. N. Hereford, | 140 |
| | | George W. Griffin, | 308 |
| | | Jones W. Burton, | 70 |
| | | Scattering, | 12 |
| | | Total, | 2,027 |
| 25th. | Caswell. | Wilson Carey, | 1,448 |
| | | P. Hodnett, | 774 |
| | | Thowas J. Brown, | 485 |
| | | William Long, | 184 |
| | | Samuel Allen, | 189 |
| | | Scattering, | 29 |
| | | Total, | 3,109 |
| 26th. | Alamance. | Henry M. Ray, | 789 |
| | | Rufus Y. McAden, | 642 |
| | | Scattering, | 1 |
| | | Total, | 1,432 |
| 27th. | Person. | William Merritt, | 788 |
| | | Robbert P. Martin, | 692 |
| | | Scattering, | 8 |
| | | Total, | 1,488 |
| 28th. | Orange. | John W. Graham, | 1,438 |
| | | Edwin M. Holt, | 1,445 |
| | | Benj. S. Hedrick, | 1,120 |
| | | Henry Jones, | 1,115 |
| | | Scattering, | 33 |
| | | Total, | 5,151 |

| Elect. Dist. | County. | Candidates. | Votes polled |
|---|---|---|---|
| 29th. | Chatham. | John A. McDonald, | 1,279 |
| | | William T. Gunter, | 1,223 |
| | | George P. Moore, | 492 |
| | | Abraham Rencher, | 579 |
| | | Kelly Mitchell, | 271 |
| | | Clabourne Justice, | 696 |
| | | John A. Hinks, | 73 |
| | | William P. Taylor, | 45 |
| | | Scattering, | 15 |
| | | Total. | 4,673 |
| 30th. | Wake. | James H. Harris, | 2,930 |
| | | Joshua P. Andrews, | 2,971 |
| | | Stokes D. Franklin, | 2,986 |
| | | B. S. D. Williams, | 2,960 |
| | | Daniel G. Fowle, | 1,895 |
| | | Priestly H. Mangum, | 1,786 |
| | | John A. McLean, | 1,787 |
| | | Bennett T. Blake, | 1,787 |
| | | Scattering, | 4 |
| | | Total, | 19,106 |
| 31st. | Granville. | John W. Ragland, | 2,453 |
| | | James J. Moore, | 2,436 |
| | | Cuffey Mayo, | 2,425 |
| | | Robert W. Lassiter, | 231 |
| | | Robert A. Jenkins, | 178 |
| | | Elijah Winston, | 97 |
| | | John Peed, | 229 |
| | | Hatchwell Freeman, | 268 |
| | | Calvin Betts, | 58 |
| | | Robert B. Gilliam, | 50 |
| | | J. J. Lansdell, | 58 |
| | | Scattering, | 357 |
| | | Total, | 8,840 |

| Elect. Dist. | County. | Candidates. | Votes polled |
|---|---|---|---|
| 32d. | Warren. | John Hyman, | 2,047 |
| | | John Read, | 1,919 |
| | | Peter R. Davis, | 572 |
| | | Daniel R. Goodloe, | 54 |
| | | Scattering, | 45 |
| | | Total, | 4,637 |
| 33d. | Franklin. | James Thomas Harris, | 1,246 |
| | | John Edward Thomas, | 769 |
| | | William R. Davis, | 811 |
| | | John H. Williamson, | 1,372 |
| | | Scattering, | 1 |
| | | Total, | 4,199 |
| 34th. | Cumberland. | W. A. Mann, | 1,607 |
| | | James H. Hood, | 1,581 |
| | | Joseph A. McArthur, | 846 |
| | | Alfred A. McKetham, | 842 |
| | | Scattering, | 29 |
| | | Informal, | 50 |
| | | Total, | 4,946 |
| 35th. | Harnett. | James M. Turner, | 729 |
| | | Benj. C. Williams. | 308 |
| | | Total, | 1,037 |
| 36th. | Moore. | Swain S. McDonald, | 632 |
| | | Charles C. Crimmon, | 141 |
| | | John Ritter, | 210 |
| | | John A. Barrett, | 60 |
| | | Adam Barrett, | 126 |
| | | Total, | 1,168 |

| Elect. Dist. | County. | Candidates. | Votes polled |
|---|---|---|---|
| 37th. | Montgomery. | George A. Graham, | 479 |
| | | Wilburn Lassiter, | 267 |
| | | Scattering and informal, | 6 |
| | | Total, | 752 |
| 38th. | Richmond. | Richmond T. Long, Sr., | 1,244 |
| | | Peter McRae, | 189 |
| | | Scattering, | 3 |
| | | Total, | 1,436 |
| 39th. | Wayne. | Hiram L. Grant, | 1,301 |
| | | Jesse Hollowell, | 1,301 |
| | | H. J. Finlayson, | 834 |
| | | E. A. Wright, | 818 |
| | | Scattering, | 2 |
| | | Total, | 4,256 |
| 40th. | Johnston. | Dr. James Hay, | 1,087 |
| | | Nathan Gulley, | 1,079 |
| | | Charles E. Preston, | 821 |
| | | Lee R. Waddell, | 830 |
| | | Scattering, | 2 |
| | | Total, | 3,819 |
| 41st. | Greene. | John M. Patrick, | 739 |
| | | James B. Faircloth, | 346 |
| | | Scattering, | 2 |
| | | Total, | 1,087 |
| 42d. | Wilson. | Willie Daniel, | 668 |
| | | J. W. Davis, | 574 |
| | | Joseph E. Tatton, | 195 |
| | | Scattering, | 4 |
| | | Total, | 1,441 |

| Elect. Dist. | County. | Candidates. | Votes polled |
|---|---|---|---|
| 43d. | Nash. | Jacob Ing, | 708 |
| | | David W. Williams, | 455 |
| | | Total, | 1,163 |
| 44th. | Halifax. | John W. Renfrow, | 2,546 |
| | | Henry Eppes, | 2,571 |
| | | J. J. Hayes, | 2,538 |
| | | Arthur McDaniel, | 737 |
| | | Wm. D. Faucett, | 744 |
| | | Silvester Wilson, | 704 |
| | | Scattering and informal, | 35 |
| | | Total, | 9,875 |
| 45th. | Northampton. | Roswell C. Parker, | 1,476 |
| | | Henry T. Grant, | 1,470 |
| | | John C. Jacobs, | 602 |
| | | Thos. W. Mason, | 425 |
| | | Benj. Franklin, | 186 |
| | | John T. Wheeler, | 96 |
| | | Scattering, | 32 |
| | | Total, | 4,287 |
| 46th. | Edgecombe. | Joseph H. Baker, | 1,665 |
| | | Henry A. Dowd, | 1,663 |
| | | Henry C. Cherry, | 1,556 |
| | | Turner W. Battle, | 154 |
| | | Nathan M. Laurance, | 139 |
| | | Isaac F. Batts, | 148 |
| | | Richmond Stattier, | 232 |
| | | D. Battle, | 294 |
| | | Scattering, | 114 |
| | | Total, | 5,965 |
| 47th. | Lenoir. | Richard W. King, | 1,101 |
| | | Henry F. Grangier, | 363 |
| | | Scattering, | 16 |
| | | Total, | 1,480 |

| Elect. Dist. | County. | Candidates. | Votes polled |
|---|---|---|---|
| 48th. | Brunswick. | Edwin Legg, | 697 |
| | | Walter G. Cushs, | 382 |
| | | Westley Hodge, | 92 |
| | | Scattering. | 1 |
| | | Total, | 1,172 |
| 49th. | Columbus. | Hayes Lennon, | 584 |
| | | M. Powell, | 468 |
| | | H. Lennon, | 24 |
| | | Scattering, | 4 |
| | | Total, | 1,080 |
| 50th. | Robeson. | O. S. Hayes, | 1,568 |
| | | Joshua L. Nance, | 1,569 |
| | | W. S. Chaffin, | 1,050 |
| | | John Leach, | 1,035 |
| | | Blank, | 1 |
| | | Total, | 5,223 |
| 51st. | Bladen. | Abial W. Fisher, | 1,112 |
| | | Frederick F. French, | 1,112 |
| | | Bertram Robeson, | 575 |
| | | R. Franklin Lewis, | 575 |
| | | Total, | 3,374 |
| 52d. | New Hanover. | Gen. Jos. C. Abbott, | 2,926 |
| | | Samuel S. Ashley, | 2,920 |
| | | Abraham H. Galloway, | 2,913 |
| | | Oscar G. Parsley, | 1,094 |
| | | William E. Freeman, | 1,093 |
| | | Solomon S. Satchwell, | 1,085 |
| | | Scattering. | 7 |
| | | Total, | 12,038 |

| Elect. Dist. | County. | Candidates. | Votes polled |
|---|---|---|---|
| 53d. | Duplin. | John Alexander Bryan, | 971 |
| | | James Warren Blount, | 964 |
| | | John W. Peterson, | 1,015 |
| | | Samuel High Smith, | 997 |
| | | Scattering, | 7 |
| | | Total, | 3,954 |
| 54th. | Sampson. | J. D. Pearsall, | 853 |
| | | Alexander Williams, | 873 |
| | | Lorenzo Dow Hall, | 357 |
| | | Sylvester Carter, | 884 |
| | | Randal Hall, | 114 |
| | | L. D. Hall, | 289 |
| | | Lorenzo D. Hall, | 60 |
| | | Ransom Hall, | 149 |
| | | Scattering and informal, | 54 |
| | | Total, | 3,633 |
| 55th. | Tyrrell and Washington. | E. W. Jones, | 774 |
| | | W. W. Walker, | 556 |
| | | Scattering, | 39 |
| | | Total, | 1,369 |
| 56th. | Martin. | Samuel W. Watts, | 787 |
| | | James E. Moore, | 570 |
| | | Scattering, | 13 |
| | | Total, | 1,370 |
| 57th. | Bertie. | Bryant Lee, | 945 |
| | | Parker D. Robbins, | 939 |
| | | Scattering, | 63 |
| | | Joseph Beasley, | 152 |
| | | Ned Outlaw, | 56 |
| | | Total, | 2,155 |

| Elect. Dist. | County. | Candidates. | Votes polled |
|---|---|---|---|
| 58th. | Hertford. | Jackson Boon Hall, | 515 |
| | | Lemuel H. Boon, | 507 |
| | | Charles H. Foster, | 174 |
| | | Total, | 1,196 |
| 59th. | Gates. | Thomas L. Hoffler, | 440 |
| | | John Brady, | 342 |
| | | Scattering, | 12 |
| | | Total, | 794 |
| 60th. | Chowan. | John R. French, | 632 |
| | | Daniel E. Ethridge, | 472 |
| | | Scattering, | 1 |
| | | Total, | 1,105 |
| 61st. | Perquimans. | Dr. Wm. Nicholson, | 851 |
| | | Scattering, | 2 |
| | | Total, | 853 |
| 62d. | Pasquotank and Camden. | Mach. A. Taylor, | 1,258 |
| | | Chas. C. Pool, | 1,273 |
| | | Geo. W. Brooks, | 609 |
| | | Wm. J. Manisett, | 547 |
| | | Total, | 3,687 |
| 63d. | Currituck. | Thomas Sanderlin, | 445 |
| | | Joseph W. Etheridge, | 412 |
| | | Scattering, | 51 |
| | | Total, | 908 |

| Elect. Dist. | County. | Candidates. | Votes polled |
|---|---|---|---|
| 64th. | Craven. | David Heaton, | 3,221 |
| | | Wm. H. S. Sweet, | 3,217 |
| | | Clinton D. Pierson, | 3,191 |
| | | Frederick Miller. | 520 |
| | | John McCotter, | 517 |
| | | McAlister Roughton, | 481 |
| | | Scattering, | 89 |
| | | Total, | 11,236 |
| 65th. | Onslow. | Franklin Thompson, | 224 |
| | | Jasper Etheridge, | 326 |
| | | David W. Scott, | 188 |
| | | Total, | 738 |
| 66th. | Carteret. | Abraham Congleton, | 809 |
| | | L. W. Martin, | 650 |
| | | Scattering, | 2 |
| | | Total, | 1,461 |
| 67th. | Jones. | David D. Colgrove, | 530 |
| | | James T. Dillihunt, | 305 |
| | | Total, | 835 |
| 68th. | Beaufort. | Wm. B. Rodman, | 853 |
| | | Wm. Stilley, | 845 |
| | | Jas. B. Stickney, | 630 |
| | | John C. Gorham, | 634 |
| | | Scattering, | 21 |
| | | Total, | 2,983 |
| 69th. | Pitt. | Byron Laflin, | 1,429 |
| | | Davis J. Rich, | 1,428 |
| | | Lomis Hilliard, | 1,044 |
| | | Wm. M. B. Brown, | 1,034 |
| | | Total, | 4,935 |

| Elect. Dist. | County. | Candidates. | Votes polled |
|---|---|---|---|
| 70th. | Hyde, | Andrew J. Glover, | 563 |
| | | Banister Midgett, | 429 |
| | | Scattering, | 9 |
| | | Total, | 1,001 |

BUREAU OF CIVIL AFFAIRS.

Citadel, Charleston, S. C., January 28, 1868.

The foregoing is a correct statement of votes cast for Delegates to Convention in the Election Districts of North-Carolica at the election held on the 19th and 20th days of November, 1867, as returned by the Superintendent of Election.

A. J. WILLARD.

*In charge of Bureau Civil Affairs.*

HEADQUARTERS SECOND MILITARY DISTRICT,
CHARLESTON, S. C., January 28th, 1868.

SIR:—I have the honor to transmit, in accordance with a resolution of the Constitutional Convention of North-Carolina, a copy of the recapitulation of the Canvass Returns for the State of North-Carolina for the election held on the 19th and 20th of November, 1867, and a statement exhibiting the number of votes cast for each of the candidates for delegates to the Convention.

Very respectfully your obedient servant,
ED. R. S. CANBY,
*Brevt. Maj. Gen. Commanding.*

*President Constitutional Convention of North-Carolina,*
*Raleigh, N. C.*

---

RECAPITULATION OF CANVASS RETURNS FOR THE STATE OF NORTH-CAROLINA.

| Election Dist. | Counties. | Recapitulation from Books. | | | Aggregate from Poll Lists. | No. Tickets Polled. | No of Tickets For a Conven'n. | No. of Tickets Against Conven | Informal Tick'ts |
|---|---|---|---|---|---|---|---|---|---|
| | | Whites. | Blacks. | Totals. | | | | | |
| 1 | Burke and McDowell, | 1,885 | 692 | 2,577 | 1,761 | 1,766 | 1,397 | 369 | |
| 2 | Rutherford and Polk, | 2,045 | 572 | 2,617 | 1,584 | 1,539 | 1,444 | 95 | |
| 3 | Yancey and Mitchell, | 1,520 | 90 | 1,610 | | 923 | 833 | 90 | |

| No. | District | | | | | | | |
|---|---|---|---|---|---|---|---|---|
| 4 | Madison, Buncombe, Henderson and Transylvania, | 3,934 | 740 | 4,674 | 2,950 | 3,014 | 2,340 | 674 |
| 5 | Haywood and Jackson, | 1,604 | 143 | 1,747 | | 1,168 | 669 | 499 |
| 6 | Macon, Clay and Cherokee, | 2,164 | 101 | 2,265 | 1,298 | 1,228 | 973 | 255 |
| 7 | Alleghany, Ashe, Surry, Watauga and Yadkin, | 5,451 | 692 | 6,143 | 3,512 | 3,505 | 2,735 | 770 |
| 8 | Caldwell, Wilkes, Iredell and Alexander | 5,840 | 1,367 | 7,207 | 4,504 | 4,680 | 3,718 | 962 |
| 9 | Davie and Rowan, | 2,862 | 1,550 | 4,412 | 3,058 | 3,054 | 2,606 | 448 |
| 10 | Cleveland, | 1,454 | 374 | 1,828 | 1,292 | 1,292 | 900 | 392 |
| 11 | Catawba, | 1,352 | 318 | 1,670 | 1,084 | 1,111 | 780 | 331 |
| 12 | Lincoln, | 897 | 417 | 1,314 | 960 | 960 | 677 | 283 |
| 13 | Gaston, | 1,053 | 442 | 1,495 | 890 | 906 | 822 | 84 |
| 14 | Mecklenburg, | 1,928 | 1,659 | 3,587 | 2,462 | 2,432 | 1,985 | 447 |
| 15 | Union, | 1,309 | 424 | 1,739 | 1,238 | 1,233 | 1,059 | 174 |
| 16 | Cabarrus, | 1,175 | 746 | 1,921 | 1,308 | 1,322 | 1,042 | 280 |
| 17 | Stanley, | 1,330 | 282 | 1,612 | 728 | 728 | 639 | 89 |
| 18 | Anson, | 1,091 | 1,076 | 2,167 | 1,785 | 1,786 | 1,182 | 604 |
| 19 | Stokes, | 1,280 | 390 | 1,670 | 645 | 620 | 547 | 73 |
| 20 | Forsyth, | 1,341 | 449 | 1,790 | 1,090 | 1,082 | 1,055 | 27 |
| 21 | Davidson. | 2,278 | 678 | 2,956 | 1,311 | 1,314 | 1,186 | 128 |
| 22 | Randolph, | 2,232 | 457 | 2,686 | 1,449 | 1,431 | 1,364 | 67 |
| 23 | Guilford, | 2,690 | 1,489 | 4,179 | 2,415 | 2,404 | 1,766 | 638 |
| 24 | Rockingham, | 1,405 | 1,349 | 2,754 | 1,440 | 1,448 | 1,074 | 374 |
| 25 | Caswell, | 1,361 | 1,703 | 3,064 | 1,964 | 1,981 | 1,485 | 499 |
| 26 | Alamance, | 1,348 | 785 | 2,133 | 1,453 | 1,444 | 872 | 572 |
| 27 | Person, | 1,007 | 882 | 1,889 | 1,513 | 1,488 | 742 | 647 |

## CANVASS RETURNS.—CONTINUED.

| Election District. | COUNTIES. | RECAPITULATION FROM BOOKS. | | | Aggregate from Poll Lists. | No. Tickets Polled. | No. of Tickets For a Convention. | No. of Tickets Against Convention. | Informal Tickets. |
|---|---|---|---|---|---|---|---|---|---|
| | | Whites. | Blacks. | Totals. | | | | | |
| 28 | Orange, | 2,004 | 1,291 | 3,295 | 2,612 | 2,605 | 1,209 | 1,396 | |
| 29 | Chatham, | 2,206 | 1,179 | 3,385 | 2,547 | 2,446 | 2,116 | 330 | |
| 30 | Wake, | 2,019 | 2,907 | 5,926 | 4,935 | 4,916 | 4,135 | 781 | |
| 31 | Granville, | 2,020 | 2,502 | 4,522 | 3,224 | 3,218 | 2,511 | 701 | |
| 32 | Warren, | 856 | 2,284 | 3,140 | 2,612 | 2,634 | 2,061 | 573 | |
| 33 | Franklin, | 1,121 | 1,487 | 2,608 | 2,241 | 2,327 | 1,460 | 867 | |
| 34 | Cumberland, | 1,579 | 1,546 | 3,125 | 2,510 | 2,485 | 1,662 | 798 | 25 |
| 35 | Harnett, | 857 | 511 | 1,368 | 1,055 | 1,037 | 744 | 292 | |
| 36 | Moore, | 1,366 | 459 | 1,825 | 1,166 | 1,161 | 975 | 186 | |
| 37 | Montgomery, | 894 | 321 | 1,215 | 762 | 758 | 752 | 6 | |
| 38 | Richmond, | 995 | 1,084 | 2,079 | 1,437 | 1,436 | 1,251 | 185 | |
| 39 | Wayne, | 1,506 | 1,229 | 2,735 | 2,100 | 2,045 | 1,317 | 828 | |
| 40 | Johnston, | 1,732 | 914 | 2,646 | 1,931 | 1,939 | 1,329 | 610 | |

| | | | | | | | | | |
|---|---|---|---|---|---|---|---|---|---|
| 41 | Greene, | 703 | 706 | 1,409 | 1,088 | 1,683 | 741 | 342 | |
| 42 | Wilson, | 1,033 | 903 | 1,936 | 1,463 | 1,456 | 885 | 571 | |
| 43 | Nash, | 1,071 | 873 | 1,944 | 1,265 | 1,258 | 860 | 398 | |
| 44 | Halifax, | 1,095 | 3,140 | 4,235 | 3,329 | 3,305 | 2,533 | 746 | 26 |
| 45 | Northampton, | 1,311 | 1,660 | 2,971 | 2,198 | 2,197 | 1,647 | 538 | 12 |
| 46 | Edgecombe, | 1,246 | 2,622 | 3,868 | | 2,908 | 2,324 | 584 | |
| 47 | Lenoir, | 922 | 1,078 | 2,000 | 1,465 | 1,483 | 1,134 | 349 | |
| 48 | Brunswick, | 740 | 728 | 1,468 | 1,174 | 1,171 | 825 | 346 | |
| 49 | Columbus, | 860 | 518 | 1,378 | 1,082 | 1,082 | 577 | 505 | |
| 50 | Robeson, | 1,584 | 1,451 | 3,035 | 2,631 | 2,632 | 1,868 | 764 | |
| 51 | Bladen, | 1,085 | 1,146 | 2,231 | 1,684 | 1,685 | 1,152 | 533 | |
| 52 | New Hanover, | 1,935 | 3,224 | 5,159 | 3,986 | 4,019 | 2,928 | 1,091 | |
| 53 | Duplin, | 1,445 | 1,181 | 2,626 | 1,972 | 1,992 | 1,055 | 937 | |
| 54 | Sampson, | 1,501 | 960 | 2,461 | 1,871 | 1,914 | 1,129 | 785 | |
| 55 | Tyrrell and Washington, | 1,280 | 790 | 2,070 | 1,374 | 1,376 | 1,028 | 348 | |
| 56 | Martin, | 971 | 799 | 1,770 | 1,361 | 1,332 | 872 | 500 | |
| 57 | Bertie, | 959 | 1,264 | 2,223 | 1,215 | 1,403 | 1,219 | 184 | |
| 58 | Hertford, | 712 | 775 | 1,487 | 1,206 | 1,209 | 706 | 503 | |
| 59 | Gates, | 723 | 469 | 1,192 | 800 | 793 | 542 | 251 | |
| 60 | Chowan, | 607 | 667 | 1,274 | 1,105 | 1,100 | 823 | 277 | |
| 61 | Perquimans, | 705 | 693 | 1,398 | 873 | 898 | 808 | 90 | |
| 62 | Pasquotank and Camden, | 1,409 | 1,511 | 2,920 | 1,894 | 1,883 | 1,331 | 552 | |
| 63 | Currituck, | 919 | 381 | 1,300 | 950 | 948 | 456 | 492 | |
| 64 | Craven, | 1,595 | 3,183 | 4,778 | 3,825 | 3,817 | 3,232 | 585 | |
| 65 | Onslow, | 816 | 402 | 1,218 | 740 | 739 | 440 | 299 | |
| 66 | Carteret, | 1,195 | 749 | 1,944 | 1,461 | 1,465 | 873 | 592 | |

CANVASS RETURNS.—Continued.

| Election Dist. | Counties. | Recapitulation from Books. | | | Aggregate from Poll Lists. | No. Tickets Polled. | No. of Tickets For a Conven'n. | No. of Tickets Against Conv'n. | Informal Tick'ts |
|---|---|---|---|---|---|---|---|---|---|
| | | Whites. | Blacks. | Totals. | | | | | |
| 67 | Jones, | 483 | 539 | 1,022 | 843 | 843 | 645 | 303 | |
| 68 | Beaufort, | 1,499 | 925 | 2,424 | 1,557 | 1,553 | 928 | 625 | |
| 69 | Pitt, | 1,450 | 1,449 | 2,899 | 2,459 | 2,480 | 1,545 | 935 | |
| 70 | Hyde, | 876 | 565 | 1,441 | 1,000 | 1,000 | 590 | 410 | |
| | | 106,721 | 72,932 | 179,653 | | 126,030 | 93,006 | 32,961 | 63 |

BUREAU OF CIVIL AFFAIRS,
Citadel, Charleston, S. C., December 26, 1868.

The foregoing is a correct statement from the Returns of the election held on the 19th and 20th days of November last, in and for the State of North-Carolina, made to these Headquarters by the canvassers, and from the returns made by the Boards of Registration for the several registration precincts of said State, it appears thereby that a majority of the votes given at said election were "For a Convention;" and, also, that at such election a majority of all the registered voters of said State voted on the question of holding said Convention.

A. J. WILLARD,
*Chief of Bureau of Civil Affairs.*

Mr. Laflin asked and obtained leave of absence for Mr. Grant of Wayne until Monday next.

Leave of absence was also granted Mr. Hollowell, also Mr. Ashley, until Monday next.

Leave of absence was also granted Messrs. Tourgee and Welker from 2 o'clock until Monday next.

Mr. Rodman presented a memorial from the citizens of Hyde County, respecting the drainage of Mattamuskeet Lake.

Referred to the Committee on Internal Improvements.

The majority and minority reports of the Committee on Legislation, were presented and ordered to be printed.

The Committee on the Judicial Department, to whom was referred the petition for divorce of Dewitt C. Wilson and Nancy C. Wilson, reported that if the Convention determines to legislate on private matters, they recommend a favorable consideration of the case.

WM. B. RODMAN, *Chairman.*

On motion the report was indefinitely postponed.

The report of the Committee on Judicial Department on a resolution introduced by Mr. Tourgee, respecting costs in criminal cases, reported through their Chairman, Mr. Rodman.

On motion the report was laid over.

Mr. Peterson introduced an ordinance making it the duty of the General Assembly to provide a Land Agency in each County of this State.

Referred to the Committee on Relief.

Mr. Renfrow introduced an ordinance for the protection of labor.

Referred to the Committee on the Judicial Department.

Mr. Congleton introduced a resolution asking for a loan of ten millions of dollars for agricultural purposes.

Made a special order for Tuesday.

Mr. Ragland offered the following resolution:

*Resolved* That the Committee appointed to confer with General Canby, be directed to inquire whether notes and bonds given since May 1st, 1865, in renewal of debts contracted prior to that date are subject to the power of General Order, 164.

On motion the rules were suspended and the resolution adopted.

Mr. Williamson introduced a resolution asking a loan from Congress.

Referred to the Committee on Finance.

The Relief Bill, No. 7, being a special order for this day, was taken up.

Mr. Welker offered an amendment.

Mr. Jones, of Washington, offered a substitute.

Mr. Graham, of Orange, also offered a substitute.

After considerable discussion,

On motion of Mr. Harris, of Wake, the whole subject was postponed until Saturday next.

On motion of Mr. Abbott, the report of the Committee on Internal Improvements, was postponed until Monday at 12 o'clock, and made special order at that time.

On motion the house adjourned.

---

## MONDAY, February 3d, 1868.

The Convention was called to order at 11 o'clock, by the President.

Prayer by the Rev. Dr. Atkinson.

The President announced a quorum.

The Journal of Saturday was read and approved.

A communication was received from the Young Men's Christian Association, asking the use of the Hall for the evening.

On motion of Mr. Watts, the request was granted.

Mr. Harris, of Wake, presented a petition for the divorce of Ann Underdue.

Laid over.

Mr. McCubbins presented a memorial from the citizens of Rowan County, regarding the usury law.

Referred to the Committe on the Judicial Department.

Mr. Ragland introduced a resolution giving certain instructions to the Committee on Judicial Department.

Referred to the Committee on Judicial Department.

Mr. Duckworth introduced an ordinance for the relief of the Sheriff of Henderson County.

Lies over under the rules.

Mr. Morton introduced the following resolution:

*Resolved*, That from and after to-day, Monday, February 3d, the Convention shall assemble at 10 o'clock, A. M., and adjourn at 2, P. M.

On motion, the rules were suspended.

Mr. Heaton moved to amend by striking out all after 10 o'clock, A. M.

The resolution, as amended, was adopted.

Mr. Glover introduced a resolution instructing the Committee on Legislature to enquire into the propriety of aboling the Bastardy law of the State.

Referred to the Committee on Legislature.

Mr. Petree introduced a resolution providing for a Committee of three to petition Congress for the reduction of the Revenue Tax on Tobacco.

Lies over under the rules.

### UNFINISHED BUSINESS.

The following resolution of Mr. Harris, of Wake, was called up, and,

On motion, was adopted:

*Resolved*, That the President of this Convention appoint a Committee of eight, one from each Judicial District, to take into consideration the Congressional Districts, and report by ordinance or otherwise.

The ordinance of Mr. Glover to revive debts, was taken up, and,

On motion, was indefinitely postponed.

The ordinance presented by Mr. Duckworth, in regard to admission to the Bar, was taken up, and,

Referred to the Committee on the Judicial Department.

The ordinance of Mr. French, of Bladen, in relation to taxes, was, with unanimous consent, withdrawn.

Mr. Candler introduced an ordinance repealing the granting of a general amnesty and pardon to soldiers, &c.

On motion, it was made a Special Order for Monday at 12 o'clock.

The vote to make the report of the Committee on Relief a Special Order for Saturday, was reconsidered, and,

On motion, the report was made a Special Order for Tuesday, at 12 o'clock.

Mr. Watts moved to reconsider the vote, on the report of the Committee on the Judicial Department in relation to a petition of divorce of Dewitt Wilson and his wife.

The motion was not sustained.

The hour of 12 having arrived,

The following report of the Committee on Internal Improvements was taken up.

The Committee on Internal Improvements, to whom was referred the ordinance in relation to the Wilmington, Charlotte and Rutherford Rail Road, have instructed me to report the ordinance with an amendment.

W. G. B. GARRETT, *Chairman.*

## AN ORDINANCE REDUCING THE AMOUNT OF BONDS AUTHORIZED TO BE ISSUED BY THE WILMINGTON, CHARLOTTE AND RUTHERFORD RAIL ROAD COMPANY.

WHEREAS, By an act of the General Assembly of the State of North-Carolina, ratified the 27th day of December, 1866, the Wilmington, Charlotte and Rutherford Rail Road Company was authorized to place upon its roadway, property and franchise, a first mortgage, to secure an issue of bonds, not to exceed in amount four millions dollars, which mortgage has been duly executed and recorded according to the provisions of said act; and whereas, the State holds a second mortgage upon the road for two millions of dollars, to protect which interest it is manifestly essential that the bonds to be issued under said first mortgage shauld be reduced in amount, and their value enhanced by the endorsement of the State, so that the Company may be enabled to complete its road; therefore,

SECTION 1. *Be it ordained by the people of North-Carolina in Convention assembled, and it is hereby ordained by the authority of the same,* That the President of this Convention, or the Governor, or the Public Treasurer of the State, or either of them, be, and they are hereby authorized and directed, in behalf of the State to endorse the bonds authorized as aforesaid to the amount of one million dollars, which endorsement shall be in the words and figures following, to wit: The principal and interest of this bond is guaranteed by the State of North-Carolina, by an ordinance of the Constitutional Convention, ratified the 3d day of February, 1868. *Provided*, that the amount of Bonds, issued by authority of the said act of the General Assembly, shall not exceed in the aggregate two millions five hundred thousand dollars, shall be delivered to the President of this Convention, or to the Governor, or to the State Treasurer, and by him or them cancelled and destroyed.

SEC. 2. *Be it further ordained*, That this ordinance shall take effect from and after its ratification.

Mr. Laflin offered to amend by adding the following to Section 1st:

"Or that said one million five hundred thousand dollars of bonds shall be cancelled and destroyed by the Trustees of said first mortgage, and a certificate shall be printed upon each of the remaining bonds certifying that two millions five hundred thousand dollars of bonds are all that are issued or are authorized to be issued under the deed of trust or mortgage, delivered to them, and that the additional one million five hundred thousand dollars of bonds have been cancelled and destroyed, and that said certificate shall be signed by each of the Trustees."

Mr. Tourgee offered the following amendment to be added to the above amendment:

*Provided further*, That five hundred thousand dollars of the remaining two millions five hundred thousand dollars of bonds, be deposited with the Treasurer of the State, as collateral security of the State for the above named endorsement, and if the said Wilmington, Charlotte and Rutherford Rail Road Company shall fail to pay either interest or principal of said endorsed bonds, so that the State shall become liable for the same, by reason of said endorsement, and shall pay the same, then the State shall become the owner of said five hundred thousand dollars of Bonds; but if the said Rail Road Company shall pay both interest and principal of said endorsed bonds, so that the State shall not become liable for the same by reason of its endorsement, to the said five hundred thousand dollars of bonds, shall be the property of said Rail Road Company."

The amendments were accepted.

The ordinance with the amendments was put upon its passage, and was adopted by the following vote:

The yeas and nays being demanded, resulted yeas 58, and nays 48.

Those who voted in the affirmative are:

Messrs. Abbott, Andrews, Aydlott, Baker, Blume, Bradley, Carey, Carter, Cherry Chillson, Daniel, Dickey, Dowd, Durham, Ellis, Eppes, Etheridge, Fisher, Forkner, French of Bladen, French of Chowan, Fullings, Galloway, Graham of Orange, Gunter, Harris of Wake, Hayes of Robeson, Highsmith, Hollowell, Holt, Hood, King of Lincoln, Laflin, Lee, Legg, Lennon, Logan, Long, May, Mayo, Marshall, McCubbins, Merritt, McDonald of Chatham, McDonald of Moore, Murphy, Nance, Newsom, Patrick, Petree, Ragland, Rich, Rodman, Stillwell Tourgee, Tucker, Watts, and Williamson—58.

Those who voted in the negative are:

Messrs. Barnes, Bryan, Candler Congleton, Duckworth, Franklin, Gahagan, Garland, George, Glover, Graham of Montgomery, Grant of Northampton, Gully, Hare, Hay, Hayes of Halifax, Heaton, Hobbs, Hodnett, Hoffler, Hyman, Ing, Jones of Caldwell, Jones of Washington, Kinney, Morton, Mullican, Nicholson, Parker, Parks, Peterson, Pierson, Pool, Ray, Read, Renfrow, Rhodes, Rose, Sanderlin, Smith,

Stilly, Sweet, Taylor, Teague, Trogden, Turner, Welker and Williams of Wake—48.

On motion the House adjourned.

---

TUESDAY, February 4th, 1868.

The Convention was called to order at 10 o'clock, by the President.

Prayer by the Rev. Dr. Hudson.

The President announced a quorum.

The Journal of Monday was read and approved.

The following communication from General Canby to the Committee appointed to consult with him on matters of public interest, was read:

HEADQUARTERS SECOND MILITARY DISTRICT,
Charleston, S. C., January 31st, 1868.

Messrs. Abbott and Ragland, *Committee,*
*Chamber Constitutional Convention:*

Gentlemen:—I have the honor to acknowledge receipt of your communication of the 28th, and of the enclosed papers from the Treasurer of the State of North-Carolina, and to state in reply that the 8th section of the law of March 3d, 1867, suplementary to the law of March 2d, 1867, to provide for the more efficient government of the Rebel States, directs that the Convention for each State shall prescribe the fees, salary, and compensation to be paid to all the delegates and other officers and agents herein authorized or necessary to carry into effect the provisions of this act, not herein otherwise provided for; and shall provide for the levy and collection of such taxes on the property of such State, as may be necessary to pay the same, and that so soon as I am advised that the Convention has provided for the levy and collection of the taxes necessary to defray its expenses, and has directed the same when collected to be paid into the State Treasury,

I will direct the payment to be made by the Treasurer upon the warrant of the President of the Convention, the taxes collected under the ordinance of the Convention to be applied to the reimbursement of the payment made from the Treasury on account of the Convention.

Very Respectfully
Your obedient Servant,
ED. R. S. CANBY,
*Brv't. Maj. General Commanding.*

On motion of Mr. Jones, of Washington, it was ordered that the Committee on Finance be directed to prepare a tax bill, in pursuance of the above communication, and report to the Convention, Thursday, A. M.

Mr. Welker presented a memorial from the citizens of Guilford County, against the distillation of grain.

Lies over under the rules.

The Committee on the Judicial Department reported as follows:

On a petition of the citizens of Rowan County, respecting usury laws recommend no action.

The report was adopted.

Also on a resolution in relation to admission "to the Bar," the committee recommend that it pass.

The report was accepted and the resolution as follows was read and put upon its passage:

*Resolved*, That any person who shall produce a certificate of admission to the bar of any State, and satisfactory evidence of good moral character, before the Supreme Court of the State, shall be admitted to the practice of law in the several courts of this State upon payment of the fees prescribed by law; and this resolution shall be in force from and after the date of its passage.

Mr. Durham demanded the yeas and nays.

The demand was sustained.

The resolution was adopted by the following vote:

Those who voted in the affirmative are:

Messrs. Abbott, Andrews, Aydlott, Barnes, Blume, Bryan,

Carey, Cherry, Chillson, Congleton, Cox, Daniel, Dickey, Duckworth, Eppes, Fisher, Franklin, French of Bladen, French of Rockingham, Fullings, Galloway, Garland, Glover, Graham of Montgomery, Grant of Wayne, Gully, Gunter, Harris of Franklin, Hay, Hayes of Robeson, Hayes of Halifax, Heaton, Highsmith, Hobbs, Hoffler, Hollowell, Hood, Hyman, Ing, Jones of Washington, King of Lincoln, King of Lenoir, Kinney, Laflin, Lee, Logan, Mann, May, Mayo, McDonald of Chatham, McDonald of Moore, Moore, Morton, Mullican, Murphy, Nance, Patrick, Parks, Petree, Peterson, Ragland, Ray, Read, Renfrow, Rhodes, Rich, Rodmon, Rose, Stilwell, Taylor, Tourgee, Tucker, Turner, Watts, Welker, Williams of Wake, and Williamson—77.

Those who voted in the negative are:

Messrs. Candler, Durham, Ellis, Etheridge, Forkner, George, Graham of Orange, Grant of Northampton, Hall, Hare, Hodnett, Holt, Jones of Caldwell, Marshall, McCubbins, Merritt, Nicholson, Parker, Pool, and Sanderlin—20.

The Committee on the Judicial Department also report as follows:

The Committee on the Judicial Department, to whom was referred a proposed ordinance for the protection of labor, respectfully report, that in their opinion, the following should be a part of the Constitution under the head of miscellaneous affairs:

The General Assembly shall provide, by law, that mechanics and laborers shall have a lien on the subject matter of their labor.

WM. B. RODMAN, *Chairman.*

The report was accepted.

The Committee on the judicial Department to whom was referred the petition of Martha A. Hopkins, wife of William T. Hopkins, to be divorced from her husband, respectfully report the following ordinance and request its passage:

*Be it ordained by the people of North-Carolina in Convention assembled*, That the bonds of matrimony between William T. Hopkins and Martha A., his wife, now of Granville

County, are hereby dissolved and each party is at liberty to marry again.

Mr. King, of Lenoir, moved to lay the ordinance on the table.

The yeas and nays were demanded and the ordinance was laid on the table by the following vote.

Those who voted in the affirmative are:

Messrs. Abbott, Aydlott, Barnes, Bradly, Bryan, Carey, Candler, Chillson, Dickey, Duckworth, Durham, Forkner, French of Bladen, Fullings, Gahagan, Garland, George, Grant of Wayne, Hall, Hay, Heaton, Hobbs, Hodnett, Hollowell, Holt, Ing, Jones of Caldwell, King of Lincoln, King of Lenoir, Kinney, Lee, Lennon, Logan, May, Mayo, Marshall, McDonald of Moore, Newsom, Petree, Pool, Ray, Renfrow, Rhodes, Rose, Stilwell, Sweet, Teague, Tourgee, Trogden, and Tucker—51.

Those who voted in the negative are:

Messrs. Andrews, Baker, Blume, Congleton, Cox, Daniel, Dowd, Eppes, Etheridge, Franklin, French of Rockingham, Galloway, Glover, Graham of Montgomery, Graham of Orange, Gunter, Hare, Harris of Wake, Harris of Franklin, Hayes of Robeson, Hayes of Halifax, Highsmith, Hood, Hyman, Jones of Washington, Long, McCubbins, Merritt, McDonald, of Chatham, Moore, Morton, Nance, Nicholson, Patrick, Parker, Parks, Peterson, Pierson, Ragland, Read, Rich, Rodman, Sanderlin, Taylor, Turner, Watts, Welker, Williams of Wake, and Williamson—49.

Mr. Forkner moved to reconsider the vote taken Monday on the ordinance in relation to the Wilmington, Charlotte and Rutherford Rail Road Company.

On motion of Mr. French, of Bladen, the motion to reconsider was laid on the table.

The yeas and nays were demanded, and the motion to reconsider was laid on the table by the following vote:

Those who voted in the affirmative are:

Messrs Abbott, Andrews Aydlott, Baker, Blume, Carey, Carter, Cherry, Chillson, Daniel, Dickey, Dowd, Durham, Ellis, Eppes, Etheridge, Fisher, French of Bladen, French of

Rockingham, Fullings, Galloway, Graham of Orange, Grant, of Wayne, Gunter, Harris of Wake, Hayes, of Robeson, Hayes of Halifax, Highsmith, Hobbs, Hoffler, Hollowell, Holt, Hood, Hyman, Ing, Jones of Caldwell, King of Lincoln, Kinney, Laflin, Lee, Legg, Lennon, Logan Long, Mann, Marshall, McCubbins, Merritt, McDonald of Chatham, McDonald of Moore, Mullican, Murphy, Nance, Newsom, Patrick, Parks, Ragland, Ray, Rhodes, Rich, Rose, Stilwell, Tucker, Watts and Williamson—65.

Those who voted in the negative are:

Messrs. Barnes, Bradley, Bryan, Candler, Congleton, Cox, Duckworth, Forkner, Gahagan, Garland, George, Glover, Graham of Montgomery, Grant of Northampton, Gully, Hare, Heaton, Hodnett, Jones of Washington, King of Lenoir, Mayo, Moore, Nicholson, Parker, Peterson, Pierson, Pool, Read, Renfrow, Rodman, Sanderlin, Sweet, Taylor, Teague, Tourgee, Trogden, Turner, Welker and Williams of Wake—39.

The following Committee was announced by the President, to report the names of persons to be recommended to Congress for relief from disabilities:

1st Judicial District, Nicholson,
2d " " R. W. King,
3d " " Hay,
4th " " Tourgee,
5th " " Hood,
6th " " C. C. Jones,
8th " " Gahagan.

### UNFINISHED BUSINESS.

The resolution of C. C. Jones, in relation to an ordinance increasing the expenses of the Convention, was taken up, and

On motion of Mr. Abbott, was referred to the Committee on Rules.

The following ordinance of Mr. Welker on distillation of grain, was taken up:

## AN ORDINANCE ON DISTILLATION OF GRAIN.

WHEREAS, In consequence of the rapid reduction of the small crop of corn in this State, the prices of food have already greatly advanced, and money being unusually scarce, great destitution already exists and starvation must inevitably follow speedily: *Therefore*, In order that all the grain still on hand may be reserved for bread, and famine at least in a degree averted,

*Be it ordained by the people of North-Carolina, in Convention assembled*, That from the first day of February, 1868, until the first day of June, 1868, it shall not be lawful for any person or persons to distill corn or any other grain into intoxicating liquors.

*Be it further ordained*, That any person or persons who shall be guilty of a violation of this ordinance, on being convicted before a competent court, shall pay a fine of $50 for the first offence, $100 for the second offence, and for the third offence his distillery shall be closed by the Sheriff, and the offender or offenders shall be punished with imprisonment in the County jail for not more than three nor less than one month, at the discretion of the court. In this ordinance, each day in which the distillery is in operation shall be counted a separate offence.

*Be it further ordained*, That all fines recovered under this ordinance, after the lawful costs are deducted, shall be paid into the Treasury of the County in which the conviction takes place, for the benefit of the poor supported by said County.

Mr. Colgrove offered an amendment which was adopted, and

On motion the vote was reconsidered.

Mr. Tourgee offered an amendment.

On motion of Mr. Graham, of Orange, the entire matter was referred to the Committee of three to consult with General Canby.

Mr. Abbott introduced the following resolution:

*Resolved*, That the Secretary be directed to prepare a list of the members of this Convention, which shall show the number of miles travelled by each, and the amount of mileage due.

On motion the Rules were suspended and the resolution was adopted.

12 oclock having arrived the report of the Committee on Relief, being made a special order for that hour, was taken up and discussed until 3 oclock and fifteen minutes,

When upon motion the house adjourned.

---

WEDNESDAY February 5th, 1868.

The Convention was called to order at 10 o'clock, by the President.

Prayer by the Rev. Mr. May.

The President announced a quorum.

The Journal of Tuesday was read and approved.

Mr. Patrick presented a petition of divorce.

Referred to the Committee on the Judicial department.

The House granted leave of absence to Mr. Benbow.

Mr. E. W. Jones, Chairman, of the Committee on corporations, reported as follows:

The Committee on Corporations, to whom was referred the resolution of Mr. Tourgee,

" That no Bank of Issue shall hereafter be established under the authority of this State,"

Ask leave to report that they have had the same under consideration, and inasmuch as they have prepared a clause to be inserted in the Constitution, which will come up in due time for consideration, ask to be discharged from the further consideration of the same.

E. W. JONES, *Chairman.*

On motion the report was adopted.

The Committee on Corporations, to whom was referred the resolution of Mr. S. S. Ashley, in regard to providing a lien for labor, ask leave to report that they have considered the same, and inasmuch as the subject matter is embraced in other Legislative and Constitutional provisions recommended to the Convention, they ask to be discharged from the further consideration of the same.

E. W. JONES, *Chairman.*

On motion, the report was adopted.

Mr. Rich introduced the following resolution:

*Resolved*, That the Committee on Finance be instructed to negotiate a loan of $500,000 for contingent expenses, and be also instructed to insert in the tax bill that amount in addition to the estimated ordinary expenses of the Convention.

On motion the rules were suspended and the resolution adopted.

Mr. Rodman introduced a resolution for the relief of the Sheriff of Halifax County.

Lies over under the rules.

On motion, the report of the Committee on Legislature was recommitted to that Committee.

On motion of Mr. Forkner, the report of General Canby of the late election, was

Referred to the Committee on Privileges and Elections.

On motion of Mr. C. C. Jones, the report of the Committee on Homesteads was recommitted to that Committee.

The following report of the select Committee on Relief was taken up:

The undersigned, a majority of the Select Committee on Relief, respectfully report the following ordinance and resolution, and recommend their passage:

## AN ORDINANCE RESPECTING THE JURISDICTION OF THE COURTS OF THIS STATE.

SECTION 1. *Be it ordained by the people of North-Carolina in Convention assembled*, That no court of law or equity of this State shall have jurisdiction of any suit or action founded on any contract made prior to the first day of May, 1865, (except actions against public officers, executors, administrators, guardians, trustees, and others acting in a fiduciary capacity, and their sureties for breach of their respective duties, by the appropriation to their own use of money or property, officially received by them, or other fraudulent acts,) or of any action or process to revive or enforce any judgment heretofore recovered on any such contract, whether such action be now pending, or shall be commenced hereafter, and whether such process has been already issued or shall be hereafter sued for; and the sheriffs, coroners and constables of this State, having in their hands any final process issued upon any judgment founded on such cause of action, are hereby commanded to stay all proceeding upon the same, and to return the same to the proper courts.

SEC. 2. This ordinance shall be in force from and after its ratification by this Convention, and shall continue in force until the first day of July, 1868, or until the Constitution, which this Convention has met to adopt, shall go into effect, whichever shall first happen.

*Resolved*, That a copy of the foregoing ordinance be sent to Major General Canby, Commanding, &c., and that he be respectfully requested to cause the same to be enforced.

Mr. McDonald, one of the Committee, agrees in recommending the foregoing ordinance, with the exception of a portion of the first section.

WM. B. RODMAN, *Chairman*.
JOHN A. McDONALD,
JOHN READ,
G. W. BRADLEY,
J. H. DUCKWORTH.

Mr. Graham, of Orange, offered the following substitute:

## AN ORDINANCE RESPECTING THE JURISDICTION OF THE COURTS OF THIS STATE.

SECTION 1. *Be it ordained by the people of North-Carolina, in Convention assembled*, That Sections 1 and 2 of the ordinance of the Convention adopted June 23d, 1866, entitled

" An Ordinance to change the jurisdiction of the Courts and the rules of pleading, therein," be and are hereby repealed.

Sec. 2. *Be it further ordained*, That Section 3 of the above entitled Ordinance be amended to read as follows: " Sec. 3. That all actions of debt, covenant, assumpsit, and account now pending in the Superior Courts shall be continued to Spring Term, 1869; and that the several Superior Courts at the Spring Term thereof only, unless otherwise herein provided, shall have exclusive original jurisdiction of all such causes of action except where jurisdiction has been or shall be given to a Justice of the Peace by the Constitution or Laws of North-Carolina. Should the defendant at the Spring Term, 1869, on writs which shall be returned to that Term or in any suit for the above causes of action then pending in the Superior Court, pay or confess judgment to the plaintiff for one-tenth of the debt and demand (principal and interest) and all costs to that time, he shall be allowed until next Spring Term to plead. At the said Spring Term should the defendant pay to the plaintiff or confess judgment for one-fifth of the residue of the said debt or demand .and cost, he shall be allowed until the succeeding Spring Term to plead. At the said Spring Term should the defendant pay to the plaintiff or confess judgment for one-half of the residue of the debt or demand, he shall be allowed until the succeeding Spring Term to plead. At the said Spring Term the pla intiff shall have judgment for the residue of his debt or demand: *Provided however*, That the plaintiff, if required, shall file his debt or demand in writing, and if the defendant shall make oath that the whole or any part thereof is not justly due, or that he has a counter demand, all of which shall be particularly set forth by affidavit, then the defendant shall only pay the instalment required of what he admits to be due, and the court shall order a jury at the same or some subsequent Term, to try the matters in dispute between the parties, and at the next Spring Term the defendant shall be allowed time to plead only upon paying or confessing judgment for one-fifth of the residue of the admitted amount, and whatever the jury finds him indebted over and above the same: *Provided further*, That should the defendent fail to pay or confess judgment for the first or any subsequent installment, then and in that case the plaintiff shall be entitled to proceed to judgment and execution for such installment, unless the defendent shall put in pleas, in which case the suit shall proceed according to the course of the court in 1860: *Provided further*, That by consent of the plaintiff the defendant at any Term of the court may confess judgment for a stipulated sum in full and final discharge of all further demand or liability upon such claim."

Sec. 3. *Be it further ordained*, That section 10 of the above recited act shall be amended to read as follows: "Sec. 10. That executions on judgments in actions of debt, assumpsit, covenant or account, or decrees for money demands in Equity, which have been, or shall be issued on judgments or decrees heretofore obtained, shall be levied on the property of the defendant and returned without sale: *Provided*, such return shall not prejudice any lien the plaintiff may acquire or then have by virtue of said *fi fa* or *venditioni exponas*. At Spring Term 1869, execution on all such judgments or decrees shall issue for only one-tenth of the amount then due; at Spring Term 1870, for one-fifth of the residue; at Spring Term 1871 for one-half of the residue; and at Spring Term 1872 for the ballance of the debt; and no execution shall issue from the Fall Term on any such judgment or decree except by consent of the defendant. That no mortgagee or trustee, shall expose to sale the property conveyed in such mortgage or trust deed, without the consent of the grantor, before first of March, 1869. Should the mortgagor, or trustor at that time pay one-tenth of the debts mentioned, the sale shall be postponed to first of March, 1870; at that time should the mortgagor or trustor pay one-fifth of the residue, the sale shall be postponed to the first of March, 1871; at that time should the trustor or mortgagor pay one-half of the residue, the sale shall be postponed to first of March 1872; and at that time the trustee or mortgagee shall sell the property or so much of it as will realize the balance of the debts: *Provided however*, That should the trustor, or mortgagor fail to pay the first or any subsequent installment, then, and in that case, the trustee or mortgagee shall sell at six months credit, so much of the property conveyed as will realize such installment."

SEC. 4. *Be it further ordained*, That section 11, of the above entitled act be amended to read as follows: "That no warrants before Justices of the Peace shall issue or be returnable until January 1st, 1869. Should the defendant upon such return pay to the plaintiff, or to the collecting officer, for his use, or confess judgment before the magistrate for one-tenth of the debt and demand, (principal and interest), he shall be allowed twelve months to plead; at the expiration of that time, should the defendant pay to the plaintiff or confess judgment for one-fifth of the residue of the said debt or demand, he shall be allowed twelve months more to plead; at the expiration of that time should the defendant pay to the plaintiff or confess judment for one-half of the residue of said debt or demand, he shall be allowed twelve months more to plead; at the expiration of that time the plaintiff shall have judgment for the residue of his debt or demand; *Provided, however*, That the plaintiff, if required, shall file his claim in writing, and if the defendant shall make oath that the whole or any part thereof is not justly due, or that he has a counter demand, all of which he shall particularly set forth by affidavit, then the defendant shall only pay the installment required of what he admits to be due, and the justice shall proceed to try the matters in dispute between the parties; and at the expiration of twelve months the defendant shall be allowed time to plead only upon payment of one-fifth of the amount admitted to be due, and whatever the justice may have found him indebted over and above the same: *Provided*, That should the defendant fail to pay or confess judgment for the first or any subsequent installment, then and in that case, the plaintiff shall be entitled to proceed to judgment and execution for such installment: *Provided further*, That by consent of the plaintiff the defendant may at any time confess judgment for a stipulated sum in full and final discharge of all further demand or liability upon such claim. That all executions on judments in actions of debt, covenant, assumpsit or account which have been, or shall be issued on judgments heretofore obtained before any magistrate, shall be levied on the property of the defendant and returned without sale; at the expiration of twelve months from such return execution on all such judgments shall issue for only one-tenth of the amount then due; at the expiration of twelve months from that time for one-fifth of the residue; at the expiration of twelve months more for one-half of the residue, and at the expiration of twelve months more for the balance of the debt."

SEC. 5. *Be it further ordained*, That Section 17 of the above entitled ordinance be amended to read as follows: "Sec. 17. That the provisions of this ordinance shall not be construed to extend to any debts or demands contracted or penalties incurred since the first day of May, A. D. 1865, or which may hereafter be contracted or incurred, except actions founded on any bond, promissory note, bill of exchange, or any other instrument of writing, or parol promise made since first May, 1865, in renewal of, or substitution for, a contract made prior to first of May, 1865, to the full amount of the principal and interest of a debt existing prior to said day, and without other consideration than such pre-existent debt; and except also, actions, suits, or process to revive, continue or enforce any judgment heretofore recovered upon any such bond, promissory note, bill of exchange or other instruments of writing or parol promise as is hereinbefore mentioned."

SEC. 6. *Be it further ordained*, That this ordinance shall be in force from and after its ratification.

The substitute of Mr. Graham, and also the substitute of Mr. Jones, of Washington, were submitted.

The Chair decided the substitute of Mr. Graham's in order.

It was discussed at length.

The question was called,

And the yeas and nays were demanded.

The substitute was lost by the following vote, yeas 18, nays 84.

Those who voted in affirmative are:

Messrs. Baker, Barnes, Bradley, Ellis, Eppes, Glover, Graham of Orange, Hare, Hodnett, Hollowell, Holt, Hyman, King of Lenoir, Lennon, Marshall, McCubbins, Merritt and Sanderlin—18.

Those who voted in the negative are:

Messrs. Abbott, Andrews, Aydlott, Blume, Bryan, Carey, Carter, Candler, Cherry, Chillson, Colgrove, Congleton, Cox, Dowd, Duckworth, Etheridge, Fisher, Forkner, Franklin, French of Rockingham, Fullings, Gahagan, George, Graham of Montgomery, Grant of Wayne, Grant of Northampton, Gully, Gunter, Harris of Wake, Harris of Franklin, Hay, Hayes of Robeson, Heaton, Highsmith, Hobbs, Hoffler, Hood, Ing, Jones of Caldwell, Jones of Washington, King of Lincoln, Laflin, Lee, Legg, Logan, Long, Mann, May, Mayo, McDonald of Chatham, McDonald of Moore, Moore, Morton, Mullican, Murphy, Nance, Newsom, Nicholson, Patrick, Parker, Parks, Petree, Peterson, Pierson, Pool, Ragland, Ray, Read, Renfrow, Rhodes, Rich, Rodman, Rose, Smith, Stilwell, Sweet, Taylor, Teague, Tourgee, Trogden, Tucker, Turner, Watts, Welker and Williams of Wake—84.

The substitute of Mr. Jones being declared in order by the President, was discussed and voted on.

The yeas and nays were demanded, and resulted yeas 21, nays 69.

Those who voted in the affirmative are:

Messrs. Baker, Barnes, Candler, Cox, French of Rockingham, Fullings, Glover, Grant of Wayne, Grant of Northampton, Hare, Hodnett, Hollowell, Hyman, Ing, Jones of Washington, King of Lincoln, King of Lenoir, Mullican, Nicholson, Parker, Pool, Renfrow, Rose, Teague, Trogden and Williams of Wake—27.

Those who voted in the negative are:

Messrs. Abbott, Andrews, Aydlott, Blume, Bradley, Bryan, Carey, Carter, Chillson, Congleton, Dickey, Dowd, Duckworth, Eppes, Etheridge, Forkner, Franklin, French of Bladen, Gahagan, Galloway, George, Graham of Montgomery, Gully, Gunter, Hay, Hayes of Robeson, Hayes of Halifax, Heaton, Hobbs, Hoffler, Jones of Caldwell, Kinney, Laflin,

Lee, Legg, Lennon, Logan, Long, Mann, May, Mayo, McCubbins, Merritt, McDonald of Chatham, McDonald of Moore, Moore, Morton, Murphy, Nance, Newsom, Patrick, Parks, Peterson, Pierson, Ragland, Read, Rhodes, Rich, Rodman, Sanderlin, Smith, Stilwell, Sweet, Taylor, Tourgee, Tucker, Turner, Watts and Welker—69.

Mr. Welker withdrew his amendment.

Mr. Tourgee offered the following amendment:

"To stay final process on all debts since May, 1865, except for laborers wages and fraud."

The yeas and nays were demanded.

And the amendment was lost by the following vote, yeas 39, nays 67:

Those who voted in the affirmative are:

Messrs. Abbott, Andrews, Blume, Bradly, Bryan, Carey, Carter, Candler, Chillson, Dickey, Franklin, George, Graham of Montgomery, Gully, Gunter, Harris of Wake, Hay, Hoffler, Legg, Lennon, Long, Mann, May, Merritt, McDonald of Chatham, McDonald of Moore, Moore, Morton, Murphy, Nance, Newsom, Patrick, Peterson, Ragland, Smith, Tourgee, Turner, Welker and Williams of Wake—39.

Those who voted in the negative are:

Messrs. Aydlott, Baker, Barnes, Cherry, Colgrove, Congleton, Cox, Dowd, Duckworth, Ellis, Eppes, Etheridge, Fisher, Forkner, French of Bladen, French of Rockingham, Fullings, Gahagan, Galloway, Glover, Grant of Wayne, Grant of Northampton, Hall, Harris of Franklin, Hayes of Robeson, Hayes of Halifax, Heaton, Highsmith, Hobbs, Hodnett, Hollowell, Hood, Hyman, Ing, Jones of Caldwell, Jones of Washington, King of Lincoln, King of Lenoir, Kinney, Laflin, Lee, Logan, Mayo, Marshall, McCubbins, Mullican, Nicholson, Parker, Parks, Petree, Pierson, Pool, Ray, Read, Renfrow, Rhodes, Rodman, Rose, Sanderlin, Stilwell, Sweet, Taylor, Teague, Trogden, Tucker, Watts and Williamson—67.

Mr. Pool offered and amendment to strike out the second "of," in the third line, and insert "to issue or enforce executions in;" also in tenth line, strike out "of" and insert "in," and strike out "or process."

The amendment was not sustained.

Mr. Tourgee moved to lay the ordinance of Mr. Rodman on the table.

The yeas and nays were demanded,

And the motion was lost by the following vote, yeas 44, nay 57.

Those who voted in the affirmative are:

Messrs. Andrews, Baker, Barnes, Blume, Candler, Cherry, Congleton, Cox, Dowd, Duckworth, Ellis, Eppes, French of Rockingham, Fullings, Gahagan, Grant of Northampton, Gully, Hayes of Robeson, Hodnett, Hoffler, Hollowell, Ing, King of Lenoir, Logan, May, Marshall, Moore, Mullican, Murphy, Nicholson, Parker, Parks, Peterson, Pool, Ray, Renfrow, Rhodes, Rose, Teague, Tourgee, Trogden, Welker and Williams of Wake—44.

Those who voted in the negative are:

Messrs. Abbott, Aydlott, Bradley, Bryan, Carter, Chillson, Colgrove, Etheridge, Fisher, Forkner, Franklin, Galloway, George, Glover, Graham of Montgomery, Grant of Wayne, Gunter, Harris of Wake, Hayes of Halifax, Heaton, Highsmith, Hobbs, Hood, Hyman, Jones of Caldwell, King of Lincoln, Kinney, Laflin, Lee, Legg, Lennon, Long, Mann, Mayo, McCubbins, Merritt, McDonald of Chatham, McDonald of Moore, Morton, Nance, Newsom, Patrick, Petree, Pierson, Ragland, Read, Rich, Rodman, Sanderlin, Smith, Stillwell, Sweet, Taylor, Tucker, Turner, Watts and Williamson—57.

The original ordinance was then placed upon its final passage.

The question was called and the yeas and nays demanded.

The ordinance was adopted by the following vote, yeas 56, nays 39:

Those who voted in the affirmitive are:

Messrs. Abbott, Aydlott, Barnes, Blume, Bradley, Bryan, Carey, Colgrove, Etheridge, Fisher, Forkner, Franklin, French of Bladen, Galloway, George, Graham of Montgomery, Grant of Wayne, Gully, Gunter, Hall, Harris of Wake, Heaton, Highsmith, Hobbs, Jones of Caldwell, Kinney, Legg, Lennon, Long, Mann, Mayo, Marshall, McCubbins, Merritt, McDonald of Chatham, McDonald of Moore, Moore, Morton, Mullican, Nance, Newsom, Patrick, Pierson, Ragland, Read, Rich, Rodman, Sanderlin, Smith, Stilwell, Sweet, Taylor, Tucker, Turner, Watts and Williamson—56.

Those who voted in the negative are:

Messrs. Andrews, Baker, Candler, Cherry, Congleton, Dowd, Duckworth, Ellis, Eppes, French of Rockingham, Fulkings, Gahagan, Glover, Grant of Northampton, Hayes of Robeson, Hayes of Halifax, Hoffler, Hollowell, Hood, Hyman, Ing, Jones of Washington, King of Lenoir, Lee, Logan, May, Nicholson, Parker, Parks, Peterson, Pool, Ray, Renfrow, Rhodes, Rose, Teague, Trogden, Welker and Williams of Wake—39.

Mr. King, of Lincoln, presented a resolution asking Congress to amend the Bankrupt law.

Referred to the Committee on the Judicial Department.

At the request of a delegate, the Hall was granted to the Conservative Convention for the evening.

On motion of Mr. Heaton, the report of the Committee on Governor and other necessary State Executive officers, as reported by the Committee of the Whole, was taken up.

The first section was read.

Mr. Heaton moved to strike out the word "two" and insert "three."

Pending which, the House adjourned.

---

## THURSDAY, February 6th, 1868.

The Convention was called to order at 10 o'clock, by the President.

Prayer by the Rev. H. T. Hudson.

The President announced a quorum.

The Journal of Wednesday was read and adopted.

Mr. Tourgee arose to a question of privilege, and desired the following protest entered on the Journal:

Whereas, We consider the ordinance entitled "an ordinance for the relief of debtors," passed by a vote of this Convention yesterday, as entirely inadequate to the wants of the people, invidious and unjust in its distinctions between debtors, affording no relief for the unfortunate debtors whose old debts have been renewed since May, 1865, and others whose present condition is equally deplorable and equally the result of war; and that it also opens the door to unlimited fraud, we respectfully protest against this action of the Convention, and ask that this protest be spread upon the Journal.

(Signed,) A. W. TOURGEE,
JAS. A. MOORE,
G. W. WELKER,
J. W. PETERSON,
ABRAHAM CONGLETON,
JOHN McDONALD,
JACOB ING.

Mr. Ray presented a petition for divorce.

Referred to the Committee on the Judicial Department.

The Committee on Finance, to whom was referred the resolution of Mr. French, of Chowan, relative to negotiating a loan to pay mileage, respectfully report that it is inexpedient to act upon the resolution, and ask to be discharged from the further consideration thereof.

JOS. C. ABBOTT, *Chairman.*

On motion the report was accepted.

The Committee on Finance, to whom was referred the resolution of Mr. Williamson, asking Congress for the loan of money, respectfully report back the resolution without recommendation; and ask to be discharged from the further consideration of the subject.

JOS. C. ABBOTT, *Chairman.*

On motion the report was accepted.

The Committee on Finance, to whom was referred the ordinance of Mr. Welker, relative to the liability of Banking institutions, report that it is inexpedient to act upon the ordi nance, as it will be a proper subject for the Legislature, and ask to be discharged from the further consideration thereof.

JOS. C. ABBOTT, *Chairman.*

On motion, the report was accepted.

The Committee report that in accordadce with the resolution of Mr. Rich, instructing the Committee to negotiate a loan of five hundred dollars for contintent expenses, they have taken the necessary steps to comply with the same.

JOS. C. ABBOTT, *Chairman.*

On motion, the report was adopted.

The Committee on Finance reported the following ordinance, which,

On motion, was adopted:

SECTION 1. *Be it ordained by the people of North-Carolina, in Convention assembled,* That for the purpose of raising moneys to pay the expenses of this Convention, according to the act of Congress in such case made and provided, a tax of one-twentieth of one per cent, shall be levied on the land in North-Carolina, according to the valuation in the year 1860, subject to such changes therein as have been since made by law, and on the personal property within said State, according to the valuation thereof to be made in the year 1868. This tax shall be collected, paid and accounted for at the Treasury of the State, at the time when, and in the same manner as other State taxes are, by law, required to be. The collecting officer shall be subject to the same penalties for failure to collect, pay and account for the taxes hereby levied, as they now are for such failure in respect to other taxes.

SEC. 2. *Be it further ordained,* That the said collecting officer shall receive the like compensation for the collection of the tax hereby levied as for the collection of other taxes.

SEC. 3. *Be it further ordained,* That this ordinance shall be in force from and after its passage.

The yeas and nays being demanded, resulted yeas 92, nays 13.

Those who voted in the affirmitive are:

Messrs. Abbott, Andrews, Ashley, Aydlott, Baker, Barnes, Blume, Bradley, Bryan, Carey, Carter, Candler, Cherry, Chilson, Colgrove, Congleton, Dickey, Duckworth, Eppes, Etheridge, Fisher, Forkner, Franklin, French of Bladen, French of Rockingham, French of Chowan, Fullings, Gahagan, Galloway, Garland, George, Graham of Montgomery, Grant of Wayne, Grant of Northampton, Gully, Gunter, Harris of Wake, Harris of Franklin, Hayes of Robeson Hayes of Halifax, Heaton, Highsmith, Hobbs, Hoffler, Hollowell, Hood, Hyman, Ing, Jones of Caldwell, Jones of Washington, King of Lincoln, King of Lenoir, Kinney, Laflin, Lee, Legg, Logan, Long, Mann, May, Mayo, Marshall, McCubbins, McDonald of Chatham, McDonald of Moore, Morton, Mullican, Murphy, Nance, Nicholson, Patrick, Parker, Parks, Petree, Pierson, Pool, Ragland, Ray, Read, Renfrow, Rhodes, Rich, Rodman, Rose, Smith, Stilwell, Taylor, Teague, Tucker, Watts, Williams of Wake and Williamson—92.

Those who voted in the negative are :

Messrs. Burham, Ellis, Graham of Orange, Hall, Holt, Lennon, Merritt, Moore, Peterson, Sanderlin, Tourgee, Turner and Welker—13.

Mr. E. W. Jones, of Washington, introduced an ordinance amending section two of an act of the Legislature of 1866-67, entitled "An act to incorporate the town of Calumbia, in the County of Tyrrell."

Referred to the Committee on Towns and Counties.

The report of the Committee on Corporations was received and ordered to be printed.

Mr. King, of Lenoir, introduced the following resolution :

*Resolved*, That the Rule of Order, No. 16, be suspended, and that all reports of Committees embracing propositions pertaining to the formation of a Constitution be taken up each day at 12 o'clock, and considered in Convention for its final action, instead of being referred to the Committee of the Whole.

On motion, the rules were suspended and the resolution adopted.

Mr. Ragland introduced the following resolution for relief :

*Resolved*, That the Committee appointed to confer with General Canby, be authorized to request him to stay the ruinous executions on new debts contracted since the 1st of May, 1865, so that property may not be sacrificed for less than its intrinsic value, and make an order to that effect, for the temporary relief of the people.

On motion, the rules were suspended.

Mr. Hood moved to postpone indefinitely.

The yeas and nays were demanded and resulted, yeas 40, nays 60:

Those who voted in the affirmative are:

Messrs. Baker, Candler, Chillson, Duckworth, Durham, Ellis, Etheridge, French of Bladen, French of Chowan, Fullings, Gahagan, Garland, Graham of Orange, Grant of Wayne, Grant of Northampton, Hall, Hayes of Robeson, Hayes of Halifax, Hodnett, Hollowell, Hood, Hyman, Jones of Washington, Lennon, Logan, Long, Marshall, McCubbins, Merritt, Murphy, Nicholson, Parker, Petree, Ray, Renfrow, Rhodes, Rose, Sanderlin, Tucker and Williams of Wake—40.

Those who voted in the negative are:

Messrs. Abbott, Andrews, Ashley, Aydlott, Barnes, Blume, Bradley, Bryan, Carey, Carter, Cherry, Colgrove, Congleton, Dickey, Eppes, Fisher, Forkner, Franklin, French of Rockingham, Galloway, George, Graham of Montgomery, Gully, Gunter, Harris of Wake, Harris of Franklin, Heaton, Highsmith, Hobbs, Hoffler, Ing, Jones of Caldwell, King of Lincoln, King of Lenoir, Kinney, Laflin, Lee, Legg, Mann, May, Mayo, McDonald of Chatham, McDonald of Moore, Moore, Morton, Mullican, Nance, Patrick, Pool, Ragland, Rich, Rodman, Stilwell, Taylor, Teague, Tourgee, Turner, Watts, Welker and Williamson.—60.

The resolution was not postponed.

Put on its passsage and adopted.

Mr. Heaton introduced the following resolution:

*Resolved*, That the President of this Convention is hereby authorized to appoint a standing Committee of three on revision and arrangement.

On motion the rules were suspended and the resolution adopted.

Mr. Turner introduced an ordinance in relation to the validity of acts of this Convention.

Lies over under the rules.

Leave of absence was granted to the following gentlemen :

Mr. Sanderlin, of Curituck for 5 days.

Mr. Galloway from Friday 12 o'clock until Monday, A. M.

Mr. Patrick until Wednesday.

Mr. Williamson until Tuesday.

Mr. Aydlott until Tuesday,

Mr. Carter for 5 days.

Mr. Peterson until Monday next.

### UNFINISHED BUSINESS.

Mr. King's resolution respecting the action of the Convention was withdrawn.

Mr. Mullican's ordinance declaring that honesty and good faith, and the Constitution of the United States requires that contracts shall be held sacred, was taken up, and,

On motion, was indefinitely postponed.

The following resolution of Mr. King was adopted :

*Resolved*, That rule 36 of the rules of order, of this Convention be amended, by striking out the word "suspended" in line 1st and 2d of said rule, and also by striking out all of rule 36 after the word "session" in 5th line of said rule.

The resolution of Mr. Gunter instructing the Committee on Relief to report an ordinance declaring void certain contracts, &c., was taken up, and referred to the Committee on Relief.

The following resolution of Mr. Read was taken up, and adopted :

*Resolved*, That on to-morrow and thence forward the Convention hold two sessions daily beginning respectively at 10 o'clock, A. M., and 4 o'clock, P. M.

Mr. Parker's resolution respecting the sessions of the Convention was taken up, and,

On motion was tabled.

Mr. Ellis's resolution in reference to the Reconstruction Acts was taken up, and,

On motion, was tabled.

The report of the Committee on Suffrage was made the special order for Monday next at 12 o'clock.

The hour of 12 having arrived the house proceeded to take up the report of the Committee on a Governor and other necessary State Executive officers, as reported on by the Committee of the Whole.

Section 1st was read.

Mr. Heaton moved to strike out the word "two" and insert "three."

Mr. Jones, of Washington, moved to amend by striking out the word "two" and inserting the word "four."

The yeas and nayes were demanded and resulted yeas 61, nays 37.

Those who voted in the affirmative are:

Messrs. Andrews, Ashley, Blume, Bryan, Carey, Carter, Cherry, Chillson, Colgrove, Congleton, Dickey, Duckworth, Eppes, Etheridge, Fisher, Franklin, French of Bladen, French of Rockingham, French of Chowan, Fullings, Gahagan, Galloway, Garland, Graham of Montgomery, Grant of Northampton, Gully, Harris of Wake, Harris of Franklin, Hayes of Robeson, Hayes of Halifax, Heaton, Highsmith, Hood, Hyman, Ing, Jones of Washington, Kinney, Laflin, Lee, Legg, Logan, Mann, May, Mayo, Moore, Murphy, Nance, Nicholson, Patrick, Parker, Parks, Pierson, Pool, Ragland, Renfrow, Rhodes, Rodman, Rose, Sweet, Taylor, Tourgee, and Williamson—61.

Those who voted in the negative are:

Messrs. Aydlott, Barnes, Bradley, Cox, Ellis, Forkner, George, Gunter, Hall, Hobbs, Hodnett, Hoffler, Hollowell, Jones of Caldwell, King of Lincoln, King of Lenoir, Long, Marshall, McCubbins, Merritt, McDonald of Chatham, McDonald, of Moore, Morton, Mullican, Newsom, Petree, Ray, Read, Sanderlin, Smith, Stilwell, Teague Trogden Tucker, Turner, Welker, and Williams of Wake—37.

The section as amended was adopted.

Section 2d was taken up.

Mr. Tourgee moved to amend by striking out the word "six" and inserting "eight," which amendment was adopted.

The section as amended was then adopted.

Section 3d was read and adopted.

Section 4th was read.

Mr. Tourgee moved to amend by striking out the word "execute" and inserting the word "perform."

The amendment was adopted.

Mr. Forkner moved to amend by inserting after the word "Constitution" the words "and laws."

The amendment was adopted.

Mr. Tourgee moved to amend by striking out all after the word "elected."

The amendment was adopted.

The section as amended was adopted.

Sections, 5th, 6th, 7th, 8th, 9th, 10th, 11th, 12th, 13th, 14th, 15th, 16th and 17th, were taken up separately and adopted as read.

On motion of Mr. Heaton, the report as amended was ordered to be engrossed and printed for a final reading on Friday at 12 oclock.

The report of the Committee on Militia as reported by the Committee of the Whole was taken up.

Sections 1st, 2d, 3d, and 4th were read and adopted.

On motion of Mr. Heaton, the report was ordered to be printed, and made as special order for final reading and passage, on Friday at 12 o'clock, M.

The petition of divorce of Ann Underdue, presented by Mr. Harris, of Wake, was taken up, and,

On motion, was referred to a committee of three to be appointed by the Chair.

The resolution introduced by Mr. Harris, of Wake, requiring immediate action on the Constitution, and a bill for the relief of the people, was taken up, and,

On motion, was laid on the table.

The resolution introduced by Mr. Harris, of Wake, providing means of Relief, was,

On motion, indefinitely postponed.

On motion the report of the Committee on a Preamblé and Bill of Rights was made a special order for Saturday at 12 o'clock, M.

The resolution of Mr. Congleton, in reference to immediate action on the Constitution and Bill of Rights, was,

On motion, laid on the table.

The resolution of Mr. Teague, "instructing the Committee of three to enquire of General Canby how far he will recognize Legislation by the Convention," was,

On motion, laid on the table.

The following Ordinance of Mr. Duckworth was adopted:

*Be it ordained by the people of North-Carolina in Convention assembled*, That William D. Justus, Sheriff of Henderson County, be allowed two years from the first day of January 1868, to collect arrears of taxes due for the year 1866.

On motion the house adjourned.

---

## FRIDAY, February 7th, 1868.

The Convention was called to order at 10 o'clock, by the President.

Prayer by the Rev. J. W. Hood.

The President announced a quorum.

The Journal of Thursday was read and approved.

Leave of absence was granted,

Mr. Dowd until Tuesday next.

Mr. Rose until Monday next.

Mr. Read until Wednesday next.

Mr. Rodman presented a petition of divorce from John Roberts.

Referred to the Committee on the Judicial Department.

On motion, the report of the Committee on Relief, was recommitted to that Committee.

The following report of the Committee on relief from disabilty, was received:

We, the Committee appointed in accordance with a resolution of this Convention, to gather such information as will enable us to report a list of persons who may be presented to Congress to be relieved from political disability, most respectfully report the following, viz:

That the delegates be invited to send to the Chairman of the Committee the names of persons who are in hearty accord with the Reconstruction Acts of Congress, whom they consider worthy of recommendation from disability, with a brief history of each person thus recommended, since May, 1861.

J. W. HOOD,
W. NICHOLSON,
G. W. GAHAGAN,
R. W. KING,
C. C. JONES,
A. W. TOURGEE,
S. FORKNER.

On motion, the report was accepted.

Mr. Durham moved to lay the report on the table, and demanded the yeas and nays.

The motion was lost by the following vote, yeas 11, nays 88:

Those who voted in the affirmitive are:

Messrs. Durham, Ellis, Etheridge, Graham of Orange, Hare, Hodnett, Hoffler, Holt, Lennon, Marshall and Merritt—11.

Those who voted in the negative are:

Messrs. Abbott, Ashley, Aydlott, Barnes, Blume, Bradley, Bryan, Carey, Candler, Chilson, Colgrove, Congleton, Cox, Daniel, Dickey, Duckworth, Eppes, Forkner, Franklin, French of Bladen, French of Rockingham, French of Chowan, Fullings, Gahagan, Garland, George, Glover, Graham of Montgomery, Grant of Wayne, Grant of Northampton, Gunter, Harris of Wake, Harris of Franklin, Hayes of Robeson, Hayes of Halifax, Heaton, Highsmith, Hobbs, Hollowell, Hood, Hyman, Ing, Jones of Caldwell, Jones of Washington, King of Lincoln, King of Lenoir, Kinney, Laflin, Lee, Legg, Logan, Long, Mann,

May, Mayo, McDonald of Chatham, McDonald of Moore, Moore, Morton, Mullican, Murphy, Nance, Newsom, Nicholson, Parker, Parks, Petree, Pierson, Pool, Ragland, Ray, Renfrow, Rhodes, Rodman, Rose, Smith, Stilly, Stilwell, Sweet, Taylor, Teague, Tourgee, Trogden, Tucker, Turner, Watts, Welker and Williams of Wake—88.

Mr. Hood moved the adoption of the report and called the previous question.

The yeas and and nays were demanded, and the report was adopted by the following vote, yeas 86, nays 9:

Those who voted in affirmative are:

Messrs. Abbott, Andrews, Ashley, Aydlott, Barnes, Blume, Bradley, Bryan, Carey, Candler, Chillson, Colgrove, Congleton, Cox, Dickey, Duckworth, Eppes, Forkner, Franklin, French of Rockingham, French of Chowan, Fullings, Gahagan, Garland, George, Glover, Graham of Montgomery, Grant of Wayne, Grant of Northampton, Gunter, Harris of Wake, Harris of Franklin, Hayes of Robeson, Hayes of Halifax, Heaton, Highsmith, Hobbs, Hollowell, Hood, Hyman, Ing, Jones of Caldwell, Jones of Washington, King of Lenoir, Kinney, Laflin, Lee, Legg, Logan, Long, Mann, May, Mayo, McDonald of Chatham, McDonald of Moore, Moore, Morton, Mullican, Murphy, Nance, Newsom, Nicholson, Parker, Parks, Petree, Pierson, Pool, Ragland, Ray, Read, Renfrow, Rhodes, Rodman, Rose, Smith, Stilly, Stilwell, Sweet, Taylor, Teague, Tourgee, Trogden, Tucker, Watts, Welker and Williams of Wake—86.

Those who voted in the negative are:

Messrs. Durham, Etheridge, Graham of Orange, Hall, Hare, Hodnett, Hoffler, Holt, and Merritt—9.

Mr. Morton introduced the following resolution:

*Resolved*, That the President of this Convention order a copy of the relief bill to be sent to the sheriffs, the County and Superior Court Clerks, of each County in the State.

On motion, the rules were suspended, and the resolution adopted.

On motion, the report of the Committee on Finance, to whom was referred the ordinance of Mr. Welker regarding the liabilities of Banks, was considered and the ordinance was placed on the Calendar.

On motion, the vote taken yesterday on the resolution of Mr. Read in regard to the sessions of this Convention, was reconsidered.

Mr. Harris, of Wake, moved that the Convention meet at 10 o'clock, A. M., and 7½ P. M., which motion was not sustained.

The yeas and nays were demanded, and resulted yeas 42, nays 58.

Those who voted in the affirmative are:

Messrs. Andrews, Ashley, Aydlott, Barnes, Blume, Bryan, Chillson, Congleton, Duckworth, Forkner, Franklin, Garland, George, Graham of Montgomery, Graham of Orange, Grant of Wayne, Grant of Northampton, Gunter, Harris of Wake, Hayes of Halifax, Hood, Hyman, Jones of Washington, King of Lincoln, Long, Mann, McCubbins, McDonald of Chatham, McDonald of Moore, Moore, Nicholson, Parker, Parks, Petree, Ragland, Read, Smith, Stilly, Teague, Tourgee, Welker and Williamsof Wake—42.

Those who voted in the negative are:

Messrs. Abbott, Bradley, Candler, Cherry, Cox, Daniel, Dickey, Durham, Ellis, Eppes, Etheridge, Fisher, French of Bladen, French of Rockingham, French of Chowan, Fullings, Gahagan, Glover, Hall, Hare, Hayes of Robeson, Heaton, Highsmith, Hobbs, Hodnett, Hoffler, Hollowell, Holt, Ing, Jones of Caldwell, King of Lenoir, Kinney, Laflin, Lee, Legg, Lennon, Logan, May, Mayo, Marshall, Merritt, Mullican, Murphy, Newsom, Pierson, Pool, Ray, Renfrow, Rhodes, Rodman, Rose, Stilwell, Sweet, Taylor, Trogden, Tucker, Turner and Watts—38.

Mr. Pool introduced an ordinance amending an act of the General Assembly.

Referred to the Committee on Relief.

The resolution of Mr. Congleton, asking Congress for a loan of money, was taken up and discussed.

Mr. Watts moved to strike out the words, " of ten millions

of dollars or what sum," and strike out "amount," and insert "loan."

The following Committee was appointed to report on a petition of divorce presented by Mr. Harris, of Wake:

Messrs. Harris of Wake, Merritt and Fisher.

The report of the Committee on Legislature was accepted, and ordered to be printed.

The hour of 12 having arrived, the House proceeded to the final reading and passage of the following report of the Committee on a Governor and other necessary State Executive Officers.

## EXECUTIVE DEPARTMENT.

SECTION 1. The Executive Department shall consist of a Governor, in whom shall be vested the supreme executive power of the State, a Lieutenant Governor, a Secretary of State, an Auditor, a Treasurer, a Superintendent of Public Works, a Superintendent of Public Instruction, and an Attorney General, who shall be elected for a term of four years by the qualified electors of the State, at the same times and places, and in the same manner, as members of the General Assembly are elected. Their term of office shall commence on the first day of January next after their election, and continue until their successors are elected and qualified: *Provided*, That the officers first elected shall assume the duties of their office ten days after the approval of the Constitution by the Congress of the United States, and shall hold their offices for four years, from and after the first day of January, 1869.

SEC. 2. No person shall be eligible as Governor or Lieutenant Governor, unless he shall have attained the age of thirty years, shall have been a citizen of the United States for five years, and shall have been a resident of this State for two years, next before the day of election; nor shall the person elected to either of these two offices be eligible to the same more than four years in any term of eight years, unless the office shall have been cast upon him as Lieutenant Governor or President of the Senate.

SEC. 3. The return of every election for officers of the Executive Department shall be sealed up and transmitted to the seat of Government by the returning officers, directed to the Speaker of the House of Commons, who shall open and publish the same in the presence of a majority of the members of both Houses of the General Assembly. The persons having the highest number of votes respectively, shall be declared duly elected; but if two or more be equal and highest in votes for the same office, then one of them shall be chosen by joint ballot of both Houses of the General Assembly. Contested elections shall be determined by a joint ballot of both Houses of the General Assembly, in such manner as shall be prescribed by law.

SEC. 4. The Governor, before entering upon the duties of his office, shall, in the presence of the members of both branches of the General Assembly, or before any Justice of the Supreme Court, take an oath or affirmation, that he will support the Constitution and laws of the United States, and of the State of North-Carolina; that he will faithfully perform the duties appertaining to the office of Governor, to which he has been elected.

SEC. 5. The Governor shall reside at the seat of Government of this State, and shall, from time to time, give the General Assembly information of the affairs of the State, and recommend to their consideration such measures as he shall deem expedient.

SEC. 6. The Governor shall have power to grant reprieves, commutations and pardons, after conviction, for all offences, (except in cases of impeachment,) upon such conditions as he may think proper, subject to such regulations as may be provided by law relative to the manner of applying for pardons. He shall annually communicate to the General Assembly each case of reprieve, commutation or pardon granted, stating the name of the convict, the crime for which he was convicted, the sentence and its date, and the date of commutation, pardon or reprieve, and the reasons therefor.

SEC. 7. The officers of the Executive Department and of the public institutions of the State, shall, at least five days previous to each regular session of the General Assembly, severally report to the Governor, who shall transmit such reports, with his message, to the General Assembly; and the Governor may, at any time, require information in writing, from the officers of the Executive Department, upon any subject relating to the duties of their respective offices, and shall take care that the laws be faithfully executed.

SEC. 8. The Governor shall be Commander-in-Chief of the militia of the State, except when they shall be called into the service of the United States.

SEC. 9. The Governor shall have power, on extraordinary occasions, by and with the advice of the Council of State, to convene the General Assembly in extra session, by his proclamation, stating therein the purpose or purposes for which they are thus convened.

SEC. 10. The Governor shall nominate, and, by and with the advice and consent of a majority of the Senators elect, appoint all officers whose offices are established by this constitution, or which may be created by law, and whose appointments are not otherwise provided for, and no such officer shall be appointed or elected by the General Assembly.

SEC. 11. The Lieutenant-Governor shall, by virtue of his office, be President of the Senate, but shall have no vote unless the Senate be equally divided. He shall, whilst acting as President of the Senate, receive for his services the same pay which shall, for the same period, be allowed the Speaker of the House of Commons, and he shall receive no other compensation except when he is acting as Governor.

SEC. 12. In case of the impeachment of the Governor, his failure to qualify, his absence from the State, his inability to discharge the duties of his office, or in case the office of Governor shall, in anywise become vacant, the powers, duties, and emoluments of the office shall devolve upon the Lieutenant-Governor until the disabilities shall cease, or a new Governor shall be elected and qualified. In every case in which the Lieutenant-Governor shall be unable to preside over the Senate, the Senators shall elect one of their own number President of their body; and the powers, duties and emoluments of the office of Governor shall devolve upon him, whenever the Lieutenant-Governor shall, for any reason be prevented from discharging the duties of such office as above provided, and he shall continue as acting Governor until the disabilities be removed or a new Governor or Lieutenant-Governor shall be elected and qualified. Whenever, during a recess of the General Assembly, it shall become necessary for a President of the Senate to administer the government, the Secretary of State shall convene the Senate, that they may elect such President.

SEC. 13. The respective duties of the Secretary of State, Auditor, Treasurer, Superintendent of Public Works, Superintendent of Public Instruction and Attorney General shall be prescribed by law. If the office of any of said officers shall be vacated by death, resignation, or otherwise, it shall be the duty of the Governor to appoint another until the disabilities be removed, or a successor be elected and qualified. Every such vacancy shall be filled by election at the first general election that occurs more than thirty days after the vacancy has taken place, and the person chosen shall hold the office for the remainder of the unexpired term fixed in the first section of this article.

SEC. 14. The Secretary of State, Auditor, Treasurer, Superintendent of Public Works, and Superintendent of Public Instructions, shall constitute, *ex officio*, the Council of State, who shall advise the Governor in the execution of his office, and three of whom shall constitute a quorum; their advice and proceedings, in this capacity, shall be entered in a journal, to be kept for this purpose exclusively, and signed by the members present, against any part of which any member may enter his dissent, and such journal shall be placed before the General Assembly when called for by either House. The Attorney General shall be *ex officio*, the legal adviser of the Executive Department.

SEC. 15. The officers mentioned in this article shall, at stated periods, receive for their services a compensation, to be established by law, which shall neither be increased nor diminished during the time for which they shall have been elected; and the said officers shall receive no other emolument or allowance whatever.

SEC. 16. There shall be a seal of the State, which shall be kept by the Governor, and used by him, as occasion may require, and shall be called "The Great Seal of the State of North-Carolina." All grants and commissions shall be issued in the name, and by the authority of the State of North-Carolina, sealed with "The Great Seal of State," signed by the Governor, and countersigned by the Secretary of State.

SEC. 17. There shall be established in the office of Secretary of State a Bureau of Statistics, of Agriculture and of Immigration, under such regulations as the General Assembly may provide.

Section 1st was read.

Mr. Graham moved to amend by striking out "Lieutenant-Governor, Superintendent of Public Works, Superintendent of Public Instruction and Attorney General."

The yeas and nays were demanded, and the amendment was lost by the following vote, yeas 13, nays 86:

Those who voted in the affirmative are:

Messrs. Durham, Ellis, Etheridge, Graham of Orange, Hall, Hare, Hodnett, Holt, Lennon, Marshall, McCubbins, Merritt and Newsom—13.

Those who voted in the negative are:

Messrs. Abbott, Andrews, Ashley, Aydlott, Baker, Barnes, Blume, Bradly, Bryan, Carey, Candler, Cherry, Congleton, Cox, Daniel, Dickey, Duckworth, Eppes, Fisher, Forkner, Franklin, French of Bladen, French of Rockingham, French of Chowan, Fullings, Gahagan, Garland, George, Glover, Graham of Montgomery, Grant of Wayne, Grant of Northampton, Gunter, Harris of Wake, Harris of Franklin, Hayes of Robeson, Hayes of Halifax, Heaton, Highsmith, Hobbs, Hoffler, Hood, Hyman, Ing, Jones of Caldwell, Jones of Washington, King of Lincoln, King of Lenoir, Kinney, Laflin, Lee, Legg, Logan, Long, May, Mayo, McDonald of Chatham, McDonald of Moore, Moore, Morton, Mullican, Nance,

Nicholson, Parker, Petree, Pierson, Pool, Ragland, Ray, Read, Renfrow, Rhodes, Rose, Smith, Stilly, Stilwell, Sweet, Taylor, Teague, Tourgee, Trogden, Tucker, Turner, Watts, Welker and Williams of Wake—86.

Mr. Tourgee moved to amend by substituting the word "this" for the word "the" before Constitution on the 14th line.

The amendment was adopted.

Mr. Durham moved to strike out the word "four" and insert "two."

The motion was not sustained.

Mr. Ashley moved the adoption of the section as amended, and called the previous question.

The call was sustained.

The yeas and nays were demanded and resulted yeas 77 nays 26.

Those who voted in the affirmative are:

Messrs. Abbott, Andrews, Ashley, Aydlott, Barnes, Blume, Bryan, Carey, Cherry, Chillson, Congleton, Cox, Dickey, Duckworth, Eppes, Fisher, Forker, Franklin, French of Bladen, French of Rockingham, French of Chowan, Fullings, Gahagan, Garland, George, Glover, Graham of Montgomery, Grant of Wayne, Grant of Northampton, Harris of Franklin, Hayes of Robeson, Hayes of Halifax, Heaton, Highsmith, Hobbs, Hood, Hyman, Ing, Jones of Caldwell, Jones of Washington, King of Lenoir, Kinney, Laflin, Lee, Legg, Logan, Long, Mann, May, Mayo, McDonald of Moore, Moore, Mullican, Murphy, Nance, Nicholson, Parker, Parks, Pierson Pool, Ragland, Ray, Read, Renfrow, Rhodes, Rodman, Stilly, Stilwell, Sweet, Taylor, Teague, Tourgee, Trogden, Tucker, Turner, Watts and Welker—77.

Those who voted in the negative are:

Messrs. Bradley, Candler, Daniel, Durham, Ellis, Etheridge, Graham of Orange, Gunter, Hall, Hare, Hodnett, Hoffler, Hollowell, Holt, King of Lincoln, Lennon, Marshall, McCubbins, Merritt, McDonald of Chatham, Morton, Newsom, Petree, Rich, Smith, and Williams of Wake—26.

The section as amended was adopted.

Section 2d was read and put upon its final passage.

Mr. Durham offered to amend so as to require the Governor and Lieutenant Governor to have been a citizen of the United States twenty years, and a citizen of North-Carolina five years and shall be able to read and write.

The yeas and nays were demanded and the amendment was lost by the following vote.

Those who voted in the affirmative are:

Messrs. Bradley, Durham, Ellis, Graham of Orange, Hall, Hare, Hodnett, Hoffler, Hollowell, Holt, Lennon, Marshall, McCubbins and Merritt—14.

Those who voted in the negative are:

Messrs. Abbott, Andrews, Ashley, Aydlott, Barnes, Blume, Bryan, Carey, Candler, Cherry, Chilson, Congleton, Cox, Dickey, Duckworth, Eppes, Fisher, Franklin, French of Bladen, French of Rockingham, French of Chowan, Fullings, Gahagan, Garland, George, Graham of Montgomery, Grant, of Wayne, Grant of Northampton, Gunter,Harris of Franklin, Hayes, of Robeson, Hayes of Halifax, Heaton, Highsmith, Hobbs, Hood, Hyman, Ing, Jones of Caldwell, Jones of Washington, King of Lincoln, Kinney, Laflin, Logan Long, Mann, Mayo, McDonald of Chatham, McDonald of Moore, Moore, Morton, Mullican, Murphy, Nance, Newsom, Nicholson, Parker, Parks, Petree, Pierson, Pool, Ragland, Read, Renfrow, Rhodes, Rich, Rodman, Smith, Stilly, Stilwell, Sweet, Taylor, Teague, Tourgee, Trogden, Tucker, Turner, Watts, Welker and Williams of Wake—81.

Mr. Holt moved to amend by inserting "be required to have a free-hold in the State of the value of two thousand dollars."

The yeas and nays were demanded and the amendment was lost by the following vote:

Those who voted in the affirmitive are:

Messrs. Bradley, Daniel, Durham, Ellis, Graham of Orange, Hall, Hare, Hodnett, Hollowell, Holt, Lennon, Marshall, McCubbins, Merritt and Rich—15.

Those who voted in the negative are:

Messrs. Abbott, Andrews, Ashley, Blume, Bryan, Carey, Candler, Congleton, Cox, Dickey, Duckworth, Eppes, Etheridge, Forkner, Franklin, French of Bladen, French of Rockingham, French of Chowan, Fullings, Gahagan, Garland, George, Glover, Grant of Wayne, Grant ot Northampton, Gunter, Harris of Wake, Harris of Franklin, Hayes of Robeson, Hayes of Halifax, Heaton, Highsmith, Hobbs, Hotller, Hood, Hyman, Ing, Jones of Caldwell, Jones of Washington, King of Lincoln, Kinney, Laflin, Lee, Logan, Long, Mann, May, Mayo, McDonald of Chatham, McDonald of Moore, Moore, Mullican, Murphy, Nance, Newsom, Nicholson, Patrick, Parker, Parks, Petree, Pierson, Pool, Ragland, Ray, Read, Renfrow, Rhodes, Rodman, Smith, Stilly, Stilwell, Sweet, Taylor, Teague, Tourgee Trogden, Tucker, Turner, Watts, Welker and Williams of Wake—80.

Mr. Ashley moved the adoption of section 2d, as read and called the previous question which was sustained and the section was adopted.

Section 3d was read and adopted.

Section 4th was read.

Mr. Graham moved to strike out the word "laws" on the 5th line.

The yeas and nays was demanded, and the motion was lost by the following vote:

Those who voted in the affirmative are:

Messrs. Abbott, Ashley, Bradley, Cherry, Daniel, Durham, Ellis, Etheridge, Fisher, French of Bladen, George, Graham of Orange, Grant of Wayne, Hall, Hare, Harris of Wake, Harris of Franklin, Hayes of Halifax, Heaton, Highsmith, Hobbs, Hodnett, Hollowell, Holt, Jones of Caldwell, Jones of Washington, King of Lincoln, Laflin, Lennon, Logan, Marshall, Merritt, Moore, Parker, Pierson, Read, Rhodes, Rich, Rodman, Stilly, Sweet, and Taylor—42.

Those who voted in the negative are:

Messrs. Andrews, Barnes, Blume, Bryan, Carey, Candler, Chillson, Congleton, Cox, Dickey, Duckworth, Forkner, Franklin, French of Rockingham, French of Chowan, Fullings, Gahagan, Garland, Glover, Graham of Montgomery, Gunter, Hayes of Robeson, Hood, Hyman, Ing, Kinney

Long, Mann, May, Mayo, McCubbins, McDonald of Chatham, McDonald of Moore, Morton, Mullican, Murphy, Nance, Newsom, Nicholson, Parks, Petree, Pool, Ragland, Renfrow, Smith, Stillwell, Teague, Tourgee, Trogden, Tucker, Turner, Watts, Welker and Williams of Wake—54.

Sections 4th, 5th, 6th, 7th, 8th, 9th, and 10th were read and adopted.

Mr. Rich moved to insert a section relative to the veto power.

Mr. Ashley moved to lay the section on the table.

Mr. Andrews moved to adjourn.

The motion was not sustained.

Mr. Ashley renewed his motion, to lay on the table, which motion was sustained.

Section 11th was read.

Mr. Tourgee moved to amend by striking out "by virtue of his office."

The amendment was adopted.

The section as amended was adopted.

Section 12th was taken up.

Mr. Rodman moved to amend by striking out the words, "Impeachment of the Governor" on 1st and 2d lines, and insert "Conviction of the Governor on Impeachment."

The amendment was lost.

The section as read, was,

On motion, adopted.

The following Committee was appointed by the Chair, on Re-districting the State:

1st District, Laflin,

2d District, Etheridge,

3d District, Fisher,

4th District, Harris, of Wake,

5th District, Trogden,

6th District, Hobbs,

7th District, Logan.

Section 13th of the Executive Department was taken up, and,

On motion, was adopted.

Section 14th was read.

Mr. Rich moved to strike out "*ex offici o*," in the 3d and 12th lines.

The motion did not prevail.

Mr. Tourgee moved to strike out "against" and insert "from" on 9th line.

The amendment was sustained, and the section as amended was adopted.

Section 15th was read and adopted.

Section 16th was read and adopted.

Section 17th was read.

Mr. Rich moved to amend by striking out the word "of" before agriculture and immigration.

The amendment was carried.

The section as amended was adopted.

Mr. Durham offered the following as section 18th:

SEC. 18. No person of African descent or of mixed blood, shall be eligible to the office of Governor, Lieutenant Governor, or any other Executive office.

The section was put to the House and the yeas and nays were demanded.

The section was lost by the following vote:

Those who voted in the affirmative are:

Messrs. Durham, Ellis, Etheridge, Graham of Orange, Hall, Hare, Holt, Lennon, Marshall, McCubbins, and Merritt—11.

Those who voted in the negative are:

Messrs. Abbott, Andrews, Barnes, Blume, Bradley, Bryan, Carey, Candler, Cherry, Chillson, Congleton, Cox, Dickey, Duckworth, Eppes, Fisher, Forkner, Franklin, French of Bladen, French of Rockingham, French of Chowan, Fullings, Gahagan, Garland, George, Graham of Montgomery, Grant of Wayne, Grant of Northampton, Gunter, Harris of Wake, Hayes of Robeson, Hayes of Halifax, Heaton, Highsmith, Hobbs, Hollowell, Hood, Hyman Ing, Jones, of Caldwell, Jones, of Washington, King of Lenoir, Kinney, Laflin, Lee, Legg, Logan, Long, Mann, May, Mayo, McDonald of Chatham, McDonald, of Moore, Moore, Mullican, Murphy, Nance,

Newsom, Nicholson, Parker, Parks, Petree, Pierson, Pool, Ragland, Ray, Read, Renfrow, Rhodes, Rich, Rodman, Smith, Stilly, Stilwell, Taylor, Teague, Tourgee, Trogden, Tucker, Turner, Watts, Welker and Williams of Wake—83.

On motion the House adjourned.

---

SATURDAY, February 8th, 1868.

The Convention was called to order at 10 o'clock, by the President.

Prayer by the Rev. Mr. Logan.

The President announced a quorum.

The Journal of Friday was read and approved.

Mr. McDonald, of Moore, presented a petition of divorce.

Referred to a special committee of three on divorces.

Mr. Abbott presented a petition for "relief" from Mr. Pearsall, of Duplin County.

Refered to the Committee on the Judicial Department.

Mr. Legg presented a petition for relief from Cooper Huggins, of Wilmington, North-Carolina.

Referred to the Committee of three to confer with General Canby.

The Committee on Privileges and Elections, to whom was referred the case of the election in the district composed of the Counties of Alleghany, Ashe, Surry, Yadkin and Watauga, respectfully report.

That by the official report John M. Marshall received 1123 votes, while John G. Marler, who at present holds a seat in this Convention, received 1030 votes; thereby entitling Marshall to a seat. The Committee therefore recommend that the Secretary of this Convention ask the attention of Major-General Canby to those facts, and if, on examination the record be as appears, to admit the said John Mr. Marshall to his seat. The Committee also report that there were 155 votes reported for James G. Marler and also 110 votes reported for Marion Marshall, and ask General Canby's attention to the same.

On motion the report was accepted.

The Committee on Privileges and Elections, also reported on the election in Sampson County.

Mr. Durham moved to lay the report on the table.

The motion was not sustained.

On motion of Mr. Pool, the report was recommitted to the Committee on Privileges and Elections with instructions to send for persons and papers.

The Committee on Enrollment respectfully report that they have examined the ordinance entitled "an ordinance reducing the amount of bonds authorized to be issued by the Wilmington Charlotte and Rutherford Rail Road Company," and find it to be properly enrolled.

C. C. POOL, *Chairman.*

On motion the report was accepted.

Mr. C. C. Jones, Chairman of the Committee on Homesteads, to whom was referred the ordinance of Mr Franklin, of Wake, "for the relief of the people," reports that the Committee have considered the ordinance in connection with their report on Homestead and beg to be discharged.

On motion the report was accepted, and the Committee discharged from a further consideration of the subject.

Mr. Jones, Chairman of the Committee on Homesteads reported.

The report was accepted.

The report of the Committee on the Judicial Department was received and made a special order for Tuesday at 11 o'clock.

Leave of absence was granted

Mr. McCubbins until Monday next.

Mr. Holt until Tuesday next.

Mr. Baker until Wednesday next.

Mr. Sweet introduced the following resolution:

*Resolved*, That the following rule be adopted as Rule 41, of the rules regulating the proceedings of this Convention, to wit:

*Rule* 41. All reports of Committees embracing propositions pertaining to the formation of a Constitution shall be read three several times, of which readings the first shall be for information only. The second for consideration and the third after engrossment and final consideration and adoption. The yeas and nays shall be entered upon the Journal, on the second and third readings of reports as above designated.

On motion the rules were suspended and the resolution adopted.

Mr. Bradley introduced an ordinance in favor of J. C. Jones, Sheriff of Alleghany County.

Lies over under the rules.

On motion the resolution of Mr. Congleton on relief, was referred to a special Committee of five.

A petition was received from the citizens of Wilkes.

Referred to the Committee on the Judicial Department.

The hour of 12 having arrived, the House proceeded to take up the following report of the Committee on a Preamble and Bill of Rights:

## REPORT OF THE STANDING COMMITTEE ON PREAMBLE AND BILL OF RIGHTS.

### PREAMBLE.

We, the people of the State of North-Carolina, grateful to Almighty God, the Sovereign Ruler of Nations, for the preservation of the American Union, and the existence of our civil, political and religious liberties, and acknowledging our dependence upon Him for the continuance of those blessings to us and our posterity, do, for the more certain security thereof, and for the better government of this State, ordain and establish this Constitution:

## ARTICLE I.

### DECLARATION OF RIGHTS.

That the general, great and essential principles of liberty and free government may be recognized and established, and that the relations of this State to the Union and government of the United States, and those of the people of the State to the rest of the American people, may be defined and affirmed, we do declare—

SECTION 1. That we hold it to be self-evident, that all men are endowed by their Creator with certain inalienable rights, among which are life, liberty, the enjoyment of the fruits of their own labor, and the pursuit of happiness.

SEC. 2. That all political power is vested in and derived from the people; that all government of right originates from the people, is founded upon their will only, and is instituted solely for the good of the whole.

SEC. 3. That the people of this State have the inherent, sole and exclusive right of regulating the internal government and police thereof, and of altering and abolishing their Constitution and form of government, whenever it may be necessary to their safety and happiness; but every such right should be exercised in pursuance of law, and consistently with the Constitution of the United States.

SEC. 4. That this State shall ever remain a member of the American Union; that the people thereof are part of the American nation; that there is no right on the part of this State to secede, and that all attempts, from whatever source or upon whatever pretext, to dissolve said Union, or to sever said nation, ought to be resisted with the whole power of the State.

SEC. 5. That every citizen of this State owes paramount allegiance to the Constitution and government of the United States, and that no law or ordinance of the State, in contravention or subversion thereof, can have any binding force.

SEC. 6. To maintain the honor and good faith of the State untarnished, the public debt regularly contracted before and since the rebellion shall be regarded as inviolable and never questioned; but the State shall never assume or pay any debt or obligation, express or implied, incurred in aid of insurrection or rebellion against the United States, or any claim for the loss or emancipation of any slave.

SEC. 7. No man or set of men are entitled to exclusive or

separate emoluments or privileges from the community but in consideration of public services.

SEC. 8. The legislative, executive, and supreme judicial powers of government ought to be forever separate and distinct from each other.

SEC. 9. All power of suspending laws, or the execution of laws, by any authority, without the consent of the representatives of the people, is injurious to their rights, and ought not to be exercised.

SEC. 10. All elections ought to be free.

SEC. 11. In all criminal prosecutions, every man has a right to be informed of the accusation against him, and to confront the accusers and witnesses with other testimony, and to have counsel for his defence, and shall not be compelled to give evidence against himself.

SEC. 12. No person shall be put to answer any criminal charge, except as hereinafter allowed, but by indictment, presentment, or impeachment.

SEC. 13. No person shall be convicted of any crime, but by the unanimous verdict of a jury of good and lawful men, in open court. The Legislature may, however, provide other modes of trial for petty misdemeanors, with the right of appeal.

SEC. 14. Excessive bail should not be required, nor excessive fines imposed, nor cruel, nor unusual punishments inflicted.

SEC. 15. General warrants, whereby any officer or messenger may be commanded to search suspected places without evidence of the fact committed, or to seize any person or persons not named, whose offence is not particularly described and supported by evidence, are dangerous to liberty, and ought not to be granted.

SEC. 16. No person ought to be taken, imprisoned, or disseized of his freehold, liberties, or privileges, or outlawed, or exiled, or in any manner destroyed, or deprived of his life, liberty, or property, but by the law of the land.

SEC. 17. Every person, restrained of his liberty, is entitled to a remedy to inquire into the lawfulness thereof, and to remove the same, if unlawful, and such remedy ought not to be denied or delayed.

Sec. 18. In all controversies at law respecting property, the ancient mode of trial by jury is one of the best securities of the rights of the people, and ought to remain sacred and inviolable.

Sec. 19. The freedom of the press is one of the great bulwarks of liberty, and therefore ought never to be restrained.

Sec. 20. The privilege of the writ of *habeas corpus* shall not be suspended in this State.

Sec. 21. The people of this State ought not to be taxed or made subject to the payment of any impost or duty, without the consent of themselves, or their representatives in General Assembly, freely given.

Sec. 22. The people have a right to bear arms for the defence of the State; and, as standing armies in time of peace are dangerous to liberty, they ought not to be kept up; and the military should be kept under strict subordination to, and governed by, the civil power.

Sec. 23. The people have a right to assemble together to consult for their common good, to instruct their representatives, and to apply to the Legislature for redress of grievances.

Sec. 24. All men have a natural and inalienable right to worship Almighty God according to the dictates of their own consciences; that no human authority can, in any case whatever, control or interfere with the rights of conscience.

Sec. 25. For redress of grievances, and for amending and strengthening the laws, elections ought to be often held.

Sec. 26. A frequent recurrence to fundamental principles is absolutely necessary to preserve the blessings of liberty.

Sec. 27. No hereditary emoluments, privileges, or honors, ought to be granted or conferred in this State.

Sec. 28. Perpetuities and monopolies are contrary to the genius of a free State, and ought not to be allowed.

Sec. 29. Retrospective laws, punishing facts committed before the existence of such laws, and by them only declared criminal, are oppressive, unjust, and incompatible with liberty; wherefore, no *ex post facto* law ought to be made.

Sec. 30. Slavery and involuntary servitude otherwise than for crimes, whereof the parties shall have been duly convicted, shall be, and is hereby forever prohibited within this State.

Sec. 31. The limits and boundaries of the State shall be and remain as they now are.

Sec. 32. All courts shall be open, and every person, for an injury done him in his lands, goods, person or reputation, shall have remedy by due course of law, and right and justice administered without sale, denial or delay.

Sec. 33. No soldier shall, in time of peace, be quartered in any house without the consent of the owner; nor in time of war, but in a manner to be prescribed by law.

Sec. 34. This enumeration of rights shall not be construed to impair or deny others retained by the people, and all powers not herein delegated, remain with the people.

DAVID HEATON, *Chairman.*
J. H. HARRIS,
WM. NICHOLSON,
JOHN R. FRENCH,
JOHN M. PATRICK,
GEO. W. GAHAGAN,
C. C. POOL,
A. W. FISHER,
J. H. BAKER,
SYLVESTER CARTER,
JULIUS S. GARLAND,
JASPER ETHERIDGE.

The report passed the first reading.

On the second reading, Mr. Heaton moved to amend section first by inserting between the words "are" and "endowed," in the second line, the words "created equal; that they are."

Mr. Tourgee offered the following amendment:

Strike out "that we hold it to be self evident," in line first, also in line second, strike out "are endowed by their creator with certain inalienable rights," and insert, "are created free and equal in rights, certain of which are inalienable."

Mr. Tourgee withdrew his amendment.

Mr. Nicholson submitted the following as a substitute:

SECTION 1st. That all men are born free and equal in natural rights, some of the rights are inalienable, and among them the right to life, to liberty, to property, and to the pursuit of happiness, none of which can rightfully be surrendered or taken away, or abridged in respect to any person, except in such measure as may be necessary to reconcile them with the equal rights of others, or in punishment for crime.

After considerable discussion, Mr. Harris, of Wake, moved the previous question.

The yeas and nays were demanded, and the substitute was lost by the following vote, yeas 10, nays 83:

Those who voted in affirmative are:

Messrs. Hare, Hodnett, Hollowell, Jones of Washington, Lennon, Merritt, Nicholson, Parker, Tourgee and Welker—10.

Those who voted in the negative are:

Messrs. Abbott, Andrews, Ashley, Blume, Bradley, Bryan, Carey, Candler, Cherry, Chillson, Congleton, Cox, Dickey, Duckworth, Durham, Ellis, Eppes, Etheridge, Fisher, Forkner, Franklin, French of Bladen, French of Rockingham, Fullings, Gahagan, Garland, George, Glover, Graham of Montgomery, Graham of Orange, Grant of Northampton, Gully, Gunter, Harris of Wake, Harris of Franklin, Hayes of Robeson, Hayes of Halifax, Heaton, Highsmith, Hoffler, Hood, Hyman, Ing, Jones of Caldwell, King of Lincoln, King of Lenoir, Kinney, Laflin, Lee, Logan, Long, Mann, May, Mayo, Marshall, McDonald of Chatham, McDonald of Moore, Moore, Morton, Mullican, Murphy, Nance, Newsom, Parks, Petree, Pierson, Pool, Ragland, Ray, Renfrow, Rhodes, Rich, Rodman, Smith, Stilly, Stilwell, Sweet, Taylor, Teague Tucker, Turner, Watts and Williams of Wake—83.

The question recurred on the amendment of Mr. Heaton, which,

On motion, was adopted.

Mr. Heaton also moved to amend by inserting in the third line, between "rights and among," the word "that;" also, to strike out "which" and insert "these,"

Which amendments were sustained.

Mr. Heaton also moved to amend by striking out the word "inalienable," and insert the word "unalienable."

The amendment was agreed to.

On motion, section first, as amended, was adopted.

On motion, the House adjourned.

---

MONDAY February 10th, 1868.

The Convention was called to order at 10 o'clock, by the President.

Prayer by the Rev. G. W. Welker.

The President announced a quorum.

The Journal of Saturday was read and approved.

A communication from a Committee on Education in Richmond, Virginia, was read, and,

Referred to the Committee on Education.

Mr. Durham introduced the following preamble and resolution:

Whereas, It is a matter of common rumor that corrupting influences have been used to secure the passage of certain ordinances which have been passed by this Convention; and whereas, if these rumors are true, it is the duty of this body to ascertain who are the guilty parties, and expose said corruption; therefore,

*Be it resolved*, That a Select Committee of three members be appointed by the President, whose duty it shall be to ascertain and report whether corrupting influences have been used to secure the passage of any ordinance, which has been passed by this Convention, and if so, the names of the guilty parties, and all the facts connected therewith. The said Committee shall have power to send for persons and papers, administer oaths and examine witnesses.

On motion, the rules were suspended and the resolution adopted.

Mr. Abbott introduced the following resolution:

*Be it resolved by this Convention*, That the thanks of the people of North-Carolina are due and are hereby tendered to

General Nelson A. Miles, the Assistant Commissioner for the Freedman's Bureau in this State, for the efficient, impartial and faithful manner in which he has discharged his duties.

*Resolved*, That the Secretary of the Convention transmit a copy of this resolution to General Miles.

On motion, the rules were suspended and the resolutions adopted.

Mr. Abbott introduced a resolution in relation to the previous question.

Lies over under the rules.

Mr. Tourgee introduced a resolution in relation to the session of the Convention.

Lies over under the rules.

Mr. Abbott moved that when this Convention adjourns, it adjourns to meet at 7½ o'clock, P. M.

The motion was not sustained.

Mr. Tourgee, Chairman of the Committee on Counties Towns, &c., reported that the Committee have considered the ordinance introduced by Mr. Jones, of Washington, entitled "an ordinance to amend section second of an act of the Legislature to incorporate the town of Columbia, in County of Tyrrell," and recommend that it should pass.

The report was adopted, and the ordinance, as follows, was adopted:

*Be it ordained by the people of North-Carolina, in Convention assembled*, That section second of the act of the Legislature passed in 1866–'67, entitled "An act to incorporate the town of Columbia, in the County of Tyrrell," be so amended as to read:

"That the said town of Columbia, shall be embraced within the following boundaries in the County of Tyrrell, to wit: Beginning at the Ferry wharf on the east side of Scuppernong river, thence running up the said river south fifty poles, then east one hundred and twenty-five poles, then north one hundred poles, then west one hundred and twenty-five poles, to the river, then by the river edge to the beginning.

The resolution of Mr. Welker, regarding the distillation of grain, was,

On motion, referred back to the House, and placed on the Calendar.

The resolution of Mr. Welker regarding the liabilities of Banking Institutions,

Was ordered to be printed, and laid over until Tuesday.

The ordinance of Mr. McDonald, of Chatham, to levy a tax f seventy five *per centum* upon old debts, was taken up.

Mr. Graham, of Orange, moved to postpone the ordinance ıdefinitely.

Mr. McDonald demanded the yeas and nays.

The motion was carried by the following vote, yeas 72, ays 13:

Those who voted in the affirmative are:

Messrs. Abbott, Ashley, Barnes, Benbow, Blume, Bradley, Bryan, Carey, Candler, Colgrove, Congleton, Cox, Daniel, Dickey, Duckworth, Durham, Ellis, Etheridge, Fisher, Forkner, French of Bladen, French of Rockingham, French of Chowan, Fullings, Gahagan, Garland, George, Glover, Graham of Orange, Grant of Wayne, Grant of Northampton, Gully, Hare, Hayes of Halifax, Heaton, Highsmith, Hobbs, Hodnett, Hoffler, Hollowell, Hood, Hyman, Ing, Jones of Caldwell, Jones of Washington, King of Lincoln, King of Lenoir, Kinney, Lee Lennon, Logan, Mann, May, Mayo, Marshall, Mullican, Nichson, Parker, Parks, Petree, Ray, Renfrow, Rhodes, Robbins, Rodman, Stilly, Sweet, Teague, Tourgee, Trogden, Tucker and Williams of Wake—72.

Those who voted in the negative are:

Messrs. Graham of Montgomery, Gunter, Harris of Wake, Hayes, of Robeson, Laflin, Legg, Long, McDonald of Chatham, McDonald of Moore, Murphy, Nance, Rich and Taylor—13.

The following resolution of Mr. Petree was adopted:

*Resolved*, That a Committee of three be appointed to draw up a memorial to be sent to the Congress of the United States praying that the revenue tax on tobacco be reduced, setting forth the reason therefore.

The resolution of Mr. Rodman for the relief of the sheriff of Halifax County, was referred to a Committee comprising the delegates of Halifax.

The resolution of Mr Bradley in favor of the sheriff of Alleghany County, was,

On motion, tabled.

On motion, the report of the Committee on Suffrage was postponed until Wednesday, at 11 o'clock, A. M.

The hour of 12 having arrived, the preamble of the report of the Committee on a Preamble and Bill of Rights was taken up.

The preamble was read.

Mr. Graham, of Orange, moved to amend by striking out the words "and the existence" in 3rd line and insert "imploring the restoration."

The amendment was not adopted.

The preamble as read was adopted.

The caption of article 1st was read.

Mr. Welker moved to amend by striking out the words "general great and" in line 1st; also in the 2d line the words "reorganized and"; also the words "and affirmed" in the 6th line.

The amendments were lost.

The caption as read was then adopted.

On motion of Mr. Heaton the report of the committee was postponed until Thursday at 11 o'clock, and made the special order for that time.

On motion of Mr. Abbott the following report of the Committee on Militia was placed upon it final reading and passage:

## MILITIA.

SECTION 1. All able-bodied male citizens of the State of North-Carolina, between the ages of twenty-one and forty years, who are citizens of the United States, shall be liable to duty in the Militia: *Provided*, That all persons who may be adverse to bearing arms from religious scruples shall be exempt therefrom.

SEC. 2. The General Assembly shall provide for the organizing, arming, equiping, and discipline of the Militia, and for paying the same when called into active service.

SEC. 3. The Governor shall be Commander-in-Chief, and have power to call out the Militia to execute the law, suppress riots or insurrections.

SEC. 4. The General Assembly shall have power to make such exemptions as may be deemed necessary, and to enact laws that may be expedient for the government of the Militia.

Mr. Graham, of Orange, moved to amend section 1st, by adding after the word "Militia" in 4th line, "but white and colored persons shall be organized into separate commands, and no white man shall ever be required to obey a negro officer."

After considerable discussion the question was called and the yeas and nays demanded.

The amendment was lost by the following vote:

Those who voted in the affirmative are:

Messrs. Bradley, Durham, Ellis, Graham, of Orange, Hall, Hare, Hodnett, Marshall, and Merritt—9.

Those who voted in the negative are:

Messrs. Abbott, Andrews, Ashley, Barnes, Bryan, Carey, Cherry, Chillson, Congleton, Cox, Daniel, Dickey, Duckworth, Eppes, Etheridge, Fisher, Forkner, Franklin, French of Bladen, French of Rockingham, French of Chowan, Gahagan, Galloway, Garland, George, Glover, Graham of Montgomery, Grant of Wayne, Grant of Northampton, Gully, Gunter, Harris of Wake, Harris of Franklin, Hayes of Robeson, Hayes of Halifax, Heaton, Highsmith, Hobbs, Hoffler, Hood, Hyman, Ing, Jones of Washington, King of Lincoln, King of Lenoir, Kinney, Laflin, Lee, Legg, Logan, Long, Mann, May, Mayo, McDonald of Chatham, McDonald of Moore, Moore, Morton, Mullican, Murphy, Newsom, Parks, Petree, Pierson, Ragland, Ray, Renfrow, Rhodes, Rich, Robbins, Rodman, Smith, Stilly, Stilwell, Sweet, Taylor, Teague, Tourgee, Tucker, Turner, Watts, Welker and Williams of Wake—83.

The section as read was then adopted.

Sections 2d, 3d and 4th as read were adopted.

On motion of Mr. Jones, of Washington, the following report of the Committee on Corporations other than Municipal, was taken up, and passed its first reading:

## REPORT OF THE COMMITTEE ON CORPORATIONS OTHER THAN MUNICIPAL.

The Committee on Corporations beg leave to submit the following Report:

SECTION 1. Corporations may be formed under general laws, but shall not be created by special act, except for municipal purposes, and in cases where, in the judgment of the Legislature, the objects of the corporations cannot be attained under general laws. All general laws and special acts passed, pursuant to this section, may be altered from time to time or repealed.

SEC. 2. Dues from corporations shall be secured by such individual liabilities of the corporations and other means as may be prescribed by law.

SEC. 3. The term corporation as used in this article, shall be construed to include all associations and jointstock companies having any of the powers and privileges of corporations not possessed by individuals or partnership, and all corporations shall have the right to sue, and shall be subject to be sued in all courts in like cases as natural persons.

SEC. 4. The Legislature shall have no power to pass any act granting any special charter for banking purposes; but corporations or associations may be formed for such purposes under general laws.

SEC. 5. The Legislature shall have no power to pass any law sanctioning in any manner, directly or indirectly, the suspension of specie payments, by any person, association or corporation issuing bank notes of any description.

SEC. 6. The Legislature shall provide by law for the registry of all bills or notes issued or put in circulation as money, and shall require ample security for the redemption of the same in specie.

SEC. 7. The Stockholders in every corporation and joint-stock association for banking purposes, issuing bank notes or any kind of paper credits to circulate as money, shall be individually responsible to the amount of their respective share or shares of stock in any such corporation or association for all its debt and liabilities of every kind.

SEC. 8. In case of the insolvency of any bank or banking association, the bill holders thereof shall be entitled to preference in payment over all other creditors of such bank or association.

SEC. 9. No bank shall receive, directly or indirectly, a greater rate of interest than shall be allowed by law to individuals lending money.

SEC. 10. The State shall not be a stockholder in any bank, nor shall the credit of the State ever be given or lent to any banking company, association or corporation, except for the purpose of expediting the construction of railroads or works of internal improvement within this State, and the credit of the State shall in no case be given or lent, without the approval of both Houses of the General Assembly.

SEC. 11. It shall be the duty of the Legislature to provide for the organization of cities, towns and incorporated villages, and to restrict their power of taxation, assessment, borrowing money, contracting debts, and loaning their credit, so as to prevent abuses in assessments, and in contracting debt by such municipal corporation.

E. W. JONES, *Chairman*,<br>
WM. MERRITT,<br>
W. A. B. MURPHY,<br>
GEORGE W. DICKEY,<br>
GEORGE TUCKER,<br>
J. H. KING,<br>
R. C. PARKER,<br>
H. T. GRANT,<br>
E. M. HOLT,<br>
J. T. HARRIS,<br>
JAMES HAY,<br>
S. S. ASHLEY.

On the second reading section 1st was taken up, and,

On motion, was adopted.

Sections 2d and 3d were read and adopted.

On motion the balance of the report was made a specia order for Friday at 11 o'clock.

On motion the House adjourned.

---

TUESDAY, February 11th, 1868.

The Convention was called to order at 10 o'clock, by th President.

Prayer by the Rev. Mr. Lennon.

The President announced a quorum.

The Journal of Monday was read and approved.

On motion of Mr. Jones, of Washington, the followin committee of three were appointed to wait on Major Genera Canby, Military Commandant of this district, and tender hir the compliments of this Convention, and invite him to vis it whenever it may suit his pleasure:

Messrs. E. W. Jones, Read, and Grant, of Wayne.

The following committee were appointed in accordaı with the resolution of Mr. Durham passed Monday:

Messrs. Durham, Ashley and Harris, of Wake.

Mr. Graham, of Orange introduced a petition of divorce.

Referred to the Special Committee on Divorce.

Mr. Ray presented a petition from the citizens of Al mance.

Referred to the Committee of three on the distillation grain.

Mr. Franklin presented a petition of divorce of Esther Todd.

Referred to the Committee on Divorce.

Mr. Harris of Wake, introduced the following preamble ar resolution:

Whereas, It is a matter of common rumor that Pla Durham, delegate "so called" from Cleveland, obtained h election by the dishonorable use of "certain official comm nications of the Freedman's Bureau surreptitiously obtained; and, whereas if those rumors are true, it is the duty of this body to expose and purge itself of this corruption, therefore, be it:

*Resolved*, That a Select Committee of three members be appointed by the President, whose duty it shall be to ascertain and report whether such corrupting procedure was adopted to secure the election of said Plato Durham as a delegate to this Convention, and if so that all the facts connected therewith, to the end that the delegate "so called," may be dealt with.

The rules were suspended.

Mr. King, of Lenoir, moved to lay the resolution on the table.

The motion was lost.

Mr. King, of Lenoir, moved to postpone indefinitely.

The motion was not sustained.

The resolution was then adopted.

The same committee to whom was referred the resolution of Mr. Tourgee in relation to the staying of certain debts, reported it back to the Convention, without recommendation, since its purpose is comprehended in another resolution, and asked to be discharged from a further consideration.

The report was on motion adopted.

The same committee to whom was referred the resolution of Mr. Ragland on relief, reported that they have transmitted the same to Major-General Canby, and asked to be discharged from the further consideration of the subject.

The report was adopted.

The same committee to whom was referred the petition of Cooper Haggins, presented by Mr. Legg of Brunswick, report the petition back to the Convention and asked to be discharged from the further consideration thereof.

The report was adopted.

Mr. Harris, of Wake, introduced an ordinance prohibiting, for a limited sum, the sale of property under mortgage or deed of trust.

Referred to the Committee on Relief, with instructions to report at an early day.

Leave of absence was granted,

Mr. Turner until Friday next, and,

Mr. Hood from Thursday until Monday next.

Mr. Harris, of Wake, introduced a resolution limiting debate.

Lies over under the rules.

Mr. Jones, of Washington, Chairman of the Committee to wait on General Canby, reported that they had called upon the General, and he stated to them that he would take pleasure in visiting the Convention on Wednesday at 11 o'clock.

The following report of the Committee on the Judicial Department was taken up for consideration:

The undersigned members of the Committee on the Judicial Department respectfully report:

That there exists among the members of the Committee wide differences of opinion on fundamental points respecting the proper organization of the Judicial Department of the State government.

The most essential points of difference are two:

1st. In respect to the mode of appointing Judges. Some gentlemen think they should be elected by the people; others by the General Assembly; and still others, that they should be appointed by the Governor, with the consent of the Senate or of the General Assembly.

2d. In respect to retaining or abolishing the distinction between action and suits in Equity, some gentlemen think such distinction should be abolished, and that there should be but one form of civil action.

It is not intended now to present any argument for or against any of these views, or even to express the opinions of the undersigned respecting them; but merely to state them.

If the opinion of the Convention can be obtained on these two points, the undersigned are of opinion that the Committee will have no further difficulty of agreeing substantially upon a plan for the organization of the Judicial Department of the government.

For the purpose of obtaining an expression of the opinion of the Convention, the undersigned herewith submit, in the shape of resolutions, affirmatives of each different view. A vote of the Convention either way, upon any one of these, will be received as a guide to the Committee upon the matter concerned, covered by the resolution, and they can then proceed to frame a plan of organization conformably.

WILL. B. RODMAN,
S. W. WATTS,
C. C. JONES,
A. W. TOURGEE,
G. W. WELKER,
A. W. FISHER,
R. W. KING,
W. H. S. SWEET,
T. L. L. COX,
E. B. TEAGUE.

1. *Resolved*, That it is the sense of this Convention; That the distinctions between actions at law and suits in Equity, and the forms of all such actions and suits shall be abolished, and there should be but one form of civil action.

2. *Resolved*, That it is the sense of this Convention; That ıe distinction between actions at law and suits in Equity, ɔw existing should not be abolished.

1. *Resolved*, That it is the sense of this Convention; That ıdges of the Supreme and Superior Courts of the State ıould be elected by the people.

2. *Resolved*, That it is the sense of this Convention; That udges of the Supreme and Superior Courts should be elected y the General Assembly.

3. *Resolved*, That it is the sense of this Convention; That ıe Judges of the Supreme and Superior Courts should be ppointed by the Governor, with the consent of the Senate, r of the General Assembly.

The resolutions in relation to the Supreme and Superior Court Judges was first taken up.

Mr. Heaton moved to substitute section third for section first.

Mr. Jones, of Washington, moved to amend by substituting section second for section third.

The yeas and nays were demanded.

The section was not adopted by a vote of yeas 30, nays 72.

Those who voted in the affirmative are:

Messrs. Abbott, Bradley, Daniel, Ellis, Eppes, Etheridge, Fisher, Forkner, Graham of Orange, Grant of Wayne, Grant of Northampton, Hall, Hare, Harris of Franklin, Hayes of Halifax, Hodnett, Hollowell, Holt, Jones of Caldwell, Jones of Washington, King of Lincoln, King of Lenoir, Laflin, Lennon, Marler, McDonald of Moore, Nicholson, Parker, Pool and Read—30.

Those who voted in the negative are:

Messrs. Andrews, Ashley, Barnes, Benbow, Bryan, Carey, Candler, Cherry, Chillson, Congleton, Cox, Dickey, Duckworth, Franklin, French of Bladen, French of Rockingham, French of Chowan, Fullings, Gahagan, Galloway, Garland, George, Glover, Graham of Montgomery, Gully, Gunter, Harris of Wake, Hayes of Robeson, Heaton, Highsmith, Hobbs, Hoffler, Hood, Hyman, Ing, Kinney, Lee, Legg, Logan, Long, Mann, May, Mayo, Moore, Morton, Mullican, Murphy, Nance, Newsom, Parks, Petree, Peterson, Pierson, Raglan[d], Ray, Renfrow, Rhodes, Rich, Robbins, Rodman, Rose, Smit[h], Stilwell, Sweet, Taylor, Teague, Tourgee, Trogden, Tucke[r], Watts, Welker and Williamson—72.

The question recurring on section third,

The yeas and nays were demanded, and resulted yeas 3[.] nays 63.

Those who voted in the affirmative are:

Messrs. Abbott, Bradley, Ellis, Eppes, Etheridge, Forkn[er], French of Bladen, French of Chowan, Graham of Orang[e], Hall, Hare, Harris of Wake, Harris of Franklin, Hayes [of] Halifax, Heaton, Hodnett, Hollowell, Holt, Hood, Hyma[n], Jones of Caldwell, Jones of Washington, King of Linco[ln], Laflin, Legg, Lennon, Mann, Mayo, Marshall, McDonald, [of]

Moore, Nicholson, Parker, Pool, Read, Renfrow, Robbins, Rodman, and Sweet—38.

Those who voted in the negative are:

Messrs. Andrews, Ashley, Barnes, Benbow, Bryan, Carey, Candler, Cherry, Chillson, Congleton, Cox, Dickey, Duckworth, Fisher, Franklin, French of Rockingham, Fullings, Gahagan, Garland, George, Glover, Graham of Montgomery, Grant of Wayne, Grant of Northampton, Gully, Gunter, Hayes of Robeson, Highsmith, Hobbs, Hoffler, Ing, King of Lenoir, Kinney, Lee, Logan, Long, May, Moore, Morton, Mullican, Murphy, Nance, Newsom, Parks, Petree, Peterson, Pierson, Ragland, Ray, Rhodes, Rich, Rose, Smith, Stilly, Stilwell, Taylor, Teague, Tourgee, Trogden, Tucker, Watts, Welker and Williamson—63.

The section was lost.

Section first was then taken up and divided.

The following portion of the section was taken up for consideration:

"That the Judges of the Supreme Courts of the State should be elected by the people."

On motion, it was adopted, yeas 56, nays 34.

Those who voted in the affirmative are:

Messrs. Andrews, Ashley, Barnes, Bryan, Carey, Candler, Chillson, Congleton, Cox, Dickey, Duckworth, Franklin, French of Rockingham, Fullings, Gahagan, Garland, George, Glover, Graham of Montgomery, Gully, Gunter, Heaton, Highsmith, Hoffler, Hood, Ing, Kinney, Lee, Logan, Mann, May, Mayo, Mullican, Murphy, Newsom, Parks, Petree, Peterson, Pierson, Ragland, Ray, Renfrow, Rhodes, Rich, Rose, Smith, Stilly, Stilwell, Taylor, Teague, Tourgee, Trogden, Tucker, Welker, Williams of Wake and Williamson—56.

Those who voted in the negative are:

Messrs. Abbott, Benbow, Cherry, Ellis, Eppes, Etheridge, Fisher, Forkner, French of Chowan, Graham of Orange, Hare, Harris of Franklin, Hayes of Halifax, Hobbs, Hodnett, Hollowell, Hyman, Jones of Caldwell, Jones of Washington, King of Lenoir, Legg, Lennon, Long, Marler, McDonald of

Chatham, McDonald of Moore, Moore, Nance, Pool, Read, Rodman, Sweet, Watts and Williams of Sampson—34.

The balance of the section, viz:

" That the Superior Court Judges be elected by the people,"

Was adopted, yeas 63, nays 15.

Those who voted in the affirmitive are:

Messrs. Andrews, Ashley, Barnes, Benbow, Bradley, Bryan, Carey, Candler, Chilson, Congleton, Cox, Dickey, Duckworth, Forkner, Franklin, French of Rockingham, Fullings, Gahagan, Garland, George, Glover, Graham of Montgomery, Grant of Wayne, Gully, Gunter, Hayes of Robeson, Heaton, Highsmith, Hoffler, Hyman, Ing, King of Lenoir, Kinney, Logan, Long, Mann, May, Mayo, McDonald of Moore, Morton, Murphy, Newsom, Parks, Petree, Peterson, Pierson, Ragland, Ray, Renfrow, Rhodes, Rose, Smith, Stilly, Stilwell, Taylor, Teague, Tourgee, Trogden, Tucker, Watts, Welker, Williams of Wake and Williamson—63.

Those who voted in the negative are:

Messrs. Abbott, Ellis, Fisher, French of Chowan, Graham of Orange, Hall, Hare, Harris of Franklin, Hayes of Halifax, Hodnett, Hollowell, Jones of Caldwell, Lennon, Marler and Pool—15.

On motion of Mr. Abbott, the Secretary was directed to send General Canby a copy of an ordinance passed by this body in relation to levying a tax to defray the expenses of this Convention.

The report of the Committee on Punishments, Penal Institutions and Public Charities, was received and ordered to be printed.

A preamble and resolutions from the Georgia Convention asking Congress for a loan of $30,000,000 dollars for the benefit of Southern planters, was received, and,

Referred to the Committee on Finance.

On motion the House adjourned.

WEDNESDAY, February 12th, 1868.

The Convention was called to order at 10 o'clock, by the President.

Prayer by the Rev. Mr. Eppes.

The President announced a quorum.

The Journal of Tuesday was read and approved.

The petition of Divorce in favor of one Hopkins, referred to the Committee on Divorce, was,

On motion, referred to the Committee on the Judicial Department.

Mr. Forkner introduced a resolution in relation to the practice of law in North-Carolina.

Lies over under the rules.

Mr. Franklin introduced a resolution granting relief to the Sherriff of Wake County.

Referred to the Committee on Finance.

Mr. Bryan introduced the following ordinance:

AN ORDINANCE IN FAVOR OF SHERIFFS.

Section 1. *Be it ordained by the people of North-Carolina in Convention assembled, and it is hereby ordained by the authority of the same,* That the Sheriffs of this State shall be allowed one year from and after the first day of January, 1868, to collect the unpaid taxes for the years 1866–'67.

Sec. 2. *Be it further ordained,* That this ordinance shall be in force from and after its passage, and that a copy of the same be printed and transmitted to each Sheriff in the State.

Mr. King, of Lenoir, moved to lay the ordinance on the table.

The motion was not sustained.

The ordinance was, on motion, adopted.

The report of the Committee on Legislature, together with that portion that was recommitted to them was made a special order for Monday at 11 o'clock.

On motion the report of the Committee on Suffrage was postponed until Tuesday next at 11 o'clock and made a special order for that time.

UNFINISHED BUSINESS.

The report of the committee on the Judicial Department considered yesterday was taken up.

General Canby at this hour, 11 o'clock, visited the Convention, was introduced to the President, who received him with an appropriate address, which was responded to by the General.

The Convention then took a recess for 15 minutes and each delegate was presented to the General.

At the expiration of the time, the house proceeded with the report of the Judicial Department.

The sense of the house as regards actions at law and suits in equity was obtained by the adoption of the following resolution :

*Resolved*, That it is the sense of this Convention that the distinctions between actions at law and suits in equity and the forms of all such actions and suits shall be abolished and there should be but one form of civil action.

The yeas and nays were demanded and the resolution was adopted by the following vote:

Those who voted in the affirmative are:

Messrs. Ashley, Barnes, Blume, Bryan, Carey, Chillson, Congleton, Cox, Dickey, Duckworth, French of Bladen, French of Rockingham, Fullings, Gahagan, Galloway, Garland, George, Graham of Montgomery, Grant of Wayne, Gully, Gunter, Hayes of Halifax, Highsmith, Hobbs, Hoffler, Ing, Kinney, Mann, May, Moore, Morton, Mullican, Murphy, Newsom, Parks, Peterson, Ragland, Ray, Renfrow, Robbins, Smith, Stilwell, Sweet, Taylor, Teague, Tourgee, Trogden, Watts, Welker and Williamson—50.

Those who voted in the negative are:

Messrs. Abbott, Aydlott, Benbow, Bradley, Candler, Cherry, Ellis, Eppes, Etheridge, Forkner, French of Chowan, Graham of Orange, Grant of Northampton, Hall, Hare, Harris of Franklin, Hodnett, Hollowell, Hyman, Jones of Caldwell, Jones of Washington, King of Lincoln, King of Lenoir, Legg, Lennon, Logan, Long, Marshall, Merritt, McDonald of Moore, Nance, Nicholson, Pierson, Pool, Read, Rhodes, Rodman and Rose—38.

Leave of absence was granted

Mr. McDonald, of Chatham, until Thursday next.

Mr. King, of Lincoln, until Monday next.

Mr. Galloway moved a recess until 7½ o'clock.

The motion did not prevail.

Mr. Harris, of Wake, called up his resolution in relation to the restriction of members in their speaking.

After some discussion,

On motion, the House adjourned.

---

THURSDAY, February 13th, 1868.

The Convention was called to order at 10 o'clock, by the President.

Prayer by the Rev. S. S. Ashley.

The President announced a quorum.

The Journal of Wednesday was read and approved.

Mr. Galloway presented a petition from the County Committee of New Hanover County.

Referred to the Committee on Suffrage.

Mr. Candler presented a petition of divorce in favor of Matilda Anderson.

Referred to the Committee on the Judicial Department.

Mr. Sweet introduced an ordinance for the appointment of a collector of taxes for the City of Newbern.

Referred to the Committee on Counties, Towns, &c.

Mr. Rich introduced an ordinance appointing a Commissioner on Immigration.

Ordered to be printed.

Mr. Cox presented a petition of divorce in favor of Archibald Harvy.

Referred to the Committee on the Judicial Department.

Mr. Rodman introduced an ordinance for the relief of the people.

Ordered to be printed.

Mr. Stilly introduced a resolution requesting Congress to reduce the tax on brandy distilled from fruits.

Referred to the Committee on Tobacco Tax.

Mr. Watts introduced an ordinance for the relief of the people.

Lies over under the rules.

UNFINISHED BUSINESS.

The following resolution of Mr. Abbott, was taken up, and,

On motion, adopted.

*Resolved*, That no one shall move the previous question except the Chairman of a Committee, whose report is under consideration, the mover of a resolution or the author of a minority report.

The following resolution of Mr. Tourgee, was taken up and adopted:

*Resolved*, That on and after Friday the 14th instant, this Convention hold two sessions daily, commencing at 10 o'clock, A. M., and 7½ P. M.

The following preamble and resolution presented by Mr. Forkner, was taken up, and,

On motion, was adopted:

WHEREAS, This Convention has passed an ordinance allowing men of legal profession, of a good moral character, by exhibiting a certificate granted by the Courts of other States, to the bar in the Courts of North-Carolina; and whereas, many of the States requiring nothing more than the establishment of a good moral character, to admit men to the bar; and that citizens of this State should be on equality with those of other States; therefore,

*Be it resolved*, That the Committee on the Judiciary be instructed to report an ordinance or clause for the Constitution, which will allow citizens of North-Carolina to practice, and plead law in the Courts of the State by establishing a good moral character and paying necessary fees.

Leave of absence was granted to,

Messrs. Hyman and Eppes until Monday evening.

Also, to Mr. Moore for two days.

On motion of Mr. Sweet, the report of the Committee on a Preamble and Bill of Rights was postponed until Friday next at 11 o'clock.

On motion, the following report of the Committee on the Legislature, its organization, &c., was taken up:

## REPORT OF THE COMMITTEE ON LEGISLATURE, ITS ORGANIZATION, &c.

A majority of the Committee on Legislature, its organization, the members, apportionment, election, tenure of office of its members, its powers, duties, except as otherwise referred, would respectfully submit the following report as the result of their deliberations:

### ARTICLE.

SECTION 1. The Legislative authority shall be vested in two distinct branches, both dependent on the people, to-wit: A Senate and House of Commons.

SEC. 2. The Senate and House of Commons shall meet annually, on the third Monday of November, and when assembled, shall be denominated the General Assembly. Neither House shall proceed upon public business, unless a majority of all the members are actually present.

SEC. 3. The Senate shall be composed of fifty Senators, biennially chosen by ballot.

SEC. 4. Until the first session of the General Assembly, which shall be had after the year eighteen hundred and seventy-one, the Senate shall be composed of members to be elected from the several districts, to consist of the Counties hereafter named, that is to say:

| | | |
|---|---|---|
| 1st | District | Perquimans and Pasquotank. |
| 2d | " | Camden and Currituck. |
| 3d | " | Gates and Chowan. |
| 4th | " | Tyrrell and Hyde. |
| 5th | " | Northampton. |

| | | |
|---|---|---|
| 6th | District | Hertford. |
| 7th | " | Bertie. |
| 8th | " | Martin and Washingtou. |
| 9th | " | Halifax. |
| 10th | " | Edgecombe and Wilson. |
| 11th | " | Pitt. |
| 12th | " | Beaufort. |
| 13th | " | Craven. |
| 14th | " | Carteret and Jones. |
| 15th | " | Greene and Lenoir. |
| 16th | " | New Hanover. |
| 17th | " | Duplin. |
| 18th | " | Onslow. |
| 19th | " | Brunswick, Bladen and Columbus. |
| 20th | " | Cumberland and Harnett. |
| 21st | " | Sampson. |
| 22d | " | Wayne. |
| 23d | " | Johnston. |
| 24th | " | Wake. |
| 25th | " | Nash. |
| 26th | " | Franklin. |
| 27th | " | Warren. |
| 28th | " | Granville. |
| 29th | " | Person. |
| 30th | " | Orange. |
| 31st | " | Alamance and Randolph. |
| 32d | " | Chatham. |
| 33d | " | Moore and Montgomery. |
| 34th | " | Richmond and Robeson. |
| 35th | " | Anson and Union. |
| 36th | " | Guilford. |
| 37th | " | Caswell. |
| 38th | " | Rockingham. |
| 39th | " | Mecklenburg. |
| 40th | " | Stanly and Cabarrus. |
| 41st | " | Rowan and Davie. |
| 42d | " | Davidson. |
| 43d | " | Forsyth and Stokes. |

| | | |
|---|---|---|
| 44th | District | Ashe, Surry, Watauga, Yadkin & Alleghany. |
| 45th | " | Wilkes, Iredell and Alexander. |
| 46th | " | Burke, McDowell and Caldwell. |
| 47th | " | Lincoln, Gaston and Catawba. |
| 48th | " | Rutherford, Cleaveland and Polk. |
| 49th | " | Buncombe, Henderson, Yancy, Madison, Transylvania and Mitchell. |
| 50th | " | Haywood, Macon, Cherokee, Jackson & Clay. |

SEC. 5. An enumeration of the inhabitants of the State shall be taken under the direction of the General Assembly in the year one thousand eight hundred and seventy-five, and at the end of every ten years thereafter, and the said Senate Districts shall be so altered by the General Assembly at the first session after the return of every enumeration taken as aforesaid, or by order of Congress, that each Senate District shall contain as nearly as may be, an equal number of inhabitants excluding aliens and Indians not taxed, and shall remain unaltered until the return of another enumeration, and shall at all times consist of contiguous territory; and no County shall be divided in the formation of a Senate District except such County shall be equitably entitled to two or more Senators.

SEC. 6. The House of Commons shall be composed of one hundred and twenty representatives, biennially chosen by ballot, to be elected by the Counties respectively according to their population, and each County shall have at least one representative in the House of Commons, although it may not contain the requisite ratio of representation. This apportionment shall be made by the General Assembly at the respective times and periods when the districts for the Senate are hereinbefore directed to be laid off.

SEC. 7. In making the apportionment in the House of Commons, the ratio of representation shall be ascertained by dividing the amount of population of the State, exclusive of aliens and Indians not taxed, and after deducting that comprehended within those Counties which do not severally contain the one hundred and twentieth part of the entire population of the State, exclusive of aliens and Indians not taxed, by the number of representatives less the number assigned to the said Counties. To each County containing the said raitio, and not twice the said ratio, there shall be assigned one representative; to each County containing twice but not three times the said ratio, there shall be assigned two representatives, and so on progressing; and then the remaining representatives shall be assigned severally to the Counties having the largest fractions.

SEC. 8. Until the General Assembly shall have made the apportionment as hereinbefore provided, the House of Commons shall be composed of members elected from the Counties in the following manner, to wit: The County of Wake shall elect four members; the Counties of Craven, Granville, Halifax and New Hanover, shall elect three members each; the Counties of Caswell, Chatham, Cumberland, Davidson, Duplin, Edgecombe, Franklin, Guilford, Iredell, Johnston, Mecklenburg, Northampton, Orange, Pitt, Randolph, Robeson, Rockingham, Rowan, Warren and Wayne, shall elect two members each; the Counties of Alamance, Alexander Allegany, Anson, Ashe, Beaufort, Bertie, Bladen, Brunswick Buncombe, Burke, Cabarrus, Caldwell, Camden, Carteret, Catawba, Cherokee, Chowan, Clay, Cleveland, Columbus, Currituck, Davie, Forsyth, Gaston, Gates, Greene, Harnett, Haywood, Henderson, Hertford, Hyde, Jackson, Jones, Lenoir Lincoln, Macon, Madison, Martin, McDowell, Mitchell, Montgomery, Moore, Nash, Onslow, Pasquotank, Perquimans Person, Polk, Richmond, Rutherford, Sampson, Stanly Stokes, Surry, Transylvania, Tyrrell, Union, Washington Watauga, Wilkes, Wilson, Yadkin and Yancey, shall elect one member each.

SEC. 9. Each member of the Senate shall be not less than twenty-five years of age; shall have resided in the State, as citizen two years, and shall have usually resided in the district for which he is chosen one year immediately preceeding his election.

SEC. 10. Each member of the House of Commons shall be not less than twenty-one years of age; shall have resided in the State as a citizen two years, and shall have usually resi ded in the county in which he is chosen, for one year immediately preceeding his election.

SEC. 11. In the election of all officers, whose appointment shall be conferred on the General Assembly by the Constitution, the vote shall be *viva voce.*

SEC. 12. The General Assembly shall have power to pass laws regulating the mode of appointing and removing militia officers.

SEC. 13. The General Assembly shall have power to pass general laws regulating divorce and alimony, but shall not have power to grant a divorce or secure alimony in any individual case.

SEC. 14. The General Assembly shall not have power to pass any private law, to alter the name of any person, or to legitimate any person not born in lawful wedlock, or to restore to the rights of citizenship any person convicted of an infamous crime; but shall have power to pass general laws regulating the same.

SEC. 15. The General Assembly shall not pass any private law, unless it shall be made to appear that thirty days' notice of application to pass such law shall have been given, under such directions and in such manner as shall be provided by law.

SEC. 16. If vacancies shall occur in the General Assembly, by death, resignation or otherwise, writs of election shall be issued by the Governor, under such regulations as may be prescribed by law.

SEC. 17. No law shall be passed to raise money on the credit of the State, or to pledge the faith of the State directly or indirectly, for the payment of any debt, or to impose any tax upon the people of the State, or to allow the Counties, Cities or Towns, to do so, unless the bill for that purpose shall have been read three several times in each House of the General Assembly, and passed three several readings, which readings shall have been on three different days, and agreed to by a majority of the whole number of members of each House, respectively, and unless the yeas and nays, on the second and third readings of the bill, shall have been entered on the Journal.

Sec. 18. The General Assembly shall regulate entails in such a manner as to prevent perpetuities.

Sec. 19. Each House shall keep a Journal of its proceedings, which shall be printed and made public immediately after the adjournment of the General Assembly.

Sec. 20. Any member of either House may dissent from and protest against any act or resolve which he may think injurious to the public, or any individual, and have the reasons of his dissent entered on the Journal.

Sec. 21. The House of Commons shall choose their own speaker and other officers.

Sec. 22. The Lieutenant Governor shall preside in the Senate, but shall have no vote, unless they may be equally divided.

Sec. 23. The Senate shall choose their other officers, and also a speaker *pro tempore* in the absence of the Lieutenant Governor, or when he shall exercise the office of Governor.

Sec. 24. The style of the acts shall be, " The General Assembly of North-Carolina do enact, as follows:"

Sec. 25. Each House shall be judge of the qualifications and elections of its own members; shall sit upon its own adjournments from day to day; prepare bills to be passed into laws, and may also jointly adjourn to any future day or other place.

Sec. 26. All bills and resolutions of a legislative nature shall be read three times in each House before they pass into laws, and shall be signed by the presiding officers of both Houses.

Sec. 27. Each member of the General Assembly, before taking his seat, shall take an oath or affirmation that to the best of his knowledge and belief, he is qualified under the Constitution of the State to take his seat; that he will support the Constitution of the United States and the laws made in pursuance thereof, and will faithfully discharge his duties as a member of the Senate (or House of Commons.)

SEC. 28. Each person elected to the Senate or House of Commons shall hold his seat from the time of his election until the next biennial election.

SEC. 29. Upon motion made, and seconded in either House by one fifth of the members present, the yeas and nays upon any question shall be taken, and entered on the journals.

SEC. 30. The election for members to the Senate and House of Commons of the General Assembly, shall be held for the respective districts and Counties, at the places where they are now held, or may be directed hereafter to be held, in such manner as may be prescribed by law, on the——— in———, in the year one thousand eight-hundred and seventy, and every two years thereafter.

All of which is respectfully submitted.

W. H. S. SWEET, *Chairman.*
MARK MAY,
SAMUEL FORKNER,
HAYNES LENNON,
LEWIS S. MULLICAN,
HENRY E. CHILLSON,
JOHN H. FRENCH,
CUFFEE MAYO,
JAMES M. TURNER,
MATCHET TAYLOR,
JERE. SMITH.

The undersigned, a minority of the Committee on Legislature, its organization, the number, apportionments, election," &c., dissent from that part of the report of the majority, which fixes actual population as the basis of representation in both Houses of the Legislature; and also to that part of said report which ignores the time honored Constitutional provision of North-Carolina, requiring a property qualification for members of the Senate and House of Commons.

JOHN G. MARLER.

The report passed its first reading.

On the second reading.

Section first was read.

Mr. Graham, of Orange, moved to strike out the word "annually," and insert "biennially."

The amendment was lost.

The section, as read, was adopted.

Sections second and third were read and adopted.

Section fourth was read.

Mr. Graham moved to amend by substituting the following as section fourth:

"The Districts shall remain as they are until the first session of the General Assembly after the year 1871, and at such session, and then every ten years thereafter, shall be laid off by the General Assembly in proportion to the public taxes paid in the Treasury of the State by the citizens thereof, and the average of the public taxes paid by each County into the Treasury of the State for three years preceeding the laying of the Districts, shall be considered as its proportion of the public taxes and constitute the basis of apportionment: *Provided*, That no County shall be divided in the formation of a Senatorial District, and when there are one or more Counties having an excess of taxation above the ratio, to form a Senatorial District, adjoining a County or Counties deficient in such ratio, the excess or excesses aforesaid shall, added to the taxation of the County or Counties deficient; and if, with such addition, the County or Counties it shall have the requisite ratio, such County and Counties each shall constitute a Senatorial District."

The yeas and nays were demanded, and the substitute was lost by the following vote, yeas 16, nays 88.

Those who voted in affirmative are:

Messrs. Bradley, Durham, Ellis, Etheridge, Graham of Orange, Hall, Hare, Hodnett, Hollowell, Holt, Lennon, Marshall, McCubbins, Merritt, Peterson and Stilly—16.

Those who voted in the negative are:

Messrs. Abbott, Andrews, Ashley, Aydlott, Barnes, Benbow, Blume, Bryan, Carey, Carter, Candler, Cherry, Chillson, Colgrove, Congleton, Cox, Dickey, Duckworth, Eppes, Fisher, Forkner, Franklin, French of Bladen, French of Rockingham, French of Chowan, Fullings, Gahagan, Galloway, Garland, George, Glover, Graham of Montgomery, Grant of Wayne, Grant of Northampton, Gully, Gunter, Harris of Wake, Hayes of Halifax, Highsmith, Hobbs, Hoffler, Hood, Hyman, Ing, Jones of Caldwell, Jones of Washington, Kinney, Laflin, Lee, Legg, Logan, Long, May, Mayo, McDonald of Chatham, McDonald of Moore, Moore, Morton, Mullican, Murphy, Newsom, Nicholson, Patrick, Parker, Parks, Petree, Pierson, Pool, Ragland, Ray, Read, Renfrow, Rhodes, Robbins, Rodman, Rose, Smith, Stilwell, Sweet, Taylor, Teague, Tourgee, Trogden, Tucker, Watts, Welker, Williams of Wake and Williamson—88.

Mr. Pool offered the following substitute to section fourth:

"The basis of representation in the Senate shall remain as at present until the year 1871, when it shall be the duty of the Legislature to apportion the Senatorial Districts upon the basis of population.

The substitute was not adopted.

Mr. Sweet corrected the report by transferring "Transylvania," from the 43d District to the 40th District.

Mr. Rich moved to recommit the fourth section to the Committee.

The motion was lost.

Mr. Ellis moved to postpone section fourth until to-morrow.

The motion did not prevail.

Mr. Rodman moved to recommit sections second, third and fourth to the Committee.

Mr. Ellis moved to amend by adding section 37th.

The amendment was accepted.

The motion as amended was lost.

Section fourth, as read, was adopted.

Sections 5th, 6th, 7th, 8th, 9th, 10th, 11th, 12th, 13th, 14th, 15th, 16th, 17th, 18th, 19th, 20th, 21st, 22d, 23d, 24th, 25th and 26th, were read and adopted.

Section 27th was read.

Mr. Graham, of Orange, moved to amend by striking out all after the word "affirmation," on the second line, down to "and," on the sixth line, and insert, "to support the Constitution of the United States, and the Constitution of North-Carolina."

The amendment was lost.

Mr. Abbott moved to amend by striking out all after the word "affirmation," in the second line, down to the word "and," in the sixth line, and insert, "That he will support the Constitution and laws of the United States and of the State of North Carolina."

Mr. Forkner moved to insert the word "Constitution," between the words "the" and "of," so as to read: "That he will support the Constitution and laws of the United States, and the Constitution of the State of North-Carolina."

The amendment was accepted, and the section, as amended, was adopted.

Section 28th was read.

Mr. Rodman moved to amend by adding to the section:

"Unless it shall be sooner vacated by death, resignation or otherwise, according to law."

The amendment was carried, and the section, as amended, was adopted.

Section 29th was read and adopted.

Section 30th was read.

Mr. Jones, of Washington, moved to fill the blank in the section by inserting, "first Monday in November,"

Which was lost.

Mr. Forkner moved to amend by inserting, "first Thursday in August,"

Which was adopted.

Mr. Rodman offered the following as an addition to section 30th:

"But the General Assembly may change the time of holding the elections. The first election shall be held when the vote shall be taken upon the adoption of this Constitution, by the voters of the State, and the General Assembly then elected, shall meet on the thirtieth day after the approval thereof, by the Congress of the United States, if it fall not on a Sunday, but if it shall so fall, then on the next day thereafter, and the members then elected, shall hold their seats until their successors are elected at a regular election."

The amendment was carried.

The section, as amended, was,

On motion, adopted.

On motion, the House adjourned.

---

FRIDAY, February 14th, 1868.

The Convention was called to order at 10 o'clock, by the President.

Prayer by the Rev. Mr. May.

The President announced a quorum.

The Journal of Thursday was read and approved.

The following communication was received from General Miles and read to the Convention:

HEADQURTERS ASSISTANT COMMISSIONERS,
State of North-Carolina,
Raleigh, N. C., February 12th, 1868.

T. A. Byrnes, *Secretary of the Constitutional Convention of North-Carolina:*

Dear Sir:—Your letter of the 10th inst., enclosing a copy of a resolution of thanks was duly received.

Please tender my grateful acknowledgements to the Convention for their kind and complimentary consideration of the services in administering the affairs of the Bureau with my ardent desires that the Convention may successfully complete its work of reconstruction and the State of North-Carolina fully restored to her place in the Union of States.

I have the honor to remain

With great respect,
Your obedient servant.
NELSON A. MILES,
*Brev't. Maj. Gen'l. U. S. A.,*
*Assistant Commissioner.*

The following order, No. 20, was received from General Canby, and read to the House:

HEADQUARTERS SECOND MILITARY DISTRICT,
CHARLESTON, S. C., February 12th, 1868.

GENERAL ORDERS,
No. 20.

The Constitutional Convention assembled in North-Carolina, under the authority of the laws of the United States, having, in conformity with the eighth section of the law of March 23, 1867, (supplimentary to the law of March 2, 1867, "To provide for the more efficient government of the rebel States,") by an Ordinance adopted in Convention on the sixth day of February, 1868, provided for the levy and collection of a tax of one-twentieth of one per cent. on the real and personal property in the State, to raise monies to pay the expenses of said Convention; and having directed that the tax so provided for shall be paid into the Treasury of the State in reimbursement for advances made from the said Treasury, for the purpose of defraying the current expenses of the Convention, the payment of its officers, members and contingent accounts; It is ordered,

*First.* That the assessors of taxes in the State of North-Carolina shall add to the assessments already made or about to be made for the year 1868 under the authority of the laws of the State, the tax levied under the ordinance before cited and hereinafter published, and the collectors of taxes will proceed to collect the same at the time and in the manner prescribed by the laws of the State for State taxes, and pay the same into the Treasury of the State.

*Second.* That the Treasurer of the State is hereby authorized and directed to pay the *per diem* and mileage of the delegates, the compensation of the officers, and the contingent expenses of the Convention, upon the warrants of the President, in the usual form.

By Command of Bvt. Major General E. R. S. CANBY:

LOUIS V. CAZIARC,
*Aide-de-Camp,*
*Actg. Asst. Adjt. Genl.*

Section 1. *Be it ordained by the people of North-Carolina, in Convention assembled,* That for the purpose of raising monies to pay the expenses of this Convention, according to the acts of Congress in such case made and provided, a tax of one twentieth of one per cent. shall be levied on the land in North-Carolina, according to its valuation in the year 1860, subject to such changes therein as have been since made by law, and on the personal property within said State according to the valuation thereof to be made in the year 1868. This tax shall be collected, paid and accounted for, at the Treasury of the State, at the times when, and in the same manner as other State taxes are required by law to be.

Sec. 2. *Be it further ordained,* That the collecting officers shall be subject to the same penalties for failure to collect, pay and account for the taxes hereby levied as they now are for such failure in respect to other taxes.

Sec. 3. *Be it further ordained,* That the said collecting officers shall receive the like compensation for collecting the tax, hereby levied as for the collection of other taxes.

Sec. 4. *Be it further ordained,* That this ordinance shall be in force from and after its passage.

Leave of absence was granted to Mr. Harris, of Franklin, until Monday next.

Mr. Jones, of Washington, presented a petition of divorce of James Overton and Charlotte Overton.

Referred to the Committee on the Judicial Department.

Mr. McDonald, of Chatham, introduced an ordinance in favor of Hugh B. Guthrie, sheriff of Orange.

Lies over under the rules.

Mr. Abbott presented an ordinance designating a depository for the State funds.

Referred to the Committee on Finance.

Mr. Congleton introduced a resolution providing for the abolishment of the Senate.

Referred to the Committee on Legislature.

Mr. McDonald, of Chatham, introduced an ordinance to repudiate all debts created prior to May 1st, 1865.

Referred to the Committee on Relief.

Mr. Rose presented a resolution in relation to debts created prior to May 1st, 1865.

Referred to the Committee on relief.

UNFINISHED BUSINESS.

The ordinance of Mr. Welker on the distillation of grain was taken up.

Mr. Welker moved to amend Section 1st by striking out "February 1st, 1868," and insert "after the passage of this act."

The amendment was accepted.

Mr. McCubbins moved to strike out "June" and insert "January."

The amendment was accepted.

Mr. McDonald, of Chatham moved to strike out the entire section.

Pending the discussion, the hour of 11 o'clock arrived, and the report of the Committee on a Preamble and Bill of Rights was taken up.

Sections 2d and 3d were read and adopted.

The President announced the following Committees:

*On Tobacco Tax.*—Messrs Petree, Read and McCubbins.

*Committee to investigate the case of Mr. Durham.*—Messrs. Harris, of Wake, Gahagan and Pool.

On motion the House adjourned to 7½ o'clock, P. M.

---

AFTERNOON SESSION, February 14th, 1868.

The Convention was called to order at 7½ o'clock by the President.

The President anounced a quorum.

The Journal of this morning was read and approved.

Section 4th of the report of the Committee on a Preamble and Bill of Rights was taken up.

The yeas and nays were demanded.

The section was adopted by the following vote:

Those who voted in the affirmative are:

Messrs. Abbott, Ashley, Aydlott, Barnes, Carter, Colgrove, Congleton, Dickey, Dowd, Duckworth, Etheridge, Fisher, Forkner, Franklin, French of Bladen, French of Rockingham, French of Chowan, Fullings, Gahagan, Galloway, George, Glover, Graham ot Montgomery, Grant of Wayne, Grant of Northampton, Gunter, Harris of Wake, Hay, Hayes of Robeson, Hayes of Halifax, Heaton, Hobbs, Hodnett, Hoffler, Hollowell, Jones of Caldwell, Jones of Washington, Kinney, Laflin, Lee, Legg, Logan, Long, Mann, Mayo, Marshall, McCubbins, McDonald of Chatham, McDonald of Moore, Mullican, Murphy, Nance, Newsom, Nicholson, Patrick, Parker, Parks, Petree, Peterson, Pierson, Pool, Ragland, Ray, Renfrow, Rhodes, Rich, Robbins, Rose, Smith, Stilly, Stilwell, Teague, Tourgee, Trogden, Watts, Welker and Williamson—77.

Those who voted in the negative are:

Messrs. Durham, Hall, Hare and Holt—4.

Section fifth was read, and the yeas and nays were demanded.

The section was adopted by the following vote, yeas 76, nays 3:

Those who voted in the affirmative are:

Messrs. Abbott, Ashley, Aydlott, Baker, Barnes, Carter, Congleton, Dickey, Dowd, Duckworth, Etheridge, Fisher, Forkner, Franklin, French of Bladen, French of Rockingham, French of Chowan, Fullings, Gahagan, Galloway, George, Glover, Graham of Montgomery, Grant of Wayne, Grant of Northampton, Gunter, Harris of Wake, Hay, Hayes of Robeson, Hayes of Halifax, Heaton, Hobbs, Hodnett, Hoffler, Hollowell, Jones of Caldwell, Kinney, Laflin, Lee, Legg, Logan, Long, Mann, Mayo, Marshall, McCubbins, McDonald of Chatham, McDonald of Moore, Mullican, Murphy, Nance, Newsom, Nicholson, Patrick, Parker, Parks, Petree, Peterson, Pierson, Pool, Ragland, Ray, Renfrow, Rhodes, Rich, Robbins, Rose, Smith, Stilly, Stilwell, Teague, Tourgee, Trogden, Watts, Welker and Williamson—76.

Those who voted in the negative are:

Messrs. Durham, Hare and Holt—3.

Section 6th was taken up and discussed.

Mr. Watts moved to amend by inserting after the word "pay," in fifth line, "or require any County, Towns, Corporations or individuals."

The yeas and nays were demanded, and the amendment was lost by the following vote, yeas 20, nays 59:

Those who voted in the affirmative are:

Messrs. Barnes, Bryan, Chillson, Congleton, Graham of Montgomery, Hay, McDonald of Chatham, McDonald of Moore, Morton, Newsom, Patrick, Petree, Peterson, Ragland, Smith, Stilly, Stilwell, Tourgee, Watts and Welker—20.

Those who voted in the negative are:

Messrs. Abbott, Andrews, Ashley, Aydlott, Baker, Carey, Carter, Cherry, Dickey, Dowd, Duckworth, Eppes, Etheridge, Fisher, Forkner, French of Bladen, French of Rockingham, French of Chowan, Fullings, Gahagan, Galloway, George, Glover, Grant of Wayne, Grant of Northampton, Gunter, Harris of Wake, Harris of Franklin, Hayes of Robeson, Hayes of Halifax, Heaton, Hobbs, Hodnett, Hollowell, Hood, Ing, Jones of Caldwell, Kinney, Lee, Legg, Logan, Mann, Mayo, McCubbins, Mullican, Murphy, Nicholson, Parker, Parks, Pierson, Pool, Renfrow, Rhodes, Rich, Robbins, Rose, Teague, Trogden and Williamson—59.

Mr. Tourgee moved to submit section 6th of the Bill of Rights to the people of the State separate from the Constitution.

The yeas and nays were demanded.

The motion was lost by the following vote, yeas 15, nays 56:

Those who voted in the affirmitive are:

Messrs. Congleton, Graham of Montgomery, McDonald of Chatham, McDonald of Moore, Morton, Murphy, Newsom, Patrick, Peterson, Ragland, Stilly, Stilwell, Tourgee, Watts and Welker—15.

Those who voted in the negative are:

Messrs. Andrews, Ashley, Aydlott, Baker, Barnes, Benbow Blume, Bryan, Chillson, Cox, Dickey, Duckworth, Etheridge Fisher, Forkner, Franklin, French of Bladen, French of Rock ingham, French of Chowan, Fullings, Gahagan, Galloway, Glover, Grant of Wayne, Grant of Northampton, Gunter, Harris of Wake, Harris of Franklin, Hayes of Robeson, Hayes of Halifax, Heaton, Hobbs, Hodnett, Hoffler, Hollowell, Hood, Jones of Caldwell, Kinney, Lee, Legg, Logan, Mayo, McCubbins, Nicholson, Parker, Petree, Pierson, Pool, Renfrow, Rhodes, Robbins, Rose, Smith, Teague, Trogden and Williamson—56.

Messrs. Andrews and Cox desired their names entered in the affirmative on sections 4th and 5th of the Bill of Rights.

On motion the House adjourned.

---

SATURDAY, February 15th, 1868.

The Convention was called to order at 10 o'clock, by the President.

Prayer by the Rev. Mr. Ellis.

The following members answered to their names:

Messrs. Abbott, Andrews, Ashley, Aydlott, Baker, Barnes, Benbow, Blume, Bradley, Bryan, Carey, Carter, Candler, Cherry, Colgrove, Congleton, Cox, Dowd, Duckworth, Ellis, Etheridge, Fisher, Forkner, Franklin, French of Bladen, French of Rockingham, French of Chowan, Fullings, Gahagan, Galloway, George, Glover, Graham of Montgomery, Grant of Northampton, Gunter, Hare, Harris of Wake, Hay, Hayes of Robeson, Hayes of Halifax, Heaton, Highsmith, Hobbs, Hodnett, Hoffler, Hollowell, Holt, Ing, Jones of Caldwell, Jones of Washington, Kinney, Laflin, Lennon, Logan, Long, May, Mayo, Marshall, McCubbins, Merritt, McDonald of Chatham, McDonald of Moore, Morton, Mullican, Murphy, Nance, Newson, Nicholson, Patrick, Parker, Parks, Petree, Peterson, Pierson, Pool, Ragland, Ray, Read, Renfrow, Rhodes, Rich, Robbins, Rodman, Rose, Stilly, Stilwell, Sweet, Taylor, Teague, Tourgee, Trogden, Tucker, Welker, Williams of Wake, and Williamson—95.

The President announced a quorum.

The Journal of Friday, P. M. was read and approved.

Mr. Etheridge was allowed to record his name in the affirmative on sections 4th and 5th of the Bill of Rights; also, in the negative on Mr. Tourgee's motion to submit section 6th to the people.

Leave of absence was granted Mr. French, of Bladen, until Tuesday next; also to Mr. Watts until Monday next.

Mr. Forkner introduced a resolution appointing a committee on adjournment.

Mr. Forkner called for a suspension of the rules.

The call was not sustained.

The resolution lies over under the rules.

### UNFINISHED BUSINESS.

The following Ordinances on the Distillation of Grain, introduced by Mr. G. W. Welker, was taken up:

## AN ORDINANCE PROHIBITING THE DISTILLATION OF GRAIN.

Whereas, In consequence of the rapid reduction of the small crops of corn in this State the prices of food have already greatly advanced, and money being unusually scarce, great destitution already exists, and starvation must inevitably follow speedily; therefore, in order that all the grain still on hand may be reserved for bread, and famine, at least in a degree averted,

Section 1. *Be it ordained by the people of North-Carolina in Convention assembled*, That after the passage of this act, until the 1st day of November, 1868, it shall not be lawful for any person or persons to distil corn or any other grain into intoxicating liquors.

Sec. 2. *Be it further ordained*, That any person or persons who shall be guilty of a violation of this ordinance, on being convicted before a competent Court, shall pay a fine of fifty dollars for the first offence, one hundred dollars for the second offence, and for the third offence his distillery shall be closed by the Sheriff. In this ordinance, each day in which the distillery is in operation shall be counted a separate offence.

SEC. 3. *Be it further ordained,* That all fines recovered under this ordinance, (after the lawful costs are deducted,) shall be paid into the Treasury of the County in which the conviction takes place, for the benefit of the poor supported by said County.

Ratified this 15th day of February, A. D. 1868.

Mr. McDonald moved to postpone indefinitely.

The motion was not sustained.

Mr. Rich moved a call of the House.

There were 96 members present.

Mr. Rich moved to lay the ordinance on the table.

The yeas and nays were demanded.

The motion was lost by the following vote, yeas 39, nays 56.

Those who voted in the negative are:

Messrs. Abbott, Ashley, Blume, Bryan, Carey, Carter, Candler, Chilson, Colgrove, Congleton, Cox, Duckworth, Etheridge, Fisher, French of Bladen, French of Chowan, Gahagan, George, Glover, Grant of Northampton, Gunter, Hare, Hay, Heaton, Highsmith, Hodnett, Hoffler, Hollowell, Jones of Washington, Kinney, Laflin, Lennon, Logan, Long, May, Mayo, Merritt, McDonald of Moore, Nance, Newsom, Nicholson, Parker, Petree, Peterson, Pool, Ray, Renfrow, Rhodes, Robbins, Rose, Taylor, Tourgee, Trogden, Tucker, Welker, Williamson—56.

Those who voted in the affirmative are:

Messrs. Andrews, Aydlott, Baker, Barnes, Benbow, Bradley, Dowd, Durham, Ellis, Forkner, Franklin, French of Rockingham, Fullings, Graham of Montgomery, Hall, Harris of Wake, Hayes of Robeson, Hayes of Halifax, Hobbs, Holt, Ing, Jones of Caldwell, Marshall, McCubbins, McDonald of Chatham, Morton, Murphy, Patrick, Parks, Pierson, Ragland, Read, Rich, Rodman, Stilly, Stillwell, Sweet, Teague, and Williams of Wake—39.

Mr. Colgrove moved to amend Section 1st by striking out "January, 1869" and insert "November, 1868."

The amendment was adopted.

Mr. Welker moved to amend Section 2d by striking out all after the word "sheriff" on the 6th line down to the word "in" on the 9th line.

The amendment was adopted.

The ordinance as amended was then adopted

The Committe on Counties, Towns, &c., reported through their Chairman as follows:

The Committee on Counties, Towns, &c., have instructed me to report the ordinance introduced by Mr. Sweet, from Craven, entitled "An ordinance for the appointment of a collector of taxes for the City of Newbern," with the accompanying amendments, and recommend its passage.

A. W. TOURGEE, *Chairman.*

Amendment to Section 1st:

That the qualified voters of the City of Newbern shall have power to elect a collector of taxes for said City and any qualfied voter resident in said City shall be eligible to such office.

Amendment to Section 3d:

Strike out "to be fixed by the Mayor and Council not to exceed," and insert instead the word "of."

Amend the title by striking out the word "appointment" and insert instead the word "election."

The report of the Committee was accepted.

The amendments proposed by the Committee were not sustained by the House.

The original ordinance, was,

On motion, adopted.

The following is the ordinance as adopted:

## AN ORDINANCE FOR THE APPOINTMENT OF A COLLECTOR OF TAXES FOR THE CITY OF NEWBERN.

Section 1. *Be it ordained by the people of North-Carolina in Convention assembled, and it is hereby ordained,* That the

Mayor and Council of the City of Newbern shall have power to appoint a collector of taxes for said City.

SEC. 2. *Be it further ordained*, That it shall be the duty of said collector of taxes to collect taxes which may be levied agreeably to law, by the Mayor and Council, and in the execution of such duty, such Collector of taxes shall have and exercise all the power given by law to sheriffs in the collection of State or County taxes.

SEC. 3. *Be it further ordained*, That the collector of taxes for the City of Newbern shall, before entering upon the duties of his office, enter into a bond with securities, approved by the Mayor of said City, in the sum of five thousand dollars, payable to the Mayor and Council of the City of Newbern with the conditions for the due collection, payment and settlement of the taxes imposed by the Mayor and Council of said City, and shall be entitled to a compensation to be fixed by the Mayor and Council not to exceed five per cent on the amount collected.

SEC. 4. *Be it further ordained*, That it shall be the duty of such collector of taxes to pay over to the Treasurer of the City of Newbern weekly all taxes collected by him.

SEC. 5. *Be it further ordained*, That all laws and clauses of laws and ordinances and clauses of ordinances conflicting with this ordinance are hereby repealed.

SEC. 6. *Be it further ordained*, That this ordinance shall take effect from the date of its ratification.

The hour of 11 o'clock having arrived, the House proceeded with the following report of the Committee on a Preamble and Bill of Rights:

## REPORT OF THE STANDING COMMITTEE ON PREAMBLE AND BILL OF RIGHTS.

### PREAMBLE.

We, the people of the State of North-Carolina, grateful to Almighty God, the Sovereign Ruler of Nations, for the preservation of the American Union, and the existence of our civil, political, and religious liberties, and acknowledging our dependence upon Him for the continuance of those blessings to us and our posterity, do, for the more certain security thereof, and for the better government of this State, ordain and establish this Constitution:

## ARTICLE I.

### DECLARATION OF RIGHTS.

That the general, great, and essential principles of liberty and free government may be recognized and established, and that the relations of this State to the Union and government of the United States, and those of the people of the State to the rest of the American people, may be defined and affirmed, we do declare—

SECTION 1. That we hold it to be self-evident, that all men are endowed by their Creator with certain inalienable rights, among which are life, liberty, the enjoyment of the fruits of their labor, and the pursuit of happiness.

SEC. 2. That all political power is vested in and derived from the people; that all government of right originates from the people, is founded upon their will only, and is instituted solely for the good of the whole.

SEC. 3. That the people of this State have the inherent, sole, and exclusive right of regulating the internal government and police thereof, and of altering and abolishing their Constitution and form of government, whenever it may be necessary to their safety and happiness; but every such right should be exercised in pursuance of law, and consistently with the Constitution of the United States.

SEC. 4. That this State shall ever remain a member of the American Union; that the people thereof are part of the American nation; that there is no right on the part of this State to secede, and that all attempts, from whatever source or upon whatever pretext, to dissolve said Union, or to sever said nation, ought to be resisted with the whole power of the State.

SEC. 5. That every citizen of this State owes paramount allegiance to the Constitution and government of the United States, and that no law or ordinance of the State, in contravention or subversion thereof, can have any binding force.

SEC. 6. To maintain the honor and good faith of the State untarnished, the public debt regularly contracted before and since the rebellion shall be regarded as inviolable and never questioned; but the State shall never assume or pay any debt or obligation, express or implied, incurred in aid of insurrection or rebellion against the United States, or any claim for the loss or emancipation of any slave.

SEC. 7. No man or set of men are entitled to exclusive or separate emoluments or privileges from the community but in consideration of public services.

SEC. 8. The legislative, executive, and supreme judicial powers of government ought to be forever separate and distinct from each other.

SEC. 9. All power of suspending laws, or the execution of laws, by any authority, without the consent of the representatives of the people, is injurious to their rights, and ought not to be exercised.

SEC. 10. All elections ought to be free.

SEC. 11. In all criminal prosecutions, every man has a right to be informed of the accusation against him, and to confront the accusers and witnesses with other testimony, and to have counsel for his defence, and shall not be compelled to give evidence against himself.

SEC. 12. No person shall be put to answer any criminal charge, except as hereinafter allowed, but by indictment, presentment, or impeachment.

SEC. 13. No person shall be convicted of any crime, but by the unanimous verdict of a jury of good and lawful men, in open court. The Legislature may, however, provide other modes of trial for petty misdemeanors, with the right of appeal.

SEC. 14. Excessive bail should not be required, nor excessive fines imposed, nor cruel, nor unusual punishments inflicted.

SEC. 15. General warrants, whereby any officer or messenger may be commanded to search suspected places without evidence of the fact committed, or to seize any person or persons not named, whose offence is not particularly described and supported by evidence, are dangerous to liberty, and ought not to be granted.

SEC. 16. No person ought to be taken, imprisoned, or disseized of his freehold, liberties, or privileges, or outlawed, or exiled, or in any manner destroyed, or deprived his life, liberty, or property, but by the law of the land.

SEC. 17. Every person restrained of his liberty is entitled to a remedy to inquire into the lawfulness thereof, and to remove the same, if unlawful, and such remedy ought not to be denied or delayed.

SEC. 18. In all controversies at law respecting property, the ancient mode of trial by jury is one of the best securities of the rights of the people, and ought to remain sacred and inviolable.

SEC. 19. The freedom of the press is one of the great bulwarks of liberty, and therefore ought never to be restrained.

SEC. 20. The privilege of the writ of *habeas corpus* shall not be suspended in this State.

SEC. 21. The people of this State ought not to be taxed or made subject to the payment of any impost or duty, without the consent of themselves, or their representatives in General Assembly, freely given.

SEC. 22. The people have a right to bear arms for the defence of the State; and, as standing armies in time of peace are dangerous to liberty, they ought not to be kept up; and the military should be kept under strict subordination to, and governed by, the civil power.

SEC. 23. The people have a right to assemble together to consult for their common good, to instruct their representatives, and to apply to the Legislature for redress of grievances.

SEC. 24. All men have a natural and inalienable right to worship Almighty God according to the dictates of their own consciences; that no human authority can, in any case whatever, control or interfere with the rights of conscience.

SEC. 25. For redress of grievances, and for amending and strengthening the laws, elections ought to be often held.

SEC. 26. A frequent recurrence to fundamental principles is absolutely necessary to preserve the blessings of liberty.

SEC. 27. No hereditary emoluments, privileges, or honors, ought to be granted or conferred in this State.

SEC. 28. Perpetuities and monopolies are contrary to the genius of a free State, and ought not to be allowed.

SEC. 29. Retrospective laws, punishing facts committed before the existence of such laws, and by them only declared criminal, are oppressive, unjust, and incompatible with liberty; wherefore, no *ex post facto* law ought to be made.

SEC. 30. Slavery and involuntary servitude otherwise than for crimes, whereof the parties shall have been duly convicted, shall be, and is hereby forever prohibited within this State.

SEC. 31. The limits and boundaries of the State shall be and remain as they now are.

SEC. 32. All courts shall be open, and every person, for an injury done him in his lands, goods, person or reputation, shall have remedy by due course of law, and right and justice administered without sale, denial or delay.

SEC. 33. No soldier shall, in time of peace, be quartered in any house without the consent of the owner; nor in time of war, but in a manner to be prescribed by law.

SEC. 34. This enumeration of rights shall not be construed to impair or deny others retained by the people, and all powers not herein delegated, remain with the people.

DAVID HEATON, *Chairman*,
J. H. HARRIS,
WM. NICHOLSON,
JOHN R. FRENCH,
JOHN M. PATRICK,
GEO. W. GAHAGAN,
C. C. POOL,
A. W. FISHER,
J. H. BAKER,
SYLVESTER CARTER,
JULIUS S. GARLAND,
JASPER ETHERIDGE.

Section 6th was taken up, and, after considerable debate the yeas and nays were called on its adoption.

The section was adopted by the following vote, yeas 72, nays 59.

Those who voted in the affirmative are:

Messrs. Abbott, Andrews, Ashley, Aydlott, Barnes, Benbow, Blume, Bryan, Carey, Carter, Candler, Chillson, Colgrove, Cox, Dickey, Dowd, Duckworth, Fisher, Forkner, Franklin, French of Rockingham, French of Chowan, Fullings, Gahagan, Galloway, Garland, George, Grant of Northampton, Gunter, Harris of Wake, Hay, Hayes of Halifax, Heaton, Highsmith, Hobbs, Hoffler, Hollowell, Ing, Jones of Caldwell, Jones of Washington, Kinney, Laflin, Legg, Logan, May, Mayo, McCubbins, McDonald of Moore, Nance, Nicholson, Parker, Parks, Petree, Pierson, Pool, Ragland, Ray, Read, Renfrow, Rhodes, Rich, Robbins, Rodman, Rose, Stilly, Stilwell, Sweet, Teague, Trogden, Tucker, Williams of Wake and Williamson—72.

Those who voted in the negative are:

Messrs. Congleton, Graham of Montgomery, Long, McDonald of Chatham, Murphy, Newsom, Taylor, Tourgee, and Welker—9.

Leave of absence was granted Mr. Tourgee until Wednesday next.

Section 7th and 8th were read and adopted.

Section 9th was read.

Mr. Bryan moved to amend by striking out the word "ought" and insert "shall."

The amendment was lost.

The section as read was adopted.

Section 10th was read and adopted.

Section 11th was read.

Mr. Tourgee moved to amend by adding "nor be compelled to pay costs or jail fees, or necessary witness fees of the defence, unless found guilty."

The amendment was adopted.

The section as amended was adopted.

Sections 12th, 13th and 14th, were read and adopted.

Section 15th was read.

Mr. Heaton moved that the following amendment be added to it:

"There shall be no imprisonment for debt in this State except for Fraud."

The amendment was adopted.

The section as amended was,

On motion, adopted.

Sections 16th, 17th and 18th were read and adopted.

Section 19th was read.

Mr. Nicholson moved to amend by adding to the section:

"But any individual shall be held responsible for an abuse of the same."

The amendment was adopted.

The section as amended was adopted.

Section 20th was read.

Mr. Rodman moved to strike out the entire section.

The motion did not prevail.

The section as read, was adopted.

Mr. Abbott moved to insert the following as a section, following section 20th:

"As political rights and privileges are not dependent upon, or modified by property; therefore no property qualification ought to effect the right to vote or hold office."

The amendment was sustained.

Sections 21st and 22d were read and adopted.

Section 23d was read.

Mr. Tourgee moved to amend by striking out "the Legislature" and inserting "any branch of the government."

The amendment was not adopted.

The section as read was adopted.

Section 24th was read and adopted.

Mr. Ashley moved the following as an additional section to section 24th:

"The people have a right to the privileges of education, and it is the duty of the State to guard and maintain that right."

The motion was sustained.

Sections 25th, 26th, 27th and 28th, were read and adopted.

Section 29th was read.

Mr. Rich moved to amend by substituting the word "acts" for "facts" in the first line.

The amendment was adopted.

Mr. Rodman moved to amend the section by adding the following:

"No law taxing retrospectively sales, purchases, or other acts previously done ought to be passed.

The amendment was adopted.

The section as amended, was,.

On motion, adopted.

Section 30th was read.

Mr Ashley moved to amend by striking out "is" on line third and insert "are"

The amendment was sustained.

Mr. McDonald, of Chatham, moved to amend by striking out "and" on line first and insert "or."

The amendment was lost.

The section as amended was adopted.

Sections 31st, 32d and 33d, were read and adopted.

Mr. Durham offered the following as a section to be inserted between sections 33d and 34th:

"The Caucassian and African races are distinct by nature, and color; therefore all intermarriages between the Caucassion or white race, and the African or black race are forever prohibited.

On motion, this amendment was laid on the table.

Section 34th was read and adopted.

On motion, the House adjourned to Monday at 10 o'clock, A. M.

---

## MONDAY, February 17th, 1868.

The Convention was called to order at 10 o'clock, by the President.

Prayer by the Rev. Mr. Hudson.

The President announced a quorum.

The Journal of Saturday was read and approved.

Mr. Abbott introduced an Ordinance relating to freights on the Wilmington and Weldon and North-Carolina Rail Roads.

Referred to the committee on Internal Improvements.

Mr. Rich, chairman of the committee on Immigration, called up the following Ordinance:

## AN ORDINANCE FOR ESTABLISHING AN IMMIGRATION AGENCY, REPORTED BY THE COMMITTEE ON IMMIGRATION.

*Be it ordained by the people of North-Carolina in Convention assembled*, That within twenty days after the ratification of the Constitution framed by this Convention, by the Congress of the United States, the Governor of the State shall appoint a suitable person to act as Land and Immigrant Commissioner, who shall serve four years, have an office in the City of New York, and be paid in quarterly installments, a salary not exceeding $2,500 per annum. It shall be the duty of the Commissioner, as far as practicable, to effect the sale of such lands as the residents of this State shall authorize him to sell. He is hereby authorized to establish in the Emigrant Depot, Castle Garden, New-York, a Southern Rail Road Agency for the purpose of selling Rail Road tickets to such Immigrants as may desire to settle in the State of North-Carolina. He shall also make arrangements with such lines of travel as may be necessary, at the lowest possible rates of passage for Immigrants; and whoever shall desire to come into the State to settle, or for the purpose of viewing such property as may be for sale, with the intention of purchasing the same, the State Treasurer is hereby authorized to pay the salary of the Commissioner appointed under this ordinance, and also such necessary expenses as may be required to carry out the purpose of this ordinance, upon the warrant of the Governor.

D. J. RICH, *Chairman.*
S. S. ASHLEY,
GEO. W. GAHAGAN,
J. W. HOOD,
*Maj. of Committee.*

Mr. Rich moved to amend section first by inserting after the word "years," on the seventh line, "under the direction of the Bureau of Statistics and Immigration."

Mr. McDonald, of Chatham, moved to amend by striking out "$2,500," on ninth line, and insert "$2,000."

The yeas and nays were demanded.

The amendment was carried by the following vote, yeas 64, nay 29:

Those who voted in the affirmative are:

Messrs. Barnes, Benbow, Blume, Bradley, Bryan, Candler, Cherry, Congleton, Cox, Dickey, Dowd, Duckworth, Durham, Ellis, Etheridge, Fisher, Forkner, French of Chowan, Garland, George, Graham of Montgomery, Grant of Wayne, Gully, Gunter, Hall, Hare, Hay, Hayes of Halifax, Hobbs, Hodnett, Hoffler, Hollowell, Holt, Jones, of Caldwell, Jones, of Washington, King of Lenoir, Lennon, Long, May, Marshall, McCubbins, Merritt, McDonald of Chatham, McDonald, of Moore, Morton, Mullican, Nance, Newsom, Patrick, Parks, Petree, Peterson, Read, Renfrow, Rose, Sanderlin, Smith, Stilly, Teague, Trogden, Tucker, Welker, Williams of Wake and Williamson—64.

Those who voted in the negative are:

Messrs. Abbott, Andrews, Ashley, Baker, Carey, Colgrove, French of Rockingham, Fullings, Gahagan, Galloway, Glover, Hayes of Robeson, Heaton, Highsmith, Ing, Laflin, Lee, Logan, Mayo, Murphy, Pierson, Ragland, Ray, Rhodes, Rich, Robbins, Rodman, Stilwell and Taylor—29.

Mr. McDonald, of Chatham, moved to amend section first by striking out on fifth line, "Governor of the State shall appoint," and insert, "People shall elect."

This amendment was discussed until the hour of 11, when,

The House proceeded with the report of the Committee on Corporations other than Municipal.

The motion to strike out and substitute by Mr. Tourgee was taken up and divided.

The motion to strike out sections 4th, 5th, 6th, 7th, 8th, 9th and 10th, prevailed.

The substitute on section fourth was put to the House, and lost.

Section 11th was read.

Wr. Welker moved to strike out the entire section.

The motion was lost.

The section, as read, was adopted.

Mr. Abbott introduced an ordinance in relation to the Dan River and Coalfield Rail Road Company.

Referred to the Committee on Internal Improvements.

Mr. Watts presented an ordinance to prohibit the collection of certain debts. Was read and ordered to be printed.

The following majority report of the Committee on Homesteads, was taken up and passed its first reading:

## MAJORITY REPORT OF THE COMMITTEE ON HOMESTEADS.

The Committee appointed to report on a Homestead, respectfully submit the following article, to wit:

Section 1. The personal property of any resident of this State, to the value of three hundred dollars, to be selected by such resident, shall be exempted from sale or execution, or other final process of any court, issued for the collection of any debt ccontracted after the adoption of this Constitution.

Sec. 2. Every Homestead not exceeding one hundred acres of land and the dwelling and buildings therewith, not exceeding in value one thousand dollars, to be selected by the owner thereof, or in lieu thereof, at the option of the owner, any lot in a city, town or village, with the dwelling and buildings used thereon, owned and occupied by any resident of this State, and not exceeding the value of one thousand dollars, shall be exempt from sale, execution, or any final process, obtained on any debt contracted from and after the adoption of this Constitution. Such exemption, however, shall not extend to any mortgage lawfully obtained; but no such mortgage or deed in the nature thereof, made by the owner ot the homestead, if a married man, and no deed of conveyance by him shall be valid without the voluntary signature and assent of his wife, signified on her private examination before a Judge of some Court of this State.

Sec. 3. The homestead of a family, after the death of the owner thereof, shall be exempt from the payment of any debt contracted by him after the adoption of this Constitution, during the minority of his children, or any one of them.

Sec. 4. The provisions of sections one and two of this Article shall not be so construed as to prevent a laborer's lien for work done and performed for the person claiming such exemption, or a mechanic for work done on the premises.

Sec. 5. If the owner of a homestead die, leaving a widow but no children, the same shall be exempt from the debts of her husband, and the rents and profits thereof shall inure to her benefit for her life.

Sec. 6. The real and personal property of any female in this State, acquired before marriage, and all property, real and personal, to which she may, after marriage, become in any manner entitled after the adoption of this Constitution, shall be and remain the sole and separate estate and property of such female, and shall not be liable for any debts, obligations or engagements of her husband, and may be conveyed, devised, or bequeathed by her as if she were a *feme sole*.

C. C. JONES, *Chairman*.
HENRY BARNES,
JESSE RHODES,
J. L. NANCE,
JOHN H. RENFROW,
ISAAC KINNEY,
SWEEN McS. McDONALD.

On motion the report was postponed until Thursday next, at 11 o'clock.

Mr. McDonald moved to call up a resolution in favor of Hugh B. Guthrie, Sheriff of Orange County.

On motion the resolution was referred to a Special Committee of five.

The ordinance of Mr. Watts, for the relief of the people, was taken up.

A motion was made to postpone the ordinance until the Constitution was framed.

The yeas and nays were demanded.

The ordinance was postponed by the following vote, yeas 54, nays 36:

Those who voted in the affirmative are:

Messrs. Ashley, Baker, Barnes, Benbow, Bradley, Bryan, Carter, Candler, Cherry, Cox, Dickey, Dowd, Duckworth, Durham, Ellis, Fisher, Forkner, French of Rockingham, Gahagan, Galloway, Garland, Glover, Grant of Wayne, Grant of Northampton, Hobbs, Hodnett, Hoffler, Hollowell, Ing, Jones of Caldwell, Jones of Washington, King of Lenoir, Kinney, Lennon, Logan, May, Mayo, Marshall, McCubbins, Mullican, Murphy, Nicholson, Parker, Parks, Petree, Pierson, Renfrow, Rhodes, Rose, Stilly, Teague, Trogden, Tucker and Williams of Wake—54.

Those who voted in the negative are:

Messrs. Carey, Chillson, Congleton, Etheridge, Franklin, French of Chowan, George, Graham of Montgomery, Gully, Gunter, Harris of Wake, Hay, Hayes of Halifax, Highsmith, Lee, Long, Merritt, McDonald of Chatham, McDonald of Moore, Morton, Nance, Newsom, Peterson, Ragland, Ray, Read, Robbins, Rodman, Sanderlin, Smith, Stilwell, Taylor, Turner, Watts, Welker and Williamson—36.

Leave of absence was granted Mr. Carey, delegate from Caswell.

Mr. Jones, of Washington, introduced the following resolution:

*Resolved*, That this Convention will not entertain any proposition of a purely legislative character after the hour of 11 o'clock, A. M., each day, until the reports of the Committees appointed to report matter looking to the formation of a Constitution shall be considered, and a Constitution framed.

Mr. Welker moved to lay the resolution on the table.

The yeas and nays were demanded.

The motion was lost by the following vote, yeas 42, nays 52:

Those who voted in the affirmative are:

Messrs. Abbott, Ashley, Barnes, Carter, Candler, Cherry, Chilson, Congleton, Etheridge, Fisher, Franklin, French of Chowan, Galloway, George, Graham of Montgomery, Gully, Gunter, Harris of Franklin, Hay, Hobbs, Hollowell, Ing, Long, Mann, McDonald of Chatham, McDonald of Moore, Morton, Murphy, Nance, Newsom, Parks, Petree, Ragland, Ray, Rodman, Rose, Smith, Stillwell, Taylor, Turner, Watts and Welker—42.

Those who voted in the negative are:

Messrs. Benbow, Blume, Bradley, Bryan, Cox, Dickey, Dowd, Duckworth, Durham, Ellis, Forkner, French of Rockingham, Fullings, Gahagan, Garland, Glover, Grant of Northampton, Hall, Hare, Hayes of Halifax, Highsmith, Hodnett, Hoffler, Holt, Hyman, Jones of Caldwell, Jones of Washington, King of Lenoir, Kinney, Lennon, Logan, May, Mayo, Marshall, McCubbins, Merritt, Mullican, Nicholson, Parker, Peterson, Pierson, Read, Renfrow, Rhodes, Robbins, Sanderlin, Stilly, Teague, Trogden, Tucker, Williams of Wake and Williamson—52.

Mr. Rodman moved to amend by adding the words, "except when there is no other business."

The amendment was accepted, and the resolution, as amended, was put upon its passage.

The yeas and nays were demanded.

The resolution was adopted by the following vote, yeas 54, nays 44:

Those who voted in affirmative are:

Messrs. Abbott, Ashley, Aydlott, Barnes, Blume, Carter, Candler, Cherry, Chillson, Congleton, Dowd, Etheridge, Fisher, Franklin, French of Chowan, George, Graham of Montgomery, Grant of Wayne, Gully, Gunter, Harris of

Wake, Hayes of Robeson, Highsmith, Ing, King of Lenoir, Kinney, Laflin, Lee, Logan, Long, Mann, Mayo, McDonald of Chatham, McDonald of Moore, Morton, Murphy, Newsom, Parks, Petree, Peterson, Pierson, Ragland, Ray, Read, Robbins, Rodman, Rose, Smith, Stilwell, Taylor, Turner, Watts, Welker and Williamson—54.

Those who voted in the negative are:

Messrs. Baker, Benbow, Bradley, Bryan, Cox, Dickey, Duckworth, Durham, Ellis, Forkner, French of Rockingham, Fullings, Gahagan, Garland, Glover, Graham of Orange, Grant of Northampton, Hall, Hare, Hayes of Halifax, Heaton, Hodnett, Hoffler, Hollowell, Holt, Jones of Caldwell, Jones of Washington, Lennon, May, Marshall, McCubbins, Merritt, Mullican, Nance, Nicholson, Parker, Pool, Renfrow, Sanderlin, Stilly, Teague, Trogden, Tucker and Williams of Wake—44.

Mr. Abbott introduced the following resolution:

*Resolved*, That the contingent expenses of this Convention, including those for labor, be not paid until audited by the Committee on Contingent Expenses, and approved by the President and Secretary.

On motion, the rules were suspended, and the resolution adopted.

The following committee of five were appointed to report on the resolution of Mr. McDonald, of Chatham, for the relief of the Sheriff of Orange County:

Messrs. McDonald of Chatham, King of Lenoir, McCubbins, Nicholson and Smith.

Mr. King, of Lenoir, introduced an ordinance concerning widows who have qualified as Executrix to the last will and testament of their deceased husbands.

Lies over under the rules.

On motion, the House adjourned.

---

## AFTERNOON SESSION, February 17th, 1868.

The Convention was called to order at 7½ o'clock by the President.

The President anounced a quorum.

Mr. Hayes, of Halifax, presented the following resolution, which was referred to the Committee on Contingent Expenses:

*Resolved*, That the servants employed by this Convention be paid two dollars per day.

Mr. Forkner called up the following resolution:

*Resolved*, That a Committee of three on adjournment be appointed and instructed to report, as in their opinion, when this Convention should adjourn *sine die*.

The resolution was, on motion, adopted.

On motion, the report of the committee on a Preamble and Bill of Rights was proceeded with.

Mr. Rodman moved to amend section 17th by adding as follows:

"The remedy shall not be suspended except in case of war, insurrection or invasion;" also to strike out section 20th.

The yeas and nays were demanded, and the amendment was lost by the following vote, yeas 6, nays 72.

Those who voted in the affirmative are:

Messrs. Abbott, Ashley, Dowd, Fisher, Rich, Rodman—6.

Those who voted in the negative are:

Messrs. Andrews, Aydlott, Barnes, Benbow, Bryan, Carter, Candler, Cherry, Chilson, Colgrove, Congleton, Cox, Dickey, Duckworth, Durham, Forkner, Franklin, French of Rockingham, Fullings, Gahagan, Geore, Glover, Graham of Montgomery, Grant of Northampton, Gunter, Hall, Hare, Harris of Wake, Harris of Franklin, Hay, Hayes of Robeson, Hayes of Halifax, Heaton, Highsmith, Hobbs, Hodnett, Hoffler, Hollowell, Jones of Caldwell, Jones of Washington, King of Lenoir, Kinney, Logan, Mayo, McCubbins, Merritt, McDonald of Chatham, McDonald of Moore, Moore, Mullican, Murphy, Newsom, Nicholson, Parker, Parks, Petree, Peterson, Pierson, Ragland, Renfrow, Rhodes, Rose, Smith, Stilwell, Taylor, Teague, Trogden, Tucker, Turner, Watts, Welker and Williamson—72.

Mr. Congleton moved to amend section 6th, by striking out all before "the State" in the fourth line.

The yeas and nays were demanded, and the amendment was lost by the following vote, yeas 10, nays 56.

Those who voted in the affirmative are:

Messrs. Congleton, Graham of Montgomery, McDonald of Chatham, McDonald of Moore, Murphy, Newsom, Parks, Taylor, Turner and Welker—10.

Those who voted in the negative are:

Messrs. Abbott, Andrews, Ashley, Aydlott, Baker, Barnes, Bryan, Carter, Candler, Colgrove, Cox, Dickey, Duckworth, Eppes, Fisher, Forkner, French of Rookingham, French of Chowan, Fullings, Gahagan, Galloway, George, Grant of Northampton, Gunter, Harris of Wake, Harris of Franklin, Hay, Hayes of Halifax, Heaton, Highsmith, Hobbs, Hollowell, Hyman, Jones of Caldwell, Jones of Washington, Kinney, Logan, Mayo, Morton, Mullican, Nance, Nicholson, Parker, Petree, Pierson, Ray, Renfrow, Rhodes, Robbins, Rose, Smith, Stilwell, Teague, Tucker, Watts and Williamson—56.

On motion the House adjourned.

---

## TUESDAY, February 18th, 1868.

The Convention was called to order at 10 o'clock, by the President.

Prayer by the Rev. Mr. Franklin.

The President announced a quorum.

The Journal of Monday was read and approved.

Mr. Read presented a petition of divorce in favor of one Edw'd Shwyer.

Referred to the Committee on Divorce.

The Committee on Contingent Expenses, to whom was referred the resolution of Mr. George, in favor of Edwin C. Bartlett, of the County of Ashe, reported as follows:

The undersigned Committee on Contingent Expenses, to whom was referred the resolution in favor of Mr. Bartlett, have had the same under consideration, and beg leave to recommend that Edwin C. Bartlett be allowed for one day's at-

attendance as a member of this Convention, and also mileage for four hundred and forty six miles, the distance from his home to the City of Raleigh and return.

| | |
|---|---|
| One day, - - - - - - - - | $ 8 00 |
| 446 miles, 20 cents per mile, - - - - - | 89 20 |
| | $97 20 |

R. W. KING,
R. F. TROGDEN,
L. C. MORTON,
JNO. READ,
J. W. HOOD.

Mr. Morton introduced a resolution to repeal an ordinance ratified June 20th, 1866.

Lies over under the rules.

The hour of 10½ having arrived, the House proceeded to take up the following report of the Committee on a Preamble and Bill of Rights, it being a Special Order at that time, and put it upon its third reading and final passage:

## PREAMBLE.

We, the people of the State of North-Carolina, grateful to Almighty God, the Sovereign Ruler of Nations, for the preservation of the American Union, and the existence of our civil, political, and religious liberties, and acknowledging our dependence upon Him for the continuance of those blessings to us and our posterity, do, for the more certain security thereof, and for the better government of this State, ordain and establish this Constitution:

## ARTICLE I.

### DECLARATION OF RIGHTS.

That the general, great and essential principles of liberty

and free government may be recognized and established, and that the relations of this State to the Union and government of the United States, and those of the people of the State to the rest of the American people, may be defined and affirmed, we do declare:

SECTION 1. That we hold it to be self-evident that all men are created equal; that they are endowed by their Creator with certain unalienable rights; among these are life, liberty, the enjoyment of the fruits of their labor, and the pursuit of happiness.

SEC. 2. That all political power is vested in and derived from the people; all government of right originates from the people, is founded upon their will only, and is instituted solely for the good of the whole.

SEC. 3. That the people of this State have the inherent, sole and exclusive right of regulating the internal government and police thereof, and of altering and abolishing their Constitution and form of government, whenever it may be necessary to their safety and happiness; but every such right should be exercised in pursuance of law, and consistently with the Constitution of the United States.

SEC. 4. That this State shall ever remain a member of the American Union; that the people thereof are part of the American nation; that there is no right on the part of this State to secede, and that all attempts, from whatever source or upon whatever pretext, to dissolve said Union, or to sever said nation, ought to be resisted with the whole power of the State.

SEC. 5. That every citizen of this State owes paramount allegiance to the Constitution and government of the United States, and that no law or ordinance of the State, in contravention or subversion thereof, can have any binding force.

SEC. 6. To maintain the honor and good faith of the State untarnished, the public debt regularly contracted before and since the rebellion shall be regarded as inviolable and never questioned; but the State shall never assume or pay any debt or obligation, express or implied, incurred in aid of insurrection or rebellion against the United States, or any claim for the loss or emancipation of any slave.

SEC. 7. No man or set of men are entitled to exclusive or separate emoluments or privileges from the community but in consideration of public services.

SEC. 8. The legislative, executive, and supreme judicial powers of government ought to be forever separate and distinct from each other.

SEC. 9. All power of suspending laws, or the execution of laws, by any authority, without the consent of the representatives of the people, is injurious to their rights, and ought not to be exercised.

SEC. 10. All elections ought to be free.

SEC. 11. In all criminal prosecutions, every man has a right to be informed of the accusation against him, and to confront the accusers and witnesses with other testimony, and to have counsel for his defence, and shall not be compelled to give evidence against himself, nor be compelled to pay costs or jail fees, or necessary witness fees of the defence, unless found guilty.

SEC. 12. No person shall be put to answer any criminal charge, except as hereinafter allowed, but by indictment, presentment, or impeachment.

SEC. 13. No person shall be convicted of any crime, but by the unanimous verdict of a jury of good and lawful men, in open court. The Legislature may, however, provide other modes of trial for petty misdemeanors, with the right of appeal.

SEC. 14. Excessive bail should not be required, nor excessive fines imposed, nor cruel, nor unusual punishments inflicted.

SEC. 15. General warrants, whereby any officer or messenger may be commanded to search suspected places without evidence of the fact committed, or to seize any person or persons not named, whose offence is not particularly described and supported by evidence, are dangerous to liberty, and ought not to be granted.

SEC. 16. There shall be no imprisonment for debt in this State, except in cases of fraud.

SEC. 17. No person ought to be taken, imprisoned, or disseized of his freehold, liberties, or privileges, or outlawed, or exiled, or in any manner destroyed, or deprived of his life, liberty, or property, but by the law of the land.

SEC. 18. Every person restrained of his liberty is entitled to a remedy to inquire into the lawfulness thereof, and to remove the same, if unlawful, and such remedy ought not to be denied or delayed.

SEC. 19. In all controversies at law respecting property, the ancient mode of trial by jury is one of the best securities of the rights of the people, and ought to remain sacred and inviolable.

SEC. 20. The freedom of the press is one of the great bulwarks of liberty, and therefore ought never to be restrained, but every individual shall be held responsible for the abuse of the same.

SEC. 21. The privilege of the writ of *habeas corpus* shall not be suspended in this State.

SEC. 22. As political rights and privileges are not dependent upon, or modified by property, therefore no property qualification ought to affect the right to vote or hold office.

SEC. 23. The people of this State ought not to be taxed or made subject to the payment of any impost or duty, without the consent of themselves, or their representatives in General Assembly, freely given.

SEC. 24. The people have a right to bear arms for the defence of the State; and, as standing armies in time of peace are dangerous to liberty, they ought not to be kept up; and the military should be kept under strict subordination to, and governed by, the civil power.

SEC. 25. The people have a right to assemble together to consult for their common good, to instruct their representatives, and to apply to the Legislature for redress of grievances.

SEC. 26. All men have a natural and unalienable right to worship Almighty God according to the dictates of their own consciences; that no human authority should, in any case whatever, control or interfere with the rights of conscience.

SEC 27. The people have a right to the privilege of education, and it is the duty of the State to guard and maintain that right.

SEC. 28. For redress of grievances, and for amending and strengthening the laws, elections ought to be often held.

SEC. 29. A frequent recurrence to fundamental principles is absolutely necessary to preserve the blessings of liberty.

SEC. 30. No hereditary emoluments, privileges, or honors, ought to be granted or conferred in this State.

SEC. 31. Perpetuities and monopolies are contrary to the genius of a free State, and ought not to be allowed.

SEC. 32. Retrospective laws, punishing acts committed before the existence of such laws, and by them only declared criminal, are oppressive, unjust, and incompatible with liberty; wherefore, no *ex post facto* law ought to be made. No law taxing retrospectively, sales, purchases, or other acts previously done, ought to be passed.

SEC. 33. Slavery and involuntary servitude otherwise than for crimes, whereof the parties shall have been duly convicted, shall be, and is hereby forever prohibited within this State.

SEC. 34. The limits and boundaries of the State shall be and remain as they now are.

SEC. 35. All courts shall be open, and every person, for an injury done him in his lands, goods, person or reputation, shall have remedy by due course of law, and right and justice administered without sale, denial or delay.

SEC. 36. No soldier shall, in time of peace, be quartered in any house without the consent of the owner; nor in time of war, but in a manner to be prescribed by law.

SEC. 37. This enumeration of rights shall not be construed to impair or deny others retained by the people, and all powers not herein delegated, remain with the people.

Mr. Watts moved to amend section 6th by inserting after the word "pay," in the fifth line, "or authorize the collection of."

The amendment was adopted.

Mr. Durham moved to amend section 20th by striking out all after the word "restrained."

The yeas and nays were demanded.

The amendment was lost by the following vote, yeas 25, nays 83:

Those who voted in the affirmative are:

Messrs. Baker, Bradley, Cox, Dowd, Durham, Ellis, Etheridge, Forkner, Graham of Orange, Hall, Hare, Hodnett, Hollowell, Holt, Jones of Caldwell, Lennon, Marshall, McCubbins, Merritt, McDonald of Chatham, Patrick, Petree, Ray, Read and Sanderlin—25.

Those who voted in the negative are:

Messrs. Abbott, Andrews, Ashley, Aydlott, Barnes, Benbow, Blume, Bryan, Carter, Candler, Cherry, Chillson, Colgrove, Congleton, Dickey, Duckworth, Eppes, Fisher, Franklin, French of Bladen, French of Rockingham, French of Chowan, Fullings, Gahagan, Galloway, Garland, George, Glover, Graham of Montgomery, Grant of Wayne, Grant of Northampton, Gully, Gunter, Harris of Franklin, Hay, Hayes of Robeson, Heaton, Highsmith, Hobbs, Hood, Hyman, Ing, King of Lenoir, Kinney, Laflin, Lee, Logan, Long, Mann, May, McDonald of Moore, Moore, Morton, Mullican, Murphy, Nance, Newsom, Nicholson, Parker, Parks, Pierson, Pool, Ragland, Renfrow, Rhodes, Rich, Robbins, Rodman, Rose, Smith, Stilly, Stilwell, Taylor, Teague, Trogden, Tucker, Turner, Watts, Welker, Williams of Wake and Williamson—83.

Mr. Durham moved to amend section 23d by adding "without representation in the Congress of the United States."

The amendment was lost.

Mr. Abbott moved to amend section 21st by striking out "in this State."

The amendment was adopted.

Mr. Graham, of Orange, moved to amend section 24th by striking out "the people have a right to bear arms for the defence of the State," and insert "a well regulated militia being necessary to the security of a free State, the right of the people to keep and bear arms shall not be infringed."

The amendment was adopted.

The report of the Committee on a Preamble and Bill of Rights as amended passed its third and final reading by the following vote, yeas 87, nays 20.

Those who voted in the affirmative are:

Messrs. Abbott, Andrews, Ashley, Aydlott, Barnes, Benbow, Blume, Bryan, Carter, Candler, Cherry, Chillson, Colgrove, Cox, Dickey, Duckworth, Eppes, Fisher, Forkner, Franklin, French of Bladen, French of Rockingham, French of Chowan, Fullings, Gahagan, Galloway, Garland, George, Graham of Montgomery, Grant of Wayne, Grant of Northampton, Gully, Gunter, Harris of Wake, Harris of Franklin, Hay, Hayes, of Robeson, Hayes of Halifax, Heaton, Highsmith, Hobbs, Hoffler, Hollowell, Hood, Hyman, Ing, Jones of Caldwell, Jones of Washington, King of Lincoln, King of Lenoir, Kinney, Lee, Logan, Mann, May, McDonald of Chatham, McDonald of Moore, Moore, Morton, Mullican, Nance, Nicholson, Patrick, Parker, Parks, Petree, Peterson, Pierson, Pool, Ragland, Ray, Read, Renfrow, Rhodes, Rich, Robbins, Rodman, Rose, Smith, Stilly, Stilwell, Teague, Trogden, Tucker, Watts, Williams of Wake, and Williamson—87.

Those who voted in the negative are:

Messrs. Baker, Bradley, Congleton, Dowd, Durham, Etheridge, Graham of Orange, Hall, Hare, Hodnett, Lennon, Long, Marshall, McCubbins, Merrit, Murphy, Sanderlin, Taylor, Turner and Welker—20.

The following report of the Committee on Suffrage and Eligibility to office was taken up:

The majority and minority reports were read to the House.

## REPORT OF THE COMMITTEE ON SUFFRAGE AND ELIGIBILITY TO OFFICE.

The Committee appointed to prepare and report to the Convention an Article of Suffrage and Eligibility to office, submit the following report:

## ARTICLE —.

### SUFFRAGE.

SECTION 1. Every male person born in the United States, and every male person who has been naturalized, twenty-one years old or upward, who shall have resided in this State twelve months next preceeding the election, and three months in the County, in which he offers to vote, shall be deemed an elector.

SEC. 2. All elections by the people shall be by ballot, and all elections by the General Assembly shall be *viva voce.*

## ARTICLE —.

### ELIGIBILITY TO OFFICE.

SECTION 1. Every voter, except as hereinafter provided, shall be eligible to office ; but, before entering upon the discharge of the duties of his office, he shall take and subscribe the following oath: "I, ——, do solemnly swear (or affirm,) that I will support and maintain the Constitution and laws of the United States, and the Constitution and laws of North-Carolina, not inconsistent therewith, and that I will faithfully discharge the duties of my office, So help me God."

SEC. 2. The following classes of persons shall be disqualified for office: 1st, All persons who shall deny the being of Almighty God ; 2d, All persons who shall have been convicted of treason, or shall have been adjudged guilty of felony, perjury, of any infamous crime, (unless such person shall have been fully pardoned,) or of corruption or mal-practice in office.

C. C. POOL,
C. C. JONES,
D. J. RICH,
J. H. HARRIS,
J. A. McDONALD,
J. P. ANDREWS,
E. BENBOW,
H. C. C. CHERRY.

## MINORITY REPORT.

We, the undersigned, a part of the committee appointed to prepare and report to the Convention an article on Suffrage and Eligibility to office, submit the following:

### ELECTIONS.

SECTION 1. In all elections by the people, the electors shall vote by ballot, and the ballot shall be deposited by the elector in person.

### ELECTION.

SEC. 2. Every citizen of the United States, who shall have resided in this State one year, and in the County in which he offers to vote, three months next preceding the day of election, shall be deemed an elector, except as hereinafter provided. 1st. Those who have been convicted of infamous crime, since becoming citizens of the United States. 2d. Those who have been judicially pronounced to be of unsound mind. 3d. Those who have prevented, or endeavored to prevent any voter from the free exercise of the elective franchise by threats, violence or bribery. 4th. Those, who are disqualified from holding office by the terms of the proposed amendment to the Constitution of the United States, known as article fourteen, and the act of Congress passed March 2d, 1867, and the several acts supplementary thereto. *Provided*, That whenever said disqualifications shall be removed, as provided in said article, the person thus relieved shall be entitled to the elective franchise in the State. 5th. Those who, during the late rebellion, inflicted, or caused to be inflicted, or were accessory to the crime of inflicting any cruel or unusual punishment upon any officer, soldier, sailor, marine, employee, or citizen of the United States, or in any manner violated the rules of civilized warfare.

REGISTRATION.

SEC. 3. It shall be the duty of the General Assembly to provide, from time to time, for the registration of all electors, but no person shall be allowed to register, vote, or hold office without having first taken and subscribed to the annexed oath:

OATH TO BE TAKEN.

I do solemnly swear, or affirm, that I will support and maintain the Constitution of the United States, and the Constitution of the State of North-Carolina; that I will never countenance or aid in the secession of this State from the United States; that I accept the political and civil equality of all men, and that I will faithfully obey the laws of the United States, and encourage others so to do; so help me God.

ELIGIBILITY TO OFFICE.

SEC. 4. Every qualified elector shall be ellgible to office.

THOMAS J. CANDLER,
ABRAHAM CONGLETON.

---

## MINORITY REPORT OF THE COMMITTEE ON SUFFRAGE.

The undersigned, a minority of the Committee on "Suffrage and Eligibility to Office," regretting that they have been unable to concur with the majority of the committee, beg leave to submit the following report:

We cannot view, without serious apprehension, the admission to all the highest rights and privileges of citizenship of a race, consisting almost entirely of those recently emerged from slavery and unfitted by previous education and habits of thought and self-reliance, for the intelligent discharge of the duties and responsibilities, which would devolve upon them.

We do not regard the right to vote as natural or inherent, but conventional merely—to be regulated in such way as will best promote the welfare of the whole community. Upon this principle, women and minors have been excluded. Is there any reason why the negro should be advanced to a higher position? While we do not deny that there are individuals of that class who might be expected to express their own convictions at the ballot-box, still the great mass of them are so ignorant and prejudiced that they easily become the dupes of designing adventurers and demagogues, and through secret associations, introduced from Northern States, merely follow instructions, and reflect the views of those who control them.

We believe that the blessings we have derived from our government have been due to the virtue, intelligence and independence of those invested with the right of suffrage, and we tremble for the safety of republican institutions, when it shall be determined to confer this trust upon those, who mentally and morally are unfit to administer it—"to confide the power of making laws to those, who have no property to protect, and to bestow the right to levy taxes upon those who have no taxes to pay."

But it is said, that the proposed alteration is demanded by Congress, and is necessary to restore our State to constitutional relations with the Federal Government. It is certainly a singular demand that we should extend the elective franchise to those who are so inexperienced and little prepared for the ordinary business of life, that the government deems it necessary, through the Freedmen's Bureau, to exercise supervision and tutelage over them.

But we deny the power of Congress to prescribe to North-Carolina who shall or shall not vote. This has always been recognized as one of those great rights reserved to the States; and, in fact, it is their privilege to prescribe, who shall vote for members of Congress, as the Constitution of the United

States, Art. I, section 2, provides: "The House of Representatives shall be composed of members chosen every second year by the people of the several States; *and the electors in each State shall have the qualifications requsite for electors of the most numerous branch of the State Legislature.*"

Congress certainly recognized North-Carolina as a State in proper constitutional relations when the ratification of the XII Amendment by the Legislature of 1865–'66, was accepted, and also when the proposed XIV Amendment was submitted to the Legislature of 1866–67, for ratification. We can, then, only regard the present measures as a punishment for our conduct on the latter occasion. Such legislation strikes us as *ex post facto*, tyrannical and unjust. We cannot consent that our State shall be degraded to an inferior position to her sisters—that she shall expunge from her Constitution clauses excluding the negro from voting and holding office, which other States have indignantly refused to strike from their own. We refer especially to their Constitutions of Ohio, Pennsylvania, Indiana, Illinois and New York. We do think that the requirement would come with much better grace if these and other States had altered the Constitutions, or if it was proposed to so amend the Constitution of the United States as to make the application universal.

Viewing the matter in every light that presents itself, and willing to extend to the negro population every right that would legitimately result from the late war, or that is necessary to their security and happiness, we yet think that the welfare of both races is best promoted by retaining our present Constitution. We consider the whole scheme as intended to advance party purposes, in the expectation that the States of the South being Africanized and Radicalized may more than counterbalance the loss of electoral votes that will occur in other sections of the Union. We advise that North-Carolina shall refuse to alter her Constitution under dictation from a Congress, composed of members who have ceased to represent their constituents, and who, in defiance of the voice of the people as expressed in recent elections, still harden their hearts and devise new tasks for us. Let us rather trust to a returning sense of justice on the part of the Northern people, and that spirit of magnanimity which will revolt at the idea of "forcing the South to accept, in a huge mass, that which the North rejects in minute quantities." Let us act upon our own conscientious convictions of what is best for North-Carolina, and while submitting patiently to the present military rule, not forget that freedom of opinion which is our birthright. If, then, negro suffrage and negro equality are forced upon us, we will not have consented to our own humiliation, and will at least, have preserved our honor and self-respect.

JOHN W. GRAHAM,
P. DURHAM.

COMMITTEE ON SUFFRAGE—MINORITY REPORT.

I concur in the report of the majority of the Committee, with this exception, that I would add to the two classes of citizens prohibiting trom holding office, a third, namely: All persons who having previously taken an oath as a member or Congress, or as an officer of the United States, or as a member of any State Legislature, or as an executive or judicial officer of any State, to support the Constitution of the United States, shall have engaged in insurrection or rebellion against the same, or given aid and comfort to the enemies thereof, until such disability be legally removed.

JOHN R. FRENCH

After an able discussion by Messrs. Pool and French, ot Chowan,

On motion, the House adjourned.

---

AFTERNOON SESSION, February 18th, 1868.

The Convention was called to order at 7½ o'clock, by the President.

The President announced a quorum.

Mr. Galloway offered a substitute for the majority and minority reports of the Committee on Suffrage and Eligibility to office.

Mr. Bynum gave notice that he would move a reconsideration of the vote on corporations other than municipal.

Leave of absence was granted Mr. Ragland for two days.

The report of the committee on Education was received, and 250 copies were ordered to be printed.

On motion, the House adjourned.

---

## WEDNESDAY, February 19th, 1868.

The Convention was called to order at 10 o'clock, by the President.

Prayer by the Rev. Mr. Pritchitt.

The President announced a quorum.

The Journal of Tuesday was read and approved.

Mr. Abbott presented a petition of Mrs. Rosa B. Quinlivan, for divorce.

Referred to the committee on the Judicial Department.

Mr. Abbott also presented a communication of John A. Richardson.

Referred to the committee on the Judicial Department.

Mr. Rodman introduced a petition of divorce of John Morgan against Nancy Morgan.

Referred to the committee on the Judicial Department.

Mr. Galloway presented a petition from the citizens of Wilmington, in relation to property bought by slaves.

Referred to the committee on the Judicial Department.

Mr. McDonald, of Chatham, presented an ordinance to divorce Winney Gribbles and James Gribbles.

Referred to the committee on the Judicial Department.

The committee on the Judicial Department report that having considered the petition of Archibald Hancy, are of the opinion that he ought to have the relief prayed for, and report an ordinance to that effect, as follows:

SECTION 1. *Be it ordained by the people of North-Carolina, in Convention assembled*, That the bonds of matrimony between Archibald Hancy and Cornelia, his wife, be, and they are hereby dissolved.

W. B. RODMAN, *Chairman.*

The report was accepted.

The committee to whom was referred the petition of James Overton, praying for a divorce from his wife, having considered the same, are of opinion that the request should be granted, and report herewith an ordinance to that effect.

SECTION 1. *Be it ordained by the people of North-Carolina in Convention assembled*, That James Overton and Charlotte, his wife, are hereby divorced from the bonds of matrimony.

The report was accepted.

Leave of absence was granted Mr. Hayes, of Halifax, until Monday next.

Leave of absence was also granted Mr. Mayo.

The hour of eleven having arrived, the House took up the report of the committee on Suffrage and Eligibility to office, which was discussed for some time.

The report of the committee on re-districting the State, was received and made a special order for Thursday, at 10½ o'clock, A. M.

On motion, the House adjourned.

---

AFTERNOON SESSION, FEBRUARY 19TH, 1868.

The Convention was called to order at 7½ o'clock by the President.

The roll was called, and the following members answered to their names:

Messrs. Abbott, Andrews, Aydlott, Barnes, Benbow, Blume, Carter, Candler, Congleton, Cox, Daniel, Duckworth, Durham, Ellis, Eppes, Etheridge, Fisher, Forkner, French of Rockingham, Fullings, George, Graham of Montgomery, Grant of Wayne, Grant of Northampton, Gunter, Hall, Harris of Wake, Harris of Franklin, Hay, Hayes of Robeson, Hayes of Halifax, Hollowell, Hyman, Jones of Caldwell, King of Lincoln, King of Lenoir, Kinney, Lee, Legg, Long, McCubbins, Merritt, McDonald of Chatham, Moore, Morton, Mullican, Murphy, Nance, Newsom, Nicholson, Patrick, Parks, Petree, Pierson, Ragland, Ray, Read, Rhodes, Rich, Robbins, Rose, Smith, Taylor, Teague, Tourgee, Trogden, Turner, Watts and Welker—69.

On motion of Mr. Abbott, the ordinance on intimidation was made a special order for 10½ o'clock, on Monday next.

The following committee were appointed on the final adjournment of this Convention: Messrs. Forkner, Blume and Taylor.

On motion, the House adjourned.

---

THURSDAY, February 20th, 1868.

The Convention was called to order at 10 o'clock, by Mr. Heaton, who nominated Mr. King, of Lenoir, to the Chair.

Prayer by the Rev. J. W. Hood.

Mr. C. J. Cowles took the Chair and announced a quorum.

The Journal of Wednesday was read and approved.

Mr. McDonald, Chairman of the Committee appointed to report on an ordinance for the relief of the Sheriff of Orange, reported.

The report was accepted.

Mr. Nicholson presented an ordinance respecting the exemption of a Homestead, &c., which was,

On motion, ordered to be printed.

Mr. Robbins, of Bertie, presented an ordinance in relation to the indenture of apprentices.

Referred to the Committee on the Judicial Department.

The hour of 10½ having arrived, the report of the Committee on the re-districting of the State as follows, was taken up and discussed:

*To the Constitutional Convention of North-Carolina:*

The undersigned Committee on re-districting Congressional Districts, respectfully report the following ordinance and recommend its passage:

BYRON LAFLIN,
JASPER ETHERIDGE,
W. H. LOGAN,
J. H. HARRIS,
A. W. FISHER,
R. F. TROGDEN,
MILTON HOBBS.

AN ORDINANCE TO DIVIDE NORTH-CAROLINA INTO SEVEN CONGRESSIONAL DISTRICTS.

SECTION 1. *Be it ordained by the people of North-Carolina in Convention assembled, and it is hereby ordained by authority of the same,* That for the purpose of electing Representatives in the Congress of the United States, the State shall be divided into seven Districts, as follows, namely: The first District shall be composed of the Counties of Currituck, Camden, Pasquotank, Perquimans, Chowan, Hertford, Gates, Northampton, Halifax, Martin, Bertie, Washington, Tyrrell, Hyde and Beaufort; the second District of the Counties of Pitt, Craven, Jones, Lenoir, Wayne, Greene, Edgecombe, Wilson, Onslow, Carteret and Duplin; the third District of the Counties of Brunswick, Columbus, Bladen, New Hanover, Cumberland, Sampson, Robeson, Richmond, Harnett, Moore, Montgomery, Anson and Stanly; the fourth District of the Counties of Wake, Franklin, Warren, Granville, Orange, Nash, Johnson and Chatham; the fifth District of the Counties of Alamance, Randolph, Guilford, Rockingham, Davidson, Forsyth, Stokes, Surry, Person and Caswell; the sixth District of the Counties of Rowan, Cabarrus, Union, Mecklenburg, Gaston, Lincoln, Catawba, Iredell, Davie, Yadkin, Wilkes and Alexander; the seventh District of the Counties of Ashe, Alleghany, Watauga, Yancey, Mitchell, McDowell, Burke, Caldwell, Rutherford, Cleveland, Polk, Henderson, Transylvania, Buncombe, Madison, Haywood, Jackson, Macon, Cherokee and Clay.

The hour having arrived, the President announced the Special Order of the day, which,

On motion of Mr. Sweet, was waived to allow the discussion on the report of the Committee on re-districting the State.

Mr. Hood moved to re-commit to the Committee with instructions to report back the Counties as re-districted by the Convention of 1865–'66.

The motion was lost.

Mr. Morton, of Stanly, moved to amend by adding Stanly County to the sixth District.

The amendment was lost.

Mr. Pool moved to re-commit with instructions to re-district the State according to the Registered voters.

The motion was lost.

Mr. Morton moved to amend by adding Stanly to the fifth District.

The motion prevailed.

The question recurred to the original report of the Committee as amended, which was adopted by the following vote, yeas 72, nays 28:

Those who voted in the affirmative are:

Messrs. Abbott, Andrews, Ashley, Benbow, Blume, Bradley, Bryan, Carey, Carter, Colgrove, Congleton, Cox, Daniel, Duckworth, Eppes, Fisher, Forkner, French of Bladen, French of Rockingham, French of Chowan, Fullings, Gahagan, Galloway, Garland, George, Grant of Wayne, Gully, Gunter, Harris of Franklin, Hay, Hayes of Robeson, Heaton, Highsmith, Hobbs, Hoffler, Hollowell, Ing, Jones of Caldwell, Jones of Washington, King of Lincoln, King of Lenoir, Kinney, Laflin, Lee, Legg, Logan, McCubbins, McDonald of Chatham, Mullican, Murphy, Newsom, Patrick, Parks, Peterson, Pierson, Pool, Ragland, Ray, Read, Renfrow, Rhodes, Robbins, Rose, Smith, Stilly, Stillwell, Sweet, Taylor, Tourgee, Welker, Williams of Wake and Williamson—72.

Those who voted in the negative are:

Messrs. Barnes, Candler, Chillson, Dickey, Durham, Ellis, Etheridge, Glover, Graham of Montgomery, Graham of Orange, Grant of Northampton, Hall, Hare, Hodnett, Holt, Hood, Hyman, Lennon, Long, Mann, Merritt, McDonald of Moore, Moore, Nance, Nicholson, Sanderlin, Teague, and Turner—28.

The report of the Committee on Suffrage was taken up.

Mr. Nicholson asked and obtained leave of absence for Mr. Grant, of Northampton.

Mr. Tourgee gave notice of a resolution to be offered by him to-morrow in relation to the pay of members.

Mr. Hood gave notice of the introduction of an ordinance in relation to Ministers of the Gospel and Magistrates of Cumberland County.

Mr. Pool gave notice that at to-morrow morning's session, he will call the previous question on Suffrage.

Leave of absence was granted Mr. Cherry until Monday next.

The President declared no quorum, whereupon the House adjourned.

---

## FRIDAY, February 21st, 1868.

The Convention was called to order at 10 o'clock, by the President.

Prayer by the Rev. Mr. Atkinson.

The President announced a quorum.

The Journal of Thursday was read and adopted.

Leave of absence was granted Mr. Newsom until Wednesday; also to Messrs. French and Barnes, of Rockingham, for the same time; Mr. Reade, of Warren, from Saturday morning to Monday afternoon; also Mr. Holt, of Orange, until Tuesday next; also Mr. E. Fullings.

Mr. Jones, of Washington, introduced the following preamble and resolution:

Whereas, By section 6th of the 104th chapter of the Revised Code of North-Carolina, it is made the duty of the Secretary of State to furnish suitable stationery and the necessary fuel for all legislative bodies of the State ; therefore

*Resolved*, That from and after this date, the Secretary of State be, and is hereby requested to supply the officers and members of this Convention with the necessary stationery and suitable fuel, and that the officers of this Convention, whose duty it is to look after the stationery and fuel, are hereby directed to call on the Secretary of State.

The rules were, on motion, suspended, and the resolution adopted.

Mr. King introduced a resolution amending the rules of order.

Lies over.

Mr. Hood presented the following ordinance:

AN ORDINANCE TO EXEMPT MINISTERS OF THE GOSPEL AND JUSTICES OF THE PEACE IN THE COUNTY OF CUMBERLAND, FROM THE PENALTY IMPOSED BY THE ACT OF THE GENERAL ASSEMBLY OF NORTH-CAROLINA FOR CELEBRATING THE RITES OF MATRIMONY IN SAID COUNTY, WITHOUT A LICENSE THEREFOR.

WHEREAS, There is no Clerk of the County Court in the County of Cumberland, (by reason of the death of the late incumbent,) and therefore no one legally authorized to issue a license to persons desiring to intermarry ; and whereas, D. G. McRae, J. W. Lett, and E. L. Pemberton, three of the Justices of the Peace in and for said County, have issued commissions to ministers of the Gospel, and Justices of the Peace, authorizing and empowering them to celebrate the rites between certain parties: now therefore

SECTION 1. *Be it ordained by the people of North-Carolina in Convention assembled, and it is hereby ordained by authority of the same*, That those ministers of the Gospel and Justices of the Peace in said County, who have or may hereafter solemnize the rites of matrimony, under a commission from the aforesaid Justices of the Peace, be, and they are hereby released from the penalty imposed by law for celebrating the rites of matrimony without having a license from the Clerk of the County Court of said County.

Sec. 2. *Be it further ordained*, That this power and authority given to said D. G. McRae, J. W. Lett, and E. L. Pemberton, shall cease and be of no effect from and after the time that a Clerk of the County Court in said County shall be appointed, and shall qualify according to law.

Mr. Benbow introduced an ordinance on Relief.

Was ordered to be printed.

Mr. Andrews introduced an ordinance taxing Theatrical and Concert companies, and moved a suspension of the rules.

Mr. Jones, of Washington, moved to lay the motion on the table.

The yeas and nays were demanded. Yeas 52, nays 50.

Those who voted in the affirmative are:

Messrs. Aydlott, Bradley, Bryan, Candler, Congleton, Cox, Daniel, Dickey, Durham, Ellis, Etheridge, French of Chowan, Gahagan, Garland, Graham of Orange, Gunter, Harris of Franklin, Heaton, Highsmith, Hodnett, Hoffler, Hollowell, Hood, Hyman, Jones of Caldwell, Jones of Washington, King of Lincoln, King of Lenoir, Kinney, Lee, Lennon, Logan, May, McCubbins, Mullican, Nicholson, Parker, Parks, Petree, Peterson, Pierson, Pool, Read, Rose, Stilly, Stilwell, Sweet, Tourgee, Trogden, Tucker, Turner and Welker—52.

Those who voted in the negative are:

Messrs. Abbott, Andrews, Ashley, Baker, Benbow, Blume, Carey, Carter, Chillson, Dowd, Duckworth, Forkner, Franklin, French of Bladen, French of Rockingham, Galloway, Graham of Montgomery, Grant of Wayne, Gully, Hall, Hare, Harris ot Wake, Hay, Hayes of Robeson, Ing, Laflin, Legg, Long, Mann, Marler, Merritt, McDonald of Chatham, McDonald of Moore, Moore, Morton, Murphy, Nance, Patrick, Ragland, Ray, Renfrow, Rich, Robbins, Rodman, Smith, Taylor, Watts, Williams of Wake and Williamson—50.

The motion was laid on the table.

The ordinance lies over.

Mr. Ashley introduced a resolution in relation to the pay of employees of this House.

Lies over under the rules.

The hour of eleven having arrived, the House took up the Suffrage Bill which was discussed until 2 o'clock P. M., when,

On motion, the House adjourned.

---

EVENING SESSION, February 21st, 1868.

The Convention was called to order at 7½ o'clock by the President.

A quorum present.

The report of the committee on Suffrage and Eligibility to office was taken up and discussed.

Leave of absence was granted Mr. Graham, of Orange, and Mr. Hare until Thursday next; and Mr. Watts obtained leave of absence until Monday.

At 10 o'clock, the House, on motion, adjourned.

---

SATURDAY February 22d, 1868.

The Convention was called to order at 10 o'clock by the President.

Prayer by the Rev. Mr. Brewer.

The President announced a quorum.

The Journal of Friday was read and approved.

Leave of absence was granted Mr. Congleton until Tuesday next.

Mr. McDonald of Chatham introduced the following resotion:

*Resolved*, That in respect to the memory and in honor to the distinguished services of General George Washington, he, who was "first in war, first in peace and first in the hearts of his countrymen," this Convention adjourn until 10 o'clock, A. M., Monday next.

Mr. Andrews moved a suspension of the rules.

Mr. King, of Lenoir, moved to lay the motion on the table, and demanded the yeas and nays.

The motion was sustained, yeas 68, nays 22.

Those who voted in the affirmative are:

Messrs. Abbott Ashley, Carter, Colgrove Cox, Daniel, Dickey, Duckworth, Durham, Ellis, Eppes, Etheridge, Fisher, Forkner, French of Bladen, French of Chowan, Gahagan, Garland, George, Grant of Wayne, Gunter, Harris of Franklin, Hay, Hayes of Robeson, Highsmith, Hobbs, Hodnett, Hoffler, Hollowell, Hood, Hyman, Ing, Jones of Caldwell, Jones of Washington, King of Lincoln, King of Lenoir, Kinney, Lee, Lennon, Logan, Long, Mann, May, Marler, McCubbins, Merritt, Mullican, Nance, Nicholson, Parker, Parks, Petree, Pierson, Pool, Ray, Rhodes, Robbins, Rodman, Rose, Stilly, Stilwell, Sweet Teague, Tourgee, Trogden, Tucker, Welker and Williams of Sampson—68.

Those who voted in the negative are:

Messrs. Andrews, Baker, Bradley, Bryan, Candler, Chillson, Dowd, Franklin, Galloway, Graham of Montgomery, Gully, Harris of Wake, Legg, McDonald of Chatham, Moore, Morton, Murphy, Patrick, Ragland, Rich, Turner, and Williams of Wake—22.

Mr. Galloway moved to adjourn until Monday at 10 A. M.

Mr. Hodnett demanded the yeas and nays.

The motion was lost, yeas 16, nays 75.

Those who voted in the affirmative are:

Messrs. Andrews, Baker, Carey, Chillson, Dowd, Franklin, French of Bladen, Galloway, Harris of Wake, Legg, Mann, McDonald of Chatham, McDonald of Moore, Ragland, Rich, and Turner—16.

Those who voted in the negative are:

Messrs. Abbott, Ashley, Aydlott, Benbow, Bradley, Bryan, Carter, Candler, Colgrove, Cox, Daniel, Dickey, Duckworth, Durham, Ellis, Eppes, Etheridge, Fisher, Forkner, French of Chowan, Gahagan, Garland, George, Grant of Wayne, Gully, Gunter, Harris of Franklin, Hay, Hayes of Robeson, Heaton, Hobbs, Hodnett, Hoffler, Hollowell, Hood, Hyman, Ing, Jones of Caldwell, Jones of Washington, King of Lincoln, King of

Lenoir, Kinney, Lee, Lennon, Logan, Long, May, Marler, McCubbins, Merritt, Mullican, Nance, Nicholson, Patrick, Parker, Parks, Petree, Pierson, Pool, Ray, Renfrow, Rhodes, Robbins, Rodman, Rose, Stilly, Stilwell, Sweet, Teague, Tourgee, Trogden, Tucker, Welker, Williams of Wake, Williams of Sampson and Williamson—75.

Mr. French, of Chowan, presented the following resolution:

*Resolved*, That with profound reverence for the memory of George Washington, we will honor the day of his birth, not by adjourning, but by proceeding to engraft upon the Constitution the great principles of justice and liberty, which have made his name illustrious.

On motion the rules were suspended, and the resolution adopted.

At 10½ o'clock, on motion, the rules were suspended to take up the Report of the Committee on Suffrage, which was discussed until 2 o'clock, P. M., when,

Mr. C. C. Pool moved to adjourn until 10 o'clock, Monday.

Mr. McDonald, of Chatham, demanded the yeas and nays.

The demand was not sustained.

The motion was adopted.

---

## MONDAY, February 24th, 1868.

The Convention was called to order at 10 o'clock, by the President.

Prayer by the Rev. J. W. Hood.

The President announced a quorum.

The Journal of Saturday was read and approved.

Mr. Harris, of Wake, presented a petition of divorce in favor of Littleton Perry.

Referred to the Committee on Divorce.

Mr. Andrews prosented a similar petition in favor of Henry G. Wood.

Referred to the Committee on Divorce.

Mr. Pool presented two ordinances on relief, which were ordered to be printed.

The following report was presented:

The Committee ordered to report to the Convention, when in our opinion this Convention should adjourn *sine die*, beg leave to submit the following report:

*Resolved*, That this Convention will adjourn *sine die*, on Tuesday the 10th day of March next, at 12 o'clock, M.

SAMUEL FORKNER,
MATCHET TAYLOR,
WM. T. BLUME.

On motion, the report was accepted.

On motion of Mr. Abbott, the report was made a Special Order for Monday next, at 10½ o'clock.

Mr. McDonald, of Chatham, introduced a resolution in relation to a Penitentiary.

Referred to the Committee on Penal Institutions.

Mr. Tourgee introduced the following resolution, notice of which having been previously given:

*Resolved*, That each member of this Convention is entitled to pay from the first day of the session, and no member shall be deprived of pay for overstaying the leave granted by this Convention, for any valid reason,

The resolution was, on motion adopted.

Mr. Abbott introduced an ordinance to incorporate the North Western North-Carolina Rail Road Company.

Referred to the Committee on Internal Improvements.

Ten and a half o'clock having arrived, the ordinance establishing an Immigration Agency, was taken up and discussed until 11 o'clock.

Mr. McDonald withdrew his amendment.

The report of the Committee on Suffrage and Eligibility to Office, was taken up.

Mr. Galloway withdrew his substitute, when the majority report was taken up and considered.

Section 1st was read.

Mr. Heaton moved to amend fifth line, by striking out "three months," and inserting "thirty days."

The amendment was adopted.

Mr. Jones, of Washington, offered an amendment.

The following amendment of Mr. French, of Bladen, to section 1st, was taken up and discussed:

After the word elector, except as hereinafter provided, viz:

1st. All persons who, prior to the year 1861, held any office under the United States Government, or held any office as a member of any State Legislature, or as an Executive or Judicial officer of any State, and afterwards engaged in insurrection or rebellion against the United States, or gave aid and comfort to the enemies thereof; but the General Assembly may, by a vote of two-thirds of each house, remove such disability.

2d. Those generally known as idiots or insane persons.

3d. All persons who shall have been convicted of any infamous crime: *Provided further*, That the first exception in this section shall not apply to those who may have their disabilities to hold office removed by the Congress of the United States, before the approval of this Constitution by that body.

Mr. Pool called the previous question, which was sustained.

Mr. French, of Bladen demanded the yeas and nays,

Which resulted yeas 23, nays 77.

Those who voted in the affirmative are:

Messrs. Bryan, Carter, Candler, Dickey, Fisher, French of Bladen, Galloway, Garland, Gully, Kinney, Logan, May, Moore, Murphy, Parks, Petree, Ray, Rhodes, Robbins, Rose, Teague, Tourgee and Turner—23.

Those who voted in the negative are:

Messrs. Abbott, Andrews, Ashley, Aydlott, Baker, Benbow, Blume, Bradley, Carey, Cherry, Chillson, Colgrove, Cox, Daniel, Dowd, Duckworth, Durham, Ellis, Eppes, Etheridge, Forkner, Franklin, French of Chowan, Fullings, George, Glover, Graham of Orange, Gunter, Hay, Hayes of Robeson, Heaton, Highsmith, Hobbs, Hodnett, Hoffler, Hollowell, Hood, Hyman, Ing, Jones of Caldwell, Jones, of Washington, King of Lincoln, King of Lenoir, Lee, Legg, Lennon, Long, Mann, Marler, McCubbins, Merritt, McDonald of Chatham, McDonald, of Moore, Morton, Mullican, Nance, Nicholson,

Parker, Peterson, Pierson, Pool, Ragland, Renfrow, Rich, Rodman, Sanderlin, Smith, Stilly, Stilwell, Sweet, Taylor, Trogden, Tucker, Watts, Welker, Williams of Sampson and Williams of Wake—77.

The amendment was not sustained.

The amendment of Mr. Jones, of Washington, was taken up and lost.

Section 1st, as amended, was then adopted.

Section 2d was read.

Mr. Jones, of Washington, moved to strike out the section, and insert as follows:

"It shall be the duty of the General Assembly to provide, from time to time, for the registration of all electors; that no person shall be allowed to register, vote, or hold office without having first taken and subscribed to the annexed oath:

OATH.

I do solemnly swear, (or affirm,) that I will support and maintain the Constitution of the United States, and the Constitution of the State of North-Carolina, not inconsistent therewith, that I will never countenance or aid in the secession of this State from the United States, that I accept the political and civil equality of all men. So help me God."

Mr. Tourgee moved to amend the section introduced by Mr. Jones, by substituting the oath of the Minority Report, or the oath prescribed in that section.

Mr. Pool moved to lay the substitute of Mr. Jones, and the amendment of Mr. Tourgee, on the table.

The yeas and nays were demanded.

The motion was not sustained by a vote of yeas 44, nays 55.

Those who voted in the affirmative are:

Messrs. Abbott, Ashley, Baker, Benbow, Bradley, Cherry, Colgrove, Daniel, Dowd, Durham, Ellis, Etheridge, Forkner, George, Graham of Orange, Heaton, Hodnett, Hollowell, Ing, Jones of Caldwell, King of Lenoir, Legg, Lennon, Long, Marler, McCubbins, Merritt, McDonald of Chatham, McDonald of Moore, Mullican, Nance, Nicholson, Parker, Peterson, Pool,

Rich, Rodman, Sanderlin, Stilly, Sweet, Taylor, Watts, Williams of Sampson and Williams of Wake—44.

Those who voted in the negative are:

Messrs. Andrews, Aydlott, Blume, Bryan, Carter, Candler, Chillson, Cox, Dickey, Duckworth, Eppes, Fisher, Franklin, French of Bladen, French of Chowan, Fullings, Galloway, Garland, Glover, Graham of Montgomery, Gully, Gunter, Harris of Wake, Harris of Franklin, Hay, Hayes of Robeson, Highsmith, Hobbs, Hoffler, Hood, Hyman, Jones of Washington, Kinney, Lee, Mann, May, Moore, Morton, Murphy, Parks, Petree, Pierson, Ragland, Ray, Renfrow, Rhodes, Robbins, Rose, Smith, Stilwell, Teague, Tourgee, Tucker, Turner and Welker—55.

The amendment of Mr. Tourgee was not sustained, by a vote of yeas 33, nays 63:

Those who voted in the affirmative, are:

Messrs. Andrews, Bryan, Carey, Carter, Candler, Chillson, Duckworth, Fisher, Franklin, French of Bladen, Galloway, Garland, Glover, Graham of Montgomery, Gully, Gunter, Harris of Franklin, Hay, Ing, Kinney, Logan, Mann, Moore, Murphy, Parks, Ragland, Ray, Rhodes, Robbins, Rose, Teague, Tourgee and Turner—33.

Those who voted in the negative, are:

Messrs. Abbott, Ashley, Aydlott, Baker, Benbow, Bradley, Cherry, Colgrove, Cox, Daniel, Dickey, Dowd, Durham, Ellis, Eppes, Etheridge, Forkner, French of Chowan, Fullings, George, Graham of Orange, Hayes of Robeson, Heaton, Highsmith, Hobbs, Hoffler, Hollowell, Hyman, Jones of Caldwell, Jones of Washington, King of Lincoln, King of Lenoir, Legg, Lennon, Long, May, Marler, McCubbins, Merritt, McDonald of Chatham, McDonald of Moore, Morton, Mullican, Nance, Nicholson, Parker, Petree, Peterson, Pierson, Pool, Renfrow, Rich, Rodman, Sanderlin, Smith, Stilly, Stilwell, Sweet, Taylor, Trogden, Watts, Williams of Sampson and Williams of Wake—63.

Mr. Abbott moved the following as a substitute:

Insert section 3d of the Minority Report in place of section 2d of the Majority Report, and attach the following:

OATH OF OFFICE.

I do solemnly swear (or affirm,) that I am truly and devotedly attached to the Union of all the States, and opposed to any dissolution of the same; that I entertain no political sympathy with the instigators and leaders of the rebellion, or with the enemies of the Union, nor approbation of their principles or purposes; that I will neither, by word or act, encourage or countenance a spirit of sedition or disaffection towards the Government of the United States or laws thereof, and that I will sustain and defend the Union of these States, and will discourage and resist all efforts to destroy or impair the same.

At 2½ o'clock, the House, on motion, adjourned.

---

EVENING SESSION, February 24th, 1868.

The Convention was called to order at 7½ o'clock, by the President.

The President announced a quorum.

The Majority Report of the Committee on Suffrage and Eligibility to Office, was taken up.

Mr. Abbott withdrew his substitute to section 2d.

The question recurred on the substitute offered by Mr. Jones, of Washington.

Mr. Heaton moved to amend the substitute of Mr. Jones, by striking out the oath therein contained and insert the following:

OATH.

I, ———, do solemnly swear, (or affirm,) that I will support and maintain the Constitution and laws of the United States, and the Constitution and laws of North-Carolina, not inconsistent therewith. So help me God.

Mr. Tourgee moved to amend the oath in substitute of Mr.

Jones, by inserting after the word " Constitution, and laws," so as to read " Constitution and laws of the United States."

Mr. Jones accepted the amendment.

After some discussion, Mr. Pool called the previous question, which was on the amendment of Mr. Heaton.

The yeas and nays were demanded, which resulted yeas 25, nay 62:

Those who voted in the affirmative, are:

Messrs. Andrews, Aydlott, Benbow, Bryan, Cherry, Cox, Forkner, George, Gully, Harris of Wake, Hayes of Halifax, Heaton, Highsmith, Hobbs, Hood, Legg, Mayo, McDonald of Moore, Petree, Pierson, Robbins, Rodman, Sweet, Trogden and Williamson—25.

Those who voted in the negative, are:

Messrs. Abbott, Ashley, Baker, Blume, Bradley, Carey, Carter, Candler, Dickey, Dowd, Duckworth, Ellis, Eppes, Etheridge, Fisher, French of Bladen, French of Chowan, Fullings, Galloway, Glover, Graham of Montgomery, Gunter, Harris of Franklin, Hodnett, Hoffler, Hollowell, Hyman, Jones of Caldwell, Jones of Washington, King of Lenoir, Kinney, Laflin, Lee, Lennon, Logan, Mann, Marler, McCubbins, Merritt, McDonald of Chatham, Moore, Morton, Murphy, Nicholson, Parker, Parks, Pool, Ragland, Read, Renfrow, Rhodes, Rich, Rose, Smith, Stilwell, Taylor, Teague, Tourgee, Tucker, Turner, Watts and Welker—62.

The amendment was not sustained.

The substitute of Mr. Jones was taken up.

The yeas and nays were demanded, which resulted yeas 39, ays 52:

Those who voted in the affirmative, are:

Messrs. Abbott, Ashley, Blume, Carter, Candler, Chilson, Dickey, Duckworth, Eppes, Fisher, French of Bladen, Fulngs, Galloway, Glover, Graham of Montgomery, Hayes of Robeson, Hayes of Halifax, Jones of Washington, Kinney, ee, Logan, Mann, Moore, Morton, Murphy, Parks, Ragland, enfrow, Rhodes, Robbins, Rose, Smith, Stilwell, Teague, ourgee, Tucker, Turner, Welker and Williamson—39.

Those who voted in the negative, are:

Messrs. Andrews, Aydlott, Baker, Benbow, Bradley, Bryan, Carey, Cherry, Cox, Daniel, Dowd, Ellis, Etheridge, Forkner, French of Chowan, George, Gully, Gunter, Harris of Wake, Hay, Heaton, Highsmith, Hobbs, Hodnett, Hoffler, Hollowell, Hood, Hyman, Jones of Caldwell, King of Lincoln, King of Lenoir, Legg, Lennon, Long, Marler, McCubbins, Merritt, McDonald of Chatham, McDonald of Moore, Nance, Nicholson, Parker, Pierson, Pool, Ray, Read, Rich, Rodman, Stilly, Sweet, Taylor and Watts—52.

The substitute was lost.

Section 2d, as read, was adopted.

Mr. Tourgee called up the following resolution of Mr. Ashley, for action:

*Resolved*, That the Committee on Contingent Expenses be instructed to allow three servants of this Convention two (2) dollars per day, for their services during the session of this Convention.

The resolution was, on motion, adopted.

Leave of absence was granted Mr. Pool for one week.

At 11 o'clock, the House, on motion, adjourned.

---

## TUESDAY, February, 25th, 1868.

The Convention was called to order at 10 o'clock, by the President.

Prayer by Rev. Mr. Fiske.

The President announced a quorum.

The Journal of Monday was read and approved.

Mr. Colgrove recorded his vote in the affirmative on section 2d of the report of the Committee on Suffrage.

Messrs. Durham, Holt and Etheridge recorded their names in the negative on the substitute for 2d section of the Majority Report on Suffrage, offered by Mr. Jones, of Washington.

Messrs. Mullican and Ing recorded their names in the affirmative on the same substitute.

Mr. Harris, of Wake, moved that when this Convention

adjourns, it adjourn to meet at 11 o'clock to-morrow, Wednesday.

Mr. Tourgee introduced an ordinance in relation to sheriff's executions, &c.

Lies over under the rules.

Mr. Tourgee moved a suspension of the rules, to take up the ordinance on Immigration.

The motion was not entertained by the President.

Mr. Tourgee appealed to the House, when the House sustained the Chair by a vote of yeas 61, nays 4.

The Committee on Rules, to whom was referred the resolution of C. C. Jones, in regard to increasing the indebtedness of the State, having had the same under consideration, respectfully report the following substitute and recommend its adoption as Rule 43 :

*Rule* 43. No ordinance shall be passed to raise a loan of money on the credit of the State, or to pledge the faith of the State directly or indirectly, for the payment of any debt, or to impose any tax upon the people of the State, other than for the necessary expenses incurred in holding this Convention; or to allow the Counties, Cities, or Towns to do so unless the ordinance for that purpose shall have been read three several times in the Convention, and passed three several readings, which readings shall have been on three different days, and agreed to by a majority of the whole number of members of the Convention, and unless the yeas and nays on the second and third readings of the ordinance shall have been entered on the Journal.

On motion, the report was adopted.

The hour of the Special Order having been announced,

The House took up the report of the Committee on Suffrage.

Article first was adopted by the following vote, yeas 76, nays 27:

Those who voted in the affirmative are:

Messrs. Abbott, Andrews, Ashley, Aydlott, Baker, Benbow, Blume, Bradley, Bryan, Carey, Carter, Cherry, Chillson, Colgrove, Daniel, Dowd, Duckworth, Eppes, Forkner, Franklin, French of Chowan, Fullings, Galloway, George, Glover,

Gunter, Harris of Wake, Hay, Hayes of Robeson, Hayes of Halifax, Heaton, Highsmith, Hobbs, Hofler, Hollowell, Hood, Hyman, Ing, Jones of Caldwell, Jones of Washington, King of Lincoln, King of Lenoir, Kinney, Lee, Legg, Long, Mann, McDonald of Chatham, McDonald of Moore, Morton, Mullican, Murphy, Nance, Newsom, Nicholson, Patrick, Parker, Parks, Petree, Peterson, Pierson, Read, Renfrow, Rich, Robbins, Rodman, Smith, Stilly, Stilwell, Sweet, Taylor, Tucker, Turner, Watts, Williams of Wake and Williamson—76.

Those who voted in the negative are:

Messrs. Candler, Cox, Dickey, Durham, Etheridge, Fisher, French of Bladen, Garland, Graham of Montgomery, Harris of Franklin, Holt, Lennon, Logan, May, Mayo, Marler, Merritt, McCubbins, Moore, Ray, Rose, Sanderlin, Teague, Tourgee, Trogden, Welker and Williams of Sampson—27.

On motion, the balance of the report of the Committee was postponed until Thursday next, at eleven o'clock.

The following report of the Committee on the Judicial Department was received, and passed the first reading:

## PLAN FOR ORGANIZATION OF THE JUDICIAL DEPARTMENT, REPORTED BY THE COMMITTEE ON THAT SUBJECT.

### JUDICIAL DEPARTMENT.

SECTION 1. The distinction between actions at law and suits in equity, and the forms of all such actions and suits shall be abolished, and there shall be in this State but one form of action, for the enforcement or protection of private rights or the redress of private wrongs, which shall be denominated a civil action; and every action prosecuted by the people of the State as a party, against the person charged with a public offence, for the punishment of the same, shall be termed a criminal action. Feigned issues shall also be abolished and the fact at issue tried by order of Court before a jury.

SEC. 2. Three Commissioners shall be appointed by this Convention to report to the General Assembly at its first session after this Constitution shall be adopted by the people, rules of practice and procedure in accordance with the provisions of the foregoing section.

SEC. 3. The same Commissioners shall also report to the General Assembly as soon as practicable, a Code of Law of North-Carolina. The General Assembly shall have power to fill vacancies occurring in this Commission.

JUDICIAL POWER.

SEC. 4. The Judicial power of the State shall be vested in a Court for the trial of Impeachment, a Supreme Court, Superior Courts, Courts of Justices of the Peace, and Special Courts.

IMPEACHMENT.

SEC. 5. The Court for the trial of Impeachments shall be the upper house of General Assembly. A majority of the members shall be necessary to a quorum, and the judgment shall not extend beyond removal from, and disqualification to hold, office in this State; but the party shall be liable to indictment and punishment according to law.

SEC. 6. The House of Representatives, solely, shall have the power of impeaching. No person shall be convicted without the concurrence of two-thirds of the Senators present. When the Governor is impeached the Chief Justice shall preside.

SEC. 7. Treason against the State shall consist only in levying war against it, or adherring to its enemies, giving them aid and comfort. No person shall be convicted of treason unless on the testimony of two witnesses to the same overt act, or on confession in open court. No conviction of treason or attainder shall work corruption of blood or forfeiture.

THE SUPREME COURT—ITS CONSTITUTION.

SEC. 8. The Supreme Court shall consist of a Chief Justice and four Associate Justices.

SEC. 9. There shall be two terms of the Supreme Court, held at the seat of Government of the State in each year, commencing on the first Monday in January, and first Monday in June, and continuing as long as the public interests may require.

SEC. 10. The Supreme Court shall have jurisdiction to review, upon appeal, any decision of the Courts below, upon any matter of law or legal inference; but no issue of fact shall be tried before this Court, and its decisions shall be remitted to the Courts below to be enforced: *Provided*, That the Court shall have power to issue any remedial writs, necessary, to give it a general supervision and control of the inferior Courts.

SEC. 11. The Supreme Court shall have original jurisdiction to hear claims against the State, but its decisions shall be merely recommendatory; no process in the nature of execution shall issue thereon; they shall be reported to the next session of the General Assembly for its action.

THE SUPERIOR COURTS.

SEC. 12. The State shall be divided into twelve Judicial Districts, for each of which a Judge shall be chosen, who shall hold a Superior Court in each County in said District, at least twice in each year, to continue for two weeks, unless the business shall be sooner disposed of.

SEC. 13. Until otherwise altered by law, the following shall be the Judicial Districts:

FIRST DISTRICT.

| | | |
|---|---|---|
| Currituck, | Camden, | Pasquotank, |
| Perquimans, | Chowan, | Gates, |
| Hertford, | Bertie. | |

SECOND DISTRICT.

| | | |
|---|---|---|
| Tyrrell, | Hyde, | Washington, |
| Beaufort, | Martin, | Pitt, |
| Edgecombe. | | |

THIRD DISTRICT.

| | | |
|---|---|---|
| Craven, | Carteret, | Jones, |
| Greene, | Onslow, | Lenoir, |
| Wayne, | Wilson. | |

FOURTH DISTRICT.

| | | |
|---|---|---|
| Brunswick, | New Hanover, | Duplin, |
| Columbus, | Bladen, | Sampson, |
| Robeson. | | |

FIFTH DISTRICT.

| | | |
|---|---|---|
| Cumberland, | Harnett, | Moore, |
| Richmond, | Anson, | Montgomery, |
| Stanly, | Union. | |

SIXTH DISTRICT.

| | | |
|---|---|---|
| Northampton, | Warren, | Halifax, |
| Wake, | Nash, | Franklin, |
| Johnson, | Granville. | |

SEVENTH DISTRICT.

| | | |
|---|---|---|
| Person, | Orange, | Chatham, |
| Randolph, | Guilford, | Alamance, |
| Caswell, | Rockingham. | |

EIGHTH DISTRICT.

| | | |
|---|---|---|
| Stokes, | Forsyth, | Davidson, |
| Rowan, | Davie, | Yadkin, |
| Surry. | | |

NINTH DISTRICT.

| | | |
|---|---|---|
| Union, | Cabarrus, | Mecklenburg, |
| Lincoln, | Gaston, | Cleaveland, |
| Rutherford, | Polk. | |

TENTH DISTRICT.

| | | |
|---|---|---|
| Iredell, | Alexander, | Wilkes, |
| Caldwell, | Burke, | McDowell. |

ELEVENTH DISTRICT.

| | | |
|---|---|---|
| Alleghany, | Ashe, | Watauga, |
| Mitchell, | Yancey, | Madison, |
| Buncombe. | | |

TWELFTH DISTRICT.

| | | |
|---|---|---|
| Henderson, | Transylvania, | Haywood, |
| Macon, | Jackson, | Clay, |
| Cherokee. | | |

SEC. 14. Every Judge of a Superior Court shall reside in his District while holding his office. The Judges may exchange districts with each other with the consent of the Governor, and the Governor, for good reasons, which he shall report to the Legislature at its current or next session, may require any Judge to hold one or more specified terms of said courts in lieu of the Judge in whose district they are.

SEC 15. The Superior Courts shall have exclusive original jurisdiction of all civil actions, whereof exclusive original jurisdiction is not given to some other court; and of all criminal actions, in which the punishment may exceed a fine of fifty dollars or imprisonment for one month.

SEC. 16 The Superior Courts shall have appellate jurisdiction of all issues of law or fact determined by a Probate Judge or a Justice of the Peace, where the matter in controversy exceeds twenty-five dollars, and of matters of law in all cases.

SEC. 17. The Clerks of the Superior Courts shall have jurisdiction of the probate of deeds, the granting of letters testamentary and of administration, the appointment of guardians, the apprenticing of orphans, to audit the accounts of executors, administrators and guardians, and of such other matters as shall be prescribed by law. All issues of fact joined before them shall be transferred to the Superior Courts for trial, and appeal shall lie to the Superior Courts from their judgments in all matters of law.

SEC. 18. In all issues of fact joined in any court, the parties may waive their right to have the same determined by jury, in which case the finding of the Judge upon the facts, shall have the force and effect of a verdict of a jury.

SEC. 19. The General Assembly shall provide for the establishment of special courts, for the trial of misdemeanors, in cities and towns where the same may be necessary.

SEC. 20. The Clerk of the Supreme Court shall be appointed by the Court, and shall hold his office for eight years.

SEC. 21. A Clerk of the Superior Court for each county, shall be elected by the qualified voters thereof, at the time and in the manner prescribed by law, for the election of members of the General Assembly.

SEC. 22. Clerks for the Superior Courts shall hold their office for four years.

SEC. 23. The General Assembly shall prescribe and regulate the fees, salaries, and emoluments of all officers provided for in this Article; but the salaries of the Judges shall not be diminished during their continuance in office.

SEC. 24. The laws of North-Carolina, not repugnant to this Constitution, shall be in force until lawfully altered.

SEC. 25. Actions at law, and suits in equity, pending when this Constitution shall go into effect, shall be transferred to the courts having jurisdiction thereof, without prejudice by reason of the change, and all such actions and suits, commenced before, and pending at, the adoption by the General Assembly, of the rule of practice and procedure herein provided for, shall be heard and determined, according to the practice now in use, unless otherwise provided for by said rules.

SEC. 26. The Justices of the Supreme Court shall be elected by the qualified voters of the State, as is provided for the election of members of the General Assembly. They shall hold their offices for sixteen years. The Judges of the Superior Courts shall be elected in like manner, and shall hold their offices for twelve years; but the Judges of the Superior Courts elected at the first election under this Constitution, shall, after their election under the superintendence of the Justices of the Supreme Court, be divided by lot, into three equal clases, one of which shall hold office for four years, another for eight years, and the third for twelve years.

SEC. 27. The Superior Courts shall be, at all times, open for the transaction of business within their jurisdiction, except the trial of issues of fact requiring a jury.

SEC. 28. A Solicitor shall be elected for each judicial district by the qualified voters thereof, as is prescribed for members of the General Assembly, who shall prosecute on behalf of the State, in all criminal actions in the Superior Courts, and advise the officers of justice in his district.

SEC. 29. In each county a Sheriff and Coroner, shall be elected by the qualified voters of the county, as is prescribed for members of the General Assembly, and shall hold their offices for two years. In each township there shall be a Constable, elected in like manner by the voters thereof, who shall hold his office for two years.

SEC. 30. All vacancies occurring in the offices provided for by this article of this Constitution, shall be filled by the appointment of the Governor, and the appointees shall hold their places until the next regular election.

SEC. 31. The officers elected at the first election held under this Constitution, shall hold their offices for the terms prescribed for them respectively, next ensuing after the next regular election for members of the General Assembly. But their terms shall begin upon the approval of this Constitution by the Congress of the United States.

On the second reading section first was adopted, yeas 73, nays 29.

Those who voted in the affirmative are:

Messrs. Abbott, Andrews, Ashley, Benbow, Blume, Bryan, Carey, Carter, Candler, Chillson, Colgrove, Cox, Dickey, Duckworth, Eppes, Fisher, Forkner, Franklin, French of

Bladen, Fullings, Galloway, Garland, George, Glover, Graham of Montgomery, Gunter, Harris of Franklin, Hay, Hayes of Robeson, Hayes of Halifax, Heaton, Highsmith, Hobbs, Hoffler, Hood, Hyman, Ing, Kinney, Lee, Legg Logan, Long, May, Mayo, McDonald of Chatham, Morton, Mullican, Murphy, Nance, Patrick, Parks, Petree, Peterson, Pierson, Ragland, Ray, Renfrow, Rich, Robbins, Rodman, Smith, Stilly, Stilwell, Sweet, Taylor, Teague, Tourgee, Trogden, Tucker, Turner Watts, Welker, and Williams of Wake—73.

Those who voted in the negative are:

Messrs. Aydlott, Baker, Bradley, Cherry, Daniel, Dowd, Durham, Ellis, Etheridge, Graham of Orange, Hodnett, Hollowell, Holt, Jones of Caldwell, Jones of Washington, King of Lincoln, King of Lenoir, Lennon, Marler, McCubbins, Merrit, McDonald of Moore, Nicholson, Parker, Read, Rhodes, Rose, Sanderlin, and Williams of Sampson—29.

Sections second and third were read and adopted.

Section fourth was read and adopted by the following vote, yeas 66, nays 17:

Those who voted in the affirmative are:

Messrs. Abbott, Andrews, Ashley, Blume, Bryan, Carter, Candler, Chilson, Cox, Dickey, Duckworth, Eppes, Fisher, Forkner, Franklin, French of Bladen, French of Chowan, Fullings, Galloway, Garland, Glover, Graham of Montgomery, Gunter, Harris of Franklin, Hay, Hayes of Robeson, Hayes of Halifax, Highsmith, Hoffler, Hood, Hyman, Ing, Lee, Logan, Long, Mann, McDonald of Chatham, McDonald of Moore, Murphy, Nance, Nicholson, Patrick, Parker, Parks, Peterson, Pierson, Ragland Renfrow, Rich, Robbins, Rodman, Smith, Stilly, Stilwell, Sweet, Taylor, Teague, Tourgee, Trogden, Tucker, Turner, Watts, Welker, Williams of Wake and Williamson—66.

Those who voted in the negative are:

Messrs. Durham, Etheridge, George, Graham of Orange, Hollowell, Holt, Jones of Caldwell, King of Lenoir, Kinney, Lennon, Marler, McCubbins, Merritt, Rhodes, Rose, Sanderlin, and Williams of Sampson—17.

Section eighth was read.

Mr. Durham moved to amend by striking out "four" and inserting "two."

The amendment was adopted, yeas 82, nays 14:

Those who voted in the affirmative are:

Messrs. Aydlott, Baker, Blume, Bradley, Bryan, Carey, Carter, Candler, Chillson, Colgrove, Cox, Daniel, Dickey, Dowd, Duckworth, Durham, Ellis, Eppes, Etheridge, Forkner, George, Glover, Graham of Montgomery, Graham of Orange, Gunter, Harris of Franklin, Hay, Hayes of Halifax, Heaton, Highsmith, Hobbs, Hodnett, Hoffler, Hollowell, Hyman, Ing, Jones of Caldwell, Jones of Washington, King of Lincoln, King of Lenoir, Kinney, Lee, Legg Lennon, Long, May, Mayo, Marler, McCubbins, Merrit, McDonald of Chatham, McDonald of Moore, Moore, Morton, Mullican, Nance, Newsom, Nicholson, Patrick, Parker, Parks, Petree, Pierson, Peterson, Ray, Read, Renfrow, Rhodes, Rose, Sanderlin, Smith, Stilley, Stilwell, Taylor, Teague, Trogden, Tucker, Turner, Watts, Williams of Sampson, and Williams of Wake—82.

Those who voted in the negative are:

Messrs. Abbott, Andrews, Ashley, French of Bladen, French of Chowan, Fullings, Garland, Hayes, of Robeson, Mann, Murphy, Rich, Robbins, Sweet and Williamson—14.

The section as amended was adopted.

Section twelfth was read and discussed.

Mr. C. C. Jones in the Chair.

Mr. Cowles moved to amend by striking out "twelve" and insert "ten"; also strike out "for two weeks" and all after that and in insert "as may be provided by act of Assembly."

After considerable discussion, Mr. Rodman called the previous question which call was sustained.

The amendment of Mr. Cowles was divided.

To strike out "twelve" and insert "ten" was put to the House.

The yeas and nays were demanded, resulting yeas 43, and nays 57.

The amendment was lost.

The second portion of Mr. Cowles' amendment, viz: to strike out "for two weeks" and all after that, and insert "as may be provided by act of Assembly," was put to the House and lost.

Section twelfth as read was adopted.

Mr. Graham, of Orange entered his vote in the negative on the substitute of Mr. Jones, of Washington, to section second of the report of the committee on suffrage.

Section twenty-seventh was read.

Mr. Heaton moved to amend by striking out after the word "elected" in the second line "the qualified voters of the State," and insert "joint Convention of the General Assembly."

The amendment was lost, yeas 36, nays 51.

The original section as read was then adopted.

On motion the House adjourned.

---

## WEDNESDAY, February 26th, 1868.

The Convention was called to order at 11 o'clock, by the President.

Prayer by the Rev. Mr. Lennon.

The President announced a quorum.

The Journal of Tuesday was read and approved.

Mr. Jones, of Washington, arose to a question of privilege, in relation to a misrepresentation of the oath in his substitute offered for section 2d, of the Bill of Suffrage in the *Sentinel* of this days issue.

Mr. Ashley arose to a question of privilege in relation to some reported remarks of Mr. Durham, as reported in the *Sentinel*.

On motion the matter was referred to a Committee of five.

Mr. Abbott arose to a question of privilege in relation to some remarks in the *Sentinel*, of that day's issue.

The report of the Committee on the Judicial Department was taken up.

Mr. Watts moved to reconsider the vote on section 8th, as amended and passed Tuesday.

Mr. King, of Lenoir, moved to lay the motion on the table.

The motion prevailed, yeas 60, nays 48 :

Those who voted in the affirmative, are:

Messrs. Aydlott, Baker, Benbow, Blume, Bradley, Bryan, Chillson, Cox, Dowd, Duckworth, Durham, Ellis, Etheridge, Franklin, Garland, George, Glover, Graham of Orange, Grant of Northampton, Gunter, Hay, Heaton, Hobbs, Hodnett, Hollowell, Holt, Jones of Washington; King of Lincoln, King ot Lenoir, Kinney, Legg, Lennon, Logan, Long, Marler, McCubbins, Merritt, McDonald of Chatham, McDonald of Moore, Moore, Mortin, Mullican, Nance, Newsom, Nicholson, Patrick, Parker, Parks, Petree, Peterson, Ray, Read, Rhodes, Rose, Sanderlin, Stilly, Taylor, Teague, Turner and Williams of Sampson—60.

Those who voted in the negative, are:

Messrs. Abbott, Andrews, Ashley, Carey, Carter, Cherry, Colgrove, Daniel, Dickey, Eppes, Fisher, Forkner, French of Bladen, French of Rockingham, French of Chowan, Fullings, Galloway, Graham of Montgomery, Gully, Harris of Wake, Harris of Franklin, Hayes of Robeson, Hayes of Halifax, Highsmith, Hoffler, Hood, Hyman, Ing, Jones of Caldwell, Lee, May, Mayo, Murphy, Pierson, Ragland, Renfrow, Rich, Robbins, Rodman, Smith, Stilwell, Sweet, Tourgee, Trogden, Watts, Welker and Williamson—48.

Mr. Abbott gave notice that on the third reading, he would introduce an amendment to section 8th.

Mr. Galloway introduced a resolution in relation to ordering an election in Wilmington.

Referred to the Committee to consult with General Canby.

On motion of Mr. Durham, the Hall was tendered to the Republican Convention for this evening.

On motion the House adjourned.

---

## THURSDAY, February 27th, 1868.

The Convention was called to order at 10 o'clock, by the President.

Prayer by the Rev. Mr. Pepper.

The President announced a quorum.

The Journal of Wednesday was read and approved.

On motion, the Convention adjourned until Friday at 10 o'clock, A. M.

---

## FRIDAY, February 28th, 1868.

The Convention was called to order at 10 o'clock, by the President.

Prayer by the Rev. Mr. Warwick.

The Journal of Thursday was read and approved.

The Chair announced a quorum.

Leave of absence was granted:

Mr. Patrick until Monday next.

Mr. Franklin, until Tuesday next.

Mr. Trogden, until Tuesday next.

The Committee on Internal Improvements asked and obtained leave to sit during the session of the Convention.

Mr. Hobbs presented a memorial for relief, from the citizens of Davidson.

Referred to the Committee on Relief.

Mr. Ellis introduced an ordinance in relation to the mail matter of the Convention.

Lies over under the rule.

Mr. Andrews introduced a resolution in favor of Solomon Bragg.

Referred to the Committee on Contingent Expenses.

### UNFINISHED BUSINESS.

The resolution of Mr. King, of Lenoir, concerning widows who have qualified as Executrix to the last will and testament of their deceased husbands, was taken up and,

Referred to the Committee on the Judicial Department.

The following ordinance presented by Mr. Andrews, was taken up:

Section 1. *Be it ordained by the delegates of the people of the State of North-Carolina in Convention assembled, and it is hereby ordained by the authority of the same,* That the State tax to be collected from Theatrical Companies, shall be five dollars per night on each exhibition, or fifty dollars tor a season of three months, and on Concerts three dollars per night, or thirty dollars for a season of three months.

SEC. 2. *Be it further ordained,* That all laws, or clauses of laws, coming in conflict with the provisions of this ordinance are hereby repealed, and that this ordinance shall go into effect from and after its passage, subject to amendment or repeal by the Legislature.

Mr. Colgrove moved to lay the ordinance on the table.

The motion was not sustained.

After some discussion the previous question was called.

The call was sustained.

The yeas and nays were demanded, yeas 61, nays 38:

Those who voted in the affirmative, are:

Messrs. Abbott, Andrews, Benbow, Blume, Carey, Carter, Candler, Chillson, Dickey, Duckworth, Eppes, Fisher, Forkner, French of Bladen, French of Rockingham, French of Chowan, Galloway, Garland, Garrett, Glover, Graham of Montgomery, Gully, Harris of Wake, Harris of Franklin, Hay, Hayes of Robeson, Hayes of Halifax, Heaton, Highsmith, Hobbs, Hyman, Ing, Jones of Washington, Kinney, Lee, Legg, Logan, Long, Mann, May, Mayo, McDonald of Chatham, McDonald of Moore, Morton, Murphy, Parks, Petree, Pierson, Ragland, Renfrow, Rhodes, Rich, Robbins, Rodman, Rose, Smith, Sweet, Taylor, Teague, Watts and Williamson—61.

Those who voted in the negative, are:

Messrs. Aydlott, Barnes, Bradley, Bryan, Colgrove, Congleton, Daniel, Ellis, Etheridge, Fullings, George, Grant of Northampton, Gunter, Hodnett, Hoffler, Hollowell, Jones of Caldwell, King of Lincoln, King of Lenoir, Lennon, Marler, McCubbins, Merritt, Moore, Mullican, Newsom, Nicholson, Parker, Peterson, Ray, Sanderlin, Stilly, Stilwell, Trogden, Tucker, Turner, Welker and Williams of Sampson—38.

The ordinance was adopted.

The hour of eleven having arrived, the report of the Committee on the Judicial Department, was taken up.

Section 5th was read and adopted.

Section 6th was amended by striking out "Representatives," and insert "Commons."

The section, as amended, was adopted.

Sections 7th, 9th, 10th and 11th were read and adopted.

Section 13th was amended by striking out "Union," in the ninth District, and inserting "Catawba."

The section, as amended, was adopted.

Sections 14th, 15th, 16th, 17th, 18th, 19th, 20th, 21st, 22d, 23d, 24th and 25th, were read and adopted.

Section 27th was read and amended by inserting the word "all" in second line, between "of" and "business."

The section, as amended, was adopted.

Section 28th was read.

Mr. French, of Bladen, moved to amend by inserting after the word "shall" on line third, "hold office for the term of four years and."

The amendment was adopted.

The section, as amended, was adopted.

Section 29th was read.

Mr. Rodman, moved to amend by adding to the section, "when there is no coroner in a County, the Clerk of the Superior Court for the County may appoint one for special cases."

The amendment was adopted.

The section, as amended, was adopted.

Section 30th was read.

Mr. Rodman moved to amend by adding after the word "Governor," on the third line, "unless otherwise provided for."

The amendment was sustained.

The section, as amended, was adopted.

On motion of Mr. Tourgee, the vote by which section 24th was adopted, was reconsidered.

Mr. Tourgee moved to amend the section by inserting after

the word "Constitution," on the second line, the words, "or the Constitution, or laws of the United States."

Mr. Graham, of Orange, moved to amend the amendment of Mr. Tourgee so as to read, "or the Constitution of the United States, and laws made in pursuance thereof."

The amendment of Mr. Graham was put to the House and lost.

The amendment of Mr. Tourgee was sustained.

The section, as amended, was adopted.

On motion of Mr. Heaton, the vote on the adoption of section 26th, was reconsidered.

Mr. Heaton moved to amend the section, by striking out "sixteen," on line fourth, and inserting "eight."

Mr. Congleton moved to amend by striking out "sixteen," and inserting "six."

The motion was not sustained.

Mr. Tourgee moved to amend the amendment of Mr. Heaton, by striking out "eight," and inserting "twelve."

Upon this amendment, the yeas and nays were called.

Which resulted yeas 45, nays 51:

Those who voted in affirmative, are:

Messrs. Ashley, Bryan, Cowles, Cherry, Cox, Dowd, Duckworth, Eppes, Ethridge, Fisher, French of Bladen, Galloway, Grant of Northampton, Gully, Harris of Franklin, Hay, Hayes of Robeson, Hayes of Halifax, Heaton, Highsmith, Hollowell, Hood, Hyman, Ing, Jones of Caldwell, Jones of Washington, King of Lincoln, King of Lenoir, Lee, Legg, Logan, Mann, McDonald of Moore, Parker, Pierson, Read, Rhodes, Rich, Rodman, Rose, Sweet, Teague, Tourgee and Welker—45.

Those who voted in the negative, are:

Messrs. Andrews, Barnes, Benbow, Blume, Bradley, Carey, Carter, Chillson, Colgrove Congleton, Daniel, Dickey, Forkner, French of Rockingham, French of Chowan, Fullings, Garland, George, Graham of Montgomery, Gunter, Hobbs, Hodnett, Hoffler, Kinney, Long, May, Mayo, Marler, McCubbins, Merritt, McDonald of Chatham, Moore, Morton, Mullican, Murphy, Nance, Newsom, Parks, Petree, Peterson,

Ragland, Ray, Renfrow, Robbins, Smith, Stilly, Stilwell, Taylor, Trogden, Tucker, Turner and Watts—51.

The amendment was not sustained.

The question recurred to the amendment of Mr. Heaton.

The yeas and nays were called,

Which resulted yeas 63, nays 33 :

Those who voted in the affirmative, are.

Messrs. Andrews, Barnes, Benbow, Blume, Bradley, Bryan, Carey, Carter, Chillson, Colgrove, Congleton, Dickey, Duckworth, Forkner, French of Bladen, French of Rockingham, French of Chowan, Fullings, Garland, Graham of Montgomery, Grant of Northampton, Gunter, Heaton, Highsmith, Hobbs, Hodnett, Hoffler, Ing, Kinney, Logan, Long, May, Mayo, Marler, McCubbins, McDonald of Chatham, McDonald of Moore, Moore, Morton, Mullican, Murphy, Nance, Newsom, Nicholson, Parker, Parks, Petree, Peterson, Pierson, Ragland, Ray, Rhodes, Robbins, Rose, Smith, Stilly, Stilwell, Sweet, Taylor, Teague, Trogden, Tucker and Turner—63.

Those who voted in the negative, are:

Messrs. Abbott, Ashley, Baker, Cowles, Cherry, Cox, Daniel, Dowd, Eppes, Etheridge, Fisher, Galloway, George, Gully, Harris of Franklin, Hay, Hayes of Robeson, Hayes of Halifax, Hollowell, Hood, Hyman, Jones of Caldwell, Jones of Washington, King of Lincoln, King of Lenoir, Legg, Mann, Read, Renfrow, Rich, Rodman, Tourgee and Welker—33.

The amendment was sustained.

Mr. King, of Lincoln, introduced the following as a new section, to follow section 26th, as section 27th :

"Any Justice of the Supreme Court, or Judge of the Superior Courts, may be removed from office for mental or physical disability, upon a concurrent resolution of a majority of both Houses of the General Assembly. The Justice against whom the General Assembly may be about to proceed, shall receive notice thereof accompanied by a copy of the causes alleged for his removal, at least twenty days before the day on which either branch of the General Assembly shall act thereon."

The section was not adopted.

18

Mr. Heaton moved to amend section 26th, by striking out "twelve," on line sixth, and insert "six."

Mr. Abbott was called to the Chair.

Mr. Hood moved to amend the amendment of Mr. Heaton by striking out "six" and insert "eight."

The amendment prevailed.

Mr. Tourgee moved to amend section 26th, by striking out all after the word "years," on sixth line.

The amendment was withdrawn by Mr. Tourgee, who offered to amend as follows:

Strike out "eight" on eleventh line, and insert "six." On twelfth line strike out "twelve," and insert "eight."

The amendment was sustained.

Mr. Hood moved to amend by striking out "three" on tenth line, and inserting "two," also strike out all after the word "years," where it occurs last in the eleventh line.

Mr. Hood withdrew his amendment.

Mr. Cowles offered to amend by striking out "three" in tenth line, and insert "four." On eleventh line strike out "four and eight," and on twelfth line strike out "twelve," and in lieu of these words, insert "two, four, six and eight years."

The amendment did not prevail.

The section, as amended, was adopted.

Leave of absence was granted Messrs. Renfrow and Moore.

On motion the House adjourned.

---

AFTERNOON SESSION, February 28th, 1868.

The Convention was called to order at 7½ o'clock, by the President.

The President announced a quorum.

The Chair announced the following Committee on Privileges: Messrs. Daniel, Nicholson, Rich, Ellis and Forkner.

On motion, the report of the Committee on the Legislature, its organization, &c., was taken up and put on its third and final reading and passage.

Sections 1st, 2d and 3d were read and adopted.

Section 4th was read.

On motion of Mr. Sweet, the County of Tyrrell was transferred from the third to the second District.

Mr. Merritt moved a division of the twenty-first District.

The motion was not sustained.

Sections 4th, 5th, 6th, 7th and 8th, were read and adopted.

Section 9th was read.

Mr. Hay offered the following amendment:

Add to the section, "and shall be possessed of a freehold in the District of the value of five hundred dollars."

The amendment was lost.

The section, as read, was adopted.

Section 10th was read.

Mr. Colgrove moved the following as a substitute:

"Each member of the House of Representatives shall be a qualified elector of the State and shall have resided in the County in which he is chosen for one year immediately preceeding his election."

The substitute was, on motion, adopted.

Sections 11th, 12th, 13th, 14th, 15th, 16th, 17th, 18th, 19th, 20th, 21st, 22d, 23d, 24th, 25th, 26th and 27th, were read and adopted.

Section 28th was read.

On motion of Mr. Abbott, it was ordered that whenever the word "Commons" occurred in the entire report, that it be stricken out, and the word "Representatives," inserted.

Mr. Sweet offered the following as a substitute for section 28th:

"The terms of office for Senators and members of the House of Representatives, shall commence at the time of their election, and the terms of office of those elected at the first election, held under this Constitution, shall terminate at the same time as if they had been elected at the first ensuing regular election."

The substitute was, on motion, adopted.

Mr. McDonald, of Chatham, offered the following as a separate section:

"No member of the Senate or House of Representatives, shall be eligible to any office within the gift of the General Assembly, during the time for which he may be elected."

The section did not prevail.

Section 29th was read and adopted.

Section 30th was read.

Mr. Sweet moved to amend by striking out on the first and second lines, the words, "To the Senate and House of Representatives."

The amendment was adopted.

Mr. Tourgee moved to amend by striking out "thirtieth," and insert "fifteenth." Strike out "adoption," and insert "ratification."

The section, as amended, was adopted.

The entire report was adopted by the following vote, yeas 69, nays 4:

Those who voted in the affirmative are:

Messrs. Abbott, Andrews, Ashley, Aydlott, Barnes, Benbow, Blume, Bryan, Carey, Carter, Cherry, Chillson, Colgrove, Congleton, Cox, Dickey, Dowd, Duckworth, Fisher, Forkner, French of Bladen, French of Rockingham, French of Chowan, Fullings, Galloway, Garland, George, Graham of Montgomery, Gunter, Hay, Hayes of Holifax, Heaton, Highsmith, Hobbs, Hyman, Jones of Caldwell, King of Lenoir, Kinney, Legg, Long, Mann, Mayo, McDonald of Chatham, McDonald of Moore, Morton, Mullican, Murphy, Nance, Newsom, Nicholson, Parker, Parks, Petree, Peterson, Ray, Renfrow, Rich, Robbins, Smith, Stilwell, Sweet, Teague, Tourgee, Tucker, Turner, Watts, Welker and Williamson—69.

Those who voted in the negative are:

Messrs. Ellis, Hodnett, Lennon and Marler—4.

Leave of absence was granted Messrs. Lennon and King of Lenoir.

On motion, the House adjourned.

SATURDAY, FEBRUARY, 29TH, 1868.

The Convention was called to order at 10 o'clock by the President.

Prayer by the Rev. S. S. Ashley.

The President anounced a quorum.

The Journal of Friday was read and approved.

A communication was received from the Republican Convention assembled at Raleigh on the 26th instant.

The communication was,

On motion, laid on the table.

Mr. McDonald, of Chatham presented a memorial from the citizens of Chatham.

Referred to the Committee on Internal Improvements.

The report of the Committee on the organization of the Judicial Department was received and ordered to be printed.

On motion of Mr. Rodman the vote on section 29th of the report of the Committee on the Judicial Department was reconsidered.

Mr. Rodman moved to amend by adding to that section as amended February 28th the following words:

"In case of a vacancy existing from any cause in any of the offices created by this section, the Commissioners for the County may appoint to such office for the unexpired term."

The amendment was ordered to be printed with the report of the Committee on the Judicial Department, its organization, etc.

On motion, the following majority report of the Committee on Homesteads was taken up, and placed upon its second reading:

## MAJORITY REPORT OF THE COMMITTEE ON HOMESTEADS.

The Committee appointed to report on a Homestead respectfully report the following Article, to wit:

SECTION 1. The personal property of any resident of this State to the value of three hundred dollars, to be selected by such resident, shall be exempted from sale or execution or other final process, of any court, issued for the collection of any debt contracted after the adoption of this Constitution.

SEC. 2. Every homestead not exceeding one hundred acres of land, and the dwelling and buildings used therewith, not exceeding in value one thousand dollars, to be selected by the owner thereof, or in lieu thereof, at the option of the owner, any lot in a city, town or village, with the dwelling and buildings used thereon, owned and occupied by any resident of this State, and not exceeding the value of one thousand dollars, shall be exempt from sale or execution or any final process, obtained on any debt contracted from and after the the adoption of this Constitution; such exemption, however, shall not extend to any mortgage lawfully obtained; but no such mortgage or deed in the nature thereof, made by the owner of the homestead, if a married man, and no deed of conveyance by him shall be valid, without the voluntary signature and assent of his wife, signified on her private examination before a judge of some court of this State.

SEC. 3. The homestead of a family after the death of the owner thereof shall be exempt from the payment of any debt contracted by him after the adoption of this Coustitution, during the minority of his children, or any one of them.

SEC. 4. The provisions of sections one and two of this article, shall not be so construed as to prevent a laborer's lien for work done and performed for the person claiming such exemption, or a mechanic for work done on the premises.

SEC. 5. If the owner of a homestead die, leaving a widow but no children, the same shall be exempt from the debts of her husband, and the rents and profits thereof shall inure to her benefit for her life.

SEC. 6. The real and personal property of any female in this State, acquired before marriage, and all property real and personal, to which she may, after marriage, become in any manner entitled, after the adoption of this Constitution, shall be and remain the sole and separate estate and property of such female, and shall not be liable for any debts, obligations or engagements of her husband, and may be conveyed, devised, or bequeathed by her, as if she were a *femme sole.*

C. C. JONES, *Chairman.*
JOHN H. RENFROW,
SWEEN M. S. McDONALD,
ISAAC KINNEY,
HENRY BARNES,
J. L. NANCE,
P. HODNETT,
HENRY EPPES.

Section first was read.

Mr. Rich moved to strike out "three" on second line and insert "five."

The amendment was sustained.

Mr. Tourgee moved to strike out all after the word "debt" in the fifth line.

After considerable discussion the amendment was adopted by the following vote, yeas 51, nays 40:

Those who voted in the affirmative, are:

Messrs. Abbott, Andrews, Ashley, Aydlott, Baker, Blume, Bryan, Carey, Carter, Chillson, Congleton, Dickey, Etheridge, Fisher, French of Chowan, George, Graham of Montgomery, Gully, Gunter, Hayes of Robeson, Hood, Hyman, Kinney, Lee, Legg, Long, Mann, May, Mayo, Marler, Merritt, McDonald of Chatham, McDonald of Moore, Morton, Murphy, Nance, Parks, Peterson, Ragland, Ray, Read, Rich, Robbins, Rodman, Smith, Stilwell, Taylor, Tourgee, Turner, Watts, Welker, and Williamson—51.

Those who voted in the negative, are:

Messrs. Barnes, Benbow, Bradley, Candler, Colgrove, Cox, Duckworth, Ellis, Eppes, Forkner, French of Rockingham, Fullings, Gahagan, Garland, Glover, Graham of Orange, Grant of Northampton, Harris of Franklin, Hayes of Halifax, Heaton, Highsmith, Hodnett, Hollowell, Ing, Jones of Caldwell, King of Lincoln, Logan, Marler, McCubbins, Nicholson, Parker, Petree, Pierson, Rhodes, Rose, Sanderlin, Stilly, Sweet, Teague, and Tucker—40.

The section as amended was adopted.

Section second was read,

Mr. Hood moved to strike out all after the word "debt" in the ninth line.

The amendment was divided, so as to strike out all after the word "debt" in the ninth line to the end of the tenth line, which

On motion, was adopted,

The balance of the amendment, viz: to strike out all after the word "Constitution" in the tenth line, was adopted.

Mr. Tourgee moved to amend by inserting after the word "debt" the following:

"*Provided*, That no sale or mortgage of the Homestead shall be of any legal force, in case the owner of the homestead is in debt to the amount of one third the value of the homestead, unless by the consent of his wife signified on her private examination before a Clerk of a Superior Court of the State."

Mr. Hood moved the following substitute for the amendment of Mr. Tourgee:

"*Provided*, That the homestead may be exchanged for other property of the same nature by the owner thereof, with the voluntary consent of his wife signified on her private examination before a Judge of some circuit of this State."

The substitute of Mr. Hood was put to the House and carried.

On motion of Mr. Abbott, the report of the Committee on Finance was made a special order for Wednesday next.

Mr. Heaton introduced the following preamble and resolution:

Whereas, It is understood that some of the Judges of the Superior Courts of this State are rendering and are about to render judgment in cases intended to be exempted by the ordinance for relief, entitled "an ordinance respecting the jurisdiction of the Courts in this State;" therefore

*Resolved*, That the President of this Convention is hereby instructed to communicate immediately with the Commanding General of this Military District and request him to issue such orders as will insure the full observance of said ordinance.

On motion, the rules were suspended, and the resolution was adopted.

On motion, the House adjourned.

---

MONDAY, March 2d, 1868.

The Convention was called to order at 10 o'clock, by the President.

Prayer by the Rev. H. T. Hudson.

The President announced a quorum.

The Roll was called and the following members answered to their names:

Messrs. Abbott, Ashley, Aydlott, Barnes, Benbow, Blume, Bradley, Bryan, Carey, Carter, Candler, Cherry, Chillson, Colgrove, Congleton, Cox, Duckworth, Ellis, Eppes, Etheridge, Fisher, Forkner, French of Chowan, Galloway, Graham of Montgomery, Gunter, Harris of Wake, Hayes of Robeson, Hayes of Halifax, Highsmith, Hodnett, Hoffler, Holt, Hood, Hyman, Jones of Caldwell, King of Lincoln, Kinney, Lee, Logan, Long, Mann, Mayo, Merritt, McDonald of Moore, Morton, Mullican, Murphy, Nance, Newsom, Nicholson, Parks, Petree, Peterson, Pierson, Ray, Read, Rhodes, Robbins, Rodman, Rose, Smith, Stillwell, Sweet, Taylor, Teague, Turner, Watts, Welker, Williams of Sampson, Williams of Wake, and Williamson—72.

The Journal of Saturday was read and approved.

A communication was received from General Canby.

Referred to the Committee on Privileges and Elections.

Mr. Abbott moved a suspension of the rules, to take up the ordinance on Immigration.

The motion was declared out of order.

Mr. Abbott appealed from the decision of the Chair.

The Chair was sustained by the House in its decision.

Mr. Abbott moved to make the ordinance a special order for Tuesday at 10 o'clock.

The President declared the motion out of order.

Mr. Andrews presented a petition of Martha Brown.

Referred to the Committee on Divorce.

Mr. Blume presented a petition of divorce of one L. S. P. Robeson.

Referred to the Committee on Divorce.

Mr. Rich presented a resolution in relation to the adjournment of this Convention.

Lies over under the rules.

Mr. Heaton introduced a resolution as a substitute for that introduced by Mr. Rich.

Mr. Heaton called for a suspension of the rules.

Declared out of order.

Lies over under the rules.

Mr. Rodman introduced a resolution concerning divorces.

Lies over under the rules.

Mr. Candler introduced a resolution tendering the thanks, of this body to the Congress of the United States for the impeachment of Andrew Johnson.

Lies over under the rules.

Mr. Harris, of Wake, introduced a resolution relating to the pay of Delegates in certain cases.

Also, one providing for a daily call of the roll of delegates, &c., both of which,

Lies over under the rules.

Mr. Jones, of Caldwell, introduced a resolution providing for an earlier daily meeting of this body.

Lies over under the rules.

On motion of Mr. Abbott, the ordinance appointing a Commissioner of Immigration was taken up and discussed.

Mr. Candler introduced the following substitute:

SECTION 1. *Be it ordained by the people of North-Carolina in Convention assembled*, That the Legislature shall have power to create the office of land and immigrant commissioners, and establish such office at such place as they may deem best for the interest of North-Carolina, and shall establish the salary for the same, and the Governor, with the consent of both branches of the Legislature, shall have power to fill said office.

On motion of Mr. Abbott, the subject was postponed and made a special order for Tuesday at 10½ o'clock.

The resolution of Mr. Heaton regarding the adjournment of this Convention, was accepted by Mr. Forkner, as an amendment to the report of the Committee on adjournment of which he is Chairman.

Mr. Rodman offered to amend by adding "that should the Convention not adjourn on the 12th, that the pay of the members cease on that day."

Mr. Candler moved the following substitute:

*Resolved*, That it be the sense of this Convention, that we adjourn on the 12th instant, but should it be the sense of this Convention on the 12th, that it was impossible to complete and finish the Constitution by the 12th, then this Convention shall have power to reconsider the question of adjournment.

The substitute was,

On motion, adopted.

The report of the majority Committee on Homesteads was taken up.

Mr. Rich moved to amend section 2nd by striking out in lines first and second, the following words: "not to exceed one hundred acres of land."

The amendment was adopted.

Mr. C. C. Jones offered to amend by adding after the word "debt" on the ninth line, "but no property shall be exempt from sale for taxes or for payment of obligations contracted for the purchase of said premises."

The amendment was,

On motion, adopted.

Mr. Graham, of Orange, offered the following substitute:

The General Assembly shall provide by law for the exemption from sale under execution or other process of a Homestead in land, in favor of any head of a family who may be the owner thereof, except for taxes.

On this the yeas and nays were demanded.

The substitute did not prevail, yeas 33, nays 61.

Those who voted in the affirmative are:

Messrs. Baker, Barnes, Benbow, Bradley, Candler, Duckworth, Ellis, Eppes, Etheridge, French of Rockingham, Fullings, Gahagan, Garland, Garrett, Glover, Graham of Orange, Hare, Harris of Franklin, Hayes of Halifax, Hodnett, Hollowell, Holt, King of Lincoln, Logan, Marler, McCubbins, Mullican, Rhodes, Rose, Sanderlin, Teague, Williams of Sampson, and Williams of Wake—33.

Those who voted in the negative are:

Messrs. Abbott, Andrews, Ashley, Aydlott, Blume, Bryan, Carey, Carter, Chillson, Colgrove, Congleton, Cox, Fisher, Forkner, Franklin, French of Chowan, Galloway, George, Graham of Montgomery, Grant of Northampton, Gully, Gunter, Heaton, Highsmith, Hoffler, Hood, Hyman, Ing, Jones of Caldwell, Jones of Washington, Kinney, Lee, Long, Mann, May, Mayo, Merrit, McDonald of Moore, Morton, Murphy, Nance, Newsom, Nicholson, Parker, Parks, Petree, Peterson, Pierson, Ray, Rich, Robbins, Rodman, Smith, Stilly, Stillwell, Taylor, Tourgee, Turner, Watts, Welker and Williamson—61.

On motion of Mr. Tourgee, the report was made a special order for Thursday evening.

On motion of Mr. Ashley the report of the Committee on Education was made a special order for Friday at 11 o'clock.

On motion of Mr. Welker the report of the Committee on Penal Institutions was made a special order for Tuesday at 11 o'clock.

On motion of Mr. Rodman, the ordinance for relief introduced by himself was made a special order for Tuesday evening at 7½ o'clock.

The report of the Committee on Counties, Cities and Towns, was received and ordered to be printed and made a special order for Thursday at 11 o'clock.

Mr. Bryan moved to reconsider the vote, striking out sections 4th to 10th inclusive of the report of the Committee on Corporations other than Municipal.

The motion was not sustained.

The following ordinance offered by Mr. Tourgee in reference to Sheriffs, Executions, &c., was taken up and passed:

SECTION 1. *Be it ordained by the people of North-Carolina, in Convention assembled*, That no sheriff or other officer in the State of North-Carolina who, in the performance of official duty, has obeyed and observed the provisions of an act of the General Assembly of the State of North-Carolina entitled, "An act to protect property sold under execution from sacrifice ratified the 26th day of February, A. D., 1867," shall be liable to amercement or any other proceedings for failure to sell any property whatsoever to satisfy any execution or other process issued from a justice of the peace or from any of the several courts of said State, and any judgments *nisi*, heretofore granted by any of such amercements, and which may still be pending in any of said courts, and any actions commenced, or which may hereafter be commenced in any of said courts for failure to satisfy execution or other process as aforsaid, shall be dismissed upon notice duly made.

On motion of Mr. Jones, of Washington, the report of the Committee on Corporations was made a special order for this evening at 7½ o'clock.

Leave of absence was granted, Messrs Ragland, and McDonald of Chatham, until Wednesday next.

The ordinance to repeal an ordinance ratified June 20th, 1868, introduced by Mr. Morton, was taken up, and,

On motion, was laid on the table.

The ordinance to prohibit the collection of certain debts, introduced by Mr. Watts, was taken up, and,

On motion, was laid on the table.

The Chair announced the following Committee on Final Revision and Arrangement:

Messrs. Heaton, Nicholson and Rodman.

Mr. Rodman moved a suspension of the rules, to take up his resolution concerning divorces.

The motion prevailed.

Mr. Candler moved to lay the resolution on the table.

The motion was not sustained.

On motion of Mr. Ing, the resolution was postponed indefinitely.

Mr. Forkner moved to adjourn.

The motion was lost.

Mr. Graham, of Orange, moved to adjourn *sine die.*

The motion was lost.

Mr. Holt moved to adjourn.

The motion prevailed.

---

EVENING SESSION, MARCH 2D, 1868.

The Convention was called to order at 7½ o'clock, by the President.

The Roll was called, forty-seven members answering to their names, viz:

Messrs. Andrews, Aydlott, Blume, Bradley, Bryan, Carey, Carter, Cherry, Chilson, Durham, Eppes, Fullings, Galloway, Graham of Montgomery, Gully, Gunter, Hay, Hayes of Robeson, Hayes of Halifax, Highsmith, Hodnett, Hood, Hyman, Jones of Caldwell, King of Lincoln, Kinney, Lee, Long, Mann, McDonald of Moore, Morton, Mullican, Murphy, Newsom, Parks, Ray, Rich, Robbins, Rodman, Rose, Smith, Stilwell, Teague, Tourgee, Tucker, Welker and Williams of Sampson—47.

Mr. Rich moved a call of the House.

Mr. Tourgee moved that the Sergeant at-Arms be sent after the absent members.

The motion was sustained.

Mr. Hodnett moved that further proceedings in the matter be suspended.

The motion was not sustained.

Mr. Hayes, of Halifax, moved a reconsideration of the vote taken on the motion of Mr. Tourgee, to send the Sergeant-at-Arms after absent members.

The motion was sustained.

A quorum being present, the House proceeded to take up the report of the Committee on Corporations other than Municipal,

Which was placed upon its third and final reading.

Section 1st was read.

Referred to the Committee on Counties, Cities, Towns, &c.

Mr. Abbott presented a petition of divorce in favor of Harmon Merritt.

Referred to the Committee on the Judicial Department.

The Committee on Privileges and Elections reported as follows:

The Committee on Privileges and Elections, to whom was referred the election returns from the Counties of Alleghany, Ashe, Surry, Yadkin and Watauga, have instructed me to report that the official returns of the various election precincts, from the district comprising said Counties, agree with the former report of Generel E. R. S. Canby, made to this Convention, which gave rise to the former action of this Convention, which declared that John M. Marshall was chosen instead of John G. Marler. Jno. M. Marshall received 1,123 votes, and John G. Marler, 1,030 votes, which shows that John M. Marshall is entitled to his seat. We, therefore, submit the following:

*Resolved*, That the seat now occupied by John G. Marler be vacated, and John M. Marshall be admitted to his seat.

The report was accepted.

The hour of 10½ having arrived, the Special Order for that hour was postponed to Wednesday at 10½ o'clock.

The following report was received from the Committee of sixteen.

The Committee of sixteen, to whom was referred the petition of certain citizens of Jones County, in relation to the change of a portion of the line between said County and the County of Lenoir, have had the same under consideration, and respectfully beg leave to to report as follows:

That the present Convention is not prepared to act upon said subject, for the following reasons:

1st. Because the Constitution now being framed, has not yet been ratified by the vote of the people.

2d. Because there will be an Article in said Constitution, pointing out the course hereafter to be taken in relation to the change of County lines, and that a remedy can be furnished at the next, or any subsequent Legislature, for the claims of said petitioners, of such a character as will enable said petitioners to accomplish the object desired.

All of which is respectfully submitted.

DAVID HEATON, *Chairman.*

On motion, the report was adopted.

Mr. Forkner moved that the report of the Committee on Privileges and Elections be adopted.

Mr. Durham moved that the report of the Committee on Privileges and Elections, be printed with the accompanying papers.

The motion was not sustained.

The hour of eleven having arrived, the Special Order for that hour was,

On motion, postponed.

Mr. Durham moved to re-commit the report of the Committee on Privileges and Election to that Committee, with instructions to communicate with General Canby, and send for the original scrolls or ballots cast in the Counties of Alleghany, Ashe, Surry, Yadkin and Watauga.

After some discussion, Mr. Forkner moved the previous question,

Which motion was sustained.

The motion of Mr. Durham was put to the House and lost.

Mr. Durham moved to lay the report of the Committee on the table.

Which motion the Chair decided out of order.

Mr Heaton moved a call of the House.

The Roll was called.

The following members present viz:

Messrs. Ashley, Aydlott, Baker, Blume, Bradley, Bryan, Carey,Carter, Candler, Chillson, Colgrove, Congleton, Cox, Dickey, Dowd, Duckworth, Durham, Ellis, Eppes, Etheridge, Fisher, Forkner, Franklin, French of Rockingham, French of Chowan, Fullings, Gahagan, Galloway, Garland, Garrett, George, Glover, Graham of Montgomery, Graham of Orange, Grant of Wayne, Grant of Northampton, Gully, Gunter, Hare, Hay, Hayes, of Robeson, Hayes of Halifax, Heaton,

Highsmith, Hobbs, Hodnett, Hoffler, Hollowell, Holt, Hood, Hyman, Ing, Jones of Caldwell, Jones of Washington, King of Lincoln, Kinney, Laflin, Lee, Legg, Lennon, Logan, Long, May, Mayo, Marler, McCubbins, Merrit, McDonald of Moore, Moore, Morton, Mullican, Murphy, Nance, Newsom, Nicholson, Parker, Parks, Petree, Pierson, Ray, Read, Rhodes, Robbins, Rodman, Rose, Sanderlin, Smith, Stilley, Stilwell, Sweet, Taylor, Teague, Tourgee, Tucker, Turner, Watts, Welker, Williams of Sampson and Williamson—89.

The Chair ordered the lobbies cleared and the doors closed,

When, on motion of Mr. Graham, of Orange, further proceedings in the matter were suspended.

The question then before the House, was on the adoption of the report of the Committee.

Mr. Durham demanded the yeas and nays.

The report was then adopted by the following vote, yeas 67, nays 17:

Those who voted in the affirmative, are:

Messrs. Ashley, Aydlott, Blume, Bryan, Carey, Carter, Candler, Cherry, Chillson, Colgrove, Congleton, Cox, Dickey, Duckworth, Fisher, Forkner, French of Bladen, French of Rockingham, French of Chowan, Fullings, Gahagan, Galloway, Garland, Garrett, Glover, Graham of Montgomery, Grant of Wayne, Gully, Gunter, Hayes of Robeson, Hayes of Halifax, Heaton, Highsmith, Hobbs, Hood, Hyman, Jones of Washington, King of Lincoln, Kinney, Laflin, Lee, Logan, Long, May, Mayo, Morton, Mullican, Newsom, Parks, Petree, Pierson, Ray, Rhodes, Robbins, Rodman, Rose, Smith, Stilwell, Sweet, Taylor, Teague, Tourgee, Tucker, Turner, Watts, Welker and Williamson—67.

Those who voted in the negative, are:

Messrs. Baker, Dowd, Durham, Ellis, Graham of Orange, Hare, Hay, Hodnett, Holt, Legg, Lennon, McCubbins, Merritt, McDonald of Chatham, Moore, Sanderlin, Stilly and Williams of Sampson—17.

Mr. Durham offered a protest, which he desired entered on the Journal of the Convention, which was granted by the House.

Mr. Marshall was properly qualified by the Secretary, and took his seat in the Convention.

Mr. Bradley moved that Mr. Marler be entitled to his per diem and mileage.

The motion prevailed.

The following report was taken up and passed its first reading:

## REPORT OF THE COMMITTEE ON PUNISHMENTS, PENAL INSTITUTIONS AND PUBLIC CHARITIES.

The Committee on Punisnments, Penal Institutions and Public Charities, would submit to the consideration of the Convention, the following report:

### ARTICLE —.

SECTION 1. The following punishments shall be known to the laws of this State, viz: Death, imprisonment, fines, removal from office and disqualification to hold and enjoy any office of honor, trust, or profit, under this State.

SEC. 2. The object of punishments being not only to satisfy justice, but also to reform the offender, and thus prevent crime, it shall not be allowed to inflict any cruel or unusual punishments; and wilful murder only shall be liable to be punished with death, while branding, cropping, whipping, and the pillory, shall never be allowed.

SEC. 3. The General Assembly shall, at its first meeting, make provision for the erection and conduct of a State's prison or penitentiary at some central and accessible point within the State.

SEC. 4. The General Assembly shall provide for the erection of Houses of Correction, where vagrants and persons guilty of misdemeanors shall be restrained and usefully employed.

SEC. 5. A House of Refuge shall also be established at an early period for the juvenile offenders, where, under proper supervision, they may be reclaimed from vicious habits and fitted for the duties of citizens.

SEC. 6. It shall be required by competent legislation that the structure and superintendence of the penal institutions of the State, the County jails, and city police prisons, secure the health and comfort of the prisoners, and male and female convicts be never confined in the same room or cell.

SEC. 7. Beneficent provisions for the poor, the unfortunate and orphan, being one of the first duties of a civilized and christian State, the General Assembly shall, at its first session, appoint and define the duties of a Board of Public Charities, to whom shall be entrusted the management of all charitable and penal State institutions, and who shall annually report to the Govornor upon their condition, with suggestions for their improvement.

SEC. 8. There shall also, as soon as practicable, be measures devised by the State for the establishment of one or more Orphan Houses, where the orphans of the poor shall be cared for, educated and taught some business or trade.

SEC. 9. It shall be the duty of the Legislature, at an early day, to devise means for the education of idiots and the cure of inebriates.

SEC. 10. The General Assembly shall provide that all the deaf-mutes, the blind, and the insane of the State shall be cared for at the charge of the State.

SEC. 11. It shall be steadily kept in view by the Legislature, and the Board of Public Charities, that all penal and charitable institutions should be made as nearly self-supporting as is consistent with the purposes of their creation.

G. WILLIAM WELKER, *Chairman.*
G. W. BRADLEY,
S. W. WATTS,
R. T. LONG,
J. S. PARKER,
W. A. B. MURPHY,
MILTON HOBBS,
T. L. L. COX,
WILLIE DANIEL,
CLINTON D. PEARSON,
BRYANT LEE,
J. H. DUCKWORTH,
ANDREW J. GLOVER.

On second reading, section 1st was adopted.

Section 2d was read.

Mr. Rodman moved to strike out all in first, second and third lines, excluding the word " Crime."

The amendment was not sustained.

Mr. Rodman moved to strike out in third and fourth lines, the words, " it shall not be allowed to inflict any cruel or unusual punishments."

The amendment was accepted by Mr. Welker, Chairman of the Committee.

Mr. Tourgee moved to strike out the word " and," in fourth line.

The motion was sustained.

Mr. Rodman moved to strike out the word " wilful," in fourth line.

The amendment was accepted by Mr. Welker, the Chairman of the Committtee.

Mr. Rodman moved to strike out the word " only," in fourth line.

Mr. Rodman withdrew the amendment, and offered the following in place thereof:

Strike out all after " crime," in line third, down to the word " while," in line fifth, and insert as follows: " Murder and also arson, burglary and rape, if the General Assembly shall so enact, shall be punishable with death.

The amendment was put to the House and lost.

On motion, the vote was reconsidered, and the amendment adopted.

Mr. Rodman moved to amend by striking out the words, " while branding, whipping, and the pillory shall never be allowed."

The amendment was adopted.

Section 2d, as amended, was adopted.

Mr. Rodman moved to reconsider the vote by which section 1st was adopted.

The motion prevailed.

Mr. Rodman moved to amend by inserting the word " only," after the word " punishments," on line first, and the words, "with or without hard labor," after the word "imprisonment," on line second.

The amendments were adopted.

The section, as amended, was adopted.

Section 3d was read.

Mr. Mullican moved the following as a substitue:

"The General Assembly shall, as soon as practicable, make provisions for the erection of a penitentiary, at some central and accessable point within the State."

The substitute did not prevail.

The section, as read, was adopted.

Section 4th was read.

Mr. Heaton moved to insert "may," instead of "shall," in line first.

The amendment was accepted by the Chairman of the Committee.

The section, as amended, was adopted.

Section 5th was read.

Mr. Jones, of Washington, moved to insert "may" instead of "shall," in line first.

The amendment was adopted.

Mr. Harris, of Wake, moved to insert after the word "House," on line first, the words, "or Houses."

The amendment was accepted by the Chairman of the Committee.

Mr. Hobbs moved to strike out the entire section.

Mr. Watts moved to adjourn.

The motion was not sustained.

The yeas and nays were granted on the motion of Mr. Hobbs, to strike out.

The House, on motion, adjourned.

---

## EVENING SESSION, March 3d, 1868.

The Convention was called to order at 7½ o'clock by the President.

The roll was called.

The following members present, viz:

Messrs. Abbott, Ashley, Aydlott, Baker, Blume, Bradley, Bryan, Carey, Carter, Chillson, Colgrove, Congleton, Cox, Dickey, Dowd, Duckworth, Durham, Ellis, Eppes, Etheridge, Fisher, Forkner, Franklin, French of Bladen, French of Chowan, Fullings, Galloway, George, Graham of Montgomery, Gully, Gunter, Hare, Hayes of Robeson, Hayes of Halifax, Highsmith, Hobbs, Hodnett, Hoffler, Hollowell, Holt, Hood, Hyman, Ing, Jones of Caldwell, Jones of Washington, King of Lincoln, Kinney, Laflin, Lee, Legg, Lennon, Mann, May, Mayo, Marshall, McCubbins, Merritt, McDonald of Moore, Moore, Morton, Mullican, Murphy, Nance, Newsom, Nicholson, Parker, Parks, Petree, Peterson, Pool, Ray, Read, Rhodes, Rich, Robbins, Rodman, Rose, Sanderlin, Smith, Stilwell, Taylor, Teague, Tucker, Turner, Watts and Welker—86.

The following ordinance introduced by Mr. Rodman, having been made a Special Order for this evening, was taken up:

## AN ORDINANCE FOR THE RELIEF OF THE PEOPLE.

SECTION 1. *It is hereby ordained by the people of North-Carolina in Convention assembled,* That no court of law or court of equity created by the Constitution, which shall be adopted by this Convention, shall have jurisdiction of any action founded on a contract made or entered into prior to the first day of May, 1865; (except actions against public officers, executors, administrators, guardians, trustees and others acting in a fiduciary capacity, founded on an appropriation to their own use of money or property officially received by them, or other fraudulent breach of trust: and except also, notes given for the purchase of land where less than half the purchase money has been paid: and except also, actions for the wages of laborers; and except also, actions against banking and rail road corporations: and except where the debt is secured by mortgage or deed in trust,) nor of any action, suit, or process to revive, continue or enforce any judgment heretofore recovered in any action founded as aforesaid, nor of any action founded on any bond, promissory note, bill of exchange or parol promise made since the 1st of May, 1865, in renewal of, or substitution for, a contract made prior to 1st of May, 1865, to the full amount of principal and interest of a debt, existing prior to said day, and without other consideration than such pre-existent debt; nor of any action, suit, or process to revive, continue or enforce any judgment heretofore recovered upon any such bond, promissory note, bill of exchange or parol promise as is heretofore mentioned: unless before or at the time of commencing any such action, proceeding or motion, or of suing out such process, or of enforcing the same, the plaintiff therein, in person or by his attorney, shall by deed, or of record, stipulate that if the defendant shall at the current or next ensuing term of the Court, to which such action shall be brought, or in which it is pending, or to which such process is returnable, pay to the plaintiff, or into Court for his use, the one-tenth part of the sum of the principal and interest, up to the first day of January, 1868, of the debt recovered, or demanded and not denied to be due, together with the taxable cost of such suit or process, and shall annually for nine years thereafter pay as aforesaid a like sum; the said plaintiff will accept such payments in full satisfaction and discharge of the demand sued for. And if the defendant shall pay the said costs and the debt in tenths annually in manner aforesaid, the action shall be continued from term to term in the Court, but the Court shall have no jurisdiction to hear, try or determine the same, or to make any other order therein. And if the defendant in any such action, shall on oath, deny that he owes to the plaintiff the sum demanded by him, or shall admit that he owes a part only of said sum, and on oath deny that he owes the residue, then the Court shall have jurisdiction of so much of the debt as is denied; and shall proceed to try and determine the suit as if brought for that portion of the claim only; and the defendant as to the portion of the claim not denied by him shall have the benefit of the provision of this ordinance. And if such defendant shall, at any time, fail to pay the costs and one-tenth annually as herein provided for, the plaintiff shall be entitled immediately to judgment and process of execution for the said costs and tenth, or for so much thereof, as shall be unpaid.

SEC. 2. If the plaintiff, in any action now pending, in any court of law or equity in this state, of which action it is enacted in the foregoing section, that no court shall have jurisdiction, unless on the performance by the plaintiff of certain conditions in said section set forth, or any person having a cause of action, of which jurisdiction is denied by the provisions of the foregoing section, shall by deed filed in the proper court, for the use of the defendant in such action, or of the person against whom such cause of action exists, or of record in such court, stipulate and agree, that if the defendant, or person against whom such cause of action exists, shall pay to the said plaintiff or person having such cause of action, or into court for his use, the cost and also one-fourth of the debt or demand of the said plaintiff, or person having such cause of action, in three equal payments, the first of which, with the costs, shall be paid in three months from the entering into such agreement, and the other two, with interest thereon, at the end of one and two years respectively, from the time of the first payment; that he, the said plaintiff or person having such cause of action, will release and discharge the defendant or person against whom the cause of action exists, from the said debt or demand, and shall have given notice to the defendant, or person against whom the cause of action exists, ten days before entering into such agreement, that he would enter into such agreement; then, and in that case, the court shall have jurisdiction to hear, try, and determine the demand of the said plaintiff or person having a cause of action, and shall give judgment for the costs of the suit, and for one-fourth of the sum found due, and execution may immediately issue, and be levied on the property of the person against whom the judgment was recorded, which levy shall be a lien on the property levied on, prior to any lien subsequently acquired; but the property shall only be sold in case of failure to pay as aforesaid.

SEC. 3. If any such plaintiff, or person having a cause of

action, shall, in manner aforesaid, agreee to receive from the defendant, or person against whom the cause of action exists in full, satisfaction and discharge of the debt or demand, a sum, which shall bear such proportion to the debt due the plaintiff, or person having cause of action as the property, rights, and credits of the defendant, or person against whom the cause of action exists, bears at the date of such agreement to the property, rights and credits of the said defendant or person, on the 20th May, 1861, or if the debt or cause of action was created after the 20th May, 1861, then on the date of its creation, the payment of the costs and of the sum to be made in the manner provided in the next preceding section for the payment of the costs and the one-fourth therein spoken of, and shall have given to the other party ten days' notice of his intention to make such agreement; then, and in that case, the court shall have jurisdiction to hear, try and determine the demand, and to ascertain according to its course and practice, what sum should be received by the plaintiff or person aforesaid, under the agreement aforesaid, and shall enter judgment for costs and for such sum, and execution may issue and be levied, and shall be a lien, in like manner as is provided for in the next preceding section.

Sec. 4. No mortgagee or trustee, under a deed in trust, made to secure debts or demands such as the courts of this State are excluded from jurisdiction of by the first section of this ordinance, and such debts or demands only, whether the said mortgage or trust-deed does or does not contain a power of sale, shall either with or without the decree of a court, sell the property conveyed in such mortgage or trust-deed, without the consent of the grantor, unless, it shall appear that the creditor has offered to accept in dscharge of his debt, payment thereof in manner, the following, viz: On the first day of January, 1869, the one-fifth of the principal and interest up to that day, and annually, on the same day for four years thereafter, the like sum, together with the interest which has accrued on the unpaid portion of the principal, since the last preceding payment, and the debtor shall have refused or failed to make such payments, and if such debtor shall so fail or refuse, he shall lose the benefit of this ordinance.

SEC. 5. No lien existing at the time this ordinance goes into effect, shall be thereby impaired. All such liens unless already registered, shall be registered within three months from the time this ordinance shall go into effect, or if acquired subsequently thereto, in thirty days after being so acquired, in the office of the Register of the County in which the property on which the lien is claimed lies. Such registration shall describe the property on which the lien is claimed, the name of the person claiming it, the name of the person against whom it is claimed, and shall show how it is claimed, or refer to some record or registered deed under which it is claimed. Upon the sale of the property subject to such liens, the proceeds shall be applied to satisfy them, according to their proper priorities.

SEC. 6. The Act of the General Assembly of North Carolina, ratified on 12th March, 1866, (ch. 39,) establishing a scale of depreciation of confederate currency; and also, the act construing the act aforesaid, ratified 24th January, 1867, (ch. 44,) are hereby re-enacted and continued in force, and shall be applied in all cases in which they are applicable, in proceedings under this ordinance.

SEC. 7. This ordinance shall be submitted to the people for ratification, at the same time and in the same manner, as the Constitution which shall be adopted by this Convention is; and if ratified by a majority of the voters, it shall go into effect upon the ratification of said Constitution, by a majority of the voters thereon.

After considerable debate the previous question was called.

The call was sustained.

The yeas and nays were ordered.

The ordinance was passed by the following vote, yeas 48, nays 42:

Those who voted in the affirmative, are:

Messrs. Ashley, Aydlott, Baker, Blume, Bryan, Carter, Cherry, Chillson, Dowd, Duckworth, Durham, Etheridge, Fisher, Franklin, French of Chowan, Galloway, George, Graham of Montgomery, Grant of Wayne, Grant of Northampton, Gunter, Harris of Franklin, Hay, Holt, Jones of

Caldwell, Laflin, Legg, Long, Merritt, McDonald of Moore, Moore, Morton, Murphy, Nance, Newsom, Read, Rich, Rodman, Sanderlin, Stilly, Stilwell, Taylor, Tourgee, Turner, Watts, Williamsof Sampson, and Williamson—48.

Those who voted in the negative are:

Messrs. Andrews, Barnes, Bradley Carey, Colgrove, Congleton, Cox, Ellis, Eppes, Forkner, French of Rockingham, Fullings, Glover, Graham of Orange, Hare, Hayes of Halifax, Highsmith, Hobbs, Hodnett, Hollowell, Hood, Hyman, Ing, Jones of Washington, King of Lincoln, King of Lenoir, Kinney, Lee, May, Mayo, McCubbins, Mullican, Nicholson, Parker, Petree, Peterson, Pool, Ray, Rhodes, Robbins, Rose, and Teague—42.

Mr. Tourgee, gave notice that on Wednesday he would call for a reconsideration of the vote.

On motion, the following preamble and resolution, introduced by Mr. Rich were taken up:

WHEREAS, It is of the utmost consequence that this Convention, in view of the importance of this State, being represented as a State in the coming Convention at Chicago, should as speedily as possible finish its work and submit the Constitution framed by it to the people for ratification or rejection:

*Be it Resolved*, That the President shall appoint a committee of two from each Congressional district, whose duty it shall be on and after Thursday the 5th day of March, to recommend to this Convention, all bills, ordinances, and Constitutional articles, which should in the opinion of that committee be acted upon by the Convention, and that no other bills, ordinances or Constitutional articles, shall be acted upon but those recommended by the committee appointed in pursuance of this resolution.

On motion the preamble was stricken out.

Mr. Tourgee moved to amend by striking out so as to read "the Committee of sixteen, of which Mr. Heaton is Chairman," instead of "the President shall appoint a committee of two from each Congressional district."

The amendment was adopted.

On motion of Mr. Heaton, Mr. Rich was added to that Committee.

The resolution as amended was adopted.

Mr. Forkner introduced a resolution limiting debate.

Lies over under the rule.

The report of the Committee on Punishment, Penal Institutions, &c., was taken up and discussed.

Pending which,

On motion the House adjourned.

---

WEDNESDAY, March 4th, 1868.

The Convention was called to order at 11 o'clock, by the President.

Prayer by the Rev. Mr. Logan.

The roll was called and the following members answered to their names:

Messrs. Abbott, Ashley, Aydlott, Bradley, Bryan, Carey, Carter, Candler, Cherry, Chillson, Congleton, Cox, Dickey, Dowd, Duckworth, Durham, Ellis, Eppes, Etheridge, Fisher, Forkner, French of Bladen, French of Rockingham, French of Chowan, Galloway, Garland, George, Graham of Montgomery, Grant of Northampton, Gully, Gunter, Hare, Harris of Wake, Hay, Hayes of Robeson, Hayes of Halifax, Highsmith, Hobbs, Hodnett, Hoffler, Holt, Hood, Hyman, Ing, Jones of Caldwell, King of Lincoln, King of Lenoir, Kinney, Laflin, Lee, Legg, Lennon, Logan, Long, Mann, May, Mayo, Marshall, McCubbins, Merritt, Moore, Morton, Mullican, Murphy, Nance, Newsom, Parker, Parks, Petree, Peterson, Pierson, Ray, Read, Rhodes, Rich, Robbins, Rodman, Rose, Sanderlin, Smith, Stilwell Taylor, Teague, Tourgee, Trogden, Turner, Watts, Welker, Williams of Sampson, Williams of Wake, and Williamson—90.

The Journal of Tuesday was read and approved.

Mr. French, of Bladen, presented a petition of relief, of James Johnson,

Referred to the Committee on Relief.

The Committee on Contingent Expenses reported as follows:

The undersigned Committee appointed on Contingent Expenses beg leave to report that they have examined the account of W. W. Holden & Son, for printing and stationery, to February 4th, 1868, amounting to the sum of nine hundred and seventy-one dollars and fourteen cents, ($971,14,) and repectfully recommend that the same be paid.

R. W. KING,
JNO. READ,
L. C. MORTON.
J. W. HOOD.

The report was received, and,

On motion, adopted.

The Committee on Privileges and Elections reported as follows:

In behalf of the Committee on Privileges and Elections, I beg leave to make the following report, in the case of the contested seat of the delegate from Sampson County, Mr. Williams:

It is the opinion of your committee that the 1,037 votes cast for Hall were intended for Lorenzo D. Hall, and that Mr. Williams received only 873 votes, leaving a clear majority for Lorenzo D. Hall of 164 votes, entitling the said Hall to the seat now occupied by Mr. Williams in this Convention; and

WHEREAS this Convention is authorized and empowered by orders received from Head Quarters second Military district to settle the matter between the contestants; therefore,

*Resolved*, That the rules be suspended and the Convention take immediate action in this case.

E. FULLINGS.
*For Committee.*

On motion, the report was received.

Mr. Ing introduced a resolution concerning petitions for divorce.

Lies over under the rules.

The hour of 10½ o'clock having arrived the Ordinance on Immigration having been made a special order for that hour, was taken up and discussed, until 11 o'clock, when the following majority report of the Committee on Finance being made a special order for that hour was taken up, and passed the first reading:

## REPORT OF THE STANDING COMMITTEE ON FINANCE.

SECTION 1. The General Assembly shall levy a capitation tax on all male inhabitants of the State over twenty-one and under fifty years of age, which shall be equal on each head to the tax on property valued at three hundred dollars in cash. The county courts (or other body which may be created for managing the municipal and local affairs of counties) may exempt from capitation tax in special cases on account of poverty and infirmity; but the State and county capitation combined, shall never exceed two dollars on the head.

SEC. 2. The proceeds of the State and County capitation tax shall be applied to the purposes of Education and the support of the poor.

SEC. 3. Laws shall be passed, taxing by a uniform rule, all moneys, credits, investments in bonds, stocks, joint stock companies or otherwise; and also, all real and personal property according to its true value in money.

SEC. 4. Until the Bonds of the State shall be at par, the General Assembly shall have no power to contract any new debt or pecuniary obligation in behalf of the State, except to supply a casual deficit, or for suppressing invasion or insurrection, unless it shall in the same bill levy a special tax to pay the interest annually.

SEC. 5. Property belonging to the State, or to municipal corporations, shall be exempt from taxation. The General Assembly may exempt cemeteries, and property held for educational, scientific, literary, charitable, or religious purposes, and also, wearing apparel, arms for muster, household and kitchen furniture, the mechanical and agricultural implements of mechanics and farmers, libraries and scientific instruments to a value not exceeding three hundred dollars.

SEC. 6. The taxes levied by County Courts, (or other body having the power to tax for County purposes,) shall be levied in the like manner with the State taxes, and shall never exceed the double of the State tax, except for a special purpose, and with the special approval of the General Assembly.

SEC. 7. Every act of the General Assembly levying a tax, shall state the specific object to which it is to be applied and it shall be applied to no other.

JOSEPH C. ABBOTT, *Chairman.*
D. HEATON,
WILL. B. RODMAN,
J. B. HARE,
C. C. JONES,
S. FORKNER,
M. HOBBS,
J. S. McCUBBINS,
R. W. KING,
R. J. LONG,
WILSON CAREY,
JOHN READ.

---

## MINORITY REPORT.

The undersigned, one of the Finance Committee, respectfully submits the following:

SECTION 1. The capitation or poll-tax shall be levied only by the General Assembly on males between the ages of twenty-one and forty-five years. It shall be equal throughout the State, and shall not exceed the sum of one dollar for any one year; and all funds arising therefrom shall be appropriated exclusively to the support of free schools.

SEC. 2. That it shall be the right of all persons, as heads of families or guardians for the benefit of minors, to own lands and tenements, or other property, of the valuation of three hundred dollars, and all other tax-payers one hundred dollars each, on which there shall be no tax levied for any purpose whatever.

SEC. 3. That all other property in this State shall be assessed and taxed in exact proportion to the valuation of such property: *Provided*, The General Assembly may exempt cemeteries and property held for educational, charitable and religious purposes.

J. W. PETERSON.

On the second reading, Mr. Tourgee moved to substitute section 1st of the minority report for section 1st of the majority report.

The yeas and nays were called, yeas 27, nays 81.

Those who voted in the affirmative, are.

Messrs. Andrews, Barnes, Blume, Bryan, Candler, Colgrove, Congleton, Duckworth, Gahagan, Garland, Graham of Montgomery, Gunter, Harris of Franklin, Heaton, Ing, Marshall, Morton, Newsom, Parker, Parks, Peterson, Rose, Smith, Stilwell, Tourgee and Welker—27.

Those who voted in the negative, are:

Messrs. Abbott, Ashley, Aydlott, Baker, Bradley, Carey, Carter, Cherry, Chillson, Cox, Daniel, Dickey, Dowd, Ellis, Eppes, Etheridge, Fisher, Forkner, French of Bladen, French of Chowan, Galloway, Garrett, George, Glover, Graham of Orange, Grant of Wayne, Grant of Northampton, Hare, Harris of Wake, Hay, Hayes of Robeson, Hayes of Halifax, Highsmith, Hobbs, Hodnett, Hoffler, Hollowell, Holt, Hood, Hyman, Jones of Caldwell, King of Lincoln, King of Lenoir, Kinney, Laflin, Lee, Legg, Lennon, Logan, Long, Mann, May, Mayo, McCubbins, Merritt, McDonald of Moore, Moore, Mullican, Murphy, Nance, Nicholson, Petree, Pierson, Pool, Ray, Read, Rhodes, Rich, Robbins, Rodman, Sanderlin, Stilly, Sweet, Taylor, Teague, Tucker, Turner, Watts, Williams of Wake, Williams of Sampson, and Williamson—81.

The motion did not prevail.

Mr. French, of Chowan, moved to amend section 2d by adding to the end of the section the following words:

"But in no one year shall more than 25 per cent. thereof be appropriated to the latter purpose."

Mr. Abbott, Chairman of the Committee, accepted the amendment.

Mr. Candler moved to amend section 1st by striking out the word "two" in line ten, and insert "one and a half."

The yeas and nays were demanded.

The amendment was lost, yeas 35, nays, 73.

Those who voted in the affirmative are:

Messrs. Andrews, Barnes, Blume, Bryan, Carter, Candler, Chillson, Colgrove, Congleton, Duckworth, Franklin, French of Rockingham, Gahagan, Garland, George, Graham of Montgomery, Gunter, Harris of Wake, Hayes of Robeson, Heaton, Hoffler, Ing, May, Mayo, Marshall, McDonald of Moore, Morton, Newsom, Parker, Parks, Peterson, Rose, Smith, Tourgee, and Welker—35.

Those who voted in the negative are:

Messrs. Abbott, Ashley, Aydlott, Baker, Benbow, Bradley, Carey, Cherry, Cox, Daniel, Dickey, Dowd, Ellis, Eppes, Etheridge, Fisher, Forkner, French of Bladen, French of Chowan, Galloway, Garrett, Glover, Graham of Orange, Grant of Wayne, Grant of Northampton, Hare, Hay, Hayes of Halifax, Highsmith, Hobbs, Hodnett, Hollowell, Holt, Hood, Hyman, Jones of Caldwell, King of Lenoir, Kinney, Laflin, Lee, Legg, Lennon, Logan, Long, Mann, McCubbins, Merrit, Moore, Mullican, Murphy, Nance, Nicholson, Petree, Pierson, Pool, Ray, Read, Rhodes, Rich, Robbins, Rodman, Sanderlin, Stilly, Stillwell, Sweet, Taylor, Teague, Tucker, Turner, Watts, Williams of Wake, Williams of Sampson, and Williamson—73.

The section as read was adopted.

Mr. Tourgee moved to amend section 2d by striking out all after the word "education" in second line.

The motion was not sustained.

The section was adopted.

Mr. Rodman moved to amend section 3d by adding "The

General Assembly may also tax trades, professions, franchises and incomes."

The amendment was sustained.

The section as amended was adopted.

Mr Tourgee offered the following as a new section to follow section 3d, to be known as section 4th.

"The General Assembly shall by appropriate legislation and by adequate taxation provide for the prompt and regular payment of the interest on the public debt, and after the year 1880, it shall lay a specific annual tax upon the real and personal property of the State, and the same thus realized shall be set apart as a sinking fund to be devoted to the payment of the public debt."

Mr. Hobbs moved to strike out "shall" and insert "may."

The motion was not sustained.

The new section as read was adopted as section 4th.

Sections 4th, 5th, 6th and 7th of the report were adopted.

The entire report as amended was adopted as a whole, yeas 83, nays 15.

Those who voted in the affirmative are:

Messrs. Abbott, Andrews, Ashley, Aydlott, Barnes, Blume, Bradley, Bryan, Carey, Carter, Candler, Cherry, Chilson, Colgrove, Congleton, Cox, Daniel, Dickey, Duckworth, Eppes, Fisher, Forkner, Franklin, French of Bladen, French, of Rockingham, French of Chowan, Fullings, Gahagan, Galloway, Garland, George, Grant of Northampton, Gunter, Harris of Franklin, Hay, Hayes of Robeson, Hayes of Halifax, Heaton, Hobbs, Hoffler, Hollowell, Hood, Hyman, Ing, Jones of Caldwell, Jones of Washington, King of Lincoln, Kinney, Laflin, Legg, Logan, Long, Mann, May, Mayo, McCubbins, McDonald of Moore, Mullican, Murphy, Nance, Nicholson, Parker, Parks, Petree, Pierson, Pool, Ray, Read, Rhodes, Rich, Robbins, Rodman, Rose, Smith, Stilwell, Sweet, Taylor, Teague, Tourgee, Tucker, Watts, Williams of Wake, and Williamson—83.

Those who voted in the negative are:

Messrs. Durham, Ellis, Etheridge, Graham of Orange, Hare, Hodnett, King of Lenoir, Lennon, Merritt, Moore, Pe terson, Sanderlin, Turner, Welker, and Williams of Sampson—15.

Mr. Rich introduced an ordinance to amend the Charter of the Chatham Rail Road Company.

Lies over under the rule.

Leave of absence was granted Mr. Jones of Washington, for five days.

The House, on motion, adjourned.

---

EVENING SESSION, MARCH 4TH, 1868.

The Convention was called to order at 7½ o'clock, by the President.

The Roll was called and the following members answered to their names:

Messrs. Andrews, Ashley, Barnes, Blume, Bradley, Bryan, Carter, Candler, Cherry, Chillson, Colgrove, Congleton, Cox, Daniel, Dickey, Duckworth, Fisher, Franklin, French of Bladen, French of Chowan, Gahagan, Galloway, George, Graham of Montgomery, Grant of Wayne, Grant of Northampton, Gunter, Hare, Hay, Hayes of Robeson, Hayes of Halifax, Hobbs, Hodnett, Hoffler, Holt, Hood, Hyman, Ing, Jones of Caldwell, King of Lincoln, Kinney, Laflin, Legg, Lennon, Logan, Long, Mann, Mayo, McCubbins, McDonald of Moore, Morton, Mullican, Murphy, Nance, Newsom, Nicholson, Parker, Parks, Petree, Peterson, Pierson, Ragland Ray, Rhodes, Rich, Rose, Sanderlin, Smith, Stillwell, Sweet, Teague, Tourgee, Turner, Welker, and Williamson—75.

The ordinance on Immigration was taken up.

The substitute of Mr. Candler was lost by the following vote, yeas 21, nays 62:

Those who voted in the affirmative are:

Messrs. Bradley, Candler, Durham, George, Graham of Orange, Gunter, Hollowell, Holt, Jones of Caldwell, Legg, Merritt, McDonald of Chatham, McDonald of Moore, Nicholson, Parker, Ray, Rhodes, Rose, Sanderlin, Smith, and Turner—21.

Those who voted in the negative, are:

Messrs. Abbott, Andrews, Ashley, Aydlott, Barnes, Blume, Bryan, Carey, Carter, Chillson, Colgrove, Congleton, Daniel, Eppes, Forkner, French of Bladen, French of Rockingham, French of Chowan, Fullings, Gahagan, Galloway, Graham of Montgomery, Grant of Northampton, Hare, Hay, Hayes of Robeson, Hayes of Halifax, Heaton, Highsmith, Hobbs, Hodnett, Hoffler, Hood, Hyman, Ing, King of Lincoln, King of Lenoir, Kinney, Laflin, Lee, Logan, Long, Mann, Mayo, McCubbins, Moore, Morton, Mullican, Murphy, Nance, Newsom, Parks, Peterson, Pierson, Ragland, Rich, Robbins, Stilwell, Sweet, Tourgee Welker, and Williamson—62.

The ordinance was put to the house and lost, yeas 31, and nays 67.

Those who voted in the affirmative are:

Messrs. Abbott, Andrews, Ashley, Barnes, Blume, Bryan, Carter, Colgrove, Forkner, Franklin, French of Bladen, French of Rockingham, Fullings, Gahagan, Graham of Montgomery, Grant of Wayne, Hayes of Robeson, Heaton, Hood, Laflin, Logan, Mann, Marshall, Morton, Murphy, Nance, Ragland, Rich, Sweet, Tourgee, and Welker—31.

Those who voted in the negative are:

Messrs. Aydlott, Bradley, Carey, Candler, Cherry, Chillson, Congleton, Daniel, Dickey, Duckworth, Durham, Ellis, Eppes, Etheridge, French of Chowan, George, Graham of Orange, Grant of Northampton, Gunter, Hare, Hay, Hayes of Halifax, Highsmith, Hobbs, Hodnett, Hoffler, Hollowell, Holt, Hyman, Ing, Jones of Caldwell, Jones of Washington, King of Lincoln, King of Lenoir, Kinney, Lee, Lennon, Long, Mayo, McCubbins, Merritt, McDonald of Chatham, McDonald of Moore, Moore, Mullican, Nicholson, Parker, Parks, Petree, Peterson, Pierson, Pool, Ray, Rhodes, Robbins, Rose, Sanderlin, Smith, Stilly, Stilwell, Taylor, Teague, Tucker, Turner, Watts, Williams of Sampson, and Williamson—67.

On motion of Mr. Tourgee, the vote on the relief ordinance introduced by Mr. Rodman, and passed by the Convention was reconsidered by the following vote, yeas 73, nays 20.

Those who voted in the affirmative are:

Messrs. Andrews, Ashley, Baker, Barnes, Bradley, Bryan, Carey, Candler, Colgrove, Congleton, Cox, Daniel, Dickey, Dowd, Duckworth, Durham, Ellis, Eppes, Etheridge, Forkner, Franklin, French of Bladen, French of Rockingham, Fullings, Gahagan, George, Glover, Graham of Orange, Grant of Wayne, Grant of Northampton, Hare, Harris of Wake, Hayes of Halifax, Heaton, Highsmith, Hobbs, Hollowell, Holt Hood, Hyman, Ing, Jones of Caldwell, Jones of Washington, King of Lincoln, King of Lenoir, Kinney, Legg, Logan, Mayo, Marshall, McCubbins, Murphy, Nance, Nicholson, Parker, Parks, Petree, Peterson, Pierson, Pool, Ray, Read, Renfrow, Rhodes, Rose, Smith, Stilly, Teague, Tourgee, Tucker, Welker, Williams of Sampson, and Williamson—73.

Those who voted in the negative are:

Messrs. Aydlott, Galloway, Graham of Montgomery, Gunter, Hay, Long, Merritt, McDonald of Chatham, McDonald of Moore, Moore, Morton, Newsom, Patrick, Ragland, Rich, Sanderlin, Stilwell, Sweet, Taylor, and Turner—20.

On motion of Mr. Pool, the ordinance was made a special order for Monday next, at 10½ o'clock, A. M.

Leave of absence was granted Mr. Gully for one day.

Mr. Tourgee presented a petition for divorce in favor of Lavina Lee.

Referred to the Committee on the Judicial Department.

The following resolution introduced by Mr. Colgrove, was taken up:

*Resolved*, That no member shall be allowed to speak more than ten minutes on any one subject except the Chairman of committees who may be allowed to speak twice on their report, and we request the Chair to enforce this rule.

Mr. King of Lenoir, moved to strike out the provision in favor of Chairman of Committees.

The motion was not sustained.

Mr. Tourgee moved to amend by adding after the word "subject" "unless by consent of the House."

Mr. Colgrove accepted the amendment.

Mr. King, of Lenoir, moved to adjourn.

Put to the House and lost.

Mr. Colgrove called the previous question on his resolution.

The resolution as amended was put to the house and lost.

On motion the House adjourned.

---

THURSDAY, March 5th, 1868.

The Convention was called to order at 10 o'clock, by the President.

The Roll was called, and ninety-one delegates present, viz:

Messrs. Abbott, Andrews, Ashley, Aydlott, Barnes, Blume, Bradley, Carey, Carter, Candler, Cherry, Colgrove, Congleton, Cox, Daniel, Duckworth, Durham, Eppes, Fisher, Forkner, Franklin, French of Bladen, French of Rockingham, French of Chowan, Galloway, Garland, Garrett, George, Graham of Montgomery, Grant of Wayne, Grant of Northampton, Gunter, Hare, Harris of Franklin, Hay, Hayes of Halifax, Highsmith, Hobbs, Hodnett, Hoffler, Hood, Hyman, Ing, King of Lincoln, King of Lenoir, Kinney, Laflin, Lee, Legg, Lennon, Logan, Long, Mayo, Marshall, McCubbins, Merritt, McDonald of Chatham, McDonald of Moore, Moore, Morton, Mullican, Murphy, Nance, Newsom, Nicholson, Parker, Parks, Petree, Peterson, Ragland, Ray, Read, Renfrow, Rhodes, Robbins, Rodman, Rose, Sanderlin, Smith, Stilwell, Taylor, Teague, Tourgee, Trogden, Tucker, Turner, Watts, Welker, Williams of Sampson, Williams of Wake and Williamson—91.

Prayer by the Rev. Mr. Eppes.

The Journal of Wednesday was read and approved.

Mr. French, of Bladen, gave notice that he would introduce a new section to the Suffrage Bill.

The Committee on Contingent Expences report that they have examined the account of Solomon Bragg, amounting to six dollars, and recommend the payment of the same.

R. W. KING,
J. W. HOOD,
L. C. MORTON.

The report was adopted.

Mr. Chillson presented an ordinance to establish a Homestead.

Referred to the Committee of Sixteen.

The Committee appointed to consider the propriety of petitioning Congress in regard to reducing the Tax on Tobacco, &c., reported as follows:

The Committee appointed to consider the propriety of petitioning Congress in regard to the Internal Revenue Tax on Tobacco and Brandy, beg leave to submit the accompanying preamble and resolutions, and respectfully ask the immediate action of the Convention thereon.

R. F. PETREE,
J. S. McCUBBINS,
JOHN READ.

Whereas, The present tax on manufactured tobacco is onerous and burdensome in the extreme, impairing the prosperity and crippling the business of a large portion of this State; and whereas, The said tax is peculiarly burdensome upon the laborers of that portion of the State, depressing the rate of wages, and decreasing the number of laborers employed; therefore,

*Be it resolved*, That this Convention do respectfully request and petition the Congress of the United States in consideration of the tax aforesaid, upon the industry of the State to reduce the tax upon all manufactured tobacco to ten cents per pound, and that of spirits distilled from fruit to fifty cents per gallon, believing, thereby, that the government would realize a larger amount of revenue.

*Resolved*, That the President of this Convention be directed to forward a copy of these resolutions to the President of the United States, Senate, and the Speaker of the House of Representatives.

The report was accepted.

On motion, the report of the Committee on Privileges and Elections, accepted Wednesday, was taken up and discussed.

The previous question was called.

The report was adopted, yeas 43, nays 35.

Those who voted in the affirmative are:

Messrs. Abbott, Ashley, Bryan, Carter, Candler, Chillson, Colgrove, Congleton, Dickey, Duckworth, Fisher, Forkner, Franklin, Fullings, Gahagan, Garland, Garrett, Glover, Graham of Montgomery, Gunter, Harris of Wake, Harris of Franklin, Hayes of Robeson, Highsmith, Hobbs, Hood, Ing, Lee, Logan, Mann, May, Marshall, Morton, Newsom, Pierson, Rhodes, Rose, Smith, Stilwell, Sweet, Teague, Tourgee and Tucker—43.

Those who voted in the negative are:

Messrs. Baker, Bradley, Daniel, Durham, Ellis, Eppes, Etheridge, French of Bladen, Graham of Orange, Grant of Wayne, Hare, Hodnett, Hollowell, Holt, Hyman, Jones of Washington, King of Lenoir, Kinney, Laffin, Legg, Lennon, Long, Merritt, McDonald of Chatham, Moore, Murphy, Nicholson, Patrick, Parks, Ray, Read, Renfrow, Sanderlin, Stilly and Welker—35.

On motion of Mr. Tourgee, Mr. Williams, of Sampson, was allowed his per diem to this day inclusive, together with his mileage.

The hour of the Special Order having arrived, the following report was taken up and passed its first reading:

## REPORT OF THE COMMITTEE ON COUNTIES, CITIES, TOWNS AND VILLAGES, THEIR OFFICERS, ORGANIZATION, GOVERNMENT AND POWERS.

SECTION 1. No Connty seat shall be changed, nor any new County organized, nor the boundaries of any County changed, but by the consent of a majority of the electors of the County, nor so as to include less than one hundred and twentieth part of the population of the State, at the last preceeeding enumeration.

SEC. 2. In each County there shall be elected biennially by the qualified voters thereof, as provided for the election of members of the General Assembly, the following municipal officers: a Sheriff, one or more Coroners, Treasurer, Register of Deeds, Surveyor and five Commissioners.

SEC. 3. It shall be the duty of the Commissioners to exercise a general supervision and control of the penal and charitable institutions, schools, roads, bridges, levying of taxes and finances of the County, as may be prescribed by law. The Register of Deeds shall be *ex officio* Clerk of the Board of Commissioners

SEC. 4. It shall be the duty of the Commissioners first elected in each County, to divide the same into convenient districts, to determine the boundaries and prescribe the names of the said districts, and report the same to the General Assembly before the first day of January, A. D. 1869.

SEC. 5. Upon the approval of the reports provided for in the foregoing section, the said districts shall have and shall thereafter possess corporate powers for the necessary purposes of local government, and shall be known as townships.

SEC. 6. In each township there shall be annually elected, by the qualified voters thereof, a Clerk and two Justices of the Peace, who shall constitute a Board of Trustees, and shall, under the supervision of the County Commissioners, have control of the schools, roads, and finances of the township as may be prescribed by law.

SEC. 7. The township Clerk shall assess the taxable property of his township, and make return to the County Commissioners as may be prescribed by law.

SEC. 8. No County, city, town, or other political corporation shall contract any debt, pledge its faith or loan its credit, nor shall any tax be levied or collected by any officers of the same, except for the necessary expenses thereof, unless by a vote of a majority of the qualified voters therein.

SEC. 9. All taxes levied by any County, city, town, or township, shall be uniform and *ad valorem* upon all property in the same.

SEC. 10. Commissioners of incorporated cities and towns may be authorized to act as Boards of Education for the same.

SEC. 11. The officers first elected under the provisions of

this Article shall enter upon their duties ten days after the approval of this Constitution by the Congress of the United States.

SEC. 12. The Governor shall appoint a sufficient number of Justices of the Peace in each County, who shall hold their places until sections 4, 5, and 6 of this Article shall have been carried into effect.

SEC. 13. All charters, ordinances and provisions relating to political corporations shall remain in force until legally changed, unless inconsistent with the provisions of this Constitution.

A. W. TOURGEE, *Chairman.*<br>
ED. FULLINGS,<br>
ABRAHAM CONGLETON,<br>
HENRY M. RAY,<br>
JESSE HOLLOWELL,<br>
A. H. GALLOWAY,<br>
JACOB ING,<br>
J. P. ANDREWS,<br>
J. S. McCUBBINS,<br>
M. J. AYDLOTT,<br>
S. D. FRANKLIN,<br>
B. LAFLIN.

---

The undersigned members of the Committee respectfully report the following additional section.

SEC. 14. No County, city, town or other political corporation, shall assume or pay, nor shall any tax be levied or collected for the payment of any debt, or the interest upon any debt contracted directly or indirectly in aid or support of the rebellion.

A. W. TOURGEE,<br>
HENRY M. RAY,<br>
ABRAHAM CONGLETON,<br>
A. H. GALLOWAY,<br>
JACOB ING,<br>
S. D. FRANKLIN,<br>
J. P. ANDREWS,<br>
B. LAFLIN.

On second reading, section 1st was adopted.

Mr. Graham, of Orange, moved to amend section 2d by striking out " and five Commissioners," on fifth line.

Mr. French, of Bladen, moved to amend by striking out " five," and inserting " three."

The amendments of Messrs. French, of Bladen, and Graham, of Orange, were put the House and lost.

Sections 2d, 3d and 4th were adopted.

Mr. Tourgee amended section 5th by inserting the words, " by the General Assembly," after the word " section."

The section, as amended, was adopted.

Section 6th was amended by Mr. Tourgee, by striking out " schools," and inserting " taxes;" also, by inserting " bridges," after " roads;" also, by adding to the section " also a school committee of three persons, whose duties shall be prescribed by law."

Mr. Colgrove amended by striking out " annually," and inserting " biennially "

The section, as amended, was adopted.

The Chairman of the Committee amended section 7th, by adding to the section, " the Clerk shall also be *ex officio* Treasurer of the township."

Mr. French, of Bladen, moved to amend by inserting " Board of Trustees," for " Clerk," and changing the word " his," to " their,"

Which was adopted.

After " Commissioners," on motion of Mr. Nicholson, " for revision," was inserted.

Section 7th, as amended, was adopted.

Section 8th was verbally amended and adopted.

Mr. Heaton offered the following as a new section, to follow section 8th :

" No money shall be drawn from any County or Township Treasury, except by authority of law."

Adopted.

Section 9th was adopted.

Section 10th was, on motion, stricken out.

Section 11th was amended by Mr. Tourgee, by inserting the word "County," between "the and officers," on line first.

The section, as amended, was adopted.

Section 12th was adopted.

Section 13th was read, when Mr. King, of Lenoir, moved the following substitute:

"The General Assembly shall have the power to change, alter, or abolish any portion, or all of the foregoing report, and to transfer all subjects therein contained, to the Justices of the Peace of each County in the State."

The yeas and nays were demanded, which resulted as follows, yeas 12, nays 81:

Those who voted in the affirmative are:

Messrs. Bradley, Durham, Ellis, Etheridge, Graham of Orange, Hare, Hobbs, Hodnett, Hoffler, Jones of Caldwell, King of Lenoir and Merritt—12.

Those who voted in the negative are:

Messrs. Abbott, Andrews, Ashley, Aydlott, Blume, Bryan, Carey, Carter, Candler, Cherry, Chillson, Colgrove, Congleton, Cox, Dickey, Duckworth, Eppes, Fisher, Forkner, Franklin, French of Bladen, French of Rockingham, French of Chowan, Gahagan, Garland, Garrett, George, Glover, Graham of Montgomery, Grant of Wayne, Grant of Northampton, Gunter, Harris of Franklin, Hay, Hayes of Halifax, Heaton, Highsmith, Hollowell, Hood, Hyman, Ing, Kinney, Legg, Logan, Long, May, Mayo, Marshall, McDonald of Chatham, Morton, Mullican, Murphy, Nance, Newsom, Nicholson, Parker, Parks, Petree, Peterson, Pool, Ragland, Ray, Renfrow, Rhodes, Robbins, Rodman, Rose, Smith, Stilly, Stilwell, Sweet, Taylor, Teague, Tourgee, Trogden, Tucker, Turner, Watts, Welker, Williams of Wake, and Williamson—81.

The substitute was lost.

Section 13th was then adopted.

Section 14th was taken up.

The Chairman of the Committee amended by striking out "political," and inserting "municipal."

Mr. Parker moved to strike out "or indirectly," on line fourth.

On this amendment the yeas and nays were called, yeas 15, nays 75.

Those who voted in the affirmative, are:

Messrs. Baker, Bradley, Dowd, Durham, Fullings, George, Graham of Orange, Hare, Hollowell, Legg, Lennon, McCubbins, Nicholson, Rodman and Sanderlin—15.

Those who voted in the negative, are:

Messrs. Andrews, Ashley, Aydlott, Barnes, Blume, Bryan, Carey, Carter, Candler, Chillson, Colgrove, Congleton, Cox, Daniel, Dickey, Duckworth, Etheridge, Fisher, Forkner, Franklin, French of Bladen, French of Rockingham, French of Chowan, Galloway, Garland, Glover, Graham of Montgomery, Grant of Wayne, Gunter, Harris of Franklin, Hayes of Halifax, Heaton, Highsmith, Hobbs, Hodnett, Hoffler, Ing, King of Lenoir, Kinney, Logan, May, Mayo, Marshall, McDonald of Chatham, McDonald of Moore, Morton, Mullican, Murphy, Nance, Patrick, Parker, Parks, Petree, Peterson, Pool, Ragland, Ray, Renfrow, Rhodes, Robbins, Rose, Smith, Stilly, Stilwell, Sweet, Taylor, Teague, Tourgee, Trogden, Tucker, Turner, Watts, Welker, Williams of Wake and Williamson—75.

The amendment was not agreed to.

Section 14th, as amended, was adopted by the following vote, yeas 85, nays 5:

Those who voted in the affirmative are:

Messrs. Abbott, Ashley, Aydlott, Barnes, Blume, Bryan, Carey, Carter, Candler, Cherry, Chillson, Colgrove, Congleton, Cox, Daniel, Dickey, Duckworth, Eppes, Etheridge, Fisher, Forkner, Franklin, French of Bladen, French of Rockingham, Fullings, Gahagan, Galloway, Garland, George, Glover, Graham of Montgomery, Grant of Wayne, Grant of Northampton, Gunter, Harris of Franklin, Hayes of Halifax, Heaton, Highsmith, Hobbs, Hodnett, Hoffler, Hollowell, Hood, Hyman, Ing, King of Lenoir, Kinney, Logan, Long, May, Mayo, Marshall, McDonald of Chatham, Morton, Mullican, Murphy, Nance, Patrick, Parker, Parks, Petree, Peterson, Pool, Ragland, Ray, Renfrow, Rhodes, Robbins, Rodman, Rose, Smith, Stilly, Stilwell, Sweet, Taylor, Teague, Tourgee, Trogden, Tucker, Turner, Watts, Welker, Williams of Wake and Williamson—85.

Those who voted in the negative are:

Messrs. Baker, Dowd, Durham, Graham of Orange and McCubbins—5.

The entire report, as amended, passed the second reading by the following vote, yeas 83, nays 10:

Those who voted in the affirmative, are:

Messrs. Abbott, Andrews, Ashley, Aydlott, Barnes, Blume, Bryan, Carey, Carter, Candler, Chillson, Colgrove, Congleton, Cox, Daniel, Dickey, Duckworth, Eppes, Fisher, Forkner, Franklin, French of Bladen, French of Rockingham, French of Chowan, Fullings, Gahagan, Galloway, Garland, George, Glover, Graham of Montgomery, Grant of Wayne, Grant of Northampton, Gunter, Hay, Hayes of Robeson, Heaton, Highsmith, Hobbs, Hoffler, Hollowell, Hyman, Ing, Jones of Caldwell, Kinney, Logan, Long, May, Mayo, Mashall, McDonald of Chatham, McDonald of Moore, Morton, Mullican, Murphy, Nance, Patrick, Parker, Parks, Petree, Peterson, Pool, Ragland, Ray, Renfrow, Rhodes, Robbins, Rodman, Rose, Smith, Stilly, Stilwell, Sweet, Taylor, Teague, Tourgee, Trogden, Tucker, Turner, Watts, Welker, Williams of Wake and Williamson—83.

Those who voted in the negative, are:

Messrs. Baker, Bradley, Dowd, Durham, Ellis, Etheridge, Graham of Orange, Hare, Merritt and Sanderlin—10.

On motion of Mr. Welker the report of the Committee on penal institutions &c., was made a special order for Saturday at 7½ o'clock.

The report of the Committee on Contingent expenses on account of Soloman Bragg was,

On motion, adopted.

On motion of Mr. Tourgee, it was ordered that the report of the Committee on Counties, Cities, Towns, &c., be placed on its third and final reading and passage, Saturday at 10½ o'clock, A. M.

On motion of Mr. Abbott, the report of the Committee on Finance was made a special order to follow the above report.

On motion of Mr. Rodman, the report of the Judicial Committee was made a special order for Friday at 7½ o'clock.

Mr. McDonald of Chatham, called up his ordinance in relation to the Sheriff of Orange County, which,

On motion, was adopted.

The following is the ordinance as adopted, with the report of the Committee to whom it was referred:

The Committee to whom was referred the ordinance for the relief of the Sheriff of Orange County have had the same under consideration, and as a substitute therefor instruct me to submit the following ordinance and ask that it be adopted.

JOHN A. McDONALD, *Chairman.*

## AN ORDINANCE FOR THE RELIEF OF THE SHERIFF OF ORANGE COUNTY.

Whereas, The Sheriff of Orange County was delinquent in paying a portion of the taxes for 1866, and judgment was obtained against him by the State for said balance, one thousand dollars penalty, and no commissions for collecting were allowed him, which commissions, if allowed, would have amounted to two hundred and sixty-seven dollars and ninety-eight cents; and whereas, all the taxes due the State for that year have since been paid, including said penalty and commissions, and owing to the extraordinary poverty of the people and difficulty of collections, in the opinion of this Convention relief should be granted said Sheriff:

Section 1. *Be it ordained by the people of North-Carolina, in Convention assembled, and it is hereby ordained by the authority of the same,* That the said Hugh B. Guthrie, Sheriff of Orange County, be allowed the sum of one thousand, two hundred and sixty-seven dollars and ninety-eight cents, ($1,267,98,) to be credited upon any taxes still owing by said Sheriff, in the order of the dates wherein the same were due.

Mr. Fullings introduced an ordinance to incorporate the "Charlotte City Hall Association."

Referred to the Committee of seventeen.

Mr. Harris, of Wake called up his resolution in relation to the pay of members, which,

On motion, was adopted

Mr. Rodman introduced an ordinance extending the time for the registration of deeds.

Lies over under the rules.

The House, on motion, adjourned.

---

EVENING SESSION, March 5th, 1868.

The Convention was called to order at 7½ o'clock, by the President.

A quorum present.

Mr. Ashley introduced a resolution providing for the election of a printer to the Convention.

Lies over under the rules.

The report of Committee on Homesteads being the special order for the same, was taken up on its second reading.

Sections 2d, 3d, 4th and 5th were read and adopted.

Mr. Jones, of Caldwell, moved an amendment to section 6th, "that the husband may insure his life for the benefit of his wife and children free of all claims," &c.

The amendment was agreed to and the section as amended was adopted.

Mr. Hood offered an additional section providing for the sale or disposal of a homestead.

Adopted.

Mr. Jones, of Caldwell, gave notice of a reconsideration of the vote by which section 2d was adopted.

The report as amended, passed its second reading by the following vote, yeas 76, nays 18.

Those who voted in the affirmative are:

Messrs. Abbott, Andrews, Ashley, Aydlott, Baker, Blume, Bryan, Carey, Carter, Cherry, Chillson, Colgrove, Congleton, Daniel, Dowd, Etheridge, Fisher, Franklin, French of Bladen, French of Chowan, Fullings, Galloway, George, Graham of Montgomery, Graham of Orange, Grant of Wayne, Grant of

Northampton, Gully, Gunter, Harris of Wake, Harris of Franklin, Hay, Highsmith, Hobbs, Hoffler, Hollowell, Holt, Hood, Hyman, Jones of Caldwell, Kinney, Lee, Long, Mayo, Marshall McCubbins, Merritt, McDonald of Chatham, McDonald of Moore, Moore, Morton, Murphy, Nance, Newsom, Nicholson, Patrick, Parks, Petree, Peterson, Pool, Ragland, Read, Renfrow, Rich, Robbins, Smith, Stilly, Stilwell, Sweet, Taylor, Tourgee, Tucker, Turner, Watts, Welker, and Williamson—76.

Those who voted in the negative are:

Messrs. Benbow, Bradley Candler, Cox, Duckworth, Ellis, Forkner, Gahagan, Glover, Hayes of Halifax, King of Lincoln, Lennon, Logan, Parker, Ray, Rhodes, Rose, and Teague—18.

On motion the report was ordered to be engrossed and made a special order for a third and final reading and passage for Friday at 7½ o'clock, P. M.

The following resolution of Mr. Forkner, limiting debate was taken up for action:

*Resolved*, That no delegate shall speak more than once on a question nor longer than fifteen minutes except it be by consent of Convention.

Mr. Hood moved to strike out "fifteen" and insert "ten." Adopted.

The resolution as amended was adopted.

Mr. Ashley called up the report of the Committee on Printing,

Pending which, the House

On motion, adjourned.

---

FRIDAY, March 6th, 1868.

The Convention was called to order at 10 o'clock, by the President.

Prayer by the Rev. Mr. Warwick.

The Roll was called, a quorum present.

The Journal of Thursday was read and approved.

Leave of absence was granted Messrs. Tourgee and Galloway until Monday next.

Messrs. Ray and Holt presented petitions of divorce.

Mr. Turner a resolution instructing the Committee on Internal Improvements.

The following report, from the Committee on the Judicial Department, was received:

"The Committee on the Judicial Department, to whom was referred a petition from sundry citizens of Wilmington respecting property purchased by slaves, respectfully report an ordinance in conformity with the views of the petitioners:

"*Be it ordained by the people of North-Carolina in Convention assembled*, That whenever it shall judicially appear that any person, while held as a slave, purchased and paid for any property, real or personal, and that a conveyance thereof was made to him or to any one for his use, such purchaser, or those lawfully representing him, shall be entitled to such property; anything in the former laws of this State forbidding slaves to acquire property to the contrary notwithstanding.

All of which is respectfully submitted,

WM. B. RODMAN, *Chairman.*"

On the adoption of this report the yeas and nays were called.

The report was adopted by the following vote—yeas 101, nays 4.

Those who voted in the affirmative, are:

Messrs. Abbott, Andrews, Ashley, Aydlott, Barnes, Benbow, Blume, Bradley, Bryan, Carey, Carter, Candler, Cherry, Chillson, Colgrove, Congleton, Cox, Daniel, Dickey, Duckworth, Ellis, Eppes, Etheridge, Fisher, Forkner, Franklin, French of Bladen, French of Rockingham, French of Chowan, Fullings, Gahagan, Galloway, Garland, Garrett, George, Glover, Graham of Montgomery, Gully, Gunter, Hare, Harris of Wake, Harris of Franklin, Hay, Hayes of Robeson, Hayes of Halifax, Heaton, Highsmith, Hobbs, Hodnett, Hoffler, Hollowell, Hood, Hyman, Ing, Jones of Caldwell, King of Lincoln, King of Lenoir, Kinney, Laflin, Lee,

Logan, May, Mayo, Marshall, McCubbins, McDonald of Chatham, McDonald of Moore, Moore, Morton, Mullican, Murphy, Nance, Nicholson, Patrick, Parker, Parks, Petree, Peterson, Pierson, Pool, Ragland, Ray, Read, Renfrow, Rhodes, Rich, Robbins, Rodman, Rose, Stilly, Stilwell, Sweet, Taylor, Teague, Tourgee, Trogden, Tucker, Watts, Welker, Williams of Wake and Williamson—101.

Those who voted in the negative are:

Messrs. Durham, Graham of Orange, Holt and Turner—4.

The Judicial Committee also reported as follows:

The Committee on the Judicial Department respectfully report the annexed ordinance, and recommend its passage:

AN ORDINANCE CONCERNING WIDOWS WHO HAVE QUALIFIED AS EXECUTRIX TO THE LAST WILL AND TESTAMENT OF THEIR DECEASED HUSBANDS.

SECTION 1. *Be it ordained by the delegates of the people of North-Carolina in Convention assembled, and it is hereby ordained by the authority of the same,* That the widow of any testator whose last will and testament has been admitted to probate in this State since the 1st day of January, 1862, and before the 1st day of May, 1865, notwithstanding such widow may have qualified to such last will and testament as executrix, be and she is hereby allowed to enter her dissent to the same according to the same forms as are now provided by law for dissent of widows.

SEC. 2. *Be it further ordained,* That in all cases, where a widow shall dissent from the last will and testament of her husband, as provided for in the foregoing section, she shall be entitled to the same rights of dower as if her husband had died intestate: *Provided, however,* That no widow shall be entitled to the benefit of this ordinance unless such dissent shall be entered within six months from and after the passage of this ordinance, nor in any case where the real estate of the deceased husband has been sold subseqnent to his death, or has been divided between his devisees or heirs at law.

Sec. 3. *Be it further ordained*, That this ordinance shall be in force from and after its adoption.

The report was received, and the ordinance was,

On motion, adopted.

The Committee on Internal Improvements, to whom was referred the ordinance in relation to the Dan River and Coalfield Railroad Company, reported that they have had the same under consideration, and recommend its passage.

The report was received and adopted.

The ordinance is as follows:

## AN ORDINANCE TO INCORPORATE THE DAN RIVER COAL FIELD RAIL ROAD COMPANY.

Section 1. *Be it ordained by the people of North-Carolina in Convention assembled, and it is hereby ordained by the authority of the same*, That a Company by the name and style of the "Dan River Coalfield Rail Road Company" be and the same is hereby incorporated, with a capital stock of twelve hundred and fifty thousand dollars, divided into shares of one hundred dollars each, for the purpose of constructing a Rail Road from some point on the Virginia line, near the town of Danville, in Virginia, to the Coalfields of Dan River.

Sec. 2. *Be it further ordained*, That for the purpose of increasing the capital stock of said Company heretofore subscribed, and renewing and sealing all former subscriptions to said Company, the following persons be and are hereby appointed general Commissioners, viz: John W. Broadnax, President, George L. Akin, Jones Burton, Wm. Carter, J. Turner Morehead, Gen. Alfred M. Scales, Marshall Black, Wm. A. Lash, Benj. Baley, Andrew H. Joyce, Reubin D. Golding, Joseph Willis, Robert Matthews, Wm. W. McCanlass and James Davis, whose duty it shall be to direct the opening of books for subscription of stock at such times and places and under such persons as they, or a majority of them, may deem proper; and said general Commissioners may have power to appoint a Chairman of their body, Treasurer, and all other officers their organization may require, and to sue for and recover all lands and sums of money that ought, under this act, be recovered by them.

SEC. 3. *Be it further ordained*, That all persons who may be hereafter by the general commissioners authorized to open books of subscription, may do so at any time after the ratification of this act, upon giving twenty days notice of the time and place when said books will be opened, and said books shall be kept open for the space of thirty days at least, and as long thereafter as the general commissioners shall direct; and that all subscriptions of stock shall be in shares of one hundred dollars in money or its value in land, the subscriber paying at the time of making his subscription five dollars on each share by him subscribed to the person or persons authorized to receive such subscriptions; and in case of failure to pay said sum all such subscriptions shall be void and of no effect; and upon closing the books all such sums as shall have been thus received of subscribers on the first cash or land instalment, shall be paid over to the general commissioners by the persons receiving the same; and in case of failure to pay as aforesaid such person or persons receiving said money or lands shall be personally liable to said general commissioners, before the organization of said Company, and to the Company itself after the organization, to be recovered in the Superior Courts of Law within this State in the County where such delinquent resides, or if he resides in another State, then in any court in such State having competent jurisdiction. The general commissioners shall have power to call on all persons empowered to receive subscriptions of stock at any time, and from time to time, as a majority of them may think proper, to make a return of the stock by them respectively received, and to make payment of all lands or sums of money paid by subscribers; that all persons receiving subscriptions of stock shall pass a receipt to the subscriber or subscribers for the payment of the first instalment, as heretofore required to be paid; and upon their settlement with the general commissioners as aforesaid, it shall be the duty of said general commissioners in like manner to pass their receipt for all sums thus received to the person from whom received, and such receipt shall be taken and held to be good and sufficient vouchers to the persons holding them; that subscriptions of stock may be received as aforesaid, or as hereinafter provided for, to the amount of twelve hundred and fifty thousand dollars.

SEC. 4. *Be it further ordained*, That it shall be the duty of said general commissioners to direct and authorize said books of subscription to be kept open until the sum of fifty thousand dollars at least shall be subscribed in the manner aforesaid, and as soon as the sum of fifty thousand dollars or upwards shall be subscribed in the manner aforesaid, and the sum of five dollars on each share paid in as aforesaid, the subscribers to said stock shall be and are hereby declared to be a body politic and corporate in fact and in law, by the name and style of "the Dan River Coalfield Rail Road Company," with all the corporate powers and authority hereby created and granted, to be held and exercised by said Company and their successors and assigns in perpetuity, and by that name shall be capable in law and in equity to purchase, hold, lease, rent, sell or convey estates, real, personal and mixed, and to acquire the same by gift, devise or otherwise, so far as shall be necessary for the purposes embraced within the scope, object and intent of this charter, and shall have perpetual succession and a common seal, which they may use, alter or renew at pleasure, and by their corporate name may sue and be sued, plead and be impleaded in any Court of Law or Equity in this State or any other State, and shall have, possess and enjoy all the rights, privileges and immunities which corporate bodies may and of the right do exercise, and may make all such by-laws, rules and regulations as are necessary for the government of the corporation, or for effecting the object for which it is created not inconsistent with the laws of this State or of the United States.

SEC. 5. *Be it further ordained*, That as soon as the sum of fifty thousand dollars or upwards shall be subscribed as aforesaid, it shall be the duty of the general commissioners to appoint a time for the stockholders to meet in Madison, in the County of Rockingham, which they shall cause to be previously published for the space of thirty days in one or more newspapers, at which time and place the said stockholders, in person or by proxy, [shall] proceed to elect by ballot nine Directors of the Company, and to enact all such regulations and by-laws as may be necessary for the government of said corporation and the transaction of business. The persons elected Directors of this meeting shall serve such period, not exceeding one year, as the stockholders may direct, and at this meeting the stockholders shall fix on a day and place or places where the subsequent election of Directors shall be held; and such elections shall henceforth be annually made, and if the day of the annual election should pass without any election of Directors, the corporation shall not thereby be dissolved, but it shall be lawful on any other day to hold and make such elections in such manner as may be prescribed by a by-law of the corporation.

SEC. 6. *Be it further ordained*, That the affairs of said Company shall be managed by a general board to consist of nine Directors, to be elected by the stockholders from among themselves at their first and subsequent general annual elections, and no stockholder shall be elected as Director, nor serve as such, unless he be, at the time of his election, the *bona fide* owner and legal holder of ten shares of said stock, and shall continue to hold the same during the term of his service.

SEC. 7. *Be it further ordained*, That the President of said Company shall be chosen by ballot by a majority of the Directors from among themselves, with a salary to be fixed by the stockholders in general meeting.

SEC. 8. *Be it further ordained*, That all stockholders being citizens of the United States shall be entitled to vote either in person or proxy, the proxy being a stockholder, at all general meetings, and the vote to which each stockholder shall be entitled according to the number of shares he may hold in the proportions following, that is to say: for one share and not more than two, one vote; for every two shares above two and not exceeding ten, one vote; for every four shares above ten and not exceeding thirty, one vote; for every six shares over thirty and not exceeding sixty, one vote; for every eight shares over sixty and not exceeding one hundred, one vote; for every ten shares over one hundred and not exceeding two hundred, one vote; and for every twenty shares over two hundred, one vote.

SEC. 9. *Be it further ordained*, That at the first general meeting of the stockholders under this act, a majority of all the shares subscribed shall be represented before proceeding to business, and if a sufficient number do not appear on the day appointed, those who do attend shall have power to adjourn from time to time until a regular meeting be thus formed; and at such regular meeting the stockholders may provide a by-law as to the number of stockholders and the amount of stock to be held by them, which shall constitute a quorum for transacting business at all subsequent regular or occasional meetings of stockholders and Directors.

SEC. 10. *Be it further ordained*, That the general commissioners shall make their return of the shares of the stock subscribed for at the first general meeting of the stockholders, and pay over to the Directors elected at their meeting, or their authorized agents, all sums of money and all lands received from subscribers; and on failure to do so they shall be personally liable to said Company, to be recovered at the suit of said Company in any of the Superior Courts of Law in this State in the County where the delinquent resides, and in case of his death the same shall be recovered of his executors or administrators.

SEC. 11. *Be it further ordained*, That the Board of Directors may fill all vacancies which may occur in it during the period for which they have been elected, and in the absence of the President may fill his place by electing a President *pro tempore* from among their number.

SEC. 12. *Be it further ordained*, That the said Board of Directors shall have power and authority to open books for further subscription to the stock of said Company, at such times and under such persons as they may designate, in the event that the whole stock be not subscribed before the first general meeting of the stockholders, and to open and keep open said books from time to time until the whole amount of the capital stock be subscribed.

SEC. 13. *Be it further ordained*, That said Company shall have power and may proceed to construct, as speedily as possible, a Rail Road, with one or more tracks, from some point on the Virginia line, near the town of Danville, in Virginia, to the Coalfields of Dan River.

SEC. 14. *Be it further ordained*, That said Company shall have the exclusive right of conveyance or transportation of persons, goods, merchandise and produce over the road constructed by them, at such charges as may be fixed upon by a majority of the Directors; and the said Company [may] farm out their right of transportation over their said Rail Road, subject to the rules above mentioned, and said Company, and every person who may have received from them the right of transportation of goods, wares and produce on said Rail Road, shall be deemed and taken to be a common carrier, as respects everything entrusted to them or him for transportation.

SEC. 15. *Be it further ordained*, That the Board of Directors may call for the payment of the sum or bond subscribed as stock in said Company, in such instalments as the interests of said Company may, in their opinion, require; the call for each payment shall be published in one or more newspapers in this State, for the space of one month before the day of payment, and on failure of any stockholder to pay each instalment as thus required, the directors may sell at public auction, on a previous notice of ten days, for cash, all the stock subscribed for in said Company, by such stockholders, and convey the same to the purchaser at said sale, discharged from all further liability, and if said sale of stock does not produce a sum sufficient to pay off the incidental expenses of the sale, and the entire amount owing by such stockholders to the Company for such subscription of stock, then, and in that case, the whole of such balance shall be held and taken as due at once to the Company, and may be recovered of such stockholder, or of his executors, administrators or assignees at the suit of said Company, either by summary motion in any court of superior jurisdiction in the County where the delinquent resides, on previous notice of ten days to said subscriber, or by action of assumpsit in any Court of competent jurisdiction, or by warrant before a Justice of the Peace, where the sum does not exceed one hundred dollars, and in all cases of assignment of stock before the whole amount has been paid to the Company, then, for all sums due on such stocks, both the original subscribers and the first and all subsequent assignees shall be liable to the Company, and the same may be recovered as above described.

SEC. 16. *Be it further ordained*, That the debt of stockholders due to the Company for stock therein, either as original proprietor or as first or subsequent assignee, shall be considered of equal dignity with judgments in the distribution of assets of a deceased stockholder by his legal representative.

SEC. 17. *Be it further ordained*, That said Company shall issue certificates of stock to its members, and said stock may be transferred in such manner and form as may be directed by the by-laws of the Company.

SEC. 18. *Be it further ordained*, That the Board of Directors shall once every year at least, make a full report of the stock of the Company and its affairs to a general meeting of the stockholders, and oftener if required by a by-law, and shall have power to call a general meeting of the stockholders when the Board may deem it expedient, and the Company may provide in their by-laws for occasional meetings being called and prescribe the mode thereof.

SEC. 19. *Be it further ordained*, That said Company may purchase, have and hold in fee, or for a term of years, any land, tenaments or hereditaments, which may be necessary for the said road or the appurtenances thereof, or for the erection of depositories, store houses, houses for the officers, servants or agents of the said Company, or for work shops or foundaries, to be used for said Company, or for procuring stone or other materials necessary to the construction of the road or for effecting transportation thereon.

SEC. 20. *Be it further ordained*, That the Company shal

have the right, when necessary, to conduct the said road across or along any public road or water course: *Provided*, That the said Company shall not obstruct any public road without constructing another equally as good and convenient.

SEC. 21. *Be it further ordained*, That when any lands or right of way may be required by said Company, for the purpose of constructing their road, and for want of agreement as to the value thereof, or for any other cause, the same cannot be purchased from the owner or owners, the same may be taken at a valuation to be made by the five Commissioners, or three of them, to be appointed by any court of record having common law jurisdiction in the County where some part of the land or right of way is situated. In making the said valuation, the said Commissioners shall take into consideration the loss or damage which may accrue to the owner or owners in consequence of the land or right of way being surrendered, and the benefit and advantage, general or special which he, she or they may receive by the general increased value of the land, or any special benefit which may arise from the location of a depot, or otherwise on said land, or any benefit which may accrue in any way whatever, by the establishment of said Rail Road or works, and shall state particularly the amount and value of each, and the excess of the loss and damage, over and above the advantage and benefit, shall form the measure of valuation of the said land or right of way: *Provided, nevertheless*, That if any person or persons, over whose land the road may pass, or if said company should be dissatisfied with the valuation of said Commissioners, then, and in that case, the party so dissatified, may make an appeal to the Superior Court, in the County where said valuation has been made, or in either County in which the land may lie, when it shall be in more than one County, under the same rules, regulation and restrictions as in other cases of appeals. The proceedings of said Commissioners, accompanied with a full description of said land or right of way, shall be returned under the hands and seal of a majority of them, to the Court from which the Commission issued, there to remain a matter of record, and the lands or right of way so valued, shall vest in the said Company so long as the same shall be used for the purpose of the Rail Road, so soon as the valuation shall have been paid, or when refused, may have been tendered: *Provided*, That on application for the appointment of Commissioners, under this section, it shall be made to appear to the satisfaction of the Court, that at least ten days' previous notice has been given by the applicant to the owner or owners of the said land, so proposed to be condemned, or if the owner or owners be infants or *non compos mentis*, then to the guardian of such owner or owners, if such guardian can be found within the County, or if he can not be so found, then such appointment shall not be made, unless notice of the application shall have been published at least one month next preceding, in some newspaper printed as convenient as may be to the Court House of the County, and shall have been posted at the door of the Court House, on the first day at least of the term of said court to which the application is made; *Provided further*, That the valuation provided for in this section shall be made on oath, or by the commissioners aforesaid, which oath any justice of the peace or Clerk is authorized to administer: *Provided further*, That the right of condemnation herein granted shall not authorize the said Company to invade the dwelling house, yard, garden or burying ground of any individual without his consent.

Sec. 22. *Be it further ordained*, That the right of said company to condemn land in the manner aforesaid, shall extend to the condemning of one hundred feet on each side of the main track of the road, measuring from the centre of the same, unless in case of deep cuts and fillings, when said company shall have power to condemn as much in addition thereto as may be necessary for the purpose of constructing said road, and the company shall also have power to condemn and appropriate lands in like manner for the constructing and building of depots, shops, warehouses, buildings for servants, agents and persons employed on the road, not exceeding two acres in any one lot or station.

Sec. 23. *Be it further ordained*, That in the absence of any contract or contracts with said company in relation to lands through which the said road may pass, signed by the owner thereof, or his agent, or any claimant or person in possession thereof, which may be confirmed by the owner thereof, it shall be presumed that the land upon which said road may be constructed, together with the space of one hundred feet on each side of the centre of the said road, had been granted to the said company by the owner thereof, shall have good right and title thereto, and shall have, hold and enjoy the same as long as the same be used for the purposes of said road, and no longer, unless the person or persons owning the said land at the time that part of the said road which may be on said land was finished, or the claiming under him, her or them, shall apply for an assessment of the value of said lands as hereinbefore directed, within two years next after that part of the said road which may be on the said land was finished; and in case the said owner or those claiming under him, his, her or them, shall not apply within two years next after the said part was finished, he, she or they shall be forever barred from recovering said land, or having any assessment or compensation therefrom: *Provided*, That nothing herein contained shall affect the rights of *feme coverts* or infants until two years after the removal of their respective disabilities.

SEC. 24. *Be it further ordained*, That all lands not heretofore granted to any person within one hundred feet of the centre of the said road, shall vest in the company as soon as the line of the road is definitely laid out through it, and any grant of said land thereafter shall be void.

SEC. 25. *Be it further ordained*, That if any person or persons shall intrude upon the said Rail Road by any manner of use thereof, or of the rights and privileges connected therewith without the permission, or contrary to the will of the said company, he, she or they may be indicted for misdemeanor, and upon conviction fined and imprisoned by any court of competent jurisdiction.

SEC. 26. *Be it further ordained*, That if any person shall wilfully and maliciously destroy or in any manner hurt or damage or destroy or obstruct, or shall wilfully or maliciously cause, or aid, or assist, or counsel, or advise any other person or persons to destroy or in any manner to hurt, damage, injure or obstruct the said Rail Road, or any bridge or vehicle used for or in the transportation thereon, any water tank, warehouse, or any other property of said company, such person or persons so offending shall be liable to be convicted therefor, and on conviction shall be imprisoned not more than six nor less than one month, and pay a fine not exceeding five hundred dollars nor less than twenty dollars, at the discretion of [the] court before which said conviction shall take place and shall be further liable to pay all expenses for repairing the same, and it shall not [be] competent for any person so offending against the provisions of this clause to defend himself by pleading or giving in evidence that he was the owner, agent or servant of the owner of the land where such destruction, hurt, damage, injury or obstruction was done at the time the same was done or caused to be done.

Sec. 27. *Be it further ordained*, That every obstruction to the safe and free passage of vehicles on the said road shall be deemed a public nuisance, and may be abated as such by any officer, agent or servant of said company, and the person causing such obstruction may be indicted for erecting a public nuisance.

Sec. 28. *Be it further ordained*, That the said Company shall have the right to take at the store-house they may establish, on or annexed to their Rail Road, all goods, wares, merchandise and produce intended for transportation, to prescribe the rules of priority and charge, and receive such just and reasonable compensation for storage as they by rules may establish, (which they shall cause to be published,) or as may be fixed by agreement with the owner, which may be distinct from the rates of transportation: *Provided*, That the said Company shall not charge or receive any storage on goods, wares, merchandise, or produce which may be delivered to them at their regular depositories for immediate transportation, and which the company may have power to transact immediately.

Sec. 29. *Be it further ordained*, That the profits of the Company, or so much thereof as the general board may deem advisable, shall, when the affairs of the Company will permit, be semi-annually divided amongst the stockholders in proportion to the stock each may own.

SEC. 30. *Be it further ordained*, That the following officers and servants, and persons in the actual employment of the said company, be, and they are hereby exempt from the jury, and ordinary militia duty: the president and treasurer the board of directors, chief and assistant engineers, the secretary and accountants of this Company, keepers of the depositories, guards stationed on the road and at the bridges and such persons as may be working the locomotive engines and traveling with the cars for the purpose of attending to transportation of produce, goods and passengers on the road.

SEC. 31. *Be it further ordained*, That for the purpose of constructing said road, the Company are hereby authorized and empowered, by a vote of the stockholders in general meeting assembled, to increase their capital stock to an amount sufficient in their opinion to effect the object, and to raise money by loan or otherwise, sufficient to complete the main track or road, upon such securities and in such a manner as the stockholders may direct.

SEC. 32. *Be it further ordained*, That for the purpose of ascertaining the best route for said road, and to locate the same, it shall be lawful for said Company, by its engineers, servants, and agents, to enter upon, examine and survey, any land or lands that they may wish to examine for such purpose, free from any liability whatever.

SEC. 33. *Be it further ordained*, That said road shall not run within twenty miles of the North-Carolina Rail Road, and if the Company hereby incorporated violate the provisions of this section, it shall work a forfeiture of their charter.

The following report was received and adopted:

The Committee on Counties, Cities, Towns, &c., having considered the ordinance presented by Mr. Fullings of Mecklenburg, entitled "an Ordinance to incorporate the Charlotte City Hall Association," have instructed me to report that in their opinion, the subject matter thereof does not in their opinion properly come before them, and ask to be relieved from its further consideration, and suggest that the same be referred to the Committee on Corporations other than Municipal.

Mr. Heaton arose to a question of privilege concerning an article published by the *North-Carolinian.*

The following report of the Committee on Education, &c., was taken up and passed first reading:

## REPORT OF THE COMMITTEE ON EDUCATION, COMMON SCHOOLS, UNIVERSITY AND THE MEANS OF THEIR SUPPORT.

The Committee appointed to prepare and report to the Convention an Article on Education, Common Schools, University and the means of their support, respectfully submit the following report:

### ARTICLE —.

#### EDUCATION.

SECTION 1. Religion, morality, and knowledge being necessary to the good government and happiness of mankind, schools, and the means of education, shall forever be fostered and encouraged.

SEC. 2. The General Assembly at its first session under this Constitution, shall provide for a general and uniform system of Public Schools, wherein tuition shall be free of charge to all the children of the State between the ages of six and twenty-one years.

SEC. 3. Each County of the State shall be divided into a convenient number of Districts, in which one or more Primary Public Schools shall be maintained at least four months in every year; and any County which shall fail to comply with the aforesaid requirement of this section shall be liable to indictment.

SEC. 4. The proceeds of all land that have been, or hereafter may be, granted by the United States to this State, and not otherwise specially appropriated by this State, or the United States: also all moneys, stocks, bonds, and other property now belonging to any fund for purposes of Education: also the net proceeds of all sales of lands and other property and effects, that may accrue to the State from sales of estrays, or from unclaimed Dividends, or from fines, penalties and forfeitures: also the proceeds ot all sales of the swamp lands belonging to the State or of any other public lands which may have been, or may hereafter be, paid over to this State, (unless forbidden by Congress:) also all money that shall be paid as an equivalent for exemption from military duty: also, all grants, gifts or devises that have been, or may hereater be, made to this State, and not otherwise appropriated by grant, gift or devise, shall be securely invested, and sacredly preserved as an irreducible educational fund, the annual income of which, together with so much of the ordinary revenue of the State as may be necessary, shall be faithfully appropriated for establishing and perfecting in this State, a system of Free Public Schools and for no other purposes or uses whatsoever.

SEC. 5. The General Assembly shall make such provisions, by taxation or otherwise, as will secure a thorough and efficient system of Public Schools throughout the State.

SEC. 6. The University of North-Carolina, with its lands, emoluments and franchises, is the property of the State, and shall be held to an inseparable connection with the Free Public School system of the State.

SEC. 7. The General Assembly shall provide that the benefits of the University, as far as practicable, be extended to the youth of the State free of expense for tuition; also, that all the property which has heretofore accrued, or shall hereafter accrue from escheats to the State, or distributive shares of the estates of deceased persons, shall be appropriated to the use and benefit of the University.

SEC. 8. The Governor, Lieutenant-Governor, Secretary of State, State Treasurer, Auditor, Superintendent of Public

Works, Superintendent of Public Instruction and Attorney General shall constitute a State Board of Education.

SEC. 9. The Governor shall be President, and the Superintendent of Public Instruction shall be Secretary of the Board of Education.

SEC. 10. The Board of Education shall succeed to all the powers and trusts of the Literary Board, and shall have full power to legislate and make all needful rules and regulations in relation to Free Public Schools, and the Educational fund of the State; but all acts, rules and regulations of said Board may be altered or amended, or repealed by the General Assembly, and when altered, amended and repealed they shall not be re-enacted by the Board.

SEC. 11. The first session of the Board of Education shall be held at the Capital of the State, within fifteen (15) days after the organization of the State government under this Constitution; the time of future meetings may be determined by the Board.

SEC. 12. A majority of the Board shall constitute a quorum for the transaction of business.

SEC. 13. The contingent expenses of the Board shall be provided for by the General Assembly.

SEC. 14. The Board of Education shall elect Trustees for the University, as follows: one Trustee from each County in the State, whose term of office shall be eight (8) years. The first meeting of the Board shall be held within ten (10) days after their election, and at this and every subsequent meeting, ten (10) Trustees shall constitute a quorum. The Trustees, at their first meeting, shall be divided, as may be, into four (4) classes. The seats of the first class shall be vacated at the expiration of two (2) years; of the second class at the expiration of four (4) years; of the third class at the expiration of six (6) years; of the fourth class at the expiration of eight (8) years; so that one-fourth may be chosen every second year.

SEC. 15. The Board of Education shall be *ex officio* members of the Board of Trustees of the University, and shall, with three (3) other Trustees to be appointed by the Board of Trustees, constitute the Executive Committee of the Trustees of the University of North-Carolina, and shall be clothed with the powers delegated to the Executive Committee under the existing organization of the Institution. The Governor shall be *ex officio* President of the Board of Trustees and Chairman of the Executive Committee of the University. The Board of Education shall provide for the more perfect organization of the Board of Trustees.

SEC. 16. All the privileges, rights, franchises and endowments heretofore granted to, or conferred upon, the Board of Trustees of the University of North-Carolina by the charter of 1789, or by any subsequent legislation, are hereby vested in the Board of Trustees, authorized by this Constitution, for the perpetual benefit of the University.

SEC. 17. As soon as practicable after the adoption of this Constitution, the General Assembly shall establish and maintain in connection with the University a Department of Agriculture, of Mechanics, of Mining, and of Normal Instruction.

SEC. 18. The General Assembly is hereby empowered to enact that every child of sufficient mental and physical ability shall attend the Public Schools during the period between the ages of six (6) and eighteen (18) years, for a term of not less than sixteen months, unless educated by other means.

S. S. ASHLEY, *Chirman.*
W. T. J. HAYES,
JNO. READ,
J. W. HOOD,
G. WILLIAM WELKER,
WM. T. BLUME,
A. W. FISHER,
W. H. LOGAN,
ALLEN ROSE,
JOHN R. FRENCH,
W. H. S. SWEET,
*Majority of the Committee.*

On second reading, section 1st was adopted.

Mr. Ashley amended section 2d by inserting in third line, after provide, " by taxation or otherwise."

Mr. French, of Bladen, moved to strike out " six," in fifth line, and insert " five."

Not agreed to.

The section, as amended, was adopted.

Mr. Ashley amended section 3d by inserting " Commissioners," after " County."

The section, as amended, was adopted.

Section 5th was, on motion, stricken out.

Mr. Durham offered the following as an additional section:

" The General Assembly shall provide seperate and distinct schools, for the black children of the State, from those provided for white children,"

When Mr. Ashley offered the following amendment:

" It being understood that this section is not offered in sincerity, or because there is any necesity for it, and that it is proposed for the sole purpose of breeding prejudice and bring-about a political re-enslavement of the colored race."

After some discussion, the previous question was called and sustained.

The amendment was adopted.

The new section, as amended, was rejected, yeas 11, nays 86.

Those who voted in the affirmative are:

Messrs. Bradley, Durham, Ellis, Etheridge, Graham of Orange, Hare, Hodnett, Holt, McCubbins, Merritt and Sanderlin—11.

Those who voted in the negative are:

Messrs. Abbott, Andrews, Ashley, Aydlott, Benbow, Blume, Bryan, Carey, Carter, Candler, Chillson, Colgrove, Congleton, Cox, Dickey, Eppes, Fisher, Forkner, Franklin, French of Bladen, French of Rockingham, Fullings, Gahagan, Galloway, Garland, Garrett, George, Graham of Montgomery, Grant of Wayne, Gully, Gunter, Harris of Wake, Hay, Hayes of Robeson, Hayes of Halifax, Heaton, Highsmith, Hobbs, Hoffler, Hollowell, Hood, Hyman, Ing, King of Lincoln, Kinney, Laflin, Lee, Legg, Logan, May, Mayo, Marshall, McDonald of Chatham, McDonald of Moore, Moore, Morton, Mullican, Murphy, Newsom, Nicholson, Parker, Parks, Petree, Peterson, Pierson, Pool, Ragland, Ray, Renfrow, Rich, Robbins, Rodman, Rose, Smith, Stilly, Stilwell, Sweet, Taylor, Teague, Tourgee, Trogden, Tucker, Watts, Welker, Williams of Wake, and Williamson—86.

Section 6th was adopted.

Section 7th was verbally amended and adopted.

Sections 8th and 9th were read and adopted.

Section 10th was read, verbally amended and adopted.

Sections 11th, 12th, 13th, and 14th were read and adopted.

Section 15th was read and amended by Mr. Ashley, by adding the President of the University to the Board of Trustees.

The section, as amended, was adopted.

Sections 16th and 17th were read and adopted.

Section 18th was read.

Mr. Graham, of Orange, offered the following amendment:

"*Provided*, That there shall be separate and distinct schools and Colleges for the white and colored races."

Mr. Tourgee offered the following substitute:

"That separate and distinct schools may be provided for any class of citizens in the State: *Provided*, That in all cases where distinct schools shall be established, there shall be as ample, sufficient and complete facilities afforded for the one class as for others, and entirely adequate for all, and in all districts where schools are divided, the apportionment to each shall be equal."

The amendment and substitute were rejected.

Section 18th, as read, was adopted.

The entire report, as amended, passed its second reading, by the following vote, yeas 88, nays 12:

Those who voted in the affirmative are:

Messrs. Abbott, Andrews, Ashley, Aydlott, Benbow, Blume, Bradley, Bryan, Carey, Carter, Candler, Cherry, Chillson, Colgrove, Congleton, Cox, Dickey, Duckworth, Eppes, Fisher, Forkner, Franklin, French of Bladen, French of Rockingham, French of Chowan, Fullings, Gahagan, Galloway, Garland, Garrett, George, Glover, Graham of Montgomery, Grant of Wayne, Grant of Northampton, Gully, Gunter, Harris of Wake, Harris of Franklin, Hay, Hayes of Halifax, Heaton, Highsmith, Hobbs, Hoffler, Hollowell, Hood, Hyman, Ing, Jones of Caldwell, Kinney, Laflin, Lee, Mann, May, Mayo, Marshall, McDonald of Chatham, McDonald of Moore, Moore, Morton, Mullican, Murphy, Nance, Newsom, Nicholson, Patrick, Parker, Parks, Petree, Pierson, Pool, Ragland, Ray, Renfrow, Rich, Robbins, Rodman, Rose, Smith, Stilly, Stilwell, Sweet, Teague, Tourgee, Watts, Welker and Williamson—88.

Those who voted in the negative are:

Messrs. Daniel, Durham, Ellis, Etheridge, Graham of Orange, Hare, Hodnett, King of Lincoln, McCubbins, Merritt, Sanderlin and Williams of Wake—12.

The following report of the Committee on the Judicial Department, was taken up.

The Committee on the Judicial Department, to whom was referred the petition of John Roberts, to be divorced from his wife Camilla, respectfully report:

That considering the peculiar circumstances of the case, and the impossibility of the petitioners obtaining adequate relief in the courts, they are of the opinion that the prayer of the petitioner should be granted, and report an ordinance to that effect.

WM. B. RODMAN, *Chairman.*

SECTION 1. *Be it ordained by the people of North-Carolina in Convention assembled*, That John Roberts, of Chowan County, be, and he hereby is, divorced from the bonds of matrimony with Camilla, his wife: *Provided*, That it shall be lawful for the said Camilla to apply to the proper court and obtain such alimony as may be proper.

SEC. 2. *Be it further ordained*, That this ordinance shall go into effect from and after its ratification.

The yeas and nays were called on the adoption of this report, yeas 51, nays 21.

Those who voted in the affirmative are:

Messrs. Abbott, Andrews, Benbow, Blume, Carey, Carter,

Cherry, Chillson, Colgrove, Congleton, Etheridge, Fisher, Forkner, Fullings, Galloway, Garland, Glover, Graham of Montgomery, Gunter, Hare, Harris of Wake, Hayes of Halifax, Highsmith, Hoffler, King of Lincoln, Laflin, Logan, Long, Mann, Mayo, Marshall, McDonald of Chatham, McDonald of Moore, Moore, Morton, Murphy, Pierson, Pool, Ragland, Read, Renfrow, Rich, Rodman, Stillwell, Sweet, Teague, Tourgee, Tucker, Watts, Welker and Williamson—51.

Those who voted in the negative are:

Messrs. Aydlott, Bradley, Bryan, Candler, Cowles, Duckworth, French of Rockingham, Gahagan, George, Graham of Orange, Hay, Hobbs, Hodnett, Ing, Jones of Caldwell, Kinney, Lennon, May, McCubbins, Trogden and Turner—21.

The report was adopted.

The Committee on the Judicial Department, to whom was referred the petition of Rosa B. Quinlivan, reported the following ordinance and recommended its adoption:

SECTION. 1. *Be it ordained by the people of North-Carolina in Convention assembled*, That Rosa B. Quinlivan, formerly Rosa B. Chatterton, now the wife of John R. Quinlivan, be, and she hereby is, divorced from the bonds of matrimony with her said husband.

SEC. 2. *Be it further ordained*, That this ordinance shall be in force from and after its ratification.

The yeas and nays were called upon the adoption of this ordinance, yeas 61, nays 23.

Those who voted in the affirmative are:

Messrs. Abbott, Andrews, Baker, Benbow, Blume, Carey, Carter, Cherry, Chilson, Colgrove, Congleton, Cox, Daniel, Eppes, Etheridge, Fisher, Forkner, Franklin, French of Bladen, French of Chowan, Fullings, Galloway, Garland, Glover, Graham of Montgomery, Gully, Gunter, Hare, Harris of Wake, Hayes of Halifax, Highsmith, Hoffler, Hollowell, Hyman, Kinney, Laflin, Long, Mann, Mayo, Marshall, McDonald of Chatham, McDonald of Moore, Moore, Morton, Murphy, Nance, Patrick, Ragland, Read, Renfrow, Rich, Rodman, Stilwell, Sweet, Teague, Tourgee, Tucker, Turner, Watts, Welker and Williamson—61.

Those who voted in the negative are:

Messrs. Aydlott, Barnes, Bradley, Bryan, Candler, Cowles, Duckworth, Gahagan, George, Graham of Orange, Hay, Hodnett, Ing, Jones of Caldwell, Lennon, May, McCubbins, Nicholson, Parks, Rose, Stilly, Trogden and Williams of Wake—23.

The ordinance was adopted.

On motion the House adjourned.

---

EVENING SESSION, MARCH 6TH, 1868.

The Convention was called to order at 7½ o'clock by the President.

The roll was called and the following members answered to their names:

Messrs. Ashley, Aydlott, Barnes, Blume, Bradley, Bryan, Carey, Carter, Cherry, Chillson, Congleton, Cox, Daniel, Dickey, Duckworth, Durham, Eppes, Etheridge, Fisher, Forkner, Franklin, French of Bladen, French of Rockingham, French of Chowan, Fullings, Gahagan, Galloway, George, Graham of Montgomery, Grant of Wayne, Grant of Northampton, Gully, Gunter, Hare, Hay, Hayes of Robeson, Hayes of Halifax, Hobbs, Hodnett, Hoffler, Hood, Hyman, Ing, Jones of Caldwell, King of Lincoln, Kinney, Laflin, Legg, Lennon, Logan, Long, May, Mayo, Marshall, McCubbins, Merritt, McDonald of Chatham, McDonald of Moore, Moore, Morton, Mullican, Murphy, Newsom, Nicholson, Parker, Parks, Petree, Peterson, Pierson, Pool, Ragland, Ray, Read, Renfrow, Rhodes, Rich, Robbins, Rodman, Rose, Sanderlin, Smith, Stilwell, Sweet, Teague, Trogden, Tucker, Turner, Watts, Welker, and Williams of Wake—89.

The report of the Committee on Homesteads having been made a special order for the evening was taken up and placed on its third and final reading and passage.

Mr. Jones, of Caldwell, moved to amend section 1st by adding to the section the words "contracted after the ratification of this constitution."

On this amendment the yeas and nays were called, yeas 34, nays 71.

Those who voted in the affirmative, are.

Messrs. Aydlott, Barnes, Bradley, Candler, Colgrove, Cox, Daniël, Ellis, Forkner, French of Rockingham, Gahagan, Glover, Graham of Orange, Grant of Northampton, Hare, Heaton, Hodnett, Hollowell, Ing, Jones of Caldwell, King of Lincoln, Logan, McCubbins, Mullican, Nicholson, Petree, Renfrow, Rhodes, Robbins, Rose, Sweet, Teague, Trogden, and Tucker—34.

Those who voted in the negative, are:

Messrs. Abbott, Andrews, Ashley, Baker, Blume, Bryan, Carey, Carter, Cherry, Chillson, Congleton, Dickey, Dowd, Durham, Eppes, Etheridge, Fisher, Franklin, French of Bladen, French of Chowan, Galloway, George, Graham of Montgomery, Grant of Wayne, Gully, Gunter, Harris of Wake, Harris of Franklin, Hay, Hayes of Robeson, Hayes of Halifax, Highsmith, Hobbs, Hoffler, Hood, Hyman, King of Lenoir, Kinney, Laflin, Legg, Long, Mann, May, Mayo, Merritt, McDonald of Chatham, McDonald of Moore, Moore, Morton, Murphy, Nance, Newsom, Patrick, Parks, Peterson, Pierson, Pool, Ragland, Ray, Read, Rodman, Sanderlin, Smith, Stilly. Stilwell, Taylor, Tourgee, Turner, Watts, Welker and Williamson—71.

The amendment was lost.

Mr. Tourgee amended by inserting the word "hereby' between "shall be" and "exempted."

Mr Graham, of Orange, moved to amend by striking out all after the word "execution."

The amendment was not sustained.

Mr. Harris, of Wake, amended by inserting "or" and striking out "under."

The section as amended was adopted by the following vote, yeas 81, nays 15:

Those who voted in the affirmative are:

Messrs. Abbott, Andrews, Ashley, Aydlott, Baker, Blume, Bradley, Bryan, Carey, Carter, Cherry, Chillson, Colgrove, Congleton, Daniel, Dickey, Dowd, Etheridge, Fisher, Franklin, French of Bladen, French of Chowan, Galloway, George, Graham of Montgomery, Graham of Orange, Grant of Wayne, Grant of Northampton, Gully, Gunter, Hare, Harris of Wake, Harris of Franklin, Hay, Hayes of Robeson, Heaton, Highsmith, Hobbs, Hoffler, Hollowell, Hood, Jones of Caldwell, King of Lenoir, Kinney, Lee, Legg, Long, Mann, May, Mayo, Marshall, McCubbins, Merritt, McDonald of Chatham, McDonald of Moore, Moore, Morton, Mullican, Murphy, Nance, Newsom, Patrick, Parks, Petree, Peterson, Pierson, Ragland, Ray, Read, Rich, Robbins, Rodman, Stilly, Stilwell, Sweet, Tourgee, Tucker, Turner, Watts, Welker, and Williamson—81.

Those who voted in the negative are:

Messrs. Candler, Cox, Forkner, French of Rockingham, Gahagan, Glover, Hayes of Halifax, Ing, King of Lincoln, Logan, Nicholson, Rhodes, Rose, Smith, and Teague—15.

Section 2d was read.

Mr. French of Bladen, moved to amend by inserting "and is hereby" before "exempted."

The amendment was agreed to.

Mr. Hood moved to insert after homestead "not to exceed-one-hundred acres of land."

Lost.

Mr. Dowd moved to amend by striking out "one-thousand" and inserting "two-thousand."

On this amendment the yeas and nays were taken, yeas 20, nay 62.

Those who voted in the affirmative are:

Messrs. Abbott, Ashley, Baker, Bradley, Cherry, Chillson, Daniel, Dowd, Etheridge, Fisher, Galloway, Graham of Orange, McDonald of Chatham, Moore, Murphy, Newsom, Patrick, Sanderlin, Turner, and Welker—20.

Those who voted in the negative, are:

Messrs. Andrews, Aydlott, Blume, Bryan, Carey, Candler, Colgrove, Congleton, Cox, Eppes, Forkner, Franklin, French of Bladen, French of Rockingham, French of Chowan, Gahagan, George, Graham of Montgomery, Grant of Wayne, Grant of Northampton, Gunter, Hare, Harris of Franklin,

Hay, Hayes of Halifax, Heaton, Hobbs, Hoffler, Hollowell, Hood, Hyman, Ing, Jones of Caldwell, King of Lincoln, King of Lenoir, Kinney, Logan, May, Mayo, Marshall, McCubbins, McDonald of Moore, Morton, Mullican, Nance, Nicholson, Parks, Petree, Peterson, Pool, Ragland, Ray, Rhodes, Rich, Rodman, Rose, Smith, Sweet, Teague, Tourgee, Tucker, and Watts—62.

The amendment was lost.

The section as amended was adopted.

Mr. Hood amended section 3d by striking out all after the word "debt" in third line to the word "constitution" in fourth line.

The section as amended was adopted.

Sections 4th, 5th and 6th, were read and adopted.

Mr. Jones amended section 7th by inserting the words "judge or."

The section as amended was adopted.

Mr Tourgee moved to reconsider the vote by which section 6th was adopted.

Agreed to.

Mr. Tourgee moved to amend by striking out the words "after the adoption of this Constitution."

Adopted.

The entire report of the Committee on Homesteads passed its third and final reading by the following vote, yeas 65, and nays 16.

Those who voted in the affirmative are:

Messrs. Abbott, Andrews, Ashley, Aydlott, Baker, Barnes, Blume, Bryan, Carey, Cherry, Chillson, Colgrove, Congleton, Daniel, Dickey, Dowd, Eppes, Etheridge, Fisher, French of Bladen, French of Chowan, Galloway, George, Graham of Montgomery, Grant of Wayne, Gunter, Harris of Wake, Harris of Franklin, Hay, Heaton, Hobbs, Hoffler, Hollowell, Hood, Hyman, Jones of Caldwell, King of Lenoir, Kinney, Long, Mayo, Marshall, McCubbins, Merritt, McDonald of Chatham, McDonald of Moore, Moore, Morton, Murphy, Nance, Newsom, Patrick, Parks, Peterson, Pool, Ragland,

Ray, Renfrow, Rich, Smith, Stilwell, Tourgee, Tucker, Turner, Watts, and Welker—65.

Those who voted in the negative are:

Messrs. Candler, Cox, Forkner, French of Rockingham, Gahagan, Graham of Orange, Hare, Ing, King of Lincoln, Logan, Nicholson, Petree, Rhodes, Rose, Sanderlin, and Teague—16.

On motion, the House adjourned.

---

SATURDAY, March 7th, 1868.

The Convention was called to order at 10 o'clock by the President.

Prayer by the Rev. Mr. Lennon.

The Roll was called and the following members answered to their names:

Messrs. Abbott, Andrews, Ashley, Aydlott, Baker, Benbow, Blume, Bradley, Bryan, Carey, Carter, Candler, Cherry, Chillson, Colgrove, Congleton, Cox, Daniel, Dickey, Duckworth, Durham, Ellis, Eppes, Etheridge, Fisher, Forkner, Franklin, French of Bladen, French of Chowan, Fullings, Gahagan, Garland, Garrett, George, Glover, Graham of Montgomery, Grant of Northampton, Gully, Gunter, Hare, Harris, of Franklin, Hay, Hayes of Halifax, Highsmith, Hodnett, Hoffler, Hollowell, Holt, Hood, Ing, Jones of Caldwell, King of Lincoln, King of Lenoir, Kinney, Lee, Lennon, Logan, Long, Mann, May, Mayo, Marshall, McCubbins, Merrit, McDonald of Chatham, McDonald of Moore, Moore, Morton, Mullican, Murphy, Nance, Newsom, Nicholson, Patrick, Parker, Parks, Petree, Peterson, Pierson, Pool, Ragland, Ray, Renfrow, Rhodes, Rich, Robbins, Rodman, Rose, Sanderlin, Smith, Stilley, Stilwell, Taylor, Teague, Tourgee, Trogden, Tucker, Turner, Watts, Welker and Williams of Wake—102.

The Journal of Friday was read and approved.

Mr. Pool, Chairman of the Committee on Enrollment and

Engrossment, gave notice that he would make a general report on all bills engrossed, on Monday next.

Mr. Durham, Chairman of the Committee on Corruption, etc., stated that the Committee, as yet, had not made up their report, but expected to be able to report on Tuesday or Wednesday next.

Mr. Renfrow introduced an ordinance relating to mechanics liens.

Referred to the Committee on Miscellaneous matters.

Mr. Turner introduced a resolution reducing the tax on Spirits Turpentine.

Referred to the Committee on Tobacco Tax.

Mr. Tourgee introduced the following resolution:

*Resolved*, That the Committee on Revision be directed and empowered to procure Parchment for the purpose of having the Constitution enrolled for signature by the members of this Convention.

On motion, the rules were snspended, and the resolution was adopted.

Mr. King, of Lenoir, moved to re-consider rule 42, of the Rules of Order, a majority of the members elect, not voting in the affirmative.

The motion was not snstained.

The following report of the Committee on Printing was taken up.

The Committee on Printing beg to report:

That to facilitate the business of this Convention, it is necesary to elect a Printer, and therefore, the Committee recommend the adoption of the following resolution, viz:

*Resolved*, That this Convention do now elect a Printer for this body.

S. S. ASHLEY, *Chairman.*
A. W. TOURGEE,
J. P. ANDREWS,
S. H. DUCKWORTH.

The report was adopted.

Mr. McDonald, of Chatham, nominated Jos. W. Holden.

Mr. Turner nominated W. W. Holden.

Mr. Durham nominated John W. Dunham.

Mr. Rodman introduced a resolution instructing the Committee on Printing, to contract with same competent person for all printing required by this Convention.

Mr. Jos. W. Holden was elected by the following vote:

For Mr. Holden—Messrs. Abbott, Andrews, Ashley, Aydlott, Benbow, Blume, Bryan, Carey, Carter, Candler, Chillson, Colgrove, Congleton, Cox, Daniel, Dickey, Duckworth, Fisher, Forkner, Franklin, French of Bladen, French of Rockingham, French of Chowan, Fullings, Gahagan, Garland, Garrett, George, Glover, Graham of Montgomery, Grant of Northampton, Gully, Gunter, Harris of Wake, Harris of Franklin, Hay, Hayes of Robeson, Hayes of Halifax, Heaton, Highsmith, Hobbs, Hoffler, Hollowell, Ing, King of Lincoln, King of Lenoir, Kinney, Laflin, Lee, Logan, Long, May, Mayo, Marshall, McDonald of Chatham, McDonald of Moore, Moore, Morton, Mullican, Murphy, Nance, Newsom, Nicholson, Patrick, Parker, Parks, Petree, Peterson, Pierson, Pool, Ray, Renfrow, Rhodes, Rich, Robbins, Rodman, Rose, Smith, Stilly, Sweet, Taylor, Teague, Tourgee, Trogden, Tucker, Turner, Watts, Welker, Williams of Wake and Williamson—90.

For Mr. Dunham—Messrs. Durham, Graham of Orange, Hare, Holt, Merritt and Sanderlin—6.

The report of the Committee on Counties, Cities and Towns, was taken up and placed on its third and final reading and passage.

Sections 1st, 2d, 3d, 4th, 5th, 6th, 7th, 8th, 9th, 10th, 11th, 12th and 13th were read and adopted.

Section 14th was read.

Mr. Baker moved to amend by adding at the close of the section:

"*Provided*, That debts contracted for benevolent and charitable purposes, shall not be considered as coming in the purview of this section."

Mr. Andrews moved to strike out "municipal," on first line.

The motion was lost.

Also, strike out "directly or indirectly."

Not adopted.

The question recurred on the amendment of Mr. Baker, which amendment was put to the House and lost.

The section, as read, was adopted.

The entire report then passed the third and final reading by the following vote, yeas 87, nays 14:

Those who voted in the affirmative are:

Messrs. Abbott, Andrews, Ashley, Aydlott, Barnes, Benbow, Blume, Bryan, Carey, Carter, Candler, Cherry, Chillson, Colgrove, Congleton, Cox, Daniel, Dickey, Duckworth, Eppes, Fisher, Forkner, Franklin, French of Bladen, French of Rockingham, French of Chowan, Fullings, Gahagan, Garland, George, Glover, Graham of Montgomery, Grant of Northampton, Gully, Gunter, Harris of Wake, Hay, Hayes of Halifax, Heaton, Highsmith, Hobbs, Hoffler, Hollowell, Hood, Ing, Jones of Caldwell, Kinney, Laflin, Lee, Logan, Long, May, Mayo, Marshall, McDonald of Chatham, McDonald of Moore, Moore, Morton, Mullican, Murphy, Nance, Newsom, Patrick, Parker, Parks, Petree, Peterson, Pierson, Ragland, Ray, Renfrow, Rhodes, Rich, Robbins, Rodman, Smith, Stilly, Stilwell, Sweet, Taylor, Teague, Tourgee, Trogden, Tucker, Watts, Welker and Williams of Wake—87.

Those who voted in the negative, are:

Messrs. Baker, Bradley, Dowd, Durham, Ellis, Etheridge, Graham of Orange, Hare, Hodnett, Holt, Lennon, McCubbins, Merritt and Sanderlin—14.

Leave of absence was granted Messrs. Grant of Wayne, Hyman and Chillson until Monday next.

The report of the Committee on Finance was taken up and placed on its third and final reading and passage.

Sections 1st, 2d, 3d and 4th were read and adopted.

Section 5th was read.

Mr. Abbott moved the following as a substitute:

"Until the bonds of the State shall be at par, the General Assembly shall have no power to contract any new debt or pecuniary obligation in behalf of the State, except to supply a casual deficit, or for suppressing invasion or insurrection, unless it shall, in the same bill, levy a special tax to pay the interest annually.

"And the General Assembly shall have no power to give or lend the credit of the State in aid of any person, association or corporation, except to aid in the completion of such Rail Roads and other works of Internal Improvement, as are unfinished, and in which the State has a direct pecuniary interest, unless the subject be submitted to a direct vote of of the people of the State, and be approved by a majority of those who shall vote thereon."

Mr. Jones, of Caldwell, moved to amend by striking out the second clause of the substitute.

Mr. Tourgee moved to amend by striking out "are," in the fifth line, and insert "may be;" insert after the word "unfinished," in the 5th line, "at the time of the adoption of this Constitution;" strike out "and" in fifth line, and insert "or."

Mr. Jones accepted the the amendment of Mr. Tourgee.

Mr. Abbott, Chairman of the Committee on Finance, accepted the amendment of Mr. Jones, as amended by Mr. Tourgee.

Mr. Candler moved to strike out all after the word "annually," in the sixth line.

The yeas and nays were demanded on the amendment of Mr. Candler.

The amendment did not prevail by the following vote, yeas 38, nays 60:

Those who voted in the affirmative are:

Messrs. Andrews, Aydlott, Baker, Barnes, Benbow, Bradley, Bryan, Candler, Cox, Dowd, Duckworth, Durham, Ellis, Etheridge, Forkner, French of Rockingham, Fullings, Gahagan, Garland, George, Glover, Hodnett, Holt, King of Lincoln, Lennon, Marshall, McCubbins, Merritt, Murphy, Patrick, Parks, Petree, Rhodes, Rose, Sanderlin, Stilly, Teague and Trogden—38.

Those who voted in the negative are:

Messrs. Abbott, Ashley, Blume, Carey, Carter, Colgrove, Congleton, Daniel, Dickey, Eppes, Fisher, French of Bladen, Graham ofMontgomery, Graham of Orange, Grant of Northampton, Gunter, Hare, Harris of Wake, Harris of Franklin, Hayes of Robeson, Hayes of Halifax, Heaton, Highsmith, Hobbs, Hoffler, Hollowell, Hood, Ing, Jones of Caldwell, King of Lenoir, Kinney, Laflin, Long, May, Mayo, McDonald of Chatham, McDonald of Moore, Moore, Morton, Mullican, Nance, Nicholson, Parker, Peterson, Pierson, Ragland, Renfrow, Rich, Robbins, Rodman, Smith, Stilwell, Sweet, Taylor, Tourgee, Tucker, Turner, Watts, Welker, and Williams of Wake—60.

Mr. Cowles moved to strike out "par," on line first, and insert "ninety per cent."

The amendment was not sustained.

The question recurred on the substitute, as amended.

The yeas and nays were demanded.

The substitute, as amended, was adopted by the following vote, yeas 62, nays 30:

Those who voted in the affirmative, are:

Messrs. Abbott, Ashley, Blume, Bryan, Carey, Carter, Colgrove, Daniel, Dickey, Duckworth, Eppes, Fisher, Franklin, French of Bladen, French of Chowan, Fullings, Graham of Montgomery, Graham of Orange, Grant of Northampton, Gunter, Harris of Wake, Harris of Franklin, Hayes of Robeson, Hayes of Halifax, Heaton, Highsmith, Hoffler, Hollowell, Hood, Ing, Jones of Caldwell, King of Lenoir, Kinney, Laflin, Logan, Long, May, Mayo, McCubbins, McDonald of Chatham, McDonald of Moore, Mullican, Murphy, Nance, Nicholson, Parker, Parks, Peterson, Ragland, Ray, Renfrow, Rich, Robbins, Rodman, Smith, Sweet, Taylor, Tucker, Turner, Watts, Welker and Williams of Wake—62.

Those who voted in the negative are:

Messrs. Andrews, Aydlott, Baker, Barnes, Bradley, Candler, Cowles, Congleton, Cox, Dowd, Durham, Ellis, Etheridge, Forkner, French of Rockingham, Gahagan, George, Glover, Hare, Hodnett, Holt, Lennon, Marshall, Merritt, Patrick, Petree, Rhodes, Rose, Sanderlin and Stilly—30.

Sections 6th, 7th and 8th were read and adopted.

The entire report of the Committee on Finance, as amended, passed its third and final reading, by the following vote, yeas 77, nays 20:

Those who voted in the affirmative are:

Messrs. Abbott, Andrews, Ashley, Barnes, Blume, Bryan, Carey, Carter, Colgrove, Congleton, Daniel, Dickey, Duckworth, Eppes, Fisher, Franklin, French of Bladen, French of Rockingham, French of Chowan, Fullings, Gahagan, George, Graham of Montgomery, Grant of Northampton, Gunter, Harris of Wake, Harris of Franklin, Hayes of Robeson, Hayes of Halifax, Heaton, Highsmith, Hobbs Hoffler, Hollowell, Hood, Ing, Jones of Caldwell, King of Lincoln, Kinney, Laflin,Logan, Long, May, Mayo, Marshall, McCubbins, McDonald of Chatham, McDonald of Moore, Mullican, Murphy, Nance, Newsom, Nicholson, Patrick, Parker, Parks, Petree, Pool, Ragland, Ray, Renfrow, Rhodes, Rich, Robbins, Rodman, Rose, Smith, Stilly, Stilwell, Sweet, Taylor, Teague, Tucker, Turner, Watts, Welker and Williams of Wake—77.

Those who voted in the negative, are:

Messrs. Aydlott, Baker, Bradley, Cowles, Candler, Cherry, Dowd, Durham, Ellis, Etheridge, Forkner, Glover, Graham of Orange, Hare, Hodnett, Holt, Lennon, Merritt, Peterson and Sanderlin—20.

Mr. Hood, by permission, introduced a report of the Committee on Political Disability.

The report was, on motion, received.

Mr. Graham, of Orange, moved the names be submitted to the people.

The motion was declared out of order.

Mr. Hood moved that the report of the Committee on Political Disability, be engrossed for final action by this Convention.

The motion was sustained.

Mr. French, of Bladen, introduced an ordinance in relation to the intimidation of voters.

On motion, the rules were suspended.

The ordinance was ordered to be printed.

Mr. Heaton presented a report of the Committee on Revision.

Ordered to be printed.

On motion, the House adjourned.

---

EVENING SESSION, March 7th, 1868.

The Convention was called to order at 7½ o'clock, by the President.

The roll was called and the following members answered to their names:

Messrs. Abbott, Andrews, Ashley, Barnes, Benbow, Blume, Bradley, Bryan, Carter, Colgrove, Congleton, Cox, Daniel, Dickey, Duckworth, Durham, Eppes, Etheridge, Fisher, French of Rockingham, French of Chowan, Fullings, Gahagan, Garrett, George, Graham of Montgomery, Grant of Northampton, Gunter, Hare, Harris of Wake, Harris of Franklin, Hayes of Halifax, Heaton, Highsmith, Hobbs, Hodnett, Hoffler, Holt, Hood, Ing, King of Lenoir, Kinney, Legg, Lennon, Logan, Long, Mann, May, Mayo, McCubbins, McDonald of Chatham, Moore, Morton, Mullican, Murphy, Nance, Newsom, Nicholson, Parker, Parks, Petree, Peterson, Pierson, Pool, Ray, Renfrow, Rhodes, Rodman, Rose, Sanderlin, Smith, Stilly, Stillwell, Teague, Tourgee, Trogden, Tucker, Turner, Watts and Welker—79.

The report of the Committee on Punishments, Penal Institutions and Public Charities, having been made a Special Order for this evening, was taken up.

Mr. Welker moved the following as a substitute for section 5th.

"A House, or Houses of Refuge, shall also be established whenever the public interest shall require it, for the correction and instruction of juvenile offenders."

Mr. Candler moved to amend section 5th, in second line, after the word "for," insert the word "such," after the word "offenders," insert the words, "as the County authorities may deem proper subjects for the same."

Mr. Candler withdrew his amendment.

The motion of Mr. Hobbs, to strike out 5th section, as amended, and insert a substitute, was put to the House and carried.

Mr. King, of Lenoir, moved to strike out the section substituted for section 5th.

The Chair decided the motion out of order.

Mr. King appealed from the decision of the Chair, and demanded the yeas and nays.

The demand was not sustained.

The House sustained the decision of the Chair.

Mr. McDonald, of Chatham, moved to reconsider the vote that struck out section 5th, and inserted the substitute of Mr. Welker.

The motion was sustained

Mr. Heaton offered the following as a substitute for section 5th.

" The Legislature shall have power to provide for the erection of such other Houses for the purposes of reformation as may be deemed necessary and proper.

Mr. Heaton withdrew his amendment to give place to the following offered by Mr. Welker, Chairman of the Committee:

Section 5. A House or Houses of Refuge may, also, be established whenever the public intersests shall require it, for the correction and instruction of other classes of offenders.

The substitute of Mr. Welker, was,

On motion, adopted.

Section 6th was read and adopted.

Sections 7th and 8th were read and adopted.

Section 9th was read.

Mr. Heaton moved to amend by striking out " at an early day," and insert " as soon as prarticable."

The amendment was accepted by the Chairman of the Committee.

The section, as amended, was adopted.

Sections 10th and 11th were read and adopted.

The entire report of the Committee on Punishments and

Penal Institutions, passed its second reading by the following vote:

Those who voted in the affirmative, are:

Messrs. Abbott, Andrews, Ashley, Barnes, Blume, Bradley, Bryan, Carey, Candler, Cherry, Colgrove, Congleton, Cox, Dickey, Duckworth, Eppes, Fisher, Forkner, French of Chowan, Fullings, Gahagan, George, Grant of Northampton, Gunter, Harris of Franklin, Hayes of Halifax, Heaton, Hollowell, Hood, Ing, Jones of Caldwell, Kinney, Laflin, Legg, Logan, Long, May, Mayo, Marshall, McCubbins, McDonald of Chatham, McDonald of Moore, Mullican, Murphy, Nance, Newsom, Nicholson, Parker, Parks, Pierson, Pool, Ray, Renfrow, Rich, Robbins, Rodman, Rose, Smith, Stilly, Tourgee, Tucker, Turner and Welker—63.

Those who voted in the negative are:

Messrs. Durham, Etheridge and Hobbs—3.

On motion of Mr. Welker, the report was ordered to be engrossed and made a Special Order for Tuesday at 11 o'clock, A. M.

Mr. Bryan gave notice that he would move to reconsider the vote on 4th section of the report of the Committee on Finance.

On motion, the House adjourned.

---

## MONDAY, March 9th, 1868.

The Convention was called to order at 10 o'clock, by the President.

Prayer by the Rev. J. W. Hood.

Members present 99.

The Journal of Saturday was read and approved.

On motion of Mr. Pool, the ordinance of relief introduced by Mr. Rodman, was postponed until Wednesday evening at 7½ o'clock.

The Committee on Internal Improvements to whom was refered the ordinance in relation to the Drainage of Mattamuskeet Lake, reported that they have had the same under consideration and recommend its passage.

On motion the report was accepted.

Mr. Rodman moved the reading and adoption of the ordinance.

The Chair declared the motion out of order.

Mr. Rodman appealed from the decision of the Chair.

The House over ruled the decision of the Chair.

The report of the Committee was then adopted.

The following is the ordinance as adopted :

## AN ORDINANCE IN RELATION TO THE DRAINING OF MATTAMUSKEET LAKE.

Whereas, The agricultural interests of Hyde County are greatly imperilled by the overflow of the waters of Lake Mattamuskeet, and whereas the value of the lands in that county belonging to the Common School fund of the State is greatly empaired thereby, therefore for the purpose of draining said lake:

Section 1. *Be it ordained by the people of North-Carolina in Convention assembled,* That David M. Carter, Jones Spencer, George W. Swindell, Riley Murrey, Joseph Mann, and William S. Carter, are hereby appointed Commissioners and invested with full power to locate one or more canals leading from lake Mattamuskeet for the purpose of draining said lake, to contract for the execution of such canals, or to have the same constructed under their own superintendence. Said Commissioners are authorized to condemn the lands through which said canals may pass to the exclusive use of such canals not to exceed one hundred feet wide, and extending from one terminus of such canal to the other; said Commissioners shall fix the price to be paid the owners of said land, who may appeal to the Superior Court of Hyde County, if dissatisfied with the price fixed by said Commissioners upon said lands, and may have the value of the lands condemned for the use of said canals, ascertained by jury, but the Commissioners, and in case of such appeal, the jury also, shall estimate the benefit accruing to the other lands of said owners in fixing the compensation for so much as is appropriated of the lands,

The title to the lands thus condemned, and to the lands and their appurtenances, shall vest in said Commissioners and their successors. A majority of said Commissioners shall constitute a quorum for the transaction of any business whatever within the scope of their duties, and a majority of that quorum shall determine all questions which may arise.

SEC. 2. *Be it further ordained*, That an annual tax is hereby levied upon all the lands in the County of Hyde of one per centum of the value of said lands as assessed for taxation in the year 1860, for the period of five years, unless the said canals are sooner completed and paid for; and also a further tax is hereby levied upon all other taxable subjects to be paid annually for the period of five years, if the same amount which the State of North Carolina may levy for State purposes on the same subjects of taxation during that period, and the money thus raised by taxation of lands and other subjects or so much as shall be necessary, shall be faithfully expended by said Commissioners in the construction of one or more canals, for the purpose of draining the waters of Lake Mattamuskeet so as to prevent the overflow, thereof.

SEC. 3. *Be it further ordained*, That it shall be the duty of the proper officer who makes out the tax list for the County of Hyde, also to make out and deliver to the Sheriff of that County, a tax list by which the taxes herein levied may be collected annually, at the same time with the other taxes, and under like penalties for any failure or neglect of duty, and it shall be the duty of the Sheriff of the County to collect and pay over to the Treasurer of the Board of Commissioners the taxes herein levied, at the same time when the taxes for the State are payable to the public Treasurer, under the same penalties for any failure or neglect of duty as are imposed in case of his failure to pay over the taxes levied for State purposes, and the securities of his official bonds are to be held liable for the same.

SEC. 4. *Be it further ordained*, That said Commissioners shall appoint one of their number President of their Board, and shall also elect a Treasurer who shall give bonds with two or more sufficient securities in the sum of ten thousand dollars, to keep safely and pay out properly under the requisition of the President, the moneys received by him from the Sheriff of Hyde County or from any other source, which are appropriated to be expended by said Commissioners, said bond shall be payable to the State of North-Carolina.

SEC. 5. *Be it further ordained*, That whenever a vacancy may happen in said Board of Commissioners by death, resignation, or expulsion for malfeasance of any of its members, by said Board of Commissioners, such vacancies may be filled by the Commissioners at their first, or any meeting thereafter. It shall also be the duty of said Commissioners to hold at least one meeting each year during the time of the construction of the canals. The president and treasurer may receive such compensation, for their services as a majority of the Commissioners shall fix.

SEC. 6. *Be it further ordained*, That said Commissioners may value all the uncleared swamp lands within two miles of said canals, and assess an amount of money to be paid for such lands in the proportion to the advantage accruing to said lands by the canals, not exceeding five per cent of their value as assessed in 1860, and in case of the refusal of the owners of said lands to pay said assessment, the said Commissioners may file their petition in the Superior Court of Hyde County, and have a judgement, condemning said lands to be sold to pay such assessment. *Provided*, That the question of the valuation of said lands may be reviewed by a jury of said Court.

SEC. 7. *Be it further ordained*, That if a majority of the whole number of said Commissioners shall be of opinion that the best plan to drain said lake is by cutting a canal from the head of Broad Creek to the head of Alligater River, then said Commissions may also expend any part of the moneys herein appropriated in cutting said canal.

SEC. 8. *Be it further ordained*, That this ordinance shall be submitted to the qualified voters of Hyde County for their approval or rejection, under the direction of the County Court of said County, or the Commissioners for said County, and shall take the proper means for that purpose and declare the result, and if approved by a majority of the qualified voters, who shall vote upon the question, shall go into force and effect from and after such approval.

The Committee on Internal Improvements to whom was referred the ordinance to incorporate the North Western North Carolina Rail Road Company, reported that they had the same under consideration, and recommend its passage.

The hour of 11 o'clock having arrived, Mr. McDonald of Chatham, moved a postponement of the general order.

The motion prevailed.

The ordinance passed its first reading.

On motion the rules were suspended and the ordinance passed its second reading.

On motion of Mr. Abbott, the rules were again suspended and the Ordinance passed its third and final reading by the following vote, yeas 84, nays 11:

Those who voted in the affirmative, are:

Messrs. Andrews, Ashley, Aydlott, Baker, Barnes, Benbow, Blume, Bradley, Bryan, Carey, Carter, Candler, Cherry, Colgrove, Congleton, Cox, Daniel, Duckworth, Durham, Ellis, Eppes, Etheridge, Fisher, Forkner, Franklin, French of Rockingham, Fullings, Gahagan, Galloway, Garland, Garrett, Graham of Montgomery, Graham of Orange, Grant of Wayne, Gully, Gunter, Harris of Wake, Harris of Franklin, Hayes of Robeson, Heaton, Hoffler, Hollowell, Holt, Hood, Ing, Jones of Caldwell, King of Lincoln, Kinney, Laflin, Lee, Legg, Logan, Long, Mann, May, Mayo, Marshall, McCubbins, McDonald of Chatham, McDonald of Moore, Morton, Mullican, Murphy, Nance, Parks, Petree, Pierson, Ray, Renfrow, Rhodes, Rich, Robbins, Rodman, Rose, Smith, Stilwell, Sweet, Teague, Tourgee, Trogden, Tucker, Watts, and Welker—84.

Those who voted in the negative, are:

Messrs, George, Grant of Northampton, Hare, Hay, King, of Lenoir, Lennon, Moore, Parker, Peterson, Sanderlin, and Turner—11.

The following is the ordinance as adopted:

## AN ORDINANCE TO INCORPORATE THE NORTH WESTERN NORTH-CAROLINA RAIL ROAD COMPANY.

Section 1. *Be it ordained by the people of North-Carolina, in Convention assembled, and it is hereby ordained by the authority of the same*, That for the purpose of constructing a Rail Road of one or more tracks, from some point on the North-Carolina Railroad, between the town of Greensboro', in Guilford County, and the town of Lexington, in Davidson County, running by way of Salem and Winston, in Forsyth County, to some point on the Northwestern Boundary line of the State, to be hereafter determined, a company is hereby incorporated, under the name and style of the North Western North-Carolina Rail Road Company, with a capital stock of two millions of dollars which shall have a corporate existence and body politic, for the space of ninety-nine years, and by that name may sue and be sued, plead and be impleaded, in any court of law and equity in the State of North-Carolina, and may have and use a common seal, and shall be capable in law and equity of purchasing, holding, leasing, and conveying estates, real and personal and mixed, and of acquiring the same by gift or devise so far as may be necessary for the objects herein contemplated, and no further, and said Company may enjoy all other rights and immunities which other incorporate bodies may lawfully exercise, and may make all necessary by-laws, and regulations for its government, not inconsistent with the Constitution and laws of the State of North-Carolina, and of the United States.

Sec. 2. *Be it further ordained*, That the capital stock of said Company may be created, by subscriptions on the part of individuals, corporations, and counties, in shares of one hundred dollars.

Sec. 3. *Be it further ordained*, That books of subscription to the capital stock of said Company shall be opened by the following Commissioners, to wit: I. G. Lash, J. A. Vogler, H. W. Tris, in the town of Salem, and Thos. J. Wilson, Jas. Masten, P. A. Wilson, in the town of Winston, and by such other persons, and in such other places, as the aforesaid Commissioners may direct, and that ten days notice of the opening of said books, shall be given in one or more newspapers of this State; and further more, that the said Commissioners or any four of them may at any time after said books have been kept open for the space of thirty days, and the sum of thirty thousand dollars has been subscribed to the capital stock of said Company and five per cent paid thereon, shall have power to call together the subscribers to said stock, for the purpose of completing the organization of said company, and the said subscribers shall be and are hereby declared incorporated into a Company by the said name and style of the North-Western North-Carolina Rail Road Company, and the said Company may from time to time receive further subscriptions to its capital stock, as it may deem proper.

SEC. 4. *Be it further ordained*, That said Company may hold annual meetings of its Stockholders, and oftener if necessary, and at its organizations and the annual meetings subsequent thereto, ten directors shall be elected to hold office for one year, or until their successors shall be elected, and any of said meetings shall have power to make or alter the by-laws of the Company. *Provided*, That in all such meetings of the Stockholders a majority of all the stock subscribed shall be represented in person or by proxy, which proxy shall be verified in the manner prescribed by the by-laws of the Company, and each share thus represented shall be entitled to one vote on all questions; that it shall be the duty of the Directors of the Company to elect one of their number as President, and to fill all vacancies in their board.

SEC. 5. *Be it further ordained*, That after the organization of said Company, and the election of the President and other necessary officers, the officers so elected shall proceed under the advice of the Directors to locate the eastern terminus of the North Western North-Carolina Rail Road, and shall proceed to construct said road with one or more tracks, as speedily as practicable, in sections of five miles each to the towns of Winston and Salem, in Forsyth County, which portion of said Rail Road when completed, shall constitute its first division. *Provided*, That if the distance from the nearest section to the towns of Salem and Winston be less than five miles, the same shall be considered a section.

Sec. 6. *Be it further ordained*, That said Company shall have the same power to call for and enforce the payment of stock subscribed, as was heretofore granted to the North-Carolina Rail Road Company, by their charter, of incorporation, and shall have power to condemn land for the use of the Company, when a contract to purchase cannot be made with the owner thereof, to the same extent, and in the same manner, and under the same rules, regulations, and restrictions, as the said North-Carolina Rail Road Company, were authoized to do by their act of incorporation.

Sec. 7. *Be it further ordained*, That all contracts made and entered into by the President or Superintendent, of the Company whether with or without seal, shall be binding upon the Company, and the President shall, under the instructions of the Board of Directors, issue certificates of stock the Stockholders, which shall be transferable in the manner prescribed by the by-laws of the Company.

Sec. 8. *Be it further ordained*, That whenever the President and Chief Engineer of said Company shall certify to the Governor of the State, that the grading of any of the sections of said road as mentioned in section 5th of this ordinance is completed, and ready for the superstructure, he shall direct the Public Treasurer, of the State to loan, in behalf of the State to said Company, the sum of fifty thousand dollars in coupon bonds, and in like manner, the Governor will direct similar loans to be made to the Company upon the completion of the grading of each and every section until the first division is graded entire, and said Company shall set aside the receipts of the road over and above its annual expenses, as a sinking fund to pay the said debts and interest on the whole amount of said debt and interest, to be paid before the said Company shall order any dividends in the stock of the Company, and that said sinking fund so produced shall be semi-annually paid into the Public Treasury.

Sec. 9. *Be it further ordained*, That no part of said loan or bonds shall be delivered to said Company, until the President and Directors thereof shall execute and deliver to the Governor of the State a mortgage on the entire Road and its property, conditioned to save the State harmless, against the loss of both principal and interest of said loan.

SEC. 10. *Be it further ordained*, That the coupon bonds loaned as aforesaid, shall be signed by the Governor, countersigned by the Treasurer, and sealed with the Great Seal of the State, bearing six per cent interest, the principal payable at the end of thirty years from the date thereof, and the coupons for interest payable semi-annually, in such form as the Public Treasurer may direct.

SEC. 11. *Be it further ordained*, That said Company may have the exclusive right of transporting persons and freight upon said Road at such rate of charge as the Board of Directors may fix, and may have power to farm, or lease the same to any person, persons or corporations.

SEC. 12. *Be it further ordained*, That the Stockholders of the said Company may pay the stock subscribed by them, either in money, labor or material, for constructing said Road, as the Board of Directors of said Company may determine, and that all Counties and Towns subscribing stock to said Company, shall do so in the same manner and under the same rules, regulations and restrictions as are set forth and prescribed in the act incorporating the North-Carolina and Atlantic Rail Road Company, for the gomernment of such Towns and Counties, as now allowed to subscribers to the capital stock of said Company.

SEC. 13. *Be it further ordained*, That the Company shall have power to construct branches to said Rail Road, one of which shall run from said towns of Salem and Winston, by way of Mount Airy, in Surry County, to the line of the State of Virginia.

SEC. 14. *Be it further ordained*, That this ordinance shall be in force from and after its ratification.

The hour of 12 having arrived, the report of the Committee on Education, &c., was placed on its third and final reading.

Sections 1st and 2d were read and adopted.

Section 3d was amended by striking out the word "Primary."

The section, as amended, was adopted.

Sections 4th and 5th were read and adopted.

Section 6th was amended by adding after the word "accrued," in fourth line, the words, "to the State;" strike out "to the State," in the fifth line; after the word "escheats," on fifth line, insert "unclaimed dividends."

The section, as amended, was adopted.

Sections 7th, 8th, 9th, 10th, 11th, 12th, 13th, 14th, 15th, 16th and 17th were read and adopted.

The report then passed its third and final reading by the following vote, yeas 78, nays 10:

Those who voted in the affirmative, are:

Messrs. Abbott, Andrews, Ashley, Aydlott, Barnes, Benbow, Blume, Bryan, Carey, Carter, Candler, Cherry, Colgrove, Congleton, Cox, Dickey, Duckworth, Eppes, Fisher, Forkner, Franklin, French of Chowan, Fullings, Gahagan, Galloway, Garland, George, Grant of Wayne, Gully, Gunter, Harris of Wake, Hay, Hayes of Robeson, Heaton, Hobbs, Hoffler, Hollowell, Hood, Ing, Kinney, Laflin, Lee, Legg, Logan, Long, May, Mayo, Marshall, McDonald of Chatham, McDonald of Moore, Moore, Morton, Mullican, Murphy, Nance, Newsom, Parker, Parks, Petree, Pierson, Pool, Ragland, Ray, Renfrow, Rhodes, Rich, Robbins, Rodman, Rose, Smith, Stilwell, Sweet, Teague, Tourgee, Tucker, Turner, Watts and Welker—87.

Those who voted in the negative, are:

Messrs. Baker, Dowd, Durham, Ellis, Etheridge, Hodnett, Lennon, McCubbins, Sanderlin and Williams of Wake.—10.

On motion of Mr. Heaton, the report of the Committee on Revision, was taken up and passed its first reading.

On the second reading.

Mr. Durham offered the following as a substitute for the entire report.

*Clause 1st.* No Convention of the people shall be called by the General Assembly, unless by the concurrence of two-thirds of all the members of each House of the General Assembly.

*Clause 2d.* No part of the Constitution of this State shall be altered, unless a bill to alter the same shall have been read three times in each House of the General Assembly and agreed to by three-fifths of the whole number of members of each House respectively; nor shall any alteration take place until the bill so agreed to, shall have been published six months previous to a new election of members to the General Assembly. If after such publication, the alteration proposed by the preceding General Assembly, shall be agreed to in the first session thereafter, by two-thirds of the whole representation in each House of the General Assembly, after the same shall have been read three times, on three several days in each House, then the said General Assembly shall prescribe a mode by which the amendment or amendments may be submitted to the qualified voters of the House of Representatatives throughout the State, and if, upon comparing the votes given in the whole State, it shall appear that a majority of the voters have approved thereof, then, and not otherwise, the same shall become a part of the Constitution.

Mr. Durham moved to strike out "two-thirds," and insert "three-fifths," after the words "agreed to in the first session thereafter."

The yeas and nays were demanded.

The call was sustained.

The amendment was lost by the following vote, yeas 22, nays 66:

Those who voted in the affirmative are:

Messrs. Baker, Bradley, Congleton, Durham, Ellis, Etheridge, French of Chowan, George, Hare, Hodnett, Hoffler, Hollowell, Holt, King of Lincoln, Lennon, Marshall, McCubbins, McDonald of Chatham, Rich, Rodman, Sanderlin and Turner—22.

Those who voted in the negative, are:

Messrs. Abbott, Andrews, Ashley, Aydlott, Benbow, Blume, Bryan, Carey, Candler, Colgrove, Cox, Dickey, Duckworth, Fisher, Forkner, Franklin, French of Rockingham, Fullings, Gahagan, Garland, Graham of Montgomery, Grant of Wayne, Grant of Northampton, Gully, Gunter, Harris of Wake, Hay,

Hayes of Robeson, Heaton, Hobbs, Hood, Ing, King of Lincoln, Kinney, Laflin, Lee, Legg, Logan, Long, May, Mayo, McDonald of Moore, Morton, Mullican, Murphy, Nance, Newsom, Nicholson, Parker, Petree, Peterson, Pierson, Pool, Ragland, Ray, Renfrow, Rhodes, Robbins, Rose, Smith, Stilwell, Teague, Tourgee, Trogden, Tucker, Watts, Welker and Williams of Wake—66.

Mr. Nicholson moved to amend by inserting after the words, "majority of the voters," the words, "voting thereon."

The amendment was adopted.

The report passed the second reading by the following vote, yeas 82, nays 7:

Those who voted in the affirmative, are:

Messrs. Abbott, Andrews, Ashley, Aydlott, Baker, Benbow, Blume, Bradley, Bryan, Carey, Carter, Candler, Cherry, Colgrove, Congleton, Cox, Dickey, Duckworth, Eppes, Etheridge, Fisher, Forkner, Franklin, French of Rockingham, French of Chowan, Fullings, Gahagan, Garland, Garrett, George, Grant of Wayne, Grant of Northampton, Gully, Gunter, Harris of Wake, Hay, Hayes of Robeson, Heaton, Highsmith, Hobbs, Hoffler, Hollowell, Hood, Ing, Jones of Caldwell, King of Lincoln, Kinney, Laflin, Lee, Legg, Long, May, Mayo, McDonald of Chatham, McDonald of Moore, Morton, Mullican, Murphy, Nance, Newsom, Nicholson, Parker, Parks, Petree, Peterson, Pierson, Ragland, Ray, Renfrow, Rhodes, Robbins, Rodman, Rose, Smith, Teague, Tourgee, Trogden, Tucker, Turner, Watts, Welker and Williams of Wake—82.

Those who voted in the negative are:

Messrs. Durham, Hare, Hodnett, Holt, Marshall, Rich and Sanderlin—7.

On motion of Mr. Heaton, the rules were suspended, and the report of the Cammittee on Revision was placed upon its third and final reading and passage.

The report was adopted by the following vote, yeas 86, nays 5:

Those who voted in the affirmative are:

Messrs. Abbott, Ashley, Aydlott, Benbow, Blume, Bradley,

Bryan, Carey, Carter, Candler, Colgrove, Congleton, Cox, Dickey, Duckworth, Eppes, Etheridge, Fisher, Forkner, Franklin, French of Rockingham, French of Chowan, Fullings, Gahagan, Galloway, Garland, Garrett, George, Graham of Montgomery, Grant of Northampton, Gully, Gunter, Harris of Wake, Hay, Hayes of Robeson, Hayes of Halifax, Heaton, Highsmith, Hobbs, Hoffler, Hollowell, Hood, Ing, Jones of Caldwell, King of Lincoln, King of Lenoir, Kinney, Laflin, Lee, Legg, Long, Mann, May, Mayo, McDonald of Chatham, McDonald of Moore, Moore, Morton, Mullican, Murphy, Nance, Newsom, Nicholson, Parker, Parks, Petree, Peterson, Pierson, Pool, Ragland, Ray, Renfrow, Rhodes, Robbins, Rodman, Rose, Smith, Stilwell, Teague, Tourgee, Trogden, Tucker, Turner, Watts, Welker and Williams of Wake—86.

Those who voted in the negative are:

Messrs. Durham, Ellis, Hare, Hodnett and Marshall—5.

Mr. Tourgee moved to reconsider the vote on the ordinance in relation to the Western North-Carolina Rail Road Company.

Mr. Abbott moved to lay the motion on the table.

The motion was sustained.

Mr. Tourgee, by permission, introduced the following resolution:

*Resolved*, That a Committee of three be appointed by vote of the Convention, to enquire whether the signature of a presiding officer who is not a registered voter under the provisions of the Reconstruction Acts, will in any way effect the validity of the Acts of this Convention, and that said Committee be required to report on Wednesday next.

On motion, the rules were suspended.

Mr. King, of Lincoln, moved to lay the resolution on the table.

The yeas and nays were demanded.

The call was not sustained.

The motion to lay on the table was lost.

The question recurred on the adoption of the resolution, which was,

On motion, adopted.

The House elected the following gentlemen as the Committee called for by the resolution of Mr. Tourgee:

Messrs. Rodman, Heaton and Pool.

On motion of Mr. Abbott, it was the sense of the Convention that the President will occupy the Chair during the session of the Convention.

Mr. Laflin introduced an ordinance vacating certain offices, and called for a suspension of the rules.

The call was not sustained.

The ordinance lies over under the rules.

Mr. Heaton introduced an ordinance to incorporate the Newbern Turpentine Company.

Mr. Hare introduced a resolution on the final adjournment.

Mr. Watts introduced an ordinance to aid the Tarboro and Williamston Rail Road Company.

Referred to the Committee of sixteen.

Mr. Ashley arose to a point of order, and stated that it was an order of the House, that all ordinances and resolutions should pass through a Committee, who should report what they thought necessary, to the House for action.

The Chair decided the point well taken.

On motion the House adjourned.

---

## EVENING SESSION, March 9th, 1868.

The Convention was called to order at 7½ o'clock by the President.

The roll was called and the following members answered to their names:

Messrs. Aydlott, Barnes, Benbow, Blume, Bradley, Carey, Carter, Candler, Cherry, Chillson, Congleton, Cox, Duckworth, Ellis, Eppes, Fisher, Forkner, Franklin, Gahagan, Galloway, George, Graham of Montgomery, Grant of Wayne, Grant of Northampton, Gully, Gunter, Hare, Harris of Wake, Hay, Hayes of Robeson, Hayes of Halifax, Hobbs, Hodnett, Hoftler, Hollowell, Hood, Hyman, Ing, King of Lincoln,

Kinney, Lennon, Logan, Long, Mayo, Marshall, McCubbins, McDonald of Chatham, Moore, Morton, Nance, Newsom, Nicholson, Parker, Parks, Petree, Peterson, Ray, Read, Rhodes, Rich, Rose, Sanderlin, Smith, Stilly, Stilwell, Teague, Tourgee, Trogden, Tucker, Turner, Watts, Welker and Williams of Wake—71.

Leave of absence was granted Mr. McDonald of Chatham.

The report of the Committee on Suffrage having been made the Special Order for the evening, was taken up.

Mr. Pool called the previous question on the Article on Suffrage.

The call was sustained.

The Article passed the second reading by the following vote, yeas 61, nays 19:

Those who voted in the affirmative are:

Messrs. Andrews, Ashley, Aydlott, Barnes, Benbow, Blume, Bryan, Carter, Cherry, Congleton, Daniel, Eppes, Forkner, Franklin, French Chowan, Fullings, Galloway, George, Grant of Wayne, Grant of Northampton, Gully, Gunter, Harris of Wake, Hay, Hayes of Halifax, Highsmith, Hobbs, Hoffler, Hollowell, Hood, Hyman, Ing, Jones of Caldwell, King of Lincoln, King of Lenoir, Kinney, Lee, Mayo, McDonald of Chatham, Moore, Nance, Newsom, Nicholson, Parker, Parks, Petree, Peterson, Pierson, Pool, Ragland, Renfrow, Rich, Robbins, Rodman, Smith, Stilly, Stilwell, Sweet, Tucker, Turner and Watts—61.

Those who voted in the negative, are:

Messrs. Candler, Cox, Dickey, Duckworth, Etheridge, Gahagan, Graham of Montgomery, Hare, Hayes of Robeson, Hodnett, Logan, May, Marshall, Merritt, Rhodes, Rose, Sanderlin, Teague and Welker—19.

The report of the Committee on Eligibility to Office was taken up.

Section 1st was read and adopted.

Section 2d was read.

Mr. Hood moved to strike out all after the words, "Almighty God," on the third line.

Mr. Candler offered to substitute exceptions first, second

and fourth of the minority report, for the exceptions in section 2d of the majority report.

After some discussion, Mr. Pool called the previous question.

The call was sustained.

The yeas and nays were granted on the substitute of Mr. Candler.

The substitute was lost by the following vote, yeas 21, nays 63:

Those who voted in the affirmative are:

Messrs. Abbott, Candler, French of Rockingham, French of Chowan, Gahagan, Galloway, Graham of Montgomery, Hayes of Robeson, Kinney, Logan, Mann, May, Marshall, Morton, Newsom, Ragland, Renfrow, Rhodes, Rose, Teague and Welker—21.

Those who voted in the negative are:

Messrs. Andrews, Ashley, Aydlott, Baker, Benbow, Blume, Bradley, Bryan, Carey, Colgrove, Congleton, Cox, Daniel, Dowd, Durham, Ellis, Eppes, Etheridge, Forkner, Franklin, George, Glover, Grant of Northampton, Gully, Gunter, Hare, Harris of Wake, Hay, Heaton, Highsmith, Hobbs, Hodnett, Hoffler, Hollowell, Holt, Hyman, Ing, Jones of Caldwell, King of Lincoln, King of Lenoir, Lee, Legg, Lennon, Long, McCubbins, Merritt, McDonald of Chatham, Nicholson, Parker, Parks, Petree, Pierson, Pool, Read, Rich, Robbins, Rodman, Sanderlin, Smith, Stilly, Stilwell, Sweet, Taylor, Turner and Watts—63.

Mr. Hood withdrew his amendment.

The section, as read, was adopted.

The Article on Eligibility to Office passsed its second reading by the following vote, yeas 51, nays 34:

Those who voted in the affirmative are:

Messrs. Andrews, Ashley, Aydlott, Baker, Benbow, Blume, Bryan, Carey, Cherry, Chillson, Colgrove, Congleton, Cox, Daniel, Dowd, Eppes, Forkner, George, Glover, Grant of Northampton, Gunter, Harris of Wake, Hay, Heaton, Highsmith, Hobbs, Hoffler, Hollowell, Ing, Jones of Caldwell, King of Lincoln, King of Lenoir, Legg, Mann, Mayo, McDonald of Chatham, Nicholson, Parker, Parks, Pierson, Pool, Read, Rich, Robbins, Rodman, Stilly, Stilwell, Sweet, Taylor, Turner and Watts—51.

Those who voted in the negative are:

Messrs. Abbott, Candler, Dickey, Durham, Ellis, Etheridge, French of Bladen, French of Rockingham, Gahagan, Galloway, Graham of Montgomery, Hare, Hayes of Robeson, Holt, Kinney, Lennon, Logan, May, Marshall, McCubbins, Merritt, Moore, Morton, Nance, Newsom, Ragland, Renfrow, Rhodes, Rose, Sanderlin, Smith, Trogden, Tucker and Welker—34.

On motion, the report of the Committee on the Judicial Department was taken up.

Section 29th was amended by adding the following words:

"In case of a vacancy existing from any cause, in any of the offices created by this section, the Commissioners for the County may appoint to such office for the unexpired term."

Mr. Tourgee moved to amend section third by striking out, "General Assembly," and insert "Governor."

The amendment was accepted.

The report of the Committee on the Judicial Department, passed its second reading by the following vote, yeas 62, nays 12:

Those who voted in the affirmative are:

Messrs. Abbott, Andrews, Ashley, Aydlott, Barnes, Benbow, Blume, Bryan, Carey, Candler, Chillson, Colgrove, Congleton, Cox, Duckworth, Eppes, Fisher, Forkner, Franklin, French of Rockingham, French of Chowan, Fullings, Gahagan, Galloway, George, Grant of Northampton, Gunter, Hay, Hayes of Robeson, Heaton, Highsmith, Hobbs, Hollowell, Hyman, Ing, Jones of Caldwell, Kinney, Laflin, Legg, Long, May, Mayo, McDonald of Chatham, Nance, Nicholson, Parker, Parks, Read, Rhodes, Rich, Robbins, Rodman, Rose, Smith, Stilwell, Sweet, Teague, Tourgee, Trogden, Tucker, Watts and Welker—62.

Those who voted in the negative are:

Messrs. Baker, Bradley, Dowd, Durham, Ellis, Etheridge, Hare, Holt, McCubbins, Merritt, Pool and Sanderlin—12.

The following remaining report of the Committee on the Judicial Department was taken up and passed its first reading:

## REPORT OF COMMITTEE.

The undersigned respectfully report the within as part of their report on the organization of the Judicial Department.

WILL. B. RODMAN, *Chairman.*
G. WM. WELKER,
A. W. TOURGEE,
E. B. TEAGUE,
A. H. GALLOWAY.

---

## JUSTICES OF THE PEACE.

SECTION 1. In each township (precinct or other subdivision) of the Counties of this State, two Justices of the Peace shall be elected by the qualified voters thereof, as is prescribed for the election of members of the General Assembly. The General Assembly may provide for the election of a larger number in Cities and Towns, and in those townships in which Cities and Towns are situated. They shall hold their offices for two years.

SEC. 2. They shall have jurisdiction under such regulations as the General Assembly shall prescribe of all civil actions founded on contract, wherein the sum demanded shall not exceed two hundred dollars, and wherein the title to real estate shall not be in controversy; and of all criminal matters arising within their Counties, where the punishment cannot exceed a fine of fifty dollars or imprisonment for one month. When an issue of fact shall be joined before a Justice, on the demand of either party thereto, he shall cause a jury of six men to be summoned, who shall try the same. The party against whom judgment shall be rendered in any civil action may appeal to the Superior Court from the same, and if the judgment shall exceed twenty five dollars, there shall be a new trial of the whole matter in the Appellate Court; but if the judgment shall be for twenty-five dollars, or less, then the case shall be heard in the Appellate Court, only upon matters of law. In all cases of a criminal nature, the party against whom judgment is given, may appeal to the Superior Court, where the matter shall be heard anew. In all cases of a criminal nature brought before a Justice, he shall make a record of the proceeding, and file the same with the Clerk of the Superior Court for his County.

SEC. 3. When the office of Justice of the Peace shall become vacant, otherwise than by the the expiration of the term, and in case of a failure by the voters of any district to elect, the Clerk of the Superior Court for the County shall appoint to fill the vacancy for the unexpired term.

SEC. 4. In case the office of Clerk of the Superior Court for a County shall become vacant, otherwise than by the expiration of the term, and in case of a failure by the people to elect, the Judge of the Superior Court for the County shall appoint to fill the vacancy until an election can be regularly held.

SEC. 5. The General Assembly may provide, by law, that the Judges of the Superior Courts, instead of being elected by the voters of the whole State, as is herein provided for, shall be elected by the voters of their respective districts.

---

Motion by Mr. Rodman to amend section 29 of report on Judicial Department by adding to said section 29, as amended on the 28th of February, the following words:

"In case of a vacancy existing from any cause, in any of the offices created by this section, the Commissioners for the County may appoint to such office for the unexpired term."

On the second reading,

Mr. Candler moved to amend section 1st by striking out "five," and insert "four."

The amendment was not sustained.

The section, as read, was adopted.

Section 2d was read.

Mr. Tourgee moved to amend by striking out "shall," on fourteenth line, and insert "may."

The amendment was accepted by the Chairman of the Committee.

The section, as amended, was adopted.

Section 3d was read and adopted.

Section 4th was read.

Mr. Sweet moved to strike out the entire section.

The motion did not prevail.

The section, as read, was adopted.

Section 5th was read and adopted.

The report passed its second reading by the following vote, yeas 56, nays 5:

Those who voted in the affirmative are:

Messrs. Ashley, Aydlott, Benbow, Blume, Bryan, Carey, Candler, Chillson, Colgrove, Congleton, Dickey, Duckworth, Eppes, Etheridge, Fisher, Forkner, French of Rockingham, Fullings, Gahagan, Galloway, George, Gunter, Hay, Hayes of Robeson, Heaton, Hobbs, Hollowell, Hood, Hyman, Ing, Kinney, Laflin, May, Mayo, Marshall, McDonald of Chatham, Morton, Nicholson, Parker, Parks, Peterson, Ragland, Ray, Read, Rhodes, Rodman, Rose, Smith, Stillwell, Sweet, Teague, Tourgee, Tucker, Turner, Watts and Welker—56.

Those who voted in the negative are:

Messrs. Baker, Dowd, Merritt, Pool and Sanderlin—5.

On motion of Mr. Rodman, the entire report of the Committee on the Judicial Department was made a Special Order Tuesday at 10½ o'clock.

Mr. Heaton introduced an Ordinance in relation to the authentication of ordinances and other acts of the Convention.

Leave of absence was granted:

Mr. Hare for three days, also,

Mr. Graham, of Orange, until Wednesday next.

On motion, the House adjourned.

TUESDAY, March 10th, 1868.

The Convention was called to order at 10 o'clock, by the President.

Prayer by the Rev. G. W. Welker.

The Roll was called, and the following members answered to their name.

Messrs. Ashley, Aydlott, Baker, Barnes, Benbow, Bradley, Bryan, Carey, Carter, Candler, Cherry, Chillson, Colgrove, Congleton, Cox, Daniel, Dickey, Dowd, Duckworth, Durham, Ellis, Eppes, Etheridge, Fisher, Forkner, Franklin, French of Rockingham, French of Chowan, Fullings, Gahagan, Galloway, Garland, Garrett, George, Graham of Montgomery, Grant of Northampton, Gunter, Harris of Wake, Hay, Hayes of Robeson, Hayes of Halifax, Highsmith, Hobbs, Hodnett, Hoffler, Hollowell, Holt, Hood, Hyman, Ing, Jones of Caldwell, King of Lincoln, King of Lenoir, Kinney, Lee, Legg, Lennon, Logan, Long, Mann, Mayo, Marshall, McCubbins, Merritt, McDonald of Moore, Moore, Mullican, Murphy, Nance, Newsom, Nicholson, Parker, Parks, Petree, Peterson, Pierson, Pool, Ragland, Ray, Read, Renfrow, Rhodes, Rich, Robbins, Rodman, Rose, Sanderlin, Smith, Stilly, Stilwell, Taylor, Teague, Tourgee, Trogden, Tucker, Turner, Watts, Welker, and Williams of Wake—99.

The Journal of Monday was read and approved.

Mr. C. C. Pool, Chairman of the Committee on Enrollment and Engrossment reported as follows:

The Committee on Enrollment respectfully report that they have examined the Enrolled Articles on Preamble and Bill of Rights, Executive Department, Legislative Department, Corporations other than Municipal and Militia, and upon careful comparison with the original ordinances find the same to be correct.

C. C. POOL, *Chairman.*

The report was accepted and adopted.

The Committee on Contingent Expenses reported that they had examined the accounts of Wm. Hardie and Isaiah Hardie, and recommend the payment to each, of seventeen dollars.

The report was adopted.

The Committee to whom the subject was referred, reported the following as a section in the Constitution :

SECTION — The General Assembly shall provide by proper Legislation for giving to Mechanics and Laborers an adequate lien on the subject matter of their labor.

Would respectfully recommend it passage,

BYRON LAFLIN,
J. H. BAKER,
MARK MAY,
M. J. AYDLOTT,
HENRY EPPES.

The report was accepted.

The Committee on Internal Improvements to whom was referred the ordinance in relation to the Fayetteville and Florence Rail Road have had the same under consideration, and have instructed me to report the ordinance back with the privilege of the introducer to withdraw it at his request.

W. G. B. GARRETT, *Chairman.*

The report was accepted.

The Committee on Internal Improvements to whom was referred the ordinance to change the manner of payment of the States subscription to the capital stock of the Western Rail Road Company have had the same under consideration and instruct me to report back to the Convention, the 1st section. They also have instructed me to report back the 2nd section and recommend its passage.

O. S. HAYES, *Acting Chairman.*

The report was on motion, accepted.

The Committee on Internal Improvements to whom was referred the ordinance to amend the Charter of the Chatham Rail Road Company, have had the same under consideration and have instructed me to report the same back to the Convention, and recommend its passage.

O. S. HAYES, *Acting Chairman.*

On motion the report was accepted.

The Committee appointed to investigate the difficulty between Messrs Durham and Ashley reported as follows:

The Committee on the subject of the difficulty between Messrs. Durham and Ashley, on account of words spoken in debate beg leave to report: That according to our understanding of Parliamentary law we have no power to act in the case, because the words to which exception was taken were not noted down by the member excepting immediately, and the attention of the Convention then and there called to the subject.

We therefore respectfully ask to the excused from further service in this matter.

WILLIE DANIEL<br>
WM. NICHOLSON,<br>
D. J. RICH.<br>
J. R. ELLIS,<br>
SAM'L FORKNER.

The report was accepted.

On motion the report of the Committee on Internal Improvement was made a special order for Wednesday at 10½ o'clock.

The report of the Committee on the Judicial Department was taken up and placed on its third and final reading and passage.

Section 1st was read.

Mr. Pool moved to amend by striking out all down to the word "and" immediately preceeding the words "every action prosecuted."

The amendment did not prevail.

The section as read was adopted.

Section 2d was read.

Mr. Rodman amended by adding to the section the following words:

"And the Convention shall provide for the commissioners a reasonable compensation."

The section as amended was adopted.

Section 3d was read.

Mr. Tourgee moved to amend by striking out "General Assembly" and insert "Governor."

The amendment was adopted.

The section as amended was adopted.

Sections 4th, 5th, 6th and 7th were read and adopted.

Section 8th was read.

Mr. Rodman moved to amend by striking out "two" and insert "four" and add to the end of the section the following:

"But the General Assembly shall have power to decrease the number after the first term of the same shall be found expedient on the expiration of the term.

The yeas and nays were demanded.

The demand was sustained.

The amendment was adopted by the following vote, yeas 49, nays 48:

Those who voted in the affirmative are:

Messrs. Abbott, Ashley, Bryan, Chillson, Colgrove, Daniel, Dickey, Eppes, Fisher, Franklin, French of Bladen, French of Chowan, Fullings, Galloway, Graham of Montgomery, Grant of Wayne, Grant of Northampton, Hayes, of Robeson, Highsmith, Hood, Hyman, Ing, Jones of Caldwell, Kinney, Laflin, Legg, Logan, Mann, Mayo, Marshall, Merritt, McDonald of Moore, Moore, Morton, Murphy, Nicholson, Patrick, Parker, Pierson, Ragland, Ray, Renfrow, Rich, Rodman, Sweet, Taylor, Tourgee, Watts, and Welker—49.

Those who voted in the negative, are:

Messrs. Aydlott, Baker, Benbow, Bradley, Candler, Congleton, Cox, Dowd, Duckworth, Durham, Ellis, Etheridge, Forkner, French of Rockingham, Gahagan, Garland, Garrett, George, Glover, Gunter, Hay, Hobbs, Hodnett, Hoffler, Hollowell, Holt, King of Lincoln, King of Lenoir, Lennon, Long, May, McCubbins, Mullican, Nance, Parks, Petree, Peterson, Read, Rose, Sanderlin, Smith, Stilly, Stilwell, Teague, Trogden, Tucker, Turner, and Williams of Wake—48.

The section as amended was adopted.

Section 9th was read.

Mr. Tourgee moved to amend by striking out the following words:

"And its decisions shall be remitted to the Courts below to be enforced."

The amendment was accepted by the Chairman of the Committee.

The section as amended was adopted.

Sections 10th, 11th, 12th, 13th, 14th, 15th and 16th were read and adopted.

Section 17th was read.

Mr. Durham moved to amend by adding:

"*Provided*, That white orphan children shall not be bound as apprentices to colored masters and no colored person shall be appointed guardian of a white ward."

The yeas and nays were demanded.

The call was not sustained.

The amendment was lost.

The section as read was adopted.

Sections 18th, 19, 20th, 21st, 22d, 23d, 24th, 25th, 26th, 27th, 28th, 29th, 30th, 31st, and 32d, were read and adopted.

Section 33d was amended by inserting after the words "they shall have" in line first the words "exclusive original."

The section as amended was adopted.

Section 34th, 35th and 36th were read and adopted.

On motion of Mr. French, of Chowan, the vote on section 26th was reconsidered.

Mr. French, moved to amend by striking out "three" and insert "four" in line ten; eleventh line strike out "four, six and eight years" and insert "two, four, six and eight years."

The amendment was adopted.

The section as amended was adopted.

The report of the Committee on the Judicial Department passed its third and final reading by the following vote, yeas 80, nays 20.

Those who voted in the affirmative are:

Messrs. Ashley, Aydlott, Barnes, Benbow, Bryan, Carey,

Carter, Cherry, Chillson, Colgrove, Congleton, Cox, Dickey, Duckworth, Eppes Fisher, Forkner, Franklin, French of Bladen, French of Rockingham, French of Chowan, Fullings, Gahagan, Galloway, Garland, Garrett, George, Glover, Graham of Montgomery, Gully, Gunter, Harris of Wake, Hayes of Robeson, Hayes of Halifax, Heaton, Highsmith, Hobbs, Hood, Hyman, Ing, Kinney, Laflin, Legg, Logan, Long, Mann, May, Mayo, Marshall, McDonald of Moore, Moore, Morton, Mullican, Murphy, Nance, Nicholson, Patrick, Parker, Parks, Petree, Peterson, Pierson, Ragland, Read, Renfrow, Rhodes, Rich, Robbins, Rodman, Rose, Smith, Stilly, Stilwell, Sweet, Taylor, Tourgee, Tucker, Welker and Williams of Wake—80.

Those who voted in the negative, are:

Messrs. Baker, Bradley, Candler, Daniel, Dowd, Durham, Ellis, Etheridge, Hay, Hodnett, Hoffler, Hollowell, Holt, Jones of Caldwell, King of Lincoln, King of Lenoir, McCubbins, Merritt, Pool, Sanderlin and Trogden—20.

Mr. Rich introduced an ordinance protecting the interest of consigners of freights.

Referred to the Commitee of Sixteen.

On motion of Mr. Heaton, the report of the Committee on Miscellaneous Affairs, was returned to that Committee to be printed and added to their regular report to be presented to the House at the next morning session.

On motion the matter of pay in regard to members, who have lately occupied contested seats, was referred to the Committee on Privileges and Elections.

The report of the Committee on Penal Institutions, Public Charities, &c., was taken up and passed on its third and final reading and passage.

Section 1st was read.

Mr. Tourgee moved to amend by inserting "only," after the word, "rape."

The amendment was adopted.

Mr. Rodman moved to amend by striking out "shall," and insert "may."

The amendment was adopted.

The section, as amended, was adopted.

Sections 2d, 3d, 4th, 5th, 6th, 7th, 8th and 9th were read and adopted.

Sections 10th and 11th were read and adopted.

The Report of the Committee on Penal Institutions, Public Charities, etc., passed its third and final reading, by the following vote, yeas 79, nays 11:

Those who voted in the affirmative, are:

Messrs. Abbott, Ashley, Benbow, Bradley, Bryan, Carey, Carter, Candler, Cherry, Chillson, Colgrove, Congleton, Cox, Daniel, Dickey, Duckworth, Eppes, Fisher, Forkner, Franklin, French of Bladen, French of Rockingham, French of Chowan, Fullings, Gahagan, Galloway, Garland, George, Glover, Graham of Montgomery, Gully, Gunter, Harris of Wake, Hay, Hayes of Robeson, Heaton, Highsmith, Hood, Hyman, Ing, Kinney, Laflin, Lee, Legg, Logan, Long, May, Mayo, Marshall, McDonald of Moore, Moore, Morton, Mullican, Murphy, Nance, Nicholson, Patrick, Parker, Parks, Petree, Peterson, Pierson, Pool, Ragland, Ray, Read, Rhodes, Rich, Robbins, Rodman, Smith, Stilly, Stilwell, Sweet, Teague, Tourgee, Tucker, Welker and Williams of Wake—79.

Those who voted in the negative, are:

Messrs. Dowd, Durham, Ellis, Etheridge, Hobbs, Hoffler, Holt, Lennon, McCubbins, Merritt and Sanderlin—11.

On Motion of Mr. French, of Bladen, the following ordinance, introduced by himself, was taken up:

SECTION 1. *Be it ordained by the people of North-Carolina, by delegates in Convention assembled, and it is hereby ordained by the authority of the same,* That any person who shall seek to intimidate or try to prevent any qualified elector from the free exercise of the elective franchise, by threats or otherwise, shall be deemed guilty of a mssdemeanor, and upon conviction thereof, shall be punished by imprisonment for not less than one month or more than six months, or by fine of not less than one hundred dollars, or more than five hundred dollars.

SEC. 2. *Be it further ordained,* That this ordinance shall be in force from and after its passage, but may be amended or repealed by the General Assembly.

Mr. George moved to amend by striking out all after the words, "by the authority of the same," down to the words, "shall be punished," and inserting, "that if any person attempts to control the vote of any person, who is an elector in this State, by threats, bribing or force, he."

Also, strike out all after the word "punished," down to "by a fine of."

On motion of Mr. Tourgee, the entire subject was committed to a Committee of three, to report Thursday next.

On motion, the following ordinance introduced by Mr. Heaton, was taken up.

SECTION 1. *Be it ordained by the Convention of North-Carolina, and it is hereby ordained by the authority of the same,* That Wm. H. S. Sweet, Chas. R. Dutton, Stephen Northrup and their associates, successor and assigns, are hereby created and constituted a body corporate and politic, by the name and style, and title of the Newbern Turpentine Company, and by that name may sue and be sued, plead and be impleaded, appear, prosecute and defend in any Court of law and equity whatsoever, in all suits and actions, may have a common seal, and alter the same at pleasure, and may purchase, hold and convey real and personal estate, to an amount not exceeding two hundred and fifty thousand dollars.

SEC. 2. *Be it further ordained,* That the first meeting of said Corporation may be called by the persons named in this ordinance, or any of them, at such time and place as they may agree upon, and at such meetings, and at all other meetings legally notified, said Corporation may make, alter and repeal such by-laws and regulations for the management of the business of said Corporation, as a majority of the stock may direct, not repugnant to the laws of this State, or of the United States.

SEC. 3. *Be it further ordained,* That the said Corporation may divide their original stock into such number of shares, and provide for the sale and transfer thereof, in such manner and form as said Corporation shall, from time to time, deem expedient, and may levy and collect assessments, forfeit and sell delinquent shares, declare and pay dividends on the shares in such manner as the by-laws shall direct.

SEC. 4. *Be it further ordained*, That it shall be the duty of the Directors, one of whom shall reside continually in the State, to have regular books of record, and transfers thereof at all times open to the inspection of the stockholders.

SEC. 5. *Be it further ordained*, That this Corporation shall continue in force thirty years from and after the passage of this ordinance.

The yeas and nays were ordered on its passage.

The ordinance was adopted by the following vote, yeas 68, nays —:

Those who voted in the affirmative, are:

Messrs. Abbott, Ashley, Bradley, Bryan, Carey, Carter, Chillson, Colgrove, Congleton, Cox, Duckworth, Etheridge, Fisher, Franklin, French of Rockingham, French of Chowan, Fullings, Gahagan, Galloway, George, Graham of Montgomery, Grant of Wayne, Grant of Northampton, Gunter, Hall, Harris of Wake, Hay, Hayes of Robeson, Hayes of Halifax, Heaton, Highsmith, Hobbs, Hodnett, Hoffler, Hollowell, Holt, Hood, Hyman, Ing, King of Lenoir, Kinney, Lee, Legg, Logan, Long, Mayo, McCubbins, McDonald of Moore, Moore, Morton, Murphy, Nance, Nicholson, Patrick, Parker, Parks, Pierson, Ray, Read, Rich, Robbins, Rose, Sanderlin, Smith, Stilwell, Tucker, Welker and Williams of Wake—68.

Mr. Morton introduced, by permission, the following resolution:

*Resolved*, That this Convention adjourn on Monday, the 16th instant, subject to the call of the President.

On motion, the rules were suspended.

After some discussion, Mr. French, of Bladen, moved to lay the whole matter on the table.

The motion was not sustained.

On motion of Mr. Harris, of Wake, the subject was postponed until 10½ o'clock Wednesday.

Mr. Rodman introduced an ordinance in relation to authenticating, etc.

Lies over under the rules.

On motion, the House adjourned.

EVENING SESSION, MARCH 10TH, 1868.

The Convention was called to order at 7½ o'clock, by the President.

The roll was called and the following members answered to their names:

Messrs. Ashley, Aydlott, Baker, Barnes, Benbow, Blume, Bradley, Bryan, Carey, Carter, Cherry, Chillson, Colgrove, Congleton, Cox, Daniel, Dowd, Duckworth, Durham, Ellis, Eppes, Etheridge, Fisher, Forkner, Franklin, French of Bladen, French of Rockingham, French of Chowan, Fullings, Gahagan, Galloway, Garland, Garrett, George, Graham of Montgomery, Grant of Northampton, Gully, Gunter, Hall, Harris of Wake, Hay, Hayes of Robeson, Hayes of Halifax, Highsmith, Hobbs, Hodnett, Hoffler, Hollowell, Holt, Hood, Hyman, Jones of Caldwell, Jones, of Washington, King of Lincoln, King of Lenoir, Kinney, Laflin, Lee, Lennon, Logan, Long, Mann, Mayo, Marshall, McCubbins, Merritt, Moore, Morton, Mullican, Murphy, Nance, Nicholson, Parker, Parks, Petree, Peterson, Pierson, Pool, Ragland, Ray, Read, Renfrow, Rhodes, Rich, Robbins, Rose, Smith, Stilwell, Sweet, Taylor, Teague, Tourgee, Trogden, Tucker, Turner, Watts and Welker—96.

The report of the Committee on Suffrage and Eligibility to Office, having been made a Special Order for the evening, was taken up and placed on its third and final reading and passage.

Section 1st was read.

Mr. French moved to amend by inserting after the word "elector," in sixth line, "except as hereinafter provided."

The amendment was adopted, yeas 54, nays 50.

Those who voted in the affirmative are:

Messrs. Abbott, Ashley, Benbow, Blume, Bryan, Carter, Candler, Chillson, Cox, Dickey, Duckworth, Fisher, Franklin, French of Bladen, French of Rockingham, Fullings, Gahagan, Galloway, Garland, Glover, Graham of Montgomery, Hall, Hayes of Robeson, Hayes of Halifax, Ing, Jones of Washington, Kinney, Laflin, Lee, Logan, Mann, May, Mayo, Marshall, McDonald of Moore, Moore, Morton, Mullican, Murphy,

Parks, Petree, Ragland, Ray, Renfrow, Robbins, Rose, Smith, Teague, Tourgee, Trogden, Tucker, Turner, Watts and Welker—54.

Those who voted in the negative are:

Messrs. Aydlott, Baker, Barnes, Bradley, Carey, Cherry, Colgrove, Congleton, Daniel, Dowd, Durham, Ellis, Etheridge, Forkner, French of Chowan, Grant of Wayne, Grant of Northampton, Gully, Gunter, Harris of Wake, Hay, Heaton, Highsmith, Hobbs, Hodnett, Hoffler, Hollowell, Holt, Jones of Caldwell, King of Lincoln, King of Lenoir, Lennon, Long, McCubbins, Merritt, Nance, Nicholson, Patrick, Parker, Peterson, Pierson, Pool, Read, Rich, Rodman, Sanderlin, Stilly, Stilwell, Sweet and Taylor—50.

The section, as amended, was adopted.

Mr. French, of Bladen, offered the following as a section, to follow section 1st:

"The General Assembly shall, at its first session, and as often thereafter as may be deemed necessary, provide for the registration of all voters, and no person shall be entitled to vote unless properly registered, and every person hereafter offering to register, shall take the following oath:

I, ———, do solemnly swear (or affirm) in the presence of Almighty God, that I am a citizen of the State of North-Carolina, that I have resided in said State twelve months next preceding this day, and in the County of ——— thirty days, that I am twenty one years old, that I have never been convicted of any infamous crime since becoming a citizen of the United States, that I am not, nor have I ever been disfranchised by what is known as the Reconstruction Acts of Congress, and that I will faithfully support the Constitution and laws of the United States and of the State of North-Carolina, not inconsistent therewith. So help me God.

"Which oath may be administered by any authorized registration officer, and any person who shall knowingly and falsely take or subscribe the above oath, such person so offending, and being thereof duly convicted, shall be subject to the pains, penalties and disabilities which, by law, are prescribed for the punishment of willful and corrupt perjury: *Provided*,

That only the last clause of the above oath, viz: (that I will faithfully support the Constitution and laws of the United States, and of the State of North-Carolina, not inconsistent therewith. So help me God.) Shall be required of any person whose disabilities to hold office under the fourteenth Article of the Constitution of the United States, (known as the Howard Amendment,) have been or may hereafter be removed by Congress, or of any person who may be (upon his own application,) declared an elector by the General Assembly, a majority of each House voting therefor."

Mr. Heaton offered the following as a substitute for the new section of Mr. French:

SECTION 2. It shall be the duty of the General Assembly to provide, from time to time, for the registration of all electors, but no person shall be allowed to register without first being required to take an oath or affirmation, to support the Constitution and laws of the United States, and laws of North-Carolina, not inconsistent therewith.

Mr. Abbott offered the following oath as a substitute for the oath of Mr. Heaton:

OATH OF OFFICE.

I am truly and devotedly attached to the Union of all the States, and opposed to any dissolution of the same, that I entertain no political sympathy with the instigators and leaders of the rebellion, or with the enemies of the Union, nor approbation of their principles or purposes, that I will neither by word or act encourage or countenance a spirit of sedition or disaffection towards the government of the United States or the laws thereof, and that I will sustain and defend the Union of these States, and will discourage and resist all efforts to destroy or impair the same.

The question was called on the amendment of Mr. Abbott.

The yeas and nays were demanded.

The amendment did not prevail by the following vote, yeas 26, nays 73:

Those who voted in the affirmative, are:

Messrs. Abbott, Ashley, Bryan, Carter, Candler, Chillson, Dickey, Duckworth, Fisher, French of Bladen, French of Rockingham, French of Chowan, Galloway, Garland, Graham of Montgomery, Hayes of Halifax, Jones of Washington, Kinney, Logan, May, Mayo, Morton, Petree, Rose, Teague and Welker—26.

Those who voted in the negative, are:

Messrs. Aydlott, Baker, Barnes, Benbow, Blume, Bradley, Cherry, Colgrove, Congleton, Cox, Daniel, Dowd, Durham, Ellis, Eppes, Etheridge, Forkner, Franklin, Fullings, Gahagan, George, Grant of Wayne, Grant of Northampton, Gully, Gunter, Harris of Wake, Hay, Hayes of Robeson, Heaton, Highsmith, Hobbs, Hodnett, Hoffler, Hollowell, Holt, Hood, Hyman, Ing, Jones of Caldwell, King of Lincoln, King of Lenoir, Laflin, Lennon, Long, Mann, Marshall, McCubbins, Merritt, Moore, Mullican, Nance, Nicholson, Parker, Parks, Peterson, Pierson, Pool, Ragland, Ray, Read, Renfrow, Rich, Rodman, Sanderlin, Smith, Stilly, Stilwell, Sweet, Taylor, Tucker, Turner and Watts—73.

The question recurred on the substitute of Mr. Heaton.

The yeas and nays were demanded.

The call was sustained.

The substitute was adopted by the following vote, yeas 74, nays 27:

Those who voted in the affirmative, are:

Messrs. Abbott, Ashley, Aydlott, Barnes, Benbow, Blume, Bryan, Carey, Carter, Chillson, Colgrove, Congleton, Cox, Duckworth, Eppes, Forkner, Franklin, French of Bladen, French of Chowan, Fullings, Galloway, George, Graham of Montgomery, Grant of Wayne, Grant of Northampton, Gully, Gunter, Hall, Harris of Wake, Hayes of Robeson, Hayes of Halifax, Heaton, Highsmith, Hobbs, Hood, Hyman, Jones of Caldwell, King of Lincoln, Laflin, Logan, Long, Mann, McDonald of Moore, Moore, Morton, Mullican, Murphy, Nance, Nicholson, Parker, Parks, Petree, Peterson, Pierson, Pool, Ragland, Ray, Read, Renfrow, Rich, Rodman, Rose, Smith, Stilly, Stilwell, Sweet, Taylor, Teague, Tourgee, Trogden, Tucker, Turner, Watts and Welker—74.

Those who voted in the negative are:

Messrs. Baker, Bradley, Candler, Daniel, Dowd, Durham, Ellis, Etheridge, Fisher, French of Rockingham, Gahagan, Garland, Hay, Hodnett, Hoffler, Hollowell, Holt, Ing, Jones of Washington, Kinney, Lennon, May, Mayo, Marshall, McCubbins, Merritt and Sanderlin—22.

Mr. French, of Bladen, moved to amend the substitute.

The Chair ruled the amendment out of order.

From which decision an appeal was taken, when the Chair was sustained.

Mr. French, of Bladen, moved to reconsider the vote on the substitute.

Pending which, the House adjourned.

---

WEDNESDAY, MARCH 11TH, 1868.

The Convention was called to order at 11 o'clock, by the President.

Prayer by the Rev. Mr. Lennon.

The Roll was called and the following members answered to their names:

Messrs. Abbott, Ashley, Aydlott, Baker, Barnes, Benbow, Blume, Bradley, Bryan, Carey, Carter, Candler, Cherry, Chilson, Colgrove, Congleton, Cox, Daniel, Dickey, Duckworth, Durham, Ellis, Eppes, Etheridge, Fisher, Forkner, French of Bladen, French of Rockingham, French of Chowan, Fullings, Gahagan, Galloway, Garland, Garrett, George, Glover, Graham of Montgomery, Grant of Northampton, Gully, Gunter, Hall, Harris of Wake, Harris of Franklin, Hay, Hayes of Robeson, Hayes of Halifax, Heaton, Highsmith, Hodnett, Hoffler, Holt, Hood, Hyman, Ing, Jones of Caldwell, Jones of Washington, King of Lincoln, King of Lenoir, Kinney, Laflin, Lee, Legg, Lennon, Logan, Long, Mann, Mayo, McCubbins, Merritt, McDonald of Moore, Moore, Morton, Mullican, Murphy, Nance, Newsom, Nicholson, Patrick, Parker, Parks, Petree, Peterson, Pierson, Ragland, Ray, Read, Renfrow, Rhodes, Rich, Robbins, Rose, Sanderlin, Smith, Stilly,

Taylor, Teague, Tourgee, Trogden, Tucker, Turner, Watts, Welker and Williams of Wake—106.

The Journal of Tuesday was read and approved.

The following ordinance to amend the Charter of the Chatham Rail Road, was taken up and passed its first reading:

## AN ORDINANCE TO AMEND THE CHARTER OF THE CHATHAM RAIL ROAD COMPANY.

SECTION. 1. *Be it ordained by the people of North-Carolina in Convention assembled*, That to enable the Chatham Rail Road Company to finish its road, the Public Treasurer is hereby authorized and directed to deliver to the President and Directors of the said Rail Road Company, the coupon bonds of the State to an amount not exceeding twelve hundred thousand dollars, ($1,200,000,) signed by the Governor, countersigned by the Public Treasurer and sealed with "The Great Seal of the State," bearing six per cent. interest, the principal payable at the end of thirty years from the date thereof and the coupons of interest payable semi-annually, in such form as the Public Treasurer may direct, to be made payable at such time and place as may be agreed upon by the Public Treasurer.

SEC. 2. *Be it further ordained*, That before the Public Treasurer shall deliver any of said bonds hereby authorized the said Chatham Rail Road Company [shall deposit] with the Public Treasurer the coupon bonds of said Company for the same amount and bearing the same interest and date, the principal and coupons payable at the same time and place as those of the State hereinbefore directed to be issued and paid over to the Chatham Rail Road Company, and to secure the principal and interest of said bonds issued by the Chatham Rail Road Company, the State of North-Carolina shall by this ordinance have a lien upon all the estate of said Company, both real and personal, which they may now have or may hereafter acquire, between the City of Raleigh and the Gulf, the terminus of said Rail Road in the Coalfields, including that at both points, together with all the rights, franchises and powers thereunto belonging or appertaining, or that may hereafter belong or appertain to said Company, which lien shall be more effectually secured by a first mortgage duly executed by said Company to the State and registered in the Register's office in the Counties of Wake and Chatham, and in case of failure of said Company to pay the semi-annual interest on its bonds for twenty four months after such interest shall become due, or to pay the principal of said bonds for twelve months after their maturity, the Board of Internal Improvements for and in behalf of the State may enter upon and take possession of all the property hereinbefore specified and dispose of the same by sale so as to protect the State.

SEC. 3. *Be it further ordained*, That the Chatham Rail Road Company may at any time before maturity take up the bonds of said Company deposited with the Public Treasurer by substituting in lieu thereof coupon bonds of the State or other indebtedness of the State.

SEC. 4. *Be it further ordained*, That the State shall have the privilege at any time within eight years from the passage of this ordinance to subscribe stock in said Company to the amount of six hundred thousand dollars ($600,000) in shares of one hundred dollars ($100) each, and upon certificate of stock being issued to the State by said Company for the same, to surrender the bonds of said Company which had previously been delivered to the State under the provisions of this ordinance.

SEC. 5. *Be it further ordained*, That this ordinance shall take effect and be in force from and after its passage.

On motion the rules were suspended.

The yeas and nays were demanded.

The ordinance was adopted by the following vote, yeas 81, nays 14:

Those who voted in the affirmative, are:

Messrs. Abbott, Andrews, Ashley, Baker, Blume, Bradley, Bryan, Carey, Carter, Candler, Cherry, Chillson, Colgrove, Congleton, Cox, Daniel, Dickey, Dowd, Eppes, Etheridge, Fisher, Forkner, Franklin, French of Bladen, French of Rockingham, French of Chowan, Fullings, Gahagan, Galleway, Garland, Glover, Graham of Montgomery, Grant of Wayne, Gully, Gunter, Hall, Harris of Wake, Harris of Franklin, Hayes of Robeson, Hayes of Halifax, Heaton, Highsmith, Hollowell, Holt, Hood, Hyman, Ing, Jones of Caldwell, Kinney, Laflin, Lee, Legg, Lennon, Logan, Long, Mann, May, Mayo, Marshall, McCubbins, Merritt, McDonald of Moore, Moore, Morton, Mullican, Murphy, Nance, Patrick, Pierson, Ragland, Read, Renfrow, Rich, Rodman, Stilly, Sweet, Taylor, Trogden, Tucker, Watts, and Williams of Wake.—81.

Those who voted in the negative, are:

Messrs. Aydlott, Duckworth, Ellis, George, Grant of Northampton, Hay, Jones of Washington, King of Lenoir, Parker, Peterson, Rhodes, Sanderlin Turner, and Welker—14.

The following report of the Committee on Internal Improvement was taken up :

## REPORT OF COMMITTEE ON INTERNAL IMPROVEMENT.

The Committee on Internal Improvement to whom was referred the ordinance relating tothe Western Rail Road Company have instructed me to report the 1st section to the Convention.

O. S. HAYES, *Acting Chairman.*

---

## AN ORDINANCE TO CHANGE THE MANNER OF PAYMENT OF THE STATE'S SUBSCRIPTION TO THE CAPITAL STOCK OF THE WESTERN RAIL ROAD COMPANY.

SECTION 1. *Be it ordained by the people of North-Carolina, in Convention assembled, and it is hereby ordained by the authority of the same,* That the Western Rail Road Company is hereby authorized to return to the Public Treasurer the sum of one million of dollars of the second mortgage bonds of the Wilmington and Rutherford Rail Road Company, which amount has heretofore been paid by the Public Treasurer to said Company, as the payment of the subscription of the State to the capital stock of said Company, under the authority of the third section of the act of the General Assembly, entitled "An act to enable the Western Rail Road Company to extend its road across the North-Carolina Rail Road to the Virginia line, near Mount Airy, in the County of Surry," ratified the 25th day of February, 1867, and in place thereof the Public Treasurer is hereby authorized and directed to make and deliver to said Western Rail Road Company, one million of dollars of the coupon bonds of the State of North-Carolina, signed by the Governor and countersigned by the Public Treasurer, bearing interest at the rate of six per cent. per annum, the principal and interest payable at such time and such manner and place as the Governor and Public Treasurer may prescribe.

---

The Committee on Internal Improvement to whom was referred the Ordinance relating to the Western Rail Road Company, have had the same under consideration and recommend the passage of the 2nd section of said ordinance.

O. S. HAYES, *Acting Chairman.*

---

SECTION 2. *Be it ordained by the people of North-Carolina in Convention assembled, &c.*, That so much of the third section of the act of the General Assembly, entitled "An act to enable the Western Rail Road Company to complete its road from the Coalfields, in Chatham County, to some point on the North Carolina Rail Road," ratified the 22d December, 1866, as prohibits said Company from negotiating its bonds "at not less than par," be, and the same is hereby repealed; and that this Ordinance shall be in force from and after its passage.

On motion, the rules were suspended.

Mr. Sweet offered the following amendment to section two:

"That no part of the $1,000,000 of bonds to the Western Rail Road Company shall be delivered to said Company, until the President and Directors thereof, shall execute and deliver to the Governor of the State, a first mortgage on the entire road and its property; conditioned to save the State harmless against the loss of both principal and interest of said loan."

Mr. Tourgee offered to amend this amendment, by adding the words after section 1st as section 2d: "and the State shall relinquish all claim to stock in said road."

Mr. Tourgee withdrew his amendment.

The amendment of Mr. Sweet was accepted by Mr. Mann.

Mr. Laflin moved to amend by striking out "one million" and insert "one half million."

The amendment was accepted by Mr. Mann.

The yeas and nays were demanded on the ordinance as amended.

The ordinance as amended was adopted by the following vote yeas 68, nays 18:

Those who voted in the affirmative are:

Messrs. Abbott, Andrews, Ashley, Baker, Benbow, Blume, Bradley, Bryan, Carey, Carter, Candler, Cherry, Chillson, Colgrove, Congleton, Cox, Dickey, Dowd, Eppes, Fisher, Forkner, French of Bladen, French of Rockingham, Fullings, Gahagan, Galloway, Garland, Graham of Montgomery, Grant of Wayne, Gully, Gunter, Hall, Harris of Wake, Harris of Franklin, Hayes of Robeson, Hayes of Halifax, Highsmith, Hobbs, Hood, Hyman, Ing, Jones of Caldwell, Kinney, Laflin, Lee, Legg, Logan, Long, Mann, Mayo, Marshall, McDonald of Moore, Murphy, Nance, Patrick, Parks, Pierson, Ragland, Read, Renfrow, Rich, Sweet, Teague, Tourgee, Trogden, Tucker, Watts, and Welker—68.

Those who voted in the negative, are:

Messrs. Aydlott, Duckworth, Ellis, George, Grant of Northampton, Hay, Jones of Washington, King of Lenoir, Lennon, McCubbins, Moore, Nicholson, Parker, Peterson, Rhodes, Rose, Sanderlin, and Williams of Wake—18.

Mr. Tourgee moved to reconsider the vote on the ordinance relative to the Western Rail Road Company.

Mr. Hood moved to lay the motion on the table.

The motion was sustained.

The following report of the Committee of Seventeen was taken up:

The Committee of Seventeen to whom was referred the ordinance entitled "an ordinance to aid the Williamston and Tarboro' Rail Road Company, have had the same under consideration and ask to report the same back to the Convention with a recommendation that said bill be passed with one amendment, viz: between the letter "a" and the word "mortgage" in the fourth line of section 2d, insert the word "first," all of which is respectfully submitted.

D. HEATON, *Chairman*,

The report was accepted and adopted.

## AN ORDINANCE TO AID THE WILLIAMSTON AND TARBORO' RAIL ROAD COMPANY.

SECTION 1. *Be it ordained by the people of North-Carolina in Convention assembled*, That whenever the President of said Company shall certify to the Governor of the State, that said road is graded, he shall direct the Public Treasurer, to loan in behalf of the State to said Company, the sum of one hundred and fifty thousand dollars in coupon bonds, and said Company shall set aside the receipts of the road, over and its annual expenses as a sinking fund to pay the said debt and interest, the whole amount of said debt and interest to be paid before the said Company shall order any dividends on the stock of the Company, and that said sinking fund so produced shall be semi-annually paid into the Public Treasury.

SEC. 2. *Be it further ordained*, That no part of said loan or bonds shall be delivered to said Company until the President and Directors thereof shall execute and deliver to the Governor of the State a mortgage on the entire road and its property, conditioned to save the State harmless, against the loss of both principal and interest of said loan.

SEC. 3. *Be it further ordained*, That the coupon bonds loaned as aforesaid shall be signed by the Governor, countersigned by the Treasurer, and sealed with The Great Seal of the State, bearing six per centum interest, the principal payable at the end of thirty years from the date thereof and the coupons for the interest payable semi-annually in such form as the Public Treasurer may direct.

SEC. 4. *Be it further ordained*, That said Company may have the exclusive right of transporting persons and freight upon said road at such rates of charges as the Board of Directors may fix, and may have power to farm or lease the same to any person or persons or corporation.

SEC. 5. *Be it further ordained*, That the stockholders of the said Company may pay the stock subscribed by them either in money, labor or material, for constructing said road, as the Board of Directors may determine, and that all Counties and Towns, subscribing stock to said Company, shall do so in the same manner and under the same rules, regulations restrictions, as set forth and prescribed in the act incorporating said Company.

SEC. 6. *Be it further ordained*, That this ordinance shall be in force and take effect from and after its passage.

Mr. Baker amended by striking out the word "said," in second line, and insert "the Williamston and Tarboro' Rail Road."

The yeas and nays were demanded.

The demand was sustained.

The ordinance passed, as amended, by the following vote:

Those who voted in the affirmative are:

Messrs. Abbott, Ashley, Baker, Benbow, Blume, Bryan, Carey, Carter, Cherry, Chillson, Colgrove, Congleton, Cox, Dowd, Fisher, Forkner, French of Bladen, French of Chowan, Fullings, Gahagan, Graham of Montgomery, Grant of Wayne, Gully, Gunter, Harris of Wake, Harris of Franklin, Hayes of

Robeson, Hayes of Halifax, Heaton, Highsmith, Hobbs, Holt, Hood, Ing, Kinney, Laflin, Legg, Long, Mann, May, Mayo, Marshall, Murphy, Nance, Pierson, Ragland, Read, Renfrow, Rich, Rodman, Stilly, Sweet, Tucker, Watts and Welker—55.

Those who voted in the negative are:

Messrs. Aydlott, Barnes, Daniel, Duckworth, Ellis, George, Grant of Northampton, Jones of Washington, King of Lenoir, Parks, Rhodes, Rose, Sanderlin and Williams of Wake—15.

Mr. Hayes, of Halifax, moved a reconsideration of the vote.

Mr. Dowd moved to lay the motion on the table.

The motion was sustained.

The following report of the Committee on inquiry on the validity of acts, etc., was received and adopted:

The Committee to whom the foregoing resolution was referred, respectfully report:

That they were not directed to enquire whether in fact the presiding officer of this Convention was a registered voter or not. They, therefore, did not enquire into these matters of fact, but assumed for the purposes of the inquiry, as seems to be assumed in the resolution, that he was not registered, and was not entitled to register. Your Committee are not aware of any way in which the authenticity or the validity of enactment can be brought into question judicially, upon the ground supposed.

They are not aware of any case in which the validity of Legislative enactment has been questioned, on the ground that any member of the enacting body was disqualified, or that the Speaker was disqualified. No one can look behind the Statute itself, if the body enacting it was possessed of Legislative power.

2d. Again, by the Reconstruction Acts of Congress, the power is conferred on the General Commanding, of the Second District, to judge of the elections and qualifications of the members of this Convention. In several cases where seats were contested, the General referred it to the Convention to decide upon these qualifications, so that this Convention possesses the power usual, if not indispensible to Legislative bodies, of deciding who are, and who are not, lawfully its members.

The General was obliged to pass on, and did pass on and decide in favor of the legal qualification of the delegate from Wilkes, who presides in this body. The decision of the General must be assumed to be correct by this Convention and by every other legislative or judicial body before whom the question may come, until it shall be reversed by this Convention, acting in the regular and accustomed manner.

This Convention has taken no such action. If it shall hereafter do so, then the seat of the delegate will be vacated by him, but the validity of no act previously passed would be thereby impaired, although it might have been passed by a majority of a single vote, which was that of the delegate whose seat was vacated. It is upon this ground that the ousted delegate is entitled to draw his pay until he is ousted.

It is a well known principle of law, that the acts of officers *de facto* cannot be collaterally impeached. This principle has been often applied to hold valid the acts of Sheriffs and other similar officers who were in office, but not rightfully so. Also, to hold valid marriages performed by Justices of the Peace and Ministers who had not been duly commissioned or licensed, but habitually performed the functions of those offices. It is conceived that this principle completely covers the case of the presiding officer of this body.

3d. Your Committee conceive that it will be the duty of this Convention, by ordinance, to provide some means by which the acts and proceedings of the body shall be authenticated. The usual method of doing this is by certificate of the presiding officer and the Secretary. But it is not the only one possible. The Convention might, if it thought proper, require its acts to be authenticated by the certificate of the President alone, or of the Secretary alone. And your Committee are of opinion that whatever mode of authentication of its acts and ordinances should be ordained by this Convention, whether it be by certificate signed by the President and Secretary, or by one of them alone, will be sufficient, and can never admit of any doubt or produce any difficulty.

And the Committee ask to be discharged from the further consideration of the subject.

WILL. B. RODMAN,
DAVID HEATON,
C. C. POOL.

On motion of Mr. Pool, the yeas and nays were demanded on the motion of Mr. Hood to lay the motion of Mr. French, of Bladen, on the table, which motion was the reconsideration of the vote on the substitute of Mr. Heaton, passed as section 2d of the Article of Suffrage.

The call was sustained.

The motion was laid on the table by the following vote:

Those who voted in the affirmative are:

Messrs. Abbott, Ashley, Aydlott, Baker, Barnes, Benbow, Blume, Bradley, Bryan, Carey, Carter, Cherry, Chillson, Col grove, Congleton, Cox, Daniel, Dickey, Dowd, Duckworth, Forkner, French of Chowan, Garrett, George, Grant of Wayne, Grant of Northampton, Gully, Gunter, Hall, Harris of Wake, Harris of Franklin, Hay, Heaton, Hobbs, Hollowell, Hood, Hyman, Ing, Jones of Caldwell, Jones of Washington, King of Lenoir, Kinney, Laflin, Legg, Logan, Long, May, Mayo, Marshall, Murphy, Nance, Nicholson, Patrick, Parker, Parks, Petree, Peterson, Pierson, Pool, Ragland, Ray, Read, Renfrow, Rhodes, Robbins, Rodman, Smith, Stilly, Sweet, Teague, Trogden, Tucker, Watts, Welker and Williams of Wake—75.

Those who voted in the negative, are:

Messrs. Candler, Durham, Ellis, Etheridge, Fisher, French of Bladen, Gahagan, Garland, Graham of Montgomery, Merritt, Rose and Sanderlin—12.

Section 3d of the Article was read and adopted.

The majority report of the Committee on Suffrage passed its third and final reading by the following vote, yeas 80, nays 8:

Those who voted in the affirmative are:

Messrs. Abbott, Ashley, Aydlott, Baker, Rarnes, Benbow, Blume, Bradley, Bryan, Carey, Carter, Cherry, Chillson, Colgrove, Congleton, Cox, Daniel, Dickey, Dowd, Duckworth,

Eppes, Fisher, Forkner, French of Chowan, George, Grant of Wayne, Grant of Northampton, Gully, Gunter, Hall, Harris of Wake, Harris of Franklin, Hay, Heaton, Hobbs, Hoffler, Hollowell, Hood, Hyman, Ing, Jones of Caldwell, Jones of Washington, King of Lenoir, Laflin, Legg, Logan, Long, May, Mayo, Marshall, McDonald of Moore, Moore, Mullican, Murphy, Nance, Nicholson, Patrick, Parker, Parks, Petree, Peterson, Pierson, Pool, Ragland, Ray, Read, Renfrow, Rhodes, Robbins, Rodman, Rose, Smith, Stilly, Sweet, Teague, Tucker, Turner, Watts, Welker and Williams of Wake—80.

Those who voted in the negative are:

Messrs. Candler, Durham, Ellis, Gahagan, Graham of Montgomery, McCubbins, Merritt and Sanderlin—8.

The Article on Eligibility to Office was taken up and placed on its third and final reading and passage.

Section 1st was read and adopted.

Section 2d was read.

Mr. Pool moved to amend by adding after the word "crime," on fifth line, the words, "since becoming citizens of the United States."

The amendment was adopted.

Mr. Marshall offered to amend by adding to the section, "or disqualified by the fourteenth Article of the Constitution of the United States."

Mr. Bryan offered to amend by inserting after the word "citizen," "those debarred from holding office by the fourteenth Article of the Constitution of the United States, known as the Howard Amendment."

Mr. Bryan withdrew his amendment.

Mr. French, of Chowan, offered the following as a substitute to the amendment of Mr. Marshall:

"All persons who have previously taken an oath as a member of Congress, or as an officer of the United States, or as a member of any State Legislature, or as an Executive or Judicial officer of any State, to support the Constitution of the United States, shall have engaged in insurrection or rebellion against the same, or given aid and comfort to the enemies thereof, until such disability be removed by the Congress of the United States."

The yeas and nays were demanded.

The substitute was not adopted, yeas 35, nays 58.

Those who voted in the affirmative are:

Messrs. Abbott, Ashley, Benbow, Bryan, Carter, Candler, Chillson, Dickey, Duckworth, Fisher, French of Bladen, French of Rockingham, French of Chowan, Fullings, Gahagan, Garland, Graham of Montgomery, Hayes of Robeson, Hayes of Halifax, Ing, Jones of Washington, Kinney, Logan, May, Marshall, Murphy, Parks, Petree, Ragland, Ray, Rhodes, Rose, Smith, Tucker and Turner—35.

Those who voted in the negative are:

Messrs. Aydlott, Baker, Barnes, Blume, Bradley, Carey, Cherry, Cowles, Colgrove, Congleton, Cox, Daniel, Dowd, Durham, Ellis, Etheridge, Forkner, George, Grant of Northampton, Gully, Gunter, Hall, Harris of Wake, Harris of Franklin, Hay, Heaton, Highsmith, Hobbs, Hoffler, Holt, Hyman, Jones of Caldwell, King of Lenoir, Laflin, Legg, Lennon, Long, McCubbins, Merritt, McDonald of Moore, Moore, Morton, Mullican, Nance, Nicholson, Patrick, Parker, Pierson, Pool, Read, Rich, Rodman, Sanderlin, Stilly, Teague, Trogden, Welker and Williams of Wake—58.

The question recurred on the amendment of Mr. Marshall.

The yeas and nays were demanded.

The demand was sustained.

The amendment was lost by the following vote, yeas 40, nays 57:

Those who voted in the affirmative are:

Messrs. Abbott, Ashley, Benbow, Blume, Bryan, Carter, Candler, Chillson, Dickey, Fisher, French of Bladen, French of Rockingham, French of Chowan, Fullings, Gahagan, Garland, Graham of Montgomery, Hall, Harris of Franklin, Hayes of Robeson, Hayes of Halifax, Ing, Jones of Washington, Kinney, Logan, May, Marshall, Mullican, Murphy, Parks, Petree, Ragland, Ray, Rhodes, Robbins, Rose, Smith, Teague, Tucker and Turner—40.

Those who voted in the negative, are:

Messrs. Aydlott, Baker, Barnes, Bradley, Carey, Cherry, Colgrove, Congleton, Cowles, Cox, Daniel, Dowd, Durham, Ellis, Etheridge, George, Grant of Northampton, Gully, Gunter, Harris of Wake, Hay, Heaton, Highsmith, Hobbs, Hoffler, Hollowell, Holt, Hood, Hyman, Jones of Caldwell, King of Lenoir, Laflin, Legg, Lennon, Long, Mayo, McCubbins, Merritt, McDonald of Moore, Moore, Morton, Nance, Nicholson, Patrick, Parker, Peterson, Pierson, Pool, Read, Rich, Rodman, Sanderlin, Stilly, Sweet, Trogden, Welker and Williams of Wake—57.

Section 2d, as read, was adopted.

The article on Eligibility to Office then passed its third and final reading by the following vote, yeas 76, nays 9:

Those who voted in the affirmative are:

Messrs. Abbott, Ashley, Aydlott, Baker, Barnes, Benbow, Blume, Bryan, Carey, Carter, Cherry, Chillson, Colgrove, Congleton, Cowles, Cox, Daniel, Dickey, Dowd, Duckworth, Eppes, Forkner, French of Chowan, Gahagan, George, Grant of Northampton, Gully, Gunter, Hall, Harris of Wake, Harris of Franklin, Hayes of Halifax, Heaton, Highsmith, Hobbs, Hoffler, Hollowell, Hood, Hyman, Jones of Caldwell, Jones of Washington, King of Lenoir, Kinney, Laflin, Long, Mayo, McDonald of Moore, Moore, Morton, Mullican, Murphy, Nance, Nicholson, Patrick, Parker, Parks, Petree, Peterson, Pierson, Pool, Ragland, Ray, Rhodes, Rich, Robbins, Rodman, Rose, Smith, Stilly, Sweet, Teague, Tucker, Turner, Welker, Williams of Wake and Williamson—76.

Those who voted in the negative, are:

Messrs. Candler, Durham, Etheridge, Garland, Graham of Montgomery, Holt, Ing, Merritt and Sanderlin—9.

Mr. Abbott introduced a petition of divorce from Joel Evans.

Referred to the Committee of seventeen.

Mr. Harris, by permission, introduced the following resolution:

*Resolved*, That no delegate of this Convention shall receive any further pay until after the adjournment, without the consent of the Convention.

Mr. King, of Lenoir, moved to lay the resolution on the table.

The motion prevailed.

Mr. Harris gave notice that he would renew his resolution in the morning.

Mr. Pool, Chairman of the Committee on Enrollment, reported:

That the Committee have compared the enrolled Articles on Homesteads, Municipal Corporation, and Finance, and certify the same to be correct.

C. C. POOL, *Chairman.*

Mr. French, of Chowan, moved to reconsider the vote on section 4th of the Article on the Judicial Department.

Pending which, on motion, the House adjourned.

---

EVENING SESSION, March 11th, 1868.

The Convention was called to order at 7½ o'clock, by the President.

The Roll was called, and the following members answered to their names:

Messrs. Andrews, Ashley, Aydlott, Baker, Benbow, Blume, Bradley, Bryan, Carter, Cherry, Chillson, Congleton, Cox, Duckworth, Ellis, Eppes, Etheridge, Forkner, Franklin, French of Bladen, French of Rockingham, French of Chowan, Fullings, Gahagan, Galloway, George, Grant of Northampton, Gully, Gunter, Hall, Harris of Wake, Harris of Franklin, Hay, Hayes of Robeson, Hobbs, Hoffler, Hollowell, Hood, Hyman, Ing, Jones of Caldwell, Jones of Washington, King of Lenoir, Kinney, Lee, Legg, Lennon, Logan, Long, Mayo, Marshall, McCubbins, Merritt, McDonald of Moore, Moore, Mullican, Nance, Newsom, Nicholson, Parker, Petree, Pierson, Ray, Robbins, Rose, Sanderlin, Stilly, Stilwell, Sweet, Teague, Trogden, Tucker, Turner, Watts, Welker and Williamson—76.

The ordinance of Relief introdnced by Mr. Rodman was taken up and discussed.

Mr. Pool offered, as a substitute for the ordinance of Mr. Rodman, an ordinance entitled

## AN ORDINANCE TO PREVENT THE SACRIFICE OF THE PROPERTY OF DEBTORS.

WHEREAS, Credit being usually extended upon the estimated value of property owned, such value, at the time, becomes of the essence of the contract, and a condition of the same; and, whereas, by reason of the present extraordinary depreciation of the value of property, owned by the citizens of North-Carolina, sales for the payment of debts, in the present condition of public affairs, would be not only unjust, but utterly ruinous to debtors, and paralyzing to every branch of industry and enterprise; therefore,

SECTION 1. *Be it ordained by the people of North-Carolina in Convention assembled, and it is hereby ordained by the authority of the same,* That hereafter, when any sheriff, constable, or other officer shall levy an execution on property for the satisfaction of any judgment, order or decree rendered, or which may hereafter be rendered, or shall have in his hands any precept for the sale of property heretofore levied upon, such sheriff, constable or other officer, shall summon three disinterested freeholders from the vicinity of such property, who shall view the same, and assess its real value at the date the contract upon which such execution or precept is based, which assessment shall be endorsed upon such execution or precept, and signed by the said freeholders.

SEC. 2. *Be it further ordained,* That no sale shall be made of property for the satisfaction of any judgment, order, or decree already rendered, or that may hereafter be rendered or made, unless the amount of said assessed value be bid or paid for the same. And, in case there shall be no bid to the amount of the said assessed value, the sheriff, constable or other officer shall make return of the fact to court to which such execution, order or precept may be returnable; and upon such return being made, either party, having given the other ten days notice in writing, may move the court to re-assess such property; and upon its appearing to the court that the assessment by the freeholders was not the true value of the property at the date of the contract, for the satisfaction of which a sale is sought to be made, the court shall proceed to hear testimony, and to re-assess the same at its true value at the date aforesaid; from which re-assessment by the court either party may appeal as now provided by law in other cases.

SEC. 3. *Be it further ordained*, That this ordinance shall be subject to amendment, modification or repeal by any future Legislature of the State.

SEC. 3. *Be it further ordained*, That this ordinance shall take effect from and after its passage.

As amended by inserting after the word "turn," in the eighth line, the following words: "return no sale for want of competition among bidders, according to law, and return the same," and striking out the words, "of the fact."

Mr. Pool also accepted the following amendment:

Insert between the words "the" and "amount," on the fourth and sixth lines, the words "three-fourth of."

Mr. Watts moved to amend section 2d by adding the following to the section:

"*Provided*, That nothing contained in the section shall be construed to prevent the debtor from consenting to the sale of the property and authenticating the execution of the title."

The amendment was accepted by Mr. Pool.

The substitute was put to the House and lost by the following vote:

Those who voted in the affirmative, are:

Messrs. Abbott, Andrews, Ashley, Barnes, Benbow, Blume, Bradley, Bryan, Carey, Cox, Duckworth, Forkner, Fullings, Gahagan, George, Glover, Grant of Northampton, Hall, Hay, Heaton, Hollowell, Jones of Caldwell, King of Lincoln, King of Lenoir, McCubbins, Mullican, Nicholson, Parker, Peterson, Pool, Ray, Renfrow, Robbins, Teague, Trogden and Tucker—36.

Those who voted in the negative, are:

Messrs. Aydlott, Baker, Cherry, Chillson, Congleton, Ellis, Eppes, Etheridge, Fisher, French of Bladen, French of Rockingham, Gunter, Harris of Franklin, Hayes of Robeson, Hobbs, Ing, Jones of Washington, Kinney, Laflin, Logan, Long, Mayo, Marshall, Merritt, McDonald of Moore, Moore, Morton, Nance, Patrick, Parks, Ragland, Read, Rhodes, Rich, Rodman, Rose, Sanderlin, Stilly, Stilwell, Sweet, Turner, Watts, Welker and Williamson—44.

The question recurred on the ordinance introduced by Mr. Rodman.

The ordinance was lost by the following vote:

Those who voted in the affirmative, are:

Messrs. Abbott, Aydlott, Blume, Chilson, Etheridge, French of Chowan, Glover, Gunter, Harris of Franklin, Hay, Laflin, Long, Mayo, Marshall, Merritt, McDonald of Moore, Moore, Nance, Newsom, Patrick, Ragland, Read, Rich, Rodman, Sanderlin, Stilly, Stilwell, Sweet, Turner, Welker and Williamson—31.

Those who voted in the negative are:

Messrs. Andrews, Barnes, Benbow, Bradley, Bryan, Carey, Colgrove, Congleton, Cox, Duckworth, Ellis, Eppes, Forkner, French of Bladen, French of Rockingham, Fullings, Gahagan, George, Grant of Northampton, Hall, Hayes of Robeson, Hobbs, Hollowell, Ing, Jones of Washington, King of Lincoln, King of Lenoir, Kinney, Logan, McCubbins, Morton, Mullican, Nicholson, Parker, Parks, Petree, Pool, Ray, Renfrow, Rhodes, Robbins, Rose, Teague, Trogden and Tucker—45.

Mr. Abbott introduced the following resolution:

*Resolved*, That the President of this Convention is authorized and directed to appoint W. H. S. Sweet a Committee to visit Charleston and confer with Major General E. R. S. Canby, Commanding the Second Military District, in relation to the approaching election, the manner of conducting the same, and what is required by this Convention in regard to the same, and report back to the body before the Convention adjourns.

On motion, the rules were suspended, and the resolution passed.

Mr. Morton gave notice that he would move to reconsider the vote on the Relief Ordinance introduced by Mr. Rodman.

On motion the House adjourned.

---

## THURSDAY, March 12th, 1868.

The Convention was called to order at 10 o'clock, by the President.

Prayer by the Rev. Mr. Branson.

The roll was called and the following members answered to their names:

Messrs. Abbott, Andrews, Ashley, Aydlott, Baker, Barnes, Benbow, Blume, Bradley, Bryan, Carey, Carter, Candler, Cherry, Chillson, Colgrove, Congleton, Cox, Dickey, Dowd, Duckworth, Ellis, Eppes, Etheridge, Fisher, Forkner, Franklin, French of Bladen, French of Rockingham, French of Chowan, Fullings, Gahagan, Galloway, Garland, Garrett, George, Glover, Graham of Montgomery, Grant of Wayne, Grant of Northampton, Gunter, Hall, Harris of Franklin, Hay, Hayes of Robeson, Hayes of Halifax, Heaton, Highsmith, Hobbs, Hodnett, Hoffler, Hollowell, Holt, Hood, Hyman, Ing, Jones of Caldwell, Jones of Washington, King of Lincoln, King of Lenoir, Kinney, Laflin, Lee, Legg, Lennon, Logan, Long, May, Mayo, Marshall, McCubbins, Merritt, McDonald of Moore, Moore, Morton, Mullican, Murphy, Nance, Newsom, Nicholson, Patrick, Parker, Parks, Petree, Peterson, Pierson, Pool, Ragland, Ray, Read, Renfrow, Rhodes, Rich, Robbins, Rodman, Rose, Sanderlin, Smith, Stilly, Stilwell, Taylor, Teague, Tourgee, Tucker, Turner, Watts, Welker, Williams of Wake, and Williamson—109.

Leave of absence was granted Messrs. Ing, Long, Garland, and Garrett.

On motion, the rules were suspended.

On motion, the order of adjournment was recinded.

The Chair announced the following Committee to report

in relation to the ordinance respecting the Intimidation of voters:

Messrs. Tourgee, Ellis, and Harris of Wake, with instructions to report at Friday evening's session.

Mr. Morton's resolution on adjournment was taken up.

Mr. Abbott introduced the following as a substitute for the resolution of Mr. Morton

Which, on motion, was adopted:

*Resolved*, That when the Convention adjourn, it be at the call of the President, or in case of his death, by the Secretary, or in case of his death, at a call signed by a majority of the delegates. This authority to re assemble the Convention shall cease after January 1st, 1869.

The following resolution introduced by Mr. Ashley was read and adopted.

*Resolved*, That this Convention will adjourn on or before Tuesday, 17th instant, at 12 o'clock, M.

The Committee to whom was referred the resolution in favor of reducing the tax on spirits of turpentine, report that they have had the same under consideration and deem further action inexpedient, and ask to be discharged from a further consideration of the subject.

The report was accepted and adopted.

The report of the Committee on Relief from Political Disabilities was received and discussed.

During the discussion Mr. Durham made use of the following language, which was ordered to be entered on the Journal:

"This report is a fraud upon the people of North-Carolina, and it is so intended to be. The Secretary may take my words down. I don't care for the Secretary or the Convention either."

Mr. Heaton introduced an ordinance in relation to the appointment of Code Commissioners.

Lies over under the rules.

Mr. Baker offered the following as a substitute for the report of the Committee on Relief from Political Disabilities:

*Resolved*, That the Congress of the United States be respectfully requested to remove the political disabilities from all persons in North-Carolina prevented by the Reconstruction Acts or the proposed 14th Article, from voting or holding office.

Mr. King, of Lenoir, offered to amend by adding to the substitute the words, " All that are in favor of universal suffrage to all male persons over twenty-one years of age, without distriction of race or color."

On motion, the amendment to the substitute was adopted.

The substitute as amended was put to the House.

The yeas and nays were called.

The call was sustained.

The substitute was lost by the following vote:

Those who voted in the affirmative are:

Messrs. King of Lenoir, Read, and Williams of Wake—3.

Those who voted in the negative are:

Messrs. Abbott, Andrews, Ashley, Aydlott, Baker, Bryan, Carey, Carter, Candler, Colgrove, Congleton, Cox, Daniel, Dickey, Dowd, Duckworth, Durham, Ellis, Etheridge, Forkner, Franklin, French of Bladen, French of Chowan, Fullings, Gahagan, Galloway, Garland, Garrett, George, Graham of Montgomery, Grant of Wayne, Grant of Northampton, Gully, Gunter, Harris of Franklin, Hay, Hayes of Halifax, Heaton, Highsmith, Hobbs, Hollowell, Holt, Hood, Hyman, Ing, Jones of Washington, Kinney, Laflin, Lee, Legg, May, Mayo, Marshall, Merritt, McDonald of Moore, Mullican, Murphy, Nance, Newsom, Parker, Parks, Petree, Pool, Ragland, Ray, Renfrow, Rhodes, Rich, Robbins, Rodman, Rose, Sanderlin, Smith, Stilly, Teague, Tourgee, Trogden, Turner, Watts, Welker and Williamson—81.

Mr. Durham offered the following substitute:

" It is the sense of this Convention that political disabilities ought to be removed from all citizens of North-Carolina without regard to political opinions or their support or opposition to universal suffrage."

Mr. Tourgee moved to amend by striking out the word "all."

Mr. Tourgee withdrew his amendment and moved to lay the substitute on the table.

By request Mr. Tourgee withdrew his motion to lay the substitute on the table and renewed his amendment.

The amendment was lost.

Mr. Hood moved to amend by striking out all after "North-Carolina."

The amendment was not sustained.

The question recurred on the substitute.

The yeas and nays were demanded.

The call was not sustained.

The substitute was put to the House and lost.

The question recurred on the original report of the Committee.

Mr. Rodman moved to amend as follows:

*Resolved*, That the Congress of the United States be respectfully requested to relieve all the people of North-Carolina from all disabilities and disqualifications imposed by the proposed fourteenth amendment to the Constitution of the United States, or by what is known as the Reconstruction Acts of Congress.

The yeas and nays were demanded.

The call was sustained.

The amendment was lost by the following vote, yeas 26, nays 75.

Those who voted in the affirmative are:

Messrs. Baker, Bradley, Daniel, Dowd, Durham, Ellis, Etheridge, Gunter, Hall, Hodnett, Hollowell, Holt, Jones of Caldwell, Laflin, Legg, Lennon, Long, McCubbins, Merritt, Read, Rich, Rodman, Sanderlin, Taylor, Turner, and Williams, of Wake—26.

Those who voted in the negative are:

Messrs. Abbott, Andrews, Ashley, Aydlott, Barnes, Benbow, Blume, Bryan, Carey, Carter, Candler, Chillson, Colgrove, Congleton, Cox, Dickey, Duckworth, Eppes, Fisher, Forkner, Franklin, French of Bladen, French of Rockingham, French of Chowan, Fullings, Gahagan, Galloway, Garland, Graham of Montgomery, Grant of Wayne, Gully, Harris of Franklin, Hayes of Robeson, Hayes of Halifax, Heaton, Highsmith, Hobbs, Hood, Hyman, Ing, Jones of Washington, King of Lenoir, Kinney, Lee, Logan, Mann, May, Mayo, Marshall, McDonald of Moore, Moore, Morton, Mullican, Murphy, Nance, Newsom, Parker, Parks, Petree, Pierson, Pool, Ragland, Renfrow, Rhodes, Robbins, Rose, Smith, Stilly, Stilwell, Teague, Tourgee, Trogden, Watts, Welker and Williamson—75.

The question recurred on the original report of the Committee, which was,

On motion, adopted.

The following is the report as adopted:

## REPORT OF THE COMMITTEE ON RELIEF FROM POLITICAL DISABILITY.

We, the undersigned Committee on Relief from Political Disability, having investigated the claims of those presented for our consideration most respectfully submit the following report:

WHEREAS, The persons hereinafter named are disqualified to hold office, by the fourteenth Article of the Constitution of the United States, known as the Howard amendment; and whereas, they have evidenced that they are in hearty accord with the Reconstruction measures of Congress: Therefore,

*Resolved*, That we petition the Congress of the United States to remove their disabilities in accordance with the provisions of the aforementioned Article of the Constitution.

J. W. HOOD, *Chairman*,
A. W. TOURGEE,
T. J. FORKNER,
C. C. JONES,
GEORGE W. GAHAGAN.
JAMES HAY,
WM. NICHOLSON,
R. W. KING.

FRAKLIN COUNTY.

A. M. Timberlake, W. S. Harris, E. A. Crudup, Green H. Grupton.

WAKE COUNTY.

Wm. H. Harrison, Albert Johnson, Hilliard J. Smith, W. R. Richardson, Wiley D. Jones, Jacob Sorrell, C. L. Harris.

PITT COUNTY.

Joseph Staten, Lewis Hilliard, Thomas Cox, James C. Laugley, Calvin Cox, Chas. J. O'Hagart, Julius C. Perkins Augustus Quimerly, Charles Roundtree.

HALIFAX COUNTY.

Chas. N. Webb, John I. Gregory, John A. Reed, John O'Brien, George W. Owens, J. T. Evans.

BEAUFORT COUNTY.

Samuel I. Carrow, Edward J. Warren, Hiram E. Stilley, Edward S. Hoyt, Wm. B. Rodman, Edmund Hodges, Luthur Ruff, Jessee G Bryan, Samuel Windley, George L. Windley, John B. Respass, Howard Wiswall, Henry Hodges, Jesse Roberson, Wm. A. Blount.

NEW HANOVER COUNTY.

Joseph H. Flanner, David Bunting, Wm. B. Flanner.

STANLY COUNTY.

Joseph Marshall, James E. Walden, Dumas Coggins, Daniel Richey, Lafayette Green, Allen Burris, Franklin A. Lafton, John W. Morton.

DAVIDSON COUNTY.

Evander Davis, Emory Davis, David Loftin, Willis Cecill, Ephraim Hampton, Henderson Adams, Green H. Lee.

PERSON COUNTY.

John D. Wilkerson.

CALDWELL COUNTY.

Lloyd L. Jones, Washington Moore, Wm M. Barber, Hosea Bradford, A. W. Austin, Robt. B. Bogle, Saml. McCall, Ja. M. Barber.

WILSON COUNTY.

George W. Blount, Newett D. Owens, Wm. D. Farmer, John Wilkerson, Francis W. Taylor.

FORSYTH COUNTY.

• Joseph S. Phipps E. A. Vogler, John G. Sides, Wm. B. Stipe, Wm. Clinard, John M. Stoltey, Allen Spack, Israel Moses, Thomas J. Wilson, Wm. F. Clafton.

TRANSYLVANIA COUNTY.

Jeremiah Osborne, Wm. R. Galloway J. C. Duckworth, Perry Orr, J. W. Clayton, Samuel Reed, Isaac A. Harris, Robert Hamilton, R. P. Kilpatrick, G. C. Neil.

HENDERSON COUNTY.

Benjamin Williams, Leander J. Pace, James M. Justice, Wm. K. Leadbetter, R. I. Allen, Thomas Osteen, S. B. O. McCall, David Stradley, G. P. Edney, Wm. D. Whitted,

Bedford Brown, James Spann, S. R. Stancill, M. Owensby, John C. Gullick, M. B. Lauce, D. M. Justice.

GUILFORD COUNTY.

Joseph Haskins, Barnabas Pane, Wyatt W. Ragsdale, John Hyatt, Robert P. Dick, George W. Bowman, David Grissom, John W. Kirkman, Fredrick Fentress, Andrew C. Murrow, Calvin Causey, Abram Clapp, Newton D. Woody, Robert M. Stafford, Wm. M. Mebane.

ALAMANCE COUNTY.

Joseph C. Thompson, Nathaniel Stout, Wm. P. McDaniel, Simpson Vestle, James Albright, Henry Boon.

LINCOLN COUNTY.

Rufus Clarke, W. P. Bynum, Henry Wilkinson.

BLADEN COUNTY.

Dugald Blue, Calvin Jones.

WILKES COUNTY.

R. M. Smith, John M. Brown, James F. Tugman, Andrew Porter, Samuel P. Smith, John F. Parlier, Isaac McCall, Harrold Hays, Ambrose Wiles, Toliver Shournate, Wm. E. Raynolds, Emanuel Harrold, James H. Hays.

CLEVELAND COUNTY.

J. O. Bridges, A. W. Goins, Andrew Parker, John Cook, David Hall, Lewis Downs, Henry Wortman, J. C. Ryers.

CUMBERLAND COUNTY.

Robert Orrell, A. G. Thornton, Duncan G. McCormick, Robert Mitchell.

SAMPSON COUNTY.

Calton Cessoms, Amos W. Hall, Clifton Ward, Robert Cain, Wm. Cessoms, Robertson Ward.

CARTERET COUNTY.

Malvin J. Davis, John C. Manson, W. J. Doughty.

DUPLIN COUNTY.

Wm. E. Hill, Thos. K. Murphy.

CURRITUCK COUNTY.

M. V. B. Gilbert, W. D. Chaddick, M. D. Lindsay,

ALEXANDER COUNTY.

Robert Carson, Daniel Moore, R. O. Bennett, Geo. W. Long, W. W. Stafford, James J. Teague, Wm. S. Teague, Thos. J. Dula, Andrew C. Watts, Elisha Bebber, F. B. Reece, Gabriel Marshall, F. A. Campbell, Wm. M. Bogle, J. W. Carson.

MECKLENBURG COUNTY.

H. N. Pritchard, Rufus Barringer, Wm. R. Myers, Jeremiah S. Reed, Wm. M. Martin, Robt. McEwen, Alexander McIver.

CAMDEN COUNTY.

Isaac Morriset, John M. Forbes, Geo. W. Spencer, James W. Chamblain, A. P. Cherry.

EDGECOMBE COUNTY.

Wm S. Battle, Joseph Cobb, Reddin S. Petway, R. W.

Proctor, Wm. H. Knight, Jesse Mercer, Exum L. Moore, Thomas Norfleet, Llewellyn Harrold, Wm. H. Johnson, John I. Killebrew, John Norfleet, R. H. Austin, Robert Norfleet, Wm. W. Parker, Henry E. Odom, John W. Johnson, Micajah P. Edwards, Lawrence Bunting.

ALLEGHANY COUNTY.

Wm. A. Brooks, Morgan Bryan, A. Marion Smith, Reuben Sparks, Hugh Hanks, John Parsons, L. M. Blackburn, Wm. Andrews, John A. Jones, Nathan Weaver, Soloman Stamper, Goldman Higgins, Alexander Black.

ASHE COUNTY.

John Williams.

HYDE COUNTY.

Sylvester McGowan, W. B. Tooley, James G. Carrowan, Joseph P. Flowers, Geo. V. Credle.

IREDELL COUNTY.

Thomas Holcomb, E. B. Stimpson.

WAYNE COUNTY.

Curtis H. Brogden.

STOKES COUNTY.

John J. Shaffer, James Harris, A. H. Joice, J. B. Young, Aquilla Moore, Ambrose Jessup, Ira E. Gentry, J. J. Martin, Wm. N. Shelton, Eaton B. Terrill, J. R. Jewell, W. B. Vaughan, Wm. M. Gordon.

PERQUIMANS COUNTY.

Nathan B. Cox, Jonathan W. Albertson, Robt. J. White.

YADKIN COUNTY.

Moses Gross, Moses Chappel, McCaus. Casteveens, S. Speere, E. C. Brown, David Hutchins, Aquilla Speere, J. S. Jones, Winston Fleming, Wm. H. Rodwell, T. L. Tulbert, John D. Holcomb, R. M. Pearson, Jesse Lackey, Thomas Hanes, Jonathan Wagoner, George Long, George Nix, Thomas F. Martin, Wm. W. Patterson, Sam'l C. Wech, Geo. D. Williams, Barnett C. Myers, H. Thomason, J. N. Vestal, Jesse Rivers, Sexton Jones, Jas. H. Myers.

HARNETT COUNTY.

James S. Harrington, John F. Shaw, Neal McLeod, Robt. A. Norden, James Hodge, John Harrington, James M. Turner, A. J. Tuddington.

NORTHAMPTON COUNTY.

Wm. Barrow, Jno. B. Odom, Noah R. Odom, Jesse Flythe, James W. Grant, Samuel Calvert, Samuel J. Calvert, David A. Barnes, George Holloman, Jesse W. Narsom.

MADISON COUNTY.

F. M. Lawson, Jas. Crowder, J. S. Dever, D. E. Freeman, James Ramsay, L. G. Brigman.

WARREN COUNTY.

Wm. A. White, John W. Patillo, John H. Bullock, John C. McCraw, James T. Russell, Nathaniel R. Jones, Wm. W. White, James T. Allston.

UNION COUNTY.

D. A. Covington, Miles A. Lemons, Wm. M. Austin, Jackson Green, Arthur Stigall, James McNeily, Thomas W.

Griffin, Robert Bivens, Richard Tarlton, Benj. F. Fincher, Asa Brumblow.

NASH COUNTY.

Geo. W. Lewis, W. W. Boddie, Absalom B. Baines, Benj. H. Sorsby.

ROWAN COUNTY.

Joseph A. Hawkins, Nathaniel Boyden, Wm. P. Atwell, Levi Trexler, Geo. W. Bernhard, Peter Williamson.

WASHINGTON COUNTY.

James A. Melson, Eli Spruill, Thomas Benbridge, W. W. Ward.

ROCKINGHAM COUNTY.

Thomas Settle, Thos. A. Ragland.

BURKE COUNTY.

Tod R. Caldwell, James H. Hall, Joseph Deaton, Asby Mull, Jeremiah Smith, Wm. Bailey, James Hildebran, Jas. R. Kincaid.

GASTON COUNTY.

D. A. Jenkins.

MONTGOMERY COUNTY.

John K. Loftin, James Batten, James W. Ressas, David Wright, John C. Nichols, James B. Ballard.

CHOWAN COUNTY,

Charles E. Robinson.

PASQUOTANK COUNTY.

John Pool, Geo. D. Pool, Frank Vaughn, F. M. Godfrey, C. W. Grandy, Jr., W. G. Pool, Geo. W. Charles, C. W. Hollowell.

BUNCOMBE COUNTY.

James Reid, P. J. Isrial, Levi Penland, Joseph P. Ellar, Amasa Roberts.

MOORE COUNTY.

Thomas W. Ritter, Samuel W. Seawell, Wm. J. King, D. W. McDonald, A. R. McDonald, John S. Ritter, John P. Cole, Benjamin Spivey, John K. McLeon, Wm. B. Richardson, Absalom Kelly, John McNeal, R. W. Barret, A. H. McNeil, M. J. Blue, Jordan Slaar.

RICHMOND COUNTY.

Oliver H. Dockery, John A. Long, Geo. McKinon, E. T. Long.

HAYWOOD COUNTY.

A. J. Murray, J. W. Harbin, Isaac Clarke, J. M. Patton, D. B. Ford, W. S. Evans, Henry Franklin, R. E. Medford, Samuel Fitzgerald, R. L. Owens.

JACKSON COUNTY.

E. D. Brindle, Wilson Ensby, L. C. Hooper, J. J. Hooper, Mordecai Zackny, A. Cope.

DAVIE COUNTY.

Uriah H. Phelps, John R. Williams, Wm. B. March.

GREENE COUNTY.

John Harvey, Rich'd J. Williams, John J. Orman, D. A. Spivey, Wm. P. Grimsley, Joseph H Dixon, Wm. T. Dixon.

MCDOWELL COUNTY.

James H. Duncan, C. S. Copeland, John Elliott, James A. McCall, John O'Brian, Thomas Ledbetter, Elijah Morgan, John T. Gregory, Chas. H. Webb.

CABARRUS COUNTY.

Victor C. Barringer.

CHEROKEE COUNTY.

Wm. McGuyre, T. R. McCombs, Phelix T. Axley, Christopher Gentry, Geo. W. Furguson, B. K. Dickey, George W. Hall.

BERTIE COUNTY.

Jonathan Taylor, Frederick Miller, Geo. N. Green, Lewis C. Bond.

GRANVILLE COUNTY.

Robt. Garner, S. G. Wilson, Eugene Grissom, E. D. Lyons.

MARTIN COUNTY.

John Watts, Wm. C. Eborn, John S. Short, F. P. Bazemore, John L. Knight.

POLK COUNTY.

Martin Hambleton, R. S. Abrams, Neslid Dinsdale, J. W. Hampton, James Jackson.

RUTHERFORD COUNTY.

G. W. Logan, Martin Walker, Rufus Williams, Willis Bradly, Israel P. Sorrell, W. G. Mode, J. E. McFarland, Edward Hawkins, A. A. Scoggins, R. J. McCraw, Smith McCurry, Eli Whisnant, C. J. Sparks, L. L. Dick, A. Hollowfield, H. H. Hopper, J. W. Morgan, J. W. Mode, B. W. Andrews, James H. Carpenter, Moses Wilkson, James McFarland, W. B. Freeman, John A. Carpenter, Thomas Long, W. G. Wilson, B. W. Barber, R. T. Carpenter, Joseph Green, W. O. Wallace, A. C. Martin, J. W. Gibson, Jerre Jackson.

LENOIR COUNTY.

Walter Dunn, Anthony Davis, James L. Canaday, Joshua Rouse, John A. Parrot, James M. Parrot.

ROBESON COUNTY.

James Sinclair, Benjamin A. Howell.

CRAVEN COUNTY.

Edward R. Stanley, Charles R. Thomas, Fredrick J. Jones.

JOHNSON COUNTY.

Thomas D. Sneed, Robert Messengale, P. P. Massey, Wm. A. Smith, B. R. Hinnent, James H. Enniss, Willie Holt, Franklin Phillips, Joh R. Coats, W. D. Holt, Samuel Woodie, Thomas Egderton, Ray Phillips, Bryan Williams, J. P. Peck, J. T. Leach.

RANDOLPH COUNTY.

John Pope, Henry Pressnel, Wm. McGee, James Latham, Alson G. Jennings, B. A. Sellars, J. R. Bulla, Alfred Julian, James T. Fox, Elijah Whitney.

BRUNSWICK COUNTY.

Robert Woodside, L. D. Thurston, D. K. Bennett, Lewis Galloway, D. L. Russell, Lorenzo Frink, P. Privlian.

CHATHAM COUNTY.

R. M. Brown, Hezekiah Henderson, W. C. B. Council, J. Howze, Wm. Griffin, H. H. Burke, Wm. Laney, Joseph Brazington, R. C. Cotton, Elias Bryan, James H. Headon.

SURRY COUNTY.

Drury McGee, John Nichols, Thomas Martin, C. H. Kepp, Joel Hurt, Wm. Hodges, Geo. A. Jarvis, James Venable, J. S. Pedigre, Isaac Armfield, Gideon Bryant, A. H. Knapp, John C. Thompson, T. J. Williams, C. C. McMichle, Martin Payne, B. F. Scott, Martin Axum, James Nations, John McCloud, Jeremiah Gay.

MACON COUNTY.

D. W. Siler, C. T. Rodgers, R. M. Henry, A. L. Parton, W. H. Higdan, A. Vaughn.

ORANGE COUNTY.

H. B. Guthrie.

The following reports of Committees were received and adopted :

We the undersigned, Committee on Contingent Expenses, having examined the within account for wood, of three hundred and fifteen ($315) dollars, recommend its payment (after deducting, as agreed upon, one dollar per cord, leaving the above balance.

We further report that on February 21st, 1868, a resolution was passed by the Convention directing the officers to call upon Secretary of State for wood, &c.

The above account is up to March 6th, 1868. As it appears that the wood was furnished we have recommended its payment; all of which is submitted.

R. W. KING, *Chairman.*

The Select Committee, to whom was referred the matter of alledged corrupting influences having been used to secure the passage of certain ordinances which have been passed by this Convention, ask leave to report that they have had the same under consideration, and that so far as their investigation has extended they have not discovered any evidence of such corruption.

P. DURHAM, *Chairman.*

Mr. Mann introduced a resolution thanking Congress for the impeachment of the President.

The rules were suspended.

Mr. Durham moved to amend section 1st by adding after the word "promptly," the words "and unconstitutionally."

The amendment was lost.

Mr. Rodman introduced the following resolution, which was, after a suspension of the rules, adopted.

*Resolved*, That a Committee of eight be appointed to take into consideration the subject of Relief of Debtors, with instructions to report some plan of relief on Friday (to morrow) at 7½ o'clock, P. M.

Mr. Durham offered the following as as an amendment to the resolution on impeachment offered by Mr. Mann.

*Resolved*, That this is a compliment to the tyranny and despotism which is being inaugurated to subvert the Constitution of the United States, and to destroy the liberties of the American people.

The yeas and nays were demanded.

The call was not sustained.

The amendment was lost.

The resolutions offered by Mr. Mann were adopted.

The following is the preamble and resolutions as offered by Mr. Mann and passed;

WHEREAS, the people of North-Carolina, through their representatives in Convention assembled, have viewed with not, less indignation than apprehension, the efforts on the part of the Executive branch of this government to throttle, circumscribe and over rule its co-ordinate and Legislative branch of the same: and whereas, in the opinion of this Convention, success in such efforts would lead to an agrarianism alike dangerous to the liberties of the people, and subversive of that good feeling and correct principle of Republicanism, which should be viewed not only with extreme jealousy and horror, but be marked by the unqualified condemnation of all lovers of good order and stable government: be it therefore

*Resolved*, That the thanks of this Convention are due, and are hereby tendered to these noble reprensentatives who have so promptly stepped forth in their power of impeachment, to check and correct the evil threatened by the acts of an usurpative Executive.

*Be it further resolved*, That a copy of these resolutions, duly engrossed, be transmitted to the Honorable, the President of the Senate, and the Speaker of the House of Representatives of the people of the United States.

*Be it further resolved*, That this Convention tender to Brevet Major General E. R. S. Canby and the officers of his command, its thanks for the bold, fearless, unprejudiced and manly manner in which they, each and all, have discharged the onerous and delicate duties devolving upon them under the Reconstruction Acts of Congress.

The House, on motion, adjourned.

---

EVENING SESSION, MARCH 12TH, 1868.

The Convention was called to order at 7½ o'clock by the President.

The roll was called, ninety-two members answering to their names:

Messrs. Andrews, Ashley, Aydlott, Baker, Barnes, Benbow,

Blume, Bradley, Bryan, Carey, Carter, Candler, Cherry, Chillson, Colgrove, Congleton, Cox, Daniel, Dickey, Dowd, Duckworth, Ellis, Eppes, Etheridge, Fisher, Forkner, Franklin, French of Bladen, Fullings, Galloway, George, Graham of Montgomery, Grant of Wayne, Grant of Northampton, Gully, Gunter, Hall, Hare, Harris of Wake, Hay, Hayes of Halifax, Highsmith, Hobbs, Hollowell, Holt, Hood, Hyman, Ing, Jones of Caldwell, Jones, of Washington, King of Lenoir, Kinney, Laflin, Lee, Legg, Lennon, Logan, Long, Mann, Mayo, Marshall, McCubbins, Merritt, Moore, Morton, Mullican, Murphy, Nance, Nicholson, Patrick, Parker, Parks, Petree, Peterson, Ragland, Ray, Read, Renfrow, Rhodes, Rich, Robbins, Rodman, Rose, Sanderlin, Smith, Stilly, Teague, Trogden, Tucker, Turner, Watts and Welker—92.

The President announced the following Committee of eight on Relief, to report an ordinance Friday evening:

Messrs. Rodman, Pool, Jones of Caldwell, Rich, Fullings, Bradley, Watts and McCubbins.

The following report of the Committee on Miscellaneous Provisions, was taken up and passed its first reading:

## REPORT OF THE STANDING COMMITTEE ON MISCELLANEOUS PROVISIONS.

### ARTICLE.

Section 1. All statute laws of this State now in force, although regarded as provisional only, not inconsistent with this Constitution, shall continue in force until they shall expire by their own limitation, or be amended or repealed by the General Assembly ; and all writs, prosecutions, actions and causes of action, except as herein otherwise provided, shall continue; and all indictments which shall have been found, or may hereafter be found for any crime or offence committed before this Constitution takes effect, may be proceded upon as if no change had taken place, except as hereinafter specified.

Sec. 2. No person shall be prosecuted in any civil action or criminal proceeding for or on account of any act by him done, performed or executed, after the first day of January, one thousand eight hundred and sixty-one, by virtue of military authority, vested in him by the government of the United States to do such act, or in pursuance of orders received by him from any person vested with such authority, and if any action or proceeding shall have heretofore been, or shall hereafted be instituted against any person for the doing of any such act, the defendant may plead this section in bar thereof.

Sec. 3. No person who shall hereafter fight a duel, or assist in the same as a second, or send, accept, or knowingly carry a challenge therefor, or agree to go out of this State to fight a duel, shall hold any office in this State.

Sec. 4. No money shall be drawn from the Treasury but in consequence of the appropriations made by law; and an accurate account of the receipts and expenditures of the public money shall be annually published.

Sec. 5. The General Assembly shall provide by proper legislation for giving to mechanics and laborers an adequate lien on the subject matter of their labor.

Sec. 6. In the absence of any contrary provision, all officers in this State heretofore elected or appointed, shall only hold their positions until other appointments are made by the Governor, or until their successors have been chosen and duly qualified according to the several provisions of this Constitution.

Sec. 7. The General Assembly shall have power to repeal or modify all ordinances adopted by any previous Convention or Conventions.

Sec. 8. The seat of government in this State shall remain at the City of Raleigh.

Sec. 9. The General Assembly shall provide by law for the indictment and trial or persons charged with the Commission of any felony in any County other than that in which the offence was committed, whenever, owing to prejudice, or any other cause, an impartial grand or petit jury cannot be impanneled in the County in which such offence was committed.

BYRON LAFLIN, *Chairman.*

On second reading,

Mr. Laflin, Chairman of the Committee, amended section 1st, by striking out all down to the word, "all," in line seventh.

Mr. Tourgee amended by adding to the section: "*Provided*, That a new trial may be granted, in the discretion of the Court, in cases where a party considers himself agrieved."

The section, as amended, was adopted.

Section 2d was read.

Mr. Tourgee moved to strike out in lines fifth and sixth, the following words: "vested in him by the government of the United States to do such act," and insert, "of the United States." Also, insert the word "the," in line fifth, between the words "of" and "military."

The amendment was put to the House and lost.

Mr. Durham moved to amend by striking out all after the word "authority," in line fifth, down to "or," in line sixth.

The yeas and nays were demanded.

The amendment was lost by the following vote:

Those who voted in the affirmative are:

Messrs. Andrews, Baker, Bradley, Daniel, Dowd, Duckworth, Durham, Ellis, Etheridge, Hare, Holt, Jones of Caldwell, Legg, Lennon, McCubbins, Merritt, Patrick, Parker, Read, Rich, Rodman, Sanderlin and Stilly—23.

Those who voted in the negative are:

Messrs. Abbott, Ashley, Aydlott, Blume, Bryan, Carey, Carter, Candler, Chillson, Colgrove, Congleton, Cox, Dickey, Eppes, Fisher, Forkner, Franklin, French of Bladen, French of Rockingham, French of Chowan, Fullings, Gahagan, George, Graham of Montgomery, Grant of Wayne, Gunter, Hay, Hayes of Robeson, Hayes of Halifax, Heaton, Highsmith, Hobbs, Hoffler, Hood, Ing, Jones of Washington, King of Lincoln, King of Lenoir, Kinney, Laflin, Logan, Long, Mann, Mayo, Marshall, Morton, Murphy, Nance, Parks, Petree, Peterson, Ray, Renfrow, Rhodes, Robbins, Rose, Smith, Teague, Tourgee, Trogden, Tucker, Turner, Watts and Williamson—64.

Mr. French, of Bladen, offered the following amendment, which, on motion, was adopted.

Add to the section :

"*Provided*, That all the benefits of this section shall be extended to all persons who were obliged to leave their homes to escape conscription."

The question recurred on the section as amended.

The yeas and nays were demanded.

The call prevailed.

The section was lost by the following vote:

Those who voted in the affirmative, are:

Messrs. Blume, Cox, Franklin, French of Rockingham, French of Chowan, Hayes of Halifax, Hood, Jones of Washington, Marshall, Parks, Petree, Ray, Trogden, Turner and Welker—15.

Those who voted in the negative are:

Messrs. Abbott, Ashley, Aydlott, Baker, Bradley, Bryan, Carey, Carter, Candler, Chillson, Colgrove, Congleton, Daniel, Dickey, Dowd, Duckworth, Durham, Ellis, Etheridge, Fisher, Forkner, Gahagan, Graham of Montgomery, Grant of Wayne, Gunter, Hare, Harris of Franklin, Hay, Heaton, Highsmith, Hobbs, Holt, Jones of Caldwell, King of Lincoln, King of Lenoir, Kinney, Laflin, Lee, Legg, Lennon, Logan, Long, Mann, Mayo, McCubbins, Merritt, Moore, Morton, Nance, Patrick, Parker, Read, Renfrow, Rhodes, Rich, Robbins, Rodman, Rose, Sanderlin, Smith, Stilly, Taylor, Teague, Watts and Williamson—66.

Section 3d was read.

Mr Durham moved to amend by striking out "no," in line first, strike out all after the word "duel," in fourth line, and insert, "shall be punished in such manner as the Legislature may by law provide."

The amendment was lost.

The section, as read, was adopted.

Sections 4th, 5th and 6th were read and adopted.

Sections 8th and 9th were read and adopted.

Mr. Tourgee offered the following as a new section:

"No amnesty act passed by any Convention or Legislature

since May, 1865, shall be of any binding force or validity after the adoption of this Constitution, except 'an act to grant amnesty and pardon to females,' ratified March 1st 1867."

Mr. Tourgee withdrew his amendment.

Mr. Laflin offered the following as a new section :

"That no person shall hold more than one lucrative office at any one time ; *Provided*, no appointment in the Militia or the office of Justice of the Peace shall be considered a lucrative office."

The section was adopted.

Mr Pool moved a reconsideration of the vote.

Mr. Jones moved to lay the motion on the table.

The yeas and nays were called.

The motion was lost, yeas 39, nays 48.

Those who voted in the affirmative are :

Messrs. Aydlott, Baker, Barnes, Blume, Carey, Candler, Dickey, Dowd, Durham, Ellis, Etheridge, Gahagan, George, Graham of Montgomery, Gunter, Hare, Hayes of Robeson, Hobbs, Holt, Jones of Washington, Laflin, Lennon, Long, Marshall, McCubbins, Merritt, Morton, Mullican, Murphy, Nance, Patrick, Parks, Petree, Rhodes, Sanderlin, Stilly, Teague, Turner and Welker—39.

Those who voted in the negative are:

Messrs. Abbott, Andrews, Ashley, Bryan, Chillson, Colgrove, Congleton, Eppes, Fisher, Forkner, Franklin, French of Bladen French of Rockingham, French of Chowan, Fullings, Grant of Wayne, Hall, Harris of Wake, Harris of Franklin, Hay, Heaton, Highsmith, Hoffler, Hollowell, Hood, Ing, Jones of Caldwell, King of Lincoln, King of Lenoir, Kinney, Legg, Logan, Mann, Mayo, Nicholson, Parker, Pool, Ray, Renfrow, Rich, Rodman, Rose, Smith, Taylor, Tourgee, Tucker, Watts and Williamson—48.

The motion to reconsider prevailed.

On motion of Mr. Tourgee, the section was recommitted to the Committee on Miscellaneous Provisions, with instructions to report the section back more carefully worded.

Mr. Heaton, Chairman of the Committee of Seventeen,

reported an ordinance, entitled "An ordinance providing for the restoration of the Public Credit."

After suspension of the rules was made a Special Order for Friday 11 o'clock, A. M.

Also, on an ordinance entitled "An ordinance to incorporate the Charlotte City Hall Association."

Mr. Abbott introduced a petition of Mrs. Amelia E. Slater, Salisbury. Referred to the Committee of Seventeen.

Mr. Tourgee introduced the following resolution:

*Resolved*, That a Committee of Three be appointed immediately, whose duty it shall be to draft an address to the people of North-Carolina, explanatory of the Constitution adopted by this Convention, which, if approved by the Convention, shall be appended to the Constitution and published therewith.

The rules were suspended and the resolution adopted.

The Committee on Enrollment and Engrossment respectfully report that they have carefully compared the enrolled ordinances on Education, Penal Institutions, Suffrage and Eligibility to Office, and the Judicial Department, with the original bills, and certify the same to be correct.

C. C. POOL, *Chairman.*

Mr. Parker introduced a resolution relating to the hours of meeting of the Convention.

On motion, the ordinance on authenticity, introduced by Mr. Rodman, was made a Special Order for Friday, at 12 o'clock.

The report of the Committee on Miscellaneous Provisions passed its 2d reading by the following vote:

Those who voted in the affirmative, are:

Messrs. Abbott, Andrews, Ashley, Aydlott, Blume, Bradley, Bryan, Carey, Candler, Colgrove, Congleton, Dickey, Eppes, Fisher, Forkner, Franklin, French of Rockingham, French of Chowan, Fullings, Gahagan, George, Grant of Wayne, Gunter, Hall, Harris of Wake, Hay, Hayes of Robeson, Hayes of Halifax, Heaton, Highsmith, Hobbs, Hood, Hyman, Ing, Jones of Caldwell, Jones of Washington, King of Lenoir, Kinney, Laflin, Logan, Mann, Mayo, Marshall, Mullican, Murphy, Nicholson, Parker, Petree, Pool, Ray, Renfrow, Rhodes, Rich, Rodman, Smith, Teague, Tourgee, Tucker, Turner, Watts, Welker and Williamson—62.

Those who voted in the negative, are:

Messsrs. Baker, Dowd, Durham, Etheridge, Hare, Holt, Merritt and Sanderlin—8.

On motion, it was ordered that the report of the Committee on Miscellaneous Provisions, be engrossed and made a Special Order for Friday, at 1 o'clock.

On motion, the house then adjourned.

---

FRIDAY, March 13th, 1868.

The Convention was called to order at 10 o'clock, by the President.

Prayer by the Rev. Mr. Logan.

The Roll was called and the following members answered to their names:

Messrs. Abbott, Andrews, Ashley, Aydlott, Baker, Barnes, Benbow, Blume, Bradley, Bryan, Carey, Carter, Candler, Cherry, Chillson, Colgrove, Congleton, Cox, Dickey, Duckorth, Durham, Ellis, Eppes, Etheridge, Fisher, Forkner, French of Bladen, French of Rockingham, French of Chowan, Fullings, Gahagan, Galloway, George, Glover, Graham of Montgomery, Grant of Wayne, Gully, Gunter, Hall, Hare, Harris of Wake, Harris of Franklin, Hay, Hayes of Robeson, Hayes of Halifax, Highsmith, Hobbs, Hodnett, Hoffler, Hollowell, Holt, Hood, Hyman, Jones of Caldwell, Jones of Washington, King of Lincoln, King of Lenoir, Kinney, Laflin. Lee, Legg, Lennon, Logan, May, Mayo, Marshall, Merritt, McDonald of Chatham, McDonald of Moore, Moore, Morton, Mullican, Murphy, Nance, Newsom, Nicholson, Patrick, Parker, Parks, Petree, Peterson, Pierson, Ragland, Ray, Read, Renfrow, Rhodes, Rich, Robbins, Rodman, Rose, Sanderlin, Smith, Stilly, Stilwell, Taylor, Teague, Tourgee, Trogden, Tucker, Turner, Watts, Welker, Williams of Wake and Williamson.

Mr. Abbott presented a memorial from the citizens of the Counties of Rowan, Mecklenburg, Iredell and Cabarrus, ask ing the formation of a new County.

Referred to the Committee of Seventeen.

Mr. Hood presented an ordinance for a Boat Charter in favor of R. M. Orrell and others.

Referred to the Committee of Seventeen.

On motion of Mr. Heaton the Preamble and Bill of Rights, presented to the Convention by the Committee, was ordered enrolled.

Mr. Candler called up his Ordinance repealing the granting of a general amnesty and pardon, etc.

Mr. Forkner moved to strike out the words "and declared null and void."

The amendment was adopted by the following vote:

Those who voted in the affirmative are:

Messrs. Abbott, Andrews, Ashley, Aydlott, Baker, Barnes, Benbow, Blume, Bradley, Carter, Colgrove, Congleton, Cox, Daniel, Dickey, Dowd, Duckworth, Durham, Ellis, Eppes, Etheridge, Forkner, French of Bladen, French of Rockingham, Gahagan, Galloway, George, Glover, Graham of Montgomery, Graham of Orange, Grant of Wayne, Grant of Northamton, Gully, Gunter, Hall, Hare, Harris of Wake, Harris of Franklin, Hay, Hayes of Halifax, Heaton, Highsmith, Hobbs, Hodnett, Hollowell, Holt, Hyman, Jones of Caldwell, Jones of Washington, King of Lincoln, King of Lenoir, Laflin, Legg, Lennon, Mayo, McCubbins, Merritt, McDonald of Chatham, McDonald of Moore, Moore, Morton, Mullican, Nance, Patrick, Parker, Parks, Pierson, Pool, Ragland, Read, Rich, Robbins, Rodman, Sanderlin, Smith, Stilwell, Trogden, Turner, Watts, Welker, and Williamson —81.

Those who voted in the negative, are:

Messrs. Bryan, Candler, French of Chowan, Fullings, Hood, Kinney, Logan, Marshall, Murphy, Newsom, Petree, Ray, Rhodes, Rose, Teague, Tourgee—16.

The ordinance as follows was adopted:

## AN ORDINANCE IN RELATION TO THE PARDON OF OFFICERS AND SOLDIERS OF THE LATE CONFEDERATE SERVICE.

SECTION 1. *Be it ordained by the people of North-Carolina, by delegates in Convention assembled, and it is hereby ordained by the authority of the same,* That an act of the General Assembly, ratified December the 22d, 1866, granting a general amnesty and pardon to all officers and soldiers of the State of North-Carolina, of the late Confederate States armies, or of the United States, or any person or class of persons to which said general amnesty was intended to apply, be and the same is hereby repealed, except so much of it as applies to females.

The ordinance was adopted by the following vote:

Those who voted in the affirmative are:

Messrs. Abbott, Andrews, Ashley, Aydlott, Benbow, Blume, Bryan, Carey, Carter, Candler, Chilson, Colgrove, Congleton, Dickey, Duckworth, Eppes, Forkner, French of Bladen, French of Rockingham, French of Chowan, Fullings, Gahagan, Galloway, George, Glover, Graham of Montgomery, Gully, Gunter, Harris of Wake, Harris of Franklin, Hay, Hayes of Halifax, Heaton, Highsmith, Hobbs, Hoffler, Hollowell, Hood, Jones of Washington, King of Lincoln, King of Lenoir, Kinney, Laflin, Lee, Logan, Mann, May, Mayo, Marshall, McDonald of Moore, Moore, Morton, Mullican, Murphy, Newsom, Parks, Pierson, Pool, Ragland, Ray, Renfrow, Rhodes, Robbins, Rose, Smith, Stilwell, Sweet, Taylor, Teague, Tourgee, Trogden, Tucker, Watts and Williamson —73.

Those who voted in the negative, are:

Messrs. Baker, Bradley, Daniel, Dowd, Durham, Ellis, Etheridge, Graham of Orange, Hare, Hodnett, Holt, Jones of Caldwell, Lennon, McCubbins, Merritt, McDonald of Chatham, Nance, Patrick, Parker, Read, Rich, Sanderlin, Turner, and Welker—24.

On motion, the report of the Committee of Seventeen on an ordinance entitled an "ordinance providing for the restoration of the Public Credit," was ordered printed and made a special order for Saturday at 10½ oclock.

Leave of absence was granted to Mr. Ellis.

On motion the following ordinance of Mr. Rodman was adopted :

## AN ORDINANCE IN RELATION TO THE PRINTING OF THE CONSTITUTION, ORDINANCES AND RESOLUTIONS.

SECTION. 1. *Be it ordained by the people of North-Carolina in Convention assembled*, That every ordinance and resolution of this Convention, when the same shall have been enrolled, shall be authenticated by the signatures of the President and of the Principal Secretary of this Convention, and the date of its final passenge shall be affixed thereto ; and such ordinances and resolutions shall go into effect from such date, unless some other be prescribed or unless such ordinance or resolution shall be required to be submitted to the people for ratification.

SEC. 2. *Be it further ordained*, That all such enrolled ordinances and resolutions, and also the Journals of the Convention, and all the papers belonging to the Convention, imimmediately upon the adjournment thereof shall be deposited by the President and Secretary of the Convention in the office of the Secretary of State for the State of North-Carolina.

SEC. 3. *Be it further ordained*, That four thousand copies of the Constitution, Ordinances and Resolutions of this Convention, and three hundred copies of the Journals, shall be printed as soon as possible after the adjournment of the Convention, under the supervision of the Principal Secretary of the Convention, and that ten copies of the Ordinances and Resolutions and one copy of the Journals shall be given to each member of this Convention, and two bound copies of the Ordinances and Resolutions to each Clerk of the Superior Court, one copy to each Judge of the Supreme Court and to each Justice of the Peace and County Commissioner elected under the provisions of this Constitution, and the residue to the Secretary of State of North-Carolina for the use of the State.

Sec. 3. *Be it further ordained*, That as soon as possible after the adjournment of this Convention there shall be printed under the same supervision ten thousand copies of the Constitution adopted, and of all Ordinances for the purpose of carrying the same into effect, or which shall be required to be submitted to the people for ratification at the same time, and that the same be distributed as rapidly as possible among them by the said Principal Secretary.

Sec. 4. *Be it further ordained*, That the Constitution shall also be published in the following named newspapers of this State once a week for three weeks: *Newbern Republican; Wilmington Post; Raleigh Standard*, Raleigh, N. C.; *Union Republican*, Charlotte; *Pioneer*, Asheville.

Sec. 5. *Be it further ordained*, That the Secretary shall receive for his services under this ordinance six dollars per day while engaged.

Sec. 6. *Be it further ordained*, That the printed copies of the Constitution, and of all the Ordinances and Resolutions of the Convention printed by authority of the Convention, or which shall be hereafter printed by authority of the General Assembly of North-Carolina, shall be admitted as evidence in all courts of this State.

The motion of Mr. French, of Chowan, to reconsider the vote on section 26th of the Bill on the Judicial Department was withdrawn.

Mr. French then moved that the Committee on Revision be instructed to amend the 26th section of the Article on Judiciary, so that the Superior Court Judges be divided into two classes instead of four, holding office for four and eight years.

The motion prevailed.

Mr. Heaton called up the ordinance in relation to Code Commissioners, which was read.

Mr. Dowd moved to strike out "A. W. Tourgee," from the names of Code Commissioners and insert "S. F. Phillips, of Orange County."

The motion was lost.

The ordinance was adopted by the following vote, yeas 60, nays 22.

Those who voted in the affirmative, are:

Messrs. Abbott, Andrews, Ashley, Aydlott, Bryan, Carey, Carter, Candler, Colgrove, Congleton, Cox, Dickey, Duckworth, Eppes, Fisher, French of Bladen, French of Chowan, Fullings, Gahagan, Galloway, Glover, Graham of Montgomery, Grant of Wayne, Gully, Gunter, Harris of Franklin, Hay, Hayes of Robeson, Hayes of Halifax, Heaton, Hood, Hyman, Jones of Washington, Kinney, Laflin, Lee, Logan, May, Mayo, Marshall, McDonald of Moore, Moore, Murphy, Nance, Patrick, Parker, Parks, Pierson, Ragland, Renfrow, Rhodes, Rich, Robbins, Rose, Smith, Stilly, Stilwell, Taylor, Williams of Wake, and Williamson—60.

Those who voted in the negative are:

Messrs. Baker, Bradley, Cherry, Daniel, Dowd, Durham, Ellis, Etheridge, George, Graham of Orange, Hare, Hodnett, Hoffler, Holt, Jones of Caldwell, King of Lincoln, Lennon, McCubbins, Merritt, McDonald of Chatham, Mullican, and Sanderlin—22.

The following is the ordinance as adopted:

## AN ORDINANCE APPOINTING COMMISSIONERS TO PREPARE A CODE OF PRACTICE AND PROCEDURE IN THE DIFFERENT COURTS OF THE STATE.

SECTION 1. *Be it ordained by the people of North-Carolina in Convention assembled, and it is hereby ordained as follows:* That Victor C. Barringer, A. W. Tourgee and Wm. B. Rodman are hereby appointed Commissioners, whose duty it shall be to prepare a Code of Practice and Procedure in the different Courts of the State, and to reduce into a written and systematic Code the whole body of law of the State, or such parts thereof as shall seem to them practicable and expedient, and consistent with the provisions of the Constitution.

SEC. 2. *Be it further ordained*, That the Commissioners shall divide the Code of Practice and Procedure into two parts, the one as a Code of Criminal Procedure, with the requisite forms, the other a Code of Civil Procedure, with forms thereof.

SEC. 3. *Be it further ordained*, That the first division of the Code of Law must embrace the laws respecting the government of the State, its civil polity, the functions of its public officers and duties of its citizens. The second must embrace the laws of personal rights and relations of property and obligations. The third shall define crimes and prescribe their punishments.

SEC. 4. *Be it further ordained*, That the Commissioners shall hold their offices for three years; but the General Assembly may continue their term if it shall be deemed necessary.

SEC. 5. *Be it further ordained*, That the Commissioners shall report to the General Assembly at its first session after the adoption of this Constitution a general analysis of the Code projected by them and the progress made by them therein, and shall continue to report at each succeeding session of the General Assembly the progress made to that time.

SEC. 6. *Be it further ordained*, That whenever the Commissioners shall have prepared the Code, or any portion of the same, they shall contract with the printer of the State for printing of the same, and cause the same to be distributed among the Justices of the Supreme Court, Judges of the Superior Courts, and other competent persons, for examination, after which the Commissioners shall re-examine their work and consider such suggestions as may have been made to them. They shall then cause the Code as finally agreed upon by them to be re-printed under the contract as aforesaid and distributed to all the Justices of the Supreme Court, the Judges of the Superior Courts and Clerks of the Superior Courts thirty days before being presented to the General Assembly; and the Penal Code in like manner to be distributed to the Solicitors of the State.

SEC. 7. *Be it further ordained*, That the Commissioners shall from time to time specify such amendments, alterations and revision of the law as to them may seem necessary to carry into effect the provisions of the Constitution, and report the same to the General Assembly.

SEC. 8. *Be it further ordained*, That each of said Commissioners shall receive a salary of two hundred dollars per month, while actually engaged in the performance of his duties as such. A suitable room in the capital shall be assigned to said Commissioners as an office, and the necessary printing and stationery allowed the same.

SEC. 9. *Be it further ordained*, That this ordinance shall be in force from and after its ratification.

Mr. King, of Lincoln, moved that the Committee on Revision be instructed to revise section 8th of the report of the Committee on plan of organization of the Judicial Department, by striking out " four associate justices " and inserting " two."

Mr. May moved to lay the motion on the table.

The yeas and nays were demanded.

The call was sustained.

The motion was carried by the following vote, yeas 50, nays 39.

Those who voted in the affirmative are:

Messrs. Abbott, Andrews, Ashley, Bryan, Carey, Carter, Cherry, Colgrove, Daniel, Dickey, Eppes, Fisher, French of Bladen, French of Chowan, Fullings, Gahagan, Galloway, Graham of Montgomery, Grant of Wayne, Harris of Franklin, Hayes of Halifax, Heaton, Hobbs, Hood, Hyman, Jones of Caldwell, Jones of Washington, Kinney, Laflin, Lee, Legg, May, Mayo, Marshall, Moore, Murphy, Nance, Parks, Pierson, Pool, Ragland, Ray, Renfrow, Robbins, Rodman, Smith, Tourgee, Watts, Welker and Williamson—50.

Those who voted in the negative, are:

Messrs. Aydlott, Baker, Barnes, Bradley, Candler, Congleton, Cowles, Cox, Dowd, Duckworth, Durham, Ellis, Etheridge, George, Graham of Orange, Gunter, Hare, Hay, Hodnett, Hoffler, Hollowell, Holt, King of Lincoln, King of Lenoir, Lennon, Mann, McCubbins, McDonald of Chatham, McDonald of Moore, Parker, Petree, Peterson, Read, Rhodes, Rose, Sanderlin, Teague, Turner and Williams of Wake—39.

The report of the Committee on Miscellaneous Provisions was taken up and placed on its 3d and final reading and pas sage.

Sections 1st, 2d, 3d, 4th, 5th, 6th, and 7th were read and adopted.

The Committee reported the following as a new section which was adopted:

No person shall hold more than one lucrative office under the State at the same time: *Provided*, That officers in the Militia, Justices of the Peace, Commissioners of Public Charities and Commissioners appointed for special purposes, shall not be considered officers within the meaning of this section.

The section was, on motion, adopted.

The report of the Committee on Miscellaneous Provisions passed its 3rd and final reading by the following vote, yeas 75, nays 6.

Those who voted in the affirmative, are:

Messrs. Abbott, Andrews, Ashley, Aydlott, Barnes, Bryan, Carey, Carter, Candler, Colgrove, Congleton, Cowles, Cox, Dickey, Duckworth, Eppes, French of Bladen, French of Chowan, Gahagan, George, Graham of Montgomery, Grant of Wayne, Grant of Northampton, Gunter, Hall, Harris of Franklin, Hay, Hayes of Halifax, Heaton, Highsmith, Hobbs, Hoffler, Hollowell, Hood, Hyman, Jones of Caldwell, Jones of Washington, King of Lincoln, Kinney, Laflin, Lee, Legg, May, Mayo, Marshall, McDonald of Chatham, McDonald ot Moore, Mullican, Murphy, Nance, Newsom, Nicholson, Parker, Parks, Petree, Pierson, Pool, Ray, Read, Renfrow, Rhodes, Rich, Robbins, Rodman, Rose, Smith, Stilwell, Teague, Tourgee, Tucker, Turner, Watts, Welker, Williams of Wake, and Williamson—75.

Those who voted in the negative, are:

Messrs. Dowd, Durham, Ellis, Etheridge, Graham of Orange, Hare, McCubbins, Merritt, and Sanderlin—9.

On motion of Mr. Jones, the report of the Committee to

whom was referred the divorce case of Overton, was taken up and adopted by the following vote:

Those who voted in the affirmative, are:

Messrs. Abbott, Andrews, Baker, Blume, Carey, Carter, Colgrove, Congleton, Daniel, Eppes, Etheridge, Fisher, French of Bladen, French of Chowan, Graham of Montgomery, Gully, Gunter, Hall, Hare, Harris of Franklin, Hayes of Halifax, Highsmith, Hobbs, Hoffler, Hood, Hyman, Jones of Washington, Kinney, Lee, Mann, Mayo, Marshall, McDonald of Chatham, Moore, Murphy, Parks, Petree, Ragland Ray, Read, Robbins, Rodman, Rose, Sanderlin, Stilwell, Tucker and Watts—48.

Those who voted in the negative, are:

Messrs. Aydlott, Barnes, Bradley, Bryan, Candler, Cowles, Duckworth, Durham, Forkner, French of Rockingham, Gahagan, George, Graham of Orange, Hay, Hodnett, Holt, Jones of Caldwell, King of Lincoln, Lennon, McCubbins, Merritt, McDonald of Moore, Nance, Peterson, Rhodes, Rich, Teague, Welker and Williams of Wake—29.

The following is the report of the Judicial Committee on the Overton case:

The Committee to whom was referred the petition of James Overton, praying for a divorce from his wife, having considered the same, are of opinion that his request should be granted, and they report herewith an ordinance to that effect.

*Be it ordained by the people of North-Carolina, in Convention assembled*, That James Overton, and Charlotte, his wife, are hereby divorced from the bonds ot matrimony.

Mr. Moore moved to reconsider the vote, which motion was laid on the table.

On motion the report of the Committee to whom was referred the petition of divorce of Mrs. Hopkins, was taken up and adopted.

The Committee on the Judicial Department, to whom was referred the petition of Martha A. Hopkins, wife of William T. Hopkins, to be divorced from her husband, respectfully report the following ordinance and recommend its passage.

WM. B. RODMAN, *Chairman.*

*Be it ordained by the people of North-Carolina, in Convention assembled*, That the bonds of matrimony between William T. Hopkins, and Martha A., his wife, now of Granville County, are hereby dissolved, and either party are at liberty to marry again.

A motion to reconsider the vote by which this report was adopted, was, on motion, laid on the table.

On motion, the following ordinance, reported by the Judicial Department, was taken up and adopted:

*Be it ordained by the people of North-Carolina in Convention assembled*, That DeWitt C. Wilson, and Nancy Wilson, his wife, of Davie County, be, and they are hereby divorced from the bonds of matrimony.

A motion to reconsider this vote, was, on motion, laid on the table.

The following ordinance, as reported by the Judicial Committee, was, on motion, adopted:

*Be it ordained by the people of North-Carolina, in Convention assembled*, That Lavinia Lee, of Guilford County, be, and she is hereby divorced from the bonds of matrimony with her husband, Wesley Lee.

A motion to reconsider the vote by which this ordinance was adopted, was, on motion, laid on the table.

The following ordinance was, on motion, adopted:

*Be it ordained by the people of North-Carolina, in Convention assembled*, That Eliza C. Wagner, of Alamance County, be, and she is hereby divorced from the bonds of matrimony with her husband, Herman Wagner.

A motion to reconsider the above vote, was, on motion, laid on the table.

The following ordinance was, on motion, adopted:

*Be it ordained by the people of North-Carolina, in Convention assembled*, That Josephine, wife of Jas. M. Emanuel, of Orange County, be, and hereby is, divorced from the bonds of matrimony with her husband.

A motion to reconsider the vote on the above was, on motion, laid on the table.

On motion, the following ordinance was adopted:

## AN ORDINANCE TO DIVORCE WINNEY GRIBBLES AND JAMES GRIBBLES.

Section 1. *Be it ordained by the people of North-Carolina, in Convention assembled*, That the nuptial tie between Winney Gribbles and James Gribbles be, and the same is hereby dissolved, and that the said Winney Gribbles be divorced from the bonds of matrimony contracted with the said James Gribbles, and that the said Winney Gribbles be from henceforth, to all intents and purposes, a *feme sole*.

Sec. 2. *Be it further ordained*, That this ordinance shall take effect from its ratification.

It was moved to reconsider the vote.

The motion was laid on the table

The following ordinance reported by the Special Committee on Divorce, was, on motion, adopted:

## AN ORDINANCE FOR THE DIVORCE OF ESTHER V. TODD AND BENJAMIN W. TODD.

Section 1. *Be it ordained by the people of North-Carolina, in Convention assembled*, That Esther V. Todd, formerly Esther V. Walton, and now the wife of Benjamin W. Todd, be, and she is hereby divorced from the bonds of matrimony with her said husband, and that she shall be at liberty to resume her maiden name; and this ordinance shall take effect from and after its passage.

A motion to reconsider the vote by which this ordinance was passed, was, on motion, laid on the table.

The following ordinance, was, on motion, adopted:

## AN ORDINANCE TO DIVORCE ADELIA E. SLATER AND JAMES A. SLATER.

Section 1. *Be it ordained by the people of North-Carolina, in Convention assembled*, That Adelia E. Slater, of Rowan County, be, and she is hereby divorced from the bonds of matrimony with her husband, James A. Slater, and that she shall be at liberty to assume her maiden name, said Adelia to have charge of her children.

A motion to reconsider the vote on the above ordinance was,

On motion, laid on the table.

The following protest was, by permission, entered on the Journal:

Being of the opinion that all cases of divorce properly belongs to the Courts, we dissent from granting the same otherwise.

J. Q. A. BRYAN,
CALVIN J. COWLES.

The following ordinance to incorporate the Charlotte City Hall Association, as reported by the Committee of seventeen, was,

On motion, adopted:

## AN ORDINANCE TO INCORPORATE THE CHARLOTTE CITY HALL ASSOCIATION.

SECTION. 1. *Be it ordained by the people of North-Carolina in Convention assembled*, That John L. Morehead, Robert M. Oates, Jonas Rudicil, Samuel Taylor, Thomas W. Dewey, Charles W. Alexander, W. I. Sater, and their associates, successors and assigns, be and they are hereby incorporated a body in law and fact, by the name and style of the Charlotte City Hall Association, for the purpose of erecting buildings and other improvements in the City of Charlotte, and shall possess and enjoy all rights and privileges in immunities of a corporation, a body politic in law necessary to carry on said business.

SEC. 2. *Be it further ordained*, That the said Company may employ such an amount of capital not exceeding one hundred thousand dollars as may be deemed necessary to carry on the business aforesaid, which may be divided into shares of one hundred dollars or such other amounts as the stockholders in general meeting may determine, for obtaining which books of subscription may be opened by the corporation aforesaid, and the sum paid in in such manner and such time as the Board of Directors may require; and if any subscriber shall fail to pay any instalment at the time required, he shall pay interest thereon at the rate of ten per cent. per annum, and his stock may be forfeited and sold by the Directors, and the proceeds applied to the payment of the aforesaid deficient instalment. Certificates of stock may be issued, and the same made transferable and assignable as the by-laws of the Company may prescribe.

SEC. 3. *Be it further ordained*, That the affairs of said Company shall be managed by a Board of five Directors, chosen from among the stockholders, who shall elect one of their number to be the President of the Company. Three of the Board shall be a quorum to transact business, one of whom shall be the President.

SEC. 4. *Be it further ordained*, That the said Company shall have power to make by laws not inconsistent with the laws of the United States and this State, appointing all necessary officers and employees, fixing salaries, taking bonds, filling vacancies and making regulations for the transaction of any matters necessary for the successful carrying on of the business of the Company.

SEC. 5. *Be it further ordained*, That as soon after the ratification of this act as they may think proper, said corporation, or a majority of them, may call a general meeting of the subscribers to the stock of said Company, for the purpose of adopting by-laws for, and electing Directors of, said Company, which Directors shall continue in office until their successors shall be elected by a succeeding meeting.

SEC 6. *Be it further ordained*, That the said corporation shall have full power and authority to purchase and hold lots and parcels of land in said city or its vicinity, and erect thereon buildings and other improvements, and to sell, rent, lease or dispose of the same as may be ordered by the stockholders of said Company.

SEC. 7. *Be it further ordained*, That the said corporation, for the purpose of carrying on their purchases of lots or lands, and of erecting buildings and other improvements, may issue bonds on the faith and credit of said corporation in such amounts, at such times and at such rates, as they may deem right and proper, and shall have power to make mortgages or deeds of trust to secure said bonds.

SEC. 8. *Be it further ordained*, That this ordinance shall be in force from and after its ratification, and continue for fifty years.

Mr. Andrews introduced a petition of divorce of Mrs. Palmer.

Referred to the Committee on the Judicial Department.

Mr. Pool, Chairman of the Engrossing Committee, reported.

Report lies over.

The following ordinance was,

On motion, adopted:

## AN ORDINANCE TO INCORPORATE THE HALCYON STEAM BOAT COMPANY.

SECTION 1. *Be it ordained by the people of North-Carolina in Convention assembled, and it is hereby ordained by the authority of the same*, That Robert M. Orrell, James A. Orrell and John R. Daily, and such others as they may hereinafter associate with them, their successors and assigns, shall be and are hereby created, constituted and declared a body corporate and politic by the name of "The Halcyon Steam Boat Company," and by that name shall be in law capable of sueing and being sued, pleading and being impleaded, shall have a common seal and be invested with all the rights and privileges and be subject to all the regulations and restrictions contained in the 26th chapter of the Revised Code, so far as the same are applicable to such a corporation, that are not inconsistent with the provisions of this act.

SEC. 2. *Be it further ordained*, That the capital stock of said Company shall consist of fifteen thousand dollars, with the privilege of increasing the same to twenty thousand dollars, divided into shares of one thousand dollars each.

SEC. 3. *Be it further ordained*, That said Company may

build another steamer or barge or flats if required for the interest of the Company.

SEC. 4. *Be it further ordained*, That said Company shall have power to hold, possess, acquire and enjoy such real estate as may be necessary for the transaction of its business, and from time to time make all necessary rules, regulations and by-laws for the government and direction of the concerns thereof, not inconsistent with the Constitution and laws of the State of North-Carolina and of the United States, and said Company to have corporate existence for twenty years, unless surrendered to the Legislature at an earlier date by a majority of the stock.

SEC. 5. *Be it further ordained*, That this ordinance shall be in force from and after its ratification.

The House, on motion, adjourned.

---

## EVENING SESSION, MARCH 13TH, 1868.

The Convention was called to order at 7½ o'clock, by the President.

The Roll was called, and the following members answered to their names:

Messrs. Andrews, Ashley, Aydlott, Barnes, Benbow, Blume, Bradley, Bryan, Carey, Carter, Chillson, Colgrove, Congleton, Cox, Duckworth, Ellis, Eppes, Etheridge, Fisher, Forkner, Franklin, French of Bladen, French of Rockingham, French of Chowan, Fullings, Gahagan, George, Grant of Wayne, Grant of Northampton, Gunter, Hare, Harris of Wake, Harris of Franklin, Hay, Hayes of Robeson, Hayes of Halifax, Hobbs, Hoffler, Hollowell, Holt, Hood, Hyman, Jones of Caldwell, Jones of Washington, King of Lincoln, King of Lenoir, Kinney, Laflin, Lee, Legg, Lennon, Mann, Mayo, Marshall, McCubbins, Merritt, McDonald of Chatham, Moore, Morton, Nance, Newsom, Nicholson, Parker, Parks, Petree, Peterson, Pool, Ragland, Ray, Read, Renfrow, Rich, Robbins, Rodman, Rose, Sanderlin, Stilwell, Taylor, Teague, Tourgee, Trogden, Tucker, Turner, Watts and Welker—85.

The Committee on Relief reported.

Mr. French, of Bladen, moved to postpone the report indefinitely.

The yeas and nays were demanded.

The motion was lost by the following vote:

Those who voted in the affirmative are:

Messrs. Barnes, Congleton, Eppes, French of Bladen, Grant of Wayne, Hood, Jones of Washington, King of Lincoln, King of Lenoir, Kinney, Lee, Petree, Ray, Renfrow, Robbins, Teague and Trogden—17.

Those who voted in the negative are:

Messrs. Abbott, Andrews, Ashley, Aydlott, Baker, Benbow, Blume, Bradley, Bryan, Carey, Carter, Cherry, Chillson, Colgrove, Daniel, Dickey, Dowd, Duckworth, Durham, Ellis, Etheridge, Fisher, Forkner, Franklin, French of Chowan, Fullings, Gahagan, Galloway, George, Glover, Graham of Orange, Grant of Northampton, Gully, Gunter, Hare, Harris of Wake, Harris of Franklin, Hay, Hayes of Robeson, Hayes of Halifax, Heaton, Hobbs, Hoffler, Hollowell, Holt, Hyman, Jones of Caldwell, Laflin, Legg, Lennon, Logan, May, Mayo, Marshall, McCubbins, Merritt, McDonald of Chatham, Moore, Morton, Nance, Newsom, Patrick, Parker, Parks, Pool, Ragland, Read, Rhodes, Rich, Rodman, Rose, Sanderlin, Stilwell, Taylor, Tourgee, Tucker, Turner, Watts, Welker and Williamson—80.

Mr. Graham, of Orange, offered a substitute for the ordinance of the Committee on Relief.

A motion to print and postpone the whole matter until Saturday at 1 o'clock, P. M., was not sustained.

On the substitute of Mr. Graham, the yeas and nays were demanded.

The substitute prevailed by the following vote:

Those who voted in the affirmative, are:

Messrs. Abbott, Baker, Barnes, Bradley, Bryan, Carey, Carter, Cherry, Chillson, Daniel, Dickey, Duckworth, Durham, Ellis, Eppes, Etheridge, Fisher, Forkner, French of Rockingham, Gahagan, Galloway, George, Glover, Graham of Orange, Gully, Hare, Harris of Franklin, Hay, Hayes of

Robeson, Hayes of Halifax, Heaton, Hobbs, Hoffler, Hollowell, Holt, Hyman, Jones of Caldwell, Jones of Washington, Laflin, Lee, Legg, Lennon, May, Merritt, Morton, Nance, Newsom, Parks, Ragland, Read, Rodman, Sanderlin, Smith, Stilwell, Taylor, Teague, Turner, Watts and Williamson—59.

Those who voted in the negative are:

Messrs. Ashley, Benbow, Blume, Colgrove, Congleton, Franklin, Fullings, Gunter, King of Lincoln, King of Lenoir, Kinney, McCubbins, McDonald of Chatham, Moore, Patrick, Pool, Renfrow, Rich, Robbins, Rose, Stilly, Tourgee, Trogden and Welker—24.

On motion the substitute of Mr. Graham, of Orange, and the report of the Committee on Relief were ordered to be printed and made a Special Order for Saturday.

Leave of absence was granted Messrs. Watts, Aydlott, King of Lenoir and Peterson.

An ordinance in relation to the intimidation of voters was introduced by the Committee on that subject.

Mr. Rich moved that the President of this Convention sign certificates of pay for members up to Tuesday next.

The motion was not sustained.

The ordinance on intimidation of voters was taken up.

Mr. Ellis offered as a substitute sections 22d and 23d, chapter 52d, of the General Assembly, entitled "an act concerning the General Assembly of the State of North-Carolina."

The substitute was not sustained.

Mr. French, of Chowan, moved to add to section 1st, the following words: "And one-half of the fine shall go to the prosecutor."

The amendment was accepted.

Mr. French, of Bladen, offered a substitute, which was lost.

The ordinance, as amended, was adopted by the following vote:

Those who voted in the affirmative are:

Messrs. Abbott, Ashley, Blume, Bryan, Carey, Carter, Cherry, Chillson, Colgrove, Congleton, Dickey, Eppes, Fisher, Forkner, French of Bladen, French of Rockingham, French of Chowan, Fullings, Gahagan, George, Glover, Gunter, Harris of Wake, Hay, Hayes of Robeson, Hayes of Halifax, Hobbs, Hyman, Jones of Washington, King of Lenoir, Kinney, Laflin, May, Mayo, Marshall, McDonald of Chatham, Morton, Nance, Newsom, Patrick, Parks, Petree, Pool, Ray, Renfrow, Rodman, Rose, Smith, Stilwell, Teague, Tourgee, Tucker, Turner, Watts, Welker and Williamson—56.

Those who voted in the negative, are:

Messrs. Baker, Bradley, Dowd, Durham, Ellis, Etheridge, Graham of Orange, Hare, Holt, Jones of Caldwell, Lennon, McCubbins, Merritt and Sanderlin—14.

The following is the ordinance as adopted:

## AN ORDINANCE TO PREVENT THE INTIMIDATION OF VOTERS.

SECTION 1. *Be it ordained by the people of North-Carolina in Convention assembled, and it is hereby ordained as follows:* Any person who shall prevent, or endeavor to prevent, any qualified elector of this State from the free exercise of the elective franchise, by violence or bribery, or by threats of violence or injury to his person or property, or by depriving an elector of employment or threatening to deprive him of employment, shall be deemed guilty of a misdemeanor, and upon conviction thereof shall be punished by imprisonment for not less than one month, nor more than six months, or by fine of not less than one hundred dollars nor more than five hundred dollars for each offence, and one half of the fine shall go to the proscutor.

SEC. 2. *Be it further ordained,* That the hiring of any laborer upon the condition that the same shall vote, or not vote, for any special candidate, or any particular party, or in any specific manner shall be deemed bribery within the meaning of this act, upon the part of the person demanding the said condition.

SEC. 3. *Be it further ordained,* That this ordinance shall be published and circulated with this Constitution for the information of voters, and shall be in force from and after the date of its passage.

Mr. Rodman introduced a resolution giving certain instructions to the Committee on Revision.

There being no quorum present, the House adjourned.

---

SATURDAY, March 14th, 1868.

The Convention was called to order at 10 o'clock by the President.

Prayer by the Rev. Mr. Lennon.

The roll was called and the following members answered to their names:

Messrs. Abbott, Andrews, Aydlott, Baker, Benbow, Blume, Bradley, Bryan, Carey, Carter, Candler, Cherry, Colgrove, Congleton, Cox, Dickey, Dowd, Duckworth, Eppes, Etheridge, Fisher, Forkner, Franklin, French of Bladen, French of Rockingham, Fullings, Gahagan, Galloway, George, Graham of Montgomery, Grant of Wayne, Grant of Northampton, Gully, Gunter, Hall, Hare, Harris of Wake, Hay, Hayes of Robeson, Hayes of Halifax, Highsmith, Hobbs, Hodnett, Hoffler, Hollowell, Holt, Hood, Hyman, Jones of Caldwell, Jones of Washington, King of Lenoir, Kinney, Laflin, Lee, Lennon, Logan, Mann, May, Mayo, Marshall, Merritt, McDonald of Chatham, McDonald of Moore, Moore, Morton, Mullican, Murphy, Nance, Newsom, Nicholson, Patrick, Parker, Parks, Petree, Pierson, Ragland, Ray, Read, Renfrow, Rhodes, Rich, Robbins, Rose, Smith, Stilly, Stillwell, Taylor, Teague, Trogden, Tucker, Turner, Welker and Williams of Wake—94.

The following Committee was appointed to prepare an address to the people: Messrs. Tourgee, Rodman and Gahagan.

The following report was taken up and discussed:

The Committee of Seventeen to whom was referred an ordinance, entitled "An ordinance providing for the restoration of the public credit," have had the same under consideration, and report the same back with a recommendation in favor of its passage after the following amendments are made, viz: *First*, Amend the title of said ordinance so as to read, "An ordinance providing for the payment ot the interest of the public debt;" *Second*, In line 8, between the words "for" and "of," strike out the words, "the resumption;" also strike out the 10th line, which reads as follows: "And the restoration of the public credit;" also, add the following as a fourth section: "This ordinance shall be in force and take effect from and after its passage."

D. HEATON, *Chairman.*

## AN ORDINANCE TO PROVIDE FOR THE PAYMENT OF THE INTEREST ON THE PUBLIC DEBT.

SECTION 1. *Be it ordained by the people of North-Carolina, in Convention assembled, and it is hereby ordained by the authority of the same*, That the first General Assembly which shall be convened under the provisions of the Constitution framed by this body, be, and the same is hereby directed to make the following provisions for the payment of the interest upon the public debt.

SEC. 2. It shall provide for the payment in cash of the interest falling due on and after the first day of January, 1869, upon that portion of the bonds of the State which are dated prior to May 20th, 1861.

SEC. 3. It shall provide for the payment in cash of the interest falling due on and after the first day of July, 1869, upon that portion of the bonds of the State which are dated on and after January 1st, 1866.

SEC. 4. It shall provide for funding all such coupons upon the above specified classes of bonds as are now due, or which may become due, prior to the time when the payment of interest shall be resumed as above directed; and for such purposes the General Assembly shall authorize the issue of bonds of the State bearing six per cent. interest, which shall be given at par in exchange for such coupons as are now due, or may become due prior to the time when such resumption of the payment of interest shall take place.

SEC. 5. This ordinance shall be in force and take effect from and after its passage.

Mr. King moved to amend by adding to section 1, "The Legislature shall have power to alter, amend or repeal this ordinance."

On this amendment the yeas and nays were demanded.

The call was sustained.

The amendment was lost by the following vote:

Those who voted in the affirmative, are:

Messrs. Aydlott, Barnes, Blume, Bradley, Candler, Daniel, Duckworth, Durham, Ellis, Etheridge, Graham of Montgomery, Graham of Orange, Grant of Northampton, Hare, Hodnett, Holt, Jones of Washington, King of Lenoir, McCubbins, Merritt, McDonald of Chatham, Moore, Mullican, Patrick, Rhodes, Rose, Sanderlin, Teague and Turner—29.

Those who voted in the negative are:

Messrs. Abbott, Andrews, Ashley, Baker, Bryan, Carey, Carter, Cherry, Chillson, Colgrove, Congleton, Cox, Dickey, Eppes, Fisher, Forkner, Franklin, French of Bladen, French of Chowan, Fullings, Gahagan, Galloway, Glover, Gully, Gunter, Harris of Wake, Hay, Hayes of Robeson, Hayes of Halifax, Heaton, Highsmith, Hobbs, Hood, Hyman, Jones of Caldwell, Kinney, Laflin, Lee, Legg, Mann, May, Mayo, Marshall, McDonald of Moore, Morton, Murphy, Nicholson, Parker, Parks, Petree, Pierson, Pool, Ray, Read, Renfrow, Rich, Robbins, Rodman, Smith, Stilwell, Taylor, Tucker and Williams of Wake—64.

The following amendment offered by Mr. Candler was put to the house and lost.

Strike out in 3d line, 2d section, "1869," and insert "1871."

The question recurred on the original ordinance as reported by the Committee, which was, on motion, adopted by the following vote:

Those who voted in the affirmative, are:

Messrs. Abbott, Andrews, Ashley, Blume, Bryan, Carey, Carter, Cherry, Chillson, Colgrove, Congleton, Cox, Dickey, Dowd, Eppes, Fisher, Forkner, Franklin, French of Bladen, French of Rockingham, French of Chowan, Fullings, Gahagan, Galloway, Glover, Gully, Gunter, Hall, Harris of Wake, Hay, Hayes of Robeson, Hayes of Halifax, Heaton, High smith, Hobbs, Hollowell, Hood, Hyman, Jones of Caldwell, Kinney, Laflin, Lee, Legg, Mann, May, Mayo, Marshall, McDonald of Moore, Morton, Murphy, Nance, Nicholson, Patrick, Parker, Parks, Petree, Pierson, Pool, Ragland, Ray, Read, Renfrow, Rich, Robbins, Rodman, Rose, Smith, Stilwell, Taylor, Trogden, Tucker and Williams of Wake—72.

Those who voted in the negative are:

Messrs. Aydlott, Bradley, Candler, Daniel, Duckworth, Durham, Ellis, Etheridge, Graham of Montgomery, Graham of Orange, Hare, Hodnett, Holt, Jones of Washington, King of Lenoir, Merritt, McDonald of Chatham, Moore, Sanderlin, Teague and Turner—21.

The Committee on Revision reported as follows:

The Committee on Revision to whom was referred the articles of the Constitution upon the Executive and Legislative Department have revised the same, and now recommend their final Enrollment.

D. HEATON,
W. B. RODMAN,
W. NICHOLSON.

The report was adopted.

The following gentlemen obtained leave to enter their names on the protest of Messrs. Bryan, and Cowles, entered on the Journal of Friday: Messrs. M. J. Aydlott, R. W. King, J. S. McCubbins, G. W. Bradley, E. B. Teague, W. H. George.

The Committee on Contingent Expenses have examined the account of Messrs W. W. Holden & Son, of five hundred and fifty-three dollars and ninety-seven cents. It appearing from the statement of the officers that the same is correct; we therefore recommend its payment. All of which is respectfully submitted.

R. W. KING, *Chairman.*

The printed ordinance of relief offered by the Committee

together with the substitute of Mr. Graham, of Orange, was taken up and discussed.

Mr. King, of Lenoir, moved an amendment to the substitute of Mr. Graham, of Orange, by adding another section, which was rejected.

The following ordinance of relief, by Mr. Graham, of Orange, was adopted.

## AN ORDINANCE RESPECTING THE JURISDICTION OF THE COURTS OF THIS STATE.

SECTION 1. *Be it ordained by the people of North-Carolina in Convention assembled*, That sections one and two of the ordinance of the Convention adopted June 23d, 1866, entitled "an ordinance to change the jurisdiction of the courts and the rules of pleading therein," be and are hereby repealed.

SEC. 2. *Be it further ordained*, That section three of the above entitled ordinance be amended to read as follows: Sec. 3. That all actions of debt, covenant, assumpsit and account now pending in the Superior Courts shall be continued to Spring Term, 1869, and that the several Superior Courts at the Spring Term thereof only, unless otherwise herein provided, shall have exclusive original jurisdiction of such causes of action except where jurisdiction has been or shall be given to a Justice of the Peace by the Constitution or laws of North-Carolina. Should the defendant at the Spring Term, 1869, on writs which shall be returned to that Term or in any suit, for the above causes of action then pending in the Superior Court, pay or confess judgment to the plaintiff for one-tenth of the debt and demand, principal and interest and all costs to that time, he shall be allowed until next Spring Term to plead. At the said Spring Term should the defendant pay to the plaintiff or confess judgment for one-fifth of the residue of the said debt or demand and cost, he shall be allowed until the succeeding Spring Term to plead. At the said Spring Term should the defendant pay to the plaintiff or confess judgment for one-half of the residue of the debt or demand, he shall be allowed until the succeeding Spring Term to plead. At the said Spring Term the plaintiff shall have judgment for the residue of his debt or demand: *Provided, however*, That the plaintiff, if required, shall file his debt or demand in writing, and if the defendant shall make oath that the whole or any part thereof is not justly due, or that he has a counter demand, all of which shall be particularly set forth by affidavit, then the defendant shall only pay the instalment required of what he admits to be due, and the court shall order a jury at the same or some subsequent term to try the matters in dispute between the parties, and at the next Spring Term the defendant shall be allowed time to plead only upon paying or confessing judgment for one-fifth of the residue of the admitted amount, and whatever the jury finds him indebted over and above the same: *Provided further*, That should the defendant fail to pay or confess judgment for the first or any subsequent installment, then and in that case the plaintiff shall be entitled to proceed to judgment and execution for such installment, unless the defendant shall put in pleas, in which case the suit shall proceed according to the course of the court in 1860: *Provided further*, That by consent of the plaintiff the defendant at any term of the court may confess judgment for a stipulated sum in full and final discharge of all further demand or liability upon such claim.

SEC. 3. *Be it further ordained*, That section 10 of the above recited act shall be amended to read as follows: Sec. 10. That executions on judgments in actions of debt, assumpsit, covenant or account, or decrees for money demands in equity, which have been, or shall be issued on judgments or decrees heretofore obtained, shall be levied on the property of the defendant and returned without sale: *Provided*, such return shall not prejudice any lien the plaintiff may acquire or then have by virtue of said *fi fa.* or *venditioni exponas*. At Spring Term, 1869, execution on all such judgments or decrees shall issue for only one-tenth of the amount then due; at Spring Term, 1870, for one-fith of the residue; at Spring Term, 1871, for one-half of the residue, and at Spring Term, 1872, for the balance of the debt; and no execution shall issue from the Fall Term on any such judgment or decree except by consent of the defendant. That no mortgagee or trustee shall expose to sale the property conveyed in such mortgage or trust deed, without the consent of the grantor, before first of March, 1869. Should the mortgagor or trustor at that time pay one-tenth of the debts mentioned, the sale shall be postponed to first of March, 1870; at that time should the mortgagor or trustor pay one fifth of the residue, the sale shall be postponed to the first of March, 1871; at that time should the trustor or mortgagor pay one-half of the residue, the sale shall be postponed to first of March, 1872; and at that time the trustee or morgagee shall sell the property or so much of it as will realize the balance of the debts: *Provided, however*, That should the trustor or mortgagor fail to pay the first or any subsequent installment, then, and in that case, the trustee or mortgagee shall sell at six months credit so much of the property conveyed as will realize such installment.

Sec. 4. *Be it further ordained*, That section 11 of the above entitled act be amended to read as follows: That no warrants before Justices of the Peace shall issue or be returnable until January 1st, 1869. Should the defendant upon such return pay to the plaintiff. or to the collecting officer, for his use, or confess judgment before the magistrate for one-tenth of the debt and demand, (principal and interest) he shall be allowed twelve months to plead; at the expiration of that time, should the defendant pay to the plaintiff or confess judgment for one-fifth of the residue of the said debt or demand, he shall be allowed twelve months more to plead; at the expiration of that time should the defendant pay to the plaintiff or confess judgment for one-half of the residue of said debt or demand, he shall be allowed twelve months more to plead; at the expiration of that time the plaintiff shall have judgment for the residue of his debt or demand: *Provided however*, That the plaintiff, if required, shall file his claim in writing, and if the defendant shall make oath that the whole or any part thereof is not justly due, or that he has a counter demand, all of which he shall particularly set forth by affidavit, then the defendent shall only pay the installment required of what he admits to be due, and the justice shall proceed to try the matters in dispute between the parties; and at the expiration of twelve months the defendant shall be allowed time to plead only upon payment of one-fifth of the amount admitted to be due, and whatever the justice may have found him indebted over and above the same: *Provided*, That should the defendant fail to pay or confess judgment for the first or any subsequent installment, then and in that case, the plaintiff shall be entitled to proceed to judgment and execution for such installment: *Provided further*, That by consent of the plaintiff the defendant may at any time confess judgment for a stipulated sum in full and final discharge of all further demand or liability upon such claim. That all executions on judgments in actions of debt, covenant, assumpsit or account which have been, or shall be issued on judgments heretofore obtained before any magistrate, shall be levied on the property of the defendent and returned without sale; at the expiration of twelve months from such return, execution on all such judgments shall issue for only one-tenth of the amount then due; at the expiration of twelve months from that time for one-fifth of the residue; at the expiration of twelve months more for one-half of the residue, and at the expiration of twelve months more for the balance of the debt.

SEC. 5. *Be it further ordained*, That section 17 of the above entitled ordinance be amended to read as follows: Section 17. That the provisions of this ordinance shall not be construed to extend to any debts or demands contracted or penalties incurred since the first day of May, A. D, 1865, or which may hereafter be contracted or incurred, except actions founded on any bond, promissory note, bill of exchange, or any other instrument of writing, or parol promise made since first May, 1865, in renewal of, or substitution for, a contract made prior to first of May, 1865, to the full amount of the principal and interest of a debt existing prior to said day, and without other consideration than such pre-existent debt; and except also, actions, suits, or process to revive, continue or enforce any judgment heretofore recovered upon any such bond, promissory note, bill of exchange or other instrument of writing or parol, or promise, as is hereinbefore mentioned.

SEC. 6. *Be it further ordained*, That this ordinance shall be in force from and after its ratification.

Mr. King, of Lincoln, offered a resolution in relation to the amalgamation of races.

Lies over under the rules.

Mr. Read offered an ordinance in relation to the Cape Fear and Deep River Navigation Company.

Referred to the Committee of Seventeen.

Mr. Harris, of Wake, introduced a report of the Committee on Divorce.

Mr. Hood introduced a resolution in relation to marriages.

Lies over under the rule.

Mr. Rodman introduced the following resolution, which was,

On motion, adopted:

*Resolved*, That for the purpose of completing the enrolment of the ordinance, and resolutions of this Convention, the Secretary be, and he is, authorized to employ one or more clerks.

On motion, the following ordinance introduced by Mr. Rodman was adopted:

## AN ORDINANCE PROVIDING FOR AUDITING THE ACCOUNTS OF THE CONVENTION.

SECTION 1. *Be it ordained by the people of North-Carolina in Convention assembled*, That Calvin J. Cowles, after the adjournment of this Convention, shall audit the accounts thereof, and also the accounts for all expenditures for the printing ordered by this Convention, and the Treasurer of this State is hereby required to pay from any money in the Treasury of the State, upon the warrant of said Cowles, any sum necessary for the purpose of paying such expenses. He shall receive for his services six dollars per day while actually employed therein, to be paid in like manner upon his own warrant. The Comptroller of the State is hereby requested to audit the accounts of said Cowles, and the said accounts so audited shall be deposited in the office of the Comptroller of the State of North-Carolina.

On motion, the House adjourned.

---

EVENING SESSION, March 14th, 1868.

The Convention was called to order at 7½ o'clock by the President.

The roll was called, the following members answering to their names:

Messrs. Andrews, Ashley, Aydlott, Bryan, Carter, Cherry, Chillson, Congleton, Daniel, Dickey, Dowd, Duckworth, Ellis, Eppes, Etheridge, Fisher, Forkner, French of Rockingham, French of Chowan, Fullings, Gahagan, Galloway, George, Graham of Montgomery, Grant of Northampton, Gunter, Harris of Wake, Hay, Hayes of Halifax, Highsmith, Hobbs, Hoffler, Hollowell, Hood, Hyman, Jones of Caldwell, King of Lenoir, Laflin, Lee, Legg, Lennon, Logan, May, Marshall, McCubbins, McDonald of Chatham, Moore, Mullican, Nance, Newsom, Nicholson, Parker, Parks, Petree, Ragland, Ray, Read, Renfrow, Rhodes, Robbins, Rose, Sanderlin, Stilwell, Teague, Tucker, Turner and Welker—67.

Leave of absence was granted Mr. Ragland until Monday next.

Mr. Hood called up the following ordinance:

## AN ORDINANCE IN RELATION TO MARRIAGES AUTHORIZED BY MILITARY AUTHORITY.

Section 1. *Be it ordained by the people of North-Carolina in Convention assembled, and it is hereby ordained by the authority of the same*, That all marriages authorized by military authority since April 1st, 1862, are hereby declared legal and valid.

Mr. Ellis offered an amendment, which was lost.

The ordinance, as read, was adopted.

The Committee on Revision reported back the following Articles, viz:

Judicial Department,

Finance,

Municipal Corporations,

With a few verbal corrections, excepting section 1st in Municipal Corporations, which was stricken out.

The report was adopted, and the Articles were ordered to be enrolled as reported by the Committee, for final action and signature.

The following ordinance was reported by the Committee of Seventeen, who recommended its adoption:

## AN ORDINANCE AMENDING THE CHARTER OF THE CITY OF WILMINGTON.

Whereas, Certain provisions of an act to incorporate the indabitants of the town of Wilmington, ratified February 1st, A. D. 1866, are inconsistent with and contrary to section 22d of the Bill of rights as adopted by the Convention, and proposed to be incorporated in the Constitution of the State ot North-Carolina:

Section. 1. *Be it ordained by the people of North-Carolina in Convention assembled*, That so much of section third of the aforesaid act to incorporate the inhabitants of the town of Wilmington, as requires a freehold situated in the city of the value of one thousand ($1,000) dollars, according to assessment for taxation, as a qualification to hold the office of Mayor and Alderman of said city, be and the same is hereby repealed.

Sec. 2. *Be it further ordained*, That so much of section fifth of the aforesaid act of incorporation, as requires the inspector of elections in each ward to be a freeholder, be and hereby is repealed.

Sec. 3. *Be it further ordained*, That within fifteen days after the organization of the State Govornment, under the Constitution adopted by this Convention, the Sheriff of the County of New Hanover, with such assistants as he may appoint, shall hold an election for Mayor, and two (2) Aldermen for each of the four wards of the City of Wilmington, which election shall be in conformity with the provisions of this ordinance, and in the manner prescribed by the seventeenth (17th) section of the beforementioned act of incorporation. The person elected Mayor shall hold office until the first Monday in January, 1869; and until his successor is qualified. Of the persons elected Aldermen of each ward, one shall hold office until the first Monday in January, 1869, and until his successor shall be qualified, and the other shall hold office until the first Monday in January, 1870, and until his successor shall be qualified. The classification of the Aldermen shall be made by the aforesaid Sheriff, in the manner prescribed by the classification of the first Board of Aldermen, by section seventeenth (17th) of the aforesaid act of incorporation.

SEC. 4. *Be it further ordained*, That this ordinance shall be in force from and after the approval by the Congress of the United States of the Constitution framed by this Convention.

The ordinance was put before the House for action.

The yeas and nays were called on its adoption.

The call was sustained and the ordinance adopted by the following vote:

Those who voted in the affirmative are:

Messrs. Abbott, Andrews, Ashley, Aydlott, Bryan, Carter, Chillson, Congleton, Dickey, Fisher, Franklin, French of Bladen, French of Rockingham, French of Chowan, Fullings, Gahagan, Galloway, George, Graham of Montgomery, Grant of Wayne, Gunter, Hall, Harris of Wake, Hay, Hayes of Robeson, Heaton, Hobbs, Hoffler, Jones of Washington, King of Lenoir, Kinney, Laflin, Legg, Logan, Mann, May, Mayo, Marshall, McDonald of Chatham, Mullican, Nance, Newsom, Nicholson, Parks, Petree, Ray, Read, Renfrow, Rich, Rodman, Rose, Stilwell, Teague, Tucker, Turner and Welker—51.

Those who voted in the negative, are:

Messrs. Baker, Durham, Ellis, Etheridge, Graham of Orange, Hare, Lennon, Merritt and Sanderlin—9.

The Committee on Divorce reported unfavorably on the following cases:

Thomas J. Hancock, Martha Brown, Elizabeth Wood and Henry G. Wood, James Bradley and Nancy Bradley, Littleton Perry and Leroy S. P. Robeson.

The Committee reported favorably on the cases of Ann Underdue and Palmer Babcock.

The petitions of Underdue and Babcock were granted.

Mr. Cherry, of Edgecombe, introduced an ordinance for the divorce of Sarah Mitchell.

Referred to the Committee of Seventeen.

Mr. Read, an ordinance for the divorce of Edward Shroyer.

The yeas and nays were granted, a majority of the members not voting, it was considered no vote.

Mr. Dowd, an ordinance to provide for the re-assessment of lands.

Referred to the Committee of Seventeen.

Mr. Abbott, an ordinance for the completion of the Western North-Carolina Rail Road, and withdrew an ordinance previously introduced.

The yeas and nays were taken.

The ordinance was adopted by the following vote:

Those who voted in the affirmative, are:

Messrs. Abbott, Andrews, Ashley, Baker, Bryan, Carter, Cherry, Chillson, Congleton, Dickey, Dowd, Durham, Ellis, Etheridge, Fisher, Forkner, French of Bladen, French of Rockingham, French of Chowan, Fullings, Gahagan, Galloway, George, Grant of Wayne, Gunter, Hall, Harris of Wake, Hayes of Robeson, Heaton, Hoffler, Hollowell, Jones of Caldwell, Kinney, Laflin, Legg, Lennon, Logan, Mann, May, Mayo, Marshall, McCubbins, Merritt, McDonald of Chatham, Mullican, Murphy, Nance, Nicholson, Parks, Petree, Ragland, Ray, Read, Rhodes, Rich, Rodman, Rose, Stilwell, Teague, Tucker, Turner and Welker—62.

Those who voted in the negative, are:

Messrs. Aydlott, Graham of Orange, Hare, Hay, King of Lenoir, Newsom, and Sanderlin—7.

## AN ORDINANCE FOR THE COMPLETION OF THE WESTERN NORTH-CAROLINA RAIL ROAD.

SECTION 1. *Be it ordained by the people of North-Carolina in Convention assembled, and it is hereby ordained by the authority of the same,* That the proceeds of no appropriations or subscriptions which the State of North-Carolina has made or may hereafter make to, or in aid of, the Western North-Carolina Rail Road Company, shall be used in the construction of any branch road except that of French Broad until the main trunk line of said Rail Road shall have been completed to Copper Mine, at or near Ducktown.

SEC. 2. *Be it further ordained,* That the General Asembly, when the interest of said corporation (the Western North-Carolina Rail Road Company) requires it, shall be and the same is hereby authorized and directed to make such further appropriation or subscription to the capital stock of said Rail Road Company as will insure the completion of said road at the earliest practicable day.

Mr. Rodman offered the following ordinance, which,

On motion, was adopted :

## AN ORDINANCE EXTENDING THE TIME FOR REGISTRATION OF DEEDS.

SECTION 1. *Be it ordained by the people of North-Carolina in Convention assembled, and it is hereby ordained by the authority of the same,* That no grant or conveyance of lands heretofore made shall be void by reason of the non-registration thereof previous to this time, but the grantees in such deeds shall have two years from the ratification of this ordinance wherein to register the same: *Provided,* That nothing herein contained shall extend to mortgages, deeds in trust or marriage settlements.

SEC. 7. *Be it further ordained,* That all persons who have

made entries of vacant land and paid the purchase money to the State for the same since the first day of January, 1861, shall have until the first day of January, 1869, to perfect titles to the same.

SEC. 3. *Be it further ordained*, That all persons who have heretofore made entries of lands according to law within the time aforesaid, and have not paid the purchase money into the Treasury, shall have until the first day of January, 1869, to make said payment and perfect their titles to said lands: *Provided*, That nothing herein contained shall be so construed as to affect the titles of persons who have heretofore obtained grants for said lands, or the rights of junior enterers, or extending to swamp lands vested in the Literary Board.

Mr. McDonald, of Chatham, obtained permission to record his name in the affirmative on the ordinances passed by the Convention in relation to the Chatham and Western Rail Road Companies.

The following are the divorce ordinances as adopted. A motion to reconsider each ordinance, was,

On motion, laid on the table:

## AN ORDINANCE FOR THE DIVORCE OF PALMER AND LUCIND C. BABCOCK.

SECTION 1. *Be it ordained by the people of North-Carolina in Convention assembled*, That Palmer Babcock be, and he hereby is, divorced from the bonds of matrimony with his wife, Lucind C. Babcock, and that this ordinance shall take effect from and after its passage.

## AN ORDINANCE FOR THE DIVORCE OF ANN UNDERDUE AND WILLIAM UNDERDUE.

SECTION 1. *Be it ordained by the people of North-Carolina, in Convention assembled*, That Ann Underdue, formerly Ann Smith, wife of William Underdue, be and she is hereby divorced from the bonds of matrimony with her said husband and that this ordinance shall be in force from and after its passage.

On motion, the house then adjourned.

MONDAY, March 16th, 1868.

The Convention was called to order at 10 o'clock, by the President.

Prayer by the Rev. Mr. Hudson.

The roll was called and the following members answered to their names:

Messrs. Andrews, Ashley, Aydlott, Benbow, Blume, Bradley, Bryan, Carey, Carter, Candler, Cherry, Chillson, Colgrove, Congleton, Cox, Daniel, Dickey, Dowd, Duckworth, Eppes, Etheridge, Fisher, Forkner, Franklin, French of Bladen, French of Rockingham, French of Chowan, Fullings, Gahagan, Galloway, George, Glover, Graham of Orange, Grant of Wayne, Grant of Northampton, Gully, Gunter, Hall, Hare, Harris of Wake, Harris of Franklin, Hay, Hayes of Robeson, Highsmith, Hobbs, Hodnett, Hoffler, Hollowell, Holt, Hood, Hyman, Jones of Caldwell, Kinney, Legg, Lennon, Logan, May, Marshall, McCubbins, Merritt, McDonald of Chatham, Moore, Morton, Mullican, Murphy, Nance, Newsom, Nicholson, Patrick, Parker, Parks, Petree, Pierson, Pool, Ray, Read, Renfrow, Robbins, Rose, Sanderlin, Smith, Stilly, Stilwell, Taylor, Teague, Trogden, Tucker, Turner, Watts, Welker and Williams of Wake—91.

The Committee of Seventeen reported the following as an amendment to Article XIII of the Constitution, which was adopted:

## ARTICLE XIII.

### AMENDMENTS.

Section 1. No Convention of the people shall be called by the General Assembly unless by the concurrence of two-thirds of all the members of each House of the General Assembly.

Sec. 2. No part of the Constitution of this State shall be altered unless a bill to alter the same shall have been read three times in each House of the General Assembly and agreed to by three-fifths of the whole number of members of each House, respectively: nor shall any alteration take place until the bill, so agreed to, shall have been published six months previous to a new election of members of the General Assembly. If, after such publication, the alteration proposed by the preceding General Assembly shall be agreed to, in the first session thereafter by two thirds of the whole representation in each House of the General Assembly, after the same shall have been read three times on three several days, in each House, then the said General Assembly shall prescribe a mode by which the amendment or amendments may be submitted to the qualified voters of the House of Representatives throughout the State; and if, upon comparing the votes given in the whole State, it shall appear that a majority of the voters voting thereon have approved thereof, then, and not otherwise, the same shall become a part of the Constitution.

The following is the vote on the adoption of the Article on Amendments:

Those who voted in the affirmative are:

Messrs. Abbott, Andrews, Ashley, Aydlott, Benbow, Blume, Bradley, Bryan, Carey, Carter, Candler, Cherry, Chilson, Colgrove, Congleton, Cox, Daniel, Dickey, Duckworth, Eppes, Etheridge, Fisher, Forkner, French of Bladen, French of Rockingham, French of Chowan, Fullings, Gahagan, Galloway, George, Glover, Graham of Montgomery, Grant of Wayne, Grant of Northampton, Gunter, Hall, Harris of Wake, Harris of Franklin, Hay, Hayes of Robeson, Hayes of Halifax, Heaton, Highsmith, Hobbs, Hoffler, Hollowell, Hood, Hyman, Jones of Caldwell, Jones of Washington, Kinney, Lee, Legg, Logan, May, Marshall, McDonald of Chatham, Moore, Morton, Mullican, Murphy, Nance, Newsom, Nicholson, Patrick, Parker, Parks, Petree, Pierson, Pool, Ray, Read, Renfrow, Rhodes, Robbins, Rose, Stilly, Taylor, Teague, Trogden, Tucker, Turner, Welker and Williams of Wake—84.

Those who voted in the negative, are:

Messrs. Durham, Graham of Orange, Hodnett, Holt, Lennon, McCubbins, Merritt and Sanderlin—9.

The following ordinance having been reported favorably by the Committee of Seventeen, was taken up, read and adopted:

## AN ORDINANCE IN RELATION TO THE CAPE FEAR AND DEEP RIVER NAVIGATION WORKS.

Whereas, The Cape Fear and Deep River Navigation Works are in a ruinous condition, and in their present condition utterly worthless to the State and highly injurious to the interests of the people residing in the valleys of said rivers; and whereas, it is expedient that said Works shall be made available in developing the resources of said valleys:

Section 1. *Now therefore be it ordained by the people of North-Carolina in Convention assembled*, That for the purpose of aiding the Chatham Rail Road Company in [the] transportation of stone for building their bridges, culverts and other masonry, and for the carriage of materials and supplies to points needed, the interest of the State of North-Carolina in said Cape Fear and Deep River Navigation Works from the Gulf Dam, on Deep River, to Northing Dam, on Cape Fear River, both inclusive, is hereby transferred to the said Chatham Rail Road Company, with liberty to said Company to repair, use and make avail of said portion of said Works, and all franchises and privileges appertenant thereto, to the same extent as is possessed by the State.

Sec. 2. *Be it further ordained*, That the President and Directors of the Chatham Rail Road Company shall have power to transfer and assign said interests herein conveyed and transferred, or any portion thereof, for the purpose of improving the valleys of said rivers.

Sec. 3. *Be it further ordained*, That this ordinance shall be in force from its passage.

The Committee of Seventeen reported the following resolution:

*Resolved*, That it is the sense of this Convention that it is impracticable to take any definite action, at this late period of the session, on the petition in relation to the formation of a new County out of Iredell, Rowan and Cabarrus Counties, and that said petition is hereby respectfully referred to the earnest attention and consideration of the next Legislature.

The resolution was, on motion, adopted.

The following resolution, reported by the Committee on Elections, was adopted:

*Resolved*, That Lorenzo D. Hall, of Sampson County, and John Marshall, of Surry County, be allowed pay and mileage from the commencement of the session, and that the President and Secretary be authorized and directed to sign vouchers for the same.

The Committee on Revision reported the following substitute for sections 2d and 5th of the Article on Suffrage and Eligibility to office:

SEC. 2. It shall be the duty of the General Assembly to provide, from time to time, for the registration of all electors, and no person shall be allowed to vote without registration, or to register, without first taking an oath or affirmation to support and maintain the Constitution and laws of the United States, and the Constitution and laws of North-Carolina, not inconsistent therewith.

SEC. 5. The following classes of persons shall be disqualified for office: First, All persons who shall deny the being of Almighty God. Second, All persons who shall have been convicted of treason, perjury, or of other infamous crime, since becoming citizens of the United States, or of corruption, or mal-practice in office, unless such persons shall have been legally restored to the rights of citizenship.

The sections were adopted.

The Article on Suffrage and Eligibility to office, as amended, was adopted by the following vote:

Those who voted in the affirmative are:

Messrs. Abbott, Andrews, Ashley, Aydlott, Blume, Bryan, Carey, Carter, Candler, Cherry, Chillson, Colgrove, Congleton, Dickey, Duckworth, Eppes, Fisher, Forkner, Franklin, French of Bladen, French of Rockingham, French of Chowan, Fullings, Gahagan, George, Glover, Graham of Montgomery, Grant of Wayne, Gunter, Hall, Harris of Wake, Harris of Franklin, Hay, Hayes of Robeson, Hayes of Halifax, Heaton, Hoffler, Hood, Hyman, Jones of Caldwell, Jones of Washington, Kinney, Laflin, Lee, May, Marshall, McDonald of Moore, Moore, Morton, Murphy, Nance, Newsom, Nicholson, Patrick,

Parker, Parks, Petree, Pierson, Pool, Ray, Renfrow, Robbins, Rose, Smith, Stilly, Stillwell, Taylor, Teague, Tourgee, Trogden, Tucker, Turner, Watts, Welker and Williams of Wake—75.

Those who voted in the negative, are:

Messrs. Bradley, Durham, Etheridge, Graham of Orange, Hare, Holt, Lennon, McCubbins, Merritt, McDonald of Chatham, Read and Sanderlin—12.

Leave of absence was granted Mr. Hodnett, Mr. May and Mr. McDonald of Chatham.

Mr. French, of Chowan, introduced an ordinance to charter the Albemarle Rail Road Company.

The ordinance passed its first reading.

A motion to suspend the rules was lost.

The following resolutions were received, and on motion, were ordered to be spread on the Journal:

CONST. CONVENTION OF SOUTH-CAROLINA,
CHARLESTON, March 14, 1868.

The following preamble and resolutions were adopted:

WHEREAS, W. H. S. Sweet, Esq., a delegate to the North-Carolina Constitutional Convention, has honored this body with a visit; therefore be it

*Resolved*, That this Convention sends greeting and good wishes to the Constitutional Convention of our sister State.

*Resolved*, That the President of this Convention is hereby requested to forward a copy of these resolutions to the Constitutional Convention of North-Carolina.

A. G. MACKEY,
*President.*

Attest:
C. J. STALBRAND, *Secretary.*

Mr. Ashley introduced the following resolution:

*Resolved*, That the Committee on Contingent Expenses be instructed to audit and allow the accounts of W. H. S. Sweet for expenses to Charleston, S. C., and return, said expenses having been incurred by order of this Convention.

The resolution, on motion, was adopted.

Mr. Rich introduced a resolution of thanks to C. J. Cowles, President of the Convention. Lies over.

Mr. Hayes, of Halifax, introduced the following resolution, which, on motion, was adopted :

*Resolved*, That it is the sense of this Convention that intermarriages and illegal intercourse between the races should be discountenanced, and the interests and happiness of the two races would be best promoted by the establishment of separate schools.

Mr. Candler moved to reconsider the vote on the ordinance legalizing marriages ordered by military authority.

The motion was laid on the table by the following vote:

Those who voted in the affirmative, are:

Messrs. Andrews, Benbow, Blume, Bryan, Carey, Carter, Cherry, Colgrove, Congleton, Cox, Dickey, Eppes, Fisher, Forkner, Franklin, French of Rockingham, Gahagan, Galloway, Gunter, Harris of Wake, Hayes of Halifax, Highsmith, Hood, Hyman, Kinney, Laflin, Marshall, McDonald of Moore, Morton, Murphy, Nance, Pierson, Pool, Ray, Renfrow, Smith, Stilly, Stilwell, Sweet andTucker—40.

Those who voted in the negative are :

Messrs. Aydlott, Baker, Bradley, Candler, Daniel, Duckworth, Durham, Etheridge, George, Glover, Graham of Orange, Hare, Hoffler, Hollowell, Holt, Jones of Caldwell, Lennon, McCubbins, Merritt, Patrick, Parks, Read, Rhodes, Rose, Sanderlin, Turner and Williams of Wake—27.

The Committee appointed to investigate the election of Mr. Durham, reported.

The report was returned to the Committee with instructions to report all the facts that have come to their knowledge.

The ordinance for the divorce of Edward Shroyer was taken up.

The yeas and nays were demanded.

They were granted.

A majority not voting, it was declared no vote.

Leave of absence was granted Mr. Sanderlin.

The following ordinance was,

On motion, adopted, yeas 69, nays 5 :

Those who voted in the affirmative, are:

Messrs. Abbott, Blume, Bradley, Bryan, Carey, Carter, Candler, Cherry, Chillson, Colgrove, Congleton, Cox, Duckworth, Eppes, Fisher, Forkner, Franklin, French of Bladen, French of Rockingham, French of Chowan, Fullings, Gahagan, George, Graham of Montgomery, Grant of Wayne, Grant of Northampton, Gunter, Hall, Harris of Franklin, Hay, Hayes of Robeson, Hayes of Halifax, Heaton, Highsmith, Hoffler, Hollowell, Hood, Hyman, Jones of Caldwell, Jones of Washington, Kinney, Laflin, Lee, McDonald of Moore, Mullican, Murphy, Nance, Patrick, Parker, Parks, Petree, Pierson, Pool, Ray, Read, Renfrow, Rhodes, Robbins, Rose, Smith, Stilly, Stilwell, Sweet, Teague, Trogden, Tucker, Watts and Welker—69.

Those who voted in the negative, are:

Messrs. Durham, Etheridge, Graham of Orange, Hare and Merritt—5.

## AN ORDINANCE FOR THE SUBMISSION OF THE CONSTITUTION TO THE PEOPLE, AND THE ELECTION OF CERTAIN OFFICERS.

SECTION 1. *Be it ordained by the people of North-Carolina in Convention assembled*, That the Constitution adopted by this Convention be submitted for ratification to the voters of this State, registered and qualified, as provided by the acts of Congress known as the Reconstruction Laws, on the 21st, 22d and 23d of April, 1868. The vote on said Constitution shall be "For the Constitution" and "Against the Constitution." The said election shall be held at the places and under the regulations to be prescribed by the Commanding General of this military district, and the returns made to him as directed by law.

SEC. 2. *Be it further ordained*, That an election shall be held at the same time and place as the ratification of the Constitution, for Senators and Representatives in the General Assembly, and for all State and County officers, who are to be elected by the people under this Constitution.

SEC. 3. *Be it further ordained*, That an election for members of the United States Congress shall be held in each Congressional District as now established, at the same time and place as the election for ratification of the Constitution. Said election shall be conducted by the same persons and under the same regulations as before mentioned in this ordinance. The returns shall be made to the President of this Convention, who shall give the persons chosen certificates of election.

SEC. 4. *Be it further ordained*, That the Commanding General of this Military District is requested to enforce this ordinance

SEC. 5. *Be it further ordained*, That the President of this Convention is hereby directed to forward a certified copy of this ordinance to the Commanding General of this Military District.

The Committee on Contingent Expenses reported as follows:

We, the undersigned, Committee on Contingent Expenses, have examined the account of W. H. S. Sweet, amounting to the sum of eighty-six dollars, and respectfully recommend that the same be paid.

JOHN READ,
J. W. HOOD,
R. F. TROGDEN.

The report was adopted.

The House, on motion, adjourned.

---

EVENING SESSION, MARCH 16TH, 1868.

The Convention was called to order at 7½ o'clock, by the President.

The Roll was called and the following members answered to their names:

Messrs. Abbott, Ashley, Aydlott, Baker, Benbow, Blume, Bradley, Bryan, Carey, Carter, Candler, Cherry, Chillson, Colgrove, Congleton, Cox, Daniel, Dickey, Duckworth, Durham, Etheridge, Fisher, Forkner,Franklin, French of Bladen, French of Rockingham, French of Chowan, Fullings, Gahagan, Galloway, Glover, Graham of Montgomery, Grant of Wayne, Grant of Northampton, Gully, Gunter, Hall, Hare, Harris of Franklin, Hay, Heaton, Highsmith, Hoffler, Hollowell, Hyman, Jones of Caldwell, Kinney, Laflin, Legg, Logan, Marshall, Merritt, Morton, Mullican, Murphy, Newsom, Nicholson, Patrick, Parker, Pool, Rhodes, Rich, Robbins, Rose, Smith, Stilly, Stilwell, Sweet, Teague, Tourgee, Trogden, Tucker, Turner, Watts, Welker and Williamson—76.

The following ordinance was adopted:

## AN ORDINANCE APPOINTING COMMISSIONERS TO INVESTIGATE THE ACCOUNTS AND AFFAIRS OF THE ALBEMARLE AND CHESAPEAKE CANAL COMPANY.

SECTION. 1. *Be it ordained by the people of North-Carolina in Convention assembled, and it is hereby ordained by authority of the same,* That E. W. Jones, C. C. Pool and Gesbourne J. Cherry, be, and the same are hereby, appointed a Committee to investigate the accounts and affairs of the Albemarle and Chesapeake Canal Company with authority to send for persons and papers, to examine and take testimony, to fill vacancies in said Commission, should any occur, and to report the result of their investigations, together with such recommendations as they may deem proper to protect the interest of the State, to the next meeting of the Convention or Legislature, and that said Commissioners be paid therefor the sum of six dollars per day each, when actually employed, together with such travelling and incidental expenses that may be incurred in prosecuting said investigation.

The following ordinance introduced by W. H. S. Sweet, was, On motion, (after a suspension of the rules,) adopted:

AN ORDINANCE TO AMEND AN ORDINANCE OF THIS CONVENTION ENTITLED "AN ORDINANCE TO CHANGE THE MANNER OF PAYMENT OF THE STATE'S SUBSCRIPTION TO THE CAPITAL STOCK OF THE WESTERN RAIL ROAD COMPANY."

SECTION 1. *Be it ordained by the people of North-Carolina in Convention assembled*, That section second of an ordinance of this Convention, entitled "An ordinance to change the manner of payment of the State's subscription to the capital stock of the Western Rail Road Company," ratified the 14th day of March, 1868, be and is hereby repealed and declared of no effect.

SEC. 2. *Be it further ordained*, That this ordinance shall be in force from and after its ratification.

The ordinance was adopted by the following vote:

Those who voted in the affirmative are:

Messrs. Abbott, Andrews, Ashley, Benbow, Blume, Bryan, Carter, Candler, Cherry, Chillson, Colgrove, Congleton, Cox, Eppes, Fisher, Forkner, Franklin, French of Bladen, French of Rockingham, French of Chowan, Fullings, Gahagan, Galloway, Glover, Graham of Montgomery, Gully, Gunter, Hall, Harris of Wake, Harris of Franklin, Hayes of Robeson, Hayes of Halifax, Highsmith, Hobbs, Hollowell, Hood, Hyman, Laflin, Lee, Legg, Logan, Mann, Marshall, McDonald of Moore, Murphy, Nance, Patrick, Parks, Pierson, Ray, Renfrow, Rich, Robbins, Rodman, Rose, Stilwell, Sweet, Taylor, Trogden, Tucker, Turner, Watts and Welker—64.

Those who voted in the negative are:

Messrs. Aydlott, Etheridge, George, Hare, Kinney, McCubbins, Merritt, Mullican and Parker—9.

The following resolution, introduced by Mr. Sweet, was,

On motion, adopted:

*Resolved*, That the President of this Convention is hereby instructed to inform Major General Canby, without delay, that the following offices have been created under the Constitution of North-Carolina, to be submitted to the registered voters of the State, on the 21st, 22d and 23d of April, at which time persons to fill said offices will be elected by the voters aforesaid, viz:

## STATE AT LARGE.

### EXECUTIVE.

One Governor.
One Lieutenant-Governor.
One Secretary of State.
One Auditor.
One Treasurer.
One Superintendent of Public Works.
One Superindent of Public Instruction.
One Attorney General.

### JUCICIARY.

One Chief Justice of the Supreme Court.
Four Associate Justices of the Supreme Court.
Twelve Judges of the Superior Court.

### LEGISLATIVE.

Fifty State Senators, to be elected in their respective Districts.

One hundred and twenty members of the House of Representatives, to be elected in their respective Counties.

Twelve Solicitors, to be elected in their respective Judicial Districts.

In each County, one Sheriff, one Clerk of the Superior Court, one Surveyor, one Register of Deeds, one Treasurer, and Five Commissioners.

Seven Representatives in the Congress of the United States, to be elected in their respective Districts.

Mr. Nicholson read to the House the Constitution as revised by the Committee and adopted by the House.

Mr. Heaton offered the following resolution, which,

On motion, was adopted.

*Resolved*, That the entire Constitution framed by this Convention be and is hereby adopted.

Upon the passage of this resolution the yeas and nays were demanded.

The demand was sustained.

The resolution was adopted by the following vote, yeas 90, nays 10 :

Those who voted in the affirmative, are:

Mr. President, Messrs. Abbott, Andrews, Ashley, Aydlott, Benbow, Blume, Bryan, Carey, Carter, Candler, Cherry, Chillson, Colgrove Congleton, Cox, Dickey, Duckworth, Eppes, Fisher, Forkner, Franklin, French of Bladen, French of Chowan, Fullings, Gahagan, Galloway, George, Glover, Graham of Montgomery, Grant of Wayne, Grant of Northampton, Gully, Gunter, Hall, Harris of Wake, Harris of Franklin, Hay, Hayes of Robeson, Hayes of Halifax, Heaton, Highsmith, Hobbs, Hoffler, Hollowell, Hood, Hyman, Jones of Caldwell, Jones of Washington, Kinney, Laflin, Lee, Legg, Logan, Mann, Marshall, McDonald of Moore, Morton, Mullican, Murphy, Nance, Newsom, Nicholson, Patrick, Parker, Parks, Petree, Pierson, Ragland, Ray, Read, Renfrow, Rhodes, Rich, Robbins, Rodman, Rose, Smith, Stilly, Stilwell, Sweet, Taylor, Teague, Tourgee, Trogden, Tucker, Turner, Watts, and Welker—90.

Those who voted in the negative, are :

Messrs. Baker, Bradley, Durham, Etheridge, Graham of Orange, Hare, Holt, McCubbins, Merritt, and Sanderlin—10.

On motion it was ordered the delegates sign the Constitution in the alphabetical order of Counties.

Before any signature was appended to the Constitution,

On motion of Mr. Heaton, the Secretary was directed to note the fact in the Journal that the following interlineations were made in the original copy of the Constitution, viz:

Article 1, section 2, line one, "power."

Article 3, section 9, line one, "have."

Article 4, section 33, line one "several."

Article 6, section 1, line four, "twelve."

Article 9, section 7, line two, "Superintendant of Public Works."

The following power of Attornies were granted Mr. T. A. Byrnes, the Secretary of this Convention, to sign the Constitution:

Messrs. R. T. Long, of Richmond County; J. S. Garland, of Yancy and Mitchell Counties; Jacob Ing, of Nash County; W. G. B. Garrett, of Haywood and Jackson Counties.

The following resolution offered by Mr. Abbott, was, on motion, adopted:

*Resolved*, That the foregoing Constitution be signed by the President and Secretary, and that the members who are absent shall have privilege of signing it between this and the first day of July next.

Mr. Abbott moved that while the Constitution was being signed by the delegates of the Convention that the capitol bell be rung.

The motion was carried.

When the Constitution was being signed by the delegates.

Mr. Tourgee moved a recess for fifteen minutes, which motion prevailed.

On motion the following resolution was adopted:

*Resolved*, That the thanks of this Convention are due and are hereby tendered to the Hon. C. J. Cowles for the impartiality, and industry, and faithfulness with which he has presided over the deliberations of this body.

The following resolution introduced by Mr. Tourgee, was, on motion, adopted:

*Resolved*, That the officers of this Convention be entitled to and receive pay from the first day of the session and until the completion of their duties.

The Committee on Contingent Expenses, to whom was referred the accounts of Messrs George O. Spooner, James Heaton, J. Howard Eldridge and J. J. Sawyer, have examined the same and find them correct and recommend their payment.

JNO READ, *Chairman*.

The House on motion, adjourned to meet at 7 o'clock, A. M., Tuesday.

TUESDAY, March 17th, 1868.

The Convention was called to order at 7 o'clock, A. M., by the President.

Prayer by the Rev. S. S. Ashley.

A quorum present.

The Journal of Monday was read and approved.

Mr. Tourgee presented an ordinance divorcing Archibald Haney from his wife, which was read and adopted:

## AN ORDINANCE OF DIVORCE IN FAVOR OF ARCHIBALD HANEY, OF RANDOLPH COUNTY.

Section 1. *Be it ordained by the people of North-Carolina in Convention assembled, and it is hereby ordained by the authority of the same,* That Archibald Haney, of Randolph County, be, and he is hereby divorced from the bonds of matrimony with Cornelia, his wife, and this ordinance shall go into effect from its ratification.

Mr. Hayes, of Halifax, then called up the following resolution:

*Resolved,* That one printed copy of the new Constitution be sent to the Secretary of State of the United States, one copy to each of the heads of the Departments of the United States, one to each member of Congress, and one to the General Commanding the armies of the United States.

The resolution, was, on motion, adopted.

On motion, the Convention took a recess until 9 o'clock, at which time the house was called to order by the President.

Mr. Andrews introduced the following ordinance which was adopted:

## AN ORDINANCE AMENDING THE CHARTER OF THE CITY OF RALEIGH.

Section 1. *Be it ordained by the people of North-Carolina in Convention assembled, and it is hereby ordained by the authority of the same,* That section 4, of the Charter of the City of Raleigh, be so amended as to read as follows:

"Sec. 4. *Be it further ordained,* That any qualified elector shall be eligible as Mayor or Commissioner, and every Commissioner shall be a resident of the Ward for which he shall be chosen."

SEC. 2. *Be it further ordained*, That this ordinance shall be in force from and after its passage.

Mr. Laflin introduced the following resolution, which was read and adopted:

*Resolved*, That the Secretary be authorized to employ a clerk to assist him in completing his duties.

Mr. Heaton introduced the following ordinance:

## AN ORDINANCE COMPENSATING C. J. COWLES.

SECTION 1. *Be it ordained by the people of North-Carolina in Convention assembled, and it is hereby ordained by the authority of the same*, That Calvin J. Cowles shall receive a compensation of six dollars per day, and mileage while engaged in the performance of the duties imposed on him by the several ordinances of this Convention, and that the same be paid by the Treasurer of the State, on the warrant of said Cowles.

SEC. 2. *Be it further ordained*, That this ordinance shall be in effect from and after its ratification.

The ordinance was adopted.

The following ordinance was on motion adopted:

## AN ORDINANCE DIVORCING EDWARD SHROYER AND MARY P. SHROYER.

SECTION 1. *Be it ordained by the people of North-Carolina, in Convention assembled, and it is hereby ordained by the authority of the same*, That Edward Shroyer be and he hereby is divorced from the bonds of matrimony with his wife, Mary P. Shroyer, and this ordinance shall be in force from and after its passage.

The following resolution was on motion adopted:

*Resolved*, That it is the sense of this Convention that the next Legislature take into consideration the condition of the landless population of this State, and if practicable devise some means by loan or otherwise so that all citizens of the State can be permanently located on a small freehold, so that all will be fully identified with the interest of the State.

On motion of Mr. Abbott, the President and Secretary were ordered to sign any ordinance remaining unsigned at the adjournment.

The following address of Messrs. Rodman and Gahagan, explanatory of the Constitution, was adopted, and ordered to be printed with the Constitution:

*To the People of North-Carolina:*

The Convention which met under the Reconstruction acts of Congress, to form a Constitution "republican in form" for the State of North-Carolina, preparatory to its re-admission into the Union, have finished their labors, and now present the Constitution to the people of the State for their ratification. The undersigned have been appointed to prepare a brief statement of its most important provisions and of the principal changes which have been made in the former system of government.

THE BILL OF RIGHTS states clearly "the general and essential principles of liberty and good government," and secures them by all the safeguards which experience can suggest. The great change introduced by the Bill of Rights is, that it removes every argument on which the doctrine of the right of secession has been advocated, and secures forever the integrity of the Union and the peace and prosperity of the United States. To the Union-loving people of North-Carolina no defence need be made for the bold assertion of this great principle.

In the EXECUTIVE DEPARTMENT the changes appear to be much greater than they really are. The names of some officers have been changed, and instead of being elected by the General Assembly as heretofore, the choice of these high agents of the people's will is giving directly to the people. This is in conformity with the acknowledged principles of

Republican government. But two new officers have been created. First, Lieutenant-Governor. The necessity for this officer to supply the place of the Governor, in case of a vacancy in his office, was so apparent that it was provided for in the proposed Constitution of 1865. No additional expense is incurred, as he will receive no pay, except while acting as Governor or presiding over the Senate. Second, A Superintendent of Public Works. A proper care of the interest of the State in the great and expensive Public Works in which it is engaged renders such an officer manifestly necessary. It is a measure of economy. The State has lost hundreds of thousands of dollars heretofore for want of the watchful attention, which this officer will give to the expenditure of the public money on internal improvements.

Under the heads of the LEGISLATIVE DEPARTMENT and SUFFRAGE AND ELIGIBILITY TO OFFICE, the change which will challenge attention is the giving the right to vote and hold office to all the male inhabitants of the State, without regard to race, color or previous condition. This change was inevitable. Without it there can be no return to the Union, no escape from the hopeless ruin which is inseparable from a continuance in our present unnatural condition. But apart from this convincing reason, reflecting men must see that a prudent regard for the welfare of both races and for the peace and harmony of society, required the extension of the great privilege of voting to the colored people, and just men must admit that all who are expected to bear their share of the manifold burdens of the government at all times, and to expose their lives for its defence in war, should be allowed a full participation in its direction. To refuse this right to any class of the people would be to continue slavery in a modified form, a course too abhorent to the spirit of the age to be permitted.

While giving suffrage to the colored people, the Convention has not been so inconsistent with itself, and with the great principles of Republican government, as to deny it to any portion of the whites. It is an undeniable monument to the wisdom, and equity, and magnanimity, of the Union people of North-Carolina, that in three years after the close of a bloody and devastating civil war, in which wrongs and outrages were endured that can never be forgotten, they have framed a Constitution, in which not a trace of animosity or vindictiveness can be found; in which the wrongs of the past are ignored for the sake of the peace of the future, and all who are now true to their country, are invited to participate in its government. Such wise forbearance is certain of its reward in the approval of reflecting men now, and of all posterity.

This may be the proper place to speak of a charge, which has been freely made against this Constitution, by those who have never seen it, and have determined to defeat it, be it what it may. The charge is, that it favors the *social* equality of the races. It is untrue, nothing can be found in the Constitution looking in that direction. With the social intercourse of life, government has nothing to do; it must be left to the taste and choice of each individual.

Some persons have been so bold or ignorant, as to allege, that white and colored people are required to be enrolled in the same militia company, and white and colored children to attend the same schools, and that intermarriages between the races are encouraged. All these assertions are false, as any reader of the Constitution will see. *All these matters are left now, as they were by the Constitution of* 1776, *by the Constitution of* 1835 *and by the proposed Constitution of* 1865, *to be regulated by the representatives of the people in the General Assembly.* Any one who denies the propriety of thus leaving them, both impeaches the wisdom of our ancestors and distrusts the people of the future.

The attempt to excite a false prejudice on these subjects, is made for partizan purposes, can only tend to excite ill will between races that are destined to live on the same soil, and ought to live together in peace, and it should be frowned down by every lover of the peace and prosperity of the country.

### JUDICIAL DEPARTMENT.

Experience will soon demonstrate that the changes made in this branch of the government taken altogether, are of great value. Some may doubt the propriety of electing Judges by the people. If the people select wisely, no harm can possibly result. The abolishment of the County Courts, rendered necessary a small increase in the number of Judges ot the Superior Courts; and it may be charged that thereby the new system will be more expensive than the old. We have considered this matter well, and we confidently assure the people of North-Carolina, that if the General Assembly shall carry out in good faith the idea of the Convention, they will save hundreds of thousands of dollars every year, by the increased despatch, cheapness and certainty of the administration of justice. We confidently invite the approval of the people to this part of the Constitution; it will stand the test of experience, and be more valued with every year of its existence.

### COUNTY GOVERNMENT.

The Republican principle of local self-government, which has been so fertile a source of good effects in the North-Eastern and North-Western States, has been applied to the administration of the local affairs of Counties and Townships. These County Legislatures, composed of five Commissioners of each County, will be schools, where the lessons of statesmanship will be learned, which may be afterwards displayed in the government of the State. By these various bodies, almost every man is brought directly to participate in public affairs. It may seem a little awkward at first, but it has approved itself elsewhere.

### EDUCATION.

The Constitution framed by our ancestors in 1776, recognized the value of education. It provided for a University.

This Constitution provides for a University *and for free public schools for all the children of the State.* All may see the difference between the success in life of the educated and uneducated man, yet as often as not, the uneducated man has been gifted with the greater degree of intellectual power; the cause of his ill success is that it has not been developed. We propose to "level upwards," to give to every child, as far as the State can, an opportunity to develop to the fullest extent, all his intellectual gifts. So noble an effort needs no vindication.

IMPRISONMENT FOR DEBT is abolished, except in cases of fraud.

A liberal HOMESTEAD is reserved to the unfortunate debtor.

The barbarous *Punishments* of whipping, branding and cropping, will be hereafter unknown. Crime is as often the result of an ignorance of the means of getting an honest living, as of a criminal disposition. Hereafter a *Penitentiary* will be at once a place for the repression of crime, and a school for teaching the useful arts, to those who are more unfortunate than criminal.

People of North-Carolina! such is the Constitution which we invite you to to adopt. Read it carefully, consider it calmly; upon you and yours, will the consequences of your decision fall. You may not approve every part of it. We can not assert that it is perfect in every part. You must allow somewhat for the differences of opinion inevitable among thinking men, and each man must yield something of his own views for the sake of harmony. If you approve the general scope and object of the Constitution, vote to ratify it. Do not be misled by the unfounded denunciation of men heated by passion and reckless of consequences. If you adopt it, the gates of the Union will be opened for your entrance, we will once again enjoy the inestimable blessings of Constitutional Liberty, and may hope for a continaance of peace and for a return of our former prosperity. With a climate and soil unsurpassed, with a people highly gifted by nature with intellect and virtue, the State of North-Carolina ought to be a great, rich and happy State. Laying aside all mutual crimination and all prejudice, and leaving the past to bear its proper burden of sorrows and guilt, let us all unite to make her what she ought to be. You have but to will it, and by the blessing of God, it will be done.

WILL. B. RODMAN,
GEO. W. GAHAGAN.

On motion, the Convention adjourned.

---

## ERRATA.

From January 21st to February 21st, inclusive, in the yeas and nays, "Marshall" should read "Marler," and "Hall" should read "Willliams of Sampson."

# INDEX.

PAGE.

General Orders, No. 165, issued by Gen. Canby, convening the Convention, - - - 3
Oath administered to delegates, - - - - - - - - - - - - - - 8
Resolution in relation to Reporters, - - - - - - - - - - - - - 15
Protest of Mr. Durham and others, - - - - - - - - - - - - - 17
" of Mr. Tourgee and others, - - - - - - - - - - - - - 141
Standing Committees, - - - - - - - - - - - - - - - 43
Additional Committees, - - - - - - - - - - - - - 52, 59, 94 129
Message from Gov. Worth, - - - - - - - - - - - - - - - 59
Communication from General Canby, - - - - - - - - - - 60, 125, 200
Communication from the Raleigh Post Commander, - - - - - - - - 68
Communication from the Public Treasurer, - - - - - - - - - - 80, 85
Statement of votes cast for delegates, - - - - - - - - - - - 99
Resolution of thanks to General Miles, - - - - - - - - - - 171
Communication from General Miles, - - - - - - - - - - - - 199
Report of the Committee on Rules, - - - - - - - - - - - 20
" " " on Contingent Expenses, - - - - - - - - - 61
" " " on Executive Department, - - - - - - - - 72
" " " on Militia, - - - - - - - - - - - - - 96
" " " on Disability, - - - - - - - - - - - 150, 414
" " " on Preamble and Bill of Rights, - - - - - - - - 165
" " " on Corporations other than Municipal, - - - - - 176
" " " on Judiciary, requesting instructions, - - - - - 180
" " " on Legislature and its organization, - - - - - - 189
" " " on Homesteads, - - - - - - - - - - - - 219
" " " on Suffrage and Eligibility to Office, - - - - - - 232
" " " on Congressional Districts, - - - - - - - - - 242
" " " on Judiciary, - - - - - - - - - - - - 258
" " " on Punishments and Penal Institutions, - - - - - 292
" " " on Finance, - - - - - - - - - - - - - 304
" " " on Counties, Towns, &c , - - - - - - - - - 314
" " " on Education, &c., - - - - - - - - - - 338
" " " on Justices of the Peace, - - - - - - - - - 376
" " " on Mechanic's Lien, . . . . . . . . . . 380
" " " on Miscellaneous Provisions, . . . . . . . 428
" " " on the Article entitled "Amendments," . . . . . 468
Address of Messrs. Rodman and Gahagan, to the people of North-Carolina, . . 483